CONSTITUTIONAL & GEOPOLITICAL PATTERNS

U.S. HISTORY
& GOVERNMENT

Authors:

Paul Stich
Susan F. Pingel
John Farrell

Editor:
Wayne Garnsey

Illustrations & Artwork:
Eugene B. Fairbanks

Cover Design:
Wayne Garnsey & Paul Stich

N & N Publishing Company, Inc.
18 Montgomery Street   Middletown, New York 10940

www.nn4text.com   (800) NN 4 TEXT   email: nn4text@nandnpublishing.com

SPECIAL APPRECIATION

Dedicated to our students, with the sincere hope that
UNITED STATES HISTORY AND GOVERNMENT – *Constitutional & Geopolitical Patterns*
will further enhance their education, encourage citizenship,
and better prepare them to participate in the American democratic systems.

SPECIAL CREDITS

To the many teachers who have contributed their knowledge, skills,
and years of experience to the making of our text, we thank you.

To these others, our researchers and readers, our deepest appreciation
for their assistance in the preparation of this manuscript.

Kenneth Garnsey   Fran Harrison
Howard VanAckooy   Maureen VanAckooy

Reference

Top-rate references are critical to consistency in word and fact. We are grateful to the authors, editors, contributors, and publishers of two of the finest resources:

The American Heritage Dictionary © – fundamental definitions and appropriate word usage
[available on CD-ROM through SoftKey Multimedia Inc, Cambridge, MA]
2000 Grolier Multimedia Encyclopedia © – date and information verifications
[available on CD-ROM through Grolier Interactive Inc, Danbury, CT]
Chicago Manual of Style © – 13th Edition – language usage and editing guidelines
[available from the University of Chicago Press, ISBN 0-226-10390-0]

© 2001, revised **February 2007**
N & N Publishing Company, Inc.
18 Montgomery Street   Middletown, New York 10940
www.nn4text.com   (800) NN 4 TEXT   email: nn4text@warwick.net

Soft Cover Edition: ISBN # 0-935487 68 9
7 8 9 0 BMP 2010 2009 2008 2007 2006

Printed in the United States of America, Book-mart Press, NJ

SAN # 216 - 4221

TABLE OF CONTENTS

STANDARDS & SKILLS

CONSTITUTIONAL ISSUES

HISTORICAL ANALYSIS

GEOGRAPHICAL INTERACTIONS

ECONOMIC DEVELOPMENT

POLITICAL SCIENCE CONCEPTS

FOREWORD

LEARNING STANDARDS

As a citizen, you are a participant in a democracy. You must make thoughtful decisions to keep the nation free, to have dignity, and to achieve happiness. Simply put, democracy dies without your participation.

To keep American democracy alive, citizens must realize that a free society evolves from struggles that people endure over many centuries. Free citizens are called upon to make rational choices. Informed decisions flow from knowing alternatives. The only realistic guide to present and future alternatives is reflection on past experience. Therefore, knowledge of the nation's history allows you to analyze and select truth, recognize bias, and avoid delusion. Knowing history gives you a point of reference from which you can make sound choices.

Of course, understanding the history of a nation is a challenge. It requires mastering basic learning standards. These are the higher levels of knowledge and skills that you need, if you are to analyze content details, ideas, and concepts that reveal patterns of human relationships. The learning standards contain basic skills to help you assume a responsible role in American society. The standards include historical interpretation, geographic awareness, economic assessment, and political analysis.

The standards provide a multidisciplinary (historic, economic, political, and geographic) awareness to grasp diversity and the unity of America's multicultural development. *U.S. HISTORY & GOVERNMENT – Constitutional and Geopolitical Patterns* reinforces the basic standards by helping you analyze information thoughtfully and think critically. Using mini-assessments and question drills enhances and hones those skills.

To apply the learning standards effectively, *U.S. HISTORY AND GOVERNMENT – Constitutional and Geopolitical Patterns* blends them into the five standards explained below.

Key Terms

governance
hypothesis (thesis)
market, command, traditional, & mixed
  systems
power
primary sources
scarcity
secondary sources
sovereignty
spatial relationships
trade-off

Throughout the book, the icon system you see below will alert you to these issues as they arise. The idea is to emphasize the drama surrounding the issue and have you reflect on its meaning.

1. CONSTITUTIONAL STRUCTURES

FEDERALISM, SEPARATION OF POWER, CHANGE AND FLEXIBILITY

Power is defined, divided, and separated in the U.S. constitutional structure. Yet, it also remains flexible enough to change as the society changes.

CONSTITUTIONAL STRUCTURES

Under **federalism**, power is divided between a strong central government and smaller units, such as the fifty states. The *U.S. Constitution* **delegates** specific power to the central government in matters concerning the whole nation. It **reserves** most of the rest of the powers for the states. At the same time, Congress gets flexibility through the Constitution's **elastic clause**. This clause of Article I gives the central government the ability (or the *flexibility*) to adapt to changing times through the idea of **implied** power.

Within the central government, the *U.S. Constitution* also **separates** the powers of the legislative, executive, and judicial branches, and it gives each branch the ability to **check and balance** the others.

Through all these devices, the Constitution gives the American government the **flexibility** to meet and deal with new situations. For more than two centuries, the government has met challenges through formal amendments and through informal adaptation by using the elastic clause, the unwritten constitution, and the process of judicial review.

2. FOREIGN POLICY

THE UNITED STATES GLOBAL RELATIONSHIPS

Since its beginning, the United States has been involved in world affairs. Although sometimes its foreign actions arouse controversy, the United States actively pursues its national interests when dealing with other nations or international organizations.

3. GROWTH OF DEMOCRACY

EXPANSION OF CONSTITUTIONAL RIGHTS, CIVIL LIBERTIES, AND EQUALITY

Basic civil liberties and individual rights in arrest and trial situations are found in the Bill of Rights and the Fourteenth Amendment. These rights are not absolute. The courts have modified and reinterpreted them in many controversial decisions. Numerous other amendments expand voting rights of citizens. The legal status of minorities has changed as a result of numerous laws, amendments, and court decisions.

4. ECONOMIC POLICY

POLITICAL DECISIONS RELATING TO MATERIAL WEALTH

The economic functions of the national government place the United States Constitution in the center of controversy relating to production, development, and management. The role of government in regulating commercial enterprise has grown increasingly complex.

5. GEOGRAPHIC INTERACTIONS

The physical environment is altered by human activities. Spatial and physical relationships modify human developmental patterns as well. Landforms, soils, climate, physical changes, water cycles, vegetation, natural resources, and population are powerful forces that influence the progress of American society.

6. REFERENCE POINTS

Awareness of the Learning Standards helps you achieve a historical point of reference. Social studies learning standards measure your abilities to analyze details and acquire a broader perspective about American society. The standards include historical analysis, graphic awareness, economic assessment, and political interpretation.

HISTORICAL ANALYSIS

In the broadest sense, **history** is knowledge of the past. To reconstruct the past, historians analyze physical evidence including oral traditions, art, folklore, written records, and even climatic changes.

History is also a perpetual dialogue among historians. New sources – unveiled through research or archeological finds – may prove or disprove long-accepted interpretations, or lead scholars to new hypotheses. A **hypothesis** is a tentative explanation that accounts for a set of facts. For example, so far there is no evidence of a separate indigenous race in the Americas. Until recently, all available evidence led anthropologists to the hypothesis that the most ancient American ancestors crossed an extinct land bridge in the area of the Bering Strait from Asia some 11,500 years ago.

However, this and any other hypotheses can be tested by new evidence found by further investigations. In recent years, new evidence in the form of remains unearthed from Peru to Virginia has provided anthropologists with a new theory of the first Americans. Evidence now

RESEARCH FOR HISTORIANS

PRIMARY SOURCES	SECONDARY SOURCES
documents	histories
journals	epic poems based on oral traditions
diaries	
autobiographies	memoirs, broad-based commentaries
eyewitness	
interviews	paintings, sculptures, monuments
artifacts	
quantitative data	songs, poems, operas
graphs	(all created after an
photos	event transpires)

indicates multiple Stone Age migrations from many regions and all earlier than the Asian-Bering one, thus challenging the old hypothesis.

Students of history must observe how differ-

ent historians use facts and interpretations to:

- support hypotheses
- identify issues, values, differences of opinion, and raise relevant questions
- formulate a position and explore its consequences

Historians look at **primary sources** (created at the time) and **secondary sources** (analysis written later – well after the events transpire – by others including historians, journalists, and government officials). Examining primary sources develops skills in determining the value of solid evidence (tests of credibility). Looking at secondary sources develops a sense of perspective and recognition of patterns and trends. Secondary sources give a "big picture" to help see how others interpret primary evidence.

SKILL ACTIVITY – THE MANHATTAN PROJECT

Below is a list of materials reviewed by a student researching the Manhattan Project, the United States' development of the atom bomb during World War II, 1939-1945:

- Groves, (General) Leslie R., *Now it Can be Told: The Story of the Manhattan Project*, New York: Harper & Brothers, 1962 (memoir, General Groves was director of the Manhattan Project)
- Fermi, Enrico, *My Observations During the Explosion at Trinity on July 16, 1945*, Collection VFA-470, Los Alamos National Laboratory Archives (Fermi was one of the scientists who developed the bomb)
- "Manhattan Project," *Encyclopedia Britannica*, Vol. 28, 1998 ed.
- Hershey, John, *Hiroshima*, New York: Alfred A. Knopf, 1946 (novel based on the aftermath of the nuclear bombing of Japan)
- Bundy, McGeorge, *Danger and Survival: Choices about the Bomb in the First Fifty Years*, New York: Random House, 1988 (foreign policy expert analyzes the impact of nuclear weapons)

Answer the following questions based on the information given above.

1 Which item is a primary source?
  1 Hershey's novel
  2 the encyclopedia article
  3 Groves' memoir
  4 Fermi's observation

2 Which item would give the student the broadest overview of the causes and effects of the U.S. development of the bomb?

_____

_____

_____

3 Why would the student bother to use the John Hershey novel? Why use Bundy's book?

_____

_____

_____

_____

_____

Note to Student: On U.S. History and Government exams, questions on stimuli (specific factual data or graphics) usually come in series. The first one usually asks for a direct idea about the item. Then, a broader essay question asks you to apply the information to a broader historical context.

You must learn to use a **multiplicity of sources** to:

- analyze the assumption(s) from which a narrative of events was constructed

- compare what authors include and exclude from a narrative

- consider multiple causes and formulate questions about interpretations

- distinguish fact from opinion

- understand the causes and consequences of people's actions

- understand the relationships that civilizations have to each other in shaping events

- see the dynamic interplay of differing interpretations

The availability, quality, and quantity of information gathered determines the scope and accuracy of the historian's investigation. No matter how pair staking the research, interpretation and presentations can be very subjective (personal). Certain data will impress one scholar more than another, resulting in a particular analysis. Often, conflicting interpretations arise and become controversial for years.

The past has powerful influences on modern life. The forces that moved Christopher Columbus to venture across the Atlantic created the world we live in just as much as Congress approving funds for space exploration. Actions taken in isolated places often have bearing on life beyond that time and place. For example, State Department foreign policy analyst George F. Kennan published an article in the journal *Foreign Affairs* in 1947 called "The Sources of Soviet Conduct." In the article, Kennan recommended a set of policies that became the basis for restraining communist governments' aggressive moves that threatened peace. His outline became the guide for U.S. containment of communism for the next four decades.

Across time and space, people face common issues and situations. Change is a powerful force in American history, but continuity is equally great. The more you read and learn history, the more you appreciate that patterns of behavior are often remarkably predictable. You begin to see patterns such as reactions to oppression, coping with geographic factors, tradition clashing with modern ways, leaders influencing events, and people migrating for economic improvement (or fleeing political oppression). Since these patterns are common and very powerful forces, they are often the focus of historians' work.

Developing a sense of time helps you grasp patterns of human interaction. Knowing the basic sequence of centuries and decades yields a sense of order. For example, the pattern of American life changed markedly with industrialization. Cities grew, the number of people feeding the nation on its more efficient farms shrank, and the mobility of people was enhanced greatly. Awareness of this evolution helps you to

SKILL ACTIVITY – U.S. TIME PERIODS

Below is a list of time periods in United States history:

- The Great Depression
- The Revolutionary Era
- The Roaring Twenties
- The Civil War Era
- The Industrial Revolution
- The Progressive Era

Answer the following questions based on the information given above.

1   Look up the dates for the periods in the list and rearrange in chronological order.

2   Which period is chronologically most distant from the others?

_____

_____

_____

_____

3   Knowing the Industrial Era came before the Progressive Era helps to explain the
    1   social impact of technology
    2   breakdown of federalism
    3   power of religion
    4   causes of economic collapse

see it as a base for more rapid change and development in later periods. Knowing major time periods helps in making time connections in narrative essays.

Besides time, historians use other theme patterns to clarify the past. Narrative essay questions on U.S. History examinations often reflect these themes:

- **multiple causation**
- **change and its effects**
- **ends** (results) **influence means** (methods of getting results)
- **role of individual and group actions**
- **comparing and contrasting differing sets of ideas** (religions, ideologies, philosophies) **and detecting linkages among them**
- **moral and / or practical consequences of decisions**

GEOGRAPHIC RELATIONSHIPS

Geography is the study of the Earth and its features. It also studies the distribution of life on the Earth, including human life and the effects produced by human activity.

Geographic features have a significant impact on where and how people live. When studying history, geography helps explain the relation of the natural environment to the human environment. Relationships to climate, water, landforms, and mineral deposits shape how people live and act toward others. Distances alter relationships, too. For example, once railroads began crossing the undeveloped western U.S., settlement increased in a very short time.

Studying the natural environment reveals much about how civilizations develop (e.g., river valleys that surround arteries of transportation often develop more rapidly than open plains). Relative location can indicate what motivates a nation. An example would be the large influx of Americans into the Texas region of northern Mexico in the beginning of the 19th century. It eventually led to annexation, a declaration of war, and conquest by the United States.

As a geographic factor, climate often plays a key role in human development. It shapes culture (e.g. Native American plains dwellers were usually nomadic). In each region of the country, the general climatic conditions govern human progress. Knowing these conditions can often help explain why things have happened in the region throughout history.

People sense spatial relationships. They identify with a place's physical characteristics or learn to adapt to them (e.g., mountaineers, islanders, forest dwellers). Their culture, music, and architecture can reflect such characteristics. An area's livelihood may spring from geographic factors (e.g., fishing has been a chief industry for New England, water power from the rapids of short rivers of the East aided industrial development, the Great Plains lent themselves to large-scale grain farming).

GEOGRAPHIC OVERVIEW OF THE UNITED STATES

PHYSICAL/CULTURAL SETTING

SIZE AND LOCATION

At over 3,700,000 square miles, the United States is just slightly smaller than the entire European continent. Only three countries (Russia, Canada, and China) have a larger land mass. The 48 contiguous (or coterminous) states (states that adjoin each other, which excludes Alaska and Hawaii) extend nearly 3,000 miles in a west-east direction, and over 1,200 miles north-south. The entire 4,000 mile northern border of the United States is with Canada, while Mexico comprises the 1,900 mile southern border. This southern boundary extends from the Gulf of Mexico to the Pacific Ocean.

Over the years, the population has continued moving westward and slightly southward. The center of population (defined as the point where the United States would balance with an even distribution of people on all sides) has moved from just east of Baltimore, Maryland in 1790 to southwest of St. Louis, Missouri 200 years later in 1990.

GEOGRAPHIC TERMS

Term - Explanation

Meridian (U.S.: approx. 67°W (Maine) – 160°W (Hawaii/ 170°W Aleutians) – An imaginary great circle passing through the North and South geographic poles; lines of longitude measured East or West to 180 degrees of the Prime Meridian (0° – running through Greenwich, England and 180° at the International Date Line)

Parallel (U.S.: approx. 18°N (Puerto Rico / Hawaii) – 72°N (Alaska) – Any of the imaginary lines representing degrees of latitude that encircle the Earth parallel to the plane of the Equator zero degrees (0°) measured North and South to 90 degrees (90° North or South – geographic poles)

Hemisphere (Western) – Either the northern or southern half of the Earth as divided by the Equator, or the eastern or western half as divided by a meridian

Continent (North America) – One of the principal landmasses of the Earth (other continents include: Africa, Antarctica, Asia, Australia, Europe, North America, and South America)

Region (New England, Middle Atlantic, Midwest, South, Southwest, Northwest) – A large portion of the country unified by physical or human characteristics such as language, culture, economic activity, or a political system

Ocean (Atlantic, Pacific) – Any of the principal divisions of the Earth's salt water surface (71%), including the Atlantic, Pacific, and Indian Oceans, their southern extensions in Antarctica, and the Arctic Ocean

Sea (Caribbean) – A relatively large body of salt water completely or partially enclosed by land

Bay (New York, Chesapeake, San Francisco) – A body of water partially enclosed by land with a mouth accessible to the sea

Gulf (Gulf of Mexico) – A large area of a sea or ocean partially enclosed by land

Lakes (Great Lakes) – A large inland body of fresh water or salt water

River (St. Lawrence, Hudson, Ohio-Missouri-Mississippi, Colorado, Columbia) – A large natural stream of water emptying into an ocean, a lake, or another body of water

Mountains (Appalachian, Rockies) – A significant natural elevation of the Earth's surface having considerable mass, generally steep sides

Plateau (Allegheny, Ozark, Intermountain) – An elevated, level expanse of land; a tableland

Plain (Eastern Coastal, Great Plains) – An extensive, level, usually treeless area of land

Peninsula (Florida, Baja Calif.) – A piece of land that projects into a body of water

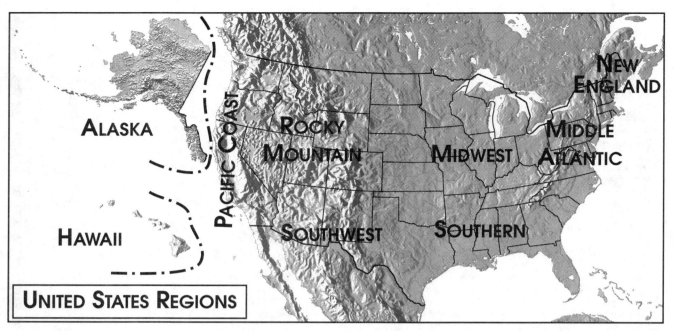

UNITED STATES REGIONS

The United States is often divided into eight regions:

New England
Middle Atlantic
Midwest
Southern
Southwest
Rocky Mountain
Pacific Coast
Alaska and Hawaii

MAJOR ZONES AND AREAS

CLIMATE ZONES

All of the coterminous 48 states are in the temperate or middle latitudes (an area defined as north of the Tropic of Cancer $23\frac{1}{2}°$N and south of the Arctic Circle $66\frac{1}{2}°$N), but the climate is enormously varied. Most of the area east of the Rocky Mountains is humid continental in the north and humid subtropical in the south, with a humid tropical region being confined to southern Florida. More varied is the area from the Rockies west. This western region includes mountain, semi-arid, and desert climates scattered throughout, and marine and Mediterranean (dry subtropical) climates along the Pacific coast.

Earth's great variety of climates has determined agricultural zones since the earliest times. Colonial Americans stayed near the moderating influence of the Atlantic. In the 19th century, settlers battled blizzards and droughts

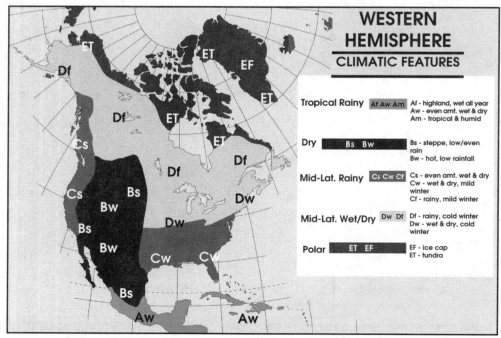

WESTERN HEMISPHERE CLIMATIC FEATURES

Tropical Rainy	Af Aw Am	Af - highland, wet all year Aw - even amt. wet & dry Am - tropical & humid
Dry	Bs Bw	Bs - steppe, low/even rain Bw - hot, low rainfall
Mid-Lat. Rainy	Cs Cw Cf	Cs - even amt. wet & dry Cw - wet & dry, mild winter Cf - rainy, mild winter
Mid-Lat. Wet/Dry	Dw Df	Df - rainy, cold winter Dw - wet & dry, cold winter
Polar	ET EF	EF - ice cap ET - tundra

in the trek west. Recently, climate has been one of the factors in the movement of people to the southern and southwestern states, popularly called the "Sunbelt."

VEGETATION ZONES

Most of the area from the Atlantic Coast to the edge of the Great Plains was at one time covered by forests. Evergreen forests dominated in the northern and mountain regions, while **deciduous forests** (broad leaf) were prevalent in much of the rest. The grasslands of the Great Plains contained prairie grasses. The area from the Rockies westward was, like the climate, more varied. Forests were predominant in the mountains, grasses and small plants in the basins and semi-arid regions, and a mixture in the coastal areas of central and southern California. Human settlement has swept away much of the naturally growing vegetation of the United States, especially in the areas east of the Rockies.

AGRICULTURAL AREAS

By the year 2000, fewer than 3% of the workers in the United States today were involved directly in agriculture, yet the nation produces enormous surpluses of food. Nearly 40% of the world's corn was grown in the United States, and between 10% - 20% of the world's cotton and wheat. The Midwest was the most productive agricultural region, while California produced the greatest value of agricultural products.

From New England to the Upper Midwest, dairy farming is common, with smaller farms growing a variety of corn, grain, and vegetables in the relatively short growing season. The Midwest and the Great Plains are the centers of America's farming region. Corn, soybeans, wheat, and oats are grown in large quantities, and pastures are filled with cattle. The longer growing season in the South permits farmers to cultivate cotton, tobacco, and in Florida and Texas, citrus fruits. Irrigation and a mild climate give California farmers the ability to grow fresh vegetables and produce a large citrus crop.

NATURAL RESOURCES

The richness in natural resources of the United States helped it become the leading industrial nation in the world. Historically, the discovery of gold and silver in places such as California, Nevada, and Alaska set off rushes in which thousands raced to a location to claim their fortune. Most came away disappointed. More important in the long run have been other resources, such as petroleum, natural gas, iron ore, and coal.

Petroleum and natural gas are found mostly in Texas, Louisiana, California, and Alaska. The Mesabi region around Lake Superior provided iron ore for steel during the years of industrial expansion. Throughout the Appalachian Mountains, coal has been mined for over 100 years. Arkansas provides most of the domestic production of bauxite, used to make aluminum. Copper comes from Arizona and Utah. Lead, phosphorus, zinc, and uranium are a few of the many other minerals that are mined in the United States.

GEOGRAPHIC FACTORS THAT SHAPED THE IDENTITY OF THE UNITED STATES

The **topography** (physical features of the Earth's surface) of the United States has greatly influenced the settlement and development of the nation. Some features served as a barrier to transportation and communication. Modern technological developments in the 20th century have helped to reduce the impact that many of these features presented in prior years.

PhotoDisc ©1996

MAJOR MOUNTAIN RANGES

Two mountain ranges have helped define the United States: the **Appalachian Mountains** in the east and the **Rocky Mountains** in the west.

SKILL ACTIVITY – *POPULATION OF U.S. CITIES*

Using the "Population in U.S. Cities" chart at the right, answer the following:

1a. Which 10 cities moved up on the list in the past 14 years?

_____
_____
_____

1b. In what regions of the country are the majority of these located? _____

2a. Which 10 cities moved down on the list in the past 14 years?

_____
_____
_____
_____

2b. In what regions of the country are the majority of these located? _____

3. What general statement can you make about urban population shifts after evaluating this data?

_____
_____
_____
_____

Population in U.S. Cities

Rank in 1994			Rank in 1980
New York, NY	(1)	New York, NY	
Los Angeles, CA	(2)	Chicago, IL	
Chicago, IL	(3)	Los Angeles, CA	
Houston, TX	(4)	Houston, TX	
Philadelphia, PA	(5)	Philadelphia, PA	
San Diego, CA	(6)	Detroit, MI	
Phoenix, AZ	(7)	Dallas, TX	
Dallas, TX	(8)	San Diego, CA	
San Antonio, TX	(9)	Phoenix, AZ	
Detroit, MI	(10)	Baltimore, MD	
San Jose, CA	(11)	San Antonio, TX	
Indianapolis, IN	(12)	Indianapolis, IN	
San Francisco, CA	(13)	San Francisco, CA	
Baltimore, MD	(14)	Washington, DC	
Jacksonville, FL	(15)	Memphis, TN	
Columbus, OH	(16)	Milwaukee, WI	
Milwaukee, WI	(17)	San Jose, CA	
Memphis, TN	(18)	Columbus, OH	
El Paso, TX	(19)	Cleveland, OH	
Washington, DC	(20)	Boston, MA	
Boston, MA	(21)	New Orleans, LA	
Seattle, WA	(22)	Jacksonville, FL	
Austin, TX	(23)	Seattle, WA	
Nashville, TN	(24)	Denver, CO	
Denver, CO	(25)	St. Louis, MO	
------------------------		------------------------	
Cleveland, OH (26)		Nashville, TN (26)	
New Orleans, LA (27)		El Paso, TX (28)	
St. Louis, MO (46)		Austin, TX (29)	

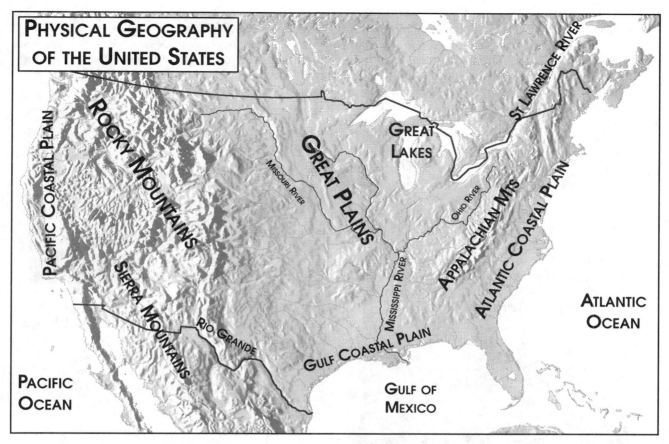

PHYSICAL GEOGRAPHY OF THE UNITED STATES

PACIFIC COASTAL PLAIN

ROCKY MOUNTAINS

SIERRA MOUNTAINS

RIO GRANDE

MISSOURI RIVER

GREAT PLAINS

GREAT LAKES

ST LAWRENCE RIVER

OHIO RIVER

APPALACHIAN MTS

MISSISSIPPI RIVER

ATLANTIC COASTAL PLAIN

GULF COASTAL PLAIN

ATLANTIC OCEAN

PACIFIC OCEAN

GULF OF MEXICO

The Appalachian Mountains extend 1,500 miles from New England, southwestward to Georgia and Alabama. These are older, eroded mountains, that are relatively low when compared to other mountain ranges around the world. However, they form a nearly continuous chain and were a formidable barrier in earlier centuries.

The Rocky Mountains extend in an irregular pattern from Canada through to northern New Mexico. The **Continental Divide** (the line that divides those rivers that flow east from those that flow west) runs through the Rockies. Many of the mountains rise above the timber line and are snow covered for much of the year.

Also in the west are the Sierra Nevada and Cascade Ranges, and adjacent to the ocean, the Pacific Coast Mountains. These mountains run in a general north-south arrangement, from the Canadian border to southern California.

In between the Rockies and the Sierra Nevada and Cascades is the Intermountain Region. This is an area which is relatively dry since moist Pacific air is stopped from advancing eastward by the mountains. Some parts of the southern region are arid deserts.

MAJOR RIVER SYSTEMS

Navigable from Minneapolis to the Gulf of Mexico, the **Mississippi River** has served as the most vital water highway in the United States. The main tributaries of the Mississippi are the Ohio to the east and the Missouri to the west. They extend the reach of the Mississippi from the Appalachians to the Rockies. The delta at the mouth of the Mississippi provides for a fertile agricultural region in Louisiana.

PhotoDisc ©1996

Rivers east of the Appalachian Mountains are generally much shorter than the great rivers of the Middle West. The Delaware, Potomac, Hudson, and Connecticut are some of the eastern rivers that flow toward the Atlantic. Also in the east is the **St. Lawrence River** that, with the construction of the St. Lawrence Seaway and other locks and canals, provides a route from the Atlantic through to the Great Lakes. In this way, cities of the Middle West such as Chicago, Cleveland, and Detroit are connected to the ocean.

Rivers west of the Rockies include the Columbia and the Colorado. They flow through large areas of desert and semi-arid lands on their way to the coast. Numerous dams have been built in the west to divert the flow of water from the rivers for irrigation.

PhotoDisc ©1996

THE GREAT PLAINS

Much of the large area between the Rocky Mountains and the Appalachian Mountains is called the Interior Plains. The eastern part of these plains are the Central Lowlands, today the Middle West. This is a fertile area with adequate rainfall. Further west, from an area west of the Mississippi to the foothills of the Rockies is the **Great Plains**. This grassland, with a slightly upward slope, is much drier than the area to the

east. Americans who saw it 150 years ago called it the "Great American Desert." Prairie grasses dominated the landscape, though today little of the native grass remains. It has been transformed for pastureland and farming.

PhotoDisc ©1996

COASTAL AREAS

The **Atlantic and Gulf Coastal Plains** extend in a broad sweep from New York to Texas. These lowlands have traditionally provided farmers with fertile soil. The gentle slope to the sea, together with the eastern rivers, give the region excellent ports for shipping.

In the west, some mountain ranges drop sharply toward the sea, providing little or no coastal plain. The battering effects of Pacific storms often make the coastline, especially in the north, a harsh place to live. The southern half of the California coast, however, is usually impacted much less by these storms.

ATLANTIC/PACIFIC OCEANS

These two oceans provided a boundary thousands of miles wide from Europe and Asia. Until the 20th century, it usually took weeks or even months to cross these oceans. The United States was often able to use the oceans as natural, protective barriers from the political, economic, and social problems of much of the world.

PhotoDisc ©1996

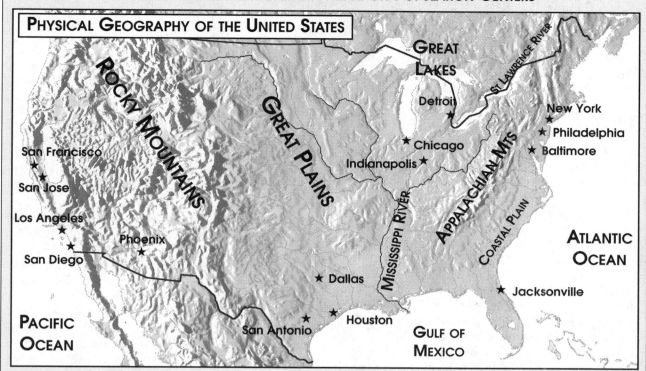

PHYSICAL GEOGRAPHY OF THE UNITED STATES

ROCKY MOUNTAINS

GREAT PLAINS

GREAT LAKES

ST LAWRENCE RIVER

Detroit

New York
★
★ Philadelphia
★ Baltimore

★ Chicago
Indianapolis ★

APPALACHIAN MTS

COASTAL PLAIN

San Francisco
★
San Jose
★
Los Angeles
★
San Diego
★

Phoenix
★

MISSISSIPPI RIVER

ATLANTIC OCEAN

★ Dallas

★ Jacksonville

PACIFIC OCEAN

San Antonio
★

★ Houston

GULF OF MEXICO

1 The importance of the Mississippi River in the history of the United States has primarily been based on the River's
1 barrier to westward movement of people
2 importance as a north-south transportation link
3 use as a source of hydroelectric power
4 only known route over the Rocky Mountains

2 The Great Plains are distinct from the Coastal Plains farther to the east, because the Great Plains
1 are much hotter in the summer and colder in the winter
2 have mountain ranges scattered throughout
3 are influenced by the Pacific marine climate
4 have a much drier climate

3 Historically, the Atlantic and Pacific Oceans
1 have been a source of hydro-electric power
2 allowed easy access to the West for settlers

3 offered protection from political problems in Europe and Asia
4 provided irrigation for dry interior plains

Answer the following questions based on the topographic (relief) map above.

Constructed Response

From the map given above, describe how geography and climate affect the distribution of people in major cities of the United States.

_____

_____

_____

_____

_____

_____

_____

_____

_____

_____

ECONOMIC DEVELOPMENT

Students beginning a U.S. history course require some understanding of economics, because it is a basic force underlying human activity. People need resources to produce the goods and services to sustain life and give comfort. The basic resources that humans use include:

- Natural resources – land, water, trees, minerals ...
- Human resources – labor, talent, organizational skills ...
- Capital resources – tools, computers, machinery, financial investment ...
- Information resources – research, ideas ...

These basic resources are vital to human existence. Yet, this is a finite world. While some resources are plentiful at certain times and in certain places, all resources have limits. This presents a very large, persistent problem in life: *all the resources listed above are limited in some way.* Economists call this the problem of **scarcity** – there are not enough resources to supply all the demands of humanity.

Since there never has been enough of anything to meet everyone's needs and desires, scarcity is a basic fact of life. It is also an uneven condition. In reality, supply never equals demand. Of course, at certain times, some people, living in some places, have had plenty. Yet, it does not take very much searching to discover that most people on the globe suffer from a lack of resources in some way.

Supply is the amount of a resource or service available for meeting a demand. **Demand** is the amount of a resource or service that people are ready and willing to consume. Simply put, on a global scale the supply of resources is finite, and the demand for resources is infinite.

DECISION-MAKING: TRADE-OFFS AND SACRIFICES

Even in a place like the United States which seems to have a great abundance of resources, scarcity forces individuals, families, communities, and nations to look at the limited resources they have and make basic decisions (and sacrifices). **Economics** is the study of how humans make such decisions:

- What to produce?
- How to produce?
- Who gets the products?

These questions seem simple enough on a personal level. Individuals assess their resources and consider their needs and desires. They decide to exchange their resources for something. Most often, they want a substantial amount of things, but only have the money for one thing. As a result, they sacrifice (trade-off) the purchase of one thing for another. That is **real cost** – the expenditure of resources *plus* the sacrifice of all the other opportunities to use those resources. (Real cost is sometimes called "opportunity cost.")

Individual decisions are often difficult, but when groups of people have to make decisions, the process becomes harder. People have different values and needs. Satisfying everyone is difficult. Evaluating the needs of the present versus the needs of the future, setting acceptable priorities, and using resources wisely becomes very complex.

For example, should a society use its natural, human, capital, and information resources to produce pasta, vacuum cleaners, mobile homes, schools, and health care, *or* should it use those resources for bread, fork lifts, computers, railroad cars, airplanes, bridges, and office buildings? (Remember, some resources, such as petroleum, are **non-renewable**. Once used, they are gone forever.) Trying to decide on this level can lead to conflict within a society. Civil wars erupt when groups feel "cut out" of the decision-making process. Conflicting desires can also lead to struggles among societies. Countries have gone to war with others over trade differences, water rights, and mineral deposits.

ECONOMIC SYSTEMS

Societies, nations, and civilizations have evolved different systems or ways to make economic choices about scarce resources. Economists see three general systems for how societies make decisions about scarce resources: **traditional**, **command**, and **market**. The kind of system found in a particular society evolves from elements such as historic experience, values, culture, the leaders' political ideology, and current conditions.

BASIC ECONOMIC SYSTEMS			
TYPE	DECISION-MAKING	CHARACTERISTICS	PROBLEMS
Traditional	based on past experience, custom, religion	common to small, primitive, isolated societies; labor-intensive, static, subsistence level, no chance to produce surplus	not equipped to deal with major change in natural, technological, or social environment; with no past patterns or guidelines to follow in emergencies, chiefs or clan elders had to issue orders to deal with dislocations until people could go back to their old ways
Market	individual producers and consumers	flexible, rapid change	business activity fluctuates, makes long-term planning difficult; sometimes insecure and unstable
Command	government planners	slow-moving, often inflexible	personal initiative not rewarded, innovation is limited to government sponsored programs; lack of competition affects quality of products

Most modern economic systems blend governmental (command) and individual (market) decision-making. These **mixed** systems vary. For example, the colonial American settlers were independent in thought and deed. They generally rejected interference in their lives from government. (Think about the economic coercion brought on the colonists by the British in the 1760s and 1770s and the colonists' reaction.) It is not unusual that a market system emerged with minimal governmental interference. The availability of critical resources, cultural values, political and religious beliefs, limitations of the natural environment, and historic experience are just some of the factors that shaped American society's mixture of market with restrained command.

INTERDEPENDENCE OF ECONOMIC SYSTEMS THROUGHOUT THE WORLD

In the modern world, especially in the age of the Internet, the choices being made every moment all over the globe mean resources are being shifted at a blistering pace. Making informed and well-reasoned economic decisions in a high-speed environment is not an easy task. Millions of individuals – producers and consumers – making resource choices daily drive global markets. Public and private organizations or institutions (e.g., various levels of government, corporations, unions, political parties) make an unending array of decisions at every moment.

The availability (or unavailability) of resources, and the transfer of them on a worldwide basis, is the foundation of modern existence. Just thinking about the array of products an individual uses in daily routines, where they come from, how they were put together, and how they arrived at the place they are being used. It shows the complexity of modern life. It also shows that interdependence is the driving force on the globe today.

Necessity links humanity; and yet, different values and perspectives divide people. Different economic systems and national agendas cause friction and conflict. Making global interdependence work demands understanding and cooperation.

POLITICAL SCIENCE CONCEPTS

Political science is the study of the structures, activities, and behavior of government. U.S. history students need to see that the political philosophies that have evolved with human existence vary greatly, and many of them were blended into our constitutional system. You must reach beyond your awareness of your own system to compare government and politics in other places and times and note the similarities and differences among them.

THE PURPOSES OF GOVERNMENT

Humans, acting in groups, devise systems to make decisions concerning their common goals. A **government** is an agency that exercises control and administration of a political unit. Governments, small and large, regulate people and speak for people to other governments.

POLITICAL CONCEPTS OF POWER, AUTHORITY, GOVERNANCE, AND LAW

Political science studies the principles on which governments rest, and whether they live up to those principles.

Historically, there have been many theories on where governments get their power and authority. The most common theories include:

- **Divine right** – the belief that power comes to an individual or group from the authority of some supernatural force
- **Physical power** – the strongest, wealthiest, or best armed holds power and offers protection to the weaker
- **Consent of the governed** – power is granted by the authority of the group being ruled

No matter what is deemed to be the source of authority, governments need two essential

---

SKILL ACTIVITY – ECONOMIC DECISION–MAKING

Centralized Decision-making	Mixed Decision-making	Individual Decision-making
Command Systems	Mixed Systems	Market Systems

Modern economic systems fall along a simple continuum based on who is answering the three basic questions about allocation of scarce resources (WHAT to produce? HOW to produce? For WHOM is it produced?). Most systems mix government (centralized) decision-making with individualized decision-making. Traditional systems are not shown on the continuum because there is no conscious dynamic of decision-making – traditions dictate the activities and allocations. If a storm were to disrupt the normal flow of activities in a traditional system, a village leader or council would have to consider the situation and consciously reallocate resources. At that point, tradition fails, and a command structure has temporarily replaced tradition.

Answer the following questions based on the information given above.

1 In the 1880s, the U.S. government began to regulate fares charged by railroads. In which direction was the system moving?
   1 tradition to command
   2 market to command
   3 market to tradition
   4 command to tradition

2 When Hurricane Blanche roared through Alabama, the governor ordered all power companies to restrict the amount of electricity supplied to residential customers, so that emergency services would have sufficient quantities. Which system change is taking place?
   1 traditional to command
   2 command to market
   3 market to command
   4 traditional to market

3 Kelly's father orders her to give up a job at the mall and devote more time to building a grade-point average that will get her into college. Explain which system seems to be operating here.

   _____

   _____

   _____

4 What factors influence the type of system, or mix of systems a society adopts?

   _____

   _____

   _____

Note to Student: On U.S. History exams, questions on specific factual data or graphics usually come in series. The first one is usually directly from the material presented. The next question(s) ask you to apply broader historical concepts and contexts to the material.

---

powers to keep control and order – the sword and the purse. First, a government must be able to **enforce** (sword) the rules and the order it desires. Second, a government must be able to **finance** (purse) its enforcement procedures and provide services. It usually does this through taxation.

Even with these two essential powers in place, a government's **sovereignty** (supreme independent authority) can be limited internally and externally. Internally, constitutions outline the power of government, but they often set forth restraints on the government's scope and authority over the people governed. Externally, other governments could compromise sovereignty (e.g., a mother country exerting authority over a colony or a federal government preempting some power of a state government).

From the clan and tribal councils of primitive times to the superpowers and international governments of today, governments come in all sizes and configurations. Until recently, there were some governments which established large empires that ruled peoples across national, language, and ethnic boundaries. Modern nation-states have governments that operate at many different levels from villages to cities, counties, provinces, and states.

Governments usually reflect the values and needs of the power groups that run them. If security and order are high priorities, a **unitary system** might evolve where all authority is linked in a seamless chain of command from the national level through the local. Where freedom and diversity are prized, but order is still important, a looser **federal system** may form. It distributes power between a central government and subdivisions (e.g., states, provinces). Where individuality is essential, a fragile **league** or **confederation** may form. It has a weak central government with only marginal power. In a confederation, the smaller units (states) retain a great deal of sovereignty.

A key function of government is to control the society by setting the rules (laws) and enforcing them. **Law** is a system of standards of conduct, obligations, and rights. Laws include written statutes, administrative rules and regulations, and judicial precedents. There are five general types of law:

- **Constitutional Law** – outlines the body of rules by which the powers of government are exercised
- **Administrative Law** – governs the organization, operation, regulations, and procedures of agencies of the government
- **Private or Civil Law** – applies rules when one person claims that another has injured his or her person, property, or reputation
- **Criminal Law** – imposes penalties for antisocial behavior
- **International Law** – sets rules on boundary disputes, warfare limits, trade

INTERNATIONAL POLITICAL SYSTEMS

History shows many attempts of nations and empires to deal with others in rational ways. Yet, only in modern times have permanent organizations been created to promote peace, cooperation, and understanding. In the *Treaty of Versailles* (WW I), the **League of Nations** (1919 to 1946) was founded as part of President Woodrow Wilson's idealism. The League actually fell apart in the 1930s but some of its support systems lasted until the **United Nations** (1945) absorbed them. Both of these voluntary organizations became forums for debate and negotiations. The U.N. has gone beyond the League by sending international peacekeeping forces to trouble spots in the world. The United Nations is an international government in theory; but in reality, nations still cling to their sovereignty and do not always cooperate for peace.

Regional associations also have a long history. From the Peloponnesian League of ancient Greek city-states to

TYPES OF GOVERNMENT (WHO HOLDS POWER?)		
GENERAL TYPE	**POWER HELD BY**	**EXAMPLE**
Monarchy	one	Louis XIV in France (absolute)
Oligarchy	an enlightened few	Ancient Sparta's Ephors or modern military juntas
Democracy	many	Ancient Athens (direct); Current U.S.A. (representative democracy)

the North Atlantic Treaty Organization (NATO) of modern times, governments have joined with others for defense and to promote trade. However, nations take their sovereignty seriously, and regional associations are often weak for this reason. In modern times, members of the **European Union** struggle to build a supranational government (transcending nations) on the basis of the earlier Common Market's economic cooperation to make Europe stronger in trade and economic competition.

RIGHTS AND RESPONSIBILITIES OF CITIZENSHIP ACROSS TIME AND SPACE

Ancient societies and kingdoms did not always perceive individuals as citizens. Today, a person becomes a citizen by virtue of birth in a country, through the citizenship status of one or both parents, or through the process of naturalization.

Citizens possess certain rights and privileges and are subject to performing certain duties. While various limits exist, in most countries a citizen has the right to

- enjoy the country's protection and its laws,
- hold and transfer all types of property,
- vote,
- seek elective office,
- hold governmental positions,
- receive welfare and social benefits, and
- be treated fairly in a legal system.

With limits, in most countries citizens have corresponding responsibilities to

- pay taxes,
- obey the laws of the nation,
- defend their nation, and
- serve jury duty.

SKILL ACTIVITY – POLITICAL SCIENCE ANALYSIS

"No happiness without liberty, no liberty without self-government, no self-government without constitutionalism, no constitutionalism without morality – and none of these great goods without stability and order."

Clinton Rossiter, introduction to *The Federalist Papers*, p. xvi (1961)

Answer the following questions based on the quotation above.

1 What does Rossiter say is the most basic function of government?	2 How do the rights and responsibilities of citizens achieve stability and order in a society?
_____	_____
_____	_____
_____	_____
_____	_____

SUMMARY

A knowledge of national history gives you a better perspective on the society in which you live. Understanding of how historians analyze facts and ideas is the beginning point. Achieving proficiency in U.S. history requires meeting standards in a broad range of the social sciences – a basic knowledge of analytical tools of historians, political scientists, economists, and geographers. These basic standards are commonly used to assess students' knowledge on history examinations. This book should help you review these standards as well as the general content of U.S. history.

PRE-COLUMBIAN CIVILIZATIONS PRE-1492
COLUMBUS' VOYAGES (1492)

1500

1600

JAMESTOWN (1607)

1625

PURITAN REVOLUTION (1648)

1650

1675

ENGLISH BILL OF RIGHTS (1689)

1700

1725

GREAT AWAKENING (1720s-1740s)

1750

FRENCH & INDIAN WAR (1754-1763)

STAMP ACT (1765)

1775

DECLARATION OF INDEPENDENCE (1776)
BATTLE OF SARATOGA (1777)
TREATY OF PARIS (1783)

1800

UNIT

1

PAGE 23

EXPLORATION & COLONIZATION OF THE AMERICAS

©1993 PhotoDisc Inc.

PRE-COLUMBIAN CIVILIZATIONS

Long before Christopher Columbus accidentally "discovered" the land of the Western Hemisphere on his journey to find an all water route to Asia, Native Americans of North and South America had already been a part of the landscape. During the pre-Columbian era (before 1492), these tribes developed diverse civilizations. Profound changes would occur with the coming of the Europeans and Africans. Relationships between these groups affected the lives and cultures of all of them.

Native Americans or **Amerindians** (earliest known inhabitants) were the first to migrate to the American continents. According to archeological finds, the first Americans migrated from the Siberian steppe in Asia about 12,000 years ago. The old theory of migration had these early American people crossing a narrow land bridge in what is now the Bering Strait. Over thousands of years, these Native American settlers slowly spread out across North America and filtered southward into Central and South America. The cold northern climate influenced southward migration. Archeological discoveries during the 1990s raise different theories. Findings in Pennsylvania and Virginia, predating 17,000 BC, suggest the migrants came by both land and sea from several regions of Asia and perhaps even from Europe.

Native Americans or American Indians are descendants of these early people. Due to the environment and other factors, they divided into hundreds of tribes with different customs, languages and dialects, and appearances. Widespread European migration to the region started after 1500 AD.

There were hundreds of pre-Columbian civilizations. Most Native American civilizations developed in isolation from the rest of the world. Not until the European Age of Discovery did some of them become known globally.

Present knowledge of the earliest Americans indicates that those who settled south of the present boundaries of the United States had more organized societies than those to the north.

After European colonization began, even the more advanced Native American civilizations disintegrated rapidly. Mexico has labored to preserve the **Mayan** and **Aztec** heritage. These people built great cities, created calendars, and constructed strong governments. They also cultivated maize (corn) which later improved the diets of millions of people outside of the Americas.

There were fewer native people north of Mexico than south, and they did not develop the same degree of civilization as those in the southern regions. The northern peoples lived in **clans** (extended families) and associated loosely in related **tribal groups**, rather than broad-based societies. Generally, these groups were hunters and gatherers and engaged in a more limited agriculture than groups to the south. They depended on food gathering – enjoying periods of feast but suffering through periods of famine.

Aztec Ruins – Tectihauacan
– ©1993 PhotoDisc Inc.

MESOAMERICAN EMPIRES: Organization & Contributions

OLMEC EMPIRE **1200 BC – 400 BC** Southern Mexico El Salvador	• formed the first truly complex Mesoamerican culture • established civic-ceremonial centers at San Lorenzo and La Venta, with temples, and palaces • built towns with clay building platforms and stone pavements and drainage systems • traded in raw materials such as jade • created large stone jade sculptures of human heads • developed rudimentary hieroglyphic writing
MAYAN EMPIRE **50 BC – 1400 AD** Southern Mexico Yucatan Guatemala Central America	• invented writing system which mixed script with ideographs and phonetics • wrote historic records on pots, stone stele (upright inscribed slabs), and palace walls • cultivated corn as staple crop • produced a complex astronomical calendar • established religious rituals which included human sacrifice, mythology, and ancestral worship • created a monarchy that united small settlements into larger states • built flat-topped pyramids as temples and rulers' tombs • built palaces, shrines, large ball courts for ceremonial sport and astronomical observatories • invented math system, including zero base
AZTEC EMPIRE **1300 AD – 1535 AD** Central Mexico	• founded island capital Tenochtitlan (modern Mexico City) • created a highly specialized, strictly hierarchal society • conquered and dominated neighbors for tribute (protection payments), not for territory • elected by nobility, ruler-emperor (tlatoani) had near god status and supreme authority • formed a powerful priestly hierarchy to administer government • produced a severe legal code of laws with judgments based on generally accepted ideas of reasonable behavior • developed a sophisticated agricultural economy, carefully adjusted to the land with crop rotation and extensive aqueduct and irrigation systems • adopted Nahuatl as a language of learning that accompanied a hieroglyphic writing system • created a 365-day solar calendar system divided into 19 months of 20 days each
INCA EMPIRE **1200 AD – 1535 AD** Andes Mountains (Peru, Ecuador parts of Chile, Bolivia, and Argentina)	• established largest empire of the Americas – at its height in the 16th century, the Inca Empire controlled 12 million people, over 100 cultures with 20 different languages • formed a strong monarchy ruled from Cuzco by using strategic resettlement of loyal "colonists" among rebellious groups • believed emperors descended from the Sun god and worshiped them as divine beings • adapted an intricate 12,000 mile road system for traveling messengers and services for traveling bureaucratic officials • created agricultural terracing and irrigation systems • adapted various "vertical climates" of the Andes' elevations for a variety of crops • built elaborate fortress cities such as Machu Picchu • developed refined spoken language (Quechua) • instituted quipu (knot-cord) record keeping system • developed a religion centered on the worship of the Sun • mined gold for use by the elite for decorative and ritual purposes

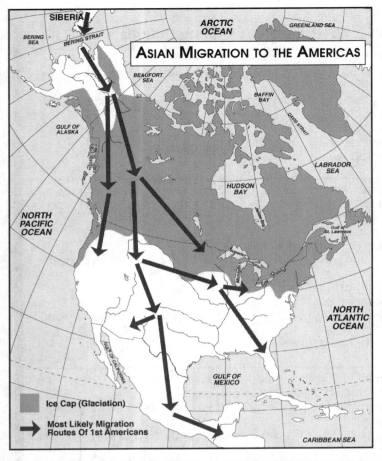

ASIAN MIGRATION TO THE AMERICAS

SIBERIA
BERING STRAIT
BERING SEA
ARCTIC OCEAN
GREENLAND SEA
BEAUFORT SEA
BAFFIN BAY
DAVIS STRAIT
GULF OF ALASKA
LABRADOR SEA
HUDSON BAY
NORTH PACIFIC OCEAN
Gulf of St. Lawrence
NORTH ATLANTIC OCEAN
GULF OF CALIFORNIA
GULF OF MEXICO
CARIBBEAN SEA

Ice Cap (Glaciation)

Most Likely Migration Routes Of 1st Americans

Even so, there was great variety among northern native tribes. They ranged from the Inuit peoples of the polar region, to the Pacific Northwest fishing cultures of the **Kwakiutl**, to the **Anasazi** and their later descendants, to the **Pueblo** people of the southwestern United States. The Anasazi irrigated their dry croplands and built distinctive dwellings. Plains people, including the **Sioux** and **Crow**, depended upon the buffalo for almost all their needs. During the hunting months, the Plains groups were nomadic and lived in tepees. For the rest of the year, they lived in villages set near rivers and streams.

Eastern woodlands Native Americans, including the **Delaware**, **Choctaw**, and **Mohawk**, established villages surrounded by cultivated fields.

In addition, eastern woodlands Native Americans hunted with bows and arrows. Skilled hands used these weapons as effectively as European muskets. A bow and arrow could be fired more rapidly than a musket. Eastern woodlands people

Anasazi, New Mexico
– ©1998 David Johnson, photographer

ANASAZI CIVILIZATION (300 AD – 1200 AD)

The Anasazi, often called the "cliff dwellers" of southwestern United States (Utah, Colorado, Arizona, and New Mexico), were known for their architectural achievements. The Anasazi built two- to three-story houses in the steep, flat top outcroppings called mesas. They used wooden poles, sandstone blocks, and mud mortar. The dwellings had many rooms for living and food storage. For protection, they often lacked doors at ground level, and the inhabitants had to use ladders to enter through the roof. By building deep inside canyons, the Anasazi allowed for air currents to cool their dwellings during the summer and provide warmth in the winter. These locations also served as protection from enemy attacks. One cliff palace had more than 200 rooms and housed over 400 people.

Scholars believe a long-term drought forced the Anasazi from the region. Present-day Pueblo tribes are their descendants. The most famous Anasazi settlements are in Mesa Verde in Colorado and Canyon de Chelly National Monument in Arizona. These are the oldest standing buildings in North America.

NORTH AMERICAN CULTURES (C 1500)

followed a pattern of division of labor more rigid than in Europe at the time. Men hunted, fished, and trapped. Women prepared the food and had primary responsibility for agriculture.

All these groups lacked technologies widely used in Europe, including the plow, the wheel, and draft animals such as horses and oxen. Native Americans' idea of land ownership differed drastically from that of the **Europeans**. The Native Americans did not understand the concept of private ownership of land. To them, the land belonged to all members of the tribe to be shared communally. Most tribes consisted of independent members joined loosely together under the leadership of a chief. Some groups did organize governments with greater authority. Examples include the **Powhatan Confederacy** in Virginia, the **Creek Confederacy** in the **Gulf Plains**, and the **Iroquois Confederacy** in upstate New York.

EUROPEAN MIGRATION TO THE AMERICAS

EARLY EXPLORATION

While there is considerable evidence that the ships of **Norse** (Viking) adventurers such as **Leif Eriksson** crossed the North Atlantic before the year 1000 AD, no Norse settlements lasted more than a few years.

Europeans moved toward global exploration as a result of the major changes occurring as they emerged from the Medieval Era. The **Christian Crusades** for possession of the Holy Lands of the Middle East, the **Renaissance**, and the **rise of nation-states** led to changes in thinking and technology that led to a period of exploration and discovery. In part, the Crusades (11th-13th C.) led to an increase in demand for spices for food preservation. Renaissance (14th-16th C.) thinking fostered a new world view and a broader scope of learning. The creation of nation-states under strong monarchs (15th-17th C.) led to increased nationalism and an interest in expanding national power.

At the same time, scientific discoveries in navigation and advances in ship design allowed sailors to venture farther from known waters. Portugal's location on the Atlantic Coast prompted it to seek an all sea route to the lucrative trade of the East. Portuguese mariners opted for a southerly route that took them around the coast of Africa. The Portuguese enjoyed a profitable gold and ivory trade with African kingdoms of **Ghana**, **Mali**, and **Songhai**. In addition, this

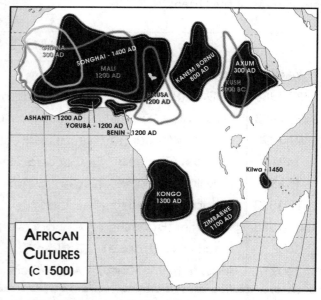

AFRICAN CULTURES (C 1500)

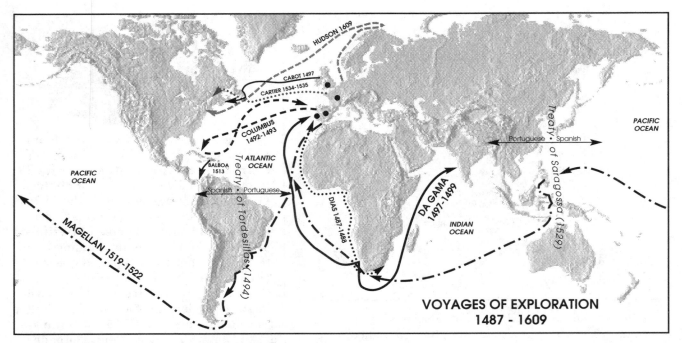

**VOYAGES OF EXPLORATION
1487 - 1609**

route avoided Muslim middlemen whose dealings decreased profits and safety.

Defeat of the Muslims and unification of Spain under monarchs **Ferdinand** and **Isabella** set the scene for competition with Portugal. Sailing under the Spanish flag, the Italian mariner **Christopher Columbus** (1451-1506) sought a different approach to the Orient. His route went westward – across the Atlantic Ocean. Many educated people had long believed that the Earth was round. Like most of them, however, Columbus greatly underestimated the circumference of the Earth, believing it was a relatively short journey westward to the rich spice areas of the Orient.

In 1492, Columbus and his crew discovered a "new world" – at least for Europeans. The region contained a wealth of natural resources. Columbus' new world included a great variety of indigenous (native) people (that he erroneously named "Indians" because he thought he was near India). Columbus never reached the mainland of North America on his four voyages. However, the voyages inspired more than a century of European exploration and colonization of the Western Hemisphere, causing dramatic changes and cultural diffusion in Europe, the Americas, and Africa.

For the native people of the Americas, European interest led to disease and death. A significant proportion of the native people died, esti-

EARLY VOYAGES OF DISCOVERY

Year	Explorer (Country)	Area
1487-1488	Dias (Portugal)	west coast of Africa, Cape of Good Hope
1492-1493	Columbus (Spain)	West Indies, Caribbean
1497-1499	Da Gama (Portugal)	east coast of Africa, India
1497	Cabot (England)	Canada, North America
1513	Balboa (Spain)	Central America, Pacific
1519-1522	Magellan (Spain)	Circumnavigates globe
1534-1535	Cartier (France)	Canada – St. Lawrence R.
1608	Champlain (France)	Eastern Canada, northern U.S.
1609	Hudson (Netherlands)	Arctic Ocean, North America

mates range as high as 90%. Most of these deaths occurred due to a lack of immunity to European viruses and germs. The chief killer was smallpox. Labor shortages in the American colonies led to the widespread development of the African slave trade. Europe and Africa acquired seeds, plants, and animals which enriched the diets of their people. The Europeans brought home crops such as potatoes and corn from the Americas. This Native American–European contact is often referred to as the **Columbian Exchange**. The provisions of the American colonies fueled the economy of Europe and changed both continents forever.

EARLY COLONIZATION

After word of Columbus' discoveries spread, many European nations grew interested in exploring the Americas. In 1494, **Pope Alexander VI** divided the newly discovered land between the Catholic monarchs of Portugal and Spain. The errors of early cartographers underpinning the provisions of the *Treaty of Tordesillas* led to Spain receiving dominion over most of the Americas with the exception of Portuguese Brazil (see map on previous page).

While the Catholic countries of Spain and France led Europe in the early explorations of the Americas, other powers joined in for more than economic reasons. The tumult of the **Protestant Reformation** (16th-17th C.) was well under way by the time England and the Netherlands commissioned explorations. The Reformation motivated some new voyages of discovery. Spreading Protestant Christianity became integrated with economic expansion among the goals of these nations.

Exploration dominated 16th century European policies. The Spanish explored and settled parts of the Americas first, but soon other European monarchs followed. England's King Henry VII sent **John Cabot** to the "new world" in 1497. The French king, Francis I, sent **Giovanni Verrazano** in 1524 and **Jacques Cartier** in 1534. The Dutch dispatched **Henry Hudson** in 1609. Rather than settlement, the first international use of North America involved long range fishing endeavors. The

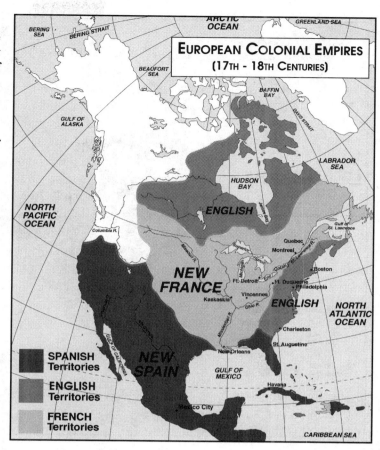

Grand Banks, teeming with fish off the Newfoundland coast (Canada), served as the first site of multinational European interest.

EUROPEAN IMPERIAL PATTERNS

By the beginning of the 17th century, Europeans developed colonial empires following several broad settlement patterns.

SPANISH SETTLEMENT

The Spanish dominated major areas of Central and South America by 1700. According to an early Aztec text, "...(the Spanish conquerors) longed and lusted for gold. Their bodies swelled with greed." The gold and silver of the Aztecs and Incas filled the treasury of Spain. Bewilderment, disease, and technology helped the Spanish defeat these centuries-old civilizations in the 1500s. Subsequently the Spanish enslaved the Aztecs and Incas. The Spanish purchased additional labor, in the form of African slaves, from Portuguese traders. Within a century, the mining boom ended and the native population was nearly destroyed. Yet, Spain dominated this area for three centuries.

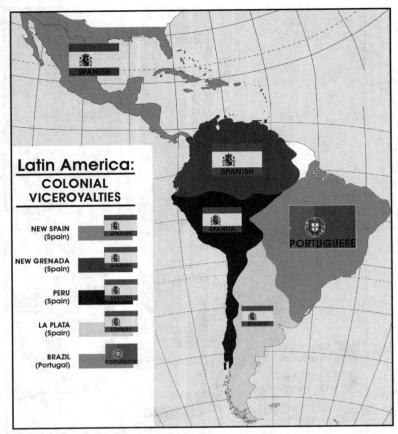

Latin America:
COLONIAL VICEROYALTIES

NEW SPAIN
(Spain)

NEW GRENADA
(Spain)

PERU
(Spain)

LA PLATA
(Spain)

BRAZIL
(Portugal)

coureurs de bois ("runners of the forest" – woodland traders and trappers) explored and settled the area around the St. Lawrence River, the Great Lakes, and the Lower Mississippi Valley area, including Louisiana. Some settled in the Caribbean islands of the French West Indies. The French did not enslave the Native Americans as had the Spanish. Rather, the French traders often served as agents between Native American trappers and European buyers.

Overall, there were few French settlers, especially in Louisiana. This is one reason for the friendliness of French-Native American relations. Most French settlers chose to go to Caribbean sugar plantations rather than to the harsher climates and rugged lands of mainland colonies.

In French North America, this resulted in a frontier environment on the mainland and a great diversity in the population. **Samuel de Champlain** (1570-1635) pioneered a series of forts in the St. Lawrence area and founded Quebec City in 1608. Catholic Jesuit missionaries, such as Father **Jacques Marquette**, carried French culture into the interior of the Great Lakes. Marquette recorded his experiences and explorations of the Mississippi (1673-1674) with mapmaker **Louis Joliet**.

Initially, Spain had little interest in the area north of Mexico. Explorations by de Soto and Coronado showed it had little mineral wealth or natives to exploit. Eventually, the Spanish settlements extended into present day New Mexico and Arizona. At **St. Augustine**, Florida in 1565, they established the first permanent European settlement in North America. Over the next two hundred years the Spanish settled in Texas and later California. But well before then, Spain's control of the world had greatly diminished.

Spreading French culture and Christianity, coureurs de bois – French trappers, traders, and missionaries explored and established outposts in the Great Lakes region and the Missouri-Mississippi river valleys.

FRENCH SETTLEMENT

The French tried to follow Spain's lead, but France did not set up permanent settlements in North America until the early 17th century. The Netherlands and Sweden did not set up their Middle Atlantic trading posts until that time either. The French experience differed greatly from the Spanish pattern of settlement. Although the French did seek gold in the north, they did not find it. Instead, their wealth came from trading in fur pelts with the Native Americans. French

French settlers, African American slaves, and American Indians created a mixed population in the lower Mississippi Valley. By 1712, **New France** (Canada) had approximately 17,000 settlers. The French built a major settlement at New Orleans in 1718.

ENGLISH SETTLEMENT

By the end of the 16th century, England's ruling **Tudor** family created a strong nation and defeated the Spanish Armada. The English accumulated an enormous amount of private wealth that funded American and other trade expeditions. Early English attempts at American colonization, such as **Sir Walter Raleigh's** Roanoke colony (North Carolina, 1587-1590) failed. Not until the first decade of the 1600s did they successfully colonize. The writings of Richard Haklyut called for English colonization to "plant religion among those infidels...enlarge the dominions of the Queen...(send) the woolen cloth of England...and (receive) commodities that we receive (now)...from Europe..." In addition, the establishment of North American colonies was proposed as a solution to England's surplus population problem.

The next phase of colonization was begun by the forerunners of today's corporations. **Joint stock companies** raised money by selling shares of stock to investors. These companies started **Jamestown** in Virginia in 1607 and **Massachusetts Bay Colony** in 1630. The crown issued **charters** (documents granting rights and privileges of ownership) to these colonies, and they became known as **charter colonies**.

Proprietary colonies began when individuals received land grants from the crown. For example in 1632, Charles I granted rights to his friend, Lord Baltimore (**Cecil Calvert**), to operate a commercial venture in Maryland. Later, Charles II, granted his brother, James Stuart, Duke of York, rights in New York (1664), and **William Penn** received a charter for Pennsylvania in 1681.

The crown took over ownership and control of most proprietary and charter colonies by the later colonial period, reorganizing them as **royal colonies**. These included eight of the original thirteen colonies.

William Penn, by Francis Place

The English came to the Atlantic colonies for a variety of reasons. Some groups and individuals came for religious freedom and some to make their fortunes. The friendly initial relations with the Native Americans soured as more settlers arrived. Disease and war took its toll on the native tribes. Yet the English colonies prospered, producing colonial wealth from tobacco, indigo, other agricultural products and naval stores.

DUTCH SETTLEMENT

Another European rival for commercial supremacy was the Netherlands. In seeking a **Northwest Passage** (all water route through North America to Asia), Henry Hudson explored the Hudson River (1609) for the Dutch East India Company and established a fur trade with the Native Americans in what is now New York State. Most of the money raised by the joint-stock company that established the New Netherlands colony came from the fur trade of the Dutch West India Company in the 1620s.

Under a land grant structure called the **patroon** system (1629-1664), the Netherlands gave enormous tracts of land to a person who transported fifty or more families to the New Netherlands colony. Few Dutch investors took advantage of this offer considering the great prosperity of Holland in the 17th century. Inadequate leadership also hurt the success of the New Netherland colony. Trading conflicts between Holland and England eventually led to the English taking control of the Dutch settlements in the 1660s. They split the New Netherland colony, renaming the sections New York and New Jersey.

1 A person studying the native groups living in North and South America before Columbus' arrival in the Caribbean in 1492 would most likely conclude that
  1 there was very little variation among the Native American tribes
  2 tribal diversity was based in part on the differences in climate and terrain
  3 Eastern woodland Indians considered themselves superior to Plains Indians
  4 the primary difference among the tribes was language

2 The "Columbian Exchange" can best be described as
  1 the enslavement or destruction of native people by Europeans
  2 a world redistribution of plants and animals
  3 the taking over of one culture by a more dominant one
  4 the use of African slave labor to meet labor shortages

3 British and Spanish colonization were similar in that both
  1 derived most of their wealth from gold mining
  2 enslaved the native populations
  3 settled families seeking religious freedom
  4 engaged in activities to enrich the mother country

Constructed Response

"There befell a great mortality among them...Their wigwams lie full of dead corpses...By this means, Christ...not only made room for his people to plant, but also tamed the hearts of these barbarous Indians."
— An early settler and historian of Puritan New England writing about the New England Indians before Puritan settlement

1 What was the author's view of the native peoples?

2 How did the Europeans' view of Native Americans affect their treatment of Native Americans during the period of exploration and colonization?

BRITISH SETTLEMENT OF THE ATLANTIC COAST

The founding and settlement of England's thirteen colonies on the middle Atlantic Coast of North America occurred in a variety of ways. **Mercantilism**, a nationalist economic policy designed to enhance the power and wealth of the mother countries, dominated all European colonization of this period.

Under mercantilism, colonies existed for the benefit of the mother country. These colonies were to supply needed raw materials and a market for finished products from the mother country. Under mercantilism, the goal of a mother country such as England was to maintain a **favorable balance of trade**. This idea meant the object of a nation's commerce with other nations was to accumulate financial wealth (gold) and not be dependent on other powers for any economic goods. To achieve this, mercantilist governments had to take an active role in supervising trade.

SETTLEMENT OF VIRGINIA

Joint stock companies funded the earliest British colonial ventures. These were enterprises with financial responsibility shared by large number of owners and run by elected directors. With a **charter** (a development license) granted by the English crown, the Virginia Company

---

BASIC MERCANTILIST PRINCIPLES

- national wealth measured in precious metals (gold and silver)
- achieve a favorable balance of trade
- acquire colonies to provide raw materials and markets
- forbid colonial manufacturing
- prohibit colonies from trading with any other country

Replicas of Colonial Ships docked
at Jamestown, Virginia   - ©1993 PhotoDisc Inc.

established Jamestown as a corporate colony in 1607. The company failed, but the Virginia colony survived. **John Rolfe**'s introduction of tobacco cultivation supplied European demand for the "noxious weed" and guaranteed the colony's success. In 1624, Virginia ceased to be a private corporate colony and became a royal colony, supervised by the government.

Virginia suffered from a labor shortage since disease cut short the life of most of its early settlers. Labor problems were partially met through the introduction of slavery (1609), and the indenture system. An indenture was a contract arrangement whereby a person was bound to work for a landholder or merchant in

exchange for passage, food, and shelter. The indenture system drew young people to settle colonial Virginia. Some individuals, primarily male, poor, and unmarried, volunteered for indentures. Others were kidnapped or deported from Europe because of indebtedness or religious dissent. After their arrival in the colonies, their contracts were sold to the highest bidders. The terms of their 4-7 year indenture were often harsh and the courts enforced the contracts.

SETTLEMENT OF MASSACHUSETTS AND NEW ENGLAND

Settlement in New England varied significantly from the commercial pattern of Virginia. Early settlement in this area involved religious freedom. In the aftermath of England's break

Puritan women working
Gallery of Masters – Trades and Industry

with the Roman Catholic Church during the Protestant Reformation, the **Pilgrims** (or Calvinist Separatists) left the **Anglican Church** (Church of England), which they saw as corrupt and hostile to their reforms. The Pilgrims felt that the Anglican Church was beyond reforming. They fled first to the Netherlands, but their supporters in England obtained a charter for them to settle in Virginia. Blown off course in 1620, they landed on Cape Cod and moved inland to establish Plymouth Colony.

Another major group of Calvinist reformers, the **Puritans**, wished to purge and purify the Anglican Church. Puritans were persecuted during the reign of Charles I (r. 1625-1649). Later, they launched a revolution which overthrew the

Replica of Mayflower at Plymouth Harbor
- ©1993 PhotoDisc Inc.

monarchy in 1649, and set up a Commonwealth government for the next 11 years under the Cromwells.

During their period of persecution under Charles I, some Puritans left England to establish a community in America. They formed the Massachusetts Bay Company and received a charter as a corporate colony. According to their governor, **John Winthrop** (1588-1649), their spiritual goal was to found "a city upon a hill." They wished this colony to be a model Christian society.

Religion had a pervasive influence over the government of the Massachusetts Bay Colony. Puritan belief in humanity's depravity due to original sin made it necessary for government to carry out the will of God. Yet, unlike the church of England in the other colonies, Puritan congregations remained separate from the state. One major exception involved taxing residents to support the churches as done in Europe. Leaders such as Winthrop and **John Cotton** (1584-1652) created a holy commonwealth that was a Puritan monopoly. They enforced discipline and adherence to Calvinistic doctrine. This idealism absorbed New England life and was promoted through the schools of the Bay Colony. They exalted hard work and perseverance. Gradually, this Puritan "work ethic" became an underpinning of the value system of America.

House of the Seven Gables, Salem, Massachusetts
– ©1993 PhotoDisc Inc.

Between 1630 and 1640, the Puritans brought 30,000 settlers in family groups to the Bay Colony. Charters created new towns. Based on the European village model, the houses clus-

ROGER WILLIAMS (1644)

INSIGHTS ON LIBERTY

"God requireth not a uniformity of religion to be enacted and enforced in any civil state; which enforced uniformity is the greatest occasion of civil war, ravishing of conscience, persecution of Christ Jesus in his servants, and of the hypocrisy and destruction of millions of souls ...To molest any person, Jew or Gentile, for either professing doctrine, or practicing worship merely religion or spiritual, it is to persecute him, and such a person (whatever his doctrine or practice be, true or false) suffereth persecution for conscience."

tered around a common village green and church, with the fields located outside of the town. The communities prospered and grew, spilling into New Hampshire and Maine. In 1636, **Thomas Hooker** (1586-1647) led a congregation into the Connecticut River Valley, creating a settlement at Hartford.

The Puritan communities were tight-knit. The members of the town worshiped together, and religious **dissidents** (nonconformists, dissenters) were not tolerated. Expulsion of some Massachusetts dissidents led to the founding of other settlements. For declaring the spiritual independence of his congregation, Massachusetts authorities banished **Roger Williams** (1603-1686). He and his followers fled to the south, founding a more tolerant colony in Rhode Island (1635), welcoming all faiths, including Jews and Quakers.

In 1638, a Massachusetts court exiled **Anne Hutchinson** (1591-1643) for questioning Calvinist doctrines. She claimed that holiness did not stem from conforming to religious laws. She argued that true grace came from inner experience. Roger Williams offered her refuge in Rhode Island. Even in that tolerant atmosphere, Hutchinson ran into conflicts over her beliefs. In 1642, she moved to the Pelham Bay area of the Dutch New Netherland colony (now, New York), where she and most of her family were killed by Native Americans the following year.

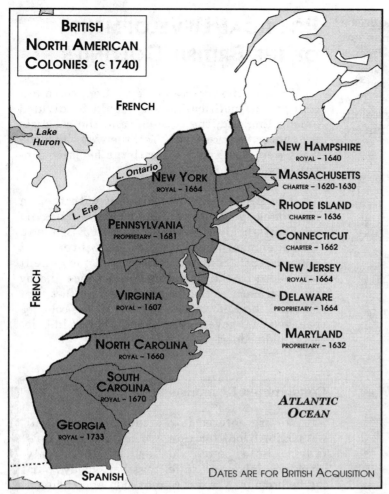

BRITISH NORTH AMERICAN COLONIES (c 1740)

FRENCH

Lake Huron

L. Ontario

L. Erie

FRENCH

NEW YORK
ROYAL – 1664

PENNSYLVANIA
PROPRIETARY – 1681

VIRGINIA
ROYAL – 1607

NORTH CAROLINA
ROYAL – 1660

SOUTH CAROLINA
ROYAL – 1670

GEORGIA
ROYAL – 1733

NEW HAMPSHIRE
ROYAL – 1640

MASSACHUSETTS
CHARTER – 1620-1630

RHODE ISLAND
CHARTER – 1636

CONNECTICUT
CHARTER – 1662

NEW JERSEY
ROYAL – 1664

DELAWARE
PROPRIETARY – 1664

MARYLAND
PROPRIETARY – 1632

ATLANTIC OCEAN

SPANISH

DATES ARE FOR BRITISH ACQUISITION

SETTLEMENT OF PROPRIETARY COLONIES

As the colonies grew and prospered, the English crown took more direct interest in colonial affairs. It granted fewer charters to joint stock company ventures. Instead, individuals or groups, known as **proprietors**, received the charters. With proprietors directly responsible to the crown, the system became similar to medieval feudalism.

In England, Quakers were free to worship, but their political rights and chances for economic advancement were restricted. Seeking a better life, some of the wealthier Quaker merchants bought land in western New Jersey in the 1670s. Repressed by the Duke of York, one of their leaders arranged for a separate grant farther west. In exchange for a debt King Charles II (r. 1660-1685) owed to his father, **William Penn** the younger (1644-1718) received a charter for land between New York and Maryland (1681).

As proprietor, the younger Penn created a "Frame of Government" which gave his **Pennsylvania** colony an elected council and an assembly with the power to legislate. Penn's government also promised complete religious freedom, and attracted German dissident groups such as the Pietists. By the early 1700s, the "Penn's Woods" colony had growing settlements of Scots-Irish Presbyterians, Catholics, and Jews.

In 1634, the second Lord Baltimore, **Cecil Calvert**, established the Maryland colony on the Chesapeake Bay land that Charles I had granted his father. Calvert's Maryland was a refuge for persecuted Catholics. Calvert tried to install a feudal manorial system. Eventually however, more Protestants settled in Maryland than Catholics. To protect the religious rights of Catholics, the Maryland assembly passed the *Act Concerning Religion* (1649). Tobacco soon became the major crop. Economically and socially, Maryland developed along lines very similar to Virginia, its Chesapeake Bay neighbor.

Farther south, colonization of the Carolinas had unique aspects as well. In 1660, when the monarchy was restored after the Puritan Revolution, King Charles II granted land to the Carolina proprietors. **North Carolina** emerged as the destination for Virginia farmers seeking free land. It developed a mixed economy based on livestock raising, foodstuff production, and processing of naval stores from the extensive pine forests.

English planters from Barbados settled coastal **South Carolina**. More exotic crops were grown in an effort to find an export base that fit into the mercantilist system. Rice, tobacco, and indigo (used for fabric dye) eventually became mainstays of the colony's economy. African slaves, first brought over from the sugar plantations of the Caribbean, became the core labor force. Thus, South Carolina began with slavery as a fully developed institution, unlike the slow start slavery got in the Chesapeake colonies.

Trouble with Spanish Florida led to the establishment of the colony of **Georgia** in 1732.

George II's advisors counseled the King to create a buffer between the prospering Carolinas and the Spanish lands. Military leader **James Oglethorpe** (1696-1785) and the other proprietors envisioned a model community for convicted English debtors to start a new life. That utopian dream faded as the prospering colony soon filled with settlers from South Carolina creating plantations and bringing in slaves.

Farther north, the commercial rivalry with the Dutch in the middle colonies led to the English taking over New Netherland in 1664. King Charles II's brother James, the Duke of York, received the land which he renamed **New York**. Trade and commercial questions concerned its diverse population more than religion or the creation of model communities. Also from the southern part of the land taken from the Dutch, the king granted to Lord Berkeley and Sir George Carteret general holdings that became the royal colony of **New Jersey**.

POLITICAL DEVELOPMENT OF THE BRITISH COLONIES

Prior to the American Revolution, the question of how political power should be divided among England, the colonies, and the colonists was never fully resolved. Yet, the way the questions were dealt with set patterns for later generations.

The British colonists brought with them a formidable political heritage that drew heavily on English civil experience and European Enlightenment liberalism. The **Enlightenment** was an 18th century intellectual movement influenced by the rise of modern science and by the aftermath of the long religious conflict that followed the Reformation. People in the colonies believed that government should protect life, liberty, and property.

MINI•ASSESSMENT (1-2)

1 The settlement of South Carolina differed from that of the other British colonies in that
   1 it was the only proprietary colony in the South
   2 its white population was very ethnically diverse
   3 slavery came to the colony as an accepted institution
   4 most English settlers chose to go there

2 In what ways were the settlers of New England most different from those of the Southern colonies?
   1 desire for religious freedom
   2 use of indentured servants
   3 tolerance of dissenters
   4 importance of agriculture

3 The significance of Maryland's *1649 Toleration Act* was its attempt to
   1 allow fair treatment of the Native Americans
   2 grant all Christians freedom of religion
   3 provide for a government based on "consent of the governed"
   4 settle differences between the French and British settlers

Constructed Response

"We are entered into a covenant [contract] with Him [God] for this work...[The Puritans must]...hold each other in brotherly affection...labor and suffer together, always having before our eyes our commission and common work, our community as members of the same body...[If this occurs]...The Lord will make our name a praise and glory, so that men shall say of succeeding plantations: "The Lord make it like that of New England." For we must consider that we shall be like a City upon a Hill; the eyes of all people are on us."

– John Winthrop, *A Model of Christian Charity*, 1630

1 According to the Puritan contract described by Winthrop, what did the Puritans owe each other?

2 If they fulfilled the terms of the contract, what could the Puritans expect?

Examples of European influence included:

- Even before the Enlightenment, the British started to put limits on absolutism with the *Magna Carta* of 1215.

- The principles of **common law** became the basis for the colonial legal system in the British colonies and the United States today. Common law draws from precedents established in earlier and similar court cases.

- The *English Bill of Rights* (1689), passed during the Glorious Revolution, limited the power of the British monarchy and established the supremacy of Parliament.

From this traditional background, there emerged a strong conviction that government should protect the rights of the individual. Many colonists had fled political persecution and resented abusive governmental power. In the free frontier wilderness, with England three thousand miles away, colonists disdained governmental authority.

The Enlightenment political philosophies of **John Locke** and French *philosophes* such as **Jean Jacques Rousseau** strengthened desires for self-government. The British kings were wary of the free environment of the colonies, and many independent charter and proprietary

colonies were reclaimed by the crown as royal colonies as the 18th century progressed.

By the American Revolution (1775-1783), eight of the thirteen original colonies were royal colonies. Within the general pattern of colonial government, great variations existed. Specific colonies or groups of colonies adapted British tradition and institutions to fit their experiences in this new land.

Governor's Palace, Williamsburg, Virginia
– ©1999 Paul Stich, photographer

- Virginia's legislature, the **House of Burgesses**, was established in 1619. Two officials representing each Virginia settlement formed the first representative body in Britain's North American colonies. This body governed local matters and made the laws for the colony.

	ROYAL	PROPRIETARY	CHARTER
GENERAL PATTERNS OF COLONIAL POLITICAL POWER			
Ownership & Power	• Crown owned land • Monarch & Parliament ruled through royal governors • All colonial laws need British Privy Council approval	• Land granted by monarch to an individual or group • Proprietors ruled through appointed governors • All colonial laws need Privy Council approval	• Land granted by monarch to a company • People's power specified in a charter
Executive Branch	• Governors appointed by monarch • Governor must approve every legislative act	• Proprietors appointed governors • Governor must approve every legislative act	• Governor elected by the colonists • Governor could veto colonial laws
Legislative Branch	• Bicameral • Upper house appointed by monarch • Lower house elected by colonists	• Bicameral • Upper house appointed by legislature • Lower house elected by colonists	• Bicameral • Both houses elected by the colonists
Judicial Branch	Court systems in all the colonies followed the British model. Generally this branch was of lesser importance than the other two.		

Plymouth Rock Memorial, Massachusetts
– ©1995 PhotoDisc, Inc.

The colonial period established important democratic principles for the later United States. These included written constitutions, popularly elected assemblies, separation of powers, guaranteed rights of the people, and the "power of the purse" (ability of locally elected legislatures to raise revenue through taxation of constituents). Colonial assemblies approved local tax policies. This kept local tax control in the hands of the colonists' representatives, rather than appointed officials. This lesson was not lost on the framers of the *Constitution of the United States* who mandated that all national revenue policies must originate in the U.S. House of Representatives.

- The Pilgrims' *Mayflower Compact* (1620) resulted from being blown off course. To overcome problems by being outside the boundaries of the land given to them by the Virginia Company, most of the Pilgrim men aboard the *Mayflower* signed an agreement to make "... just and equal laws for the general good of the colony." While not a constitution (written framework of government), it did establish the people as the source of political power.

Even in colonial times, the concern of Americans over freedom of the press was evident. In 1733, a New York newspaper editor, **John Peter Zenger**, was arrested for printing articles critical of the Royal Governor of New York. Under existing British law, Zenger, criticism had been an act of libel, even if the charges turned out to be true. A New York jury acquitted Zenger. The jurors had concluded that the charges were true and libel could not have occurred, regardless of the British legal code.

- The *Fundamental Orders of Connecticut* (1639) comprised the first written constitution in the colonies. It granted all Connecticut men the right to vote, not just church members. It provided for judges and the governor to be elected annually.

Not all aspects of colonial government were democratic. Only in Rhode Island and Connecticut did colonists elect their governors. In most colonies, the British monarchs claimed the power to review and veto any colonial laws. Voting rights were limited, too. Many colonies had religious qualifications for voting. All colonies had property qualifications to vote.

- **New England town meetings** began in Massachusetts Bay. Puritan leaders gave ownership of new towns to a group of freemen. While not all men could vote, all could take part in the meeting. Free discussion of public matters became common practice in New England. Those who owned property and belonged to the established church could vote for town officials, colonial assemblymen, and local matters.

- **County** or **parish** governments became more important in the Southern colonies. A sparse population spread out over a large area called for a different method of organization than New England's town model. Colonial governors appointed county officials and the colonists selected the burgesses for larger areas.

FUNDAMENTAL ORDERS OF CONNECTICUT – 1639

INSIGHTS ON LIBERTY

"It is decreed that the election of magistrates shall be in this manner: every person present and qualified for choice shall bring in one single paper with the name of him written in it whom he desires to have governor, and he that hath the greatest number of papers shall be governor for that year ... It is ordered ... that no person be chosen governor above once in two years, and that the governor be always a member of some approved congregation."

Distance from the polls and proving property claims made voting difficult for frontier settlers.

While under British rule before the American Revolution, there was little success in trying to unite the colonies. In 1754, concern over French colonial policies led Benjamin Franklin to draft a "plan of union" for the British colonies. Neither Britain nor the colonies supported the scheme. The **Albany Plan of Union** failed. Rivalry between the colonies and geographic isolation contributed to its failure.

ECONOMIC DEVELOPMENT OF THE COLONIES

BRITISH MERCANTILE POLICY

Mercantilism was the basic economic framework for Britain's Atlantic colonies. The early adventurers and proprietors were supposed to uncover new sources of the elusive gold and silver to fill Britain's coffers. As the colonies developed, they supplied raw materials and staple crops to Britain. In return, the colonies bought goods produced in Britain. Theoretically, this mercantile system worked to the advantage of both the colonies and the mother country. However, in Britain's eyes, it was more important to keep the mother country independent and able to accumulate wealth.

Weak enforcement of mercantile regulation and lack of clear direction for British economic policy prior to the end of the **French and Indian War** in 1763 left the colonies with a great deal of economic independence. Reasons for Britain's "benign neglect" or "salutary neglect" (lax attention) included distance, struggles between king and Parliament (which eventually led to an English civil war), and politically appointed customs agents who were both inept and corrupt. As early as 1650, the British were trying to regulate

---

MINI•ASSESSMENT (1-3)

1 The chief institution of New England local government was the
   1 town meeting
   2 county government
   3 House of Burgesses
   4 Albany Plan of Union

2 New England colonies and Southern colonies differed politically because
   1 only New England colonies had requirements for voting
   2 the population distribution pattern differed
   3 New England colonies were under more British control
   4 religion was more important in the Southern colonies

3 Which of the following was a democratic aspect of the colonial governments?
   1 colonial governors' taxing power
   2 voting for all ethnic groups
   3 unwritten constitutions
   4 belief in the rights of Englishmen

Constructed Response

"The rise of representative assemblies [lower houses of the colonial legislatures] was perhaps the most significant political and constitutional development in the history of Britain's overseas empire before the American Revolution. [The king and the proprietary owners of colonies] had obviously intended the governor [to be the most powerful]...But...[after] the Glorious Revolution, the lower houses [began to successfully] restrict the authority of the executive, [and] undermine the system of colonial administration laid down by imperial and proprietary authorities..."
   – Jack P. Greene, *The Role of the Lower Houses of Assembly in Eighteenth Century Politics*, 1961

1 What change in power occurred in the American colonies after the Glorious Revolution?

2 Why would the lower houses of the colonial legislatures challenging the governors be considered a democratic aspect of colonial government?

3 What critical power did colonial legislatures possess?

IMPERIAL STRUGGLES IN NORTH AMERICA

YEARS	WAR	RESULTS
1652-54, 1664	Anglo-Dutch Wars	Arguments involved control of trade; British took New Amsterdam (NY, NJ)
1689-1697	King William's War	No major territorial changes
1702-1713	Queen Anne's War	British made major territorial gains in Hudson Bay and Nova Scotia
1739-1748	King George's War	French fortress of Louisbourg captured but returned to French for British gains in India
1756-1763	French and Indian War	British gained control of Canada and land west to Mississippi River; French left North America (temporarily)

American trade more carefully. Parliament passed a series of **Navigation Acts** that

- banned foreign shipping from the colonies,
- forbade the colonies from exporting certain "enumerated goods" to anywhere but England, and
- routed all European and Asiatic trade with the colonies through England.

At first rigidly enforced, the *Navigation Acts* cut down on colonial smuggling, but allowed British merchants to accumulate sizeable fortunes. Not everyone benefited from these acts. New England shipbuilders prospered, but Chesapeake tobacco growers suffered from depressed prices.

As time went by, the system's enforcement weakened. Colonists paid little attention to the later acts such as the *Molasses Act* (1733) which restricted rum distillers, and the *Iron Act* (1750)

which prohibited colonial manufacturing so as not to compete directly with British producers.

These policies partly caused England to fight a number of wars between 1689 and 1763 to determine which European nation would control North America. Combatants included Spain, France, and France's Native American allies.

DIFFERENT ECONOMIC REGIONS DEVELOP

Although joined together within Britain's colonial framework, the Atlantic colonies developed along different economic lines. Differences in geography including climate, terrain, and population patterns contributed significantly to somewhat unequal development.

In the South, single crop export plantation agriculture dominated. The plantations included more than the main house (initially little more

REGIONAL COMPARISONS IN BRITISH ATLANTIC COLONIES

NEW ENGLAND COLONIES	MIDDLE COLONIES	SOUTHERN COLONIES
• rugged terrain • rocky soil • irregular coastline containing numerous harbors • abundant fishing • abundant forest land for shipbuilding and lumbering Eventually led to emphasis on shipping and trading, including the famed triangular trade.	• fertile soil • temperate climate • harbors Production of abundant foodstuffs, including grains such as barley and wheat, led to the label "Bread Colonies."	• fertile soil • abundant, navigable rivers • wide coastal plain • warm, semi-tropical climate Conditions led to the development of the plantation system based on slave labor and export of single staple crops.

than a shack) and the fields. They bustled with activity producing virtually everything that its inhabitants needed. These included a laundry, smoke house, kitchen, and buildings to house the plantation artisans, usually slaves. This type of economic development, unknown in England, flourished first in the Caribbean colonies, especially with sugar cane.

On the American mainland, the warmer, humid climate allowed for tobacco cultivation in the Chesapeake colonies, with rice and indigo in South Carolina and Georgia.

Upland back country settlers in the South relied less on the Atlantic trade than the coastal planters. Many Germans and Scots-Irish settled in the frontier areas.

Family farms dominated the North. Land ownership was more widespread than in the South. This partly resulted in a smaller gap between rich and poor than in Europe or the South. Generally fifty-acres became the normal size of a family farm in many areas. They grew a wider variety of crops than a typical plantation. Exports from the middle colonies included corn, wheat, beef, and pork.

Although less than 5% of the colonial population lived in towns and cities, coastal towns were at the center of the commercial and intellectual life of the colonies. The major ones, Boston, New York, Philadelphia, and (to a lesser extent) Baltimore and Charleston provided direct commercial links with England. The merchants reigned in these seaport towns. In a time before banks, the merchants linked producers and consumers. Among other economic activities, merchants extended credit, built ships, and traded goods.

SELECTED ESTIMATED URBAN POPULATION (JUST PRIOR TO THE REVOLUTION)	
CITY	POPULATION
Philadelphia	28,000
New York City	22,000
Boston	16,000
Charleston	11,000
Baltimore	6,000

THE QUESTION OF LABOR

By the end of the 1600s, the overall population growth rate in the English Atlantic Coast colonies of North America was greater than in any other area of the world. The death rate slowed after the early years of malnutrition and deadly diseases (especially malaria and typhoid fever). Yet, while the death rate was lower in America than in England, it was not enough to solve the labor shortage in some sparsely populated colonies.

Although slave and indentured labor was used in every colony, New England did not have the severe labor shortage problems experienced in the South. New England's settlement pattern – families in a town setting and the development of shipping and trading – created less demand for labor than in the Southern colonies.

Early Virginia depended heavily on the labor of indentured servants to ensure the success of the colony. These poor individuals signed contracts to work for terms of four to seven years in return for their passage. Many indentured servants died before their contracts expired, especially in the early years of colonization.

Throughout the colonies, indentured servants who survived eventually acquired land on the frontier and pushed American settlement westward. Conflicts later occurred between the former indentured servant farmers of the inland areas and the Chesapeake planters. Those on the frontier believed that the Chesapeake planters controlled the government and were reluctant to give them protection or political power. **Nathaniel Bacon** of Virginia led one such rebellion in 1676 for expansion of rights for the lower classes.

Following a similar pattern, poor immigrants from Germany and Switzerland agreed to sell their labor to gain passage. Ships' captains marketed their services upon arrival to the colonies. These people were called **redemptioners**. Together, such colonial bonded servants totalled more than half of all white immigration.

The introduction of **slavery** provided another response to the shortage of labor. Initially, the European colonists were unsuccessful at enslaving the native populations. Differences in culture and knowledge of the area made Native American slavery unsuccessful. However, African slavery increased throughout the colonial period.

In 1619, the first known Africans sent to Virginia were sold as indentured servants. However, by 1640 slavery-for-life became the norm for most Africans forced to migrate to the Americas. Of the estimated 9 to 12 million Africans imported to the Americas over 350 years, only 4.5% entered Britain's 13 Atlantic Coast colonies. Most were shipped to Caribbean plantations and Brazil.

After enduring horrid conditions connected with the transatlantic voyage – often referred to as "the middle passage" – individuals worked in every colony, but the larger numbers provided labor for Southern plantations. Many West Africans brought with them valuable knowledge of the cultivation of rice and indigo. Despite the repression and brutality connected with slavery, the slaves developed a culture which mixed

JOHN WOOLMAN ON SLAVERY – 1754

INSIGHTS ON LIBERTY

"Placing men on the ignominious Title, Slave, dressing them in uncomely Garments, keeping them to servile Labour, in which they are often dirty, tends to gradually fix a notion in the mind, that they are a sort of people below us in Nature..."

African, European, and American elements.

Opposition to slavery arose early in the colonial era. Pennsylvania Quakers, such as **John Woolman** (*Some Considerations on the Keeping of Negroes*, 1754), organized against it on moral grounds. Even as the slave trade peaked in the 1770s, the Enlightenment concept of equality challenged slavery. Infrequent slave rebellions, such as the **Nat Turner Uprising** (Virginia, 1831), met with little success. More common and disruptive slave resistance included work slow-downs and temporarily running away.

MINI•ASSESSMENT (1-4)

1   During the early decades of English settlement, the labor force on most plantations consisted of
   1   African slaves
   2   Native American slaves
   3   indentured servants
   4   wage labor

2   Opposition to African slavery
   1   grew most in the South
   2   grew because it was economically unprofitable
   3   resulted in many successful American slave rebellions
   4   developed along with the institution of slavery

3   The relative importance of the Caribbean colonies as compared to the North American British colonies within the mercantilist system could *best* be determined by analyzing
   1   migration and settlement patterns
   2   the number of slaves in each area
   3   the political system each area set up
   4   the amount of exports and imports to each area

Constructed Response

DESTINATION OF AFRICAN SLAVES 1526-1810
Source: Curtin, *The Atlantic Slave Trade*

British North America	427,000
Mexico & Central America	224,000
West Indies	4,040,000
Spanish America	746,000
Portuguese America	3,647,000

1   Geographically, which Western Hemisphere area received the greatest number of slaves?

2   How did the numbers of African slaves brought to the British North American colonies compare to other Western Hemisphere destinations?

SOCIAL DEVELOPMENT OF THE COLONIES

Although influenced by Europe, the 13 British Atlantic Coast colonies acquired a distinctive American culture. Certain social developments reflected a gradual transformation in cultural patterns and traits.

POPULATION EXPANSION

By the time of the American Revolution (1775), the population of the thirteen colonies approximated 2.7 million people. Just 130 years earlier, the non-Native American population stood at 27,000. A number of factors accounted for that change including a high birth rate, comparatively low death rate, continued migration, and the founding of new settlements by diverse European groups.

RELIGION AND EDUCATION

Out of the upheaval of the Protestant Reformation in Europe, many religious groups came to America seeking freedom from religious persecution. As noted earlier, little religious tolerance existed at the beginnings of the colonial period, especially in Massachusetts. Later, colonies provided broader religious freedom, especially Rhode Island and Pennsylvania.

Christianity was central to the beliefs of most European settlers. Puritans especially considered reading of the Bible essential to their religious salvation. Thus, religious groups often created schools for children. As a result, early New England education stressed reading. The present public school system has its roots in a Massachusetts law of 1647 requiring every town of fifty families to establish a school. The children who attended paid tuition. The South had few schools. Planters employed private tutors to teach their children. Generally, Africans, and Native Americans did not attend schools, but some reading filtered into their lives through churches and missionaries. Overall, American literacy was high compared to Europe.

Early colonies established colleges to train clergy of various denominations. These early colleges included Harvard (Boston, 1636) and Yale (New Haven, 1701). Anglican Virginia plantation families established the College of William and Mary (Williamsburg, 1693) to broaden the education of sons unable to go to England.

THE AMERICAN MIND

Two major events lifted colonial American thinking out of strictly European channels – the Great Awakening and the Enlightenment.

The **Great Awakening** consisted of a number of Calvinist religious revivals that swept across the colonies between the 1720s and 1740s. Certain evangelical ministers believed that religion was on the decline. Leaders included **William** and **Gilbert Tennent** among Pennsylvania's Presbyterians, **Theodorus Frelinghuysen** among the Dutch Reformed churches in New Jersey, and **Jonathan Edwards** (1703-1758) among Massachusetts' Congregational churches. They promoted religious revivals to rekindle the faith they saw waning as life became more settled. Emotional sermons threatened sinners with burning in hell if they did not repent.

George Whitefield (1714-1770), the touring British preacher was seen by thousands of people at what were later called "camp meetings" in the late 1730s. Many attendees were common folk who felt that the established clergy and churches did not meet their needs.

In the aftermath of the Great Awakening new Protestant churches were founded by British missionaries. They were **evangelical** groups such as Baptists and Methodists; they stressed renewed interest in the gospels, ardent personal conversion, and living a zealous life by faith. These new groups established new schools to train ministers. Some schools evolved into prestigious colleges such as Rutgers, Brown, Dartmouth, and Princeton universities. The revivalist movement also intensified the Christianizing of African Americans and Native Americans. This religious conversion did not include an end to slavery or any measure of equality in the 1700s. Still, African American congregations and ministers deepened the sense of community and promoted awareness of suppression among slaves.

The Great Awakening did not strengthen moral and religious fervor as its leaders intended. Instead, doctrinal controversies deeply split parishes and congregations and new sects formed, diluting the strength of older churches. However, the Awakening gave birth to even greater religious diversity, and in the process, broadened tolerance.

As the rigidity of theological influences diminished, the more open spirit of scientific questioning of the European Enlightenment broadened American intellectual life. The new laws of science proclaimed by English physicist **Sir Isaac Newton** (1643-1727) dispelled many medieval myths and opened new avenues of experimentation and learning.

The Enlightenment also influenced political thought immensely. In *Two Treatises of Government* (1690) English philosopher John Locke (1632-1704) established the concepts of natural laws and rights that made sense in the less restrictive atmosphere of the American colonies. Locke's theories paved the way for the American Revolution itself. Born in England's Glorious Revolution (1688), Locke's idea was that a repressed people could righteously overthrow an unjust monarch. The idea was openly embraced by colonial assemblies struggling with autocratic governors.

Locke's ideas, coupled with the ideas of French *philosophe* Jean-Jacques Rousseau (gov-

ernment as a social contract) strengthened resourceful Americans' belief in the rational capability of humans to solve their own problems. New experiences in America encouraged resourcefulness and experimentation, influencing the colonies' emerging political leadership. **Benjamin Franklin** is considered the most notable American Enlightenment figure. An inventor, philosopher, publisher, and statesman, Franklin sang the praises of intellectual freedom throughout the later colonial era that ushered in the tumult of the American Revolution.

SOCIAL STRUCTURE

Compared to Europe, America was a land of fluid economic and social opportunity. Slavery was a notable exception. No one was born a slave in England. Hereditary class distinctions based on the European model did not take root in the American colonies, but a distinct social structure emerged nonetheless.

- A wealthy, influential aristocracy developed. Southern planters, large landowners, and Northern merchants numbered in its ranks.

- The majority of the population were **yeomen** (small independent farmers), skilled artisans, shopkeepers and laborers.

- American women enjoyed broader property rights than their European counterparts, especially in the North. However, women had secondary status to men.

- At the bottom of the social ladder were slaves and Native Americans.

MINI•ASSESSMENT (1-5)

1   Which statement best applies to colonial education?
    1   Free, public education was widely available throughout the colonies.
    2   Colonial education was valued little, especially in New England.
    3   Colonial education was generally left to religious groups or private tutors, rather than the government.
    4   Colonial education, following the European model, provided for a series of schools based on heredity and wealth.

2   The concept that the universe is based on certain scientific laws which govern behavior and can be learned is part of
    1   the Enlightenment
    2   religious revivalism
    3   Puritan belief
    4   mercantilism

3   Literacy was high in the colonies because
    1   free, public education was available
    2   most colonists lived in urban areas
    3   education followed the English model
    4   Protestant beliefs required Bible reading

Constructed Response

"The colonies grew fast in the 1700s. English settlers were joined by Scotch-Irish and German immigrants. Black slaves were pouring in; they were 8 percent of the population in 1690; 21 percent in 1770. The population of the colonies was 250,000 in 1700; 1,600,000 by 1760. Agriculture was growing. Small manufacturing was developing. Shipping and trading were expanding. The big cities – Boston, New York, Philadelphia, Charleston – were doubling and tripling in size...Through all that growth, the upper class was getting most of the benefits and monopolized political power."

– Howard Zinn, *A People's History of the United States 1492-Present*, 1995

1   What changes were occurring in British-American colonies from 1700-1770?

2   What impact would these changes have on the diversity of the colonies?

3   What is Zinn's point of view regarding the significance of these changes?

COLONIAL DISCONTENT AND REVOLUTION (1763-1781)

CHANGES IN COLONIAL RELATIONS
THE FRENCH AND INDIAN WAR

Warfare among the major European powers spilled into North America during the 18th century. In **King George's War** (1744-1748), colonists battled the French at Louisbourg in Nova Scotia. Later from 1754-1763, the **French and Indian War** (known in Europe as the Seven Years' War) had momentous impact upon colonial America. Victory over the French gave the British a vastly enlarged empire in North America. The end of the French and Indian War also saw a shift in the relationship between Britain and its American colonies. This changed attitude resulted in a series of events leading up to revolution and independence a decade later.

During the French and Indian War, colonists fought with British troops and, in many instances, against Native Americans allied to the French. Opposing armies met in Western Pennsylvania, Western and Northern New York, and Eastern Canada. In 1755, British General **Edward Braddock** suffered a major defeat at Fort Duquesne (present-day Pittsburgh). Other failures followed, but by 1758, Britain avenged its losses. The British returned and defeated the French at Fort Duquesne.

Quebec fell to the British in 1759, and Montreal the next year. By 1763, the War was over, and France lost nearly all its colonies in North America. Large parts of Canada and the Mississippi region came under British control. With Florida also temporarily under British control, all lands east of the Mississippi, and much of Canada, became part of the British Empire.

To strengthen defenses during the War, some British and colonial officials attempted to unify the colonies at the Albany Congress in 1754. With seven colonies represented, some delegates discussed the need for a continental legislature and an executive. However, the independent colonial assemblies had little enthusiasm for the plan, and nothing came of it.

NEW REGULATIONS IMPOSED ON THE COLONIES

The cost of the War, combined with administering the new colonial areas, was a large financial burden for Britain. Residents of England already bore a large tax burden, and the national debt increased each year. Some members of Parliament demanded that the colonists pay a greater share of the costs. Parliamentary leaders decided that revenue could be raised through new taxes and stricter enforcement of existing trade laws.

Most British ministers and members of Parliament held the view that colonists should be subordinate to Parliament. They believed that the colonists had to conform to the will of the British government. This included laws of navigation, trade, and taxation.

Yet for many years, elected colonial legislatures controlled most of the internal affairs of the colonies. They rarely looked to London to solve problems. Now, after many years of "salutary neglect," colonists resented taking orders from Parliament and the King. This was especially true concerning taxation. The British began a series of actions which gradually increased tensions between the colonists and the mother country.

COLONIAL RESISTANCE TO THE NEW REGULATIONS

As in any protest, the main obstacle facing the American colonists was their lack of unity. Rarely had they ever cooperated on anything. Though in many instances, cultures and ways were similar among the thirteen colonies, numerous differences existed. Opposition to the new British taxes and regulations brought about unprecedented unity among the colonies.

ORGANIZED PROTESTS

Colonists swiftly organized to oppose the *Stamp Act.* **Patrick Henry** (1736-1799) passionately convinced the Virginia House of Burgesses to denounce Parliament's power to impose the tax. Similar declarations by other colonial legislatures followed.

In 1764, Boston lawyer James Otis moved the Massachusetts General Court (the colonial

ROAD TO REVOLUTION – ACTIONS AND REACTIONS OF THE 1760S

PARLIAMENTARY ACT	PURPOSE	COLONIAL REACTION
Navigation Acts (18th century)	Act forced colonists to trade with Britain and its possessions. Parliament imposed **customs duties** (tariffs) to enforce the regulations.	Colonists engaged in widespread smuggling, importing foreign items, and bribing colonial officials.
Writs of Assistance – 1760	Parliament provided British officials with Writs of Assistance – general search warrants – to find smuggled goods. Officials searched colonial homes and businesses, even if no probable cause for suspect activity was present.	Attempts by Massachusetts colonists to convince the British to halt the random searches failed. For the first time, the British took enforcement of trade regulations seriously.
Proclamation of 1763	Uprisings led by the Native American leader Pontiac made life on the frontier dangerous and deadly. To diminish the cost of frontier defense, British Finance Minister George Grenville issued a proclamation that banned white settlement west of the Appalachian Mountains.	Colonists (land speculators and farmers) defied the order, and continued westward.
Sugar Act – 1764	Grenville cut the duty on sugar in half to take the incentive out of bribing customs officers. British naval vessels strictly enforced the new regulations in and around American waters. Violators were to be tried in vice-admiralty courts, instead of civil courts with local juries.	Colonists continued smuggling sugar and molasses to make rum.
Stamp Act – 1765	For the first time, Parliament imposed an "internal tax" – a tax on goods bought and sold within the colonies. The tax required colonists to purchase specially stamped paper for documents, licenses, papers, pamphlets, almanacs, and playing cards. Once again, vice-admiralty courts were to try any violators.	Mobs destroyed the houses of those who were to sell and supervise distribution of stamps. Riots and threats of mob violence spread to other colonies. Stamp Act Congress issued a declaration of grievances.
Quartering Act – 1765	At the end of the French and Indian War, the British kept a standing army in America to minimize conflicts between colonists and Native Americans. To defray the military cost, Parliament forced colonists to provide certain supplies, rations, and shelter for the troops.	Samuel Adams and others wrote protests against the tyranny of a standing army in peacetime.
Townshend Acts – 1767	Parliament imposed new import taxes on glass, lead, paint, paper, and tea, and a Board of Customs Commissioners in Boston for enforcement and levying fines.	Colonists pressured merchants to halt importation of British goods.

legislature) to write to other colonies urging opposition to the *Sugar Act*. Massachusetts also became the hotbed of protest against the 1765 *Stamp Act* tax. The groups who led the protests began calling themselves the **Sons of Liberty** – the loose organization became popular and spread throughout the colonies.

A **Stamp Act Congress** met in New York City in October of 1765. It issued a *Declaration of Rights and Grievances*, stating that colonists could only be taxed by their elective representatives, the colonial legislatures. The Stamp Act Congress condemned the use of British admiralty courts, and called for repeal of both the *Stamp Act* and the *Sugar Act*. By the time distribution of stamps was to begin on November 1st, all stamp tax agents had resigned or fled. For a brief period, widespread confusion existed in the colonies, as no stamped paper was available. By the start of 1766 however, most business conducted by royal officials returned to normal, without any tax collected.

Some members of Parliament saw the tax as a mistake. Parliament repealed the tax in 1766, but simultaneously passed the ***Declaratory Act***. This act stated that Parliament reserved the right to make all laws in the colonies, tax and otherwise.

BOYCOTTS AND NON-IMPORTATION

To force repeal of the *Stamp Act*, colonial merchants joined together and boycotted those items with stamps. Such action threatened the livelihood of British businessmen who traded with American colonists, and they protested to Parliament.

In response to the *Townshend Acts of 1767*, protesters pressured merchants to halt importation of British goods. The Sons of Liberty and other leaders organized a propaganda campaign to convince people to give up these imports. They urged patriotic Americans to make their own clothes rather than buying them from England. Most colonial assemblies supported non-importation. Trade with Britain eventually fell by at least one third.

LEADERS ARISE

A small but influential number of colonists began to express their ideas about the difficulties with Britain in writing. Lawyer **John Dickinson** (1732-1808) wrote ***Letters from a Farmer in Pennsylvania***, which most newspapers printed. Dickinson said that Parliament had no right to tax commerce if the sole intent was to raise revenue.

In 1768, **John Hancock** (1737-1793), a prominent Boston merchant had a shipload of wine seized by customs officials. Crowds gathered in a quiet protest. Hancock became a wealthy backer of the Sons of Liberty and an outspoken critic of Parliamentary action to suppress trade.

The *Townshend Acts* moved **Samuel Adams** (1722-1803), a Boston brewer-merchant and Sons of Liberty agitator, to renew the "Committees of Correspondence" network. Adams authored a letter to other colonial legislatures condemning taxation without representation. In the *Journal of the Times*, Adams aroused the citizens of Boston with stories (often exaggerated) of abuse committed by British troops and customs officers.

Colonials Protest – Colonial Woodcut

PENNSYLVANIA FARMER'S LETTER

INSIGHTS ON LIBERTY

"I hope, my dear countrymen, that you will, in every colony, be upon your guard against those who may at any time endeavour to stir you up, under pretenses of patriotism, to any measures of disrespectful to our Sovereign and our mother country. Hot, rash, disorderly proceedings, injure the reputation of a people, as to wisdom, valor and virtue, without procuring them the least benefit... We cannot act with too much caution in our disputes. Anger produces anger; and differences, that might be accommodated by king and respectful behavior, may, by imprudence, be enlarged to an incurable rage... If, however, it shall happen, by an unfortunate course of affairs, that our applications to his Majesty and the parliament for redress, prove ineffectual, let us then take another step, by withholding from Great Britain all the advantages she has been used to receive from us..."

– John Dickinson, *Letters from a Farmer in Pennsylvania,* 1767.

For all the reactions in the colonies, it was again the merchants in England who altered the situation. They complained to Parliament that the colonial protests threatened them with financial ruin. In 1770, Parliament repealed most of the duties imposed by the *Townshend Acts*. Only a small tax on tea remained. Animosity between most of the colonies and Britain temporarily declined.

MINI • ASSESSMENT (1-6)

1 The French and Indian War changed the relationship between Britain and the colonists because Parliament
   1 gave direct representation to the colonists in America
   2 for the first time encouraged American settlement in the western lands
   3 voted for new colonial taxes and stricter enforcement of laws
   4 allowed the colonists to decide all revenue matters for themselves

2 The purpose of the *Navigation Acts* was to protect
   1 New England merchants
   2 economic interests of the British Empire
   3 colonial trade with the West Indies
   4 the slave trade between England and the colonies

3 Colonists hoped that boycotts and non-importation would be effective by
   1 teaching colonists to make their own cloths
   2 raising additional revenue for the colonies
   3 pressuring Parliament through British merchants
   4 increasing the amount of money available in America

Constructed Response

Event A: June 1767: *Townshend Revenue Act* is passed by Parliament.

Event B: August 1768: Merchants in Boston and New York sign non-importation agreements.

Event C: (graph below)

Value of Imports from Britain by New York

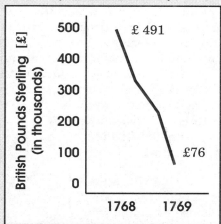

1 What happened to the value of imports from Britain to New York between 1768 and 1769?

2 How did the actions in *Events A* and *B* cause the result in *Event C*?

Boston Massacre - Colonial Woodcut

MOVING TOWARD WAR (1770-1775)

BOSTON MASSACRE

Inspired by John Dickinson's *Letters from a Farmer in Pennsylvania* and Sam Adams' *Journal of the Times,* colonial legislatures vehemently protested British policies. Customs commissioners felt increasingly threatened by hostile crowds in Boston, stirred up by Adams and the Sons of Liberty. In response, Britain sent troops to Boston in 1768 to protect its officials. Bostonians saw this as a threat to civil liberties. They associated standing armies with tyranny.

On 5 March 1770, a disturbance outside the Boston customs house escalated into a violent confrontation between colonists and British soldiers. The hostile crowd threw garbage, rocks, and snowballs at the troops.

After attempts to restrain the crowd failed, the troops fired back, killing five colonists. The soldiers sus-
pected of firing were brought to trial. A jury found them not guilty of murder. The damage, however, had been done. Sam Adams wrote extensively to the other colonies, propagandizing the incident as a "massacre."

COMMITTEES OF CORRESPONDENCE

In 1772, the British ship *Gaspee* ran aground while enforcing trade laws off Rhode Island. Colonists, angry at the way laws were enforced, boarded and burned the stranded schooner. British authorities failed to find the guilty parties, but their announced plan to send any suspects to England for trial would have violated the basic rights and liberties of colonists.

Though no one ever stood trial, colonists felt threatened by the possibility of being sent to England. The Massachusetts and Virginia legislatures wrote to each other about their concerns. Other colonial assemblies informally reorganized the Committees of Correspondence that they used during the *Stamp Act* controversy. The purpose of these new committees was to communicate with other colonies about threats to liberty.

BOSTON TEA PARTY

After Parliament repealed the *Townshend Acts* in 1770, only a small duty remained on tea, an important colonial import. In 1773, Parliament passed the *Tea Act* to allow the

Boston Tea Party - Colonial Woodcut

British East India Tea Company to sell surplus tea directly to the colonists. For tea drinking colonists, this eliminated middlemen and lowered the price of tea, but it hurt the business of colonial merchants who normally sold tea. Merchants like Boston's John Hancock organized the colonists and turned back ships with tea on them.

In Boston, Lt. Governor Thomas Hutchinson wanted the law enforced. He refused to let ships leave Boston without unloading the tea. One night in December, 1773, a group of colonists disguised as Native Americans boarded the tea-bearing ships and dumped the cargo overboard in protest. This illegal Boston "Tea Party" infuriated British authorities.

Independence Hall,
Philadelphia, Pennsylvania
© Wildside Press

THE INTOLERABLE ACTS

In response to the Bostonians' act, British Prime Minister Lord North urged Parliament to pass the *Boston Port Bill*. This act closed Boston Harbor until colonists paid for the tea. A new *Quartering Act* extended the right of troops to demand housing on private property. Another act gave new powers to the governor and limited the number of town meetings. Together, the colonists called these acts the "**Intolerable Acts**" or the "**Coercive Acts**."

Another separate Parliamentary move in 1774, the *Quebec Act*, extended the boundaries of the British province of Quebec to the Ohio River and limited self-government in the area. The *Quebec Act* also allowed continuance of French law and protected Catholic Church properties. Once again, British colonists saw this as a threat to their liberties.

Boston quickly alerted other colonies to the harsh action. Volunteer militias of **Minutemen** began forming in towns and villages. Several assemblies called for a general congress of colonies to discuss the British actions and a response.

THE FIRST CONTINENTAL CONGRESS – SEPTEMBER 1774

Representatives from twelve of the thirteen colonies met at Philadelphia in the Fall of 1774. (The royal governor of Georgia deftly blocked sending delegates.) Most delegates to this **First Continental Congress** still hoped for reconciliation with Great Britain. Though unhappy with Parliament, they were basically loyal to England. Still, a majority decided to support the Bostonians and urged repeal of the *Intolerable Acts* by passing the ***Declaration of Rights and Grievances***. In it, the Congress demanded that colonists have the rights to assemble and petition, to be tried by one's peers, and to be free of a standing army. The Declaration also stated that Parliament could not tax the colonies except to regulate external commerce. Congress sent a separate letter to King George stating its view that Parliament, not he, was the problem.

The First Continental Congress then organized a boycott of British goods. Members urged colonists to form committees to enforce the non-importation, non-consumption, and non-exportation agreements of British goods. They hoped that British merchants, suffering from such a boycott, would pressure Parliament to alter its pattern of coercion. Congressional delegates agreed to a second meeting in May 1775 to re-evaluate the situation.

OUTBREAK OF FIGHTING – 1775

The British commander in Massachusetts, General **Thomas Gage**, was ordered to arrest the leading troublemakers of the colony. With little hope of catching them, he attempted to seize military weapons the colonists had hidden at Concord.

On 19 April 1775 after some brief encounters with the colonists at Lexington, the British moved onto Concord, but found few weapons. Enraged colonists mistakenly thought the British were burning the town. Angry Minutemen arrived on the scene and harassed the British on their sixteen mile march back to Boston. The British lost 273 men to enemy fire.

Over the next several weeks, a growing number of armed colonists surrounded the British army in Boston. At the same time, **Ethan Allen** (1738-1789) captured Fort Ticonderoga on Lake Champlain on 10 May 1775. Many of the cannons captured at the Fort were transported through the mountains to Boston to help with the siege.

In June, the British defeated the colonists at the **Battle of Bunker Hill** (actually, Breed's Hill) in Boston. However, it was a costly victory. British casualties numbered more than one thousand.

General Washington Takes Command

THE SECOND CONTINENTAL CONGRESS – MAY 1775

The delegates to the Second Continental Congress (this time with all colonies represented) gathered at Philadelphia three weeks after the outbreak of fighting at Concord. Though they composed a petition to the King seeking peace, most realized the need to prepare for war.

The Continental Congress took control of the army surrounding Boston. The unanimous selection as Commander-in-Chief was Virginian **George Washington** (1732-1799). Attempts were made to keep Native Americans neutral during the conflict. The Congress also urged the individual colonies to designate Committees of Safety to supervise security and defense.

COMMON SENSE FROM TOM PAINE

INSIGHTS ON LIBERTY

"As much has been said of the advantages of reconciliation, which, like an agreeable dream, has passed away and left us as we were, it is but right that we should examine the contrary side of the argument, and inquire into some of the many material injuries which these colonies sustain, and always will sustain, by being connected with and dependent on Great Britain.

"I challenge the warmest advocate for reconciliation to show a single advantage that his continent can reap by being connected with Great Britain. I repeat the challenge; not a single advantage is derived. Our corn will fetch its price in any market in Europe, and our imported goods must be paid for, buy them where we will.

"But the injuries and disadvantages which we sustain by the connection, are without number; and our duty to mankind at large, as well as to ourselves, instruct us to renounce the alliance...

"A government of our own is our natural right: and when a man seriously reflects on the precariousness of human affairs, he will become convinced, that it is infinitely wiser and safer, to form a Constitution of our own in a cool deliberate manner, while we have it in our power, than to trust such an interesting event to time and chance."

– Thomas Paine, *Common Sense*, 1776

THE DECLARATION OF INDEPENDENCE

Even after fighting began, there was a reluctance to blame the King for colonial troubles. Most continued to condemn Parliament for their difficulties. The publication of the pamphlet *Common Sense*, by **Thomas Paine**, altered this view. In simple language, Paine condemned monarchies, saying they had no right to rule others. He urged that an independent America be established.

At the Second Continental Congress, **John Adams** (MA) and **Richard Lee** (VA) called for a complete break with England. Though some still hoped for compromise with Britain, support for independence grew. Congress urged the individual colonies to form their own governments. Members of Congress wanted a written statement to rally the people. Adams joined Pennsylvania's Benjamin Franklin, **Thomas Jefferson** (VA), **Robert Livingston** (NY), and **Roger Sherman** (CT) in composing one. Jefferson did most of the writing.

Rendition of the signing of the *Declaration of Independence*
© Wildside Press

SOURCES USED BY JEFFERSON

The earlier Enlightenment thinkers of Europe provided Thomas Jefferson with many of the ideas used in the ***Declaration of Independence***. Most influential were the ideas of 17th century British philosopher John Locke. He had applied the theory of natural reason to justify Parliamentary leaders unseating James II and bringing William and Mary to the England's throne in the Glorious Revolution (1688). Locke stated that people have natural rights to life, liberty, and property, and that people can remove a government from power if it fails to protect these rights.

Jefferson was also influenced by other important government documents and practices. These included: the *Magna Carta*, English common law, the *English Bill of Rights*, the *Mayflower Compact*, and the Virginia House of Burgesses.

THREE MAIN PARTS

The *Declaration of Independence* did not set up a framework for a new government. Its basic philosophy on government, however, reflected

---

THE UNANIMOUS DECLARATION OF THE THIRTEEN UNITED STATES OF AMERICA

GROWTH OF DEMOCRACY

"When in the course of human events, it becomes necessary for one people to dissolve the political bonds which have connected them with another, and to assume, among the powers of the earth, the separate and equal station to which the laws of nature and nature's God entitle them, a decent respect to the opinions of mankind requires that they should declare the causes which impel them to the separation. ---- We hold these truths to be self-evident, that all men are created equal; that they are endowed by their Creator with certain unalienable rights; that among these are life, liberty, and the pursuit of happiness. ---- That, to secure these rights, governments are instituted among men, deriving their just powers from the consent of the governed; ---- That, whenever any form of government becomes destructive to these ends, it is the right of the people to alter or to abolish it, and to institute a new government, laying its foundation on such principles, and organizing its powers in such form, as to them shall seem most likely to effect their safety and happiness. ..."

– Thomas Jefferson, *Declaration of Independence*, 1776

---

later designs for the American government, including the Constitution. Three parts of the Declaration are

- a proclamation of democratic ideals, embodying the natural rights ideas of John Locke,

- a statement of grievances against King George III of England, and

- a concluding statement declaring the break with Britain.

Congress made several changes in Jefferson's original document. On 4 July 1776, Congress formally approved the document. The Declaration was signed by fifty six members of the Continental Congress on 2 August 1776. (full text on pages 364 to 366)

THE AMERICAN REVOLUTION MILITARY ASPECTS

AMERICAN ADVANTAGES AND DISADVANTAGES

In rebelling against the world's foremost power, the American colonists took on a nearly impossible task. Britain's population was nearly four times that of the colonies' 2.5 million (some of whom were Loyalists and others slaves). Britain's army was formidable, having fought the Seven Years' War in Europe. Its wealth also allowed it to supplement its veteran forces with German mercenaries. Britain also ruled the oceans. No European power could equal its prowess.

MINI•ASSESSMENT (1-7)

1 Which British action helped bring about the Boston Tea Party?
1 doubling the tax on tea sent to the colonies
2 giving the East India Company a monopoly to distribute tea in America
3 cutting the amount of tea sent to the colonies by half
4 placing colonial governors in charge of the tea distribution system

2 Through his pamphlet *Common Sense*, Thomas Paine urged Americans to
1 compromise with the British Parliament concerning taxes
2 rid themselves of monarchy rule
3 ask King George to appoint new ministers
4 petition Parliament for the right to elect colonial governors

3 In writing the *Declaration of Independence*, Thomas Jefferson based his argument for American independence on the idea that
1 people have natural rights as human beings
2 the British refused to import colonial raw materials
3 monarchy was evil by nature
4 Britain was too far away to rule the colonies effectively

Constructed Response

"...That whenever any Form of Government becomes destructive of these ends, it is the Right of the People to alter or to abolish it, and to institute a new Government ... Prudence, indeed, will dictate that Governments long established should not be changed for light and transient causes....But when a long train of abuses and usurpations ... evinces a design to reduce them under absolute Despotism, it is their right, it is their duty, to throw off such Government and to provide new Guards for their future security."

– Thomas Jefferson, *Declaration of Independence*, 1776

1 Under what circumstances does Thomas Jefferson justify the overthrow of a government?

2 What were some of the British actions in the years before the *Declaration of Independence* that justified the "throwing off" of the British government in America?

(Look at a complete copy of the *Declaration of Independence* for the list of abuses itemized by Jefferson, page 364)

Yet, the American rebels had some advantages. Although they had little in the way of funds, and depended on individual states to support their army, the Americans fought on familiar territory. With over 90% of the population rural, British capture of most cities meant little. Over time, the Americans hoped to wear the British down through fighting in the vast poorly-mapped countryside. Early in the war, American forces under General Richard Montgomery and Benedict Arnold invaded Canada but failed to convince the Canadians to join the American cause.

George Washington constantly struggled to keep his army together. Short enlistment periods made it impossible to have a unified fighting force for any length of time. Food, supplies, weapons and powder were always in short supply. Congress paid troops in nearly worthless Continental currency. Raw, undisciplined militia made the job more difficult.

Marquis de Lafayette

Despite these difficulties, the Americans under Washington succeeded in wearing down the British. Washington relied on the assistance of military figures from Europe. The **Marquis de Lafayette** (1757-1834) from France and **Baron von Steuben** (1730-1794) from Germany led and trained American troops.

France was eager to see its imperial rival suffer defeat. France sent large quantities of supplies, and eventually thousands of troops.

BRITISH ADVANTAGES AND DISADVANTAGES

The British had superior weapons, battle seasoned officers, and extensive training. They had a long established, unified government, as opposed to the cautious, struggling Continental Congress.

The British navy overwhelmed the tiny American fleet. American naval commanders such as Captains **John Barry** (1745-1803) and **John Paul Jones** (1747-1792) primarily succeeded in harassing British shipping and raiding ports. The British land forces were aided by 30,000 Hessian (German) mercenary soldiers.

However, the vast distance from England and unfamiliar territory hampered the effectiveness of the war effort. British commanders were often indecisive and careless in moving forces and in battle. Americans also used backwoods guerrilla tactics and knowledge of the terrain to surprise their enemy. The British were more used to open-field engagements. Even in defeat, most of the Continental army usually escaped and avoided capture.

MAJOR BATTLES

In 1776, the British evacuated Boston and invaded New York. They pushed Washington out of Brooklyn and White Plains. The Continental Army retreated into New Jersey and Pennsylvania. Washington gained a singular victory when he surprised Hessian troops with a Christmas night assault on Trenton (NJ).

In early 1777, Washington defeated the British at Princeton (NJ) but failed to stop British General Howe from taking Philadelphia that spring. In October, a three-prong attack by the Americans at Saratoga (NY) on a British col-

Washington Crossing the Delaware River
Arms, Armor & Battles – © Wildside Press

umn marching south from Canada proved to be a decisive victory. The surrender of British General John Burgoyne's army thwarted an attempt to cut New England off from the rest of the country. Saratoga also proved to the French that the Americans could win. In Paris, Benjamin Franklin and Silas Dean were able to negotiate an alliance to aid the Americans with funds and armed forces.

The British took many Southern coastal towns with little difficulty. Savannah (GA) and Charleston (SC) fell to British sea power. However, in 1781, Washington marched his Continental Army south and combined with a powerful land and sea force supplied by the French. He trapped the main British army under General **Cornwallis** at Yorktown (VA), and forced a surrender.

POLITICAL ASPECTS

AMERICA DIVIDED – PATRIOTS AND LOYALISTS

Not all residents of the colonies supported the Revolution. Apathy affected part of the population. Others, known as **Loyalists** or **Tories**,

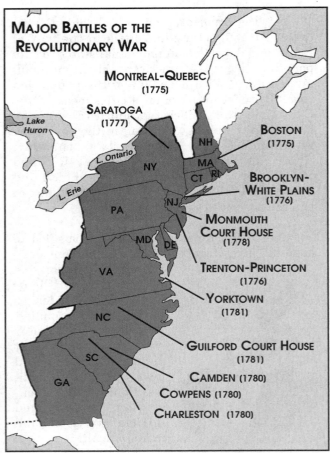

MAJOR BATTLES OF THE REVOLUTIONARY WAR

MONTREAL-QUEBEC (1775)
SARATOGA (1777)
Lake Huron
L. Ontario
L. Erie
NH
MA
CT RI
NY
NJ
PA
MD DE
VA
NC
SC
GA
BOSTON (1775)
BROOKLYN-WHITE PLAINS (1776)
MONMOUTH COURT HOUSE (1778)
TRENTON-PRINCETON (1776)
YORKTOWN (1781)
GUILFORD COURT HOUSE (1781)
CAMDEN (1780)
COWPENS (1780)
CHARLESTON (1780)

Washington at Yorktown
©Wildside Battles

pledged loyalty to King George. They opposed the Revolution. Some of the Middle colonies, especially New York, were centers of Loyalist activity. An estimated 19,000 fought on the side of the British.

Families divided over the question of independence. Often, Loyalists faced the hostility of Patriot colonists, sometimes being forced out of the community. Patriots confiscated vast amounts of Loyalist property during the Revolution. In the end, nearly 100,000 Loyalists fled to Canada, the West Indies, or back to Britain.

FOREIGN HELP FOR THE AMERICANS

Eighteenth century Britain had numerous enemies in Europe. France was especially bitter after being humiliated in the Seven Years' War a decade earlier. American leaders sought military and economic help from these nations. At first, France expressed reluctance toward becoming involved in a colonial dispute, and it provided secret aid. However, by 1777, the French believed that war with England was inevitable. Helping America now would distract the British from a war in Europe. The French did not want to support a losing proposition, however, and wanted proof that America could win.

This proof came in the fall of 1777 when the the Americans forced the surrender of a large British army at Saratoga. Any hope of a quick British victory ended. American representatives in France, led by Benjamin Franklin, negotiated the *Treaty of Alliance* in which the French government formally recognized American independence.

In the *Treaty of Alliance*, France promised to fight Britain until American independence was won. Also, a peace treaty had to be agreeable to both parties. In return, the Americans agreed to come to the aid of France in future wars with Britain. This last provision caused difficulty in Franco-American relations in the 1790s. Britain declared war on France as a result of the alliance. Spain later joined the War to aid France, but aside from a few small loans, never committed any military force to the Americans' cause.

DEFEAT OF GREAT BRITAIN

Partly because of mediocre British commanders, military efforts in America proved more and more difficult. Foreign aid in the form of French money, equipment, and troops (Spain and Holland provided some money, also) strengthened America's resolve and ability to wage war. French naval forces battled Britain where the Americans could not. In England, public support for the War declined over time.

In the West, **George Rogers Clark** captured a number of British forts. American victories in the area also helped quiet Native Americans, who often sided with the British.

The tiny American navy under daring commanders such as Jones and Barry, combined with privateers, disrupted British merchant shipping. British ship owners lost huge sums. The Americans posed little threat to the regular British navy, however.

In 1781, combined American-French forces trapped the main British army at Yorktown (VA). Though fighting continued into the next year, Cornwallis' surrender was the major defeat that caused the British government to lose the desire to continue fighting. Britain agreed to American independence, and peace treaty negotiations started.

AN INDEPENDENT NATION

Independence did not signal an end to America's difficulties. Though fighting ended, a formal peace treaty had to be signed. Benjamin Franklin, John Adams, and **John Jay** (1745-1829) represented the new nation in Paris. Congress instructed the negotiators to consult with the French before they concluded any agreement. However, the American representatives distrusted the French, and they made an agreement with Britain without consultation with the French.

The **Treaty of Paris**, signed in 1783, gave America most of its demands. Besides recognition by Britain, the western boundary was set at the Mississippi River. Americans also secured fishing rights off the Canadian coast. The British agreed to remove all troops from American soil. In return, America promised that attempts would be made to restore Loyalist property. The new nation also agreed not to interfere with Britons who attempted to collect debts owed by Americans.

SUMMARY

THE COLONIAL EXPERIENCE

Nearly two hundred years under British colonial rule greatly influenced America. While Britain's thirteen colonies on the Atlantic seaboard evolved from diverse circumstances, the hybrid British culture created more similarities than differences.

The new nation's written laws, elected legislatures, and separation of government power among the branches reflected common Anglo-Saxon traditions. While royal governors and the British Crown exerted powerful vetoes on colonial legislatures, the new nation's government checked that kind of power. Property and religious qualifications restricted those who could vote, slavery still existed, and there was no expansion of rights for women. The diversity of colonial religion voided out the power of any one church. Property ownership did grow when the states seized and auctioned lands belonging to fleeing Loyalists, but most of that land was bought by the wealthier groups in the new society.

The new American nation, born of revolution, turned to making independence work. It could apply to that problem an experience built on almost two hundred years of sociopolitical evolution and experimentation.

MINI•ASSESSMENT (1-8)

1 An American advantage in the Revolutionary War was
1 naval superiority
2 better trained officers and troops
3 fighting on familiar soil
4 a stable currency

2 Historians call the Battle of Saratoga a turning point in the War because
1 Parliament refused to send any more troops to the colonies after this battle
2 it showed the British could successfully fight the Americans in the wilderness
3 it convinced the French to openly aid the Americans
4 it was the first major American naval victory of the war

3 The *Treaty of Paris* (1783) set the western boundary of the United States at the
1 Appalachian Mountains
2 Mississippi River
3 Ohio River
4 Continental Divide

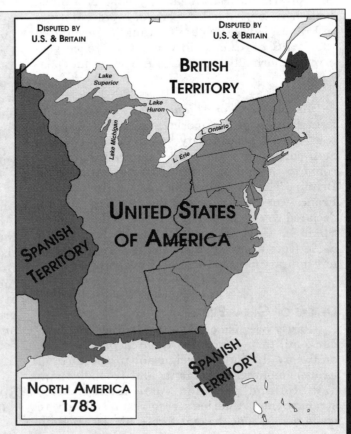

DISPUTED BY U.S. & BRITAIN

DISPUTED BY U.S. & BRITAIN

BRITISH TERRITORY

Lake Superior

Lake Huron

Lake Michigan

L. Ontario

L. Erie

UNITED STATES OF AMERICA

SPANISH TERRITORY

SPANISH TERRITORY

NORTH AMERICA 1783

Constructed Response

1 The map above shows the borders of the United States in 1783. Insert the following labels on the map:

Atlantic Ocean
Mississippi River
Florida
Canada

2 How does the map indicate why Americans were still concerned over European threats even after 1783?

UNIT ASSESSMENT

MULTI-CHOICE QUESTIONS

1 An example of colonial American economic development during the 18th century is
  1 tremendous development of inland cities west of the Appalachian Mountains
  2 decreasing use of slave labor
  3 development of coastal cities
  4 greater emphasis on agriculture in New England's economy

2 Colonial women were generally
  1 better educated than men
  2 employed in the home
  3 able to vote and hold office
  4 employed as ministers and church deacons

Base your answer to question 3 on the the map below and your knowledge of social studies

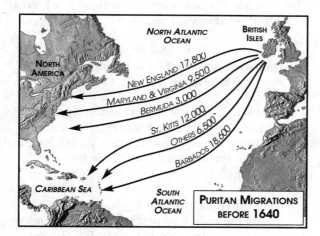

PURITAN MIGRATIONS BEFORE 1640

3 The migration pattern illustrated in this map seems to support the generalization that
  1 there were more Puritans in Virginia than in New England
  2 no immigrants to New England came from Africa
  3 the Caribbean was a major destination for English immigrants
  4 a greater number of Puritans fled to Holland than the Americas

4 The *Mayflower Compact* and the *Fundamental Orders of Connecticut* are both similar in that they
  1 are written constitutions
  2 allowed universal suffrage
  3 guaranteed the rights of men
  4 believed in the consent of the governed

5 Due to factors such as Britain's distance from North America, British domestic concerns, and continued war with other European countries, British control of the American colonies
  1 did not develop under a strong and centralized plan
  2 had little long term effect on United States political development
  3 was extremely tight and effective from the 1600s
  4 changed little during the colonial period

6 Historian Mechal Sobel entitled her work *The World They Made Together: Black & White Values in 18th Century Virginia.* The most likely focus of her book is
  1 the equality given white and African women in Virginia
  2 the effects of African and Euro-American culture on each other
  3 a description of the coming of the American Revolution
  4 a defense of the institution of slavery

7 An important difference between French and English colonization of North America in the 17th century was that
  1 the French discovered more mineral wealth
  2 the French settled all along the Atlantic Coast
  3 lesser number of French led to easier relations with the natives
  4 the English defeated the Spanish for control of New England

8 The *Proclamation of 1763* had the greatest impact on those who lived
  1 in New England
  2 right on the Atlantic Coast
  3 near the Appalachian Mountains
  4 next to the Canadian border

9 One of the results of the end of the French and Indian War in 1763 was
1 the British were deeply in debt and needed to raise more money
2 the removal of the French from North America led to removal of British troops from the colonies
3 British officials gave the Americans more responsibility in running their own affairs
4 the French strengthened their control over Canada

10 Which statement best explains French involvement during the American Revolution?
1 They believed the American colonists were about to lose the War after Saratoga.
2 The beliefs of the French Revolution supported those of the American Revolution.
3 The English were their historic enemy.
4 They planned to regain territory in North America.

11 Which is an important reason that the American colonists rebelled against England in the 1770s?
1 The colonists desired the right to control the basic aspects of their economy.
2 An overwhelming majority of the colonists favored rebellion.
3 England did not adequately protect America from attack by other European nations.
4 England had reduced the number of colonial representatives in Parliament.

12 The writs of assistance permitted colonial authorities to
1 punish suspects without trials
2 search homes of suspected violators
3 levy fines against suspected smugglers
4 send suspects back to Great Britain for trial

13 In the post-1763 era, Britain sought new revenue sources from the colonies in order to
1 expand its Empire in Asia
2 pay for the enormous costs of war
3 build new factories in Great Britain
4 increase the size and strength of its merchant fleet

14 The *Stamp Act* tax differed from earlier taxes imposed on the colonies because
1 the tax affected only wealthy individuals
2 the tax was an internal tax placed on colonists' everyday activities
3 with a valid stamp, trade with France was permitted
4 the colonists had voted for this tax themselves

15 Charles Townshend attempted to create a fund to pay royal officials in the colonies in order to
1 get officials with higher qualifications to apply
2 increase the amount of money in circulation in the colonies
3 lessen the influence of Parliament in the colonies
4 reduce the power colonial legislatures had over some officials

Base your answers to questions 16 to 18 on the Speaker's statements below and your knowledge of social studies

Speakers A, B, C, and *D* are discussing relations between Great Britain and the American colonies in early 1776.

Speaker A: Let me say quite simply that making laws is not a basic right of the colonies. We are a part of the British Empire and should obey the laws made by Parliament.

Speaker B: Let us first try to have our wrongs set right by just and peaceful means – by boycotting British goods, for example – before we take a step so extreme as to fight our mother country.

Speaker C: A government of our own is our natural right, and it is better to form one now, when we have the power, than to wait until we may have such a chance again.

Speaker D: Let us behave like obedient children, who have received unjust blows from a beloved parent. Let us complain to our parent, but with words, not guns.

16 Which two speakers disagree most with each other about colonial relations with Great Britain?
   1 A and B
   2 A and C
   3 B and D
   4 B and C

17 Which two speakers would have been most opposed to the *Declaration of Independence* when it was issued?
   1 A and C
   2 A and D
   3 B and C
   4 C and D

18 What does this discussion indicate about the colonies in the mid 1770s?
   1 The British Empire had resolved most of its problems concerning colonial resistance.
   2 Most colonists supported the idea of revolution.
   3 The colonists believed they had been granted full rights as British citizens.
   4 Conservatives, moderates, and radicals competed for power in the colonies.

19 A result of the Boston Tea Party was
   1 the Boston Massacre
   2 repeal of all tea taxes
   3 repeal of the Townshend duties
   4 passage of the Intolerable Acts

20 Which feature of government was developed most fully during the colonial era?
   1 separation of church and state
   2 an independent court system
   3 universal suffrage
   4 representative assemblies

21 In the *Declaration of Independence*, Thomas Jefferson said the people
   1 should obey all laws made by legislative bodies
   2 have the right to overthrow tyrannical government
   3 if uneducated, are not ready for self-government
   4 should overthrow any government with which they are unhappy

22 Which heading for the outline below would fit most appropriately in the blank space?

I. _____
   A Stamp Act Congress
   B Committees of Correspondence
   C Boston Tea Party
   D Declaration of Rights and Grievances

   1 British Attempts to Unify the Colonies
   2 Colonial Support of King George
   3 French Interference in Colonial America
   4 Colonial Responses to British Attempts at Control

23 "These are the times that try men's souls. The summer soldier and the sunshine patriot will, in this crisis, shrink from the service of their country…"

   Which attitude is best reflected in this quotation?
   1 neutrality
   2 nationalism
   3 colonialism
   4 imperialism

24 In which pair is the second event or development a direct result of the first?
   1 British surrender at Saratoga – signing of a treaty of alliance with France
   2 *Intolerable Acts* – Boston Massacre
   3 Battles of Lexington and Concord – Boston Tea Party
   4 British surrender at Yorktown – Publication of *Common Sense*

25 The colonial and revolutionary experience made the new nation very distrustful of
   1 legislative bodies
   2 state militias
   3 monarchies
   4 foreign military leaders

THEMATIC ESSAY

Theme:

> **The road to independence**
>   Actions undertaken by Great Britain during the colonial period caused increasing
>   concern in the American colonies, especially after 1760. The protests against these
>   actions eventually led to the American Revolution.

Task:

> Using your knowledge of United States history and government, write an essay in which you
> select *three* specific controversial actions taken by the British government toward the
> American colonies after 1760. For *each* action
>
> - identify the action taken by Great Britain,
> - explain why the American colonists were upset by the action, and
> - describe what the American colonists did in response to the British action.

Suggestions:

You may use any controversial action from your study of U.S. history and government within the
specified time period. Some suggestions you might wish to consider include: the writs of
assistance, the *Proclamation of 1763*, the *Stamp Tax*, the *Townshend Acts*, the *Tea Act*, or the
Intolerable Acts. **You are not limited to these suggestions.**

_____

DOCUMENT BASED QUESTION

The following task is based on the accompanying documents. The documents may have been
edited for the purposes of this exercise. This task is designed to test your ability to work with
historical documents. As you analyze the documents, take into account both the source of the
document and the author's point of view.

Directions:

Read the documents in Part A and answer the question after each document. Then read the
directions for Part B and write your essay.

Historical Context:

The United States is one nation composed of many states. It is a representative democracy, with
people who cherish their freedom. The development of these ideals can be traced to colonial
history.

Task:

Using the information from the documents and your knowledge of United States history and
government, write an essay in which you

- describe the difficulties of unifying colonial Americans, and
- discuss the concerns of colonial Americans on democracy and freedom.

PART A - SHORT ANSWER

Analyze the documents and answer the questions that follow each document.

Questions for Document 1

1 What is democratic about this selection process?

2 What were some of the restrictions imposed on the office of governor?

DOCUMENT 1

"It is decreed that the election of magistrates shall be in this manner: every person present and qualified for choice shall bring in one single paper with the name of him written on it whom he desires to have governor, and that he that has the greatest number of papers shall be governor for that year... It is ordered...that no person be chosen governor above once in two years, and that the governor be always a member of [an] approved congregation [church group]."

– *Fundamental Orders of Connecticut* (1639)

Question for Document 2

What are Williams' views on religious liberty?

DOCUMENT 2

"God requireth not a uniformity of religion to be enacted and enforced in any civil state; which enforced uniformity is the greatest occasion of civil war, ravishing of conscience, persecution of Jesus Christ in his servants, and of hypocrisy and destruction of millions of souls... To molest any person, Jew or Gentile, for either professing doctrine, or practicing worship merely religion or spiritual, it is to persecute him, and such a person (whatever his doctrine or practice be, true or false) suffereth persecution for conscience."

– Roger Williams (1644)

Question for Document 3

Why were there differences in the numbers of representatives?

DOCUMENT 3 – ALBANY PLAN OF UNION, 1754

COLONY	EST. POPULATION IN 1750	REPRESENTATIVES
Massachusetts	188,000	7
New Hampshire	28,000	2
Connecticut	110,000	5
Rhode Island	33,000	2
New York	77,000	4
New Jersey	71,000	3
Pennsylvania	120,000	6
Maryland	141,000	4
Virginia	231,000	7
North Carolina	73,000	4
South Carolina	64,000	4

Question for Document 4

According to the resolution, what right of Englishmen was being violated by the British?

DOCUMENT 4

"...it is inseparably essential to the freedom of a people and the undoubted rights of Englishmen, that no taxes be imposed on them but with their own consent, given personally or by their representatives."

– Resolution of the *Stamp Act* Congress (1765)

Question for Document 5

Why does Dr. Church want all the colonies to set up Committees of Correspondence?

Question for Document 6

This 1754 illustration was used again in 1776. What does it say about colonial unity in 1776?

DOCUMENT 6

JOIN or DIE

GO ON TO PART B

Part B - Essay

Directions:
- Write a well organized essay that includes an introduction, several paragraphs, and a conclusion.
- Use evidence from the documents to support your response.
- Do not simply repeat the contents of the documents.
- Include specific related outside information.

Historical Context:
The United States is one nation composed of many states. It is a representative democracy, with people who cherish their freedom. The development of these concepts – unity, democracy, and freedom – can be found in the days of colonial history.

Task:
Using the information from the documents and your knowledge of United States history and government, write an essay in which you

- describe the difficulties of unifying colonial Americans, and
- discuss the concerns of colonial Americans on democracy and freedom.

Be sure to include specific historical details. You must also include additional information from your knowledge of United States history and government.

CONSTITUTIONAL FOUNDATIONS

1650 **ENLIGHTENMENT** (1640-1740)
    LOCKE
    MONTESQUIEU
    ROUSSEAU

1675

ENGLISH BILL OF RIGHTS (1689)

1700

1725

1750

ALBANY PLAN OF UNION (1754)

1775

AMERICAN REVOLUTION (1775-1783)

ARTICLES OF CONFEDERATION (1781-1789)

CONSTITUTION OF THE U.S. (1789)

WASHINGTON AS PRESIDENT (1789-1797)

BILL OF RIGHTS (1791)

1800

Independence Hall,
Philadelphia, PA
– ©1993 PhotoDisc Inc.

FORGING A NEW NATION

The United States was the first nation in modern times to have a government designed and run according to democratic principles. Those principles came from many earlier democratic traditions. America's colonial experience altered some of these traditions, and the experiences of the young nation changed others.

THE ARTICLES OF CONFEDERATION 1781-1789

Even in the midst of a war against British authority, the rebelling colonists knew they needed a new government responsive to the people. Starting in 1776, colonial assemblies converted themselves into state governments and replaced colonial charters with written constitutions.

Constitutional historians believe the idea of habitual (frequent and regular) elections in the new states flowed from John Locke's concept of "right of revolution." In theory, allowing the people to regularly cast ballots provides opportunity to express satisfaction or dissatisfaction with governmental performance. Most states broadened participation by changing property requirements for voting.

Every state except Pennsylvania kept the bicameral legislatures (two chambers) of their colonial past. They made the legislators responsible to the **electorate** (voters) instead of the King or the Parliament. Legislators had short terms to make them more responsible to the voters. Also, the new states showed their fear of tyrants by giving very limited executive authority to governors, making them stand for popular election every two years. Most states made their legislative branch supreme by giving over-

Early Shield of the 13 States
– ©1995 DeskGallery

whelming power to their elected representatives.

The new state constitutions also protected individual rights. Each state added a bill of rights to its constitution. These documents guaranteed freedom of speech and freedom of worship, and they safeguarded property ownership. The constitutions also preserved bail and trial rights for accused persons.

It was no easy task to preserve the new power and authority of the states while establishing a central government to administer national affairs (such as conducting a revolutionary war). Pennsylvania delegate **John Dickinson** drew up the first system of national government for the Continental Congress. In 1777, Dickinson submitted a document called the ***Articles of Confederation***. The new states were so protective of their authority and land claims that they took almost four years just to ratify the *Articles*.

As a constitutional structure, the *Articles* created a **confederation** – a loose union with power shared between states and the national (central) government. It was a weak government, but the *Articles* accurately reflected the former colonists' suspicion of large-scale, distant authority. The *Articles* assured the people that power remained as close to home as possible. These few powers allowed the national government were difficult to exercise. Simple legislation required a two-thirds majority. Amendments to the *Articles* had to be approved unanimously. However, the new government had some essential powers. It could make war and negotiate treaties. It could borrow money and resolve disputes between states.

Still, the government under the *Articles* lacked the most fundamental of all powers –

> **Note: Items marked with an * are listed in the *Landmark Supreme Court Decisions* chart in Appendices.**

"the power of the purse." It could not levy taxes. Also, the *Articles* limited the national government's **sovereignty** (independent power). The national government could not regulate commerce nor raise troops. It had no separate executive officers, only secretaries appointed by and responsible to Congress to manage financial (Robert Morris, PA) and foreign affairs (John Jay, NY). With no power to raise funds and virtually no enforcement power (the "power of the sword"), the national government had to depend on the good will of the states to contribute funds and to make its laws work. The *Articles* provided no national courts in which to prosecute offenses or settle disputes.

THE CRITICAL PERIOD

The *Articles of Confederation* were in effect from 1781 to 1789. Historians now call those years the "Critical Period" in American history. The national government did successfully conclude the Revolutionary War. It negotiated a favorable end to the war (*Treaty of Paris*, 1783). It also created a model for the admission of new territories and the orderly admission of states to the Union (**Northwest Ordinance**, 1785). However, it was too weak to give the new nation the firm basis it needed for growth (see the chart below for an overview of the weaknesses of the *Articles*, and how the new **Constitution of the United States** of 1787 remedied them).

Merchant traders experienced financial difficulties in the Critical Period. Prior to the American Revolution, Parliament officially restricted their business to Britain and British colonies of the Caribbean. After the Revolution, the amount of new, freer trade with China, France, the French West Indies, and other European powers did not equal the amount of pre-Revolutionary trade with Britain.

On the frontier, poorly equipped army units could not protect the new settlers who swarmed into the Ohio Valley from violence sometimes stirred up by the British forces still lingering in the region.

When the Revolutionary War ended, the economy was in disarray. With no taxing power, the money issued by the national government never gained much acceptance. States issued their own paper money, but people lacked confidence in it. They placed more value in the British, French, and Dutch coins that circulated throughout the country. Actually, Spanish gold coins became the most valued (and scarcest) form of money.

WEAKNESSES OF THE ARTICLES / CONSTITUTIONAL CHANGES	
WEAKNESSES OF THE ARTICLES	**CONSTITUTIONAL CHANGES**
• unicameral legislature; each state had equal vote no matter size of population	• bicameral legislature; representation proportional in House, states equal in Senate
• two-thirds majority needed to pass laws	• simple majority could pass laws
• no control of interstate or foreign trade	• Congress regulates interstate and foreign commerce
• Congress could levy but could not collect taxes	• Congress could levy and collect taxes
• no executive department to enforce laws	• executive department headed by a single president
• no national judicial branch, only individual state courts	• national judiciary, headed by a Supreme Court
• unanimous vote of states needed to amend the constitutional structure	• two-thirds vote of Congress, then three-fourths of the states must approve

Debtors – mostly farmers – were pressured by merchants and creditors to pay their bills in hard currency (coin). The crisis came to a head in 1785, when New England merchant-lenders pressed overtaxed farmers toward bankruptcy. The poor farmers of Western Massachusetts rallied around **Captain Daniel Shays** (1747-1825), a Revolutionary War veteran threatened with imprisonment for debt. Captain Shays' followers held political meetings and sent petitions to the Massachusetts General Court (the state assembly) for tax relief and the printing of more paper money. Their requests were ignored by the merchant-dominated General Court in Boston. Mobs began to threaten tax collectors and foreclosure courts.

Shays' Rebellion spread and Massachusetts' Governor Bowdoin sent troops to disperse the mobs. There were a few skirmishes and some of the rebels were captured and released. Shays and his followers fled to Vermont and were not prosecuted.

While the Massachusetts General Court later enacted some tax relief, the outburst in New England frightened people. George Washington and other leaders felt the weakness of the central government, disputes between states, the economic crisis, and mob outbursts such as the Shays' incident threatened the future of the nation.

About the same time as the disturbances in Massachusetts, the states of Virginia and Maryland sponsored a meeting in Alexandria to resolve border problems. At the meeting, the delegates' discussions broadened to general national problems. A short while later, General Washington agreed to reconvene the meeting at his Mount Vernon home and invited representatives from Pennsylvania and Delaware. That group asked the Maryland and Virginia legislatures to sponsor a meeting open to all states in Annapolis (MD) the following year.

Only five states were represented at this September 1786 meeting, and little was accomplished. However, the Annapolis meeting launched another effort by younger leaders such as **James Madison** (VA, 1751-1836) and **Alexander Hamilton** (NY, 1755-1804) to assure full attendance at a proposed Convention for revision of the *Articles* in Philadelphia in 1787.

News traveled slowly in the 18th century, and even more slowly in the sprawling, less developed terrain of America. As knowledge of the Shays episode spread, so did fear that more incidents could lead to a general civil war. Pressure from propertied groups grew. Patriots who had sacrificed much for independence fighting the Revolution agreed that the country's future was endangered. Yielding to increasing concern, Congress endorsed the Annapolis meeting's call and authorized a convention in Philadelphia for the purpose of revising the *Articles of Confederation*.

INDEPENDENCE HALL

THE CONSTITUTIONAL CONVENTION

The gathering in Philadelphia that late May of 1787 was a formidable one. Twelve states chose their most distinguished citizens. Only Rhode Island declined to send a delegation, fearing the Convention would strip states of sovereignty (independent power). Only fifty-five of the seventy-two appointees attended. They were all white males – mostly lawyers, large landholders, and a few merchants.

The common people – yeoman farmers and frontiersmen – were not well represented. Some major figures of the Revolution were away on diplomatic missions (Thomas Jefferson in France and John Adams in England).

The delegates' charge was to revise the *Articles*, yet the delegates eventually drafted an entirely new form of government. While waiting for a quorum, informal discussions among early arrivals created firm support for a more powerful national government. This advance group included Virginia delegates Governor **Edmund**

Randolph (1753-1813) and James Madison, New York delegate Alexander Hamilton, and **James Wilson** (1745-1798) of Pennsylvania.

When the Convention finally met, it chose George Washington (VA) to preside. His prestige and dignity lent legitimacy to the meeting, but he also supported a strengthening of the national government. Since the Convention proceedings were secret, James Madison's notes are the main source of knowledge of how the gathering created the *Constitution of the United States*.

Not everyone agreed with a total reforming of the government. Some delegates, such as Robert Yates and John Lansing of New York, left in the midst of the Convention rather than lend their presence to an unauthorized, radical transformation of the national government. Three of the delegates – Edmund Randolph and George Mason of Virginia and Elbridge Gerry of Massachusetts – refused to sign the final document, claiming the group had gone too far.

CONSTITUTIONAL BACKGROUND

The Philadelphia delegates were well educated men of affairs. They brought to Philadelphia a wealth of background on government, politics, and history. Their ideas on government flowed from several sources: the ancient world, the European Enlightenment, and the colonial experience in America.

CLASSICAL THOUGHT

The delegates were educated in the classical tradition revitalized by Renaissance studies. Their 18th century education traced Western political thought back to the ancient Greek contributions (direct democracy, juries, and salaries for public officials). They studied the *Republic* of **Plato** (428-347 BC) and the *Politics* of **Aristotle** (384-322 BC). They translated Cicero and Caesar and knew the Roman contributions (representative government, vetoes, and codified law) well. These classical ideas were Anglicized (assimilated into English culture) over several centuries in British universities and were integrated into the Anglo-Saxon legal system (or common law) that the English brought to the colonies of North America.

ENLIGHTENMENT THOUGHT

The European Enlightenment of the 17th and 18th centuries (sometimes called the "Age of Reason") is also a major part of the background for the new republican form of government. While the Philadelphia delegates had studied the ancient classical ideas, the works of later European scholars also influenced them. Among them were:

- **John Locke** (1632-1704), an English theorist who set out influential principles in his *Two Treatises on Government*. His beliefs included: an optimistic and rational view of human nature; natural rights (life, liberty, and property); social contract (that government's authority stems from the people); right of revolution (that government may be abolished or redesigned if it does not meet the peoples' needs).

- **Voltaire** (François Auguste René Rodin, 1694-1778), the leading "philosophe" (intellectual figure) of the French Enlightenment, advocated religious tolerance, growth of material prosperity, natural rights, and abolition of torture in works such as his *Philosophical Dictionary* (1764).

- **Baron de Montesquieu** (Charles de Secondat, 1689-1755), another French "philosophe," wrote *The Spirit of the Laws* in 1748. He contributed the idea that power in the modern state must be limited. Montesquieu held that separation of powers among different parts of a government was a necessary means to achieve such limitation. He recommended assigning fundamental

government functions to separate legislative, executive, and judicial branches.

- **Jean-Jacques Rousseau** (1712-1778) a later French "philosophe," expanded Locke's ideas and made them more popular in Europe. He spoke against the contemporary theory of the divine right of kings. In his utopian work, *The Social Contract* (1762), Rousseau favored democratic self-rule, and, like Locke, claimed that rulers must serve the wishes of the people.

AMERICAN INDIAN CONTRIBUTIONS

Not all of America's political ideas came from Europe. Before the arrival of European settlers, Native American people of the Seneca, Cayuga, Onondaga, Oneida, Mohawk, and Tuscarora nations had set up an **Iroquois Confederation** (also called the Haudenosaunee Union). Located mostly in what is now New York State, the confederation met periodically to deal with common problems.

Benjamin Franklin and other colonial figures were aware of such Native American ideas at the time of American independence. In the summer of 1754, Representatives of seven colonies (NY, PA, MD, MA, CT, RI, NH) and of the five Iroquois nations met in Albany to discuss British colonial defenses against the French. Franklin unveiled his **Albany Plan of Union** proposing a self-governing federation under the British crown with elected representatives. The plan failed because of inter-colonial jealousy, lukewarm response from the Crown, and refusal of the Iroquois to offer a firm commitment.

COLONIAL EXPERIENCE

The nearly two hundred years of British colonial rule undoubtedly influenced the Philadelphia Convention delegates. While Britain's thirteen colonies on the Atlantic seaboard evolved from several different situations, their written law, elected legislatures, and separation of government power among the branches reflected common Anglo-Saxon traditions.

Of course, not all colonial experiences were democratic. Royal governors and the British Crown exerted powerful vetoes on colonial legislatures. In some colonies, property and religious qualifications restricted voting eligibility.

CONFLICT AND COMPROMISE

At the 1787 Philadelphia Convention, delegates generally agreed to the need for

- a stronger central government,
- legislative power to tax, regulate commerce, and raise an army,
- separate executive and judicial branches, and
- better guarantees of property rights.

There were many long arguments about how these general points of agreement would be implemented. The differences were extensive and compromise became essential. In fact, the *Constitution of the United States* has been called a "bundle of compromises."

THE GREAT COMPROMISE

Representation in Congress was a major problem at the Convention. Virginia led the states with large populations. Edmund Randolph's **Virginia Plan** called for a bicameral body with the number representatives in the lower house to be apportioned to a state according to the number of free people a state had. The upper house would be chosen by the lower house from a list of nominees submitted by the state legislatures. The small states rallied behind William Paterson's **New Jersey Plan**, calling for a unicameral legislature with the number of representatives per state to be equal. After a number of heated debates, a committee was formed to seek a solution. Headed by Benjamin Franklin (PA), Oliver Ellsworth and Roger Sherman (CT), the committee hammered out a compromise: a bicameral legislature with equal representation (2 per state) in the upper house (Senate) and representation determined by population in the lower house (House of Representatives).

THREE-FIFTHS COMPROMISE

Determining representation by population in the House led to another problem. The Southern states had sizable slave populations. The Southern states wanted the slaves counted to determine their representation in the House, but not for taxation. The Northern states felt slaves (considered as property) should be taxed but not represented. It was finally agreed that five slaves would be counted as only three persons for both purposes.

SLAVE TRADE

Slavery itself became an issue when its opponents tried to have it abolished. They did succeed in having the importation of slaves forbidden after 1808, but slavery itself was allowed to continue.

TARIFFS

Southern agricultural exporters disapproved of any federal tariffs (foreign trade taxes). Northern business interests wanted tariffs as protection against foreign competition. In the end, the Constitution gave Congress authority to tax imports but forbade taxing exports.

THE PRESIDENCY

Proposals on the Chief Executive's term of office ranged from three years to life. Some delegates wanted direct election, but others mistrusted the judgement of uneducated people. Compromises worked out a four year term and indirect election through the "electoral college" system.

THE DOCUMENT

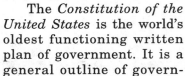

(See the Appendix for full text)

The *Constitution of the United States* is the world's oldest functioning written plan of government. It is a general outline of government, not an intricate plan. The final document contained seven brief articles that outlined governmental structure but left much room for flexible interpretation of power. Careful attention was paid to keeping power limited within each branch, and procedures were included for each of the branches to block the others from overstepping their bounds. Several features deserve special focus:

- The **Preamble** (preface) lists the purposes of the U.S. government: "...to form a more perfect union, establish justice, insure domestic tranquillity, provide for the common defense, promote the general welfare, [and] secure the blessings of liberty..."

- **Limited Government** is a basic principle threaded throughout the Constitution's framework. It specifies what the national and state governments can and cannot do.

- **Representative Government** is another basic principle that provides a process by which the people directly and indirectly choose their leaders and deal with issues.

- **Federalism** is a refinement of confederation. A federal union is a compromise between a unitary system's concentration of power and a decentralized confederation structure. In a federal union, the states accept the overall sovereignty of the national government but they retain power in local matters. A federal union sets up a dual system of government.

- **Separation of Power** is a principle that sets up limits among three distinct branches (legislative, executive, and judicial). The Constitution specifically assigns different functions and powers to each branch.

- **Checks and Balances** is a system assuring that each branch has limited power by giving each one special controls to block the other branches from illegally expanding their powers.

RATIFICATION

The Philadelphia Convention delegates took a radical step when their work was done in mid-September 1787. They did not ask the Continental Congress' approval of their work. Article VII of their new Constitution bypassed Congress. The delegates sought approval of the new Constitution directly from the states. Article VII was also radical in a second sense – it required ratification by only nine states, not all thirteen.

Since the new Constitution would change government considerably, ratification became a controversial issue in the new nation. The debate divided the people into two groups.

- **Federalists** (supporters of the new Constitution) were mainly from the business and propertied interests. They were well organized and financed. Their arguments were that a strong, stable government was the key to peace and economic growth, and that guarantees of personal liberty were unnecessary because they were protected in state constitutions.

BRITISH TERRITORY

CLAIMED BY GREAT BRITAIN
CLAIMED BY GREAT BRITAIN
Lake Superior
Lake Huron
Lake Michigan
Mississippi River
L. Ontario
L. Erie
Ohio R.
MAINE (TO MASS.)
N.H. JUNE 1788
MASS. FEB. 1788
NEW YORK JULY 1788
R.I. MAY 1790
PENNSYLVANIA DEC. 1787
CONN. JAN. 1788
NEW JERSEY DEC. 1787
DELAWARE DEC. 1787
VIRGINIA JUNE 1788
CLAIMED BY VIRGINIA
MARYLAND APRIL 1788
CLAIMED BY NORTH CAROLINA
N. CAROLINA NOV. 1789
S. CAROLINA MAY 1788
SPANISH LOUISIANA
CLAIMED BY GEORGIA
GEORGIA JAN. 1788
SPANISH FLORIDA

CONSTITUTIONAL RATIFICATION 1787-1790

- **Anti-Federalists** (opponents of the new Constitution) were generally the less well-to-do and less educated groups (frontiersmen, laborers, and yeomen). They feared a conspiracy of the rich. Anti-Federalists were not a cohesive group. Some wanted only the addition of a bill of rights. Others, including old revolutionaries such as New York's Governor **George Clinton** (1739-1812), Virginia's Patrick Henry, and Massachusetts' Sam Adams and John Hancock were all suspicious. They feared a loss of local power to a tyrannical central government.

During the ratification campaigns in Pennsylvania and several less populous states, the Federalists rushed through the voting before their opponents became organized. In the larger, more populous states, the process was drawn out, and passage occurred by much smaller margins.

Bitter ratification battles raged in the pivotal states of Virginia and New York. Their geographic positions made them critical to keeping the new union together. At Virginia's ratifying convention, Anti-Federalists such as Patrick Henry and George Mason could not offset the prestige of Washington and the arguments of Madison and John Marshall. Once these towering figures managed to turn Governor Edmund Randolph's opinion, victory was close. In the midst of Virginia's debate, New Hampshire became the 9th state to ratify, and the union was officially formed. This turned the tide, and Virginia voted to become the 10th state.

In New York, Governor George Clinton, John Lansing, and Robert Yates led the Anti-Federalist forces. Still, the Federalists were better organized. Earlier, Alexander Hamilton and John Jay had joined James Madison of Virginia in writing a series of eighty-five persuasive articles. They were published in newspapers throughout the states under the pen-name "Publius." They were later collected into a volume called the *Federalist Papers*. They are still considered among the best analyses of the American constitutional system. The pressure of the earlier New Hampshire and Virginia decisions also helped the Federalists win New York. By a narrow victory (30-27) at the ratifying convention in Poughkeepsie, New York became the 11th state to ratify. Anti-Federalists in North Carolina and Rhode Island blocked ratification for several months, but by 1790 they reluctantly joined the union.

THE SCOPE OF THE NEW CONSTITUTION

Once ratified, the new *Constitution of the United States* had to be put into practice. Each state selected two Senators and elected

James Madison
(U.S. National Archives)

ARGUMENT FOR A STRONGER GOVERNMENT

"(Patrick Henry) informs us that the people of the country are in perfect repose; that is, every man enjoys the fruits of his labor peaceably and securely, and that everything is in perfect tranquility and safety. I wish sincerely that this were true. If this be their happy situation, why has every state acknowledged the contrary? Why were deputies from all states sent to a general convention? Why have complaints of national and individual distresses been echoed and reechoed throughout the continent? ... A government is formed for the protection of its individual members. Ours (the Confederation) has attacked itself with impunity. Its authority has been disobeyed and despised.

– James Madison, *In Favor of the Federal Constitution*, Virginia Ratification Convention, Richmond, VA, 6 June 1788

CONSTITUTIONAL STRUCTURES

MINI•ASSESSMENT (2-2)

1 Which belief was generally held by the delegates to the Constitutional Convention of 1787?
  1 A strong central government is necessary to maintain order.
  2 Slavery should be abolished.
  3 The principles of government should be firm and unchangeable.
  4 Rule of men is superior to the rule of law.

2 During the debates over the ratification of the *Constitution of the United States*, Federalists and Anti-Federalists disagreed most strongly over the
  1 division of powers between the national and state governments
  2 provision for admitting new states to the Union
  3 distribution of powers between the Senate and the House of Representatives
  4 method of amending the Constitution

3 "In framing a government which is to be administered by men over men, the great difficulty lies in this, you must first enable the government to control the governed; and in the next place, oblige it to control itself."

This passage from the Federalist papers refers to the need for a(n)
  1 strong executive
  2 system of checks and balances
  3 independent military
  4 national education system

Constructed Response

"On erection of the eleventh pillar of our National Dome... The foundation is good – it may yet be saved."

1 In the above 1788 political cartoon, to what do the words "National Dome" refer?

2 Explain why you think the cartoonist is a Federalist or an Anti-Federalist.

Representatives according to their estimated population. According to the Constitution's "electoral college" process, the states also chose Electors who then selected George Washington to be President and John Adams to be Vice President. In the spring of 1789, Congress began passing laws to create a new federal government and President Washington began implementing them. Throughout this early stage, Congress and the Vice President set **precedents** (initial procedures that became models for succeeding administrations). Some of these precedents became an underpinning for practices that scholars sometimes call the "unwritten constitution."

THE *BILL OF RIGHTS*

One of the major criticisms of the original *Constitution of the United States* by the Anti-Federalists was its lack of specific guarantees of individual civil liberties. Opponents felt that Congress' **enumerated powers** or delegated powers (those specifically mentioned in the Constitution) would be too broadly interpreted.

They claimed this broadness would lead to laws that could infringe on citizens' rights.

Reacting to this argument, Representative James Madison (VA) offered a group of amendments to safeguard personal freedoms. Although modified, Madison's ideas became the basis for the first ten amendments proposed by Congress and sent to the states for ratification in 1789. Officially adopted in 1791, this first group of ten amendments to the *Constitution of the United States* became known as the **Bill of Rights**.

Many of the civil liberties granted in the Bill of Rights flow directly from problems encountered during the colonial experience. For example, the Fourth Amendment (see chart on next page) was drawn up in response to the British authorities' use of **writs of assistance** (blanket search warrants).

The Bill of Rights was originally intended to guarantee citizens protection from abuse by the national government. Most of the original state constitutions already listed their own guarantees for their citizens.

MAJOR PROVISIONS OF THE BILL OF RIGHTS

INSIGHTS ON LIBERTY

I. Congress *shall not* pass laws infringing on freedoms of speech, press, peaceful assembly; free exercise of religion and separation of church and state.

II. Congress *shall not* pass laws infringing on the right to bear arms so that a well regulated militia can be maintained.

III. Congress *shall not* pass laws quartering troops in private homes in peacetime.

IV. Congress *shall not* pass laws authorizing unreasonable searches, seizures; warrants only on probable cause.

V. Congress *shall not* pass laws abusing legal proceedings. This amendment requires:
1. indictment by grand jury in felony cases
2. no double jeopardy (being tried a second time after acquittal)
3. self-incrimination cannot be forced
4. due process must be used (proper and equal legal procedures)
5. property cannot be taken without just compensation

VI. Congress *shall not* pass laws abusing accused citizens. This amendment requires:
1. speedy and public trial
2. impartial jury of peers
3. informing of charges
4. confrontation by accusers
5. calling of supportive witnesses
6. guarantee of counsel

VII. Congress *shall not* pass laws denying jury trials in certain civil (non-criminal) cases.

VIII. Congress *shall not* pass laws requiring excessive bail; cruel, or unusual punishment.

IX. Congress *shall not* pass laws denying other rights not listed in the Constitution.

X. Congress *shall not* pass laws denying to the states other powers not listed in the Constitution. (As part of the theory of federalism, powers not specifically assigned to the central government are reserved for the states.)

The Bill of Rights has not changed for over 200 years. However, the federal courts have interpreted its words in different ways over those years. For example, in recent years court rulings have frequently applied Bill of Rights guarantees to protect individuals from the actions of state governments. A later Amendment, the Fourteenth, guarantees equal protection of the laws for all citizens. The federal courts use the Fourteenth to make sure the Bill of Rights is fairly and properly applied to all citizens.

THE AMENDMENT PROCESS

While thought of as a unit, the Bill of Rights is really ten separate additions to the Constitution. When the first Congress proposed these amendments and sent them to the states for ratification, it followed the procedures built into the Constitution for change. The writers of the Constitution knew the document was not perfect and would need refinement as it went into

effect. Also, they knew that times changed and government must be able to change. Yet, they did not want the fundamental law of the land to be changed too easily.

It is a testimony to the work and foresight of the delegates of the Philadelphia Convention that the Constitution has been altered only two dozen or so times in more than two centuries of operation. All of the amendments emerged from Congressional vote and state ratification. The special national convention method has never been used (see chart on next page).

FEDERALISM

CONSTITUTIONAL STRUCTURES

As a basic element in U.S. government, federalism (division of power between the states and the national government) required a statement in the Constitution. Protection of the **reserved powers** of states in

TWO STEPS TO AMEND THE *UNITED STATES CONSTITUTION*	
STEP ONE	**STEP TWO**
Proposed amendments can be offered by either a two-thirds vote of Congress, or by a special national convention called by Congress at the request of two-thirds of the state legislatures. (The latter procedure has never been used.)	Proposed amendments must then be ratified either by: *a* sending them to the state legislatures, and gaining approval of three-fourths of them for ratification; or *b* setting up special conventions in the states, in which case three-fourths of them must approve the amendment for it to become part of the Constitution.

the Tenth Amendment (see chart) provides this – but not clearly. The powers left to the states were modified by two sections of Article I. Section 10 of Article I places many specific restrictions on the states. Section 8 of Article I contains the famous "elastic clause." This clause gives Congress a great deal of implied power to do things not restricted in the Constitution.

The concept of federalism is complex and dynamic. In a way, federalism created a perpetual power struggle between states and the national government. In the 19th century, debates in Congress, Supreme Court cases, and the eventual War Between the States revolved around the issue of federalism. Right down to the present day, the struggle continues over hundreds of issues such as welfare spending and highway regulations.

In many cases, Congress' use of the elastic clause has lessened state power. For example, making educational policy used to be the exclusive domain of the states. However, more recent federal aid programs and federal civil rights protections provide a base for federal rules and regulations, thus limiting state education powers.

BASIC STRUCTURE AND FUNCTION OF GOVERNMENT

The theories of Locke and Rousseau were influential at the time of the Philadelphia Convention. These Enlightenment thinkers held that all government power resides with the people. In practicality, the U.S. is an *indirect* democracy or a **democratic republic**. This means when the people vote, they give the power to govern to their representatives.

Powerful as the influence of Enlightenment thinkers was, the delegates at Philadelphia were reluctant to let the people directly elect all national government officials. Under the original *Constitution of the United States*, the only official that the people could choose *directly* was their local member of the House of Representatives. Originally, Senators, the President and Vice President, and federal judges were chosen *indirectly*. The Philadelphia delegates believed that voters could be swayed too easily. For all their Enlightenment rhetoric, the Constitution's framers had doubts about the education and the wisdom of the general population in 1787.

Capitol Building – Home of the U.S. Congress
– ©1993 PhotoDisc Inc.

The uncertainty about people and power led the framers to use Montesquieu's idea about separating and limiting power. They separated federal powers into three branches. According to constitutional design, each of the branches has a primary purpose described at length in the first three articles of the Constitution.

CONSTITUTIONAL STRUCTURES

ARTICLE I: THE CONGRESS

The framers described Congressional structure and power in Article I. It was first because they saw Congress as the base of U.S. government. Because Congress writes the nation's laws, the framers saw it as the core of power in the nation. It is the "peoples' branch" – the gathering place for the ideas of elected local representatives from every corner of the country. The Seventeenth Amendment (direct election of Senators) and the Twentieth Amendment (moving the date for starting sessions of Congress to January) are the only formal changes to Article I since 1789. Of course, the intricate operation and rules of Congress evolved over time. The Senate and the House of Representatives have different rules, but still check each other's work, and must cooperate to produce laws.

While their function is the same, the constitutional design of the two houses made them different. Elected directly from small districts for only two years, members of the House were closer to the people. By reflecting local needs and desires, and hearing everyday opinions, the House was designed to be – and still is – more reflective of change. On the other hand, the Senate was designed originally to represent broader statewide interests. U.S. Senators were originally chosen by the state's legislature, and with six year terms, they were to be more stable, farsighted, and temperate in nature. If the House reflected change, the Senate was to represent continuity. The comparative table on the following page shows this in clearer detail.

The powers used by Congress to rule the United States fall into three categories: delegated power, implied power, and concurrent power.

First, the basic source of Congressional authority is Section 8 of Article I where seventeen enumerated or **delegated powers** are listed. For

CONGRESSIONAL BICAMERAL ORGANIZATION

HOUSE OF REPRESENTATIVES (reflects *change*)	SENATE (reflects *continuity*)
Membership: • Total of 435 (set by law); each state's delegation is determined by its population relevant to the others **Qualifications:** • At least 25 years of age, U.S. citizen for 7 years, resident of state represented **Term:** • 2 years, entire House must be elected every two years **How Elected:** • Directly by the voters of a district **Presiding Officer:** • Speaker of the House elected by the members (voting along party lines) **Special Powers:** • Brings impeachment charges • May choose the President if there is no majority in the electoral system • Must start all revenue bills	**Membership:** • 2 per state (currently 100 from 50 states) **Qualifications:** • At least 30 years of age, U.S. citizen for 9 years, resident of state represented **Term:** • 6 years with staggered elections, one-third of the members elected every 2 years **How Elected:** • Directly by voters of a state (*17th Amendment*); Originally, each state legislature chose its two U.S. Senators **Presiding Officer:** • Constitution assigns the Vice President of the U.S. to be "President of the Senate"; a "President Pro-Tempore" is also chosen by the Senate members **Special Powers:** • Acts as jury in impeachment trials (two-thirds vote needed) • May choose the Vice President if there is no majority in the electoral system • Must ratify treaties with foreign nations by two-thirds vote • Must approve Presidential appointments (majority needed)

example, the list includes:

- levying and collecting taxes
- borrowing on the credit of the U.S.
- declaring war
- establishing immigration rules
- maintaining the court system
- maintaining a postal system
- regulating interstate and foreign commerce
- governing patents and copyrights
- coining money and punishing counterfeiters
- maintaining an army and navy

The list of delegated powers is clear and to the point. The framers intended to give Congress the powers governments most commonly exercised in the 18th century and those that would solve the problems experienced in the "Critical Period."

Yet, the framers had a vision of a changing world and a fluid American society. They knew they had to build some flexibility into the governmental system without resorting to formal amendment. The final clause of Article I, Section 8 skillfully provided a window of flexibility for the future. The eighteenth power listed is the famous **elastic clause**. It allows Congress to stretch the meaning of the other seventeen powers to cover new situations. The 18th clause states that Congress "...shall have the power to make all laws necessary and proper to carry into effect the foregoing powers..."

The elastic clause is the basis of a second type of Congressional power – the doctrine of **implied power**. The doctrine has both proponents (loose constructionists) and enemies (strict constructionists). **Loose constructionists** believe Congress should liberally stretch

FEDERALISM

Delegated Powers
(national government only)

interstate & foreign commerce
foreign relations
declares war
coins money
immigration
postal service

&

Implied Powers
Congress can stretch
the delegated
powers

Concurrent Powers
(both governments)

taxation
borrowing
court systems
penal systems
law enforcement agencies
general welfare of citizens
charter banks and
corporations

Reserved Powers
(state governments only)

intrastate commerce
local governments
public health
voter qualification
supervise elections
supervise education
license occupations

AMERICANS ARE CITIZENS UNDER TWO GOVERNMENTS:
NATIONAL (U.S. FEDERAL) GOVERNMENT AND THE STATE IN WHICH THEY RESIDE

the 17 delegated powers to meet any and all the problems confronting society. **Strict constructionists** believe Congress should conservatively stretch the 17 delegated powers only when absolutely necessary to meet only the most serious problems confronting society.

The doctrine of implied power continues to cause some of the most controversial questions in our society – how much power should the federal government have? The loose and strict viewpoints have battled continuously in U.S. history. Often, the Supreme Court has been asked to judge whether Congressional laws have employed the elastic clause too liberally. In some cases the Court has declared that Congress acted unconstitutionally.

A third type of Congressional power is **concurrent power**. This is shared power. All governments use two basic powers to operate. Any government needs the **"power of the purse"** – the power to raise the money to operate. Because governments need **revenue** (income), taxes are necessary and so are tax collection agencies. Also, all governments must have the **"power of the sword"** (the power to enforce their laws). Federal, state, and local governments all have this police power. The Constitution assigns the powers of the purse and the sword to the Congress and the Vice President respectively. To function, the states must have these powers too.

According to the Tenth Amendment, all powers not delegated, implied, or concurrently granted to the federal government in the Constitution are **reserved** (set aside) for the states. According to this reserved power theory, most **intrastate** activities (those that take place within a state) are governed by state and local authority. Examples include intrastate transportation, health, education, professional licensing, and business and employment regulations.

Over the years since the Constitution was set in place, there have been many conflicts over this theory of reserved power. As technology and industrialization changed the country, many activities crossed state borders (e.g., interstate railroads, federal aid to schools), Congress used the elastic clause (doctrine of implied power) to stretch into many of the areas originally thought to belong exclusively to state power. This conflict of state versus federal power caused some of the great constitutional debates of American history.

The *Constitution of the United States* specifically denies certain powers to the federal government. It cannot suspend **writs of habeas corpus** (speedy arraignment) except in times of rebellion and invasion. It cannot pass **bills of attainder** (legislative acts declaring people guilty without trials) nor can it make **ex post facto laws** (laws that declare an act a crime after the act has been done). The federal govern-

Representative introduces bill. Speaker sends to proper committee.

Committee studies bill and may change provisions.

Rules Committee arranges for discussion by entire House.

House debates bill. If passed, bill goes to Senate.

Bill is considered by Committee and debated by entire Senate. If different from House version, bill goes to Conference Committee.

HOW A BILL BECOMES A LAW

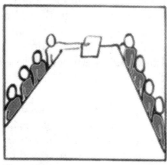

Conference Committee of House and Senate resolves differences. Compromise bill is sent to House and Senate.

If both pass compromise, it goes to President for signature.

President signs. If he vetoes, Congress may override veto by two-thirds vote in each house.

ment cannot levy direct taxes on people. (The Sixteenth Amendment – income tax – is an exception.) It cannot tax exports, spend money without appropriation, nor grant titles of nobility.

Congress operates by taking **bills** (proposed laws) submitted by its members and processing them through committees and public debates. As the diagram on the facing page shows, the process is lengthy and involved, but the idea is to be deliberate (careful) and meticulous. Congress must avoid unworkable or unjust laws that encumber the society. (Note: Article I requires that revenue [tax] bills can only be started in the House, because it was originally closest to the people.)

White House – Home of the U.S. President
– ©1993 PhotoDisc Inc.

ARTICLE II: THE PRESIDENCY

The executive branch is outlined in Article II. The Twelfth, Twentieth, Twenty-second, Twenty-third, and Twenty-fifth Amendments focus on the executive branch as well. Article II names only two officials – a President and a Vice President. Simple qualifications for these executive positions exist. A person must be at least 35 years of age, a native born citizen, and a resident of the United States for at least 14 years.

The presidential term of office is four years. Removal is possible through the **impeachment process**. Impeachment means to accuse an official of serious misconduct – "high crimes and misdemeanors." Official charges must be voted by the House of Representatives. Subsequently, a trial takes place in the Senate, and the Chief Justice of the Supreme Court presides over the

trial. The Senate acts as a jury with a two-thirds vote necessary to remove.

The Constitution outlines a number of official roles or duties for the President: **chief executive** (implements and administers laws and programs legislated by Congress), **chief of state** (represents the country on ceremonial occasions, **chief diplomat** (conducts affairs with other nations), and **commander-in-chief** (supervises the military forces). Presidents also play the role of **chief legislator** (propose legislation and filter it into the legislative branch through friendly members of Congress, lobby other members of Congress to vote for or against a bill, and finally sign or veto all legislation).

As with Congress, there is much more to the Presidency than the Constitution outlines. Much about the office evolved over time. Presidents picked up "extra-constitutional roles" as time progressed: world leader, emergency director, manager of prosperity, voice of the people, and head of a political party.

As the international power and prestige of the United States grew, Presidents became more than diplomatic representatives for the U.S. alone. As **world leader** a President often plays a powerful role in influencing international events. An example would be President Bush's organization of an international coalition (under U.N. authority) to liberate Kuwait from Iraqi aggression in 1990-1991.

As **emergency director**, a President often mobilizes federal action in case of floods, earthquakes, and storms. Although the free enterprise economy shuns governmental interference, as **manager of prosperity** a President often takes corrective action in recessions and depressions. The mass media can project an image of a President as **voice of the people**, indicating the President's words project the feelings and opinions of the entire nation.

As the holder of the highest elected office, the President has also evolved into a **head of political party** role. Elections are much more complex today than the framers of the Constitution ever imagined. With the exception of George Washington, every President has had to campaign for the office. Through the first quarter of the 19th century, **caucuses** ("insider

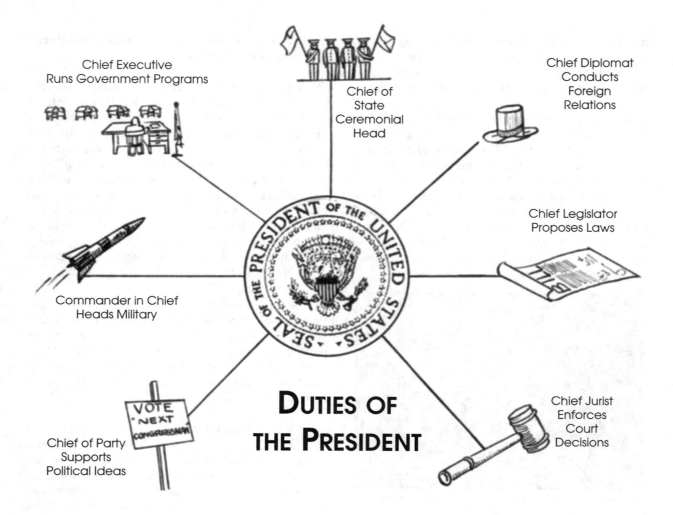

Chief Executive
Runs Government Programs

Chief of
State
Ceremonial
Head

Chief Diplomat
Conducts
Foreign
Relations

Chief Legislator
Proposes Laws

Commander in Chief
Heads Military

DUTIES OF
THE PRESIDENT

Chief Jurist
Enforces
Court
Decisions

Chief of Party
Supports
Political Ideas

groups") of party leaders chose presidential candidates.

In modern times, political campaigns have become difficult and expensive tasks. Presidential candidates begin campaigning for office years before the election. A complex system of local caucuses and primary elections choose delegates to national party nominating conventions. The delegates then officially nominate party candidates at the conventions. The candidates of each party then face each other in a general election.

PRESIDENTIAL ROLES	
CONSTITUTIONAL ROLES	**EXTRA-CONSTITUTIONAL ROLES**
• Appoints all important gov't. officials • Commander-in-Chief • Grants pardons and reprieves • Recommends legislation • Delivers State of the Union address • Executes federal laws and programs • Receives ambassadors • Makes treaties with foreign nations • May call special sessions of Congress	• World Leader • Voice of the People • Director of Emergency Actions • Manager of Economic Prosperity • Head of Political Party

In keeping with the reluctance of the Constitution's framers to place too much power in the hands of the people, Article II provides for *indirect* election of the President and the Vice President by special officers chosen by each state called **Electors of the President**. Each state sets its own rules for choosing these electors.

Each state is entitled to a number of electors equalling its total Congressional delegation (= the number of census-based apportioned representatives + 2 Senators). U.S. territories do not have electors, but the District of Columbia is granted a minimum of three (Twenty-third Amendment, 1961).

Although they never all meet in one place, the electors are often collectively referred to as the **electoral college**. There are 538 **electoral votes** (= 435 representatives + 100 senators + 3 for DC). No state can have fewer than three (3) votes (= at least 1 representative + 2 senators).

To win the presidency, a candidate must receive a majority (270) of the 538 electoral votes. In most states, the "unit rule" operates. This means that if a party's candidate wins the greatest amount of the popular vote of a state, *all* of the state's electors will be chosen from that party. (Electors customarily cast a "rubber stamp" vote for their party's candidate).

For candidates, the system is unequal. This "winner takes all" in a state actually makes it possible to win a majority of the national total popular votes but lose the electoral vote. A candidate can lose by devastating margins in some small vote states, but barely win in enough big electoral vote states (such as CA, NY, TX, FL, etc.) and get enough total electoral votes to win the presidency. On a national scale, a large majority of the total popular vote could be for one person, but the electoral vote might determine another person as the winner. In 1888, incumbent President Grover Cleveland won in total popular votes, but lost the electoral vote to Benjamin Harrison.

The electoral college system creates inequalities for citizens, too. The possibility of winning certain very populous states makes the votes of citizens there more important to candidates than those of voters in small-vote states. With high electoral votes at stake, candidates spend more time and money campaigning in big-vote states. Just barely winning the popular vote in five states – California (55), New York (31), Texas (34), Florida (27), and Pennsylvania (21) – gives a candidate 31% of the total electoral votes and 61% of the 270 majority needed to win. With the stakes so high in the big states and campaigns so expensive, candidates often ignore voters in states with a small number of electoral votes.

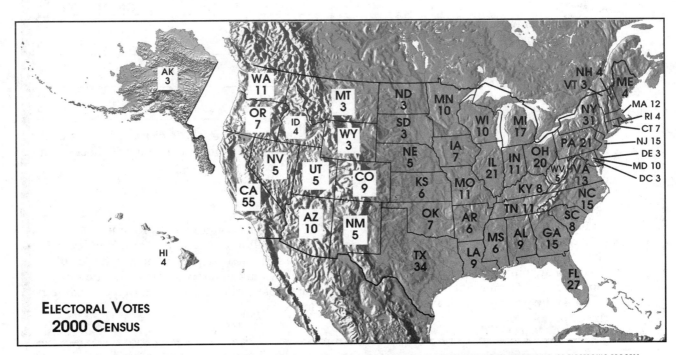

ELECTORAL VOTES
2000 CENSUS

According to Article II of the Constitution, if a vacancy occurs through the President's death, disability, retirement, or resignation, the Vice President takes over. If there is no Vice President to succeed the President, Congress can set the order of succession. In 1947, Congress enacted the **Presidential Succession Act** setting the order after Vice President as: Speaker of the House, President Pro Tempore of the Senate, then Secretaries of the Cabinet, starting with the Secretary of State.

However, the adoption of the Presidential Disability and Succession Amendment (Twenty-fifth Amendment, 1967) makes it unlikely that there will be a vacancy in the Vice Presidency ever again. It requires the President to nominate a new Vice President with the approval of both houses of Congress if that office becomes vacant. This Amendment also says that in the event of the disability of the President, the Vice President may become "Acting President."

The Twentieth Amendment (1933) moved the inauguration of the President from the March 4 to the January 20th after election. At the inauguration, the President takes an oath to "preserve, protect, and defend the *Constitution of the United States of America.*"

ARTICLE III: THE JUDICIAL BRANCH

The writers of the Constitution described the national courts in Article III. The courts interpret the nations' laws. The Constitution refers to only *one* court by name – the **Supreme Court of the United States**. Congress has to pass laws to create other courts in the federal system. The first Congress did this under the **Judiciary Act of 1789**. All federal judges are appointed for life tenure by the President with the approval of the Senate. Federal judges serve while in "good behavior," and they are subject to the same Congressional impeachment process as the President. The diagram on the next page shows the federal court system.

MINI•ASSESSMENT (2-4)

1 The President vetoes a bill and then Congress overrides the veto by a two-thirds vote of both houses. This situation is an example of the operation of
   1 checks and balances
   2 federalism
   3 legislative compromise
   4 direct democracy

2 Which action demonstrates the President's role as chief legislator?
   1 asking members of the Cabinet to serve as members of Congress
   2 asking executive department staff to propose and support legislation
   3 selecting chairpersons of congressional committees
   4 participating in Congressional debates

3 Which feature of the Presidency is a result of a constitutional amendment?
   1 two term limit in office
   2 power to appoint ambassadors
   3 duty to act as Commander-in-Chief
   4 responsibility to nominate Justices to the Supreme Court

Constructed Response

1 Complete the following study chart.

POWER IN THE U.S. FEDERAL STRUCTURE		
POWERS	STATE OR FEDERAL?	WHERE IN THE CONSTITUTION
Delegated		
Implied		
Reserved		

2 Using the *How a Bill Becomes a Law* chart (page 80), describe an example of checks and balances.

3 Although the committee system is not mentioned in the *Constitution of the United States*, it has become an important part of the law making process. Describe the role of congressional committees in the law making process.

Supreme Court Building
– ©1993 PhotoDisc Inc.

The Supreme Court's main power is **judicial review** (deciding cases involving local, state, and federal statutes and governmental actions to determine if they violate the *Constitution of the United States.*

If the Supreme Court finds such a conflict, it will declare a law or action "null and void" or "unconstitutional." This power is not specified in Article III, but was assumed by the Court in the famous *Marbury v. Madison* decision (1803) under Chief Justice **John Marshall** (1755-1835). This is a unique power and has often placed the Supreme Court at the center of controversy in American history.

CONSTITUTIONAL STRUCTURES

U.S. SUPREME COURT

1 Chief Justice & 8 Associate Justices (has original & appellate jurisdiction hearings on Constitutional issues)

U.S. CIRCUIT COURTS OF APPEAL (11)

have only appellate jurisdiction, operate as hearing panels, decisions are final in most cases

U.S. DISTRICT COURTS (94)

have original jurisdiction, operate using normal jury trial procedure

FEDERAL BUREAUCRACY

While the Constitution describes the basic elements of government, a broader structure of power has evolved since 1789. Today, several million people work for a government that has grown enormous in size and scope, especially in recent times. The **bureaucrats** are the civil servants and appointees who do everything from delivering the mail to processing income tax returns. Without this army of workers, the President could not hope to carry out the thousands of laws and programs that Congress sets up. At the same time, these civil servants have long careers. They serve under different administrations. How efficiently they work reflects on the success of programs. They also have to work with Congressional committees giving them information on programs. Their efforts can speed up or slow down progress. They have the power to help or hinder the government.

PAID CIVILIAN EMPLOYEES OF THE UNITED STATES GOVERNMENT*	
1816	4,837
1861	36,672
1881	100,000
1935	780,582
1945	3,816,310
1960	2,421,000
1970	2,881,000
1980	3,021,000
1990	2,985,000

* If military employment was added, the figure for 1990 would be over 4.1 million. (Source: Historical & Statistical Abstracts of U.S.)

COMPARISON TO OTHER NATIONAL GOVERNMENTS

The table on page 86 indicates some of the basic similarities and differences between our national government and those of Great Britain and China.

SUMMARY

Over the course of a turbulent fifteen year period from 1776 until 1791, the people of the new United States created a series of new governments based on principles untried in the

NATIONAL GOVERNMENTAL STRUCTURES			
	U.S.A.	**GREAT BRITAIN**	**CHINA**
Characteristic	representative democracy	representative democracy	totalitarian
Type	federal	unitary	unitary
Executive	President elected independently, but indirectly	Prime Minister chosen by Parliament	Premier selected by Communist Party oligarchy
Constitution	written: guaranteed civil liberties	unwritten: common law plus precedent plus documents (*Magna Carta*)	no written guarantee of civil liberties
Political Parties	2 major (Democrat and Republican) plus several minor	2 major (Labour and Conservative) plus several minor	only Communist Party is allowed

modern world. While fighting the American Revolution, U.S. leaders created new state and national constitutions based on republicanism, limited government, and the consent of the governed. Although the first attempt at a national government under the *Articles of Confederation* failed, the development of the *Constitution of the United States* proved to be a lasting achievement. Its principles of separation of powers and the creation of a federal system of government have survived for over two hundred years.

MINI•ASSESSMENT (2-5)

1 The main purpose of granting life tenure to federal judges is to
  1 help bring about impartiality in their decision making
  2 permit them to obtain judicial experience
  3 assure that they will follow the President's wishes
  4 reward them for their political loyalties

2 Justices of the U.S. Supreme Court
  1 are directly elected by the people
  2 serve six-year terms as do U.S. Senators
  3 can be impeached
  4 must be members of the same political party as the President

3 The efficiency of the federal bureaucracy determines the
  1 impartiality of the courts
  2 the kind of government states have
  3 due process in criminal cases
  4 effectiveness of government programs

Constructed Response

"... a constitution does not in itself imply any more than a declaration of the relationship which the different parts of the government bear to each other, but does not, in any degree, imply security to the rights of the individual."

– Agrippa (20 January 1788)

1 What is the relationship of the "parts" to the "whole" in the *Constitution of the United States*?

2 How was "Agrippa's" concern over individual rights addressed ?

UNIT ASSESSMENT
MULTI-CHOICE QUESTIONS

1   Thomas Jefferson's use of the phrase "… certain unalienable Rights … Life, Liberty, and the Pursuit of Happiness …" in the *Declaration of Independence* illustrates his familiarity with the
1   political legacy of ancient Rome
2   governmental structures of Montesquieu
3   philosophy of John Locke
4   Haudenosaunee or Iroquois political system

2   Under the *Articles of Confederation*,
1   the states were the ultimate source of authority and power
2   the national government had absolute sovereignty
3   new legislation was passed by simple majority
4   a unanimous decision was needed to levy taxes

3   Governmental achievements under the *Articles of Confederation* included
1   a statement of John Locke's basic philosophy of government
2   self-government for the Iroquois
3   establishment of a national court system
4   successful conclusion of the Revolutionary War

4   The system of federalism was adopted by the writers of the *Constitution of the United States* due primarily to their fear of
1   powerful radical groups
2   an overly strong national judiciary
3   aggressive foreign leaders
4   an overpowering central government

5   Which is the best example of the concept of checks and balances?
1   The Senate passes a tax bill approved by the House of Representatives.
2   The President sends an envoy to negotiate a peace settlement in the Middle East.
3   A U.S. District Court hears a case involving drug smuggling from Columbia.
4   The Senate ratifies an arms treaty negotiated with Russia by the President.

6   An Enlightenment idea found in American governmental structure is government by
1   confederation
2   direct democracy
3   consent of the governed
4   divine right

7   Federalism is best defined as a system of government based on
1   branches within a government checking each other's power
2   written guarantees of personal civil liberties
3   passage of legislation by majority vote
4   division of power among levels of governments

8   Which is the basic principle underlying the *Constitution of the United States*?
1   The executive branch should determine the type of government the nation has.
2   Interests of the state are more important than those of the citizens.
3   Government must maintain law and order by any means.
4   Basic power rests with the people.

9   "The proposed Constitution, so far from implying an abolition of the State governments, makes them constituent parts of the national sovereignty, by allowing them a direct representation in the Senate, and leaves in their possession certain exclusive and very important portions of their sovereign power." - *Publius*
The author of this statement believed the
1   *Articles of Confederation* was superior to the *Constitution of the United States*
2   states' power was properly preserved in the *Constitution of the United States*
3   fears of the Anti-Federalists were well founded
4   power of the central government was too weak compared to the states

10   A major objection to the *Constitution of the United States* when it was presented for ratification in 1787 was that it
1   reserved too much power for the states
2   contained too many compromises
3   required the approval of all the states to ratify it
4   provided insufficient guarantees of civil liberties

Base your answer to questions 11 and 12 on the chart below and your knowledge of U.S. history and government.

PAID CIVILIAN EMPLOYEES OF THE UNITED STATES GOVERNMENT*

1816	4,837
1861	36,672
1881	100,000
1935	780,582
1945	3,816,310
1960	2,421,000
1970	2,881,000
1980	3,021,000
1990	2,985,000

* If military employment was added, the figure for 1990 would be over 4.1 million. (Source: Historical & Statistical Abstracts of U.S.)

11 The chart indicates the
1 total number of federal, state, and local government employees
2 non-military national bureaucracy since 1816
3 civilian and military government work force
4 national and state civil service growth for more than 170 years

12 Which statement is best supported by information in the chart?
1 The growth slowed after World War I.
2 The bureaucracy grew at its fastest rate in the 1861-1881 period.
3 In recent years the size of the federal bureaucracy has diminished.
4 States took over many federal functions in the 19th century.

13 The United States is a democratic republic because
1 the government maintains a national court system
2 power rests with citizens and is exercised by representatives
3 the executive branch can veto laws passed by the legislative
4 the chief executive is elected directly by the people

14 In 1787, the authors of the *Constitution of the United States* originally provided for an indirect rather than direct election of United States Presidents and Senators primarily because they believed that
1 only the upper classes should be given citizenship
2 the people could not be fully trusted
3 the checks and balances system could not be fully trusted
4 the electoral college should control elections for both

15 The President of the United States is exercising extra-constitutional powers when
1 appointing a new ambassador to Ireland
2 increasing naval forces in the Persian Gulf region
3 helping a Senator campaign for re-election
4 sending a State of the Union Address to Congress

THEMATIC ESSAY QUESTION

Theme:

checks and balances

With the development of the *Constitution of the United States*, the Founding Fathers created a government based on the rule of law and the belief that power should be checked in a number of ways. In addition to the checks of one branch on another, there is also provision for the citizenry to check the government.

Task:

Using your knowledge of United States history and government, write an essay in which you:

> - Select *three* specific examples of how the provisions of the *Constitution of the United States* provide for a system of checks and balances;
> - Explain how the checks and balances system works in your three examples using specific examples from the *Constitution of the United States*; and
> - Illustrate your explanation with specific historical examples of the checks and balances chosen.

Suggestions:

You may use any examples of checks and balances provided for in the *Constitution of the United States*. You may wish to focus on how the legislative branch may check the executive branch or how the executive branch may check the judicial branch. You may focus on the "advise and consent" role of the Senate or the powers of the Presidency. **You are not limited to these suggestions.**

DOCUMENT BASED QUESTION

The following task is based on the accompanying documents. The documents may have been edited for the purposes of this exercise. The task is designed to test your ability to work with historical documents. As you analyze the documents, take into account both the source of the document and the author's point of view.

Directions: Read the documents in Part A and answer the question after each document. Then read the directions for Part B and write your essay.

Historical Context:

The development and ratification of the *Constitution of the United States* and the Bill of Rights took place over four years from 1787-1791. The new Constitution was controversial from its very beginning. The documents below identify some of the main controversies surrounding the development and ratification of the Constitution.

Task:

Using information from the documents and your knowledge of United States history and government, write an essay in which you

- Identify the main controversies surrounding the development and ratification of the *Constitution of the United States,*
- Explain the reasoning underlying these controversies, and
- State the resolution of the controversies.

Part A - Short Answer (begin on the next page)
Analyze the documents and answer the questions that follow each document.

Questions for Document 1

1   State two principles Madison believed the new national government should possess.

2   Why did Madison believe the people must approve of the new government?

DOCUMENT 1

"Dear Sir,

...I would propose...that in addition to the present federal powers, the national Government should be armed with positive and compleat [complete] authority in all cases which require uniformity; such as the regulation of trade...taxing...imports, the fixing of the terms of naturalization...A Government composed of such extensive powers should be well organized and balanced...To give a new System its proper validity and energy, a ratification must be obtained from the people..."

– James Madison in a letter to George Washington, April 16, 1787

DOCUMENT 2

one figure = 50,000 slaves

Counted for representation and taxation   Not counted for representation and taxation

Question for Document 2

How does the graph represent a solution to a key controversy at the Philadelphia Convention?

Question for Document 3

What does Mason find missing in the Constitution?

DOCUMENT 3

"There is no Declaration of Rights, and the Laws of the general government being paramount to the laws and constitution of the several states, the Declaration of Rights in the separate States are no security."

– George Mason, 1787

Question for Document 4

Why would New Jersey object to representation based on population?

DOCUMENT 4

"To proclaim a national legislature with representation based on population is to proclaim tyranny for New Jersey and small states like it."

– Anonymous delegate, Philadelphia Convention, 1787

Question for Document 5

Explain why the passage from Article I represents a great compromise of the Philadelphia Convention.

GO ON TO PART B

Part B - Essay

Directions:
- Write a well organized essay that includes an introduction, several paragraphs, and a conclusion.
- Use evidence from the documents to support your response.
- Do not simply repeat the contents of the documents.
- Include specific related outside information.

Historical Context:
The development and ratification of the *Constitution of the United States* and the Bill of Rights took place over four years from 1787-1791. The new Constitution was controversial from its very beginning.

Task:
Using information from the documents and your knowledge of United States history and government, write an essay in which you

- identify the main controversies surrounding the development and ratification of the *Constitution of the United States*,
- explain the reasoning underlying these controversies, and
- state the resolution of the controversies.

Be sure to include specific historical details. You must also include additional information from your knowledge of United States history and government.

NO PERMISSION HAS BEEN GRANTED BY N&N PUBLISHING COMPANY, INC TO REPRODUCE ANY PART OF THIS BOOK BY ANY MECHANICAL, PHOTOGRAPHIC, OR ELECTRONIC PROCESS.

N&N©   *UNIT 2 – CONSTITUTIONAL FOUNDATIONS*   Page 91

1800

LOUISIANA PURCHASE (1803)
MARBURY V. MADISON (1803)

1810

WAR OF 1812 (1812-1814)

CONSTITUTIONAL CONFLICTS

1820 MISSOURI COMPROMISE (1820)

1830 TARIFF CONFLICT (1828-1833)
ABOLITIONIST CRUSADE (1830-1860)

1840

MEXICAN WAR (1846-1848)
1850 COMPROMISE OF 1850 (1850)

DRED SCOTT DECISION (1857)

1860

CIVIL WAR (1861-1865)

President Abraham Lincoln
Civil War CD, Digital Stock ©1995

STRUGGLES OF A NEW REPUBLIC

During the Era of the New Republic (1789-1865), the theories behind the new *Constitution of the United States* were put into action. A new government based on a federal union began operation. The actions of the early Presidents and other governmental figures set **precedents** (initial actions that become patterns for future procedures) still in effect today. Taken together, these precedents make up a body of procedures that governmental scholars call the "**unwritten constitution**." Gradually, precedents added specific structure to the ideas that were only vaguely outlined or barely implied in the original *Constitution of the United States*.

DOMESTIC PRECEDENTS: DEVELOPMENT OF THE UNWRITTEN CONSTITUTION

Under the first three Presidents – Washington, John Adams, Jefferson – several procedures became part of the unwritten constitution. These precedents range from the Cabinet, political parties, and powerful law enforcement to judicial review and lobbying.

THE CABINET

In the summer of 1789, Congress created three executive departments to assist the President: Departments of State, Treasury, and War. Washington then appointed Alexander Hamilton to head the Treasury, Thomas Jefferson to serve as Secretary of State (foreign affairs), and Revolutionary general **Henry Knox** (1750-1806) to be Secretary of War. He also named Edmund Randolph to serve as Attorney General (the government's chief prosecutor).

Although the *Constitution of the United States* mentioned establishing "executive departments," there was no reference to their heads forming a special advisory group for the President. Following the custom used in Britain, President Washington called them together as a **cabinet** (an advisory committee) when making executive decisions. All subsequent Presidents

have followed the precedent of having a cabinet. In the first cabinet, Hamilton and Jefferson often disagreed on policy issues. At the core of these conflicts was a perpetual question in U.S. government – how loosely or strictly to interpret the *Constitution of the United States*?

POLITICAL PARTIES

The writers of the *Constitution of the United States* had a distaste for party politics, or what they called government by "competing factions." Yet, such political groups began forming almost immediately. Individuals began to join with others into parties to achieve common goals including:

- electing officials
- influencing the public
- conducting campaigns
- framing solutions to political issues
- monitoring the other groups in power

KEY TERMS

Unwritten Constitution	Sectionalism
Separation of Power	Compromise
Limited Government	Popular Sovereignty
Manifest Destiny	Federalism
Judicial Review	Neutrality
States' Rights	Secession
Due Process	

CURRENT U.S. DEPARTMENTS UNDER THE PRESIDENT

1 State - 1789
2 Treasury - 1789
3 Justice (Attorney General) -1789
4 Interior (federal lands) - 1849
5 Agriculture - 1889
6 Commerce - 1903
7 Labor - 1913
8 Defense - 1947
9 Housing & Urban Development - 1965
10 Transportation - 1966
11 Energy - 1977
12 Health & Human Services - 1977
13 Education - 1979
14 Veterans Affairs - 1989
15 Homeland Security - 2002

Note: Items marked with an * are listed in the *Landmark Supreme Court Decisions* chart in Appendices.

The first two formal political parties emerged during Washington's administration: the **Federalists** and the **Democratic-Republicans**. They began to influence how congressional committees and voting were organized. Eventually, parties determined whom the candidates would be for each elected office at every level of government. Although only indirectly related to today's Democratic and Republican Parties, the Federalists and Democratic-Republicans of the new republic were their forerunners.

LAW ENFORCEMENT

Another early precedent was set in 1794. Western Pennsylvania distillers and farmers seized the federal marshals who were charging them with evading the new federal excise tax. Treasury Secretary Hamilton persuaded Washington to let him ride west with 13,000 militia against this "insurrection" on the frontier. There was no fighting. Only a few protesters were arrested, and they were pardoned afterwards. The use of a large armed force to suppress resistance to federal law set a precedent not covered in the Constitution's Article II on the powers of the executive branch.

The aggressive crackdown of this **Whiskey Rebellion** was criticized as an an overreaction. Yet, it was popular with Federalists for it demonstrated the power of the federal government to enforce the law. However, Hamilton's overblown military action was very unpopular in the remote back country (frontier – region away from the coasts). It nudged many frontier dwellers toward the Democratic-Republican Party which had opposed the use of such governmental force.

COMPARISON OF THE FEDERALISTS AND THE DEMOCRATIC-REPUBLICANS

THE FEDERALISTS

Leaders:

Alexander Hamilton   John Adams

Advocated:
- loose construction
- stronger central gov't.
- central control of economic affairs, pro-national bank & protective tariffs

Supporters:
Wealthy & propertied groups merchants & manufacturers

Foreign Affairs:
. pro-British

THE DEMOCRATIC-REPUBLICANS*

Leaders:

Thomas Jefferson   James Madison

Advocated:
- strict construction
- stronger state governments
- less central control of economic affairs; against a national bank & high tariffs

Supporters:
"Common People" – small farmers, city labor, frontier people

Foreign Affairs:
pro-French

*For a while after 1800, the group was called "Republicans," but is no relation to the modern Republican Party which formed in the 1850s. By the 1830s, the group took the permanent name of "Democrats."

JUDICIAL REVIEW

CONSTITUTIONAL STRUCTURES

The complex power of judicial review was a fourth major precedent to emerge in this early period. **Judicial review** is the power of the Supreme Court to determine if local, state, and federal statutes and governmental actions violate the *Constitution of the United States*. The Constitution grants the Supreme Court some original jurisdiction (cases involving ambassadors, international treaties) but most hearings are brought up on appeal from cases tried in lower state or federal courts.

The power of judicial review grew out of a Supreme Court decision involving job appointments by the President. Just before leaving office in 1801, Federalist President John Adams made a series of appointments of federal judges. Adams did not complete the process. He did not have his Secretary of State deliver the appointments to the appointees. The new Democratic-Republican President, Thomas Jefferson, would not allow his Secretary of State, James Madison, to deliver the appointments. One of Adams' appointees, William Marbury, sued in federal court to force Secretary Madison to deliver his appointment.

The issue went to the Supreme Court in 1803. In *Marbury v. Madison**, the Supreme Court decided for Madison (and indirectly for Jefferson's position).

But in the long run, the Court decided for itself. In the decision, Chief Justice John Marshall overturned a congressional law, the *Judiciary Act of 1789*. In that act, Congress gave the Supreme Court the power to give orders to the President. Chief Justice Marshall said this violated the constitutional principle of separation of power. The Court declared that portion of the *Judiciary Act* unconstitutional. In doing so, the *Marbury* decision set the precedent for judicial review. Marshall served as Chief Justice from 1801-1835, and he strengthened this power of judicial review in a number of famous cases (see chart below). To this day, judicial review remains the Supreme Court's most important – and most controversial – power.

EXECUTIVE AND LEGISLATIVE SEPARATION

Another precedent set by Washington altered the relationship between Congress and the President. Congress wanted to monitor Washington's presidential decisions. It asked for frequent reports by his department heads. This annoyed Washington, and he limited how often his cabinet officers appeared to testify before Congress. This underlined the independence and separation of the executive branch. How far the President could carry this idea of **executive privilege** is still questionable. Recent history shows that Congress and the President still clash over separation of power (see the the "Watergate" and "Iran-Contra" affairs).

LOBBYING

Another precedent set in the early stages of government under the Constitution concerned influence groups. Using the First Amendment's

SIGNIFICANT DECISIONS OF THE SUPREME COURT UNDER CHIEF JUSTICE MARSHALL		
YEARS	DECISIONS	SIGNIFICANCE
1810	Fletcher v. Peck*	Supreme Court established its power to review state laws.
1819	Dartmouth College v. Woodward*	Set precedent that states may not pass laws impairing private contracts.
1819	McCulloch v. Maryland*	Upheld the constitutionality of the Bank of the United States by denying the state of Maryland's attempt to tax a federal institution.
1824	Gibbons v. Ogden*	Established broad interpretation of the federal government's authority over interstate commerce.

"right to petition" clause, many early groups pressured government officials to see their side of an issue. These pressure groups from outside government began to exercise tremendous influence on Congress. It became customary for these individuals and groups to approach Congressional representatives in the entrances of the Capitol. Hence, the name "lobbyists" emerged.

By the year 2000, there were 4,000 registered professional **lobbyists** (hired agents for pressure groups) in Washington D.C. They represent every major business, economic group, foreign nation, and other special interest. Many members of Congress believe that lobbyists present vital information they would not be able to obtain otherwise. Opponents of the influence of lobbyists say the information is always biased, and that lobbyists even lean toward unethical behavior (bribes) to get their way. A number of laws have been passed to monitor and control this practice. Lobbyists must now register with the federal government and publicly report their financial activities.

CREATING DOMESTIC STABILITY: HAMILTON'S FINANCIAL PLAN

ECONOMIC POLICY

Washington's Secretary of the Treasury, Alexander Hamilton, had the formidable challenge of putting the shaky U.S. economy on a firm footing. His basic goals were to: establish the credit of the U.S. among the other nations; provide a sound currency; strengthen the central government; and secure the support of the propertied classes. To do this, Hamilton proposed five key actions:

- repay the foreign debt
- assume debts still unpaid by states from the Revolutionary War
- raise revenue through excise taxes on luxury items (liquor and jewelry) and tariffs
- impose a protective tariff to encourage domestic industries
- create a Bank of the United States to coordinate public and private financial activities

After much debate, negotiation, and **log-rolling** (pressuring and trading of votes), Congress passed most of Hamilton's proposals. One of the most controversial actions was the creation of a national bank (The Bank of the United States). Strict constructionists (taking the Constitution literally) opposed the Bank. They claimed the Constitution delegated no power to Congress to do this. Loose constructionists argued that the "elastic clause" allowed the Bank. They said such a bank was "necessary and proper" to allow Congress to carry out financial responsibilities delegated in Article I Section 8 of the Constitution. The establishment of the Bank of the United States became one of Congress' first uses of the doctrine of implied power.

PRECEDENTS IN FOREIGN POLICY: WASHINGTON THROUGH MONROE

Early presidential administrations also set precedents in foreign affairs. Many of these policies guided America's behavior in the world into the 20th century.

FOREIGN POLICY

NEUTRALITY

Realizing that the new nation was militarily and economically weak, President Washington adopted policies which kept the United States out of unstable European politics. While the Atlantic Ocean provided realistic protection in a time of slow-moving transportation, the United States was still surrounded by British and Spanish possessions. France's revolutionary politics had wide-ranging effects on America.

President Washington tried to keep the United States politically neutral. Still, the U.S. was economically linked to major European trading powers. In order to avoid being drawn into the conflicts between Britain and France, Washington issued a *Proclamation of Neutrality* in 1793. Later, as he left the presidency, Washington advised the new nation to "steer clear of permanent alliances with any portion of the foreign world." This advice in the *Farewell Address* became a cornerstone of a long-standing American isolationist tradition.

1 The establishment of a Cabinet and political parties during the administration of George Washington best illustrates
  1 the use of the amending process to the Constitution
  2 the early development of the "unwritten constitution"
  3 the application of specific provisions of the *Constitution of the United States*
  4 efforts to maintain a division of power between the three branches of government

2 In 1794, President George Washington sent federal troops into Western Pennsylvania to deal with an uprising known as the Whiskey Rebellion. The significance of President Washington's action is that it
  1 strengthened the power of local and state governments
  2 forced Congress to pass the Bill of Rights
  3 showed the strength of the federal government under the Constitution
  4 weakened the power of the federal government to collect sales taxes

3 "The Constitution is what the Supreme Court says it is!"
  This statement refers to the idea that
  1 the original Constitution was framed by judges and lawyers
  2 the Supreme Court interprets the meaning of the Constitution
  3 amendments must receive the Supreme Court's approval before they are enacted
  4 decisions of the Supreme Court cannot be reversed

Constructed Response

"I consider the foundation of the Constitution as laid on this ground – that all powers not delegated to the United States, by the Constitution, nor prohibited by it to the states, are reserved to the states, or to the people [Tenth Amendment]. To take a single step beyond the boundaries thus specially drawn around the powers of Congress, is to take possession of a boundless field of power, no longer susceptible of any definition."

– Thomas Jefferson (1791)

A modern day depiction of "Alexander Hamilton's view of the Constitution"

1 What two opposing views of the Constitution are expressed in the passage and the picture above?

2 How were these views expressed in the arguments over the creation of the Bank of the United States during the Washington Administration?

ECONOMIC PRESSURES

In this early period, the country's economic needs often determined the path Presidents took in foreign affairs.

JAY'S TREATY (1795)

Britain did not live up to its promises in the *Treaty of Paris* (1783) which ended the American Revolution. The British kept troops in the western regions of the U.S. They also ignored financial claims of American merchants.

While at war with France, Britain's commanders harassed U.S. ships and impressed American seamen into the British Navy. (**Impressment** is the act or policy of seizing people or property for public service or use.) Washington sent Chief Justice John Jay – an accomplished diplomat – on a mission to Britain to try to settle these problems. As a result of **Jay's Treaty** (ratified in 1795), a number of issues were settled. Jay's Treaty made many concessions about trade, and it was unpopular in the U.S. Yet, it did improve relations with Britain, and the threat of war subsided.

PINCKNEY'S TREATY (1795)

Around the same time, Ambassador **Thomas Pinckney** negotiated a useful treaty with Spain. The *Treaty of San Lorenzo* (ratified in 1795), or *Pinckney's Treaty*, settled American rights on the Mississippi. Western farmers received the **right of deposit** to transship goods through the Spanish port of New Orleans safely.

JEFFERSON'S EMBARGO (1807)

In the first decade of the 19th century, when the Napoleonic Wars broke out in Europe, the United States stayed neutral. Britain blockaded the European continent and choked off supplies to France. Also, the British continued to pester U.S. ships and impress sailors. At the same time, the French launched a counter blockade of the British Isles. United States trade across the Atlantic and in the Caribbean suffered. By the middle of the decade, the annoying incidents multiplied to the point that President Jefferson took action. He successfully pressed Congress to pass an *Embargo Act*. It forbade all U.S. foreign trade. The embargo was extremely unpopular with trading interests. It was quickly repealed in favor of a law which restricted trade only with warring Britain and France.

THE WAR OF 1812

President James Madison (term: 1809-1817) inherited the neutrality problems from Jefferson. He failed at diplomatic efforts to keep the United States from being drawn into the European conflict.

The neutral United States became a pawn in the British struggle with Napoleon. The British set up an effective naval blockade to force all neutral trade to Europe through their ports. France condemned neutral shipping that obeyed British regulations. Madison protested that neutrals' rights on the seas were being violated by both nations. Also, the British impressed any British sailors who were serving on American merchant ships. Frequently, they impressed Americans along with English sailors.

British actions threatened economic depression. Some Americans wanted a declaration of war. In Congress, a group of young Western and Southern Congressmen (**John C. Calhoun**, SC and **Henry Clay**, KY) – all Democratic-Republicans – blamed the British for inciting the Native Americans in their region and patriotically called for war. Among these young **"War Hawks"** there was an underlying desire to take British lands from Canada. Federalists in New England opposed the drive toward war, claiming the area had suffered from the 1808 Embargo, and a war would totally destroy the economy.

By 1812, the War Hawks managed to get control of Congress. They pressured Madison into asking Congress for a declaration of war against Britain. Congress declared war in June, 1812. Madison was forced to follow through and conduct a war for which the United States was unprepared.

American hopes of conquering Canada collapsed in disastrous campaigns in 1812 and 1813. Attacks were uncoordinated. Detroit surrendered to the British in August 1812 and American troops lost the Battle of Queenston Heights in October and withdrew from Lake Champlain in November.

"We have met the enemy and they are ours."
Oliver Perry Defeats the British on Lake Erie,
September 1813   – ©1996 Wildside Press

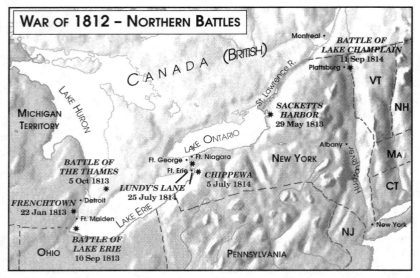

On the oceans, American ships won a series of battles with the British. However, the British were successful in tightening a blockade around America's coasts, ruining American trade.

In 1813, American attempts to invade Canada failed again. The only success was in the West. Americans won control of the Detroit frontier region when the ships of Oliver Hazard Perry destroyed the British fleet on Lake Erie.

The British defeated Napoleon in Europe in 1814 and began to transfer large numbers of troops to the fighting in America. The British appeared near success in the late summer of 1814. In August, they marched into Washington, D.C. and burned most of the public buildings. President Madison fled into the countryside.

In 1815, even though the War had officially ended, the British attacked New Orleans and isolated naval actions continued for a few months. In January 1815, Gen. Andrew Jackson won a decisive victory at New Orleans over the attacking British forces.

Peace came with the ***Treaty of Ghent*** late in 1814. The treaty acknowledged the war was a draw and none of the causes were addressed. However, relations with Britain improved throughout the next decade.

TERRITORIAL EXPANSION

CONSTITUTIONAL DILEMMA OF LOUISIANA (1803)

In 1800, the vast Louisiana Territory west of

the Mississippi was ceded by the Spanish government to France. The French leader, Napoleon, envisioned using Louisiana as part of a new French Empire based in the Caribbean. President Jefferson, content with a weak Spain in control of Louisiana, grew alarmed at the prospects of dealing with the much more powerful French. Westerners worried that the previously negotiated right of deposit at New Orleans would end.

Jefferson authorized James Monroe and Robert Livingston to travel to France and attempt to purchase New Orleans and some of adjacent West Florida. Napoleon, having failed in his new attempts at an empire in Santo Domingo, offered all of Louisiana to the Americans. Negotiations between the two sides settled the purchase price at $15 million.

Jefferson did not expect to be offered the entire territory. He had doubts about the constitutionality of the purchase. The Constitution is vague on the acquisition of new territory, and Jefferson

CONSTITUTIONAL STRUCTURES

was for strict interpretation of the Constitution. He even considered an amendment to carry out the purchase, but he feared that delay would lead Napoleon to change his mind. Jefferson saw the need this one time for a loose interpretation of the Constitution. He put the Louisiana

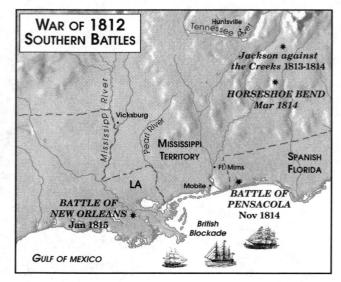

WAR OF 1812 SOUTHERN BATTLES

Purchase in a treaty between the two nations, which the Senate soon ratified.

The Louisiana Territory doubled the size of the United States, and it extended the western boundary of the nation to the Rocky Mountains. Jefferson desired information about the new land and directed **Meriwether Lewis** and **William Clark** to lead an expedition into the new territory. During the 1804-1806 trip, **Sacajawea** (1784-1812), a Shoshone Native American, gave valuable assistance to the explorers on their journey westward to the Columbia River and the Pacific Coast. Stories of the trip helped spark added interest in western lands, though large scale settlement was still decades away.

In recognition of her valuable assistance to the Lewis and Clark Expedition, the Sacajawea "Golden" Dollar was issued by the U.S. Mint in 2000.

In the next decade, the War of 1812 increased Americans' interest in western lands, both in settlement and investment. A surging nationalism swept the country in the postwar years.

The interest in western lands spurred road and canal building. The **Cumberland** (**National**) **Road** was financed by Congress, and New York State built the **Erie Canal**. The Canal made Buffalo a major western port by connecting it to Albany and New York City.

DEMOCRATIC IDEALISM IN FOREIGN POLICY: THE MONROE DOCTRINE

FOREIGN POLICY

Also during this national period, President **James Monroe** (1758-1831, term 1817-1825), set another major foreign policy precedent, a cornerstone that eventually bore his name. In 1823, Imperial Russia was intruding on United States' Pacific territorial claims in the Oregon region. In addition, an alliance of European powers (Austria, France, Prussia, and Russia) sought to reclaim Latin American colonies that had declared their independence during the Napoleonic Wars.

President Monroe's Secretary of State, **John Quincy Adams** (1767-1848), urged

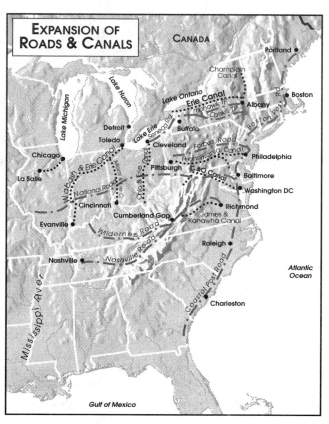

EXPANSION OF ROADS & CANALS

MINI•ASSESSMENT (3-2)

1 Which foreign policy advice did George Washington give in his *Farewell Address* of 1796?
   1 A new and weak nation should ally itself with the stronger nations of Europe.
   2 European countries would not try to establish new colonies in the Western Hemisphere.
   3 The United States has the right to intervene in a Latin American nation when necessary.
   4 The new nation should avoid permanent alliances with any other nation of the world.

2 Jefferson's embargo policy can best be explained as
   1 favoring the British over the French
   2 favoring the French over the British
   3 an attempt to keep out of the Napoleonic Wars
   4 a violation of the loose construction of the *Constitution of the United States*

3 In 1823, the Monroe Doctrine was established mainly because the United States wanted to
   1 keep control of Alaska and Hawaii
   2 establish more colonies in Latin America
   3 support England's attempt to keep its empire in Central America
   4 warn Europe against any further colonization in Latin America

Constructed Response

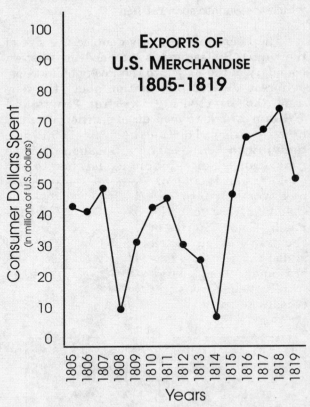

EXPORTS OF U.S. MERCHANDISE 1805-1819

Consumer Dollars Spent (in millions of U.S. dollars)

Years

1 What two years from the chart were the lowest in the dollar value of exports?

2 Explain how foreign events helped account for the two sharp declines in the first two decades of the 19th century.

---

the President to take action in the form of a warning to Europe that there would be no more colonization of the Western Hemisphere. The United States pledged it would not interfere with existing colonies, and repeated its determination to remain neutral in European affairs. Part of Monroe's December 1823 annual message to Congress outlined this policy which later became known as the **Monroe Doctrine**. Britain, wanting to keep its trade with the new American republics flourishing, quietly backed Monroe. The policy was successful in discouraging the European alliance. The Monroe Doctrine became a cornerstone of United States foreign policy throughout the 19th and 20th centuries.

THE CONSTITUTION TESTED

SECTIONAL DIFFERENCES DEVELOP

An "Era of Good Feeling" followed the War of 1812. It was a short-lived period of national harmony and political cooperation. Perhaps it is symbolic of the era that when President Monroe ran for his second term in 1820, he was unopposed and received all but one electoral vote. Despite the harmony, there were differences of opinion developing that soon caused deep divisions among the leaders of sections of the country. Tense national debates evolved over the

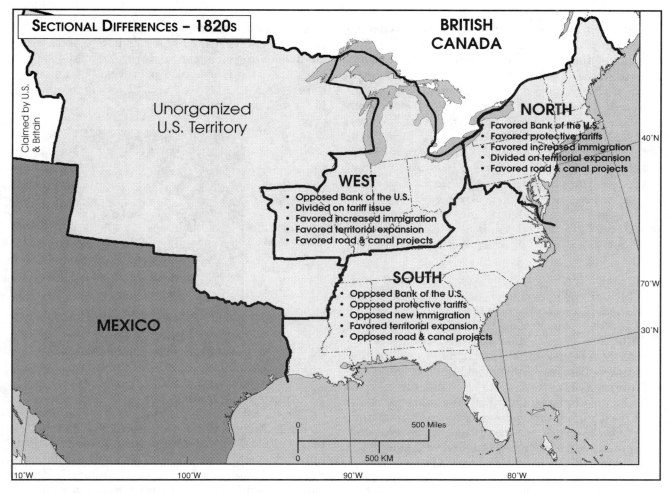

SECTIONAL DIFFERENCES – 1820s

BRITISH CANADA

Claimed by U.S. & Britain

Unorganized U.S. Territory

NORTH
- Favored Bank of the U.S.
- Favored protective tariffs
- Favored increased immigration
- Divided on territorial expansion
- Favored road & canal projects

WEST
- Opposed Bank of the U.S.
- Divided on tariff issue
- Favored increased immigration
- Favored territorial expansion
- Favored road & canal projects

SOUTH
- Opposed Bank of the U.S.
- Opposed protective tariffs
- Opposed new immigration
- Favored territorial expansion
- Opposed road & canal projects

MEXICO

40°N

70°W

30°N

0   500 Miles

0   500 KM

10°W   100°W   90°W   80°W

power of the central government, states' rights, and slavery. Those arguments escalated into a bloody civil war forty years later.

By the late 1820s, the "Era of Good Feeling" fell victim to **sectionalism** (giving primary loyalty to a state or region rather than to the nation as a whole). For example, in the South, supporters of states' rights proclaimed the states were supreme over the federal government. The different life styles in the sections of United States became more pronounced with the economic development and population shifts after the War of 1812:

- The commercial North favored policies which would protect its industries from foreign competition, increase trade, and provide a strong banking system.

- The agricultural South hoped to increase its cotton exports and generally favored less interference from the federal government.

- The agricultural West wanted federal protection and transportation improvements but was against regulated banking.

THE TARIFF CONTROVERSY

In 1828, Congress passed a very high protective tariff (Southerners called it the "**Tariff of Abominations**"). While its aim was to protect infant Northern industries from foreign competition, Southerners felt that the tariff could ruin their economy. High rates would increase the cost of foreign manufactured goods in the South and lead to **reciprocation** (retaliation by foreign nations raising their tariffs against Southern cotton exports).

CONSTITUTIONAL STRUCTURES

The South's most gifted spokesman was the brilliant senator from South Carolina, John C. Calhoun, who later served as Jackson's Vice President. In 1828, Senator Calhoun secretly wrote the *South*

Carolina Exposition and Protest denouncing the *Tariff of 1828*. In the essay, Calhoun spelled out the **doctrine of nullification**. He claimed that states, like the Supreme Court, could proclaim acts of the federal government unconstitutional. Calhoun said a state could declare such federal laws "null and void" inside its borders. Also, the Senator said that states have the "right to secede" (leave the Union). This doctrine of nullification was in direct opposition to Article VI of the *Constitution of the United States*. Known as the "supremacy clause," Article VI says that laws made by the federal government must be adhered to by the states. It also says that states cannot pass laws that contradict federal law.

STATES' RIGHTS

Other national leaders rejected Calhoun's arguments concerning the rights of states. In 1830, the U.S. Senate became the site of an intense debate over the doctrine of nullification between **Daniel Webster** (MA, 1782-1852) and **Robert Y. Hayne** (SC, 1791-1839), successor to Calhoun's Senate seat. Hayne championed the state's rights or state supremacy position. Senator Webster theorized that the federal government is not an agent of individual states, but an agent of the people at large. He argued that only the Supreme Court could declare laws unconstitutional. He said that if the states could nullify federal laws, the Union would become a mere "rope of sand."

This debate over the relationship of power between state governments and the federal government was not new. The writers of the Constitution had argued over the concept of federalism at the Philadelphia Convention in 1787.

Andrew Jackson (1767-1845) became President in 1829. He was born in the South and raised in the West. Jackson was a Tennessee farmer whose military exploits in the War of 1812, made him a hero of the common people. He despised the "old aristocracy" of the North – the powerful merchants and financiers who controlled the central **Bank of the United States**. As a Westerner, Jackson also disliked the Tariff of 1828.

Still, President Jackson was sworn to defend the *Constitution of the United States* and the federal law. In the controversy over the tariff, he had to make a choice between his oath and his roots. At a Jefferson Day party in 1830, Jackson let his feelings be known in an official toast: "Our Union – it must be preserved!" Calhoun countered with his own toast: "The Union – next to our liberty, most dear!"

Andrew Jackson (Library of Congress)

The situation grew into a constitutional crisis. Anger grew against the tariff and against the President. Finally, a confrontation occurred in 1832. Despite Congress passing the Jackson-backed *Tariff Act of 1832* which substantially reduced tariff rates, Vice President Calhoun resigned. South Carolina invoked Calhoun's doctrine of nullification. A special state convention officially declared the tariff "null and void" and refused to abide by it. The Convention defiantly stated that if the federal government tried to enforce the tariff law, South Carolina would secede (leave) from the Union.

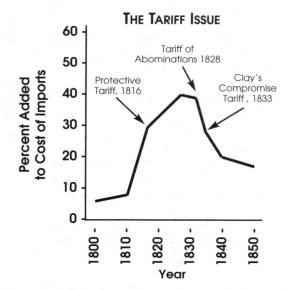

THE TARIFF ISSUE

Henry Clay
(Chicago Historical Society)

South Carolina's action incensed President Jackson. He prepared to send federal troops to enforce the law. A compromise offered by Kentucky's Senator **Henry Clay** (1777-1852) averted armed confrontation. Senator Clay introduced a bill to gradually reduce the tariff to levels acceptable to both the North and the South. Congress passed Clay's compromise and the constitutional crisis subsided. Still, the issue of states' rights was not resolved. It plagued the nation for another generation, and it was the main cause of the Civil War in the 1860s.

THE BANK CONTROVERSY

In another states' rights issue, the South succeeded in opposing the powerful financial interests of the North. This time, President Jackson took the South's side. He had long believed that the Bank of the United States was a financial monopoly and made life difficult for debt-ridden farmers. In the eyes of agrarian Southerners and Westerners, the Bank was a corrupt tool of Northern financiers that kept interest rates high and made borrowing difficult. In its place, the Bank's opponents wanted numerous state-chartered banks that would be more sensitive to the needs of each region.

The congressional charter of the Bank of the United States was not up for renewal until 1836. To embarrass Jackson and hurt his chances for reelection, Whig Party candidate Henry Clay and his supporters tried to have it renewed in 1832.

The Bank had always been controversial. Originally, the authority of Congress to set up such a national bank as part of Alexander Hamilton's financial plan in 1791 was questioned. Opponents said the power was not specifically mentioned in the Constitution. Proponents claimed it was a proper use of the elastic clause (implied power), because the Constitution gives Congress power over the nation's currency.

MCCULLOCH V. MARYLAND

Congress allowed the Bank's charter to lapse in 1811, but rechartered it for another 20 years in 1816. Its authority was challenged in the Supreme Court in 1819. In *McCulloch v. Maryland**, Chief Justice John Marshall said that Congress is given implied power in the Constitution's Article I, Section 8 – the "elastic clause" – to do what is "necessary and proper" to carry out its delegated powers. According to Marshall, the Bank of the United States was a constitutionally proper use of the elastic clause. In the same landmark case, Marshall also ruled on the supremacy of the federal law, saying that a state (in this case, Maryland) had no right to interfere with the functioning of a federal agency like the Bank.

Despite all this, President Jackson blocked the Bank recharter bill in early 1832. In his veto message, Jackson claimed Congress stretched its power too far. He said the Bank was a misuse of government power to create privileges for the rich at the expense of "the humble members of the society."

Ultimately, Jackson's Bank veto proved to be a disaster not only for the economy but for Jackson's political followers. In actuality, the Bank provided considerable economic stability for the country. After the veto, unregulated "wildcat" state banks proceeded to issue paper securities of little value. They made unwise loans and speculated in Western lands with depositors' money. The country entered a long and dismal depression as Jackson left office in 1837. Unregulated banking, triggered by the Bank veto and combined with changes in foreign investment, sent the economy into a downward spiral. Jackson required gold or silver to purchase federal land, contributing to the depression. Jackson's successor, **Martin Van Buren** (NY) had to preside over this disaster, and it cost him re-election in 1840.

Martin Van Buren
(Library of Congress)

DEMOCRACY EXPANDS

GROWTH OF DEMOCRACY

Prior to and during the presidency of Andrew Jackson, the number of Americans able to take part in the democratic process expanded. When the Constitution took effect in 1789, most of the original thirteen states limited voting and office holding to persons owning a specific amount of property. Participation in the democratic process began to change in the first half of the 19th century. Frontier states beyond the Appalachian Mountains were admitted to the Union. In these new states, nearly everyone owned property. With no older, aristocratic establishment dominating the economic and political life, equality was closer to reality. As a result, **suffrage** (the right to vote) in the Western states was generally extended to all white males. By 1830, most eastern states had followed the lead of the West, dropping most property requirements.

Another political reform in what some historians call the "Age of Jacksonian Democracy" was in the presidential election process. The Constitution makes no mention of either political party or how to select presidential candidates.

Soon after the Constitution was adopted, a two party system emerged. Prior to 1828, candidates for the presidency were selected by party **caucuses** (small groups of party members) in Congress. The general party membership played no part in the selection process. Voters began to demand a greater voice in party affairs. Beginning in 1832, a new system emerged: the **national nominating convention**. Prior to an election, party members in each state selected delegates to represent them at these national conventions to choose candidates.

Another democratic reform was in how Electors of the President were chosen. The Constitution left this up to the states. In most states before the 1830s, caucuses within the state legislatures chose the Electors. By the 1830s, most states were letting the voters choose the Electors directly.

These election reforms greatly increased the interest in Presidential politics among average citizens. Campaigning among the masses became necessary if a candidate wanted to gain support of the increasing number of voters.

VOTING EXPANDS		
YEAR	POPULAR VOTE	TOTAL POPULATION VOTING (%)
1824	356,000	3.3 %
1828	1,155,000	9.5 %
1840	2,404,000	14.1 %

From the chart above, it is evident that while the popular vote was increasing, most people still did not go to the polls. The political reforms affected only white males. It would be many decades before women, African Americans, or Native Americans would be permitted to cast ballots.

Democracy bypassed Native Americans in the 19th century. As the frontier moved westward, settlers put increasing pressure on the federal government to remove Native American groups from the land. Previously, the government had officially dealt with the Native Americans as if they were separate foreign nations, making treaties which were often broken. In the 1830s, President Jackson proposed that eastern groups of Native Americans should be moved to a special Indian Territory, west of the Mississippi (the location of the present state of Oklahoma). Here, he claimed they would be free to practice their own ways and free of harassment by white settlers. Those Native American nations refusing to go peacefully were to be forcibly moved by the U.S. Army.

The **Cherokee Nation** sought to fight this removal policy in the U.S. Supreme Court. Despite the fact that Chief Justice Marshall ruled (**Worcester v. Georgia***, 1832) that the state of Georgia could not take their lands, Congress took no supportive action for the Cherokee. The takeover, and the forced removals continued. By the 1850s, settlers were streaming across the Mississippi, and more restrictions and violence were in store for the Native Americans.

AN AMERICAN CULTURE EMERGES

After the War of 1812, domestic affairs became the focus of American life. To outside observers, such as French writer **Alexis De Tocqueville** (*Democracy in America*, 1835), everyone in this bustling society seemed to be in motion. Americans were aware that change was an essential part of their lives. The fluid first half of the 19th century produced a variety of reform movements. New ideas flowed freely in religion, education, and literature. Reformers worked to discourage alcohol consumption, abolish slavery, promote women's rights, and improve treatment of the mentally ill. While some praised the reformers as humanitarians who wanted to improve society, others viewed them as fanatics who tried to force their beliefs on everyone. The Northern and Midwestern

---

MINI•ASSESSMENT (3-3)

1 Sectional differences developed in the United States largely because
   1 the federal government adopted a policy of neutrality
   2 economic conditions and interests in each region varied
   3 only Northerners were represented at the Constitutional Convention
   4 early Presidents favored urban areas over rural areas

2 The South objected to the 1828 "Tariff of Abominations" because the tariff
   1 encouraged increased trade with nations that had outlawed slavery
   2 placed taxes on agricultural exports grown in the South
   3 increased the cost of imported goods and reciprocation could ruin of Southern plantation agriculture
   4 increased the power of the Bank of the United States by giving it more funds

3 Before the Civil War, one example of increased democracy was the
   1 elimination of property ownership as a requirement for voting in national elections
   2 granting of the right to vote to women

3 elimination of the electoral college system for electing the President
4 extension of suffrage to most African Americans

Constructed Response

House vote on the Tariff of 1828 (Tariff of Abominations)

Section	For	Against
New England	16	23
Middle Atlantic	55	11
West (OH, IN, IL, MO)	17	1
South	3	50
Southwest (TN,KY)	12	9

1 What two sections were most clearly for the tariff? What section was in near total opposition?

2 How does the 1828 vote show the different economic concerns of the various sections?

---

states were home to most of these efforts. The South was less a part of this national movement. The Southern leaders created laws to protect slavery from any reformers protecting agrarian life to ward off attacks on slavery.

RELIGIOUS REFORMS

In the 1820-1860 period, Northern religious revivalists created what has been called the **Second Great Awakening**. (The original Great Awakening took place in Colonial America during the 1740s.) The movement challenged Calvinist beliefs of predestination, and the practices of more traditional religions, such as Congregational, Presbyterian, and Episcopalian. Some new preachers proclaimed the imminent second coming of Christ. Many held religious revivals that were characterized by emotional conversions. In Rochester (New York), evangelist **Charles Grandison Finney** (1792-1875) preached that men and women controlled their own destinies, and could choose not to sin. During the revival era, Baptists and Methodists grew into two of the largest American denominations.

Two religions that emerged outside mainstream 19th century American society were the Mormons and the Shakers. **Joseph Smith** (1805-1844) of Palmyra, NY founded the Church of Jesus Christ of Latter-day Saints in the 1830s. **Mormonism** held that Jesus had appeared in Pre-Columbian America. This and other Mormon beliefs were found in Smith's

Joseph Smith, Jr.
(courtesy of "All About Mormons, www.mormons.org)

translation of the newly discovered *Book of Mormon*. Many Americans condemned the new scriptural revelation and also the Mormon practice of polygamy. Discouraged by their hostile reception in many towns in the 1840s (Smith was murdered in Illinois), the Mormons continued moving west. In 1846, under the leadership of **Brigham Young** (1801-1877), they journeyed to the Great Salt Lake in Utah territory. Their cooperative, strictly ruled communities tamed the desert, controlled water supplies, and prospered in relative isolation.

Another group became known as **Shakers** for their gyrations during meetings. Formally the Millennial Church (or the United Society of Believers in Christ's Second Appearing), they were originally a Quaker reform sect in England. By 1776, **Mother Ann Lee** emigrated to upstate New York to form a religious community that practiced celibacy and believed the world would soon end. Through revivals, membership increased, though it never approached the large numbers of other religions. Prior to 1860, membership peaked at 6,000 and began to decline afterwards. Shakers rejected Calvinist beliefs and operated in small, self-sufficient agrarian communities supported through sales of craft items.

EDUCATIONAL CHANGES

Formal education underwent major changes in the first half of the 19th century. Rural schools typically educated all ages in one room in primitive conditions. Corporal punishment was common, attendance sporadic, and teachers poorly trained. The privileged and upper classes usually sent their children to private schools, to tutors, or in some cases, to Europe for classical education.

In the 1830s, the democratic spirit that broadened political participation in the Jacksonian Era swept in changes in education. As secretary of the Massachusetts State Board of Education from 1837-1848, reformer **Horace Mann** (1796-1859) pushed for change. He called for state funded schools with separate grades, a longer school year, standard texts, and teacher training schools. **Henry Barnard** (1811-1900) sought similar reforms in Rhode Island and Connecticut. Supporters of school reform praised the emphasis on punctuality, the competitive

Emma Hart Willard
(New York Public Library)

NATIONAL LITERATURE APPEARS

The period from 1800-1860 saw the blossoming of American literature. A number of creative individuals from New England and New York became known as the "American Romantics." They produced a vigorous new national literature that became famous throughout the world.

New England intellectuals contributed a diverse range of work. **Henry Wadsworth Longfellow**'s (1807-1882) historical poems such as *Evangeline* (1847) and *Song of Hiawatha* (1855) celebrated the uniqueness of American experience. **Ralph Waldo Emerson** (1803-1882) promoted transcendentalist thought through lectures and essays (*Nature, Representative Man*). In *Civil Disobedience* (1849) and *Walden* (1854), **Henry David Thoreau** (1817-1862) criticized American government, society in general, and supported an individual's right to disobey unjust laws.

atmosphere, and an informed electorate. Opponents included farmers and the poor who needed children to work and Catholics who cited a Protestant bias in the curriculum. Educational improvements spread rapidly throughout much of New England, the Middle Atlantic, and Midwestern states but were adopted much more slowly in the South.

During this time, reformers also made the first efforts to provide formal education for women. **Emma Willard** (1787-1870) opened a school for girls in Troy (NY) in 1795, and **Mary Lyon** (1797-1849) founded what later became Mt. Holyoke College in Massachusetts (1837), one of the oldest women's colleges in America. In 1833, Oberlin College in Ohio became the first co-educational college in the United States. However, few young women were able to take advantage of these initial educational opportunities.

From the banks of New York's Hudson River, **Washington Irving** (1783-1859) created the mythical lives of Rip Van Winkle and Ichabod Crane in his *Sketch Book* (1820). Another New Yorker, **James Fenimore Cooper** (1789-1851), wrote the "Leatherstocking Tales" – novels of the colonial American frontier including *The Last of the Mohicans* (1847), *The Deerslayer* (1841), and *The Spy* (1847).

Signet Classic

James Fenimore Cooper
THE LAST OF THE MOHICANS

Boston-born **Edgar Allan Poe** (1809-1849) spent a tumultuous life writing and editing in New York, Virginia, and Baltimore. His poems (*The Raven*, 1845 and *The Bells*, 1849) and short stories (*The Fall of the House of Usher*, 1845), while sometimes macabre, gave American literature a rich heritage. Other authors during this near "golden age" penned what have become American classics. Among them were the poems of **Walt Whitman** (1819-1892; (*Leaves of Grass*, 1855), and the novels of **Nathaniel Hawthone** (1804-1864; *The Scarlet Letter*, 1850 and *The*

House of the Seven Gables, 1851), and **Herman Melville** (1819-1891; *Moby Dick*, 1851).

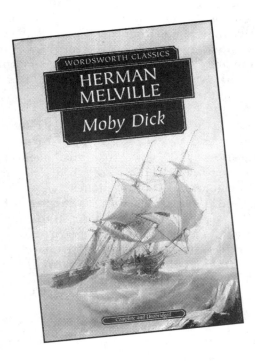

Walt Whitman
(National Portrait Gallery, Smithsonian Institution, Washington, DC)

SOCIAL REFORMS

In the expanding, prosperous society of the Pre-Civil War Era, there were many attempts to purify the defects of society. Alcohol consumption surged dramatically in the first decades of the 19th century. Excessive drinking resulted in abuse at home and poor performance at work. Wages spent on alcohol kept many in poverty. The concern over alcohol abuse led to the rise of the temperance movement. Its followers sought to limit, and later ban, alcohol consumption.

Reverend **Lyman Beecher** (1775-1863), a religious revivalist from Connecticut, was one of the first to call for total prohibition of alcohol in 1825. The American Temperance Society, founded in 1826, urged total abstinence. Factory owners supported the temperance movement, hoping for a more reliable workforce. By the 1840s, the movement for a legal prohibition of alcohol was growing. Maine became the first state in 1851 to ban the sale of alcohol, and other states soon followed with their own restrictions. Although not everyone agreed with the goals and methods of the temperance

movement, it succeeded in reducing consumption of alcohol by mid-century.

Of course, abolition of slavery was the burning social and political issue of the time. Abolitionists had limited success in the North and even less in the South. Initial efforts included the work of the American Colonization Society, founded in 1817. Its goal was gradual emancipation and the return of freed African Americans to Africa. The Society was instrumental in establishing what became the nation of Liberia in West Africa (1822) for this latter purpose. Few actually gained freedom, however, and even fewer freed African Americans returned to Africa.

Liberian Flag
Shows American influence with star and stripes.

By 1831, abolitionists were becoming more militant and radical. Boston editor **William Lloyd Garrison** (1805-1879) led the movement for immediate emancipation. Garrison wrote in *The Liberator*, "I am in earnest. I will not equivocate. I will not excuse. I will not retreat a single inch and I will be heard." Others in the abolition movement included the **Grimke** sisters (**Angelina**, 1792-1873 and **Sarah**, 1805-1879), who lectured throughout the North for the American Anti-Slavery Society in the 1830s and 1840s. The Grimke sisters also demanded equality for women. **Harriet Tubman** (1821-1913), along with **Frederick Douglass** (1817-1895) and **Sojourner Truth** (1797-1883), worked with abolitionists to form the "underground railway" – a secret network of operatives and "safe houses" to smuggle escaped slaves to Canada in the 1850s.

Abolitionists petitioned Congress year after year to end slavery in Washington D.C. In 1836, Congress passed the "gag rule," which forbade any discussion of slavery. Former President John Quincy Adams, a member of the House from Massachusetts after his term in the White House, forced the repeal of the gag rule in 1845.

Dorothea Dix
(Library of Congress)

Many militants in the early women's rights movement, including **Lucretia Mott** (1793-1880), **Elizabeth Cady Stanton** (1815-1902), and the Grimke sisters, started as abolitionists. In 1848, leading American women met at Seneca Falls (NY) to issue the ***Declaration of Sentiments***. This statement, patterned after the *Declaration of Independence*, declared that all men and women are created equal. In all, the women at Seneca Falls passed twelve resolutions demanding equality.

Dorothea Dix (1802-1887), a Unitarian school teacher, led a crusade to improve the horrible treatment of the insane and mentally ill. In her 1846 report to the Massachusetts legislature, Dix described the deplorable conditions of the insane. The report helped to persuade state lawmakers to appropriate money for public mental institutions and provide more humane conditions.

Symbolic of the optimistic spirit in American society at this time were a small number of visionaries fostering utopian communities. They believed that small perfect societies could be achieved. After emigrating from Scotland, **Robert Owen** (1771-1858) founded New Harmony, Indiana in 1825. It failed after two years because, while it offered excellent educational facilities, it attracted many

Frederick Douglass
(Civil War CD, Digital Stock ©1995)

individualists who were not willing to work hard for each other's survival. Other experimental communities were planned based on the premise that suffering and evil would vanish if social conditions could be controlled and perfected. Another community – popular with intellectuals such as Emerson and Hawthorne – was Brook Farm (1841-1846) in Massachusetts. Unfortunately, New Harmony, Brook Farm, and most other similar communities soon failed amidst bickering and disagreements.

In the decades before the Civil War, idealism and restlessness blended to forge the American character. The desire to perfect life through new ideas and reforms was an outward sign of this character. The quest for equality, the searching for religious satisfaction, and the probing for intellectual innovation shaped the American mind and attitude.

TERRITORIAL EXPANSION AND MANIFEST DESTINY

The first phase of territorial expansion took place in 1803, with the purchase of Louisiana (see pg. 100). Explored by Lewis and Clark, most of the region saw few settlers until the mid 19th century. However, events in the 1840s led to increased settlement and the desire to extend American control westward to the Pacific Ocean.

THE WEST PRIOR TO AMERICAN EXPANSION: SPANISH, MEXICAN, NATIVE AMERICAN

Spanish control of Western lands lasted until the early 19th century. Through a network of missions, the Spanish language and Roman Catholic faith spread through the region. Mexican independence in the 1820s resulted in the control of western lands by Mexico. Through routes such as the Santa Fe Trail, Americans carried on trade with Mexicans who lived in these lands. Some of the Native Americans in these western lands were residents of the missions. Others were used as forced labor by the Mexicans, while some remained free of Spanish and Mexican control and carried on a nomadic lifestyle. The Comanches, Apaches, and Navahos often came into conflict with Mexicans in the sparsely settled region.

MANIFEST DESTINY

During the 1840s, New York journalist John O'Sullivan created the term "Manifest Destiny." He wrote that it was the United States' "divine

---

MINI•ASSESSMENT (3-4)

1 Many of the religious revivals of the early 19th century included the belief that
   1 only the Church hierarchy could live relatively free of sin
   2 men and women could control or eliminate sin
   3 the Bible was not important in the practice of religion
   4 men and women were predestined by God to sin

2 Advocates of school reform saw their efforts even more necessary as immigration increased because the reforms would
   1 discourage new immigrants from coming to America
   2 provide teaching jobs for the immigrants
   3 help assimilate the immigrants into American society
   4 provide the schools with a more diverse atmosphere

3 The main goal of the Seneca Falls Convention (1848) was to
   1 organize the first labor union in the United States
   2 correct the abuses of big business
   3 make the public aware of environmental problems
   4 obtain equal rights for women

Constructed Response

"We hold these truths to be self evident: that all men and women are created equal."
Declaration of Sentiments, Seneca Falls, 1848

1 What earlier document from American history is this patterned after?

2 What conditions in American society in the first half of the 19th century made it necessary for this statement to be issued?

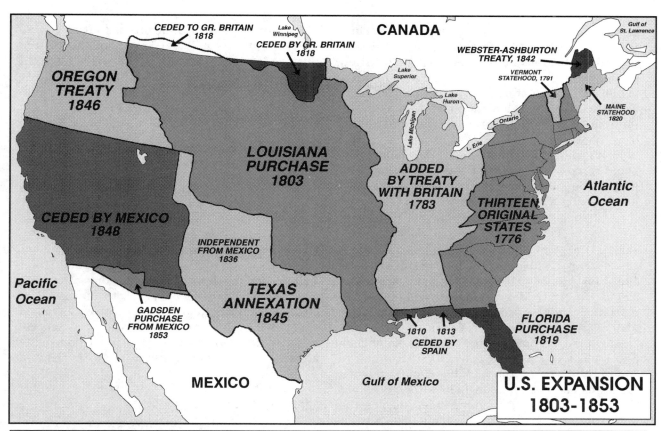

U.S. EXPANSION 1803-1853

UNITED STATES TERRITORIAL EXPANSION	
U.S. TERRITORY	**ACQUISITION**
1803 Louisiana	Purchased from France for $15 million; doubled U.S. territory, secured port of New Orleans.
1818 Northern Border	Negotiation with British set western U.S.-Canadian border at 49th parallel; exchange of territory in Great Lakes.
1818 Western Florida	Native American uprising quelled by General Andrew Jackson; United States claimed Spanish lands.
1819 Florida	Adams-Onis Treaty: U.S. paid $5 million for Florida Peninsula; U.S. gave up claim to Texas 42nd parallel as boundary with Spanish Mexico.
1842 Northern Maine	Webster-Ashburton Treaty settled disputed boundary with Great Britain.
1845 Texas	An independent republic since 1836, Congress agreed to Texas' request to be annexed.
1846 Oregon	Treaty with Britain extended the 49th parallel border from the Rockies to the Pacific.
1848 Mexican Cession	War broke out with Mexico over Texan boundary; U.S. paid $15 million for southwest region which included New Mexico, Arizona, California, Utah, Nevada, and Colorado.
1853 Gadsden Purchase	Bought from Mexico to complete a southern transcontinental rail line.

mission" to spread democracy from "sea to shining sea." Most understood this to mean that expansion to the Pacific was inevitable. A few even had sights set on Canada and Mexico. While the spread of democracy became an ideal, the practical expansionists hoped to make profits from trade and settle rich agricultural lands.

The map and chart (page 113) shows the rapid territorial growth of the U.S. in the first half of the 19th century. Expansion was almost an obsession with many Americans at the time.

TEXAS

By the 1820s, American settlers led by **Stephen Austin** (1793-1836) began moving into Texas. At first, Mexico encouraged American migration into the region. However, in the 1830s, Mexico tried to stop further American settlement. Controversies erupted over the existence of slavery in Texas and the growing influence of Americans, who by the mid 1830s outnumbered Mexicans nearly 10 to 1. In 1836, after a defeat at the Alamo, Texans proclaimed independence and organized a provisional government. The Texans under **Sam Houston** captured Mexican dictator Santa Anna at San Jacinto in April 1836 and established the Republic of Texas.

Texas requested annexation by the United States, but this met opposition in the United States. Many, especially in the North, feared Texas would become a slave state and add to Southern influence in Congress. However, support for annexation slowly grew. In 1845, Congress admitted Texas, which soon became the 28th state.

OREGON

American settlement beyond Texas was slow. Geographic obstacles and harsh climate deterred many. The availability of fertile land was motivation for most who traveled west. The **Oregon Trail** led settlers to Oregon, which was jointly occupied by the United States and Great Britain. As the American population of Oregon grew, some wanted the U.S. to claim all of Oregon – to latitude 54° 40' N. War was avoided when Britain and America agreed to a compromise at the 49th parallel, which extended the already existing boundary between the United States and Canada.

MEXICAN WAR (1846-1848)

By the mid 19th century, a number of disagreements existed between the United States and Mexico:

- U.S. annexation of Texas
- disputes over the Texas-Mexico boundary
- increased American settlement in the Mexican territory of California
- debt disputes between Americans and the Mexican government

American diplomatic attempts to settle the disputes failed. A border skirmish near the Rio Grande River in 1846 led President Polk to request from Congress a declaration of war against Mexico. Congress agreed, and American armies soon invaded Mexico. Generals **Zachary Taylor** and **Winfield Scott** led American forces to important victories. By the end of 1847, Mexico City was occupied, and Captain John C. Fremont's conquests ended Mexican rule in California.

UNITED STATES MEXICAN WAR 1846-1848

Battle of Chapultepec, 1847
(Arms, Armor, Battles, Wildside Press ©1996)

THE GREAT CONSTITUTIONAL DEBATES

The expansion of democracy and the intellectual quest for equality through the 1830s, 1840s, and 1850s intensified constitutional debates in the nation's political life. Slavery accentuated the issue of states' rights, and it eventually tore the country apart.

When the Constitution was written in 1787, many people believed that the institution of slavery would become unprofitable and gradually die out in the U.S. While this is what occurred in the North, the South saw the demand for slaves increase in the last decade of the 18th century and the early decades of the 19th century. The invention of the cotton gin, the expansion of territory, and the increased demand from the North and from overseas for raw cotton, all contributed to this rejuvenation of slavery. Article I, Section 9 of the Constitution officially ended the slave trade, but not slavery itself, in 1808.

A defeated Mexico had no choice but to agree to the *Treaty of Guadalupe Hidalgo* in 1848. The Treaty established the Rio Grande as the border of Texas and gave California and the New Mexico Territory (known as the Mexican Cession) to the United States. In return, the United States paid Mexico $15 million and agreed to settle any disputed debts.

IMPACT OF WESTERN EXPANSION UPON MEXICANS AND NATIVE AMERICANS

The new territory added tens of thousands of Spanish-speaking people to the United States. Many found the adjustment difficult as more and more Americans moved into the region. Problems of discrimination, poor economic opportunities, and lack of respect and understanding of traditional ways caused resentment for those of Spanish ancestry for many years. The new territory also included hundreds of thousands of Native Americans, who soon had their hunting grounds broken up and their lands confiscated.

TRANSITORY COMPROMISES

As the sectional differences grew after 1820, slavery became a thorny issue, increasing the animosity among Northerners, Southerners, and Westerners. As with the tariff issue, legislative compromises on slavery played an important part in temporarily keeping peace among the sections. Two specific issues related to the controversy were balancing the Senate representation between free and slave states, and allowing slavery in new federal territories.

Southern states demanded that the states having abolished slavery be balanced with those allowing slavery, so that there would be equal representation in the U.S. Senate. The free states of the North had almost twice the population of the slave states of the South. Therefore, control of the House of Representatives was never at issue.

In 1820, the question of the admission of Maine as a new free state aroused the South. Senator Henry Clay (KY) offered the *Missouri Compromise*. The compromise admitted Missouri to the Union as a slave state and

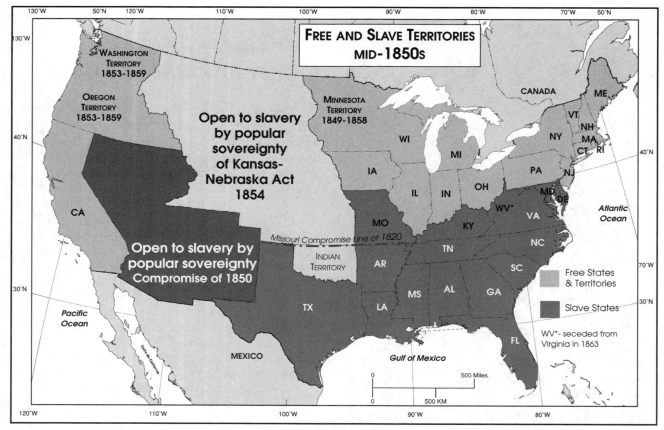

FREE AND SLAVE TERRITORIES MID-1850S

WASHINGTON TERRITORY 1853-1859

OREGON TERRITORY 1853-1859

Open to slavery by popular sovereignty of Kansas-Nebraska Act 1854

MINNESOTA TERRITORY 1849-1858

CANADA

CA

Open to slavery by popular sovereignty Compromise of 1850

Missouri Compromise Line of 1820

INDIAN TERRITORY

Pacific Ocean

MEXICO

Gulf of Mexico

Atlantic Ocean

Free States & Territories

Slave States

WV*- seceded from Virginia in 1863

0   500 Miles

0   500 KM

Maine as a free state. Simultaneous free state and slave state admissions continued for the next thirty years. By the *Missouri Compromise*, territories north of 36° 30" latitude would henceforth be considered free, those to the South, slave (Missouri being the exception).

In the late 1840s, the new lands acquired in the Mexican War re-opened the controversy. The now sickly and aging "Great Compromiser," Henry Clay, once again offered a series of resolutions that became the ***Compromise of 1850***. California was admitted as a free state, but the slavery question in the rest of the new southwest territories would be determined by vote of the inhabitants under what became known as **"popular sovereignty."** The compromise included a new ***Fugitive Slave Act*** allowing runaway slaves to be hunted down and captured more rapidly in the North.

By 1850, both positions on slavery had grown stronger. The extremists nearly defeated Clay's efforts. Moderates such as Senators **Stephen Douglas** (IL) and Daniel Webster (MA) managed to scrape enough votes together to pass the compromise. However, Clay's solution was very short lived.

THE STRUGGLE INTENSIFIES

Abolitionism became more and more militant after 1830. An increasing number of Americans began to oppose slavery not as a political problem but as a moral wrong. Britain abolished the institution throughout its worldwide empire in the 1830s. Reformers wanted it abolished throughout the United States. In the 1840s, abolitionists railed against it as an institution that violated religious teaching and the basic human rights stated in the *Declaration of Independence*. The arguments continued and grew more commonplace over the next two decades.

Abolitionists fell into two categories: moderate and extreme. Moderate abolitionists wanted gradual elimination of slavery. Moderates realized that the South was economically dependent and politically committed to slavery. they attempted to seek compromise solutions.

Extreme abolitionists wanted an immediate end to slavery with no economic compensation to owners. They argued that because slavery was such a horrible wrong, it had to be ended regardless of the consequences. Boston's William Lloyd Garrison constantly stirred up the controversy through his newspaper (*The Liberator*). While Frederick Douglass was somewhat more moderate in his frequent lecture tours throughout the country, he still called for immediate abolition.

SOUTHERN POPULATION 1800-1860

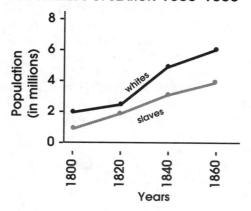

The extremists gained little popular support until the 1850s. Northern textile interests were afraid of a rise in cotton prices, and Northern laborers feared a drop in wages if freed slaves began to enter the labor market. Most Northerners accepted gradual abolition, first in the territories, then slowly in the states. As expected, Southerners rejected any talk of abolition. Prior to 1830, some in the South did accept the moderate idea of gradual elimination. A series of aborted minor slave revolts (the most notable by **Nat Turner** in Virginia, 1831) struck fear into even the most moderate of Southerners. From Boston, Garrison's writing and the stirring oratory of the American Anti-Slavery Society's **Wendell Phillips** (1811-1884) unleashed a steady barrage of calls for immediate emancipation throughout the 1840s and 1850s.

Most Southerners defended the institution of slavery. They pointed out that African American slaves had been civilized by their white masters who Christianized them, educated them, and gave them better living conditions than many Northern factory workers. Of course, economic prosperity in the South depended on labor-intensive cotton exports. Actually, less than 25% of white Southerners owned slaves. Nevertheless, some white Southerners supported the system, because they someday hoped to own slaves, or because such an inferior status system had become an accepted part of their culture.

After 1850, abolitionists boldly launched organized attempts to smuggle runaway slaves out of the South and into Canada. They created the "**Underground Railway**," a series of secret "safe-houses," where runaways could hide in the daytime and receive care. Harriet Tubman, a former slave, was one of the most active organizers of the movement. Although relatively few slaves managed to escape, Southerners were enraged after 1850, when many Northern states refused to enforce the *Fugitive Slave Act*.

SPIRIT OF COMPROMISE DISINTEGRATES

The sides in the slavery argument became more rigidly drawn in the 1850s. A newspaper barrage of extreme abolitionists and "hard-line" states' rights positions made compromise less and less feasible. In the North, the abolitionist crusade gained even more momentum in 1852 after Harriet Beecher Stowe (1811-1896) published her novel of harsh treatment on the plantations, ***Uncle Tom's Cabin*** (1852).

In 1854, Congress passed the ***Kansas-Nebraska Act*** to allow the slavery issue to be settled by popular sovereignty. Militant "free soilers" and anti-slavery groups rushed to the Kansas Territory. Their struggle to create rival territorial legislatures led to five years of intermittent bloodshed which killed over 200 settlers.

The two national political parties of the era, the **Democrats** and the **Whigs**, tried to avoid alienating voters by refusing to take a stand on the slavery issue. As Whig leaders Clay and Webster faded from the political scene, the party disintegrated. As a result, abolitionists were drawn first to the **Free Soil Party**. Then, in the mid-1850s, they joined what became the modern **Republican Party**. Generally, the Republicans were moderates who opposed the extension of slavery into the new territories but did not seek full emancipation.

President James Buchanan pressed the Supreme Court for a solution but the Court only managed to make things worse. In ***Dred Scott v. Sanford*** (1857), the Court ruled that slaves were property. It said the Fifth Amendment to the Constitution forbids Congress from depriving citizens of life, liberty, or property without due process of law. It held that slaves were property. Therefore, the *Missouri Compromise* and

John Brown
(Civil War CD, Digital Stock ©1995)

THE SEPARATION BEGINS

After the election, Southern leaders decided that the policies of the Republicans under Lincoln would ruin the South. South Carolina seceded on 20 December 1860. In the two months that followed, Mississippi, Florida, Alabama, Georgia, Louisiana, and Texas followed suit. In February, the seceding states met in Montgomery, Alabama to form a weak, loosely organized nation called the **Confederate States of America**. The former U.S. Senator from Mississippi, **Jefferson Davis** (1808-1889), was chosen to be President, and Alexander H. Stephens of Georgia became Vice President. The Confederate Constitution did not give President Davis much power and raising money for military expenses constantly hampered his effectiveness.

When secession began in December 1860, **James Buchanan** (1791-1868) was still the "lame duck" President of the United States. (A **lame duck** is an officeholder who has not been reelected. The lame duck's political influence is reduced because his/her successor is not bound to follow the lame duck's policies.) Buchanan declared that actions by the Southern states were unconstitutional, yet he also believed the Constitution gave him no power to stop the

other actions taken over the years to forbid slavery in some areas were unconstitutional. As a result of the *Scott* decision, all territories were open to slavery. Southerners and pro-slavery groups praised the decision. Abolitionists urged disobedience to the Court's ruling.

In 1859, some extreme abolitionists helped the radical **John Brown** of Kansas launch a raid on the federal arsenal at Harper's Ferry (VA). Brown hoped that the arms he captured would help to launch a widespread slave insurrection. Ironically, the garrison at Harper's Ferry was rescued by a U.S. Army unit led by Col. **Robert E. Lee** (1807-1870) who later commanded the Confederate Army. Brown was tried for treason and executed. The episode focused greater attention on the divisions between the North and the South.

By 1860, the Democrats were badly split into many different factions. The Republicans were able to gain enough electoral votes in the North to elect their candidate, **Abraham Lincoln** (1809-1865) of Illinois.

Abraham Lincoln
(Civil War CD, Digital Stock ©1995)

Jefferson Davis
(Civil War CD, Digital Stock ©1995)

states from seceding. With this situation, it was doubtful that Buchanan could have done anything to bring about a peaceful solution to the problem between December and March. To make things worse, Confederate leaders ordered forts and other federal facilities seized, yet Buchanan did nothing.

James Buchanan
(*People & Portraits*, Wildside Press ©1997)

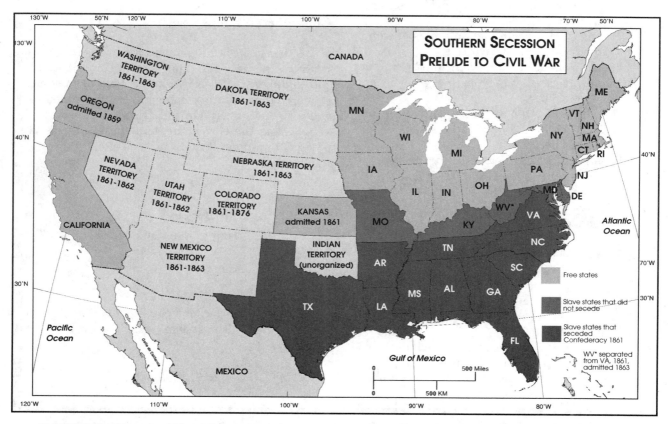

SOUTHERN SECESSION
PRELUDE TO CIVIL WAR

WASHINGTON TERRITORY 1861-1863

OREGON admitted 1859

DAKOTA TERRITORY 1861-1863

CANADA

NEVADA TERRITORY 1861-1862

UTAH TERRITORY 1861-1862

NEBRASKA TERRITORY 1861-1863

COLORADO TERRITORY 1861-1876

CALIFORNIA

NEW MEXICO TERRITORY 1861-1863

KANSAS admitted 1861

INDIAN TERRITORY (unorganized)

MN

WI

MI

IA

IL

IN

OH

MO

KY

TN

AR

MS

AL

GA

TX

LA

ME

VT

NH

NY

MA

CT

RI

PA

NJ

MD

WV*

VA

DE

NC

SC

FL

Pacific Ocean

Atlantic Ocean

Gulf of Mexico

MEXICO

500 Miles

500 KM

Free states

Slave states that did not secede

Slave states that seceded Confederacy 1861

WV* separated from VA, 1861, admitted 1863

On 4 March 1861, Abraham Lincoln was inaugurated as the 16th President of the United States. Addressing the nation that day, Lincoln said he wished to preserve the Union. He promised not to interfere with slavery in the states where it already existed. The South rejected Lincoln's offers. The attack on the federal **Fort Sumter** in Charleston (SC) harbor took place just six weeks later (12 April 1861). Fort Sumter's surrender the next day was a turning point in the secession crisis. Between 14 April and 8 June, Virginia, Arkansas, North Carolina, and Tennessee joined the Confederacy. The surrender of Ft. Sumter made Northerners realize that political solutions were impossible, and war was necessary. The tragedy of the American Civil War began.

THE CONSTITUTION IN JEOPARDY: THE AMERICAN CIVIL WAR

While slavery was a leading cause of the Civil War, it was by no means the only cause. The issue of states' rights, differing economic and cultural patterns, the territorial expansion issue, and the rising power of the industrial North all contributed to the breakdown of unity. While initially fighting to preserve the Union, the North was later led by Lincoln into making abolition of slavery a major aim. Slavery was abolished at the end of the War, but bitterness between the North and the South remained long after the last shot was fired.

MINI•ASSESSMENT (3-5)

1 "By the 1850s, the Constitution, originally framed as an instrument of national unity, had become a source of sectional discord." This quotation suggests that
  1 vast differences of opinion existed over the issue of states' rights
  2 the federal government had become more interested in foreign affairs than in domestic problems
  3 the Constitution had no provisions for governing new territories
  4 the Southern states continued to import slaves

2 The United States Supreme Court decision in *Dred Scott v. Sanford* (1857) was important because it
  1 strengthened the determination of abolitionists to achieve their goals
  2 caused the immediate outbreak of the Civil War
  3 ended the importation of slaves into the United States
  4 increased the power of Congress to exclude slavery from the territories

3 Which event was the immediate cause of the secession of several Southern states from the Union in 1860?
  1 the Dred Scott decision, which declared that all prior compromises on the extension of slavery into the territories were unconstitutional

  2 the Missouri Compromise, which kept an even balance between the number of free and slave states
  3 the raid on the Federal arsenal at Harper's Ferry, which was led by the militant abolitionist John Brown
  4 the election of President Abraham Lincoln, who opposed the spread of slavery into the territories

Constructed Response

"...the right of property in a slave is distinctly and expressly affirmed in the Constitution. The right to traffic in it, like an ordinary article of merchandise and property, was guaranteed to the citizens of the United States...for twenty years...And the Government in express terms is pledged to protect it in all future time."
– Chief Justice Roger Taney,
Dred Scott v. Sanford (1857)

1 What concept in the Constitution is the Court referring to in its defense of slavery?

2 How did this decision cause greater conflict than ever in the struggle over slavery?

Artist: Eugene Fairbanks

Others in the North, called **"Copperheads,"** demanded an immediate, negotiated settlement and were constant critics of the President and Congress.

LINCOLN STRETCHES POWER

For the most part, President Lincoln acted within constitutional guidelines as Commander in Chief, but he did exceed his authority on a number of occasions. Congress was not in session when the South began hostilities, and Lincoln did not call a special session. Most Americans realized the need for quick action and did not question Lincoln's actions. Ultimately, Congress gave its approval to most of what he did, but his arbitrary implementation of martial law in the border states was later ruled unconstitutional by the Supreme Court (*Ex parte Milligan*, 1866).

THE NATION DIVIDES

As hostilities began, volunteers from both the North and the South rushed to join their respective armies. The most difficult decisions were made by those in the **border states** – where slavery existed, but which remained loyal to the Union (Delaware, Maryland, Kentucky, and Missouri in 1861, and West Virginia in 1863). Although much of the population in these states leaned toward the Confederate side, Lincoln was able to convince them, sometimes by force, to remain in the Union.

People were mainly loyal to their section, but support was by no means unanimous. It is doubtful that a majority of Southerners really favored secession, and a number joined the Union forces. While most Northerners were willing to fight to preserve the Union, the goal of abolishing slavery was not universally supported at the outset of the War.

Congress stretched its powers, too. By using the doctrine of implied powers under the elastic clause (Art. I, sec. 8) Congress passed a military conscription act (draft) when the first flurry of volunteers subsided. The draft was later a cause for discontent. For a fee of $300, a draftee could hire a substitute. Poor Northerners, especially recent Irish immigrants, objected to this discrimination. Severe anti-draft riots broke out in New York City in 1863. To protect Northern business and raise war revenue, Congress passed a high tariff in 1861. Also to defray the cost of the war, the government implemented the nation's first income tax.

CONSTITUTIONAL STRUCTURES

Lincoln Memorial - Washington, DC
(PhotoDisc ©1997)

At first, Lincoln did not commit the Union to a War goal of abolishing slavery. His

PRESIDENT LINCOLN AND THE UNITED STATES CONSTITUTION

THE CONSTITUTION STATES:	LINCOLN'S ACTIONS WERE:
Congress is given the power to raise and support armies.	Increased the size of the army without Congressional authorization.
No money can be taken from the treasury unless approved by law.	Withdrew $2,000,000 for military purposes without authorization.
The Writ of Habeas Corpus shall not be suspended, except in cases of rebellion or invasion.	Arrested and jailed anti-Unionists giving no reason. No permission was obtained from Congress.
No law shall be made abridging freedom of speech or the press.	Censored some anti-Union newspapers and had editors and publishers arrested.
Accused persons have the right to a speedy trial and impartial jury in the state or district where the alleged act was committed.	Even though U.S. civil courts were operating, he set up military courts to try Confederate sympathizers.

only goal was to save the Union. In his inaugural speech, he promised not to interfere with slavery in the states where it already existed (the border states). Lincoln strengthened the Union cause late in 1862 by issuing the *Emancipation Proclamation*. This executive order declared slaves in the states in rebellion to be free. This kept the border states tenuously in the Union.

The *Emancipation Proclamation* did not abolish slavery, but it did give the Union a "moral cause" for victory. Internationally, the proclamation strengthened popular support in Europe for the North. This support discouraged Britain's government from giving financial aid to the Confederate states that were its longtime source of cotton for its textile mills.

Although foreign aid never materialized, the idea that European powers would openly help the South in its drive for independence was real. Some European autocrats had hoped the American "experiment in democracy" would crumble at last. Others hoped for trade advantages in the new, weaker political states that would emerge if the Union dissolved. Foreign actions to help the Confederacy consisted of trading war and food supplies for cotton, tobacco, rice, and indigo. However, one of the results of Lincoln's Proclamation – making the Civil War a moral as well as a Constitutional struggle – was the diminishing of foreign aid to the South.

THE FIGHTING BEGINS

THE TWO SIDES

When the War Between the States began in 1861, the North's resources were superior to the South's. The North had a population of 22 million – 2 1/2 times that of the South. It had more than 100,000 acres of diversified cropland, more than 21,000 miles of railroads, and 120,000 factories with nearly 2 million workers. While not rapidly mobilized, the North's superiority in finance, food, and munitions production was developed gradually and became an advantage as the War progressed.

However, the North's population and resources were spread over a vast area that reached westward to the frontier. All during the War, the North sent troops to the frontier to fight Native Americans.

The South's resources were less than half those of the North: population of 9 million (of which almost 3.5 million were slaves), just over 56,000 acres of cropland – much of which devoted to cotton and tobacco, nearly 9,000 miles of railroads, and only 20,000 factories with 112,000 workers. The South had the army and excellent commanders who could have won a short war in a few decisive battles. However, the War dragged on for over four years, and the shallowness of the South's resources added up to defeat.

Battlefield Memorial - Gettysburg, PA
(PhotoDisk ©1996)

The African American population served both sides. Southern slaves were used in military construction and supply operations. In 1862, the U.S. Congress passed laws allowing African Americans to serve in segregated units, "U.S. Colored Troops" in the Union Army. Many of the 209,000 African Americans who served received less pay and were issued inferior equipment. African Americans took part in more than 200 battles and skirmishes. The Confederacy at first refused to recognize African Americans as soldiers. Unlike other Union troops who were captured, African American soldiers were at first not allowed to surrender. Many were shot. Nearly 20,000 gave their lives as Union soldiers. In all, 68,178 African Americans died in the War as a result of wounds or disease.

STRATEGIES

As hostilities began, the U.S. Army General-in-Chief, 76 year-old Winfield Scott, cautioned Lincoln to prepare for a long struggle. While methodical preparation irked Congressmen who wanted a fast, aggressive strategy, the President bought time for the Union. He ordered the U.S. Navy to blockade the Confederacy's Atlantic and Gulf of Mexico coastlines to cut off vital trade with Europe. Within months, nearly all the South's export of its cotton crops to Britain's textile mills ceased. The Union goals also included controlling the Mississippi River and capturing the Confederate capital at Richmond, VA.

Unlike the North, the South did not have to launch an offensive war to "quell the rebellion." The Southern strategy was defensive. The Confederacy hoped to wear out the Union Army and force the North to abandon the idea of conquering the South. Confederate leaders also counted on the North's military resources being strained in launching far-flung invasions, carrying out prolonged sieges, maintaining blockades, and occupying conquered territories.

THE COMMANDERS

Military officers on both sides had training at the service academies. But, aside from frontier duty, most had not seen combat since the Mexican War thirteen years before, and then only as small unit commanders. To compound the problem on both sides, men with no military training used political influence to gain appointments as officers. Clashes of ego between regular army officers and these political appointees led to problems of command.

The South had a greater number of experienced, highly qualified military officers, including **Robert E. Lee, Joseph E. Johnston, Albert Sidney Johnston, Thomas "Stonewall" Jackson, A.P. Hill, Braxton Bragg,** and **John B. Hood**. Even Confederate President Jefferson Davis – a West Point graduate – had served in the Mexican War. But, brilliant as these commanders were, some were unlucky in battle. Jackson, Hill, and A.S. Johnston were killed while Joe Johnston, Bragg, and Hood were all seriously wounded during the War.

On the Union side, Lincoln lacked the education and experience of some previous Presidents, yet he had the ability and patience to deal effectively with the crisis of the Civil War. He had many critics in both Congress and his own cabinet, but the Commander in Chief role gave the Lincoln's enormous power, and Lincoln used it well.

One of President Lincoln's biggest problems was organizing and training a volunteer army with largely inexperienced officers at all levels. From 1861 to 1864, Lincoln went through difficult times with a number of commanders (McDowell, McClellan, Halleck, Burnside, Hooker) before finding those who could aggressively and consistently achieve victory: Generals **Ulysses S. Grant, Philip Sheridan, William T. Sherman, George H. Thomas,** and **George G. Meade**.

ENGAGEMENTS OF THE AMERICAN CIVIL WAR 1861 - 1865

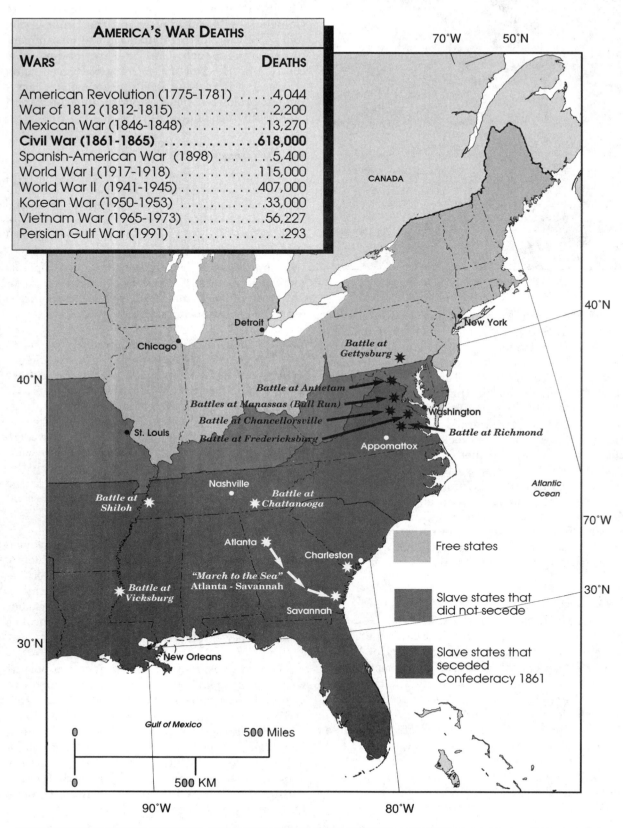

AMERICA'S WAR DEATHS

WARS	DEATHS
American Revolution (1775-1781)	4,044
War of 1812 (1812-1815)	2,200
Mexican War (1846-1848)	13,270
Civil War (1861-1865)	**618,000**
Spanish-American War (1898)	5,400
World War I (1917-1918)	115,000
World War II (1941-1945)	407,000
Korean War (1950-1953)	33,000
Vietnam War (1965-1973)	56,227
Persian Gulf War (1991)	293

CANADA

70°W 50°N

40°N

Detroit

Chicago

Battle at Gettysburg

New York

Battle at Antietam

Battles at Manassas (Bull Run)

Battle at Chancellorsville

Washington

Battle at Fredericksburg

Battle at Richmond

St. Louis

Appomattox

Atlantic Ocean

70°W

Nashville

Battle at Shiloh

Battle at Chattanooga

Atlanta

Charleston

"March to the Sea" Atlanta - Savannah

Battle at Vicksburg

30°N

Savannah

Free states

Slave states that did not secede

30°N

New Orleans

Slave states that seceded Confederacy 1861

Gulf of Mexico

500 Miles

500 KM

90°W

80°W

Engagement
Manassas, VA (Bull Run) – July 1861

Commanders
Irvin McDowell (USA)
P.G.T. Beauregard (CSA)
Thomas "Stonewall" Jackson (CSA)

Action
Between Richmond, VA and Washington, DC. McDowell engaged Beauregard with success the first day. The arrival of Stonewall Jackson's fresh troops turned this into a Confederate victory that shook the Union's confidence in its superior supplies and weapons. Lincoln replaced McDowell with General George B. McClellan.

Thomas "Stonewall" Jackson
(Civil War CD, Digital Stock ©1995)

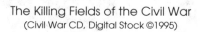

The Killing Fields of the Civil War
(Civil War CD, Digital Stock ©1995)

Engagement
Shiloh, TN – April 1862

Commanders
P.G.T. Beauregard (CSA)
Albert Sidney Johnston (CSA)
Ulysses Grant (USA)

Action
The Union navy moved up the Mississippi River while Confederate forces under Beauregard and Johnston sped west to surprise Ulysses Grant's troops at Shiloh. The bloody battle ended with Confederate forces withdrawing southward and leaving Memphis open for attack. Memphis, New Orleans, Baton Rouge, and Natchez surrendered. Except for Vicksburg, MS, the Mississippi River came under Union control.

Engagement
Antietam, MD – Sept. 1862

Commanders
Robert E. Lee (CSA)
Thomas "Stonewall" Jackson (CSA)
George B. McClellan (USA)

Action
McClellan attacked Lee's Army near Sharpsburg (MD): Sept. 17th was the bloodiest day of the war – 4800 killed, 18,000 wounded. The battle was a draw, but it temporarily stopped Lee's northward momentum. It was even more important because it cost the South so dearly in men and scarce resources.

James Ewell Brown Stuart
(Civil War CD, Digital Stock ©1995)

Ambrose Everett Burnside
(Civil War CD, Digital Stock ©1995)

George Brinton McClellan
(Civil War CD, Digital Stock ©1995)

Engagement
Fredericksburg, VA – Dec. 1862

Commanders
Robert E. Lee (CSA)
Thomas "Stonewall" Jackson (CSA)
Jeb Stuart (CSA)
Ambrose Burnside (USA)

Action
Lincoln picked Burnside to replace the timid McClellan. Burnside's drive on Richmond was thwarted by Jeb Stuart's intelligence gathering that allowed Lee's well entrenched forces to soundly defeat a superior army. Lincoln replaced Burnside with Hooker.

Engagement
Chancellorsville, VA – May 1863

Commanders
Robert E. Lee (CSA)
Thomas "Stonewall" Jackson (CSA)
Joseph Hooker (USA)

Action
Hooker tried to surprise Lee by moving a sizeable force straight at him, while sending the rest of the Union troops to hit Lee from behind. Stuart's scouts caught the move and Lee ordered Jackson to attack Hooker's weaker force, then Lee smashed Hooker's main line. Hooker fell back on the defensive. The Union lost 12,000, the South lost 10,000. Chancellorsville was Lee's greatest victory. It renewed his confidence to move up the Shenandoah Valley into Maryland and Pennsylvania. Lee lost his most daring commander when Stonewall Jackson was accidentally killed here.

Davis, Lee, & Jackson
Stone Mountain Confederate Memorial
(W.H. Garnsey ©1999)

Engagement
Vicksburg, MS – July 1863

Commanders
Joseph E. Johnston (CSA)
Ulysses Grant (USA)

Action
In April 1863, Grant bluffed an army-navy attack on Vicksburg, then withdrew and seemed to move on Jackson, MS, to split Confederate forces. In May, the Union troops pushed Johnston's forces to the north, drawing Confederate defense forces out of Vicksburg, and Grant intensified his siege against the weakened city and forced its surrender in early July. The victory gave the Union control of the Mississippi River, and combined with the success at Gettysburg, revitalized the Union cause.

Engagement
Gettysburg, PA – July 1863

Commanders
Robert E. Lee (CSA)
George B. Meade (USA)

Action
As Lee advanced into Maryland, Meade's army paralleled his northern drive and finally engaged him at Gettysburg, outside Harrisburg, PA. Lee's bold charges could not break Meade's defenses and artillery barrages. With nearly 36,000 losses, Lee retreated. Gettysburg was a slaughter. There were some 23,000 Union losses, but it was also a turning point. The Confederates abandoned the hope of recognition and aid from European countries. During the six week campaign into the North, Lee's army lost nearly 60,000 troops, and he retreated southward. However, Meade did not pursue.

Robert E. Lee
(Civil War CD, Digital Stock ©1995)

Ulysses Simpson Grant
(Civil War CD, Digital Stock ©1995)

Engagement
Chattanooga , TN – Nov. 1863

Commanders
Joseph Johnston (CSA)
Braxton Bragg (CSA)
William Rosecrans (USA)
George H. Thomas (USA)
Ulysses Grant (USA)

Action
CSA Generals Bragg and Johnston routed Union Gen. Rosecrans at Chickamagua Creek, GA. They surrounded the Union forces in Chattanooga, where General Thomas held the CSA forces at bay for nearly a month. In late November, Grant rushed troops by rail from the west to aid Thomas. The Union commanders attacked at Lookout Mountain and Missionary Ridge outside Chattanooga. These victories allowed Grant to complete his hold on Tennessee. It also opened the opportunity for a Union drive southward through Georgia.

William Tecumseh Sherman
(Civil War CD, Digital Stock ©1995)

Engagement
Atlanta – Savannah, GA – May-Dec. 1864

Commanders
Joseph E. Johnston (CSA)
John B. Hood (CSA)
William T. Sherman (USA)

Action
Sherman's 100,000-man force advanced from Chattanooga pushing Johnston's 65,000-man Confederate army through Georgia. Sherman laid siege to Atlanta by the end of July 1864. Neither Johnston nor Hood could halt Sherman's advance. On 31 August, Hood evacuated Atlanta. In the fall of 1864, Sherman fanned his army out 50 miles and launched a three week "March to the Sea," plundering, tearing up railroads, and destroying property. In early December, he captured Savannah and turned north through the Carolinas forcing General Johnston to surrender in April 1865.

Engagement
Richmond, VA – April 1865

Commanders
Robert E. Lee (CSA)	Ulysses Grant (USA)
A.P. Hill (CSA)	Philip Sheridan (USA)
John B. Gordon (CSA)	George B. Meade (USA)

Action
Grant, Meade, and Sheridan relentlessly pounded Lee's army in battle after battle in central Virginia, wearing him down and pursuing him toward Richmond and beyond. On 9 April, a week after the fall of Richmond, Lee surrendered to Grant 50 miles west at Appomattox Court House, VA.

Appomattox Surrender
(*Arms, Armor & Battles -* Wildside Press ©1996)

SUMMARY

From its beginnings under Washington to the crisis under Lincoln, the young nation tested the durability of its new constitutional structure. The experiences altered and strengthened the structure. The changing patterns of life in America probed the weaknesses and strengths of the system. At the close of this era, moderates failed to make compromises work. Extremists on both sides came to the forefront, until war between the states was inevitable. Though the Union won the resulting Civil War, it came at a great cost. Suffering on both sides was immense. Just a week after the Confederate surrender in April 1865, President Abraham Lincoln was assassinated by Southern sympathizer John Wilkes Booth. The War concluded with great sadness among the victors, bitterness for the defeated South, and an uncertain future for 3.5 million former slaves.

MINI•ASSESSMENT (3-6)

1 Early in his Presidency, Abraham Lincoln declared that his primary goal as President was to
  1 enforce the *Emancipation Proclamation*
  2 preserve the Union
  3 end slavery throughout the entire country
  4 encourage sectionalism

2 The existence of abolitionists in the South and Copperheads in the North during the Civil War indicated that
  1 there was no dissent in either region
  2 foreign nations played a major role in the war's outcome
  3 with rigid military discipline, desertion was a minor problem
  4 not everyone supported the leaders of their section

3 The basic constitutional issue resolved by the Civil War was the
  1 expansion of the President's war powers
  2 extension of the right to vote to all adults
  3 supremacy of federal authority over the states
  4 civil liberties of citizens during wartime

Constructed Response

"That on the first day of January, in the year of our Lord one thousand eight hundred and sixty three, all persons held as slaves within any State or designated part of a State, the people whereof shall then be in rebellion against the United States, shall be then, and thenceforward, and forever, free..."

– Abraham Lincoln, *Emancipation Proclamation*, September, 1862

1 How did this document indicate a shift in Lincoln's purpose for fighting the Confederacy?

2 What did Lincoln hope to accomplish by making this Proclamation?

UNIT ASSESSMENT
MULTI-CHOICE QUESTIONS

1 In an outline, one of these entries is a main topic and three are subtopics. Which is the main topic?
   1 Alexander Hamilton's Economic Program
   2 The Rise of National Political Parties
   3 The Constitution's First Tests
   4 John Adams' Stormy Presidency

2 Actions and policies of the government under President George Washington generally resulted in the
   1 establishment of strong political ties with other nations
   2 liberation of many enslaved persons
   3 failure to create a sound financial program for the country
   4 strengthening of the federal government

3 Alexander Hamilton's argument that the government has the power to create a National Bank is based on which part of the Constitution?
   1 the Preamble
   2 the elastic clause
   3 guarantees to the states
   4 the Bill of Rights

4 Which view of the power of the federal government is most consistent with the philosophy of Alexander Hamilton and his supporters?
   1 The government which governs least governs best.
   2 The government may exercise only those powers specifically given to it by the governed.
   3 The government should give up most of its authority to the states.
   4 The government may exercise all powers necessary and proper to meet its responsibilities.

5 The 19th century belief in a "divine mission" to expand U.S. territory is known as
   1 the *Monroe Doctrine*
   2 strict constructionism
   3 Manifest Destiny
   4 neutrality

6 "The great rule of conduct for us in regard to foreign nations is, in extending our commercial relations, to have with them as little political connection as possible."

   Which foreign policy flows from these words of President Washington?
   1 supporting a particular faction in an internal conflict
   2 avoiding permanent trade agreements with other nations
   3 providing military aid to developing nations
   4 signing a mutual defense pact

7 In deciding to purchase the Louisiana Territory, President Thomas Jefferson had to overcome the problem of
   1 obtaining the support of western settlers
   2 passing the constitutional amendment necessary to authorize the purchase
   3 avoiding a possible war with England over the purchase
   4 contradicting his belief in a strict interpretation of the Constitution

8 The significance of the case *Marbury v. Madison* (1803) is that it
   1 established the principle of judicial review
   2 declared the *Alien and Sedition Acts* to be legitimate laws
   3 demonstrated the supremacy of the national government over the states
   4 attempted to place the judiciary outside the impeachment power of the House of Representatives

9 Any part of the unwritten constitution may become a formal part of the *Constitution of the United States* by
   1 Congressional statute
   2 amendment
   3 tradition
   4 referendum

10 When John Marshall was Chief Justice, United States Supreme Court decisions tended to strengthen the power of
   1 the national government
   2 state and local governments
   3 labor unions
   4 trusts and monopolies

11 Slavery did not become a lasting institution in the Northern states primarily because
1 it was always considered morally wrong by the residents of the North
2 anti-slavery societies were formed in the North
3 traders never brought any slaves to the North
4 it was unprofitable on small farms of the North

12 Armed confrontation in the constitutional crisis over the *Tariff of 1828* was avoided when Henry Clay
1 proposed a gradual reduction in the tariff rates
2 proposed the *Missouri Compromise*
3 agreed to change the "supremacy clause" of the Constitution
4 traded lower tariff rates for re-chartering the Bank of the United States

13 In the period between 1820 and 1860, Southerners wanted slavery extended to the Western territories so that the South could
1 continue to elect Southern Presidents
2 continue to dominate the Supreme Court
3 keep enough strength in the Senate to protect Southern interests
4 use slave labor to expand Southern industries

14 The growth in democratic procedures in the 19th century can best be attributed to the
1 equality of the Western frontier
2 social structure of the Southern plantations
3 increasing numbers of European immigrants
4 inability of the federal government to control the slave controversy

15 Mormons aroused much controversy in the 19th century because they
1 were vocal supporters of slavery in the territories
2 used new scripture translations and practiced polygamy
3 moved westward in search of new land
4 sought capital for their new businesses from Europe

16 Utopian communities of the mid 19th century hoped to achieve a perfect society by
1 establishing a completely agrarian lifestyle
2 carefully controlling the conditions under which man lived
3 banning the practice of religion
4 separating social classes based on wealth

17 Many factory owners in the 19th century supported the work of the temperance movement because
1 sober workers meant a more reliable work force
2 factory owners and temperance supporters had similar political ideology
3 both groups were most numerous in the slave-owning South
4 alcohol abuse resulted in increased business taxes

18 The *Missouri Compromise*, the *Compromise of 1850*, and the *Kansas-Nebraska Act* attempted to solve the issue of
1 extension of slavery into the Western territories
2 equitable distribution of frontier lands to the owners of small farms
3 placement of protective tariffs on foreign imports
4 need for internal improvements in transportation

19 At the heart of the tariff issue of 1828 and the secession of the Southern states in the 1860s was the constitutional issue of
1 the federal-state relationship
2 popular sovereignty
3 checks and balances
4 representation in Congress

20 Southern defenders of slavery said that most slaves
1 received a better education in the South than in the North
2 were allowed to take part in the political process
3 had the right to buy their freedom
4 were better cared for than Northern factory workers

21 The Southern states were opposed to the election of Lincoln in 1860 because he
    1 proposed immediate emancipation of all slaves
    2 stepped up federal enforcement of the Fugitive Slave Law
    3 proposed the Thirteenth Amendment to abolish slavery
    4 hoped to stop slavery from spreading into new territories

22 What action of President Lincoln during the Civil War was considered unconstitutional?
    1 replacement of Union army commanders
    2 removing money from the Treasury without Congressional approval
    3 buying weapons from foreign governments
    4 selecting a Vice Presidential running mate from a slave state

23 During the Civil War, Congress authorized a draft by using
    1 delegated powers
    2 reserved powers
    3 implied powers
    4 concurrent powers

24 By suspending the right to a writ of habeas corpus, the government can
    1 arrest individuals and hold them without disclosing the reason
    2 tax individuals without passing congressional acts
    3 station troops in private homes
    4 compel a person to be a witness against himself

25 Which statement about the results of the Civil War is most accurate?
    1 Federal supremacy was strengthened.
    2 Constitutional government was proven ineffective.
    3 Universal suffrage was generally accepted.
    4 Sectional disputes ceased to exist.

THEMATIC ESSAY

Theme:

Federalism

Between 1787-1865, the United States was under constant stress from two opposite forces: those who wanted the federal power to be strengthened and those who wanted the states to retain as much power as possible.

Task:

Based on your knowledge of United States history and government, write an essay in which you
* define federalism,
* give specific historical evidence to prove that federal power helped to strengthen the United States in the period 1789-1865, and
* show through specific examples how those supporters of state power thought the federal government was abusing its authority.

Suggestions:
Examples of federalism and the federal-state conflict were shown in the Bank controversy, the tariff controversy of 1828, the debate over interstate commerce, and the expansion of slavery. **You are not limited to these suggestions.**

DOCUMENT BASED QUESTION

The following question is based on the accompanying documents. Some of the documents have been edited for the purpose of this exercise. The question is designed to test your ability to work with historical documents. As you analyze the material, take into account both the source of the document and the author's point of view.

- Write a well organized essay that includes an introduction with a thesis statement, several paragraphs explaining the thesis, and the author's point of view.

Historical Context:
Sectional differences between the North and the South increased throughout the first half of the 19th century. The growing conflict eventually led to the Civil War from 1861-1865.

Task:
Using information from the documents and your knowledge of United States history and government, write an essay in which you discuss the growth of sectional disputes between the North and the South in the period from 1800-1860. Show how these disputes led the country closer to disunion.

Part A - Short Answer
Examine each document carefully and then answer the question which follows it.

made 1 millions of dollars

Question for Document 1

On what basis did the author justify opposition to the tariff?

DOCUMENT 1
"The Senate and House of Representatives of South Carolina ... do solemnly protest against the system of protecting duties, lately adopted by the federal government,...because the good people of this commonwealth believe that the powers of Congress were delegated to it in trust for the accomplishment of certain specified objects which limit and control them"

– South Carolina Exposition and Protest - December 19, 1828

cotton

Questions for Document 2

1 How important was the production of cotton to the South?

2 What was the relationship between cotton exportation and slavery?

DOCUMENT 2

	AMERICAN COTTON EXPORTS			
YEAR	POUNDS (IN MILLIONS)	DOLLAR VALUE (IN MILLIONS)	PERCENT OF TOTAL EXPORTS	SLAVES (IN MILLIONS)
1800	17	5	7	1.5
1820	127	22	31	2.0
1840	743	63	53	3.2
1860	1,767	191	57	4.0

Question for Document 3

Why does Douglass call the July 4th celebration "a sham"?

DOCUMENT 3
"What, to the American slave, is your 4th of July? I answer: a day that reveals to him, more than all other days in the year, the gross injustice and cruelty to which he is the constant victim. To him your celebration is a sham; your boasted liberty, an unholy license;...your sounds of rejoicing are empty and heartless... You glory in your refinement and your universal education, yet you maintain a system as barbarous and dreadful as ever stained the character of a nation – a system begun in avarice, supported in pride, and perpetuated in cruelty."

–Frederick Douglass, 4 July , 1852

Questions for Document 4

1 What defense of slavery is being made by Senator James Hammond?

2 Why might there be disagreement to this view?

DOCUMENT 4

"Our slaves are black, of another, inferior race. The status in which we have placed them is an elevation. They are elevated from the condition in which God first created them, by being made our slaves...They are happy, content, uninspiring, and utterly incapable, from intellectual degradation, ever to give us any trouble by their aspirations."

– Senator James H. Hammond (SC) - Speech, 4 March 1858.

Question for Document 5

Which phrase in this pamphlet would disturb law-abiding citizens?

DOCUMENT 5

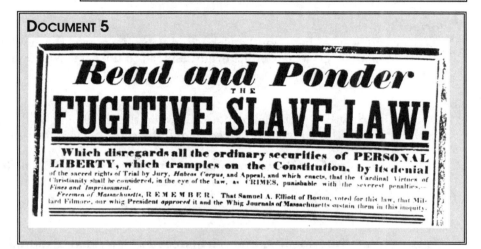

Read and Ponder THE **FUGITIVE SLAVE LAW!**

Which disregards all the ordinary securities of PERSONAL LIBERTY, which tramples on the Constitution, by its denial of the sacred rights of Trial by Jury, Habeas Corpus, and Appeal, and which enacts, that the Cardinal Virtues of Christianity shall be considered, in the eye of the law, as CRIMES, punishable with the severest penalties,—Fines and Imprisonment.

Freemen of Massachusetts, REMEMBER, That Samuel A. Elliott of Boston, voted for this law, that Millard Filmore, our whig President *approved* it and the Whig Journals of Massachusetts sustain them in this iniquity.

DOCUMENT 6

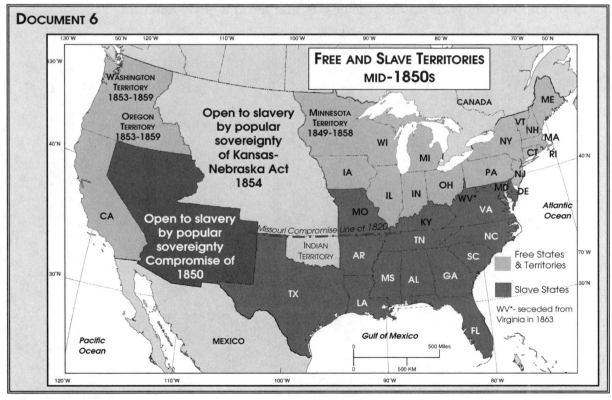

FREE AND SLAVE TERRITORIES MID-1850s

Questions for Document 6
1 According to the map, in what areas was slavery permitted?
2 Which citizens would object to popular sovereignty?

Part B: Essay Response
Directions:

- Write a well-organized essay that includes and introduction, several paragraphs, and a conclusion.
- Use evidence from the documents to support your response.
- Do not simply repeat the contents of the documents.
- Include specific related outside information.

Historical Context:

Sectional differences between the North and South increased throughout the first half of the 19th century. The growing conflict eventually led to the Civil War from 1861-1865.

Task:

Discuss the growth of sectional disputes between the North and South in the period from 1800-1860. Show how these disputes helped to pull the country closer to disunion.

Using information from the documents and your knowledge of U.S. history and government, write an essay which shows how constitutional conflicts brought the country toward disunion from 1800-1860.

Be sure to include specific historical details. You must also include additional information from your knowledge of U.S. history and government.

1865 RECONSTRUCTION (1865-1877)

JOHNSON'S IMPEACHMENT (1868)
TRANSCONTINENTAL RAILROAD (1869)
GRANT SCANDALS (1869-1876)
1870 JIM CROW LAWS (1870s)

1875
LITTLE BIGHORN (1876)
MUNN V. ILLINOIS (1877)

1880
CHINESE EXCLUSION ACT (1882)
CIVIL SERVICE ACT (1883)

1885
AF OF L UNION FOUNDED (1886)
INTERSTATE COMMERCE ACT (1887)

1890 *SHERMAN ANTI-TRUST ACT* (1890)
WOUNDED KNEE (1890)

POPULIST PARTY (1892)

PULLMAN STRIKE (1894)
1895
PLESSY V. FERGUSON (1896)

SPANISH-AMERICAN WAR (1898)
CARNEGIE STEEL CORP. (1899)
1900

NAACP (1909)
1905

INDUSTRIALIZATION
OF THE
UNITED STATES

The Brooklyn Bridge, NYC – built 1869-1883
(PhotoDisc ©1995)

FOREWORD

THE RECONSTRUCTION ERA

The Civil War ended with a human cost of over half a million lives. Despite the military victory of the Union forces, important questions remained unanswered. How to deal with Confederate leaders? What should be the economic and political fate of the freed slaves? What path should the recovery of the South take? What role should the national government take in responding to these and other questions? The answers to these complex questions offered by the political leaders of the day often led to conflict. The results of the struggles for answers led one historian to call the Reconstruction Era "America's Unfinished Revolution."

POLITICAL STRUGGLES OVER RECONSTRUCTION

Reconstruction refers to the period from 1865-1877 when the nation was rebuilding after the Civil War. The two main political tasks became readmitting the Southern states to the Union and granting rights to the newly freed slaves.

CONSTITUTIONAL STRUCTURES

Before the War ended, Congress claimed authority over Reconstruction in the *Wade-Davis Bill* (1864), but Lincoln vetoed it. President Lincoln started to plan the nation's Reconstruction. However, certain members of Congress did not agree with the President's philosophy. After Lincoln's assassination in April 1865, conflict deepened between Congress and Lincoln's successor, President Andrew Johnson. Congress then took greater authority in Reconstruction planning.

LINCOLN'S PLAN FOR RECONSTRUCTION
Lincoln's plan flowed from his belief that the Union had not been broken, therefore the Southern states should not be treated harshly. Under this plan, regained Southern states (those that were taken over by Union troops)

Key Terms	
Cultural Pluralism	Reservations
Social Darwinism	Monopolies
Laissez-Faire	Segregation
Urbanization	Unionism
Gilded Age	Populism
Assimilation	Nativism
Immigration	Socialism

could establish new state governments as soon as 10% of those people who voted in 1860 took an oath of loyalty to the Union. High-ranking Confederates would not be allowed to vote.

In March of 1865, before Congress adjourned for the summer, it created – with the President's approval – the Bureau of Refugees, Freedmen, and Abandoned Lands. It was soon known as the **Freedmen's Bureau**. This welfare agency was to provide relief supplies (food, clothing, shelter and medical supplies) to both African American and white Union refugees. At first, it could resettle freedmen on confiscated lands. This was later weakened when most lands were restored to their original owners. The Bureau also provided a local court system and negotiated labor contracts between freedmen and planters. Its greatest success was establishing thousands of schools across the South for the former slaves.

After the War, **Radical Republicans** controlled Congress. They believed the Union had been broken and the South should be punished harshly. They did not favor Lincoln's mild "ten percent" plan. Prior to his death, Lincoln approved of Secretary of War Edwin Stanton's policy for temporary military authority and provisional governments to be set up in the South. After Lincoln's assassination, Vice President **Andrew Johnson** (1808-1875) took control of Reconstruction planning.

JOHNSON'S PLAN FOR RECONSTRUCTION
President Johnson's plan generally followed Lincoln's. He wanted to grant amnesty to most Southerners who took loyalty oaths to the Union. He outlined steps for instituting new

Note: Items marked with an * are listed in the *Landmark Supreme Court Decisions* chart in Appendices.

civilian governments. These steps included drawing up new state constitutions that prohibited slavery and secession and the ratification of the Thirteenth Amendment which prohibited slavery.

Johnson's plan did not work. The Radical Republicans claimed it was too lenient. They cried out when white pre-War leaders regained power in the Southern states and used the **Black Codes** (segregationist employment contracts and legal status restrictions) to block civil rights for African Americans.

CONGRESSIONAL RECONSTRUCTION

In late 1865, Radical Republican leaders in Congress swept aside Johnson's work and took over Reconstruction. Radical Republicans in Congress set clearly defined goals

- establish democracy in the South,
- ensure voting and civil rights for all, including African Americans, and
- confiscate and redistribute land ("40 acres and a mule").

Not all of these were worked into the final Congressional Reconstruction plan. The Republican-controlled Congress finally passed the **Military Reconstruction Plan of 1867**. Its provisions included

- the U.S. Army would have control until new governments could be established,
- former slaves would be guaranteed the right to vote in state elections,
- each Southern state had to ratify the Fourteenth Amendment, and
- each Southern state had to ratify a Congressionally approved state constitution.

POST CIVIL-WAR AMENDMENTS

Three Amendments to the *Constitution of the United States* were ratified during the Reconstruction years. Ironically, in each case, ratification would not have occurred without the mandatory approval of the Southern states.

The **Thirteenth Amendment** (1865) abolished slavery in the United States.

The **Fourteenth Amendment** (1868) made African Americans citizens by stating, "All persons born or naturalized in the United States...are citizens of the United States..." It prohibited states from abridging citizens' "privileges and immunities," depriving them "due process under the law," or denying "equal protection of the laws." This Amendment also declared the Confederate debt null and void, excluded former Confederate officials from holding office, and reduced representation proportionally for those states that denied African Americans the right to vote. As a result of these clauses in the Fourteenth Amendment, powers in areas such as voting procedures and education, once reserved to the states under the Tenth Amendment, increasingly came under federal control. In the second half of the 20th century, Supreme Court interpretations of the Fourteenth Amendment have caused federal actions to prevent states from denying individuals their basic civil rights.

The **Fifteenth Amendment** (1870) prohibited states from denying the right to vote "on account of race, color, or previous condition of servitude."

IMPEACHMENT OF ANDREW JOHNSON

President Johnson and the Republican-controlled Congress did not cooperate. Relations between the two became strained as Congress enacted provisions designed to silence and restrict the President. One of these was the *Tenure of Office Act* (1867) through which the Senate maintained the power to interfere with presidential changes of Cabinet personnel. This act, passed over Johnson's veto, was designed to protect Secretary of War Stanton, who sympathized with the Radical Republicans.

When Johnson tried to remove Stanton without Senate approval he technically violated the *Tenure of Office Act*. The Radicals on the

PRESIDENTIAL VETOES & CONGRESSIONAL OVERRIDES		
	VETOES	OVERRIDES
All Presidents (1789-1865)	36	6 (16.6%)
Andrew Johnson (1865-1869)	21	15 (71.1%)

CONSEQUENCES FOR ANDREW JOHNSON

CONSTITUTIONAL STRUCTURES

"... The members (of the House of Representatives) collected in groups ... wondering how Mr. Johnson grew so daring. He must have weighed the consequences of his action, and he must have known as well as anyone that he has openly violated the Tenure of Office Bill. It is no use arguing that he himself considers this law unconstitutional, because, until the Supreme Court has given its opinion, the President is bound to put into execution the laws which Congress passes. It is impossible to see what the President is driving at, for he knows that Article 6 of this bill states that any removal from office or any appointment made contrary to the provisions of this law will be considered a misdemeanor, and the Constitution states the President can be deposed for high crimes and misdemeanors ..."

(Library of Congress)

– Georges Clemenceau, *American Reconstruction and the Impeachment of President Johnson*, Washington, DC, February, 1868

House Judiciary Committee called for his impeachment and a trial to remove him from office. Finding enough evidence to go to trial, the House of Representatives indicted Johnson in 1868. After a three-month trial in the Senate, removal from office was one vote short of the necessary two-thirds.

The acquittal established the precedent that removal from office should occur only in serious violation of constitutional law. Johnson, quietly completed the few months left in his term. Tennessee returned him to the U.S. Senate in 1875, but he died later that year. In 1887, the basis for charges that the Radicals used against

MINI•ASSESSMENT (4-1)

1 The most accurate definition of Reconstruction is
   1 the period after the Civil War when the South was rebuilding its industrial base
   2 increased purchasing by the federal government aiding industry
   3 efforts of the South to develop economically according to the North's pattern
   4 "picking up the pieces" after the Civil War to reunify the country

2 The main difference between the Congressional Reconstruction Plan and Johnson's plan was
   1 mandatory ratification of a Constitutional amendment
   2 role of the military in implementing Reconstruction policy
   3 development of new state constitutions
   4 prohibiting slavery and granting civil rights to former slaves

3 The post-Civil War amendments illustrate the
   1 growing power of the federal government to regulate Southern state governments
   2 continued use of the doctrine of nullification by the South
   3 federal government's power to insure the political equality of former slaves
   4 failure of the *Constitution of the United States* to adjust to changing circumstances

Constructed Response

"With malice toward none, with charity for all, with firmness in the right as God gives us to see the right, let us strive on to finish the work we are in, to bind up the nation's wounds, to care for him who shall have borne the battle and for his widow and his orphan, to do all which may achieve a just and lasting peace among ourselves and with all nations."

– Abraham Lincoln, *Second Inaugural Address*, 1865

1 According to the text, what were President Lincoln's beliefs on how the South should be treated during Reconstruction?

2 How did the Radical Republicans' Reconstruction planning compare to President Lincoln's?

Johnson – the *Tenure of Office Act* – was repealed. In 1926, the Supreme Court declared that the *Tenure of Office Act* had been unconstitutional.

FEDERAL, STATE, AND INDIVIDUAL RELATIONSHIPS

In the Reconstruction era, changes occurred in the way the federal and state governments related to one another. One of the major questions leading to the Civil War – states' rights and a state's ability to secede – was decided in favor of the Union. As a result of the post-War amendments, military occupation, and federal civil rights legislation, there was a growing federal (national) presence in state affairs. Much of the involvement revolved around the individual's right to use the federal government as an intermediary in state versus individual conflicts. The idea of federal protection of the individual was not fully accepted and developed until the mid-20th century. The issue of the extent of states' rights continues today (i.e., modern civil rights movement, and highway aid).

THE POST-WAR NORTH

ECONOMIC POLICY

In the post-Civil War period, the North became more industrialized with the number of non-agricultural workers and factories increasing dramatically. From 1875-1900, the United States enjoyed a favorable balance of trade, exporting more goods than it imported. Markets included Europe, Latin America, and the Far East.

INDUSTRIAL DEVELOPMENT

The Civil War mobilized Northern industries to design, invent, and implement an entire range of new products. In addition, businesses developed new practices of record keeping and distribution to meet the huge demands made on them. The last half of the 19th century signaled a period of tremendous growth for American business.

Initially, the Civil War hurt businesses in the North and the South as transportation and communication systems were disrupted.

INDUSTRIAL ERA IMPORTS & EXPORTS 1860-1900

Import / Export Dollars (in millions)

1400, 1200, 1000, 800, 600, 400, 200, 0

Years: 1860, 1870, 1880, 1890, 1900

• • • Exports of U.S. Goods
——— Imports of Foreign Goods

By 1862, the federal government created an enormous market for war-connected goods, munitions, and ready-made clothing. Vast profits were made. This capital was then used for future investment. Congress passed higher tariff legislation which promoted Northern industries.

Although the Civil War did not give birth to the Industrial Revolution, it did stimulate technological development. In December 1861, the magazine *Scientific American* reported, "Sixty-six new inventions relating to engines, implements, and articles of warfare have been illustrated in our columns..." for that year alone, not including non-war connected inventions. Business looked for quicker ways to mass produce the desired goods. In industry and agriculture, the shortage of labor also contributed to mechanization. Sewing machines, which had been invented before the Civil War, became widely used to produce the massive amounts of clothing needed. Repeating rifles, the steam engine, and the use of iron-clad ship hulls gave rise to new industries and changed the course of warfare. The transcontinental railroad was built from 1862-1869. The gauge of railroad track was standardized, making for universally connected transport. In 1851, industrialist **William Kelly** of Pittsburgh (1811-1888) patented a method for blowing a blast of air through molten pig iron

American Railroads used European steel to build lighter weight, stronger bridges enhancing and accelerating America's industrial development.
(Civil War CD, Digital Stock ©1995)

THE NEW SOUTH

After Radical rule ended, Southern government and politics became dominated by industrialists, merchants, and bankers. The "**New South**" refers to the growing industrialization of the South after the Civil War. However, much of this industrial growth was tied to agricultural products, (e.g., textile mills). Many Southern industries were subsidiaries of Northern firms and dependent upon capital from Northern banks.

to oxidize its impurities. In England, Sir Henry Bessemer set up an identical system that took Europe by storm. The **Kelly–Bessemer Process** made steel for railroads plentiful, less expensive, and more desirable than the softer and weaker iron.

DEVELOPING LABOR NEEDS

The skilled and unskilled labor needed to fuel these technological changes were readily available after the Civil War. Immigrants, unrestricted for most of the 19th century, provided a constant supply of cheap labor. In 1861, most workers in the United States were involved in agricultural work. By 1900, over 60% of American workers were in non-agricultural jobs.

Industrialization and the spread of the factory system changed workers' lives drastically. Machinery replaced the need for skilled artisans, and the workplace shifted from the home to the factory. Within the new factory system, workers' actions were dictated by the work bell and time clock. **Real wages** (amount of goods and services income buys) rose between 1860 and 1890. However, working conditions were less than ideal. Safety precautions were often non-existent. Ten and twelve hour work days and six day work weeks were the rule. Wages were so low that workers were forced to live in tenements and slum conditions. Most children went to work full-time before they were 14 years old.

AGRICULTURE: LAND AND LABOR

The devastation as a result of the Civil War caused a significant change in Southern agriculture. The number of property owners remained stable while the number of farms doubled and the acreage per farm decreased. The new agricultural system was one of tenant farming or sharecropping. This **sharecropping system** perpetuated the plantation system. In return for the lease of farm land, a sharecropper would agree to turn over a portion of his crops (usually one third for land and one third for use of tools). By 1920, over two thirds of Southern farmers, both African American and white, were sharecroppers.

Since currency was in short supply in the postwar South, farmers would borrow on their only asset, their expected harvest, agreeing to pay a portion of their crops in return for credit. This is known as the **crop lien system**. High prices for seed, tools, and fertilizer caused the farmers and the South to go deeper and deeper into debt. A single cash crop, cotton, was still the norm. As cotton production increased, cotton prices dropped causing further hardship for farmers.

STATUS OF FORMER SLAVES

Most former slaves remained in agricultural occupations as sharecroppers or tenant farmers, the same occupations as before the Civil War. Thus, they experienced limited economic opportunity. Those seeking work in textile mills and other factory jobs were often refused employment. Although slavery was abolished and the franchise (vote) was granted by new constitutional amendments, there were many restrictions on African Americans' political rights.

Southern state governments began instituting procedures to decrease the political power of African Americans. **Poll taxes** of one or two dollars were assessed on those wishing to vote. Poor African Americans and whites were unable to pay and therefore could not vote. **Literacy tests** were given. **Grandfather clauses** exempted from the literacy tests whites whose grandfathers had been eligible to vote prior to the Civil War. Socially, segregation continued. Separation of the races had been a long-standing custom in the South. By the 1870s and the 1880s, state governments passed a number of formal segregation laws. These became known as **Jim Crow laws**, named after an early minstrel show character. Segregation by law or statute is know as **de jure segregation**. African Americans began leaving the South, but not in tremendous numbers until the great exodus of the World War I era.

POLITICAL CONTROL IN THE NEW SOUTH

Exercising their power under the "Civil War Amendments" (13th, 14th, 15th), African Americans elected many African American people to public office (including fourteen Congressmen and two United States Senators). A white **backlash** (vicious reaction) developed. Organized efforts to quiet the African American political voice developed. Through intimidation and terrorism, such groups as the **Ku Klux Klan** sought to keep African Americans in a subjective, inferior position. Federal legislation was passed to outlaw the activities of the Klan.

THE NEW REPUBLICANS: AFRICAN AMERICAN LEADERS DURING RADICAL RECONSTRUCTION

During the Radical Reconstruction in the South following the end of the Civil War, new Southern state laws enfranchised large numbers of African Americans. Republican leaders encouraged African Americans to enter politics. (Photos – Library of Congress)

Robert Smalls

Blanche Kelso Bruce

Pinckney Benton Stewart Pinchback

• **Robert Smalls** was born a slave and became a Civil War naval hero. Following the War, he was elected from South Carolina on the Republican ticket to the U.S. House of Representatives (1875-79; 1881-87).
• **Blanche Kelso Bruce**, reared in slavery, graduate of Oberlin College, Ohio, became a planter in Mississippi after the Civil War. Elected in 1874, he was the second African American to serve in the U.S. Senate. Later, President Garfield appointed him register of the treasury.
• **Pinckney Benton Stewart Pinchback**, whose mother was an emancipated slave and whose father was white, raised a company of African American volunteers called the Corps d'Afrique during the Civil War. In 1871, he was elected to the Louisiana Senate and served as its president pro tempore, later becoming the Louisiana lieutenant governor.

African Americans usually supported the Republicans ("the party of emancipation"), but they played a limited role in party politics. In the South, the Democratic Party leaders refused membership to African Americans. State legislation and private groups kept African Americans disenfranchised. With the end of Reconstruction and the fall of Radical Republican state governments, African Americans lost political power. New "**redeemer governments**" (Southerners who took power back from the "northern carpet-baggers") worked with the planter class to insure their own economic, social, and political goals at the expense of African Americans.

Ulysses S. Grant, 18th U.S. President
(Library of Congress)

THE GRANT ERA

In a close popular vote, the popular Civil War general, **Ulysses S. Grant** (1822-1885), won his first election as President in 1868. A better warrior than President, his administration became known for political scandals and corruption.

NATIONAL AND LOCAL POLITICAL CORRUPTION

During Grant's administration (1869-1877), a number of major political scandals became public. In 1869, financial speculators **Jay Gould** (1836-1892) and **Jim Fisk** (1834-1872) sought to dominate the gold market by purchasing all available gold and selling it at higher prices. Through Grant's brother-in-law, they convinced the President that it would be unwise for the Treasury Department to sell any United States gold. Grant agreed to the proposal for a time. When he reversed his position, the price of gold fell so low, it caused a financial panic on 24 September 1869, "**Black Friday**."

The **Credit Mobilier Scandal** also came to light during Grant's first administration. During the building of the transcontinental railroad, the Union Pacific Railroad had contracted with the Credit Mobilier Company to do the construction. This company swindled over 23 million dollars from the bulk of Union Pacific stockholders. To block a Congressional investigation, stock was distributed at ridiculously low prices to members of Congress and even to Vice President Colfax.

The **Salary Grab Scandal** (1873) involved a Congressional act doubling the pay of the President and raising its own salary by 50% for the previous two years. It was later repealed.

The **Whiskey Ring Scandal** (1873-1877) involved revenue collectors and liquor distillers cheating the federal government out of tax revenue in St. Louis, Milwaukee, and Chicago.

In the **Indian Service Scandal** (1876), a House investigation found that Secretary of War William Belknap had accepted bribes in assigning trading posts in Indian Territory.

Corruption occurred even more frequently at the state and local level. One of the most infamous groups was the **Tweed Ring** in New York City. Political boss **William Marcy Tweed** (1823-1878) embezzled some 200 million dollars through kickbacks, and rent padding.

Political cartoonist **Thomas Nast** (1840-1902), a German immigrant, gained fame depicting issues of social and political significance. One of his cartoons dealing with the corruption of Tweed helped to apprehend and extradite Tweed from Spain. Nast's barbed comments on political corruption popularized the political cartoon in America.

THE END OF RECONSTRUCTION

By the mid-1870s, Reconstruction was gradually ending, Radical leaders had died or left office, reformers had lost momentum, and others were looking to a new industrial focus.

DISPUTED ELECTION OF 1876

In the presidential election of 1876, the Democratic candidate was **Samuel Tilden** (1814-1886), reform governor of New York. The Republican candidate was **Rutherford B. Hayes** (1822-1893), reform governor of Ohio. Tilden won the popular vote by a slim margin (under 275,000), but he was one electoral vote short of the needed majority. There were a number of disputed electoral votes, primarily in South Carolina, Florida, and Louisiana. The *Constitution of the United States* provided no procedure to decide these votes. Congress appointed a bipartisan (both Republicans and Democrats) electoral commission which decided the election in favor of Hayes.

Some scholars suggest a compromise was secretly worked out between the Republicans and Democrats. They claim the Democrats agreed to support Hayes and treat African Americans equitably. They claim the Republicans agreed to remove federal troops from the South, appoint a Southerner to the Cabinet, and provide federal money for Southern railroads. Other scholars feel that the Democrats realized that they did not have enough support. In any case, Hayes became the nation's 19th President in 1877.

END OF MILITARY OCCUPATION IF THE SOUTH (1877-1878)

Although the greatest demobilization of federal troops from the South occurred within one year of the end of the Civil War (from 1 million to 57,000), the last troops were removed in April of 1877. With their removal, the last Radical Republican state government collapsed. It signaled a return to conservative, Southern Democratic control.

RESTORATION OF WHITE CONTROL IN THE SOUTH (1870s AND 1880s)

The passage of Fourteenth and Fifteenth Amendments and the actions of the Radical governments were designed to minimize the political power of conservative Southern Democrats. Yet, white Southerners ("redeemers") quickly regained control. The activities of the Ku Klux Klan prompted Congress to pass two *Force Acts* and an *Anti-Klan Law* in 1870 and 1871. These gave law enforcement officials the power to take action against the Klan. Prosecution was rigor-

ous, but conviction was minimal. Nevertheless, the Klan was forced underground.

Congress passed the *Amnesty Act* in 1872, which pardoned most of the remaining Confederates. Eight Southern states were "redeemed" by 1876. Conservative Democratic politicians were in control. Regaining of political control by white Southerners is also referred to as "home rule." Southern attitudes of racial inferiority and discrimination were legitimatized by the passage of Jim Crow laws in the 1870s and 1880s. Later known as de jure segregation, these laws mandated segregation in virtually every situation.

FOURTEENTH AMENDMENT: SUPREME COURT INTERPRETATIONS

The Fourteenth Amendment guarantees "equal protection under the laws" and "due process" of the law to all citizens. In the later 19th century, Supreme Court decisions established the precedent that the Fourteenth Amendment protected citizens' rights only against infringement by state governments. The precedents set in these civil rights cases remained in existence until the desegregation decisions in the 1950s and 1960s.

PLESSY V. FERGUSON*

In 1890, Louisiana passed a Jim Crow law requiring railroads to provide equal but separate accommodations for African American and white passengers. As a test case to challenge the constitutionality of this legislation, Homer Adolph Plessy, a mulatto (a person of mixed race), sat in an all white car. He was arrested and found guilty. The case was eventually appealed to the Supreme Court because the issue involved a constitutional conflict: Did a state's reserved rights to pass legislation (Tenth Amendment) contradict the "equal protection" guarantee of the Fourteenth Amendment?

In *Plessy v. Ferguson** (1896), the Supreme Court ruled against Plessy. It said Louisiana's creation of "separate but equal accommodations" was a "reasonable use of state power." The Court never considered the physical equality of African American and white facilities. This judicial precedent remained in effect until the 1954 decision in *Brown v. the Board of Education of Topeka, Kansas.**

CITIZENS' RIGHTS – COURT DECISIONS		
YEAR	CASE	DECISION
1873	Slaughterhouse Cases	Decided that the basic rights under the Bill of Rights were not guaranteed by the federal government against state action. State and national citizenship were separate.
1876	U.S. v. Cruikshank	Decided the Fourteenth Amendment guarantees did not cover the actions or misdeeds of private individuals against other individuals.
1883	Civil Rights Cases*	Declared unconstitutional the 1875 Civil Rights Act which outlawed segregation. Stated the federal government had no jurisdiction over the behavior of private groups in race relations.
1896	Plessy v. Ferguson*	"Separate but equal" doctrine upheld – equal protection requirements met if separate facilities were provided (in this case, railroad cars).
1899	Cumming v. County Board of Education	"Separate but equal" doctrine extended to public education.

THE NATIONAL DEBATE OVER PROPER ROLE OF AFRICAN AMERICANS

During the last quarter of the 19th century, there came from the African American community a number of voices addressing the proper role of African Americans in society. **Booker T. Washington** (1856-1915), a former slave and self-made man, called for "realistic accommodation" and a policy of self-help. In 1881, he founded the **Tuskegee Institute**, a vocational school for African Americans.

Washington argued that political equality could only be achieved after economic and property rights were secured. To achieve these, African Americans needed to "dignify and glorify common labor" and promote their own communities. When African Americans achieved and proved themselves, their political rights would follow. Whites generally supported this policy of accommodation.

The African American critics of Washington's accommodation policy included **W.E.B. DuBois** (1868-1963), a New Englander with a Harvard doctorate. He called for a more militant approach to secure equal voting rights and economic opportunities. In 1905, a meeting of supporters near Niagara Falls gave rise to the **Niagara Movement**, a call for increased agitation. According to DuBois, African American

leadership was to come from the **Talented Tenth**, 10% of the African American population, who were highly educated and able.

In 1909, a group of Progressives, both African American and white, founded the **National Association for the Advancement**

W.E.B. DuBois
(Library of Congress)

of Colored People. The major focus of the **NAACP** was the protection of civil rights and an end to the disenfranchisement of African Americans. DuBois served as its major spokesman. The group appealed mostly to middle class, educated African Americans and had little or no contact with rural, sharecropping families. By 1914, the NAACP had over 6,000 members joined in 50 branch offices. Despite their differences, both Washington and DuBois agreed that African Americans should develop basic middle class values of family and work.

NEW POLITICAL ALIGNMENTS

After the Civil War, neither major political party was intensely reform-minded (with the exception of the Radical Republicans). Since the Republican and Democratic parties were composed of a number of special interests, they tended to shy away from specific stands on issues.

Republicans, who won the majority of postwar presidential elections, were supported by Northern industrialists and urban workers, Western farmers, veterans, and the newly enfranchised African American voters. The African American vote, although made impotent (weakened) by state and local actions, remained basically Republican until a major realignment occurred during the New Deal of the 1930s.

The Democratic Party's major supporters were from the South and those industrialists and workers who did not favor Republican policies such as high tariffs.

THE "SOLID SOUTH"
Political alignments became very distinct in the post-Civil War South. Although African Americans associated with the Republican party, white Southerners became staunchly Democratic especially after the disputed 1876 election. The **Solid South** refers to the consistent and overwhelming Democratic majorities in elections for almost a century.

THE NATURE OF CITIZENSHIP
According to the Fourteenth Amendment, all people born or naturalized in the United States are citizens of the United States, and no state may deny them either **due process** or **equal**

protection of law. This amendment was initially designed to make the recently freed African Americans into citizens. In actuality, the Southern states passed Jim Crow legislation that severely curtailed the civil rights and equality of African Americans.

The Fifteenth Amendment granted the right to vote to citizens regardless of race, color, or previous condition of servitude. However, African American and white women were not given the voting rights by this amendment. African American voting rights were curtailed further by the use of poll taxes, literacy tests, and grandfather clauses.

FEDERAL-STATE RELATIONSHIPS

Passage of the three post-Civil War amendments and the *Civil Rights Act* (1875) gave the federal (national) government the possibility of increased control of state affairs.

However, several decisions by the Supreme Court in the late 19th century trimmed this control considerably. The *Civil Rights Act of 1875* was declared unconstitutional when its narrow interpretation of the Fourteenth Amendment was implemented.

Strides in technology required policies of a national dimension. Developments in communication and transportation made the various geographic areas of the United States more accessible to each other. Now, the mechanisms were in place for the federal government to grow increasingly stronger.

THE RISE OF AMERICAN BUSINESS, INDUSTRY, AND LABOR (1865-1920)

CAPITALISM AND TECHNOLOGY

The **Industrial Revolution** changed the way goods were produced. Goods mainly produced in the home were now produced in the factories which utilized machinery, new power sources, and more unskilled than skilled labor.

ECONOMIC POLICY

1   Sharecropping is said to have perpetuated the plantation system because the
    1   slaves and sharecroppers were both owned by the landowner
    2   slaves and sharecroppers were exclusively African American
    3   plantation owners were as wealthy and successful after the Civil War, as before the War
    ④   sharecroppers in reality had as little economic independence as the slaves

2   Labor market changes immediately after the Civil War included a greater
    1   reliance on imported raw materials
    2   demand for equal pay for women
    3   proportion of the population becoming involved in agriculture than before 1860
    ④   demand for cheap immigrant labor

3   Opponents of the Fourteenth Amendment's guarantees were pleased with the decision
    1   in the Civil Rights cases (1883) which prohibited segregation in public places
    2   in *Plessy v. Ferguson* (1896) which allowed de jure racial separation
    ③   of President Garfield to veto the amendment
    4   of Congress to deny federal funds to any state which had Jim Crow laws

Constructed Response

"All persons born or naturalized in the United States and subject to the jurisdiction thereof, are citizens of the United States and of the State wherein they reside. No State shall make or enforce any law which shall abridge the privileges or immunities of citizens of the United States; nor shall any State deprive any person of life, liberty, or property, without due process of law; nor deny to any person within its jurisdiction the equal protection of the laws."

– Section 1, Amendment XIV to the *Constitution of the United States*, ratified July 9, 1868

1   According to this amendment, how is United States' citizenship determined?

You have to be born or naturalized.

2   How did the Southern states respond to these provisions of the Fourteenth Amendment?

Jim crow laws

Industrialization first occurred in England then spread to other nations. There are still countries in the world which have not yet undergone industrialization.

Fundamentally, industrialization was driven by **capitalism** – an economic belief that the means of production must be privately owned. Capitalism is a dynamic system based on continued growth and improvement of living standards.

In a capitalist-market structure, supply and demand guide business organizations' decisions in producing goods for the marketplace. Progress in a capitalist system rests on efficient production linked to borrowing, accumulating, and reinvesting money (capital) gained in free exchange (market).

In 1776, philosopher Adam Smith explained capitalism in his book, *The Wealth of Nations* (full title: *An Inquiry into the Nature and Causes of the Wealth of Nations*). Marketplace signals help businesses estimate what to produce, who will produce it, how to produce it, and how to distribute the rewards. Unlike command systems, Smith's capitalist market has no central control (unless monopolies emerge or government interferes).

In addition to the development of the factory system and the focus on capitalism, many other changes occurred within the industrializing nations. Population growth rates increased due to both an increasing birth rate and decreasing death rate. Changes in diet as a result of the agricultural revolution and changes in medicine contributed to these population trends.

ENGLAND

In England, a new group developed out of the growing middle class. They were neither factory owners nor workers, but managers who began to exercise increasing economic and later political power. England's early industrialization (18th century) was made possible by an agricultural revolution which increased production and used less labor. This freed up workers who migrated to cities. The cotton textile industry was the first to be mechanized. Later inventions shifted the workplace from the home to the factory where production increased. This led to a decrease in prices and an increase in the demand for cotton cloth.

Much of the cotton for England's textile industry came from the southern United States. Water power eventually gave way to steam power. Better transportation systems developed – roads, canals, and later railroads. Numerous inventions by Europeans and Americans encouraged industrialization in Western Europe and the United States. Wars and a lack of one or more of the factors of production (land, labor, capital, and infrastructure) inhibited rapid industrialization in some countries (France, Italy, and Russia).

GERMANY

Germany's industrialization came later than England's, partly because of political disunity. In the late 1870s, the policies of the "Iron Chancellor," Otto von Bismarck, unified the country and German industry made use of the best technology available. German government policies encouraged the growth of business by creating uniform banking and currency regulations, centralizing postal and telegraph services,

and imposing high protective tariffs. As in Japan, government encouraged businesses to develop **cartels** (immense organizations which acted to monopolize industries). By 1900, Germany was rivaling both the United States and England in world markets.

JAPAN

As a result of the **Meiji Restoration** in the 1860s, Japan began a period of modernization. Foreign finance and economic experts were invited to Japan. Scholars from Japan went to Europe and America to study all manner of things, including industry, the military, and educational systems. They copied the best that the Western nations had to offer. By the turn of the century, Japan caught up to the Western industrial states. This caused problems of overpopulation in the cities and led to increased emigration and shortages of available raw materials. These needs eventually led to aggressive Japanese imperialist policies in the 20th century.

TECHNOLOGICAL DEVELOPMENTS: SCOPE OF DEVELOPMENT 1750-1860

Developments, such as those listed in the chart below, encouraged industrialization in many nations.

TECHNOLOGICAL DEVELOPMENTS		
DATE	TECHNOLOGY	INVENTOR
1764	spinning Jenny increased thread production	James Hargreaves (Br)
1769	water Frame increased thread production	Richard Arkwright (Br)
1769	first modern steam engine	James Watt (Br)
1785	power loom increased cloth production	Edmund Cartwright (Br)
1793	cotton gin	Eli Whitney (USA)
1800	1st battery with a steady stream of electricity	Alessandro Volta (It)
1800	magnetic effects of electric current	Andre Ampere (Fr)
1807	application of steamboat	Robert Fulton (USA)
1814	perfected the locomotive engine	George Stephenson (Br)
1839	vulcanization of rubber	Charles Goodyear (USA)
1853	Bessemer steel process	Henry Bessemer (Br) & William Kelly (USA)

PRE-CIVIL WAR INDUSTRIAL GROWTH: IRON AND TEXTILES

GEOGRAPHIC INTERACTIONS

In America, one of the most important commercial enterprises in the early development of the English colonies was the iron industry. The valleys of the Appalachian Mountains were a rich source of iron ore. The dense forests of this region provided the fuel needed to smelt the ore. The English colonists provided the skill to process the ore and manufacture useful tools.

IRON

The competition of the small colonial iron industry caused the British Parliament to pass a mercantilist *Iron Act* in 1750. The mercantilist system was designed to have colonies compliment the mother country's economy. The *Iron Act* forbade iron finishing mills in the colonies. Like many other mercantilist regulations, the act was ignored by the colonists. By the time of the American Revolution, iron foundries existed in every colony.

Still, the iron and steel industry could not develop into a substantial enterprise until increased sources of ore were found, transport made easier, and cheaper, faster production methods were developed. By the mid-1800s these things were beginning to happen. Iron ranges like the massive **Mesabi**, in the Lake Superior region, were discovered. In 1855, the **Sault Sainte Marie Canals** (also called the Soo Canals) were completed, connecting Lake Superior and Lake Huron. As a result, Mesabi became the key iron supply for the nation's manufacturers.

Early in the 19th century, Englishman William Bessemer and American William Kelly invented a process for iron to be converted to steel. The Bessemer/Kelly Process was implemented in Pittsburgh factories in the mid-1800s, and spread rapidly. As a result, iron production (only 30,000 tons in 1776) was at the 1.1 million ton level by 1864. As production increased, industry developed more machinery to shape and roll the steel, thereby increasing its usefulness.

TEXTILES

America's textile industry was virtually nonexistent during the colonial times due to a more strictly enforced set of mercantilist regulations. The first textile mill was built in the United States in 1790, in Pawtucket, Rhode Island, using plans smuggled out of England by **Samuel Slater** (1768-1835). This technology and the invention of the cotton gin in 1793 heralded the growth of the American textile industry. At first, the needed power came from New England's swift streams and rivers, and early production centered on making thread. Later, steam-powered looms were developed to produce finished cloth.

FORMS OF BUSINESS ORGANIZATION		
FORM	**ADVANTAGES**	**DISADVANTAGES**
Proprietorship	• owner close to customers and workers • has total control of management • receives all profits	• owner assumes all risks • limited capital available • one manager's perspective
Partnership	• more capital can be raised • risks are shared • more management perspective	• profits must be shared • unlimited liability for owners • dissolves if one partner leaves
Corporation	• increased capital through sale of shares (stocks) • losses limited to investment • increased number of managers • ownership transferable • larger growth potential • research facilities possible • risks shared	• state & federally regulated • subject to corporate taxes • management removed from customers & workers

In 1813, the Boston Manufacturing Company, operated by **Francis Cabot Lowell** (1775-1817), and industrial designer Paul Moody, set up a textile factory in Waltham, Massachusetts. It was the first factory to house all the textile operations under one roof. Lowell's system also included the large scale employment of young women, who were housed in dormitories. It provided farm girls with a way to earn a marriage dowry. This system hit its peak in the 1830-1840 period. Eventually, immigrant labor took the place of native labor, and Lowell's system and the salaries decreased. When the source of Southern cotton was lost in the Civil War, the Lowell factory system died out.

MAJOR AREAS OF GROWTH IN BUSINESS AND INDUSTRY

Although the major basic industries were developing rapidly before the Civil War, much of the investment capital came from adventurous Europeans. Domestic investment capital – accumulated during the War – made the industrial era a time of massive growth and expansion.

BUSINESS ORGANIZATIONS

Before the industrial revolution, **proprietorships** (single owner) and **partnerships** (small group of owners) were the most common forms of business organization. These forms were basically for small scale business operations.

Nationwide operations demanded a more efficient form of ownership and management which provided wider sources of capital and gave protection to investors. The **corporation** was the answer. It allowed for limited sharing of ownership through stock sales. Corporations are chartered by state authority and regulated as legal entities. Therefore, they can own property, lend and borrow money, sue and be sued, and pay taxes.

THE ECONOMICS OF SCALE

National territorial and population increases spurred corporate industrial expansion. Access to foreign markets was made easier, first with the fast clipper ships of the 1830s and then the steamship. Better roads, canals, and developing

railroads made widespread distribution of goods possible. Increased profits resulted from large scale production and lowered per item costs. Communication technologies allowed for rapid transfer of ordering information and projection of production quotas.

Mass production, the increase of consumers, and better distribution led to changes in merchandising. Department stores emerged to replace specialty shops. **John Wanamaker**'s, **R.H. Macy**'s and **Marshall Field**'s became leading retail stores in the nation's major cities. Most transactions were "cash and carry."

Gradually, some businesses began to make limited amounts of credit available to customers, and began rail delivery services. In 1869, the **Great Atlantic & Pacific Tea Company** applied department store retailing techniques to food. To reach a more rural clientele, companies, such as **Montgomery Ward** and **Sears, Roebuck, & Co**. created mail order (catalog) merchandising.

TRANSPORTATION

Mass transportation allowed cities and the nation to grow. Prior to 1870, horses and mules pulled the main modes of urban transit. After

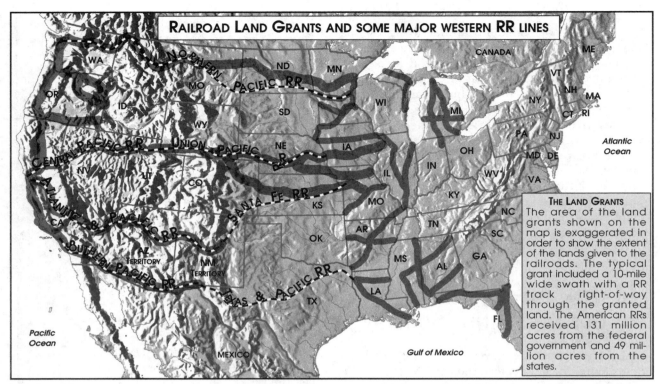

THE LAND GRANTS
The area of the land grants shown on the map is exaggerated in order to show the extent of the lands given to the railroads. The typical grant included a 10-mile wide swath with a RR track right-of-way through the granted land. The American RRs received 131 million acres from the federal government and 49 million acres from the states.

1870, steam (and later electricity) would power trains and street cars to provide commuter and merchandise transport.

From the 1830s, railroads developed rapidly, and soon supplanted river and road transport. By 1850, there was 9,000 miles of track in the country, mostly in the eastern sector. A northern transcontinental route was being planned when the hostilities of the Civil War intervened. Rail travel was crude until post-Civil War technology refined it. **George Westinghouse**'s air brakes and **George Pullman**'s sleeping cars were major contributions. On 10 May 1869, at Promontory Point, Utah, the **Central Pacific** and **Union Pacific** railroad companies drove the "golden spike" joining the rails of the nation's first transcontinental rail line. Trackage increased rapidly after that historic meeting. In 1865, there were 35,000 miles of track in the country. By 1890, there were 200,000 miles. By 1900, transcontinental and regional rail networks had created a nationwide market. It caused standardization of time zones (Eastern, Central, Mountain, and Pacific) to accommodate scheduling.

In the 1890s, **Henry Ford** (1863-1947), an electrical engineer in Detroit's Edison Company, spent his spare time developing a gasoline internal combustion engine. In 1903, he opened the Ford Motor Company and applied mass production and mass marketing techniques to automobile production. By 1908, his Model T Ford was selling 10,000 cars per year.

BUILDING MATERIALS

New factories and office buildings of huge proportions demanded newer, stronger building materials. Masonry, concrete, and steel soon supplanted wood and stone. America's steel industry had blossomed during the heavy demand years of the Civil War, once localized industries were bought out or consolidated. The largest corporation in the world was formed in 1901, when **J.P. Morgan** (1837-1913) bought out the Carnegie Steel Corporation and merged it with other steel manufacturers to form the United States Steel Corporation.

J.P Morgan

MINI•ASSESSMENT (4-3)

1 Which had a favorable impact on the development of the steel industry in the United States during the last half of the 19th century?
   1 development of the urban department store
   2 discovery of the Mesabi Range resources
   3 the inventions of James Hargreaves and Richard Arkwright
   4 creation of the Lowell System

2 Markets for American goods broadened during the 19th century because
   1 local proprietors offered "cash and carry" service
   2 partnerships had limited capital resources
   3 corporations could be taxed as legal individuals
   4 national transportation networks emerged

3 Which statement is an OPINION, rather than a FACT?
   1 Most early oil was used to make kerosene as a replacement for whale oil.
   2 By 1900 the U.S. emerged as the world's largest steel producer.
   3 Even if the Civil War had not happened, the transcontinental railroad would have been built along a Northern route.
   4 Development of heavy industry in the United States is directly tied to the increase in coal usage.

Constructed Response

INCREASE IN SIZE OF THE INDUSTRIAL WORK FORCE, 1860-1900 (SOURCE: U.S. BUREAU OF THE CENSUS) AVERAGE NUMBER OF WORKERS PER ESTABLISHMENT		
INDUSTRY	1860	1900
cotton goods	112	287
iron and steel	65	333
carpets and rugs	31	213
meat packing	20	61
agricultural implements	8	65

1 What is the general trend in the average number of workers per establishment 1860-1900 as shown in the chart?

it increased

2 Of those industries listed, which had the largest increase in the number of workers per establishment?

Iron & steel

3 Explain factors that would account for the trend shown in this chart.

ENERGY SOURCES

COAL

Commercial coal mines started in 18th century America. The consumption of coal began to increase as factories turned to steam driven machinery. Steel mills demanded massive amounts of coal for the smelting processes. Railroads needed coal for their locomotives. After the Civil War and into the 20th century, coal provided 90% of America's energy needs. Mining became a major industry and the increased demands made on miners made it an extremely hazardous line of work. It is not surprising that major labor disputes of the age centered on this industry. (See Labor Unionization on page 157.)

OIL

The first oil well in America was drilled in 1859 near Titusville, Pennsylvania. An oil boom followed. The major industrial use was not as a fuel at this stage, but as a lubricant for machinery. Pipelines and refineries were built rapidly. Refining oil into kerosene for lighting and heating fuel made the demand for petroleum grow. In 1870, a young man,

John D. Rockefeller

John D. Rockefeller (1839-1937), organized what would become the major monopoly of the Industrial Age – the Standard Oil Company of Ohio. In 1901, at Spindletop, Texas, the richest oil well ever drilled gushed forth, opening rich fields in the southwest in time to start providing petroleum for the automobile revolution.

ELECTRICITY

In 1882, **Thomas Alva Edison** (1847-1931) started America's first electric power generating station in Washington, D.C. However, direct current could not be transmitted over vast distances. Invention and innovation overcame this difficulty. George Westinghouse developed alternating current. His electrical transformers made it possible to transport this current over long distances. In 1892, the General Electric Company was formed. In 1895, an international group of scientists recommended a hydroelectric plant to harness the power of Niagara Falls.

COMMUNICATIONS

In the early 19th century, a practical telegraph was made possible by the development of electric storage batteries and improvements to electromagnets. **Samuel F.B. Morse** (1791-1872), a landscape artist, developed the first telegraphic sending devices and a telegraphic signal code which bears his name. Starting in 1843, the federal government's support spread the use of Morse Code rapidly. The Western Union Telegraph Company was formed in 1856. Ten years later, a permanent transatlantic cable linked the communications systems of Europe and America for the first time.

Alexander Graham Bell (1847-1922) first transmitted the human voice over wire in 1876. The Bell Telephone Company, created the following year, set up local telephone systems throughout the Northeast. By 1900, the Bell System grew into the American Telephone and Telegraph Corporation.

REPRESENTATIVE ENTREPRENEURS

The business leaders of the post-Civil War era have been called both "robber barons" and "captains of industry," depending on the speaker's point of view. Supporters of the term captains of industry point to the new, highly efficient industries they created. They cite the selection of new products and the industrialists' donations to charities as positive accomplishments of these men. Those who call the industrialists, "robber barons," concentrate on the negative actions of the businessmen: exploitation of workers, unscrupulous business practices, and political corruption. In addition to those profiled below, other leaders included J.P. Morgan (money trust), **Philip Armour** (meat packing), and **Charles Pillsbury** (flour milling).

JOHN D. ROCKEFELLER (OIL)

In 1859, John D. Rockefeller and his associates built a small refinery in Cleveland, Ohio, laying the foundation for an oil empire. In 1870, he formed the Standard Oil Company of Ohio. Using a variety of business tactics, including price-cutting, railroad rebates, and manipulating the effects of the Depression of 1873, he increased his position in the oil industry. By 1880, Rockefeller had control of nearly all U.S. oil shipping and refining facilities. This control over a limited aspect of one industry is called **horizontal integration**. Rockefeller also acquired interest in related businesses, such as barrel making, pipelines, railroads, and oil storage facilities. His goal was to pay no one a profit except his company.

The Standard Oil Trust was formed in 1882 only to be dissolved ten years later by the Ohio Supreme Court. The trust was replaced by the Standard Oil Company of New Jersey, a holding company. This was dissolved in 1911, by the United States Supreme Court and separated into 34 units. John D. Rockefeller retired in 1897, as the richest man alive with a worth of one billion dollars. He then engaged in philanthropic endeavors, including creation of the Rockefeller Foundation.

ANDREW CARNEGIE (STEEL)

Carnegie's story is a classic example of "rags to riches." **Andrew Carnegie** (1835-1919), a Scottish immigrant, began his career in railroads. He later entered the steel business, in which he saw real potential for the post-Civil War period. The company he created secured major aspects of the entire industry, as well as iron ore deposits and steamships to transport ore to steel mills. This control over all aspects of an industry is called **vertical integration**.

Andrew Carnegie

By 1900, Carnegie Steel Company produced over one-half of the nation's steel. In 1901, Wall Street financier J.P. Morgan bought out Carnegie and formed the United States Steel Company. Carnegie retired and donated over 450 million dollars for libraries and other philanthropic works.

HENRY FORD (AUTOMOBILES)

Henry Ford, a mechanical genius, produced his first car in 1892 and created the Ford Motor Company in 1903. In 1908, he designed the Model T, a durable, economical automobile. Using assembly line and mass production techniques, he produced a car that the average American could afford. Like Rockefeller and Carnegie, Ford sought to control the total enterprise from raw materials to distribution of the final product. Although Ford paid high wages, he tolerated no opposition and refused to recognize labor unions.

HORATIO ALGER AND AMERICAN WORK ETHIC

Early America's Calvinist virtues included hard work, an emphasis on self-reliance, and the shunning of idleness, extravagance, and vanity. These "Puritan values" included emphasis on the lessons of the Bible and thrift. In the late 19th century, these values were compatible with the ideas of laissez-faire economics. Hard workers would get ahead. **Horatio Alger** (1834-1899) popularized these ideas in his books. Alger's "rags to riches" stories featured heroes who achieved great wealth through hard work, honesty, and thrift.

The industrial leaders commanded vast power and control over resources, production, and distribution. As corporate power grew, critics began to question their business practices and right to control America's resources. As corrupt business practices became more publicized, people looked increasingly to the government to reassert itself to protect the public good.

BUSINESS PRACTICES AND GOVERNMENT

In an effort to deal with America's business expansion and a "roller coaster" business cycle (boom periods followed by depressions or panics), businesses began to develop new methods of organization and combination.

ECONOMIC POLICY

LAISSEZ-FAIRE AND GOVERNMENT SUPPORT

Laissez-faire implies little or no government regulation of business beyond providing an atmosphere conducive for business development. This would include maintaining a stable currency, passing protective tariffs, and providing a stable domestic situation. The federal government – from Alexander Hamilton's financial plan forward – basically supported and promoted American business. The guarantees of the Fourteenth Amendment were interpreted by the Supreme Court to protect, not only individuals, but also "corporate persons."

COMPETITION AND ABSORPTION: MERGERS AND TRUSTS

The last few decades of the 1800s saw businesses merging and combining to eliminate competition, increase profits, and reduce inefficiency. The mergers were caused in part by the desire of business to secure itself from dramatic swings in the economy. There were several major financial panics in the last half of the 19th century and larger businesses could withstand them better.

- **Pools** were voluntary combinations in which a number of similar industries would agree to control output, set prices, and break competition. Agreements were often violated by members.

- **Mergers** created monopolies when industries, usually the strongest in the field, would buy out their rivals.

- **Trusts** were a more common form of combination. Chartered by a state, trusts had a board of directors which held the stock or trust certificates of its members. This allowed for greater control of members' practices.

After 1890, other forms of combination were developed:

- **Interlocking directorates** occur when one or more persons serve on the board of directors for several corporations.

- **Holding companies** control one or more companies by holding a controlling number of voting shares in these companies.

RAILROAD POOLING

Railroad managers in a certain section of the United States would meet to decide what percentage of business each would receive. They then fixed prices, established rebates for large volume customers and engaged in other inequitable practices. Farmers distrusted these policies, organized politically, and demanded government action.

CHANGING ATTITUDES ON TRUSTS

Many Americans began to question the tactics of big business. They looked to government for leadership. The public accused business of destroying competition, the basis free enterprise. In his book, *The Wealth of Nations* (1776), economist Adam Smith said, "Competition and the ability to purchase goods and services freely in the market place are the bases of the market system." Smith said the two enemies of a properly functioning market are artificial restrictions through government regulation and monopolistic business practices. The simple interaction of supply and demand should determine the free choices of consumers and producers. As the nation became industrialized, one of Smith's negative market forces – government regulation – had to be used to restrain the other – monopolies. Achieving a sane balance between these two demons proved difficult.

In the 1870s, farmers of prairie and Western states were at the mercy of monopolistic railroad shippers in getting their produce to market. The states enacted laws to regulate railroad abuse, but railroad owners quickly challenged these **Granger laws**. The Supreme Court of the United States initially upheld some Granger laws in 1876 (*Munn v. Illinois*). The Court reasoned that the government could regulate private business when it was in the public interest to do so. *Wabash R.R. v. Illinois** (1886) changed this ruling. It said states could regulate the railroads only within their state boundaries. *Wabash* said Congress alone could regulate interstate

MINI•ASSESSMENT (4-4)

1   Which correctly pairs the industrialist with his industry?
    1   Andrew Carnegie – oil
    2   John D. Rockefeller – steel
    3   Philip Armour – steel
    4   Charles Pillsbury – flour

2   Many industrialists of the Gilded Age
    1   sought to abolish monopolistic practices
    2   built diversified corporations – owning steel mills and oil refineries, car plants, and flour mills
    3   controlled their fields vertically – owning many of the businesses used to produce a product: refineries, pipelines, distribution centers
    4   amassed fortunes with no conscious plan on how to achieve their goals

3   The goal of various types of consolidation during the late 19th century was
    1   the creation of a monopoly
    2   the increase of government regulation
    3   diversification (to acquire different types) of holdings
    4   closer relationships with the people business served

4   During the latter years of the 19th century, people began to feel that the industrialists were
    1   without equal, creating a heaven on earth here in the United States
    2   out of control, amassing vast fortunes at the expense of the common people
    3   nothing out of the ordinary in the nation at that time
    4   the saviors of the United States

Constructed Response

"…Our first combination was a partnership and afterwards a corporation in Ohio. That was sufficient for the local refining business. But dependent solely upon local business we should have failed years ago. We were forced to extend our business and to seek for export trade. This latter made the seaboard cities a necessary place of business, and soon we discovered that manufacturing for export could be more economically carried on at the seaboard, hence refineries at Brooklyn, at Bayonne, at Philadelphia, and [we formed] necessary corporations in New York, New Jersey, and Pennsylvania."

– John D. Rockefeller (1908), quoted in *Government and the American Economy, 1870–Present* (1950)

1   What does Rockefeller claim saved him from failing in business?

2   Was the national and international corporate growth Rockefeller describes helpful or harmful to U.S. society?

commerce. Farmers and the public turned to Congress for action. In 1887, Congress passed the **Interstate Commerce Act**. It regulated railroad rates and prohibiting railroad pools.

Shortly afterwards, Congress passed the **Sherman Anti-trust Act** (1890). It outlawed monopolies and forbade "combinations in restraint of trade" (trusts, pools, holding companies, etc.).

Almost immediately, the conservative Supreme Court weakened the *Sherman Act*. In *United States v. E.C. Knight** (1895), the Court took a narrow view of "commerce." It ruled that under Article I of the Constitution, Congress could only make laws regulating distribution of manufactured goods. The *Knight* decision said that manufacturing was an entirely different economic activity. The *Sherman Act* could only be applied to transportation between states. Ten years went by before the Court took a broader view of business activities that restrained trade.

LABOR UNIONIZATION

In the industrial era, labor organizations developed rapidly. **Craft unions** organized workers by a particular skill and **industrial unions** organized all workers in a particular industry. Although a study of unionism is important to an understanding of American history, only a small percentage of the work force was unionized. By 1900, there were only one million union members from a total work force of 27.6 million.

EFFORTS AT NATIONAL LABOR UNIONS

As industry grew, owners demanded more of their workers. As management became increasingly distanced from its workers, employees organized to gain recognition and better conditions. They established unions. Workers realized the strength of acting together and engaging in **collective bargaining** (workers uniting to seek common demands instead of doing it individually).

The **Knights of Labor Union** was organized by **Uriah Stephens** in 1869. It admitted all workers, from skilled to unskilled. Under the leadership of **Terence Powderly** in the 1880s, the Knights urged a number of basic reforms including an eight hour day, no child labor, equal pay for men and women, and establishment of cooperatives. During the McCormick Reaper strike in Chicago in 1886, a bomb went off and violence erupted.

The Knights of Labor were not part of the incident known as the **Haymarket Riot**. However, in the public's mind, their support of the McCormick strike associated them with the violence. The Knights' strength peaked prior to 1885. A series of unsuccessful strikes, failure of cooperatives, and the Haymarket Affair turned public opinion against the group. The Knights lost their membership to the American Federation of Labor.

Samuel Gompers (1850-1924) founded the **American Federation of Labor** (AFL) in 1881. The AFL emphasized "bread-and-butter unionism." Gompers' movement concentrated on higher wages, insurance, and working conditions of its membership, as opposed to trying to reform the entire industrial system. Gompers believed workers are concerned with **real wages**, the amount of goods and services that can be purchased by one's wages. The AFL accepted the system of industrial capitalism and sought to improve conditions. It organized along craft lines, accepting only skilled workers. Local units set their own course of action, while the national organization lobbied for legislation, handled public relations, and provided the general direction for the locals. AFL membership went from 140,000 at its start, to one million by 1901.

The **International Ladies Garment Workers Union** (ILGWU) is an example of an industrial union. It sought to organize an entire industry and not distinguish among separate crafts within the industry. Eighty percent of the garment workers were women.

Efforts to organize garment workers were helped by the "Uprising of the 20,000," a general strike called by shirtwaist workers in 1909, and the tragic **Triangle Shirtwaist Company Fire** in New York City in 1911. The dismal conditions in the garment **sweat shops** were publicized, and the ILGWU won public support. This primarily female and immigrant union was strong and successful in achieving its goals.

In general, organized labor insisted on a free and public system of education as a foundation for democracy. In addition, they stressed inclusion of the practical as well as the liberal arts. Compulsory school attendance was another goal. By removing children from the work force, job competition was lessened.

CHILD LABOR IN THE MINES
Investigators for the National Child Labor Committee photographed a young boy standing outside the Turkey Knob Mine in MacDonald, West Virginia in 1908. Often young children were used in mines to push coal cars and operate tipples used to empty the coal cars at the end of rail piers.
(Library of Congress)

Immigrants, women, and African Americans were largely shut out of the early unions. Immigrants were excluded from many unions, although there were many immigrants involved in various trades. Some unions were openly hostile to women workers. Women were competing for the number of available jobs at lower wages. Some saw women as unfit to work. African Americans were usually excluded from union membership during this time period. They were often employed as **scabs** (strike breakers). The Knights of Labor's policies included restrictions on all these minority groups.

THE RADICAL FRINGE

Opponents of capitalism believed that large-scale means of production should cease to be private property, becoming instead the property of the community. Others advocated as little government interference with business as possible.

The **IWW** (Industrial Workers of the World or "Wobblies") emerged from Western mining struggles in 1905. It emphasized worker solidarity and used strike and sabotage. The Wobblies wanted to seize industries and run them without either capitalists or politicians. They emphasized class struggle. Radical socialist leaders included **Big Bill Haywood**, **Elizabeth Gurley Flynn**, and **Eugene V. Debs**. The IWW rapidly declined in 1917, due in part to negative public reaction to the Russian Revolution.

MAJOR STRIKES

In an effort to secure their demands, unions went on strike. Labor violence sometimes erupted which caused fear in the public and decreased public support for unionism.

THE HOMESTEAD STRIKE (1892)

An AFL affiliated (connected) union, the Amalgamated Association of Iron and Steel Workers, went on strike in a refusal to accept pay cuts at Carnegie's Homestead, Pennsylvania plant. Company President **Henry C. Frick** refused to back down and called in **Pinkerton Guards** (a private security agency). Violence erupted and the governor called in the state militia. The strike collapsed and the union was smashed. Union money was gone, likewise public

support. Other steel mills refused to recognize unions in the steel industry until the United Steelworkers Union emerged in the 1930s.

THE PULLMAN BOYCOTT (1894)

George Pullman provided everything for his workers (at cost, of course) but would not negotiate with his workers. In 1894, in response to the Panic of 1893, wages were cut 25-40%, but prices charged for supplies in the company store, and rent were not cut.

The **American Railway Union**, under the leadership of Eugene V. Debs (1855-1926), organized a boycott. The boycott spread nationwide and stopped the delivery of the federal mail. Pullman got a court injunction (stop action order). So, President Cleveland called out federal troops to end the illegal action. Management used provisions from the *Sherman Anti-trust Act* ("no combinations in restraint of trade") to secure the injunction. This illustrates the power of the courts to break a strike. Debs was jailed for six months, and the Supreme Court upheld his conviction (*In Re Debs**, 1895).

THE LAWRENCE TEXTILE STRIKE (1912)

This strike, led by the Wobblies, was their most notable and successful. A reduction in wages for Lawrence, Massachusetts textile workers and speedups led to the strike. The strictly disciplined strike and its songs, pickets, and rallies focused national attention on Lawrence. The American Woolen Company offered terms which met virtually all union demands, including wage increases and overtime pay.

MANAGEMENT'S POSITION

Management's goals are to manage their companies without outside interference, increase productivity and profit with minimal cost, and maintain an open shop (right to hire any workers – union or nonunion).

Most labor-management agreements are decided through the process of collective bargaining. If negotiations break down, mediation or arbitration may be sought. A disinterested third party seeks to work out a solution in **mediation**. The mediator's recommendations are non-binding. In **arbitration**, both parties pledge to abide by the decision of a disinterested third party.

POWERFUL WEAPONS USED ON BOTH SIDES	
UNIONS	**EMPLOYERS**
strike	lockout (keeping workers out)
boycott	hiring scabs (strikebreakers)
strike fund - $ for strikers	injunction (court stop action order)
picketing	yellow-dog contract - workers agree not to unionize as a condition of employment
publicity	blacklist

UNIONS AND ROLE OF GOVERNMENT

The federal and state governments passed legislation designed to curb the abuses of big business. Often these same laws, especially the *Sherman Anti-trust Act*, were used to curb union activities. The federal government also used injunctions and troops against unions.

MIDDLE CLASS SUPPORTERS

The middle class, not only the working class, supported the betterment of working conditions. The **Women's Trade Union**, organized in 1903, was the first broad-based women's union. It lobbied for protective legislation, engaged in educational activities, and advocated women's suffrage and an equal rights amendment. It was dominated by middle class women. Generally non-militant, it dissolved by 1930. The **Consumers' Union**, founded in the 1930s, is comprised of groups who support and purchase only those goods produced by factories which had approved conditions. This group still publishes *Consumer Reports* magazine.

SOCIETY ADJUSTS TO INDUSTRIALIZATION

The massive changes going on in America during the latter half of the 19th century required major adjustments in American life.

MINI•ASSESSMENT (4-5)

1   The industrialists of the late nineteenth century were philosophically opposed to
    1   the ideas of laissez-faire capitalism
    2   the development of labor unions
    3   controlling the many components of their businesses
    4   ridding themselves of business competition

2   Which is a valid statement based on the history of the labor movement in late nineteenth and early twentieth century America?
    1   The majority of workers were unionized.
    2   The primary objective of labor unions was to eliminate class differences.
    3   The federal government consistently supported union efforts.
    4   Union organization and tactics differed considerably.

3   Why were early unions unpopular with the public?
    1   Their tactics seemed to support violence.
    2   They endorsed laissez-faire ideas.
    3   They employed strikebreakers.
    4   They were anti immigration.

Constructed Response

"...[Mayor Carter Harrison] was present at the [Haymarket] meeting ... leaving for home a short time before the meeting was to end. He later declared on the witness stand that he heard nothing that would warn of lawless acts. But within a few moments after he left, several hundred policemen marched out of the Desplains Station and headed for the Haymarket Square crowd. The captain of the police ordered the meeting to break up and some person – neither court proceedings nor any other record tells us who – threw a bomb into the midst of the policemen. Seven were killed instantly and another died soon after. ...After a long trial seven were found guilty and hanged. One was sentenced to 15 years in prison for distributing the handbills announcing the Haymarket meeting."

– Joseph Buchanan, *The Story of a Labor Agitator*, 1903

1   Who threw the bomb that caused the Haymarket Riot?

2   Why was there such fierce reaction if fault for the bombing could not be proven?

IMPACT OF INDUSTRIALIZATION ON PEOPLE

Urbanization, immigration, and the demise of the American frontier left their mark on American life. Industrial cities grew rapidly. By 1900, New York, Chicago, and Philadelphia each had more than a million inhabitants.

Cultural offerings – including libraries, museums, and symphonies – were available to the urban public. Urban schools, larger than their rural counterparts, offered a wider range of subjects and had a greater heterogeneous student population. The cities became the manufacturing centers of America, drawn to the vast labor supply and transportation hubs. Therefore, the jobs industrial America had to offer were plentiful in the cities.

URBAN & RURAL POPULATION 1860-1920

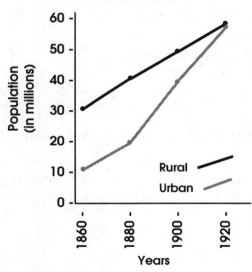

PROBLEMS

Despite attractions, cities were riddled with problems, especially for the lower classes. Into the late 1800s, a child born on a farm could expect to live a decade longer than one born in a city. Two of the biggest problems were lack of clean drinking water and a sewage system. Many of the cities were using the same body of water for drinking and disposing of raw sewage. Urban pollution also came from the main mode of transportation, the horse. Those and overcrowded living conditions caused tremendous health problems, including epidemics of tuberculosis and typhus. Acceptance by the 1890s of the "germ theory of disease" slowly brought about

the needed reforms. Increased crime rates were also a problem. Gangs, pick-pockets, and worse bothered America's urban dwellers. Since many of America's urban population were immigrants, they were blamed for the crime problem. Police forces became larger during this period.

TECHNOLOGY

During the last half of the 19th century, America's cities were transformed from "walking cities" to sprawling centers (over 5-6 miles) with suburbs. They also grew in altitude with the rise of **skyscrapers** of five stories or more. Urban expansion also came as a result of streetcars and omnibuses that were electrified by the 1880s. **Elevated railroads** ("Els") and **subways** (underground rail systems) appeared in Boston and New York City before 1900.

Cast iron skyscrapers of up to five stories gave way to steel framed structures which could soar to ten stories or more. Major buildings often housed departments stores such as Macy's and Wanamaker's. Lack of adequate housing, especially for the lower classes, led to the development of tenement houses. It was possible to house up to 4,000 people on one city block (see illustration below). Bridge building technology accelerated the growth of cities. In 1883, the **Brooklyn Bridge** connected Manhattan Island and Long Island. The link became so strong that Brooklyn and New York merged into Greater New York City in 1898.

IMPROVEMENTS IN URBAN TENEMENT BUILDINGS

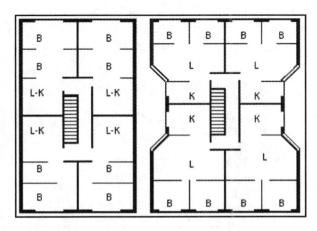

1860s, 4-apartment Tenement Building 1-window per flat.

1900s, 4-apartment Tenement Building 4-windows per flat.

THE GILDED AGE IN AMERICA (1877-1900)

Author **Mark Twain** (Samuel Clemens, 1835-1910) called the industrial era the **Gilded Age**. Rather than a true golden age, Twain and other social critics saw the society as having only a thin gold coating (gilding) hiding coarseness and hypocrisy. On the surface, the age glittered with great fortunes, industrial miracles, urbanization, and new philosophies. Beneath the surface, the critics saw a ruthlessness, a "piratic" air of profit-taking, exploitation of workers and corruption. This coarseness and vulgarity marred the achievements of the age and made them seem superficial.

During this time, Englishman **Herbert Spencer** (1820-1903) developed a philosophy that scientifically approached the study of humans from an evolutionary point of view. Later this philosophy became popularly known as **Social Darwinism**. American **William Graham Sumner** (1840-1910), a Yale professor, created a sociology that applied Spencer's and Darwin's ideas on evolution and "the survival of the fittest" to the industrial experience. According to this philosophy, power and wealth go to those most capable. The laissez-faire government policies fit perfectly into this idea. Supporters said people should be completely free to accumulate and dispose of wealth as they see fit. John D. Rockefeller summed it up, "I believe it is my duty to make money and still more money and to use the money I make for the good of my fellow man according to the dictates of my conscience."

Some of the wealth of the upper classes was used to help others. **Philanthropy** was a matter of individual choice, although the upper classes believed they had a social responsibility to help those less fortunate than themselves. Following the philosophy that he expounded in his book, *The Gospel of Wealth,* multi-millionaire Andrew Carnegie distributed his vast fortune in various ways, including building public libraries across the United States.

The wealth of the upper classes was apparent in the spending and decorating habits of wealthy Americans. **Conspicuous consumption** called for those who had money to spend it in ways that would be obvious. Large, elaborate homes and furnishings, summer "cottages" in Newport, Rhode Island, and elaborate parties were a part of this conspicuous spending.

WORK AND WORKERS

GEOGRAPHIC, ECONOMIC, AND SOCIAL CONSIDERATIONS

Working class people and immigrants tended to concentrate in inner-city neighborhoods. This provided ready access to jobs and association with others of the same socio-economic background.

Political bosses, such as William Marcy Tweed, and political machines actively sought the support of these groups by providing jobs and favors in return for votes.

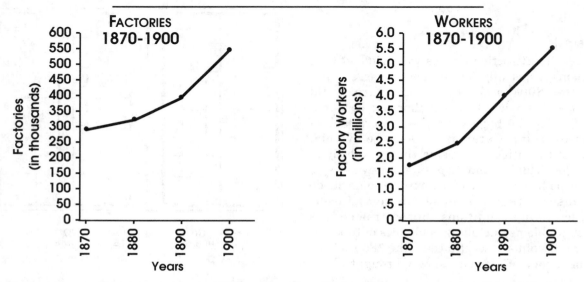

Working Conditions

Division of labor and mechanization made work monotonous (tedious repetitions). **Sweatshops**, with many people working together in crowded and unsafe conditions for long hours, were common. Unemployment, both seasonal and structural (shutdowns for unspecified periods of time) could be disastrous since most workers had no alternatives.

Machinery and practices such as speedups contributed to the hazards of factory work. Death and maiming occurred frequently. Hours were long, averaging ten hours per day – six days a week. Children and women were employed at wages much lower than those for men.

Critics of the industrial system referred to the inadequate salaries of factory workers as "wage slavery." Prices began to rise faster than incomes leading to a decline in real wages (purchasing power).

Living Conditions

Many factories, mines, and the like set up company towns where food, housing, and supplies were bought directly from the company, often at inflated prices. In the cities, the working class often lived in tenements. Although the working class standard of living rose for many, there was widespread poverty. Entire households often worked to bring in enough money for essentials. Extra money was made by taking in boarders. Many of the new conveniences made possible by industrialization, including the washing machine and telephone, were well beyond the reach of working class pocketbooks.

Women, Families, And Work

Traditional Roles

The Victorian ideal placed women on a pedestal, making them the "light of the home," protectors of family and hearth, and little beyond that. The reality of women's roles during the Gilded Age depended on class.

Upper class and middle class women most fitted the ideal. New labor saving devices allowed middle class women more free time. Many women from these classes were involved in reform movements. Some sought employment as teachers and social workers. Women seeking employment in the traditionally male fields of law and medicine often met with public disapproval. Lower working class women often had to work just to survive.

Job Availability

Between 1880 and 1910, the number of working women grew from some 2.5 million to 8 million. These mostly lower class and immigrant women comprised 15-20% of the American work force during the age of industrialization. Employment opportunities were limited and women earned substantially less than their male counterparts. About one quarter of all working women labored in factories. Many sought employment as domestics. During this time, some traditionally female occupations such as seamstressing initially decreased with the development of new machinery. Clerical work became increasingly dominated by female employees.

Family Patterns

Most families were **nuclear family units** (mother + father + children), although extended families existed. The average number of children declined to three or four per family as birth rates declined. The divorce rate was low, but still grew during this time. The median age in the United States was twenty-one in 1880. It was a young nation with a young population.

Problems of Child Labor, the Elderly, and Disabled

With most members of the family working, few families could care for elderly or disabled relatives. Child labor prevented significant numbers of children from being educated. As the 20th century opened, more and more people looked to the government to provide facilities and care which had been accepted traditionally as the family's responsibility.

Role of Religion in a Pluralistic Society

White Anglo-Saxon Protestants (**WASPs**) made up most of the population. The influx of predominantly Catholic and Jewish immigrants in the late 1800s brought a variety of ethnic groups and religious beliefs to the United States. Religious tolerance developed slowly, assisted by the presence of a diversity of beliefs.

THE GROWING MIDDLE CLASS

EMERGING STANDARDS OF CULTURAL VALUES

In the late 19th century, managers and unskilled workers alike benefited from the industrialization of the United States. They enjoyed increased leisure time and an improved standard of living. These contributed to an increase in consumerism. Middle class salaries (approximately $1,000 yearly) could provide relatively comfortable housing.

Industrialization provided a range of new products for middle class consumers. Enterprising manufacturers found ways of mass-producing imitations of hand-crafted goods designed for the rich. Pressed glass imitated expensive crystal. Silver plate items looked like sterling silver. Advertising in magazines such as *McClure's*, *The Saturday Evening Post*, and *The Ladies' Home Journal* spread practical information about new home products.

MIDDLE-CLASS MATERIALISM AND MORALITY

The growing middle class provided the purchasing power to fuel American industrial growth. Middle class values mixed certain moral beliefs with materialism. The middle class of the Gilded Age blended Christian charity and strong family loyalties with devotion to laissez-faire capitalism.

LEISURE ACTIVITIES

As urban leisure time increased, so did the number of ways to spend it. Organized sports increased in popularity. People participated in baseball, croquet, football, and basketball. They ran track, rowed, swam, and cycled. Many also watched as spectators. Professional baseball teams first formed in Cincinnati and Pittsburgh. Teams from eight cities from Boston to St. Louis formed the National League in 1876. The railroads brought circuses, musical comedies, and vaudeville performances to small cities and towns.

ART AND LITERATURE

RISE OF THE POPULAR PRESS

Joseph Pulitzer's *New York World* and **William Randolph Hearst**'s *New York Journal* popularized newspapers with the techniques of **yellow journalism** (sensationalism), exploiting lurid scandals, disasters, and crimes to sell papers. Advertising became a major industry. **Dime novels** (low-priced, adventure paperbacks) were the most widely read print material in the United States. Stories were primarily about the wild west, detectives, or science fiction. Horatio Alger's *"rags to riches"* stories were very popular.

REGIONAL LITERATURE

The lifestyles and flavor of particular geographic areas was captured by certain authors, using local expressions and dialects. **Joel Chandler Harris'** *Uncle Remus' Stories* romanticized the old South while **Hamlin Garland**'s *Son of the Middle Border* realistically portrayed the farm life of the Midwest.

The Western writers included **Bret Harte** (*The Luck of Roaring Camp*) and **Mark Twain** (*Tom Sawyer*, 1876, and *Huckleberry Finn*, 1884). But the realistic and ruthless side of life also emerged in **Stephen Crane**'s *Maggie, Girl of the Streets*, **Theodore Dreiser**'s *Sister Carrie* and *An American Tragedy*, and **Jack London**'s *The Call of the Wild*.

JOHN J. MCGRAW

Hall of Famer (elected in 1937), McGraw began his professional baseball career as 3rd baseman for the Baltimore Orioles. One of his accomplishments was achieving a career (1891-1906) batting average of .334. However, he is better known for having managed the New York Giants for three decades. During his 30-year management career, the Giants won 3 World Series and only finished out of the first division (top half) twice. Perhaps McGraw is best known for his frequent feuding and verbal battles with umpires and his players.

– source: ©1999 Grolier Interactive Inc.

Mark Twain's Boyhood Home
Hannibal, MO
– ©1993 PhotoDisc Inc.

ART AND MUSIC

Donations by the wealthy opened art museums and symphonies to the public during the Gilded Age. The Metropolitan Museum of Art opened in 1880 in New York City.

CRAFTSMANSHIP VALUED AS ART

Industrially produced goods did not mean progress to everyone. Some people rejected ornate, mass produced items. An Arts and Crafts Movement developed. It emphasized quality, simplicity, and hand-craftsmanship. The **Roycroft Movement** began in East Aurora, NY. It manufactured quality designed items and ran a publishing business. **Gustav Stickley**, a founding member of the Arts and Crafts Movement, crafted simple oak furniture known as Mission Oak. Stickley's sleek, simple designs still enjoy popularity.

IMMIGRATION: CHANGING PATTERNS

The United States is a "nation of nations." With the exception of Native Americans, everyone in the United States can trace their families back within 400 years to one or several immigrants or forced migrants. In particular, many people living in the United States can trace their heritage back to those who came through the **Castle Garden** station or, after 1890, the **Ellis Island** immigrant processing center located in New York harbor in the 19th and early 20th centuries.

EARLY COLONIZATION (1609-1776)

From the arrival of the European settlers in the 17th century until the United States declared its independence in 1776, certain characteristics of these immigrants emerge. Settlers from England made up the largest number of these immigrants. Scotch-Irish, Germans, Swedish and Dutch settlers also immigrated in significant numbers. A large number of Africans became part of the forced migration to the Atlantic colonies.

Many European governments had official state religions and persecuted other sects. Groups such as English Catholics and Quakers; German Mennonites, Baptists, and Jews; French Huguenots; Spanish and Portuguese Jews; and Scandinavian Catholics and non-Lutheran Protestants fled religious persecution. English, German and Scots-Irish dissenters, for example the Puritans, fled oppression and civil war. Famines and wars in Europe caused many people to flee economic hardship.

Not all European immigrants came to the colonies as free and independent citizens. A labor shortage in the New World was met in a number of ways. Those who had means found their own passage to the New World.

Poor people – sometimes petty criminals – who could not pay their passage, entered into a contractual agreement working from four to seven years in return for passage. Poor parents sometimes sold their children into such contracts. These were known as indentured servants. Impoverished Swiss and German immigrants, sometimes called redemptioners, agreed to have their services sold in the New World to pay for their fare.

Not all early immigration was voluntary. The labor shortage was alleviated through the use of African slaves, especially after 1670. Their brutal, crowded journey to the New World was known as "the middle passage." By the 1800s, there were approximately one-half million slaves in the United States, mostly in the South. (The Constitution outlawed the import of slaves after 1808.)

"OLD IMMIGRATION" (1776-1880)

The term "old immigration" generally refers to the period from the creation of the new nation to the decades after the Civil War. People who fall into this category generally arrived in the United States before 1890. Most of the immigrants came from Northern and Western European countries. Ireland, Germany, and Scandinavia supplied a major number of immigrants. In addition, these immigrants supposedly assimilated into the existing Anglo-Saxon dominated culture easily since their customs and traditions were similar.

Massive famine in the 1840s caused by the repeated failure of the potato crop in Ireland, led many Irish to seek a better quality of life in the United States. Revolutions and political upheaval in Germany led to a search for political stability. Millions of others sought economic opportunity. Not all were from Europe. Some quarter of a million Chinese, mostly men, came to the United States between 1860 and 1900 as contract laborers. They sought to leave depressed economic conditions in China. Overall, the desire for a better standard of living and to leave unemployment, crop failures, or a depressed economy has been the major motivation for immigration.

NATIVIST REACTION

Since immigration is so prevalent in United States society, the country has had to deal with frequent bouts of anti-immigrant sentiment, or nativist reaction. Prior to the Civil War, the most vocal nativists were some minority parties, especially the **American Party** (or "Know-Nothings") of the 1840s. This viciously anti-Catholic party increased in strength as large numbers of Catholics, especially Irish and German, began to enter the country. They sought to restrict immigration and office-holding by naturalized citizens. To this day, much nativist reaction is connected to fear of economic competition, because impoverished immigrants often take jobs at low pay to survive.

ABSORPTION BY CONQUEST AND ANNEXATION

As the United States expanded westward, it not only annexed land, but also the people on that land. French-speaking people came with the Louisiana Purchase. Those of Hispanic culture came with territorial acquisitions of Florida, Texas, the Mexican Cession, and the Gadsden Purchase.

ETHNIC AND GEOGRAPHIC DISTRIBUTION CIRCA 1870

- total continental U.S. population - 39,818,440
- almost even male-female split (slight male edge)
- Almost 5 million non-whites (4.8 million African Americans, Indians, Chinese, and very few others)
- 12.3 million people in the Northeast, 13 million in the North Central states, 12.3 million in the South, and approximately 1 million in the West
- vast majority of Americans (c. 82%) of Northern and Western European ancestry

---

THE "NEW IMMIGRATION" 1890-1924

THE IMPULSES ABROAD

In the late 1800s, Southern and Eastern Europeans began fleeing high taxes, poor soil, and high land rents. Poles fled the wars and politics that led their country to be divided by foreign powers. Other Eastern Europeans fled harsh imperialist governments. Jews fled religious, economic, and political persecution.

ATTRACTIONS HERE

The American Industrial Revolution created a tremendous demand for cheap labor. Settlers were needed to develop the West. Many industries and states advertised in Europe for workers and settlers. New immigrants encouraged family and friends to come.

URBANIZATION

While most of these peasant peoples dreamed of farms in the interior of America, poverty forced the "new" immigrants of the post Civil War period to settle in cities, especially in the Northeast. They formed ethnic neighborhoods and enclaves which became ghetto areas

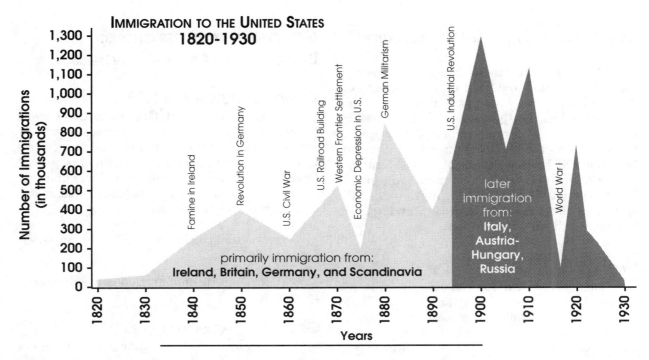

IMMIGRATION TO THE UNITED STATES 1820-1930

Number of Immigrations (in thousands)

Famine In Ireland

Revolution in Germany

U.S. Civil War

U.S. Railroad Building

Western Frontier Settlement

Economic Depression in U.S.

German Militarism

U.S. Industrial Revolution

World War I

primarily immigration from:
Ireland, Britain, Germany, and Scandinavia

later immigration from:
Italy, Austria-Hungary, Russia

Years

("Little Italys," "Chinatowns," and "Little Polands").

AMERICANIZATION PROCESS

Gradually, they learned the ways of their new home. Street life, work in factories, night school for adults, public, and private school for children, immigrant newspapers, and ethnic organizations combined to acculturate the immigrants.

FAMILY, RELIGION, EDUCATION, & POLITICS

Many of the "new" immigrants were Catholics and Jews entering a predominantly Protestant country. Initially, many of the immigrants were men that travelled alone. Families were reunited after the men had secured enough money to pay their passages.

Many took advantage of the free public education America offered. (Jews were often denied access to public education in Russia and the Austro-Hungarian Empire.) The influx of immigrants in the cities attracted the attention of the political machines, such as New York City's **Tammany Hall**. In effect, both the bosses and immigrants benefited from this relationship. In return for favors ranging from finding apartments ("flats") and food to jobs, the immigrant gave his political loyalty to the boss and political party that helped him.

CONTRIBUTIONS

Immigrant contributions to the United States are enormous. Each and every ethnic group has helped to build America, either through hard, physical labor, the use of special skills or aptitudes, or the discovery of a new or different way to do things.

EXAMPLES OF IMMIGRANT CONTRIBUTIONS
FIELD
Building of transportation systems . . . . .Chinese, Irish, Italians, Slavs (railroads, roads, canals)
Mining . . . . .Welsh, Poles, Slavs
Textiles/Garment Trades . . . . .English, Jews
Optical Equipment . . . . .Germans
Chemical Industry . . . . .French
Stone masons / sculptors . . . . .Italians

REACTIONS TO THE "NEW IMMIGRATION"

Adapting to the American culture by acquiring new customs and traditions (sports, holidays, slang, and food) is a process called **acculturation**. This process was accelerated by educational institutions, immigrant organizations, such as the "Polish National Alliance" or the "Sons of Italy," and legal naturalization. **Assimilation** occurs when an immigrant blends into the society. Assimilation is much more difficult to attain than acculturation and seldom happens in the first generation.

NATIVIST REACTION

Reasons for nativist reaction include job competition, the belief that immigrants could not be readily assimilated into America, and the belief that the "new" immigrants were mentally and physically inferior to the "old." **Stereotyping** (repeated distortion of reality based on ignorance) occurred. Religion also became an issue. After 1890, many groups sought immigration restrictions. Groups such as the **Ku Klux Klan** and **American Protective Association** agitated against Catholic immigration. They argued that if greater Catholic political power continued, the Pope would be dictating American policies. Nativists were also anti-Semitic (against Jews categorically), anti-Asian, and anti-any other minority groups. Agitation by such groups often led to Congressional legislation which formally restricted the flow of immigration to the United States.

THEORIES OF AMERICANIZATION

- **Homogeneous Culture Theory** is based on newcomers being changed into English-speaking and -acting Americans.

- **Melting Pot Theory** holds that all immigrants are different, but are transformed (melted) into a new homogeneous, yet ever-changing society.

- **Cultural Pluralism Theory** emphasizes the diversity of the inhabitants of the United States, but recognizes a common center of political and economic institutions, including language. Synonyms include: cultural symphony, cultural mosaic, and "salad bowl."

GOVERNMENTAL RESTRICTIONS: BACKGROUND AND EFFECTIVENESS

CHINESE EXCLUSION ACT (1882)

Background: West Coast Chinese were regarded as cheap labor, strikebreakers, possessing strange customs and unlikely to assimilate. Many local and state governments passed laws discriminating against them, including segregated schooling. Boycotts of Chinese businesses occurred; violence flared.

Provisions: Prohibited Chinese immigration for 10 years.

Effect: Drop in immigration caused violence to subside.

GENTLEMEN'S AGREEMENT (1907)

Background: Nativist fear over job losses resulted in violence erupting in the San Francisco area. President Theodore Roosevelt negotiated the Gentlemen's Agreement with Japan.

Provisions: Japan denied passports to Japanese workers intending to go to the United States. San Francisco promised to desegregate its schools.

Effect: Anti-Japanese agitation continued, but Japanese immigration ceased.

LITERACY TEST ACT (1917)

Background: World War I fueled fear of foreigners and called for immigration restrictions. Previous literacy test bills had been successfully vetoed. This one was not.

Provisions: Immigrants had to pass a literacy test in English or their own language before they could receive a visa to come to the United States.

Effect: Kept very few immigrants out.

EMERGENCY QUOTA ACT (1921)

Background: As war refugees streamed into the country, Americans upset by the **Bolshevik Revolution** in Russia and the spread of communism in Europe feverishly suspected communist infiltration of the United States. There was a belief that revolutionaries were active in the immigrant community. After a series of bombings in 1919,

U.S. Attorney General **A. Mitchell Palmer** conducted nationwide raids to round-up suspected communists. Denials of civil liberties occurred.

Provisions: Quotas were set for each country at 3% of the number of each nationality living in the United States in 1910. A general limit was set at 350,000 immigrants a year.

Effect: Decreased number of immigrants.

EMERGENCY QUOTA ACT (1924)

Background: Some people believed the 1921 Act's immigration numbers were too high.

Provisions: Quotas set at 2% of the number of each nationality living in the United States in 1890; prohibited Asian immigration.

Effect: Lowered immigration from Southern and Eastern Europe.

THE LAST FRONTIER (1850-1890)

THE FRONTIER AS IDEA AND REALITY: 1607-PRESENT

GEOGRAPHIC INTERACTIONS

A frontier can be defined as the furthermost area of settlement. In 1893, American historian **Frederick Jackson Turner** presented a paper entitled *The Significance of the Frontier in American History*. He argued that the chief influence in shaping the American character was the frontier. His thesis was that the frontier provided: social equality through easy purchase of cheap land; political equality; rise in nationalism; optimistic spirit; independence; and a safety valve for out of work industrial workers.

MINI•ASSESSMENT (4-6)

1 Which statement regarding the working class in the Gilded Age is valid?
 1 They tended to concentrate in suburban neighborhoods.
 ② The number of industrial workers decreased as more and more machinery was being used.
 3 Urban political machines actively sought the support of the working class.
 4 Rising wages helped most factory workers to move into the middle class.

2 Which statement concerning immigration to the United States is best supported by historical evidence?
 1 The diversity of the immigrant population created a pluralistic society.
 2 The quota laws were designed to prevent discrimination in immigration.
 3 Organized labor generally favored unrestricted immigration.
 4 Industrial growth led to a decreased demand for cheap labor.

3 Which is an example of nativist activity?
 1 immigrants settling in ethnic ghetto areas
 2 government passing the *Chinese Exclusion Act*

 3 political bosses helping immigrants in exchange for votes
 4 government creating receiving stations for immigrants

Constructed Response

"Give me your tired, your poor,
Your huddled masses yearning to breathe free,
The wretched refuse of your teeming shore.
Send these, the homeless, the tempest-tost to me.
I lift my lamp beside the golden door!"

– Emma Lazarus "The New Colossus" (1883)

1 What type of immigration policy would Emma Lazarus support? Why?

2 Which federal act of the late 19th century is in opposition to Lazarus' point of view?

3 Describe the relationship between the immigrants and the economy of the United States of the late 19th century.

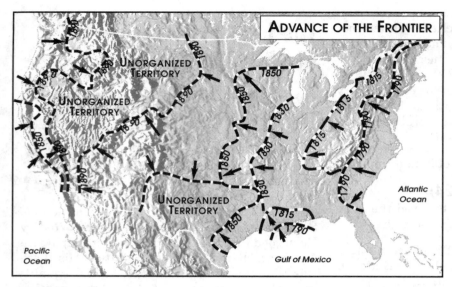

ADVANCE OF THE FRONTIER

Unorganized Territory

Unorganized Territory

Unorganized Territory

Pacific Ocean

Atlantic Ocean

Gulf of Mexico

LAND WEST OF THE MISSISSIPPI

Under the *Homestead Act* (1862), one hundred and sixty acres of free federal land would be given to any homesteader who would work and live on it for at least five years. Thousands took advantage of this offer.

By 1900, four hundred million acres were settled under this program. Homesteaders and other settlers increased the need for the railroad and for farm machinery.

THE IMPACT OF INDUSTRIALIZATION

FOOD SUPPLY SHIPPED EAST

Railroad connections made it possible to ship more and more food eastward. Chicago became a major terminal for cattle shipments and center of America's meat-packing industry. Eastern cities received grain and other foodstuffs from the American heartland.

THE SPREAD OF IMMIGRANTS

The West lured many immigrants from their homelands and from their earliest jobs on the East Coast. Railroad agents often met them in the major eastern cities with offers to move westward. In some cases, the agents recruited settlers in Europe. Many Western states opened up immigration bureaus in European countries.

POTENTIAL FOR INVESTMENT

There was opportunity in the West. Railroad development, lumbering, and mining employed many people. American and foreign investors earned fortunes. Gold, silver, and less glamorous minerals (copper, lead) attracted hundreds of thousands of people westward. Some ventures prospered, such as Montana's Anaconda Copper Mine. Most fared worse. Cattle ranching also drew thousands of investors, future President Theodore Roosevelt among them. Oil development spread westward, too. The largest oil strike of the era occurred at Spindletop, Texas (1901).

DEVELOPMENT OF KEY URBAN CENTERS

Railroads accelerated the development of urban centers at hubs and along cattle routes. Omaha, Kansas City, Cheyenne, Los Angeles, Portland, and Seattle became bustling transportation terminals and commercial centers. (See railroad map page 152.)

NATIVE AMERICAN PEOPLES: STATUS SINCE 1607

Native Americans had close relationships with nature. However, they actively altered and controlled their environment as well. Many Indian tribes engaged in farming. Major ways they altered the environment was through the use of fire for communication, scrub removal, and

Prairie Bison (PhotoDisc ©1995)

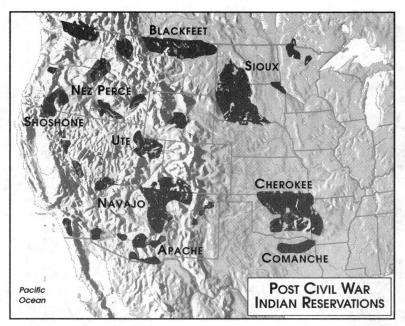

POST CIVIL WAR INDIAN RESERVATIONS

NORTHWEST ORDINANCE (1787)

The Northwest Ordinance governed the area from the Great Lakes, to the Ohio and Mississippi Rivers. This congressional law said the U.S. government would treat Native Americans in good faith. It said the government would never take land without their permission. In reality, it proved meaningless.

INDIAN REMOVAL ACT (1830)

The *Indian Removal Act* authorized President Jackson to send the U.S. Army to move thousands of Native Americans. Native Americans remember the forced march from the Southeast to areas west of the Mississippi as the **Trail of Tears**. Large numbers died during the episode. Federal agents often bribed Native American leaders to agree to the removal treaties.

farming practices. Native Americans often made full use of the supplies nature provided. The buffalo provided virtually everything the Plains Indians needed. Still, Native Americans suffered from the seasonal scarcity of food supplies.

ADVANCING SETTLEMENT PRESSURES

As more and more white settlers came to the New World, problems developed. Native-Americans did not understand European ideas of private ownership or the buying and selling of land. They believed in communal or tribal ownership. Cultural differences caused problems. Whites eventually won the struggle with modern technology, immunity to diseases and complex military and political organizations.

TREATIES

Prior to the development of the United States, the British tried to successfully solve the problem of hostilities with the Indians by passing the *Proclamation of 1763*. It prohibited colonial settlement west of the Appalachian Mountains, reserving that area for the Native Americans. It failed. After American independence, many conflicts continued to arise. United States government relations with the Native Americans included passage of the following:

CHEROKEE NATION V. GEORGIA (1831)

Gold was discovered on the Cherokee reservation in Georgia in 1828. As prospectors moved in, the state of Georgia claimed authority over the federal land and the Cherokee objected. In 1831, they took their case to the Supreme Court. Chief Justice John Marshall ruled that the Cherokee nation was a "dependent state" but that the Court itself had no constitutional jurisdiction to stop Georgia. He also said that only the federal government, not the states, had power over Native American nations. Congress took no action.

LEGAL STATUS

By the 1840s, comparatively few Native Americans lived east of the Mississippi River. With the coming of the California Gold Rush, the development of the transcontinental railroad and the increased demand for additional farmland, American settlement moved further westward into Native American territory.

Sitting Bull (Chief Tatanka Lyotake, 1831-1890), a great Sioux leader, helped with the defeat of General George Custer at Little Bighorn. Later captured, he toured for a short time with William F. "Buffalo Bill" Cody's Wild West Exhibition. The show toured throughout the United States and Europe from 1883-1913. (Library of Congress)

INDIAN WARS (1850-1890)

From the 1850s to the 1890s a series of Indian Wars broke out as the Native Americans reacted to the increased settlement pressure from the East. Westward migration increased tremendously with the discovery of gold at Pike's Peak, Colorado in 1858. As more and more settlers disrupted the Native Americans' lifestyle and livelihood, the clashes between the two cultures increased. Although some tribes moved to government reservations with little protest, others such as the Nez Perce, the Apaches, and the Plains Comanches resisted.

Despite winning some battles, including the defeat of General George Custer by Chief Sitting Bull at Little Bighorn in 1876, Native Americans did not win the war in the end. The result was a near genocide. The last battle was a one-sided massacre (200 Sioux and 8 soldiers) at Wounded Knee, South Dakota in 1890.

LEGISLATING NATIVE AMERICAN LIFE

By the 1880s, most Native American nations were relocated on reservations, usually on undesirable land. The people became wards of the federal government. **Helen Hunt Jackson**'s 1881 book, *A Century of Dishonor*, brought attention to the plight of the Native Americans. In response, Congress passed the *Dawes General Allotment Act* (1887). It was designed to give each Indian family head a 160-acre farm and American citizenship when they "civilized." It also provided for the selling of "surplus" reservation land. The Act did not work. The land was poor and the Native Americans were unused to farming. Under the Act, Native Americans lost over one-half of their reservation land.

THE CATTLE FRONTIER

THE CATTLE KINGDOM

The Spanish introduced cattle ranching to the New World. Eventually, the concept spread to other European settlers. By buying small acreage adjoining public land, the rancher had access to an enormous range for his cattle. This was known as the open range.

Cattle ranching increased rapidly from in the late 19th century. Investors rushed to cash in on its profits. It reached its peak in the late 1880s. Overgrazing, disease, severe winters, and falling prices eventually took their toll, forcing all but a few giant concerns out of business.

HOMESTEADERS AND TECHNOLOGY

After the Civil War, homesteaders (farming settlers) arrived in large numbers. The railroad, the "Iron Horse," brought settlers and cut through cattle grazing and buffalo hunting lands. Disputes over land rights occurred frequently between the settlers and the ranchers and between the cattle ranchers and sheep ranchers. The development of barbed wire allowed vast tracts of land to be inexpensively enclosed, cutting down on the amount of open range acreage. Enclosure of the range angered the ranchers, but it increased the settlers.

JUSTICE ON THE FRONTIER

The frontier towns usually lacked an organized police force to keep order and control their citizens. Violence erupted frequently over land and mining claims. **Vigilante groups** (unauthorized secret citizen groups) were sometimes organized to maintain order. Claiming to represent law and order, they engaged in mob violence and often threatened the peace and safety of people.

THE FARMING FRONTIER

As the heyday of cattle ranching declined, farming increased in the Western frontier territories.

NATURE'S WILL

The prairie sod encountered by homesteaders and other settlers was difficult to plow and plant. There was little lumber. The tough layer of sod they peeled from the prairie became the primary building material. Homesteaders stacked the sod to build the walls of their primitive houses ("soddies"). For heat, they burned buffalo and cattle manure. Harsh sun, blizzards, drought, flooding, insects, and high winds brought the settlers many problems. The most

The Western Prairie   (PhotoDisc ©1995)

common phenomena of prairie life was loneliness, especially for the women who were responsible for maintaining the home and nurturing the children.

TECHNOLOGICAL EFFECTS

Inventions allowed for successful development of the Great Plains. Windmills provided much needed water. Previously, plains farmers practiced centuries old dry farming techniques. A reliable steel plow was developed to cut through the tough sod. Mechanical reapers allowed for quicker harvesting while utilizing fewer people. In 1862, the *Morrill Land Grant Act* provided for the sale of federal land to fund agricultural colleges and quicken the pace of scientific agricultural development.

NATURE'S CHANGES

Farmers had to battle nature's changes each day on the prairie. Insect plagues, droughts, windstorms, and tornadoes made Western farm life difficult and dangerous. Loneliness was a constant problem. Farm families joined churches and clubs for social contact. In the 1870s, mail order houses such as Montgomery Ward and Sears, Roebuck & Co. arose. They changed the primitive existence of Great Plains farmers. Farm families could enjoy the new manufactured goods of the industrial age without long trips to the cities.

AGRICULTURE'S PERSISTENT PROBLEMS

By the 1880s, the farmers were confronted by a number of persistent problems. High middleman charges and falling prices caused by foreign grain and cattle competition (Canada and Argentina) made the farmers dependent upon market conditions. Railroad pricing policies were charging "what the market would bear." Rates were high on short hauls while fraud and cheating were common. Rebates and price fixing occurred. Preference was given to long-haul shippers and those with large tonnage. The banks were reluctant to grant loans to farmers, and charged high interest rates when they did. Farm debt was usually very high. Because of the distance from the manufacturing centers, the farmers paid dearly for goods, credit, and supplies, while receiving low prices for the fruits of their labor.

Although the American farmers enjoyed a relatively prosperous period during the Civil War years, afterward they complained of low prices for their goods, high industrial prices, high railroad charges, and lack of credit. The farmers began to organize and demand action from the government to counteract these forces.

THE GRANGE MOVEMENT

The **Grange Movement,** formally known as the National Grange of the Patrons of Husbandry, founded in 1867, started out as a series of farm clubs. The farmers became politically active as

their discontent increased. They elected their own candidates for state and local political office and passed state laws to regulate railroads (Grange laws). They also used the idea of **cooperatives,** farmers acting together to purchase major equipment and acting as their own middlemen buying and selling in quantity. Grange cooperatives were not very successful due in part to a lack of organization and training. However, grain elevators (moving and storage of grain) operated by the Grange achieved some success.

LEGAL EFFORTS

Farmers frequently saw the railroads as their biggest problem. From 1875-1900, farm state legislatures tried to regulate the railroads. The railroad companies challenged the state laws and several wound up in the U.S. Supreme Court. The basic issue involved in these cases: *Did the states (government) have the right to regulate a private business for the public's good?*

FARMERS V. RAILROADS: KEY CASES

- *Munn v. Illinois* (1877)
  The Supreme Court ruled that states could regulate private property engaged in the public interest (the Grange laws were upheld).

- *Wabash, St. Louis, and Pacific R.R. v. Illinois** (1886)
  The Supreme Court changed its Munn ruling. It said that states could regulate the railroads only within their boundaries (only Congress could regulate interstate commerce).

- *Chicago, Milwaukee & St. Paul R.R. Co. v. Minn.* (1889)
  The Supreme Court overturned a Minnesota law which denied the right of businessmen to appeal freight rates set by the state government.

Gradually, the Supreme Court introduced the idea that the due process clause of the Fifth and Fourteenth Amendments gave the courts the power to review the substance of legislation, for example, the railroad rate legislation.

NATIONAL GOVERNMENT RESPONSE

The federal government passed the *Interstate Commerce Act* (1887) which stated, "all charges...shall be fair and reasonable." This act created the **Interstate Commerce Commission (ICC).** It regulated the railroads by prohibiting pools, rebates, high rates for short hauls, and rate discrimination. It investigated any alleged violations.

POPULISM

The Grange movement declined in power and other "farm" parties appeared. The most significant political party was the **Populist** or **People's Party,** established in 1892. Farmers were looking to "raise less corn and more hell." The Populists also sought the support of union members.

On the silver question, farmers believed that their problems stemmed from the lack of money in circulation. They wanted inflation in order to make their debts worth less. Until 1873, the United States was on a bimetallic standard, using both gold and silver to determine the value of money.

THE POPULIST PARTY PLATFORM

- more government control of the railroads
- graduated income tax
- secret ballot
- direct election of Senators
- 8-hour work day
- government ownership of telephone and telegraph
- restriction of immigration
- free and unlimited coinage of silver at the rate of 16:1

However in 1873, as silver prices rose over the government's price, a law was passed by Congress to stop the issue of silver coins. This upset the farmers who believed money with only a gold backing would become even more scarce. They called it "**The Crime of '73**." Hence, they believed the free coinage of silver would increase the amount of money in circulation and end their economic woes.

In the 1892 Presidential election, the Populists made a strong showing, garnering one million votes. They increased their support in the 1894 Congressional elections. The 1896 Presidential election represented the Populist Party's best hope for high national support. The Republicans selected **William McKinley** (1843-1901) as their candidate.

The Republicans stood for high tariffs, the gold standard, and no free coinage of silver. The Democrats nominated **William Jennings Bryan** (1860-1925) who awed audiences with his anti-Republican/business interest "Cross of Gold" speech.

The Democrats advocated free coinage of silver. Bryan won the Populist nomination as well. The candidates campaigned strenuously. The modern presidential campaign can be traced to this election. McKinley won the Northeast, Midwest, California, and Oregon by narrow margins. Bryan won the less populous South and the West by large margins, but nonetheless lost the election in the electoral college. In 1900, the gold standard was formally adopted.

MINI•ASSESSMENT (4-7)

1 "Many, if not most, of our Indian wars have had their origin in broken promises and acts of injustice on our part."
   The author of this statement would most likely agree that the history of the United States treatment of American Indians was primarily the result of
   1 prejudice toward Native American religions
   2 the desire for territorial expansion
   3 a refusal of Native Americans to negotiate treaties
   4 conflicts over trade

2 Which person would have been most likely to support the Granger movement and the Populist Party in the 1890s?
   1 a banker in Philadelphia
   2 a farmer in Kansas
   3 a factory worker in Pittsburgh
   4 a small business owner in New York City

3 A belief in Manifest Destiny, the passage of the Dawes Act, and the completion of the transcontinental railroad are most closely associated with the
   1 rise of big business
   2 growth of the labor movement
   3 abolitionist movement
   4 expansion and settlement of the West

Constructed Response

"The great common people of this country are slaves, and monopoly is the master. The West and South are bound and prostrate before the manufacturing East...We want money, land, and transportation."

– Mary Elizabeth Lease, 1890

1 What are Mary Elizabeth's Lease's complaints?

2 Explain Lease's point of view regarding the relationship between the West, the South, and the East.

3 Would Lease support the Populist Party? Why?

SUMMARY

As America turned into the 20th century, changes were occurring which would make it a world leader. The American population moved from the rural areas to the nation's new urban centers and from the farms to the factories. According to the census, the frontier, as a recognizable line of Western settlement, had disappeared in 1890. As of the 1920 census, over fifty percent of the nation's population lived in cities having more than 2,500 people.

From 1870 to 1910, America's urban population increased by 400%. With the influx of huge waves of immigrants, Americans began to emphasize their own culture. Public schooling, the immigrant press, and immigrant aid societies assisted in the acculturation process.

American business drew on the nation's rich supply of natural resources, the growing labor force, and the wealth of inventions to shape a society and economy which would become a dominant force in the world. During most of the late 1800s, the economic energy conquered the American West and expanded domestic markets. With the close of the frontier, American businessmen looked beyond our borders, first to the Western Hemisphere, and then to Asia.

Nonetheless, many people believed there were better ways to achieve progress than were currently being done. Major critics of industrialism and exploitation included:

• **Henry George** (1839-1897) believed inequality stemmed from a few people cashing in on rising land values as a result of increased demand for land. His proposal to relieve this inequality called for a tax on the rise of land values not attributable to the owner's improvements. All other taxes would be abolished. Simply, it was a single tax to remove undue profits from the sale of land. These ideas he set down in *Progress and Poverty* (1879).

• **Edward Bellamy** (1850-1898) advocated a socialist government which owned all the means of production and distribution and set moral laws. As he described in *Looking*

Backward (1888), unless a fully nationalized state was set up, catastrophe would result.

• **Henry Demerest Lloyd** (1847-1903) was a reformer and one of the early "muckraker" journalists (see Unit 5). In *Wealth Against Commonwealth* (1894), he criticized the unethical tactics of John D. Rockefeller and all the robber barons. He proposed an alternative commonwealth similar to Bellamy's.

UNIT ASSESSMENT
MULTI-CHOICE QUESTIONS

1   By late 1865, Congress took control over Reconstruction planning because
    1   President Johnson had been impeached and subsequently removed from office
    2   the Radical Republican Congress did not favor the President's lenient policies
    3   President Johnson had run out of ideas and asked Congress for leadership
    4   Congress succeeded in vetoing the main policies of President Johnson

2   The term "redeemer governments" is best defined as
    1   a biased term referring to more conservative Southern governments
    2   the conversion of thousands of African Americans to the Republican party
    3   carpetbaggers' attempts to institute more democratic Southern governments
    4   the election of great numbers of Southern Protestants to office

3   Which is an accurate statement about Southern agriculture in the late 19th century?
    1   Crop diversification led to large increases in farm income.
    2   A large number of farmers had liens on their crops.
    3   A decline in the world cotton supply caused a rise in prices and profits.
    4   Agricultural profit depended mainly on Southern textile mills.

4   During the years 1861-1866, Northern industry
1   made vast profits which could be invested back into business
2   was hurt by a lack of adequate protective tariff legislation
3   was devoting much of its production capacity to overseas trade
4   halted new product development due to the fighting of the Civil War

Base your answers to question 5 on the cartoon below and your knowledge of U.S. history and government.

5   The cartoonist is indicating that
1   large numbers of officials make government decision-making very difficult
2   it is impossible to tell who is responsible for taking the people's money
3   builders are corrupt and should not be involved in politics
4   political bosses swindled the people of New York City

6   Proprietorships and partnerships proved to be inadequate for the needs of growing American business because
1   they maintained too close a relationship with consumers
2   they responded quickly to innovations in production and merchandising
3   transportation and communication techniques were inadequate
4   their sources of capital were limited

7   Thomas Nast's cartoons made the public most aware of
1   political corruption
2   racial segregation
3   the violence of the Ku Klux Klan
4   unethical business tactics

8   The South began to vote overwhelmingly Democratic after the 1870s because
1   pardoned Confederates voted against the party of Lincoln
2   African American voters were being helped by the Southern Democrats
3   Congress was in the hands of the Democratic Party
4   Democrats were free from the political corruption that plagued the Republicans

9   The decision in *Plessy v. Ferguson* (1896) is significant because
1   it declared the *1875 Civil Rights Act* unconstitutional
2   it upheld the constitutionality of the "separate, but equal" doctrine
3   the federal government overturned a state law
4   it showed the weakness of the Southern economy 25 years after the Civil War

Base your answers to question 10 on the statements below and your knowledge of U.S. history and government.

"(African Americans) …do not expect that the free right to vote, to enjoy civic rights, and to be educated, will come in a moment; they do not expect to see the bias and prejudices of years disappear at the blast of a trumpet; but they are absolutely certain that the way for a people to gain their reasonable rights is not by voluntarily throwing them away and insisting they do not want them…"

10 To achieve racial equality, the author would most likely advocate
1   the philosophy of Booker T. Washington
2   increased agitation for basic political rights
3   greater reliance on the policy of accommodation
4   a revival of the Ku Klux Klan

11 Mail-order companies began to emerge in the late 19th century to
1 bring mass merchandising to rural areas
2 overcome the lack of urban mass transit
3 tap the overseas markets for American goods
4 maintain personal contact between proprietors and customers

Base your answers to questions 12 and 13 on the the speakers' statements below and your knowledge of U.S. history and government.

SPEAKER A: These men are a pox on America. They have bled it dry for their own personal glory and fortunes. To come out from their domination, something has to be done.

SPEAKER B: Business competition has been destroyed and the consumers have suffered.

SPEAKER C: An American beauty rose is created by sacrificing the smaller buds so that one large, strong one may result.

SPEAKER D: American business is changing and so is America. Both are growing and doing so admirably at this time.

12 Which of the speakers would most likely label the Gilded Age industrialists as "robber barons"?
1 *A* and *D*
2 *B* and *C*
3 *A* and *B*
4 *B* and *D*

13 Speaker *A* would most likely support the
1 continuation of laissez-faire policies
2 philanthropic work of Andrew Carnegie
3 creation of U.S. Steel Company in 1901
4 dissolution of the Standard Oil Trust by the Ohio Supreme Court in 1892

14 By the end of the 19th century, which of these forms of business combination were laws trying to regulate?
1 interlocking directorates and mergers
2 interlocking directorates and holding companies
3 holding companies and trusts
4 pools and trusts

15 Many of the industrial leaders of the late 19th century
1 channeled some of their fortunes back into the community through charitable causes
2 retired as millionaires who did not engage in any philanthropic work
3 were part-time ministers in addition to their roles as industrial leaders
4 devoted their energies to improving their workers' lives while still in control of their businesses

16 By tracing the business ventures of John D. Rockefeller, it is accurate to state that
1 the federal government supported all of Rockefeller's business practices
2 his methods differed significantly from those used by other industrialists
3 he used a variety of techniques, many questionable, to achieve his empire
4 he supported increased government regulation of business

17 Between 1865 - 1900, labor-management disputes were marked by
1 a willingness to arbitrate on both sides
2 violence on both sides
3 public sympathy for strikers
4 government mediation

18 In the Granger cases of the 1870s involving railroad regulation, Supreme Court decisions said
1 racial segregation on transportation facilities is unconstitutional
2 the regulation of business is solely a state power
3 government can regulate private business in the public interest
4 an end to the influence of the Populists was near

19 At the end of the nineteenth century, the United States of America was a nation
1 with an older population struggling with industrialization
2 with a highly sophisticated system of government care for the elderly
3 where man and women were on equal footing economically
4 where traditional family patterns were changing in the face of industrialization

Base your answer to question 20 on the graph below and your knowledge of U.S. history and government.

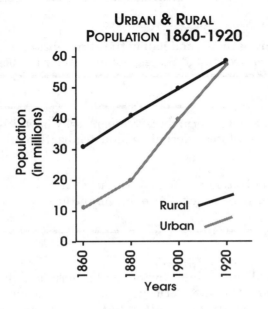

URBAN & RURAL
POPULATION 1860-1920

20 Which statement would provide a correct interpretation of the information in the graph?
1   During the Gilded Age, the total population of the U.S. decreased significantly.
2   Urban population growth exhibited a greater increase from 1860-1920 than did rural population growth.
3   For most of the latter half of the 19th century, the United States was an urban rather than an agrarian nation.
4   After the turn of the 20th century, urban population growth leveled off.

21 For which reason did most early-20th century immigrants to the United States settle in large cities?
1   Cities provided a wide variety of cultural activities.
2   Immigrants encountered little prejudice in cities.
3   Peasant backgrounds made immigrants comfortable in urban environments.
4   Jobs were available in urban factories.

22 Negative reaction to the immigrants coming to America at the turn of the 20th century was based on
1   the feeling that immigrants supplied necessary industrial labor
2   the idea that diverse cultures broaden the sense of equality
3   a belief that new groups were inferior to earlier settlers
4   the political unity of most national groups

23 The basic premise of historian Frederick Jackson Turner's work is
1   the frontier is one of a number of important factors influencing the development of American society
2   the frontier is a major factor which explains the American character
3   American development has been motivated first by a European heritage and second by the frontier
4   the role of the frontier in American history has been grossly exaggerated

24 In the last half of the 19th century, the Western frontier
1   was settled slowly since the demand for urban workers was so great
2   remained virtually inaccessible to prospective settlers
3   was considered too risky for substantial business development
4   disappeared rather quickly due to the availability of cheap land

25 Which action was supported by the farmers as a way to alleviate their problems?
1   development of cooperatives
2   the open range for cattle grazing
3   the Republicans' gold standard for currency
4   high interest rates on loans

THEMATIC ESSAY QUESTION

Theme:

> ### Technological Impact
>
> The industrialization of the United States during the second half of the 19th century (1850-1900) had a tremendous impact on the entire United States, not always for the best.

Task:

> Using your knowledge of United States history and government, write an essay in which you identify three groups of people of the United States affected by industrialization at this time. For each group or area:
>
> - describe with detail the impact of industrialization on the group or area, and
> - explain whether industrialization had a positive or negative effect on the group or area.

Suggestions:

You may use any group or area from your study of United States history and government during this time frame. You may choose to include workers, Native Americans, immigrants, farmers, or different geographic regions of the United States. **You are not limited to these suggestions.**

DOCUMENT BASED QUESTION

The following task is based on the accompanying documents. The documents may have been edited for the purposes of this exercise. The task is designed to test your ability to work with historical documents. As you analyze the documents, take into account both the source of the document and the author's point of view.

Directions: Read the documents in Part A and answer the question after each document. Then read the directions for Part B and write your essay.

Historical Context:

During the second half of the 19th century, tremendous changes were taking place in the United States. The urban landscape provided the setting for many of those changes. Cities in the United States were undergoing major transformations. Not all the change was welcome.

Task:

Using information from the documents and your knowledge of United States history and government, write an essay in which you

- describe some of the changes occurring in the cities of 1850-1900 (explain why these changes were happening), and
- discuss the impact of these changes on life in the United States during this period.

Analyze the documents and answer the questions that follow each document.

Question for Document 1

Compare the urban population to the rural population for this time period. What trends are indicated by the information in the chart?

DOCUMENT 1

URBAN - RURAL POPULATION AND NUMBER OF URBAN PLACES, 1850-1890

Source: Historical Statistics of the United States

YEAR	NUMBER OF URBAN PLACES	TOTAL URBAN POPULATION (IN MILLIONS)	TOTAL RURAL POPULATION (IN MILLIONS)
1850	236	3.5	19.6
1860	392	6.2	25.2
1870	663	9.9	28.7
1880	939	14.1	36.0
1890	1348	22.1	40.8

Question for Document 2

How does Olmstead think life has changed in rural America by 1871?

DOCUMENT 2

"...It used to be a matter of pride with the better sort of our country people that they could raise on their own land or manufacture within their own households almost everything needed for domestic consumption. But if now you leave the rail, at whatever remote station...and make your way to the house of any long-settled and prosperous farmer, and the intimacy of his family with the town will constantly appear, in dress, furniture, viands [food], in all conversation...[For example:]...If the baby has outgrown its shoes, the measure is to be sent to town..."

– Frederick Law Olmstead, 1871,
quoted in Hoogenboom and Hoogenboom [ed.], *The Gilded Age*

Questions for Document 3

1 What problems did city life have?

2 How has city life improved?

DOCUMENT 3

"Before 1895 the streets [of New York City] were almost universally in a filthy state. In wet weather they were covered with slime, and in dry weather the air was filled with dust. Artificial sprinkling in summer converted the dust to mud...Rubbish of all kinds, garbage, and ashes lay neglected in the streets, and in the hot weather the city stank with the emanations of putrefying organic matter. It was not always possible to see the pavement, because of the dirt that covered it...[Now]...New York is...clean...Few realize [the changes]...For example, there is far less injury from dust to clothing, to furniture...children make free use as a playground of streets which were formally impossible to them. "Scratches" a skin disease of horses due to mud and slush...is now almost unknown..."

– NYC Commissioner George E. Waring, Jr., 1897,
quoted in Hoogenboom and Hoogenboom [ed.], The Gilded Age

Questions for Document 4

1　How did urban life make Americans more interdependent?

2　What role did technology play in this interdependence?

DOCUMENT 4

"...By 1900 [urban Americans] found themselves living in a communal setting...they now turned toward the impersonal government or corporation to provide them with water and heat, sewerage and light, elevators and elevateds, machine-made clothes and factory-canned goods. It was a life of interdependence accentuated by technology, rather than a life of independence assured by [rural] distance..."

– Robert H. Walker, "The Changing Community,"
The Age of Enterprise, 1865-1900, 1971

Questions for Document 5

1　What new form of politics did cities create?

2　What was the relationship between immigrants and urban political machines?

DOCUMENT 5

"The sheer size of cities helped create a new form of politics...Many city problems were handled by local political bosses who traded in patronage favors and graft. Big-city political machines were not altogether sinister in their effects: they provided food and money for the poor, fixed problems at city hall, and generally helped immigrants in their adjustment to a new life..."

– Tindall & Shi, "City Politics" *America, A Narrative History,* 1999

Questions for Document 6

1　How did urban geography change in the last half of the 19th century?

2　Describe the role technology had in that change.

DOCUMENT 6

"By the last quarter of the nineteenth century, [the walking city, so named for the necessity of walking to work] disappeared. Where once substantial houses, businesses, and small artisan dwellings had stood side by side, central business districts emerged...Few people lived downtown, although many worked or shopped there. Surrounding the business center were areas of light manufacturing and wholesale activity with housing for workers. Beyond these working-class neighborhoods stretched middle class residential areas. Then came the suburbs...Scattered throughout the city [was] industrial activity surrounded by crowded working-class housing...Better transportation increasingly allowed middle- and upper-class residents to live away from their work and from grimy industrial districts..."

–Nash, et. al., *The American People,* 1998

Questions for Document 7

1   How do the diagrams represent a change in urban living?

2   Explain if the change is beneficial or harmful to urban residents.

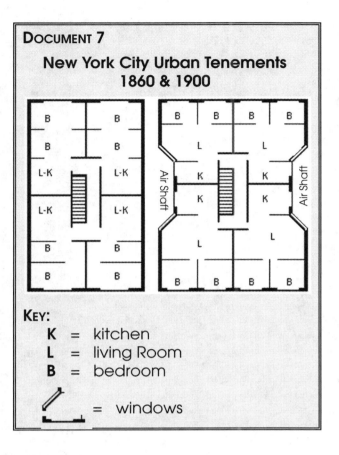

DOCUMENT 7

New York City Urban Tenements 1860 & 1900

KEY:

K = kitchen
L = living Room
B = bedroom

⟋⟍ = windows

GO ON TO PART B
Part B - Essay

Directions:
• Write a well organized essay that includes an introduction, several paragraphs, and a conclusion.
• Use evidence from the documents to support your response.
• Do not simply repeat the contents of the documents.
• Include specific related outside information.

Historical Context:
During the second half of the 19th century, tremendous changes were taking place in the United States. The urban landscape provided the setting for many of those changes. Cities in the United States were undergoing major transformations. Not all the change was welcome.

Task:
Using information from the documents and your knowledge of United States history and government, write an essay in which you

• describe some of the changes occurring in the cities of 1850-1900 (explain why these changes were happening), and
• discuss the impact of these changes on life in the United States during this period.

Be sure to include specific historical details. You must also include additional information from your knowledge of United States history and government.

THE PROGRESSIVE MOVEMENT & THE GREAT WAR

1900

THEODORE ROOSEVELT AS PRESIDENT (1901-1909)

PANAMA CANAL TREATY (1903)

NORTHERN SECURITIES CO. V. U.S. (1904)

1905

PURE FOOD AND DRUG ACT (1906)
MEAT INSPECTION ACT (1906)
GENTLEMEN'S AGREEMENT (1907)

1910

WOODROW WILSON AS PRESIDENT (1913-1921)
INCOME TAX AMENDMENT (1913)
FEDERAL RESERVE SYSTEM (1913)

WW I IN EUROPE (1914-1918)

1915

U.S. ENTERS WW I (1917)

PROHIBITION AMENDMENT (1919)

1920

VERSAILLES TREATY REJECTED (1920)

WOMEN'S SUFFRAGE (1920)

RED SCARE (1920)

1925

REFORM IN AMERICA
THE REFORM TRADITION

Reform is a part of American tradition. Although addressing different issues or concerns, Americans, individually and in groups, worked to improve the quality of life in the United States. American reform movements sought a number of different goals from expanding rights to changing the patterns of life in the United States. Some movements focused on very narrow ideals. At other times, general reform movements drew a broad range of causes together.

THE AMERICAN REVOLUTION

The American Revolution resulted in the creation of a democratic republic. Not since ancient times was there a government based on the idea that its power came from the people. Conquest, divine right, or heredity were bases of medieval governments rejected by the framers of the American system. The Constitution forbade granting titles of nobility. No legalized special privileges would create a stifling class structure as had occurred in Europe.

Land reform also broadened democracy after the American Revolution. Land ownership determined who could vote. There were two causes of this expansion. First, state governments seized the estates of Loyalists or Tories who fled after the Revolution. States sold their lands to others, increasing the number of land-holders (and voters). Second, states abolished **primogeniture** under which all inheritance went to the oldest male offspring. Other children became eligible to claim parts of a family's lands. This also increased the number of land owners as well as voters.

THE ABOLITION MOVEMENT

Many reform movements appeared in antebellum (pre–Civil War) America. The Abolitionist Movement to end slavery became a crusade in the 1830–1860s. As seen in Unit 3, abolitionist fervor spread rapidly throughout the North.

Key Terms

Internationalism	Imperialism
Trust Busting	Suffragettes
Progressivism	Muckrakers
Disarmament	Diplomacy
Consumerism	Neutrality
Conservation	Sedition
Intervention	Reform
Isolationism	

It became a sectional issue and reached a peak as the slavery question became connected to the admission of new states into the union. In the first half of the 19th century, the issue of the states' rights to permit slavery split the nation and brought on the Civil War. The abolitionists achieved their goal in 1865 with the passage of the Thirteenth Amendment. It completely abolished slavery in the United States.

WOMEN'S RIGHTS

During the mid–1800s, women began to agitate collectively for equal rights, including the right to vote. The desire for social, political, and economic equality tied this early women's rights movement with the abolition movement.

In 1848 at Seneca Falls, New York, the first women's rights convention met under the direction of Lucretia Mott and Elizabeth Cady Stanton. The convention issued the *Declaration of Sentiments* which was modeled after the *Declaration of Independence*.

In matters of economics, legality, education, and politics, women had second class citizenship. The laws gave fathers or other male relatives control over unmarried women's lives. Husbands had legal superiority over wives. During this time, women seldom had any legal control of their property or even authority over their own children.

The Civil War resulted in the abolition of slavery and new voting rights for former slaves, but no similar rights for women. **Suffragist** leaders (women organized to gain the right to vote) focused on gradual lobbying in state and

Note: Items marked with an * are listed in the *Landmark Supreme Court Decisions* chart in Appendices.

Woman Suffrage Headquarters, Cleveland, Ohio, 1912
(Library of Congress)

Another women's rights (or liberation) movement developed in the 1960s. Economic equity, including comparable worth (equal pay for equal work) and a proposed Equal Rights Constitutional Amendment rallied women to the liberation movement.

CIVIL SERVICE

The spoils system traces its roots to the Jacksonian Era of the 1830s. Successful politicians gave political jobs to party loyalists. Many unqualified and incompetent persons received government jobs. After the Civil War, the system resulted in widespread corruption in government. In the 1870s, President Hayes and others called a new system of hiring based on civil service examinations.

However, Congress did not take action until 1881 after a disgruntled office-seeker assassinated President **James A. Garfield** (1831-1881). Political bosses and their machines tried to block this reform. *The Pendleton Act* (1883) created a civil service commission which administered the civil service examinations and made appointments based on the scores received. This law provided the basis for the civil service system we have today.

federal legislatures. In the late 1860s, **Lucy Stone** (1818-1893), **Susan B. Anthony** (1820-1906), and Stanton formed organizations to campaign for the ballot. In 1869, the Wyoming Territorial Legislature gave female residents the right to vote, and in 1872, **Victoria Woodhull** (1838-1927) became the first woman presidential candidate. In 1878, Anthony's group proposed a right to vote amendment to the Constitution. In 1890, the key organizations merged into the National American Woman Suffrage Association (NAWSA).

During the **Progressive Era** (1900–1920), NAWSA suffragists took direct action through marches and civil rights demonstrations. Wyoming was the first territory and state to grant women suffrage. By 1919, fifteen states allowed the female population the franchise. In 1920, seventy-two years after the Seneca Falls meeting, the Nineteenth Amendment gave all American women the right to vote.

THE INDUSTRIAL AGE: PRESSURES FOR REFORM

The changing character of America in the later 19th and early 20th century caused a number of people to demand reform.

IMPACT OF DEVELOPING TECHNOLOGIES

As industry grew larger, its relations with workers and consumers grew more impersonal. In an effort to stem this tide, organizations developed such as unions, professional organizations, and social clubs. The increase in leisure time contributed to growth of such organizations.

FAIR STANDARDS

With the United States becoming increasingly urbanized and industrialized, more people were directly affected by the poor working conditions than ever before in the nation's history. Many groups and individuals became involved in the reform. Their goal was to standardize practices and improve working conditions within industries to the benefit of the workers.

INEQUITIES OF WEALTH AND POVERTY

Historians adopted Mark Twain's term "Gilded Age" for the Industrial Era because, while it was an era of vast wealth for a few, it became a time of grinding poverty for many. Late in the 19th century, critics of the excessive wealth of the upper classes were appalled at conspicuous consumption. This blatant display of wealth caused more people to demand various methods of redistributing wealth.

RISING POWER AND INFLUENCE OF THE MIDDLE CLASS

A well educated group among the middle class (businessmen, lawyers, social workers, doctors, clergy, educators) became the core of the Progressive movement. Concentrated in urban areas, this new middle class had a sizable impact on the reform movements. They had the moral training that stressed a "Christian duty" to help those less fortunate, and often the leisure time to devote to these pursuits.

MASS COMMUNICATION MEDIA

Development of mass communication technologies such as the telephone, the telegraph, teletype, and faster, more efficient mail delivery made it possible for reformers to exchange information and coordinate activities. This led to the spread of nationwide organizations, many with reform motivations, including the American Bar Association and the National Consumers League. Mass production techniques utilized in the

publishing and printing industries also helped to mobilize public opinion.

SOCIAL AND ECONOMIC CHANGE

Public outcries against big business tactics came from a number of different voices with a number of different goals. Government at all levels was spurred into action by concerned citizens or the press. Progressive reform had begun.

INFLUENCE OF THE MUCKRAKERS

Compulsory public education became more widespread in the 19th century. As literacy grew in America, the power of the media grew. Many Progressive reformers worked with journalists who wrote articles exposing the evils of big business. Theodore Roosevelt likened these journalists to a character in John Bunyan's *A Pilgrim's Progress*. Obsessed with profit making, he ignored the salvation of his soul. Muckrakers seemed to be obsessed with turning up the seamier side of American life and often stirred public opinion with their exposés.

In the early 1900s, several magazines began to feature muckraking articles. *McClure's* (1893-1933) was among the notable magazines focusing public attention onto social problems. Writers included: **Ida Tarbell** (1857-1944) who wrote a series of exposés on the Standard Oil Company; **Lincoln Steffens** (1866-1936), who had a series on *The Shame of the Cities*; and others whose works ranged from child labor to corruption in politics.

Novelists employed muckraking too. **Upton Sinclair** (1878-1968) described the unsanitary conditions in Chicago's meat packing plants in *The Jungle* (1906). Its publication mobilized public demand for government regulation of the industry. **Frank Norris** described the farmers' plight resulting from railroad abuses in *The Octopus* (1901).

He showcased the Chicago wheat exchange in *The Pit* (1903). Even earlier, **Jacob Riis'** *How the Other Half Lives* (1890), the first book specifically about urban problems (immigrant slums in NYC), stimulated housing reform.

ECONOMIC POLICY

The articles and novels stimulated public demand for governmental action. The work of these writers and other Progressive reformers resulted in the passage of many state and congressional laws.

• ***The Meat Inspection Act*** (1906) – the first consumer protection law passed by Congress. It used the interstate commerce clause to subject all meat crossing state lines to strict inspection by federal employees.

• ***The Pure Food and Drug Act*** (1906) – forbade the sale of adulterated goods or those fraudulently labeled. Congressional passage of this law was based on the commerce clause (a delegated power) of the Constitution's Article I.

Muckraking journalism faded after the election of 1912. Public weariness with crusades and intense exposés caused the decline. Political reforms led by Theodore Roosevelt, Robert LaFollette, and Woodrow Wilson answered the muckrakers calls for action.

Yet, in a larger sense, the muckrakers reformed journalism itself. Today's investigative reporters follow the muckraking tradition. Investigative reporters triggered protest action on Vietnam (*The Pentagon Papers*), the Watergate Scandal, the Iran-Contra Affair, and the Savings & Loan Crisis of the 1980s.

OTHER PROGRESSIVE CONCERNS

Besides the muckrakers, many private individuals and organizations became catalysts for change. They also worked for social reform during the Progressive Era.

SETTLEMENT HOUSES

The plight of the urban poor (often immigrants) came to the public's attention in a num-

At the time of her death, *The New York Times* wrote about Jane Addams, "Perhaps the world's best-known and best-loved woman."
(Courtesy of *Ladies' Home Journal* "100 Most Important Women of the 20th Century," Meredith Corp ©1999)

ber of exposés such as Riis' *How the Other Half Lives*. Individuals such as **Jane Addams** (1860-1935) sought to provide accessible help to those living in urban slums. In 1889, she created **Hull House** in Chicago as a social service center. These **settlement houses**, located right in slum neighborhoods, offered adult education classes, job training, clinics, child care, and Americanization classes, among other things. This concept originated in England and spread to urban America, especially the Northeastern cities.

WOMEN'S RIGHTS AND EFFORTS FOR PEACE

During the Progressive Era, women agitated for suffrage and equal rights. **Margaret Sanger** (1879-1966), a nurse working primarily with immigrant expectant mothers in New York City, gave up her job in 1912 to promote the use of birth control. Her actions violated existing obscenity statutes (laws) and brought her into conflict with the law. She coined the term "birth control."

Many men and women followed **pacifism** (opposition to all war). **Jeannette Rankin**

(1880-1973) of Montana became the first female member of the House of Representatives. She served one term in 1916-1917. As a pacifist, she voted against the United States entry into World War I. Serving a second term in 1940-1941, she cast the lone dissenting vote against U.S. entry into World War II.

THE SEARCH FOR RACIAL JUSTICE

The movement for racial equality and equity of treatment was divided over the policies and programs of Booker T. Washington and W.E.B. DuBois. Racist lynching increased in the South in the late 19th century and continued to gain strength in the decade that followed World War I. Although several anti-lynching bills were introduced in Congress, filibustering (endless debate used to postpone a vote) by Southern Senators blocked passage of these laws. Around the period of World War I, Jamaican-born **Marcus Garvey** (1887-1940) founded the

Universal Negro Improvement Association. The UNIA sought to create free and independent nations in Africa. Garvey hoped that African Americans would help to populate these new nations. Garvey is regarded as one of the first African American nationalists, although his dreams were not fulfilled. He was jailed for mail fraud and later deported.

TEMPERANCE AND PROHIBITION

Originally calling for moderation in the consumption of alcohol, the temperance movement eventually turned to the goal of prohibition. Groups such as the National Prohibition Party (1869), the **Women's Christian Temperance Union** (1874), and the **Anti-Saloon League** (1895) believed drink was the primary factor in crime, poverty, and vice. Prohibitionists' goals were reached when the Eighteenth Amendment was passed in 1919 banning the sale, manufacture, and distribution of alcohol.

MINI•ASSESSMENT (5-1)

1 The major reasons for the rise of Progressive Reform include
  (1) the growing middle class indignation and desire for reform
  2 increasing equality in the distribution of wealth in the United States
  3 the desire to return to an agrarian culture
  4 the responsiveness of business to public demands for safety

2 At their outset, which two American reform movements were tied together?
  1 abolition and temperance
   women's suffrage and civil service reform
  3 care of the elderly and abolition
  4 women's suffrage and abolition

3 Generally, reform movements in America have tended to
  1 seek better conditions for people in rural environments
  (2) broaden the voting base and increase the standard of living for all
  3 concentrate geographically in the Midwest and Western states
  4 be a direct result of reform movements in Europe

Constructed Response Question:

"...If woman would fulfill her traditional responsibilities to her own children...if she would educate and protect factory children and] bring cultural forces to bear upon our materialistic civilization; and if she would do it with all the dignity and directness fitting one who carries on her immemorial duties, then she must bring herself to the use of the ballot – that latest implement for self-government. May we not fairly say that American women need this implement in order to preserve the home?"

– Jane Addams, "Why Women Should Vote,"
Ladies Home Journal (January 1910)

1 Is Jane Addams a suffragist? Why or why not?

2 How does Addams connect the preservation of the home with the ballot for women?

PROGRESSIVISM INFLUENCES AMERICAN POLITICS

Progressive reform was primarily an urban, middle class movement which influenced many other groups in society and every level of government.

STATE AND LOCAL REFORMS

Initially, much of the government reform movement was aimed at the municipal and state level, especially cities where the problems of urbanization and industrialization seemed most intense.

In an effort to root out municipal and state government corruption, reformers sought to make governments run more efficiently and more professionally. They called for civil service reform, an end to bossism, and the creation of city commissions and city managers.

The rapid growth of the urban population magnified the inadequacies in various basic services. Reformers called for government ownership of public utilities, including electricity, gas, telegraph, and telephone, so that these services would be accessible and affordable to the general public, not just the rich.

On the state level, reformers looked to the governors for leadership. Goals often differed by regions (West – railroad regulation, South – anti-big-business, North – political corruption and labor conditions).

In Wisconsin, Republican-Progressive Governor **Robert LaFollette** (1855-1925) eventually became the state's U.S. Senator (1905-1925). Before he left the governorship (1900-1905), "Fighting Bob's" Wisconsin became synonymous with progressive reform including direct primaries, equitable taxes, and regulation of railroads. One way reform was achieved hinged on the activities of commissioners who reported directly to the governor. They used a scientific approach to collect data and make reports.

After the **Spanish-American War** of 1898, **Theodore Roosevelt** (1858-1919) was elected Governor of New York State. He championed

social legislation including improving conditions in urban tenements and taxing public utility corporations.

Following the lead of the Midwestern states and New York in the East, Massachusetts limited women's working hours to 60 per week. Twelve years later in 1900, Massachusetts created a commission empowered to recommend minimum wages for women and expose employers who did not comply.

STATE REFORMS

Initiative – process where voters can suggest new laws and constitutional amendments

Referendum – people allowed to vote directly on legislation

Recall – process where voters can remove officials from office before their term is up

Secret Ballot – voters could make their choices in privacy

States began using their police powers to regulate the health and safety of their citizens. Reforms undertaken using these powers included: factory inspections, insurance to cover job accidents, minimum employment age, maximum hours for child labor (usually 8–10 hours per day), limit on hours for women, and old age pensions.

NATIONAL REFORMS: THEODORE ROOSEVELT AND THE SQUARE DEAL

Theodore Roosevelt's 1904 campaign theme demanded that business and government give consumers a **Square Deal**. He saw a new economic role evolving for the presidency. Later his policies became known as the **New Nationalism**. The dynamic president indicated trusts were necessary evils and part of American life, therefore controls were needed to curb the more flagrant monopolistic tendencies. He saw the presidency as a "stewardship of the people" meaning that the president controlled and wielded power in the best interests of the people. The public good must be the overriding concern of the holder of the executive office.

REFORM IN THE SQUARE DEAL

ECONOMIC POLICY

PROGRESSIVE LEGISLATION

Many programs were pushed through Congress during Roosevelt's tenure as chief executive.

- The **Commerce Department** (1903) was created to collect information necessary to enforce existing anti-trust legislation.

- The *Elkins Act* (1903) expanded powers of the **Interstate Commerce Commission** (**ICC**) and made rebates illegal.

- The *Pure Food and Drug Act* and *Meat Inspection Act* (1906).

- The *Hepburn Act* (1906) strengthened the *Elkins Act* and gave the ICC power to reduce objectionable railroad rates subject to court approval. It also allowed the ICC to regulate interstate commerce (i.e., done by oil pipelines, railroad terminals, sleeping car companies, and bridges).

"TRUST BUSTING" POLICY

Due in large part to the energetic activities of the Commerce Department, Theodore Roosevelt took action against over forty American trusts. As a result, Roosevelt was often referred to as a "trust buster." In 1904, in the ruling on the ***Northern Securities Co. v. U.S.****, the Supreme Court ordered the breakup of one of Wall Street titan J.P. Morgan's railroad monopolies in the Pacific Northwest. In 1911, the Supreme Court ordered the dissolution of Rockefeller's Standard Oil Company of New Jersey, declaring the monopoly represented an "unreasonable restraint of trade." Under the High Court's "rule of reason," trusts were not automatically condemned. Instead, their actions had to be analyzed as to their effects on trade in general.

REFORMING WORKING CONDITIONS

In the 1890s, many states used their police powers to regulate and improve working conditions for laborers. Not all agreed with these reforms. Two Supreme Court decisions illustrate the battle for judicial acceptance of legislative reform.

Theodore Roosevelt, 26th President of the U.S.
(White House Historical Association, National Geographic Society)

- ***Lochner v. New York**** (1905) involved a progressive New York State law limiting bakers' hours to 10 a day, 6 days a week to ensure the health of the bakers and protect consumers. Lochner, a bakery owner, was found guilty of violating this law and appealed to the Supreme Court. In a split decision, the law was found unconstitutional. The Court's reasoning held that the law violated due process guarantees of the Fourteenth Amendment infringing on workers' rights to work more than 10 hours a day. Justice Oliver Wendell Holmes wrote a classic dissenting opinion on this case.

- In ***Muller v. Oregon**** (1908), an Oregon laundry owner was found guilty of violating an Oregon law limiting women workers to 10 hours work a day. He appealed the decision to the Supreme Court. The lawyer for Oregon, **Louis D. Brandeis** (who later was a Supreme Court Justice himself, 1916-1939), entered a groundbreaking form of arguments (legal brief). Instead of long citations of judicial precedents, Brandeis' argument focused on a wealth of scientific data and statistics to show this occupation was unhealthy. This format came to be known as the "Brandeis Brief."

Oregon won the case and two important precedents were set: non-legal data could be used and admitted as evidence, and certain circumstances justified the use of a state's police powers.

In the Square Deal, the government began playing a stronger role in labor mediation. In 1902, anthracite coal miners went on strike demanding higher pay, shorter working hours, and union recognition. The strike began to affect Americans when the colder weather approached. President Theodore Roosevelt took action by calling union leaders and mine owners to Washington. When discussions broke down, he threatened to use troops to get the mines producing again. The operators finally agreed to binding arbitration. The union saw some of their demands met, including half the wage increase sought. Public support for Roosevelt increased dramatically as a result of his mediation.

CONCERN FOR THE ENVIRONMENT

The great waste caused by industrialization made Americans aware of the dangers of environmental deterioration rather belatedly.

In 1907 Roosevelt said, "We are prone to think of the resources of this country as inexhaustible; this is not so." He used his presidential powers to add 150 million acres to national forests and preserves belonging to all. He sought a well conceived plan for resource management.

Going back to 1891, Congress authorized the President to remove United States owned timber land from sale. Roosevelt used these provisions enthusiastically.

- The **Newlands Act** (1902) used money from the sale of Western lands for irrigation and created the National Forest Service.

- The **Antiquities Act** (1906) provided that sites of historic and/or scientific interest be placed under national protection and control, including the Grand Canyon and Niagara Falls.

- The **Inland Waterways Act** (1907) planned control and improvement of river systems.

Yosemite National Park, California
(PhotoDisc ©1994)

Niagara Falls National Park, New York
(PhotoDisc ©1994)

Snake River, Grand Teton National Park, Wyoming   (PhotoDisc ©1994)

1 Which best explains why the Progressive Movement became nationwide?
  (1) An accessible, and national system of communications had developed.
  2 There were great disparities between the very rich and the very poor.
  3 Most Americans were farmers.
  4 The problems were regional in nature.

2 The Progressive movement of the early 20th century represented an attempt to
  1 repeal the antitrust laws
  2 protect the rights of racial minorities
  3 destroy the capitalistic system of the United States
  (4) deal with the problems created by industrialization

3 Which statement is true of Progressivism at the state level?
  (1) Many of its ideas grew out of the reform philosophy at the local level.
  2 Most Progressives were from minority groups.
  3 It achieved few of its goals at the state level.
  4 Progressive governors proved weak and ineffectual at instituting change.

Constructed Response

"While making it clear that we do not intend to allow wrongdoing by one of the captains of industry any more than by the humblest private in the industrial ranks, we must also in the interests of all of us avoid cramping a strength which, if beneficially used, will be for the good of all of us. The marvelous prosperity we have been enjoying for the past few years has been due primarily to the high average honesty, thrift, and business capacity among our people as a whole; but some of it has also been due to the ability of the men who are the industrial leaders of the nation. In securing just and fair dealing by these men let us remember to do them justice in return, and this not only because it is our duty but because it is our interest – not only for their sakes, but for ours. We are neither the friend of the rich man as such nor the friend of the poor man as such; we are the friend of the honest man, rich or poor; and we intend that all men, rich and poor alike, shall obey the law alike and receive its protection alike."

– Theodore Roosevelt, *Dealing with the Big Corporations*, Cincinnati, OH, 20 September 1902

1 What factors does President Roosevelt say contributed to American prosperity?

2 Why could the nickname "trust buster" for President Roosevelt be considered misleading?

Under Roosevelt, chief of the Department of Agriculture's Division of Forestry **Gifford Pinchot** (1865-1946) played a large role in the national conservation movement of his day. Pinchot was instrumental in calling the National Conservation Congress (Association) in 1908. It pressed to expand the national forest reserve and get Congress to pass the *Waterpower Act* (1920). Another naturalist, Scottish born **John Muir** (1838-1914) was the founder and first president of the Sierra Club (1892). He was instrumental in bringing the Yosemite area into the **National Park System** in 1891. Muir wrote many wilderness books including *The Mountains of California* (1894) which focused public attention on the value of American forests.

THE NEW FREEDOM: PROGRESSIVISM AT ITS ZENITH

The 1912 Presidential election featured three candidates, all with reform credentials. One reason to account for the Democratic electoral victory was the split within the powerful Republican Party. Theodore Roosevelt, unimpressed with the policies of his successor **William Howard Taft** (1857-1930), entered the race seeking the Republican nomination. Roosevelt called for a New Nationalism - vigorous government action from all branches to address society's problems.

Woodrow Wilson during the 1912 Presidential Campaign against William Howard Taft and Theodore Roosevelt. (Library of Congress)

Wilson became the first Democrat to be elected president in 20 years. He was a relative newcomer politically, but a true progressive reformer. Under his program, the **New Freedom**, Wilson viewed trusts as fundamentally evil entities and sought to break them and restore free competition in the marketplace.

UNDERWOOD TARIFF AND GRADUATED INCOME TAX

Over Congressional opposition, Wilson secured the passage of the **Underwood Tariff** (1913) and a federal income tax. Many people saw international competition as another way to combat trusts. They believed lowering tariffs would increase this competition. The Underwood Tariff reduced duties on imported goods from 38% to approximately 26% of the product's value.

The Populist–inspired income tax was finally achieved by Progressive reformers. A **progressive income tax** (one in which tax rate increased as the amount of income increased) took the tax burden off those who could least afford to pay it – the lower classes. Previous revenue tariffs were said to be **regressive** (placing an unfair tax burden on those who could not afford to pay it).

The ratification of the **Sixteenth Amendment** in 1913 gave Congress the authority to tax personal and corporate income. The *Revenue Act* (1913) placed a 1% tax on incomes over $3,000 and surcharges on those over $20,000. The bulk of Americans did not pay any tax.

CLAYTON ANTI-TRUST ACT AND FEDERAL TRADE COMMISSION

In an effort to curb trust activities, Congress passed the *Clayton Antitrust Act* and created the **Federal Trade Commission** (FTC) in 1914. *Clayton* was designed to strengthen the *Sherman Antitrust Act* of 1890.

Factionalism at the Republican Convention led Roosevelt and his liberal supporters to form the Progressive Party (also known as the Bull Moose Party). Conservative Republicans supported the incumbent, William Howard Taft. Roosevelt's third party gained more votes than Taft's Republicans but the split allowed Democrat **Woodrow Wilson** (1856-1924) to win a slim plurality, and an overwhelming electoral majority.

1912 PRESIDENTIAL ELECTION RESULTS			
CANDIDATE & PARTY	POPULAR VOTE	PERCENT OF POPULAR VOTE	ELECTORAL VOTE
Woodrow Wilson (Democratic)	6,296,547	41.9	435
Theodore Roosevelt (Progressive)	4,118,571	27.4	88
William H. Taft (Republican)	3,486,720	23.2	8
Eugene V. Debs (Socialist)	900,672	6.0	0
Eugene W. Chafin (Prohibition)	206,275	1.4	0

The new *Clayton Act* specified the abuses considered monopolistic, including rebates, certain interlocking directorates, and exclusive sales contracts. It exempted labor unions and agricultural cooperatives, but hostile court decisions rendered this exemption meaningless.

The FTC strengthened anti-trust legislation. It could investigate monopolistic practices and "kill a monopoly in the seed." The FTC could issue "cease-and-desist orders" when monopolistic tactics were found. Unfair practices included: mis-branding and adulterating products; spying and bribery; and misleading advertising. In the 1920s, a series of corporate challenges in the Supreme Court led to conservative decisions that hurt the FTC's effectiveness. Actions in the 1930s and 1970s strengthened the Commission.

ECONOMIC POLICY

THE FEDERAL RESERVE SYSTEM

Reform in the banking system was designed to wrest power away from controlling eastern banks. People believed that financial instability was caused by banking policies, especially their reluctance to lend money.

The Federal Reserve System, established by Congress in 1913, under the *Federal Reserve Act*,

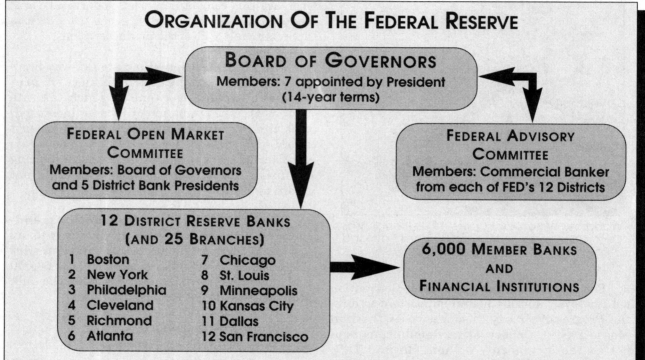

ORGANIZATION OF THE FEDERAL RESERVE

BOARD OF GOVERNORS
Members: 7 appointed by President
(14-year terms)

FEDERAL OPEN MARKET COMMITTEE
Members: Board of Governors and 5 District Bank Presidents

FEDERAL ADVISORY COMMITTEE
Members: Commercial Banker from each of FED's 12 Districts

12 DISTRICT RESERVE BANKS (AND 25 BRANCHES)
1 Boston
2 New York
3 Philadelphia
4 Cleveland
5 Richmond
6 Atlanta
7 Chicago
8 St. Louis
9 Minneapolis
10 Kansas City
11 Dallas
12 San Francisco

6,000 MEMBER BANKS AND FINANCIAL INSTITUTIONS

The Board of Governors in Washington consults with the presidents of the FED's 12 district banks and supervises banking operations, regulates the money supply, and establishes credit rules for the nation. The 12 district banks are nonprofit "bankers' banks" owned by the member banks. They perform many services for the banking community:

- make low interest loans to member banks to keep proper reserves
- hold reserves on account for member banks
- modify and administer the policies set by FED's Board of Governors to meet the needs of banks in their district
- computer process (credit/debit) the 40 billion checks written in the country
- transfer funds among the 12 districts
- make loans to the government, especially for disaster aid (floods, earthquakes, hurricanes, etc.)
- disburse new U.S. currency (and destroy old, worn currency)
- regulate the money supply rules set by the Board of Governors

The 12 district banks "customize and fine-tune" the basic regulations set down by the Board of Governors to the particular circumstances in their region of the country.

set up a government-controlled banking system designed to allow for an **elastic currency** (one which could expand or contract as the economy required). It is a three-tiered system:

1 At the top is the **Board of Governors**. Members are appointed by the President to supervise and regulate the activities of the system, or "The Fed."

2 Twelve **regional banks**, which act as "banks' banks" hold reserves and lend money to

3 **member banks** (all nationally-chartered banks and other banks who wish to join the system).

VICTORY FOR WOMEN'S SUFFRAGE

At the beginning of the Progressive Era, more militant national leaders emerged in the

Alice Paul, 1920, a leader of radical tactics of the women's suffrage movement, later drafted the first *Equal Rights Amendment.* (Library of Congress)

women's suffrage movement. The National American Woman Suffrage Association had relied on gradual legislative lobbying and court actions up to that time. In 1913, NAWSA President **Alice Paul** (1885-1977) resigned to form the National Woman's Party. She led the party in mass marches and hunger strikes. By 1915, **Carrie Chapman Catt** (1859-1947) was leading a more militant NAWSA. Jeannette Rankin (MT) became the first female member of the House of Representatives in 1916-1917. Universal suffrage for women was finally achieved in 1920, with the ratification of the Nineteenth Amendment. It forbade denial of voting rights to anyone because of their gender.

WORLD WAR I AND ITS EFFECTS ON DOMESTIC REFORM

Domestic reform programs may be crippled by wartime priorities. By 1916, the Progressive movement had run its course. Concern over the growing conflict in Europe and the eventuality of American participation required coordination of the government and cooperation by all involved, not conflict between various groups. The enemy was now "over there." Government regulations were dropped or relaxed to stimulate war production.

CHANGING FOREIGN POLICY
INDUSTRIAL – COLONIAL CONNECTION

During the second half of the 19th century, expansion of American industry propelled the United States to look beyond its borders for markets and raw materials. The resulting American colonial empire, though not as large as those of European powers, was geographically far flung and ethnically diverse. While many Americans supported expansionist policies, concern was voiced over the growing global involvement of the United States.

ECONOMIC IMPERIALISM

UNITED STATES INDUSTRIAL PRODUCTIVITY
American industry experienced tremendous growth in the decades after the Civil War. Americans with surplus capital looked beyond North America for new places to invest. They

1   The programs of the Progressive movement
    (1900-1920)
    1   emphasized the expansion of civil rights
        for African Americans and other
        minority groups
    2   were passed by Congress despite strong
        opposition by the President and other
        party leaders
    3   took effect during periods of extended
        economic depression
    4   resulted in a greater involvement of the
        federal government in the daily lives of
        Americans

2   Which statement regarding the end of the
    Progressive reform movement is correct?
    1   All reforms sought by Progressive
        reformers were enacted.
    2   Preparation for a wartime economy took
        attention away from reform.
    3   Power of the trusts overwhelmed
        democratic government.
    4   There was no leadership in the White
        House.

3   Wilson's New Freedom differed from
    Roosevelt's New Nationalism in that
    1   Wilson tried to help the monopolies deal
        with increasing government restriction
    2   Roosevelt's policies accepted the
        continued existence of monopolies
    3   Wilson's program is not considered part
        of the Progressive Era
    4   Roosevelt attempted to completely
        eradicate business monopolies

Constructed Response

"The conscience of the people, in a time of grave national problems, has called into being a new party, born of the nation's sense of justice. We of the Progressive party here dedicate ourselves to the fulfillment of the duty laid upon us by our fathers to maintain the government of the people, by the people, and for the people whose foundations they laid...

"We hold with Thomas Jefferson and Abraham Lincoln that the people are the masters of their Constitution...

"It is time to set the public welfare in the first place."

– The Progressive Party Platform of 1912

1   Why would the Progressive Party use the phrase "of the people, by the people, and for the people" and make reference to Thomas Jefferson and Abraham Lincoln in this document?

2   Based on the opening paragraphs, what specific policies or programs would the Progressive Party support?

looked overseas for new markets and new sources of raw materials. The "closing" of the frontier in 1890 indicated to many that it was time to expand abroad. Pursuing these policies, government and business leaders hoped to strengthen America's position as a leading industrial nation.

DEVELOPMENT OF COMMERCIAL AND NAVAL POWER

Between 1870 and 1900, the value of American agricultural and industrial exports more than tripled. The ever increasing output of factories and farms could not be consumed within the nation. American merchant and naval fleets were strengthened and modernized to give the nation a greater role in international commerce.

In 1890, **Captain Alfred Thayer Mahan** (1840-1914) of the Naval War College, authored *The Influence of Sea Power Upon History, 1660-1783*. Mahan's book tried to show that throughout history, nations with sea power dominated the world. Mahan urged that it was time for Americans to "look outward" for naval bases, markets, and raw materials. Modernization of the Navy was already underway. By 1900, the U.S. Navy was ranked third in the world.

Technological advances spurred a growing interest in international affairs. The increased speed of steamships made trade more profitable, and the need for "coaling stations" forced Americans to take an interest in Pacific Islands.

Trans-oceanic telegraph cables brought the hemispheres closer together. Continued industrial growth required new sources of raw materials, and improved military weapons made conquest easier.

CULTURAL PATERNALISM: EUROPEAN IMPERIALISM AND MISSIONARY IMPULSE

Led by Britain and France, European nations rushed to gain control of colonies in the second half of the 19th century. Nearly all of Africa, India, and Indochina came under the domination of Europe. The Europeans attempted to justify their conquests by claiming it was the "White Man's Burden" to bring the benefits of western civilization to less developed regions.

Early in the 19th century, Christian missionaries ventured into various parts of Asia and the Pacific to find Christian converts. Hawaii was of particular interest to New England Congregationalists. By the close of the 19th century, many Americans came to believe that it was the "divine mission" of the United States to spread the benefits of democracy, liberty, and Christianity to the less civilized. A number of authors, including the **Rev. Josiah Strong**, (*Our Country*, 1885) popularized the belief that it was the duty of Americans to uplift the less fortunate. Such popular ideas made it easier for Americans to accept an imperialistic role for the United States.

THE TARIFF CONTROVERSY: FREE TRADE V. PROTECTIONISM

One of the more hotly debated political issues of the 19th century was the tariff. **Protectionists**, usually Republicans and their business backers, argued that high tariffs protected the wages and jobs of workers as well as the profits of capitalists. **Free trade** supporters advocated lower tariffs (and eventual elimination of all tariffs). They were often Democrats and claimed that high rates raised the price of manufactured goods for consumers, benefited only a few, and interfered with America's ability to sell goods overseas. The tariff rose and fell depending on the party in power.

Throughout American history, high protective tariffs have been used as an expression of economic nationalism. The high rates have not always helped the economy, because the benefits of foreign trade were lost. But lower tariffs, while promoting trade, have combined with other economic factors to cause trade deficits and loss of American jobs.

During the 20th century, the government resorted more frequently to the use of quotas rather than high tariffs in an effort to control foreign imports. The **General Agreement on Tariffs and Trade** (GATT), signed in 1967, reduced the tariffs in the major industrial nations by as much as fifty percent. By the 1980s, large U.S. trade deficits piled up and protectionist voices rose once again.

EMERGING GLOBAL INVOLVEMENT

The Civil War, Reconstruction, and internal growth limited American interest in foreign affairs for much of the 19th century. While Americans prospered from the benefits of foreign trade, efforts at expansion were often ridiculed (Alaska, 1867). However, the last decades of the century saw a change as public support increased for overseas adventures.

MANIFEST DESTINY AND EXPANSION TO THE PACIFIC

GEOGRAPHIC INTERACTIONS

In the first part of the 19th century, Americans made their way across the continent spurred on by the belief in Manifest Destiny, that America had a "divine mission" to conquer the entire continent (see map page 200). The annexation of Texas, settlement of the Oregon dispute, and the spoils of the Mexican War brought the Americans to the Pacific by 1850. The new west coast ports increased interest in Far Eastern trade.

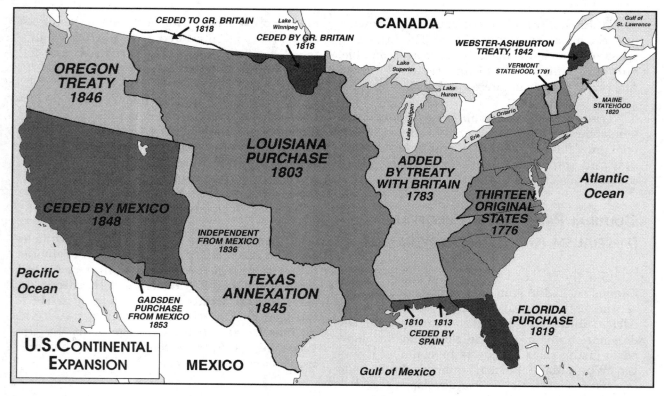

Map labels:
- CEDED TO GR. BRITAIN 1818
- Lake Winnipeg
- CEDED BY GR. BRITAIN 1818
- CANADA
- Gulf of St. Lawrence
- OREGON TREATY 1846
- Lake Superior
- WEBSTER-ASHBURTON TREATY, 1842
- VERMONT STATEHOOD, 1791
- Lake Huron
- MAINE STATEHOOD 1820
- Lake Michigan
- LOUISIANA PURCHASE 1803
- L. Ontario
- L. Erie
- ADDED BY TREATY WITH BRITAIN 1783
- Atlantic Ocean
- CEDED BY MEXICO 1848
- THIRTEEN ORIGINAL STATES 1776
- INDEPENDENT FROM MEXICO 1836
- Pacific Ocean
- GADSDEN PURCHASE FROM MEXICO 1853
- TEXAS ANNEXATION 1845
- 1810 1813 CEDED BY SPAIN
- FLORIDA PURCHASE 1819
- U.S. CONTINENTAL EXPANSION
- MEXICO
- Gulf of Mexico

JAPANESE CONTACTS (1857–1900)

Japan had isolated itself in the mid-17th century, having little to do with Western civilization. In 1853, disputes over American whaling rights and an interest in trade led to a visit by Commodore **Matthew C. Perry** (1794-1858). In 1854 – with an impressive show of U.S. naval force in Tokyo Bay, Perry persuaded the Japanese to open several ports to American commerce. This was soon followed by European powers making similar demands. The Japanese were impressed by modern technology and the military power of the Westerners. By 1900, Japan had a modern government, a thriving textile industry, and rapidly growing heavy industries. Japan also modernized its military and began its own era of imperialism.

THE CHINA TRADE:
INTEREST SINCE COLONIAL TIMES

Despite a distance of over 12,000 miles, American East coast merchants carried on a profitable trade with China from the 1780s. The opening of additional ports following Britain's victory in the Opium War in the mid-1800s, the speed of American clipper ships, and the addition of the Pacific ports contributed to an increase in the China trade prior to the Civil War.

While Americans were interested primarily in trade and missionary activity, imperialist nations annexed territory and established economic control (spheres of influence) over large parts of China toward the end of the 19th century. While not wanting territory, the United States was fearful of losing trading privileges, and began to play a role in Asian politics.

THE OPEN DOOR POLICY

At the end of the 19th century, foreign spheres of influence and possible annexations threatened U.S. trade with China. In 1899 and 1900, Secretary of State **John Hay** (1838-1905) sent two notes to major powers with trading interests with China. In them, he declared principles which became known as the **Open Door Policy**. The policy tried to create an atmosphere of equal opportunity for all nations in trade, investments, and profits. The second note warned the imperialistic nations of Europe and Japan not to annex any Chinese territory. China appreciated American efforts on its behalf, but the Open Door Policy proved difficult for the United States to effectively enforce.

THE BOXER REBELLION

Foreign nations exerted increasing control over the domestic affairs of China. In 1900, a

MINI•ASSESSMENT (5-4)

1   A nation will often restrict the importation of foreign products to
   1   protect domestic jobs
   2   reduce prices on domestically produced goods
   3   increase tariff revenues
   4   widen the variety of products available to consumers

2   In the late 19th century, many of the leading industrial nations began a policy of imperialistic expansion, because of
   1   a desire to gain control of strategic locations in preparation for World War I
   2   the need for allies in other global regions
   3   a desire to obtain supplies of raw materials and expand markets for trade
   4   the need for a place to put surplus population

3   Which statement best reflects the attitude of British, German, and French leaders toward Africa and Asia during the 19th century?
   1   We should not become involved with people who are different from us.
   2   These lands are sources of raw materials and markets for our products.
   3   There are many advantages to sharing and learning from other cultures.
   4   The political power and wealth of these areas are threats to our position in the world.

Constructed Response

"Whether they will or not, Americans must now begin to look outward. The growing production of the country demands it. An increasing volume of public sentiment demands it. The position of the United States, between the two Old Worlds and the two great oceans, makes the same claim, which will soon be strengthened by the creation of the new link joining the Atlantic and Pacific. The tendency will be increased by the growth of European colonies in the Pacific, by the advancing civilization of Japan, and by the rapid peopling of our Pacific states."

– Alfred Thayer Mahan, "The United States Looking Outward"
Atlantic Monthly, 1890

1   According to Captain Mahan, what geographic factors should change Americans' view of the world?

2   Why would views like Mahan's prompt Congress to build up U.S. naval forces?

---

group of patriotic Chinese went on a violent rampage, killing foreigners and destroying property (the **Boxer Rebellion**). After several months, an international military force, which included U.S. troops, ended the rebellion, and an indemnity was assessed on the Chinese government. (The United States eventually gave much of its share back to China).

PEACE IN CHINA

"...the policy of the government of the United States is to seek

FOREIGN POLICY

a solution which may bring about permanent safety and peace to China, preserve Chinese territorial and administrative entity, protect all rights guaranteed to friendly powers by treaty and international law, and safeguard for the world the principle of equal and impartial trade with all parts of the Chinese Empire."

U.S. Secretary of State John Hay,
Open Door Notes: A Circular Letter - 3 July 1900

ACQUISITION OF HAWAII

American interest in Hawaii began with missionary activities early in the 19th century. As sugar growers also flocked to the islands, Americans gradually dominated affairs. In 1893, American settlers engineered a successful overthrow of the Queen **Liliuokalani** (1838-1917). The new rulers requested annexation by the United States, but President **Grover Cleveland** (1837-1908) determined that most native Hawaiians opposed annexation, and the matter was dropped.

Five years later, the fighting in the Philippines during the Spanish American War convinced those with imperialist leanings that Hawaii was needed to send supplies and men across the Pacific. President William McKinley and Congress quickly approved the annexation of Hawaii in 1898. In addition to agricultural benefits, Hawaii also provided the American military with the important Pearl Harbor naval base.

NAVAL BASE: SAMOA

The Samoan Islands in the South Pacific served as a coaling station for the United States beginning in 1872. Britain and Germany also showed interest in the islands. In 1889, after much diplomatic haggling, the United States and Germany each annexed part of Samoa, with Britain receiving other considerations.

THE SPANISH AMERICAN WAR

The Spanish American War in 1898 had a number of causes:

- harsh treatment of Cubans by Spanish rulers

- desire by investors to continue a profitable agricultural trade

- **yellow journalism** – false and exaggerated stories published by American newspapers

- explosion of the battleship *Maine* incorrectly blamed on the Spanish

With the American public clamoring for war, McKinley requested a recognition of Cuba's independence and a declaration of war, which Congress passed on 25 April. The fighting lasted until August. Serious deficiencies in the nation's military preparedness were exposed. Poor planning, rotten food, and unsanitary conditions killed many more than combat. In the ***Treaty of Paris***, concluded on 10 December 1898, a humiliated Spain yielded to American imperialism. The Spanish ceded Puerto Rico, Guam, and the Philippine Islands. Cuba was given independence but agreed to cede territory for U.S. naval stations.

The War established the United States as a major power in the Far East and the dominant power in the Caribbean. Although Filipino nationalists fought a bitter four-year struggle for immediate independence, the United States

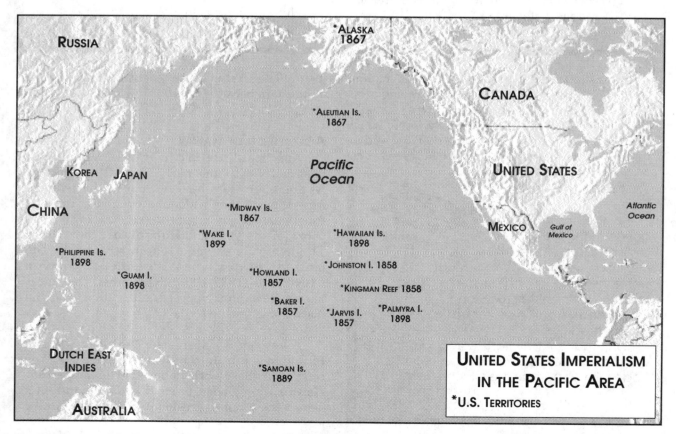

UNITED STATES IMPERIALISM IN THE PACIFIC AREA
*U.S. TERRITORIES

THE SPANISH AMERICAN WAR
April - August 1898

PACIFIC ACTION

In April, the newer steel-hulled cruisers of the U.S. Pacific Squadron commanded by Commodore **George Dewey** were on assignment off the Chinese coast. On orders from Assistant Secretary of the Navy Theodore Roosevelt, Dewey sped to the Spanish Philippines Islands. Within several hours on 1 May, he bottled up and defeated the aging Spanish fleet in Manila Bay. Dewey then laid siege to the colony's capital.

Nearly 11,000 U.S. troops were landed in the next two months. Under General Wesley Merritt, they joined with Filipino rebels to force the surrender of Manila on 13 August. Meanwhile, another of Spain's Pacific island colonies, Guam, was taken in July.

CARIBBEAN ACTION

The navy under Rear Admiral William T. Sampson quickly launched a blockade of Cuba and Puerto Rico. It took Gen. William R. Shafter nearly two months to mobilize the U.S. Army's first overseas expeditionary force in Tampa, Florida. In late June, 17,000 U.S. troops landed at Daiquiri and Siboney and moved toward Santiago. The regular army, under field commanders

such as Nelson Miles and Leonard Wood, was supported by special volunteer regiments, such as the "Rough Riders," led by Col. Theodore Roosevelt. (Roosevelt had resigned his post as Assist. Navy Secretary to form the unit.). The American forces were victorious at the battles of El Caney and San Juan Hill on 1 July.

On 3 July, the new battleships and cruisers commanded by

U.S. Army Archive

Sampson and Commodore Winfield Scott Schley sank most of the Spanish ships trying to leave Santiago harbor. On 17 July, the Spanish commanders in Santiago surrendered. The Spanish diplomats in Washington asked for peace terms shortly after this victory.

---

clung to the archipelago because it seemed a portal to the China market. Puerto Rico became an American colony.

THE DISCOMFORT OF IMPERIALISM

As the United States extended its control over several new areas, some Americans felt uneasy about having colonies. These anti-imperialists pressured Senators to vote against the *Treaty of Paris*, ending the Spanish-American War and annexing the Philippines. Prominent members of the **Anti-Imperialist League** included social welfare leader Jane Addams, labor leader Samuel Gompers, educator John Dewey, author Mark Twain, and industrialist

Andrew Carnegie. The anti-imperialists in Congress were primarily Democrats, but there were some Republicans in their ranks. They argued that the taking of overseas territory was contrary to the principles of American democracy.

Like the advocates of Manifest Destiny a generation before, the imperialists proclaimed the vigorous new mission of the United States was to spread democracy, western civilization, and Christianity. Imperialists emphasized the need to move toward trade in the Pacific. They wanted to challenge the imperialistic nations already there. By a close vote, the Senate ratified the *Treaty of Paris* in February 1899.

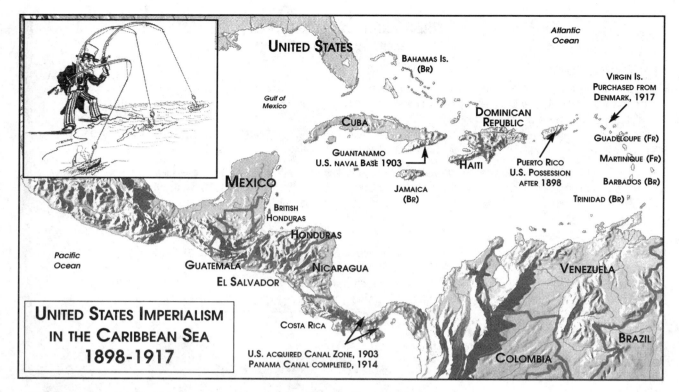

UNITED STATES IMPERIALISM IN THE CARIBBEAN SEA 1898-1917

UNITED STATES EMPIRE

The fruits of the Spanish-American War gave America a small but widely spread overseas empire. United States expansion coincided with a renewal of European imperialism.

CUBA

For nearly a generation after the overthrow of the Spanish, Cuba existed as a satellite of the United States. Some highlights of that period included:

- The **Teller Resolution** in 1898 made Congress promise not to annex Cuba;

- The *Platt Amendment* (1901) set up terms for withdrawal from Cuba of U.S. occupation troops from the Spanish American War. It granted a modified independence. The Cubans included political, economic, and military concessions to the U.S. in their constitution. The agreements made Cuba an informal U.S. protectorate until 1934; and,

- **Franklin Roosevelt's Good Neighbor Policy** led to Congress' repeal of the *Platt Amendment* (a symbol of "Yankee imperialism") in 1934 and gave the Cuban people total independence.

PUERTO RICO

After the Spanish-American War, Puerto Rico became a U.S. colonial possession and eventually received special status as a commonwealth. Key steps in this evolution included

- The *Foraker Act* (1900) granted territorial status to Puerto Rico, with limited self-government,

- The *Jones Act* (1917) extended American citizenship to residents, and

- Under **Commonwealth Status** (1952), residents were permitted to elect their own legislature and governor, but were not represented in Congress nor in the Electoral College. It was also stipulated that Puerto Rico could become a state if the Puerto Rican people desired and had U.S. Congressional approval.

PHILIPPINES

Located over 7,000 miles from the U.S. mainland, the Philippines presented greater difficulties. A number of Americans claimed the islands were too far away, too hard to defend, and populated by an alien race. Following the American annexation in 1899, a bloody three year guerrilla war was launched by **Emilio**

Aguinaldo's rebels. The same forces that had helped the American troops overthrow Spanish rule were crushed into submission by the U.S.

During U.S. control of the islands, sanitation programs, economic development, literacy, and democratic ideas were all put in place. Filipinos continued to ask for independence, and the *Tydings–McDuffie Act* freed the islands in 1946.

Territorial expansion prior to the 1890s consisted mostly of sparsely inhabited areas on the North American continent. It was fully expected that these areas would eventually achieve statehood. Acquisitions after 1890, however, were far from the mainland and populated by foreign peoples, with little possibility of statehood. A constitutional question arose: Are the people in these new areas protected by the *Constitution of the United States*? (Does the Constitution follow the flag?)

In the **Insular Cases** (1901), the Supreme Court decided that areas not likely to become states (unincorporated areas) were under the authority of Congress. While certain civil liberties were guaranteed by the Constitution, most Constitutional protections, such as citizenship, voting, and representation could be legislated by Congress.

LATIN AMERICAN AFFAIRS
INFLUENCE OF *THE MONROE DOCTRINE* (1823–1898)

In 1823, President James Monroe stated that the European nations would be prohibited from any further colonization in the Western Hemisphere, and that the U.S. would stay out of European affairs. It was to the political and economic benefit of America for the newly independent nations of Latin America to be weak and

PROTECTION OF NATURAL RIGHTS?

"Fundamental (natural rights) are protected in all areas controlled by the United States, but other rights can be withheld "until Congress shall see fit to incorporate the territory into the United States."
- Excerpt from the *Insular Cases* (1901, 1904, 1905)

FOREIGN POLICY

detached from Europe. Realistically, the United States was not powerful enough to enforce the Monroe Doctrine, but Britain accepted the policy, hoping for trade opportunities in Latin America. This was enough to keep anyone from challenging the Doctrine for forty years. (During the Civil War, an indirect attempt by France to control Mexico through a puppet emperor – the **Maxmilian Affair** of 1864-1865 – was condemned by the United States and eventually abandoned by the French.)

Latin American nations initially welcomed the Monroe Doctrine, but increased American meddling in their internal affairs began causing resentment. Beginning in the 1890s, recurrent American intervention led to frequent friction and increased distrust.

United States influence and intervention in the domestic affairs of many Latin American nations grew tremendously in the decade following the Spanish-American War. In creating an "American Lake" in the Caribbean, U.S. policy makers felt they were meeting the strategic and economic demands of the nation. However, many Latin American nations harbored increasing resentment toward U.S. meddling in their affairs.

ROOSEVELT'S "BIG STICK" POLICY

President Theodore Roosevelt believed in an aggressive foreign policy. He felt it was important for the U.S. to wave a "big stick" – make a strong show of force in foreign affairs. He believed the policy would keep Europeans out of the Western Hemisphere and bring the Latin American nations in line with U.S. wishes.

During Roosevelt's administration, the "big stick" was used in Venezuela to end the English and German blockade (1902), the Dominican Republic (1903-05) to collect debts, and in Cuba to end a rebellion (1906).

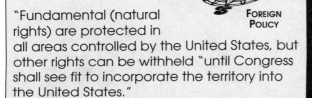

Although many Latin American nations were poorly governed, they nonetheless resented the "big stick" policies, and similar interventions by later presidents.

PANAMA CANAL:
ACQUISITION AND CONSTRUCTION

In the 1850s, American settlement of California aroused interest in a Central American canal connecting the Atlantic and Pacific. The water route from New York to California was 13,000 miles but would be cut in half with a canal. The French company that built the Suez Canal tried to do the same in Panama, but failed. With the addition of territories in the Caribbean and the Far East, a canal became a vital strategic and commercial necessity for the United States.

The United States paid the French company 40 million dollars for the land rights in Panama, and in 1901 negotiated a treaty with Colombia, which controlled Panama at the time. When the Colombian Senate refused to ratify the treaty, U.S. naval ships helped the Panamanians stage a revolt that led to independence. A U.S. Panamanian treaty was then finalized with Roosevelt boasting of having "taken the canal." After ten years of construction, the two oceans were joined in 1914.

As part of the agreement, the United States took title to a ten mile wide strip of land and paid Panama annual rent for its use. A small, affluent American community resided in the **Panama Canal Zone**, in contrast to the poverty of most Panamanians. Growing resentment to the U.S. ownership surfaced as riots erupted in 1964. After years of negotiations, a 1977 treaty provided for the gradual return of the area to Panama.

MONROE DOCTRINE UPDATE

The original intent of the Monroe Doctrine (1823) was to prevent the reappearance of European colonialism in the Western Hemisphere. By the 1890s, it was being interpreted to extend American political and economic influence over Latin America.

British refusal to submit a boundary dispute between Venezuela and British Guiana to arbitration led to American intervention in 1895. Secretary of State **Richard Olney** warned Britain to

---

THE INTERNATIONAL POLICEMAN

FOREIGN POLICY

"If a nation shows that it knows how to act with reasonable efficiency and decency in social and political matters, if it keeps order and pays its obligations, it need fear no interference from the United States. Chronic wrongdoing ... may ... ultimately require intervention by some civilized nation, and in the Western Hemisphere the adherence of the United States to the Monroe Doctrine may force the United States, however reluctantly, in flagrant cases of such wrongdoing or impotence, to the exercise of an international police power."

– Theodore Roosevelt, *Annual Message - Dec. 6, 1904, Washington, DC.*

---

reconsider, claiming that "the United States is practically sovereign on the [South American] continent." Hostilities were averted when Britain agreed to arbitration of the disputed area.

President Theodore Roosevelt went further, stating that in cases of "chronic wrongdoing," the United States can use "international police power" in Latin America. This became known as the **Roosevelt Corollary** to the Monroe Doctrine. It was applied in 1905 to the Dominican Republic when it was unable to repay debts to European nations. To keep Europe out of the Americas, the United States took over the economy of the Dominican Republic (1905) and supervised the debt repayment. This approach was used by the United States in a similar instance in Haiti in 1916.

Monroe Doctrine

Many Latin Americans grew increasingly suspicious of the domineering "help and protection" given to them by the United States. During the Venezuelan Claims Crisis of 1902, an Argentine official proclaimed the **Drago Doctrine**, condemning the use of force by foreign powers to collect debts. While few American leaders considered the wishes of Latin American nations, Presidents continuously involved the U.S. militarily, politically, and economically well into the 1920s.

TAFT AND DOLLAR DIPLOMACY

President William Howard Taft expanded America's "international police power" in Latin America. Nicaragua, Haiti, and the Dominican Republic were all occupied by U.S. military forces in order to protect American investments and loans. This policy approach was called **"Dollar Diplomacy"** by critics and met with considerable protest in Latin America, but it was enthusiastically supported by American business interests.

PRESIDENT WILSON AND THE MEXICAN REVOLUTION

A revolution against Mexican dictator **Porfiro Diaz** in 1910 initiated nearly a decade of civil war in that country. American businessmen watched with concern as the government changed hands several times and threatened to end foreign investment.

President Wilson applied a policy of "Watchful Waiting," resisting calls for American military intervention but also refusing to recognize a Mexican government with questionable authority. This worked for a time, but when rival Mexican leader **Pancho Villa** (1878-1923) crossed the border and killed American citizens in 1916, U.S. troops led by General **John Pershing** (1860-1948) pursued him into Mexico. Order was finally restored to Mexico after 1917, but Villa was never captured.

MINI•ASSESSMENT (5-5)

1 As Western trade with China expanded during the 19th century, U.S. policy was to
   1 establish and maintain a colony in East Asia
   2 partake in the international division of Chinese territory
   3 increase and strengthen American trading privileges
   4 encourage Chinese emigration

2 Which reflects a foreign policy of Presidents Monroe and Theodore Roosevelt?
   1 Close economic ties with Asia must be maintained.
   2 Non-involvement in world affairs is the wisest policy for the United States.
   3 U.S. influence in Latin America must be accepted by other nations.
   4 The United States should help in the settlement of internal European disputes.

3 The most important reason for the construction of the Panama Canal was the need to
   1 increase the security of the United States
   2 spread the United States way of life to less developed nations
   3 encourage the economic development of Central America
   4 prevent European colonization of Latin America

Constructed Response

1 The cartoon's title is "Policeman of the Western World." What events would prompt a cartoonist to portray President Roosevelt this way?

2 Why would this new role disturb some Americans?

RESTRAINT AND INVOLVEMENT: 1914-1920

In contrast to Latin America and the Pacific, the United States avoided involvement in European political affairs. America prospered from European trade and became a refuge for millions of immigrants, but abstained from the "entangling alliances" as George Washington had counseled in his *Farewell Address*. Although Wilson struggled to preserve neutrality at the beginning of World War I, as a major world power, the United States would eventually be drawn into the conflict.

EUROPEAN BACKGROUND TO WORLD WAR I

NATIONALISTIC RIVALRIES

European nations had formed several alliances in order to maintain a balance of power on the continent. In the late 19th century, Germany, Austria-Hungary, and Italy formed the **Triple Alliance**, while France, Great Britain, and Russia comprised the **Triple Entente**. Each was pledged to help the other members of the alliance in event of war. An intense atmosphere of nationalism in Europe convinced people to support their government, regardless of the consequences.

A tremendous build-up of military forces and weapons took place in the early part of the century. New weapons, such as submarines, tanks, poison gas, artillery, machine guns, and airplanes made warfare much more deadly and expensive.

Nationalism caused dissension and turmoil in Europe. Some ethnic groups, especially in the Balkans and central Europe, sought freedom from Germany, Austria–Hungary, and Russia.

COLONIALISM AND THE SPREAD OF WAR

The rush to colonize Africa and Asia led to numerous disputes among the European nations over matters such as boundaries and trade. Germany and Italy, having few colonies, wished to create colonial empires of their own. With large military forces available and national pride very strong, Europe was a "powder keg." It

EUROPE AT THE START OF WORLD WAR I

ALLIED POWERS

CENTRAL POWERS

erupted when a Serbian patriot assassinated the Austrian Archduke Franz Ferdinand in 1914. Austria retaliated against Serbia, and within a week, the promises made within each alliance brought all the major powers of Europe into the conflict.

THE GREAT WAR BEGINS

As World War I began, the nations maneuvered for position. Italy dropped out of the Triple Alliance, but the Ottoman Empire (Turkey) and Bulgaria joined Germany and Austria-Hungary to form the **Central Powers**. The rival Triple Alliance (France, Great Britain, Russia) evolved into a larger group of nations, including Serbia, Romania, Portugal, Italy, and eventually the U.S., calling themselves the **Allied Powers**.

CONTROL OF SEA ROUTES

At the start of hostilities, Britain attempted to choke off Germany by blockading the European coasts. To retaliate, Germany used submarine warfare against shipping in the Atlantic. This threatened the shipping rights of neutral nations. Traditional rules of warfare, which required enemy ships to identify themselves before sinking a merchant ship, were impossible for the submarine, which needed to remain underwater to be effective.

This **unrestricted submarine warfare** killed many innocent people. The most deadly attack occurred against the *Lusitania* (7 May 1915), when over 1,000 lives were lost at sea. Germany, though widely condemned, defended her actions as the only way to break the British blockade.

The German government agreed to halt these attacks when they issued the *Sussex Pledge* (May 1916). A few months later, Germany renewed its unrestricted submarine warfare and sank four American merchant ships. The *Zimmerman Note* (March 1917) angered Americans when British intelligence announced a plot by minor German diplomats to persuade Mexico to declare war against the United States.

UNITED STATES INVOLVEMENT

EFFORTS AT NEUTRALITY AND "PREPAREDNESS"

Upon the outbreak of hostilities in Europe (1914), President Wilson issued a *Proclamation of Neutrality*, but most citizens favored the Allied Powers: Britain, France, Russia, and Italy.

America's English heritage, belief in democracy, trade, and investment with the Allies all influenced the nation's thinking. Although both sides violated American rights on the seas, unrestricted submarine warfare of the Germans was much more deadly and costly to the United States. While official government policy was neutrality, Germany complained of America's aid to the Allies, especially shipments of arms and extension of credit.

The American military was unprepared to wage war. It was understaffed and short of supplies. A few farsighted Americans urged the establishment of officer training camps, but Congress reacted slowly. In 1916, a slight increase in manpower and equipment was authorized, but the United States was still far behind its European counterparts.

CAUSES OF UNITED STATES ENTRY INTO THE WAR

For over two years, the American government maintained neutrality, and Wilson campaigned for re-election in 1916, as the candidate "who kept us out of war." Still, hostility had been building toward Germany for several years, and the events of early 1917 dragged the United States into war.

Early in 1916, Wilson demanded an end to Germany's random sinking of merchant ships.

Wilson, no longer able to ignore the outward acts of aggression, asked Congress for a declaration of war. On 6 April 1917, Congress overwhelmingly approved (Senate vote: 82-6, House Vote: 273-50).

WILSON'S REASONS FOR WAR

"It is a war against all nations. American ships have been sunk, American lives taken...the ships and people of other neutral and friendly nations have been sunk and overwhelmed in the waters in the same way...Our motive will not be revenge or the victorious assertion of the physical might of the nation, but only the vindication of right."

WILSON'S AIMS: THE 14 POINTS

Early in 1918, President Wilson announced America's war aims and proposed a plan for world peace: *The 14 Points*. The plan included the following provisions:

- an end to secret diplomacy
- freedom of the seas
- free and open trade
- reduction of armament
- consideration for native populations in colonial areas
- self-determination for subject nationalities of Europe, including Poland, Czechoslovakia, and Alsace-Lorraine
- a general association of nations to protect the political independence and territorial integrity of all nations

The idealistic *14 Points* were distributed to all nations. The Central Powers, especially Germany, were hopeful for them becoming the basis for a just peace. The proposals met with objections from some of the Allied Powers, who hoped to gain strategic and economic benefits from the spoils of the war. These conflicting goals proved fatal for Wilson's plan.

THE AMERICAN EXPEDITIONARY FORCE

As in most of its wars, America was unprepared to send troops overseas in 1917. General John Pershing began organizing, equipping, and training 42 divisions of the nearly 4 million soldiers raised from volunteers and the *Selective Service Act* (May 1917 draft). Pershing and some administrative units of the **AEF** (American Expeditionary Force) arrived in Europe in June. It took over six months before the first complement of 87,000 combat troops were transported across the Atlantic.

By 1917, the European war was at stalemate. With brutal but indecisive battles being fought desperately in the trenches of France, the Allies were starting to run out of men. Unrestricted submarine warfare was severely damaging Allied supply lines from America. Tsar Nicholas abdicated in March 1917. The Provisional Republican government, under Aleksandr Kerensky, pledged to fight on. By November 1917 when Lenin and Trotsky took over, discipline in the Russian Army collapsed. The **Bolshevik** (Marxist communists) government withdrew from the War; Russia formally surrendered to Germany in March of 1918.

Yet, the Central Powers were no better off for Russia's elimination. The British blockade choked off supplies. Austria could barely defend itself and made no headway against Italy or in the Balkans. In Mesopotamia, Palestine, and the Caucasus Mountains, the Ottoman Empire's forces were collapsing.

With Russia out of the War,

Jeannette Rankin
(©1998 National Woman's Hall of Fame)
www.greatwomen.org

German commanders Hindenburg and Ludendorff shifted thousands of troops to the Western Front, severely pressing Britain and France. However, the United States had a substantial fighting force on European soil by the spring of 1918. The AEF helped to stop the German advances at St. Mihiel, Chateau-Thierry, and Belleau Wood. Near the end of the War, American troops suffered heavy casualties leading the Allied counter offensive at Argonne Forest. America suffered 116,000 war deaths and 204,000 were wounded. The Great War took 8.5 million lives worldwide, and twice as many were wounded. Germany surrendered as the Allies neared the German border in November 1918.

WARTIME CONSTITUTIONAL ISSUES

Opposition to American involvement developed in varying degrees during every war that the United States has entered. World War I was no exception. A small but vocal group of Americans protested. The government instituted a tremendous propaganda campaign aimed largely at denouncing the Germans and uniting the American public. In the interest of national security, certain limits had to be placed on civil liberties. This resulted in the arrest of a number of individuals. Some ardent supporters of the war effort criticized the government for placing restrictions on basic constitutional freedoms.

THE PEACE MOVEMENT

A number of women's organizations opposed war in general and American entrance into the League of Nations in particular. Representative **Jeannette Rankin** (MT) voted against the declaration of war against Germany, and organized the American Women Opposed to the League of Nations. Another group, the **Women's International League for Peace and Freedom** opposed the League of Nations, because it still permitted war in certain cases. They also protested the use of income tax monies for military purposes.

ESPIONAGE AND SEDITION ACTS

To prevent obstruction of the war effort, Congress passed the *Espionage Act* (1917) and the *Sedition Act* (1918). The *Espionage Act* attempted to halt acts of disloyalty and closed the mails to publications that printed such material. The *Sedition Act* stipulated jail terms for those who disrupted the government's war effort, and prohibited the use of disloyal language. A number of patriotic Americans who supported the War were critical of these measures, citing them as unconstitutional restrictions on civil liberties.

OPPOSITION AND PATRIOTISM: THE DRAFT ISSUE

When the U.S. Congress declared war, not everyone believed that Americans should be forced to "make the world safe for democracy." Mention of a draft evoked bitter memories of Civil War riots and visions of German militarism. The urgent need for men convinced Congress to pass the *Selective Service Acts* in 1917 and 1918 which required registration of all men between the ages of 18 and 45. By the end of the war, nearly 5 million served in the military, 3 million of whom were draftees.

SCHENCK V. UNITED STATES* (1919): CLEAR AND PRESENT DANGER

Charles Schenck, secretary of the Socialist Party, printed and distributed pamphlets that discouraged young men from registering for the draft. This antiwar effort violated the 1917 *Espionage Act*. Schenck was arrested, convicted, and jailed. He appealed his conviction, claiming his First Amendment right to freedom of the press had been violated. The Supreme Court

I WANT YOU FOR U.S. ARMY
NEAREST RECRUITING STATION

accepted his appeal. A unanimous Court ruled against Schenck, pointing out that his actions were a "clear and present danger" to the security of the American people in wartime. This "clear and present danger" rule set a judicial precedent that has often been used to determine the constitutionality of measures which restrict free speech and press.

RADICAL ACTIVITIES

Socialists, communists, and anarchists were under close surveillance during the War. Socialist-Labor Party leader Eugene Debs spoke out against what Socialists called "the capitalist war" and was convicted under the *Espionage Act*. The Industrial Workers of the World (IWW) organized a number of strikes in mining industries during the War, delaying government production schedules. IWW leader "Big Bill" Haywood, and over 100 other "Wobblies," received jail sentences of up to 20 years for hindering the war effort. **Emma Goldman**, an anarchist from Russia, opposed militarism and the use of force. She received a two year jail sentence for speaking out against the draft, and was later deported to Russia.

RED SCARE – 1918-1919

As the Russian Revolutions developed in 1917, many Americans were not sorry to see an end to the autocratic rule of the Tsar. Yet the sudden withdrawal of Russia from the War and its takeover by the Bolsheviks presented new problems. At the end of World War I, some American troops were among the Allied forces sent to Siberia and other parts of Russia to prevent a German capture of Russian arms and to keep an eye on imperialistic Japan. The United States also tried to keep the communist Bolsheviks from gaining control of any military supplies. Fighting between the rival White Army (anti-communists) and Red Army (communists) continued for several years after the War. The United States give limited but ultimately unsuccessful aid to the White Army.

The Bolshevik Revolution and communist triumphs in the following years concerned many Americans. Some believed that the Bolsheviks' next move would be in the United States, and many blamed the small Communist and Socialist parties for a number of disruptive strikes. Several unexplained explosions between 1919-1921 were also blamed on these two groups.

In trying to stem the communist "red tide," several actions of questionable constitutionality occurred. As a result of a series of raids staged by U.S. Attorney General **A. Mitchell Palmer**, over 5,000 revolutionaries, anarchists, socialists, and communists were searched and detained without warrants. Civil rights and liberties were blatantly violated. Nearly 250 people – mostly Russian immigrants with American-born children – were forced to sign papers which the government used at summary immigration hearings with no counsel and led to deportation. Some states passed "criminal syndicalism" laws, which made it unlawful to advocate violent change. While the threat of a communist takeover in America was remote, the hysteria of the Red Scare made the possibility seem real.

MINI•ASSESSMENT (5-6)

1 At the outbreak of World War I, the U.S. government favored a policy of
   1 remaining neutral
   2 entering the War on the side of the Allies
   3 invading Europe in order to acquire territory
   4 settling conflict through an international peace organization

2 By implementation of the *14 Points*, President Wilson hoped to
   1 weaken Germany so it could never fight another war
   2 divide the territory of the Central Powers among the Allies
   3 formulate a peace which would help prevent further war
   4 set up democratic governments throughout Europe

3 Restrictions of constitutional guarantees during wartime most often involve
   1 free speech and press
   2 the quartering of soldiers
   3 the right to bear arms
   4 excessive bail

4 The fact that people opposed the draft during World War I indicated that
   1 German agents had infiltrated the government
   2 the American army was of adequate strength
   3 some Americans opposed mandatory military service
   4 France was not supplying her share of troops in the War

Constructed Response

"In ordinary times the defendants, in saying all that was said in the circular [that Schenck distributed] would have been within their constitutional rights. But the character of every act depends on the circumstances in which it is done ...The most stringent protection of free speech would not protect a man in falsely shouting "Fire!" in a theater and causing a panic...

"When a nation is at war, many things that might be said in a time of peace are such a hindrance to its efforts that their utterance will not be endured so long as men fight ..."

– Justice Oliver Wendell Holmes, Jr., Majority Opinion in *Schenck v. United States*, 1919.

1 According to Holmes, when would free speech not be protected by the First Amendment to the Constitution?

2 Why do courts take circumstances into account when determining justice?

EUROPE AT THE END OF WORLD WAR I

New States (Results of WWI Peace Treaties)

Norwegian Sea

NORWAY

SWEDEN

FINLAND

ESTONIA

DENMARK

Baltic Sea

LATVIA

LITHUANIA

GER.

North Sea

IRELAND

UNITED KINGDOM

BEL.

NETH.

LUX.

GERMANY

POLAND

Russia (U.S.S.R. after 1922)

CZECHOSLOVAKIA

FRANCE

SWITZ.

AUSTRIA

HUNGARY

Bay of Biscay

ITALY

YUGOSLAVIA

RUMANIA

BULGARIA

Black Sea

Caspian Sea

PORTUGAL

SPAIN

ALBANIA

GREECE

TURKEY

Mediterranean Sea

SYRIA

League of Nations Mandates

IRAN

French

PALESTINE

JORDAN

IRAQ

Italian

EGYPT

ARABIA

SEARCH FOR PEACE AND ARMS CONTROL: 1919-1930

President Wilson hoped to negotiate a fair and just peace, but power rivalries among the European nations frustrated attempts to implement many of his moral ideas. Ultimately, Wilson failed to get any treaty approved in the United States. Several political blunders, illness, and stubbornness resulted in Senate defeat of the *Treaty of Versailles*.

FOREIGN POLICY

Though disappointed with the results of World War I, the United States continued to have a limited involvement in international matters, especially measures to promote peace and arms control. The nation could have played a much larger role in foreign affairs between 1920-1940, but isolationist sentiment was strong.

TREATY OF VERSAILLES: WILSON'S ROLE

Amid some objections at home, President Wilson personally represented the United States at the **Versailles Peace Conference** near Paris. Especially critical were Senate Republicans, with whom the Democratic Wilson barely consulted during the negotiations. This was a fatal blunder. The Republicans controlled the Senate which would have to ratify any treaty President Wilson signed.

President Wilson, **David Lloyd George** (Britain), **Georges Clemenceau** (France), and **Vittorio Orlando** (Italy) dominated the Versailles Conference. Wilson soon discovered that secret treaties had been made at the start of the War, parceling out territory to the victors. Wilson decided compromise was the only solution, even if some of his *14 Points* had to be shelved. After several months at Versailles, a treaty was completed.

Wilson's most important goal, the creation of a League of Nations, was included in the Treaty, as well as self determination for several European nationalities. However, the President was unable to secure the adoption of his other points. The European powers demanded huge reparations from Germany, German disarmament, and in France's case, German territory. Colonial areas were put under League of Nations mandate, but still dominated by Europe.

Historians generally agree that Wilson did the best he could under the circumstances, at least in softening some of the Allies' more extreme demands. Fifteen years later, the vengeful *Treaty of Versailles* would come back to haunt the European powers as Hitler used the Germans' resentment to build his Third Reich.

LEAGUE OF NATIONS
HENRY CABOT LODGE & SENATE REJECTIONS

Despite its drawbacks, Wilson urged Senate ratification of the *Treaty of Versailles* in 1919. Led by **Henry Cabot Lodge** (MA, 1850-1924), the Republicans regained control of the Senate in the 1918 Congressional elections. They were especially opposed to American entrance into the League of Nations, which would require the U.S. to support the European members against acts of aggression. Opponents of the *Treaty of Versailles* also feared loss of sovereignty and the possibility of entangling alliances.

Although there were isolationist "irreconcilables" who would have nothing to do with the *Treaty of Versailles* or the League, Lodge and other moderate Republicans were willing to support the *Treaty of Versailles* "with reservations." They hoped these limits would protect the

United States and give Congress the final say on military commitments to Europe. Wilson refused to compromise with the Senators.

Instead, he embarked on a nationwide tour to gain public support for the treaty. Halfway through the tour, the exhausted Wilson suffered a stroke and remained in seclusion for the rest of his term of office.

The Senate took several votes on the Treaty, but political fighting led to rejection. The Republicans refused to approve the *Treaty of Versailles* as presented by President Wilson and Wilson directed the Democrats in the Senate to vote down any version of the Treaty which included the Lodge group's reservations.

Historians have blamed both the power-hungry Senate and Wilson's stubbornness as reasons for the failure to ratify the Treaty. Separate

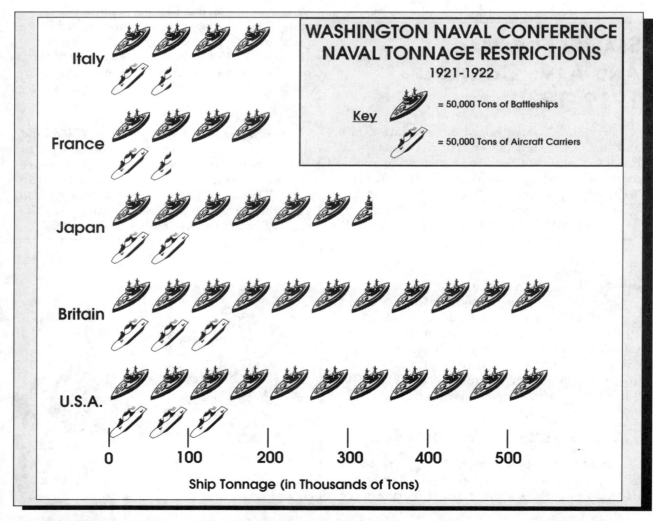

WASHINGTON NAVAL CONFERENCE NAVAL TONNAGE RESTRICTIONS
1921-1922

Key:
= 50,000 Tons of Battleships
= 50,000 Tons of Aircraft Carriers

Ship Tonnage (in Thousands of Tons)

peace agreements were finally made with Germany and other Central Powers in the 1920s.

WASHINGTON NAVAL ARMS CONFERENCE

While participation in the League was undesirable to U.S. leaders, the goal of avoiding war was not. In 1921 and 1922, Harding's Secretary of State, **Charles Evans Hughes** (1862-1948), sponsored an international meeting to address disarmament and peace issues.

During World War I, the United States and other nations embarked on major shipbuilding programs. The cost was a burden to taxpayers and complaints increased after the War ended. Growing demands for disarmament and questions about colonies and mandates in the Pacific led to support for a meeting of the great powers.

At the **Washington Conference** (1921-22), the United States, Great Britain, Japan, France, and Italy produced a *Five Power Naval Armaments Treaty* (1922). It put a 10-year moratorium on the construction of major ships (10,000 tons or more – battleships, cruisers). It also limited the gross tonnage of these ships that each nation could maintain to a 5-5-3-1-1 ratio. No limits were placed on smaller ships (destroyers, subs), and Japan continued to build these at a rapid pace.

While there was no enforcement machinery for the *Five Power Treaty*, it did slow the growth of the arms race, at least temporarily. Due to the expense of the War, most nations did not have the resources to devote to military construction. To meet the tonnage limit, Britain and the U.S. even scuttled some existing ships and some under construction (66 and 30 respectively). In 1930, the Washington agreement was expanded to other classes of ships at the 1930 London Naval Conference, but the system fell apart with the rise of militarism in the 1930s.

Hughes' Washington Conference also produced a *Four Power Treaty* (1921) to keep the peace among colonial powers in the Pacific. Signers of the *Nine Power Treaty* formally pledged recognition of the Open Door policy towards China. The treaties temporarily slowed Japan's burgeoning territorial expansion by guaranteeing the independence of China.

REPARATION AND WAR DEBTS

In the 1920s, U.S. diplomats remained active in other areas as well. As a result of the tremendous amount of money loaned by the United States during World War I, the nation changed from a debtor nation to a creditor nation – that is, foreign nations owed money to the United States. The U.S. government had loaned the Allies over 10 billion dollars, and expected repayment after the War.

With high tariffs restricting trade during the 1920s, the foreign governments found it difficult to raise money. While the United States extended payment time and lowered interest rates, much of the debt was still outstanding in 1930.

European governments claimed that they should not have to repay the debt since the U.S. did not experience physical destruction during the War, and suffered fewer casualties. In addition, the Allies pointed out that Germany had not paid war reparations levied in the *Treaty of Versailles*, a bill of nearly 33 billion dollars.

The American government still demanded payment in full, and eventually denied further loans to those still in arrears. No further payments were made, however, and the issue was eventually dropped as the Great Depression deepened.

KELLOGG–BRIAND PACT (1928)

One idealistic attempt to prevent war was the *Kellogg–Briand Pact* negotiated by the United States and France in 1928. The agreement, eventually signed by over 60 nations, outlawed war and required settlement of disputes by peaceful methods. However, the *Kellogg-Briand Pact* did permit the use of military force in the case of self defense. Since it endorsed the idea that war would have to be used to prevent war, the agreement had little practical value. *Kellogg-Briand* had League of Nations' backing, but like other agreements of this type, it had no enforcement apparatus and could not be implemented.

THE WORLD COURT

In an effort to settle international disputes, the League of Nations helped establish an independent **World Court** in 1920. It was suggested

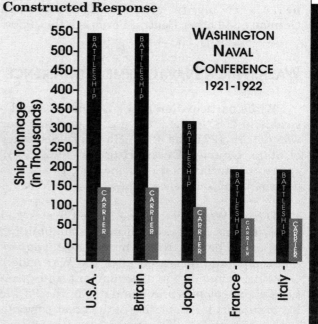
by Presidents **Warren Harding** (1865-1923) and **Calvin Coolidge** (1872-1933) that the United States become a member, but the Senate once again feared foreign entanglements. In 1926, an attempt to join was rejected by the World Court itself when the Senate added several "reservations" to United States membership. Franklin Roosevelt tried again in the 1930s but to no avail. By that time, the Senate reflected the deepening isolationist sentiments of the American public.

SUMMARY

America rolled into the 20th century with a great burst of industrial energy. The Progressives slowly gained momentum in assault on the abuses of big business and government corruption. Reformers made headway in banking and trade reform, safer and better working conditions, voting rights, and even control of alcoholic beverages. At the same time, laissez-faire faltered with each new commercial regulation and commission.

World War I officially brought the United States into the realm of European power politics. Nearly a generation of building naval power, acquiring colonies, and developing a worldwide trade were not enough to convince Americans that they need not play the power game in Europe. Rejecting the *Treaty of Versailles* and the League of Nations showed that the new power role was uncomfortable. The emotional reaction to the Red Scare unveiled a lingering public sentiment suspicious of the Old World. As the next decade would show, Americans' ideal of peace and prosperity lacked a global perspective.

UNIT ASSESSMENT

MULTI-CHOICE QUESTIONS

1 Civil service reform basically called for
   1 a system modeled after the one used by Andrew Jackson
   2 continuation of the spoils system
   3 issuance of jobs based on merit rather than political patronage
   4 increasing the federal bureaucracy

2 The abolitionists achieved their goal when which was ratified?
   1 Thirteenth Amendment
   2 the *Pendleton Act*
   3 Nineteenth Amendment
   4 primogeniture

3 Which is generally characteristic of a nation undergoing the process of industrialization?
   1 less opportunity for social mobility
   2 conflicts between religions
   3 shifts in the population from urban to rural areas
   4 increased reliance on the extended family to supply basic needs

4 The impact of the muckrakers finally decreased because
   1 their activities were eventually outlawed by the national government
   2 the cost of printing such journals became prohibitive
   3 Progressive politicians began instituting some changes
   4 there were very few muckrakers of note

5 Which statement best describes Progressive era support?
   1 Progressive supporters were predominantly from the rural, Western areas.
   2 Progressive support cut across political divisions, but was predominantly middle class.
   3 There are no general characteristics to describe those who advocated Progressivism.
   4 Progressive reformers were predominantly women of all social classes.

6 Publication of *The Jungle* by Upton Sinclair lead to
   1 creation of the Interstate Commerce Commission
   2 increased support for Margaret Sanger's activities
   3 ratification of the Nineteenth Amendment
   4 passage of the *Meat Inspection Act*

7 "Crouched over the (coal) chutes, the boys sit hour after hour, picking out the pieces of slate and other refuse...I once stood in a breaker for half an hour and tried to do the work a twelve-year-old boy was doing day after day, for ten hours at a stretch, for sixty cents a day. The gloom of the breaker appalled me..."   – John Spargo, 1906

   The author of this passage is most likely a(n)
   1 muckraker
   2 industrialist
   3 Populist
   4 supporter of W.E.B. DuBois

Base the answer to questions 8 and 9 on the chart below and your knowledge of U.S. history and government.

$0 – $3,000 = 0%
$3,001 – $20,000 = 1%
$20,001 – $30,000 = 2%

8 A tax based on the chart above is called a
   1 regressive tax
   2 progressive tax
   3 tariff
   4 poll tax

9 The authority for the United States Congress to pass such a tax was based on
   1 an amendment and a law
   2 a congressional statute
   3 a treaty
   4 voluntary approval of the states

10 The Federal Reserve Board has great control over the United States economy because it has the power to
   1 regulate the money supply
   2 increase and decrease income taxes
   3 determine the federal debt ceiling
   4 determine the value of the dollar abroad

11 Progressive reforms prompted the passage of a number of amendments to the Constitution including
1 prohibition of alcohol and creation of the Interstate Commerce Commission
2 protective tariffs and the Federal Reserve System
3 anti-trust prosecution and workers compensation
4 income tax and direct election of United States Senators

12 Theodore Roosevelt's attitude toward government control of business was that
1 only state governments had the authority to control business
2 a strict policy of laissez-faire should be followed
3 business at this point was uncontrollable
4 the federal government should eliminate bad business practices

13 Which statement is accurate regarding local and state Progressive reform?
1 It included such measures as referendum and recall which put more power in the hands of the voters.
2 It had little impact on national politics since the issues were regional rather than national.
3 It provided a training ground for radicals who led socialist revolutions in the 1930s.
4 It led to technological reform in agriculture.

14 The conquest of colonial areas was made easier in the second half of the 19th century because
1 most native populations were willing to be ruled by Europe
2 the native populations were usually Christian
3 new weapons and technology made conquests easier
4 European Christianity easily assimilated native religions

15 "We must bring the benefits of Western civilization and Christianity to the less fortunate." This idea has been used to justify
1 imperialism
2 socialism
3 nationalism
4 feudalism

16 The major goal of the U.S. Open Door Policy was to
1 aid the Chinese in the fight against communism
2 prevent Japan from invading China
3 weaken the Chinese Emperor
4 protect United States trading rights in China

17 "In our infancy we bordered upon the Atlantic only; our youth carried our boundary to the Gulf of Mexico; today, maturity sees us upon the Pacific. Whether they will it or not, Americans must now begin to look outward."

This late 19th century quotation best reflects a United States policy of
1 imperialism
2 militarism
3 isolationism
4 neutrality

18 During the early part of the 20th century, the basic goal of U.S. policy toward the nations of Latin America was to
1 spread democratic ideas throughout the area
2 provide the United States with more territory
3 support United States economic and political interests
4 form military alliances to counteract the growing power of European nations

19 The Dollar Diplomacy of the Taft Administration resulted in
1 the forming of military alliances to fight communism
2 increased animosity between the U.S. and Latin America
3 huge investment in the U.S. by Latin American nations
4 military takeover of most of the Latin American republics

20 Although the President is responsible for foreign policy, Wilson had to ask Congress
1 for a Proclamation of Neutrality
2 to sever relations with Germany
3 to condemn the sinking of the Lusitania
4 for a declaration of war against Germany

21 The Washington Naval Conference (1921-1922), was an attempt at
1 arms limitation
2 imperialism
3 free trade
4 mercantilism

22 In the case of *Schenck v. United States*, the Supreme Court ruled that an individual's
1 opposition to the draft during wartime must be tolerated
2 rights can be compromised if there is a clear and present danger to society
3 opposition to the draft is permitted by the constitutional guarantee of free speech
4 right to due process of law does not apply to the military

23 The "Red Scare" in the U.S. was indirectly a result of a communist revolution in
1 Germany
2 France
3 Russia
4 China

24 Which statement about the League of Nations is an opinion?
1 Senator Lodge was a leader in the fight to keep the U.S. out of the League.
2 President Wilson traveled widely to gather support for U.S. entry into the League.
3 The Senate's rejection of the *Treaty of Versailles* also blocked entry into the League.
4 Wilson's unwillingness to compromise kept the U.S. from joining the League.

25 Wilson should probably have worked more closely with the Senate during peace negotiations because
1 all treaties must be approved by a 2/3 vote of the Senate
2 Wilson needed Senate support to run for another term in 1920
3 the Senate was controlled by his own political party
4 the Senate was responsible for the war debts of the Allies

THEMATIC ESSAY QUESTION

Theme:

> **Reform**
>
> The patterns of American history show reform movements frequently altering society.

Task:

> Using your knowledge of United States history and government, write an essay in which you choose *three* major reforms that altered American society. For *each* one chosen:
>
> • describe the existing economic, social, or political conditions that caused the reform, and
> • discuss the impact of the change on American society.

Suggestions:
You may wish to focus on reforms concerning the working conditions, political equality, economic fairness, public welfare, or consumer protection. **You are not limited to these suggestions.**

DOCUMENT BASED QUESTION

The following task is based on the accompanying documents. The documents may have been edited for the purposes of this exercise. The task is designed to test your ability to work with historical documents. As you analyze the documents, take into account both the source of the document and the author's point of view.

Directions: Read the documents in Part A and answer the question after each document. Then read the directions for Part B and write your essay.

Historical Context:

As the 19th century came to a close, American leaders pursued a controversial policy of imperialism.

Task:

Using information from the documents and your knowledge of United States history and government, write an essay in which you

- discuss the advantages and disadvantages of an overseas empire for the United States, and
- compare and contrast the different viewpoints of late 19th and early 20th century on the appropriateness of an overseas empire for the United States.

Part A - Short Answer

Analyze the documents and answer the questions that follow each document.

DOCUMENT 1

"I walked the floor of the White House...and I went down on my knees and prayed to Almighty God...and one night late it came to me this way...that we could not give them back to Spain – that would be cowardly and dishonorable; that we could not turn them over to France or Germany, our commercial rivals in the Orient – that would be bad business and discreditable; that we could not leave them to themselves they are unfit for self-government...; and that there was nothing left to do but to take them all, and to educate the Filipinos, and uplift and Christianize them..."

– President McKinley to a group of Methodist ministers, October, 1898

Question for Document 1

Why would McKinley not want to see France or Germany take over the Philippines?

DOCUMENT 2

Question for Document 2

How is the cartoonist representing Uncle Sam's activities?

DOCUMENT 3

"The Anti-Imperialists were especially shocked about the situation in the Philippines. The Filipinos did not want to be ruled by the United States any more than by Spain. Led by Emilio Aguinaldo, they fought against the Americans. Guerrilla warfare went on for three years. The United States used more troops and spent more money than in the entire war against Spain."

– Daniel Boorstin, *A History of the United States Since 1861* [Ginn & Co., 1981]

Question for Document 3

Why were the Anti-Imperialists shocked?

Question for Document 4

Why does Denby think influence in the Far East is so important for America?

DOCUMENT 4

"If we give up the Philippines, we throw away the splendid opportunity to assert our influence in the Far East. We do this deliberately; and the world will laugh at us. Why did we take Manila [Philippine capital]? Why did we send 20,000 troops to Luzon [largest island]? There was no purpose in the conquest...if we did not intend to hold [them]. The Philippines are a foothold for us in the Far East. Their possession gives us standing and influence. It also gives us valuable trade in both imports and exports."

– Charles Denby, U.S. Commission on the Philippines, 1898

Questions for Document 5

1 Why were U.S. business people interested in expanding trade with China?

2 What areas were the most valuable trading partners for the United States in 1900?

DOCUMENT 5

U.S. FOREIGN TRADE IN 1900 (IN THOUSANDS OF DOLLARS)
SOURCE: HISTORICAL STATISTICS OF THE UNITED STATES

REGION	EXPORTS	IMPORTS	NET TRADE*
Europe	$1,040,168	$440,567	+ $599,601
North America	187,595	130,036	+ 57,559
Asia	67,554	145,814	– 78,260
Oceania	40,751	28,640	+ 12,111
South America	38,946	93,667	– 54,721
Africa	19,470	11,218	+ 8,252
Total	$1,394,483	$849,941	+ $552,794

Question for Document 6

Why does Twain say that U.S. behavior in the Philippine Insurrection contradicted our role as a nation?

DOCUMENT 6

"We have crushed and deceived a confiding people; we have turned against the weak and the friendless who trusted us; we have stamped out a just and intelligent and well-ordered republic; we have stabbed an ally in the back; we have robbed a trusting friend of his land and his liberty; we have invited our clean young men...to do bandits' work...; we have blackened [America's] face before the world."

– Mark Twain, *On the Philippine Insurrection*, 1898

GO ON TO PART B (on the next page)

Part B - Essay

Directions:
- Write a well organized essay that includes an introduction, several paragraphs, and a conclusion.
- Use evidence from the documents to support your response.
- Do not simply repeat the contents of the documents.
- Include specific related outside information.

Historical Context:
As the 19th century came to a close, American leaders pursued a controversial policy of imperialism.

Task:
Using information from the documents and your knowledge of United States history and government, write an essay in which you

- discuss the advantages and disadvantages of an overseas empire for the United States, and
- compare and contrast the different viewpoints of late 19th and early 20th century on the appropriateness of an overseas empire for the United States.

Be sure to include specific historical details. You must also include additional information from your knowledge of United States history and government.

UNIT

6

PAGE 223

ECONOMY: PROSPERITY, THEN, THE GREAT DEPRESSION

1920-

BABBITT (1920-1922)

HARDING SCANDALS (1924)

1925- *THE GREAT GATSBY* (1925)

"TALKIES" (1926)

LINDBERGH FLIES ATLANTIC (1927)

GREAT DEPRESSION (1929-1941)
NATIONAL ORIGINS ACT (1929)
STOCK MARKET CRASH (1929)
HAWLEY-SMOOT TARIFF (1930)

1930-

BONUS ARMY (1932)
FDR ELECTED (1932)

FDIC CREATED (1933)
"THE HUNDRED DAYS" (1933)
NRA ESTABLISHED (1933)
CCC ESTABLISHED (1933)
AAA FOUNDED (1933)

1935- *NATIONAL LABOR
RELATIONS ACT* (1935)
SOCIAL SECURITY (1935)

COURT PACKING (1937)

GRAPES OF WRATH (1939)

1940-

Pre-WW II upper middle class vacationers motor to a summer
resort in their 1937 General Motors Pontiac Sedan
(Retro-Americana, ©PhotoDisc)

FOREWORD

WAR ECONOMY AND PROSPERITY

In the years between the two world wars, America rode a roller coaster of economic highs and lows. The upswings were partly due to demand for goods from war-devastated Europe, but the instability was the result of human blunder and ignorance. The worldwide actions and inactions of governments, business leaders, and private individuals contributed to the massive economic collapse that came in the 1930s. Out of that sorry state of human misery, dictatorships arose that plunged the world into a second world war. This unit shows the complex economic interdependence of public and private institutions which shaped these events.

WAR ECONOMY

In April 1917, a reluctant President Woodrow Wilson went before Congress to ask for a declaration of war against the Central Powers. The moment Wilson dreaded had come; as Commander in Chief, he would now have to recruit, train, and send an American Expeditionary Force (AEF) to Europe. Congress granted him enormous emergency powers to mobilize the economy to support not only the AEF, but the allies as well. In doing so, Congress temporarily converted the United States into a partial **command economy**.

The basic U.S. system is a **market economy**. In a market, the aggregate (total) decisions of consumers and businesses give the economy its general direction with minimal governmental interference. In a command economy, a governmental authority plans and makes the basic economic decisions for the public.

GOVERNMENT BOARDS AND CONTROLS

The government began to command substantial sectors of the economy under its wartime authority. Wilson created a **Council of National Defense** made up of cabinet officers and civilian advisors. The Council established a number of agencies to organize economic forces of the home front. To run them, he also recruited experienced public servants, such as Food Administration head **Herbert Hoover** (1874-1964), and private businessmen, such as Wall Street financier **Bernard Baruch** (War Industries Board).

MOBILIZATION OF LABOR AND ARMED FORCES

Organized labor was represented on the Council of National Defense in the person of the A.F.of L. president, **Samuel Gompers**. He worked with Wilson to rally labor to a no-strike pledge and set up a War Labor Board to mediate disputes and grievances. Some of the labor force was siphoned into the military. Nearly half of all who served in the armed forces were volunteers, but Congress also passed the *Selective Service Act* (1917) which drafted nearly three million men by the end of the War.

GOVERNMENT OPERATION: RAILROADS, COMMUNICATION

Although arteries of transportation like railroads and the shipping industries were virtually

Note: Items marked with an * are listed in the *Landmark Supreme Court Decisions* chart in Appendices.

commandeered by the government, they were operated efficiently and were managed profitably. Official government communication was managed through the Committee on Public Information by Wilson advisor **George Creel**. Creel launched a massive propaganda campaign featuring anti-German news releases, posters, and slogans.

REVENUE SOURCES
AND FINANCIAL MANAGEMENT

 ECONOMIC POLICY

To pay for all of this, Congress raised taxes and authorized bond drives. The chart below indicates the extent of the government's management of the American economy during World War I.

WAR'S IMPACT ON
GENDER ROLES AND ON BLACKS

Volunteer enlistment and the draft combined to create a labor shortage. This increased the already large number of African Americans leaving the segregated South and migrating to industrial cities of the North. The accelerated pace of wartime industrial production easily absorbed nearly half a million African Americans. The increasing flow northward continued into the 1920s.

Women also filled some of the gaps, working in factories, and doing many jobs previously reserved for men. Many married women were forced into the labor market because of the lack of income when their husbands and fathers were drafted into military service.

RECONVERSION AND "NORMALCY"
1918-1920

As the War ended, the government began to **demobilize**, dropping its demand for war material. This caused a general **economic contraction** (decline), leading to production cuts, plant closings, layoffs, and widespread unemployment.

Freed from the restrictions of "wartime no-strike pledges," labor unions began a long series of bitter and sometimes violent strikes. However, the massive growth of industry during the War, along with the vast profits made, allowed most of the larger firms to manage through the conversion. Seeking to pull their lives back together, civilian workers and returning servicemen cashed in war bonds and began spending their savings on homes, autos, and other consumer goods. This new consumer demand gradually pulled the economy out of the postwar conversion depression.

In 1920, Presidential candidate **Warren G. Harding** (1865-1923) captured this mood when he accidentally coined a phrase indicating that a public weary of war, depression, and reform crusades now wanted a return to "normalcy."

ELEMENTS OF ECONOMIC COMMAND DURING WORLD WAR I	
FEDERAL AGENCIES	**ECONOMIC SECTORS MANAGED**
War Industries Board	allocated raw materials; supervised war production
War Labor Board	mediated labor disputes to prevent strikes
Shipping Board	built transports for men and materials
Railroad Administration	controlled and unified railroad operations
Fuel Administration	increased production of coal, gas, and oil; eliminated waste
Food Administration	increased farm output; public campaigns to conserve supplies
Raising funds for the War effort	Increased income and excise taxes; "Liberty Bond" and "Victory Bond" Drives

MINI•ASSESSMENT (6-1)

1 In general, the major economic problems of the 1917-1940 period were caused by the
 1 recovery from World War I devastation and reactions to the peace settlement
 2 high military expenditures for U.S. armed forces in the 1920s
 3 expense of implementing the Progressive Era consumer protection laws
 4 dictatorial way government managed the economy during World War I

2 In which type of economy is the primary decision-making power placed in the hands of government planners?
 1 free enterprise
 2 market
 3 command
 4 underdeveloped

3 What caused the 1919-1921 economic contraction?
 1 an increase in minority groups in the labor force
 2 investment of war profits by businesses
 3 people cashing in war bonds
 4 a decrease in government spending

Constructed Response

"To conserve fuel for winter use, on and after July 10, the nights of Monday, Tuesday, Wednesday, and Thursday of each week will be lightless...After July 15 all elevator service will be curtailed between 6:30 PM and 7:30 AM."

– Orders of the War Industries Board, 1 July, 1918

1 Why was the War Industries Board issuing these orders? [handwritten answer] to give fte to the soilders

2 Why was it unusual for a U.S. government agency to issue such an order? [handwritten answer] Being they put the war infrmb of the ppl.

THE 1920s

BUSINESS BOOM OR FALSE PROSPERITY?

Americans entered the 1920s disillusioned with world politics and wanting to put the experience of recent years behind them. They responded to the kind of sentiment Harding expressed with his "normalcy" phrase.

There was an intense desire to achieve the **American Dream** – to seek personal satisfaction, material wealth, and a trouble-free life. In such a mood, Americans were receptive to the unleashing of market forces by business which would characterize the wild, wonderful, but structurally uneven prosperity of the Twenties.

POST-WORLD WAR I RECESSION

The conversion from wartime to peacetime production was not smooth. It resulted in a short, but deep contraction (depression), which caused a great deal of discord at home and abroad.

WAR DEBT CONTROVERSY

Overseas, the situation was far more serious. All of the major industrial nations suffered economic devastation. Actually, the European Allies were victorious in name only. Against the vanquished Germans, they leveled **reparations** (harsh financial penalties), took away its colonies, and crippled its chances for recovery.

The long years of war savagely drained national treasuries. Both sides owed very large debts (chiefly to the United States). To pay the debts, governments levied increased taxes on already broken economies. This made recovery a longer and more painful experience.

AVARICE AND SCANDAL: TEAPOT DOME

At home, Americans did their best to forget the War and the problems in Europe. In an atmosphere which seemed to be a reaction to Progressivism and Wilsonian idealism, most wanted to forget political affairs altogether and to enjoy the promise of American prosperity.

Harding's *normalcy* shifted political leadership toward Congress, and without a watchful press and public, special interest groups easily got their way. Harding unwittingly allowed unscrupulous individuals to take advantage of the public's mood of apathy. The result was a number of unsavory scandals involving the "Ohio Gang"; associates to whom Harding generously gave jobs. As the scandals emerged, Harding died from an embolism (blocked blood vessel) during a trip to Alaska.

The most famous scandal was the **Teapot Dome Affair**. Harding's Secretary of the Interior, Albert Fall, was convicted in 1924 of accepting bribes to lease government oil reserves in California and Wyoming to private companies. The Custodian of Alien Property, Thomas Miller, was found guilty of fraud in 1925. Also in 1925, the Director of the Veterans Bureau, Charles Forbes, was convicted of mishandling funds for hospital supplies. Finally in 1927, Harding's Attorney General, Harry M. Daugherty, was tried on conspiracy charges.

COOLIDGE PROSPERITY

After the brief **post-war contraction** (1919-21), American business began to take advantage of new production and distribution ideas developed during the war to focus on the consumer market. Business improved on assembly-line patterns set up earlier in the century by Henry Ford.

Electricity, more available as a result of expanded war production, changed factory production and working hours. Mass advertising campaigns became widespread. Industry adopted the scientific analysis theories developed by efficiency expert **Frederick Winslow Taylor**.

Corporations sometimes streamlined their operations by questionable mergers that brought them into conflict with government antitrust laws. Harding's administration tried to return to the laissez-faire attitude of the pre-Progressive Era. Government officials tended to "look the other way" when they could have been bringing anti-trust suits against many of these mergers.

Both Harding and his successor, Calvin Coolidge, believed firmly that the leadership and prosperity of America was best left in the hands of the businessman. They wanted to keep government out of the way of business as much as possible. The principal business regulatory agencies (Interstate Commerce Commission [ICC], Federal Reserve Board, and Federal Trade Commission) were run by bureaucrats who reflected the laissez-faire attitude.

Even the Supreme Court announced that it would apply the "rule of reason" in anti-trust prosecutions. This meant it adopted a more lenient attitude toward business activities than it had in the Progressive Era.

PROBLEMS ON THE FARM

Agriculture did not follow the pattern of prosperity. During the War, farmers greatly expanded production to feed our allies. After the War, American farmers continued to feed millions through the international relief effort headed by Herbert Hoover. However, by the mid-1920s, Europe's recovery cut back this profitable demand.

American farmers had to pay off new machinery purchased during the War. They continued to produce more. However, world demand for their produce declined, and even technology began to work against them. Refrigeration and transportation improvements, which allowed larger farmers to compete in far off markets, ran smaller local farmers out of business. To fight back against high U.S. tariffs, many nations reciprocated (responded in similar fashion) with high tariffs of their own. This diminished the chances of U.S. farmers to sell their surplus overseas.

THE MELLON TAX REDUCTIONS, TARIFF MANIPULATIONS, AND RECIPROCATION

While adopting a laissez-faire attitude toward mergers, the government stimulated business through its tax policies. It encouraged investment by reducing corporate taxes. It also stimulated consumer spending by reducing personal income taxes. This stimulation policy was mainly the idea of millionaire financier **Andrew Mellon** (1855-1937), Secretary of the Treasury for both Harding and Coolidge.

Mellon also pressured Congress to pass the enormously high protective tariffs (*Fordney-McCumber Act*, 1922 and the *Hawley-Smoot Act*, 1930). These acts aimed at shielding American manufacturing European competition as it recovered after World War I. This protectionism backfired when the Europeans and Japanese reciprocated with their own high tariff duties against American goods.

SPECULATIVE BOOM IN STOCKS

During the 1920s, Americans were optimistic about the material changes in society and their personal lives. Although the increase in wealth was far less dramatic than commonly believed, the optimism led many to blindly risk their life savings in stocks and real estate.

Brokers on Wall Street were enjoying a boom in stock purchases and profits. They called it the "Big Bull Market" as stock prices rose rapidly. Many brokers accepted **margin** purchases (paying only a fraction of the stock's value). Some banks allowed customers to borrow money just to buy the stocks on margin. The result of all this fractional transacting was overvalued stock prices. This was an over inflated market. But a giddy optimism kept things afloat. With no government oversight, unscrupulous characters drew unsuspecting people into deceptive stock schemes. Real growth and productivity was nowhere near the prices of the stocks of many companies. People invested blindly, and the economy grew more unstable as the decade continued.

CONSUMERISM AND CLASH OF CULTURE

The Twenties was an age of bewildering contrasts. New inventions were changing daily life at a rapid pace. In the fast-moving society, personal beliefs and long-held traditions were ques-

---

MINI•ASSESSMENT (6-2)

1 Which aided business growth in the early and middle 1920s?
   1 technological advancement, mergers, and efficiency
   2 progressive legislation by Congress
   3 government anti-trust prosecutions
   4 generous wage agreements with labor

2 The widespread stock speculation in the 1920s revealed that
   1 the government strictly enforced financial regulations
   2 efficiency studies improved industrial production
   3 farming income declined
   4 over confidence made investors reckless

3 Secretary of the Treasury Mellon's tax policies
   1 favored big business
   2 aided European economic recovery
   3 were opposed by the Supreme Court
   4 improved farm production

Constructed Response

Harding (Republican)
Total Electoral Votes = 404
Total Popular Vote = 16,143,000

Cox (Democratic)
Total Electoral Votes = 127
Total Popular Vote = 9,130,000

0   500 Miles

1 How was the election divided geographically?

2 What was the margin of victory in the popular vote? In the electoral vote?

tioned. The mood was a combination of strange uneasiness, optimism, and over confidence. It produced an underlying social tension which showed itself in a variety of ways.

CONSUMERISM

The economy became focused on the middle class consumer, and nothing was more symbolic of this new consumer society than the automobile. Wartime demand had forced many of the older, custom-built auto manufacturers to adopt Ford's mass-production techniques. Production surpassed demand. Cars were available, but too expensive for the middle class. Instead of dropping prices to keep the market alive, manufacturers and banks popularized credit-buying. With the **installment plan**, they made it easy for consumers to borrow for a high priced item and then make small payments (with interest) over a period of time.

The installment plan revolutionized the auto industry, and the registration of autos tripled. The auto changed middle class lifestyles dramatically. As road construction and tourism increased, many Americans saw in the auto a chance to have their families live away from the noise, congestion, and fast pace of the cities. The auto allowed people to commute to work and live a more peaceful life in the open spaces of suburbia. A suburban real estate boom began in the middle 1920s. Like the stock market, however, low down payments and long-term mortgages fueled the speculative nature of this real estate boom. It became another staging ground for dishonest schemes. Many lost vast sums of hard-earned money.

Charlie Chaplain

A better life-style for the middle class meant more leisure time, and a host of technical advancements led to the entertainment business becoming a major part of the American economy. No longer was entertainment centered in the vaudeville theatres of the big cities. The film industry took movies into every town. By decade's end, the "silents" gave way to "talkies." Over the air waves, radio shows aggressively promoted sponsors' products in nearly everyone's parlor.

Educational advances changed the publishing industry. Readership of newspapers and older popular magazines, such as *The Saturday Evening Post*, and *Colliers*, multiplied. Many new periodicals including *Time, Newsweek, Reader's Digest, Life, The New Yorker*, and others began and flourished during the inter-war period.

CONSTITUTIONAL AND LEGAL ISSUES

During World War I, propaganda and fear made Americans more suspicious of subversive activities. Intolerance against German sympathizers grew, but it also spread to any groups that reflected foreign influences (immigrants, Catholics, Jews, African Americans, and radicals). The fear and emotionalism of wartime continued in the economic and political turmoil of 1918-1920. In times of emotional stress, individual rights can be trampled in the "best interest" of the state.

As the World War I drew to a close, nearly 3,600 strikes broke out nationwide. Workers sought to hold on to the wage and hour gains they made during the War. A wave of fear generated by radical labor groups made the situation worse. Radicals urged American workers to follow the lead of the Bolsheviks who had just taken power in Russia. Strike-plagued employers played on public fears by condemning all strikes as revolutionary. In the spring of 1919, radicals were blamed for a series of nationwide terrorist bombings aimed at public officials. During this "Red Scare," Wilson's Attorney General, A. Mitchell Palmer (1872-1963), sanctioned a series of Justice Department raids against the headquarters of radical groups in thirty-three cities. In these Palmer Raids, over 3,000 people were denied due process rights such as habeas corpus, reasonable bail, defense lawyers, and jury trials. Over 550 aliens among them were arrested and eventually deported.

Denial of due process and anti-immigrant sentiment were also issues in the celebrated **Sacco-Vanzetti Trial**. The two Italian immigrants, avowed anarchists, were arrested by Massachusetts officials and tried for robbery and murder on weak, circumstantial evidence. By the time they were executed in 1927, the case and its appeals had come to symbolize the atmosphere of repression in the country.

Xenophobia (emotion-ridden anti-foreign feeling) was also at the heart of the unusual resurgence of the Ku Klux Klan (KKK) in the 1920s. The new version of the Klan (its predecessor had been outlawed in the South during Reconstruction) attracted thousands of Americans throughout the nation to its racist, anti-foreign teachings. It was influential in pressuring Congress to pass a series of restrictive immigration acts. The tense years after World War I saw a renewal of the massive waves of immigrants and anti-immigrant sentiment grew. Congress passed the *National Origins Act* in 1929, which limited immigration with a set of quotas aimed at restricting Southern and Eastern Europeans and Asians.

Repression of ideas became an issue in the celebrated **Scopes Monkey Trial** in 1925. A young teacher was prosecuted for violating a state law forbidding the teaching of Darwin's theories of evolution in Tennessee. **William Jennings Bryan** (1860-1925) successfully championed the views of fundamentalist groups trying to stop the teaching of evolution. Scopes' defense under **Clarence Darrow** (1857-1938) failed. The Supreme Court later overturned Scopes' conviction and declared similar state laws unconstitutional in 1968.

The deep social divisions in the nation in the 1920s were also illustrated by passage of the Eighteenth Amendment to the Constitution. Long desired by reformers, prohibition cut down the nation's alcohol consumption, but it also caused a substantial rise in crime.

Prohibition aimed at regulating moral alcohol abuse. In the rapidly changing society of the 1920s,

it failed. There was no general agreement on what proper moral behavior was. Prohibition was repealed by the Twenty-first Amendment in 1933.

SHIFTING CULTURAL VALUES

In the 1920s, American culture was rapidly transformed by technology and science. The genteel traditions of a rural society fell away as those of a new, fast-paced urban society took hold.

The younger generation was disillusioned by the bloody experience of war in Europe. Young people seemed to openly reject the past and embrace the new life-style which placed material pleasure and personal wealth above patriotism or service to others. The rise of the entertainment industry, the popularity of the phonograph, the growth of night clubs, and the faster pace of ragtime and jazz music along with dances like the Charleston, showed a changing pace of life.

By 1920, a powerful combination of factors had begun to break down earlier **Victorian ideals** about the status of women. Broader educational opportunity for women gradually took hold in the industrial era. During the War, women put that education to use in playing new, vital economic roles. The Nineteenth Amendment, women's suffrage, gave them a new political status. This combination of changes in economic and political status created a feeling of female emancipation. It showed itself in new fashions: short skirts, slacks, and shorts. It also showed itself in the break-down of old social restrictions: disappear-ance of chaperones, increasing participation in sports, and co-ed schools.

This re-evaluation of the role of women raised moral questions. It caused a more open discussion of sexual behavior, which often shocked and embar-rassed the older gener-ation. It changed thinking about marriage, and divorce rates rose in the 1920s.

The 1920s produced literature that reflected the unsettled mood of the times. Among the works portraying disillusion and frustration are those of novelists **F. Scott Fitzgerald** (*The Jazz Age, The Beautiful and the Damned, The Great Gatsby*), **Ernest Hemingway** (*The Sun Also Rises*), and **Sinclair Lewis** (*Main Street, Babbitt*), and poets and playwrights such as **T.S. Eliot** (*The Waste Land*) and **Eugene O'Neill** (*Emperor Jones*).

In the opening decades of the 20th centu-ry, many African-Americans moved north, escaping the Jim Crow system of the South. The freedom of the Jazz Age also saw a new cultural consciousness among them as they expressed their hopes and frustrations in the arts. The novels of **Langston Hughes** and **Jean Toomer**, along with the poetry of **Claude McKay** and **Countee Cullen**, and the music of **Duke Ellington**, **Louis Arm-strong**, and **Bessie Smith** became the cen-ter of a movement known as the **Harlem Renaissance**.

THE GREAT DEPRESSION

ONSET OF THE DEPRESSION

To those groups that did well during the 1920s, the technological and social advance-ments made it seem like a golden age. In 1928,

---

MINI•ASSESSMENT (6-3)

1   Which invention had the greatest socio-economic change on American life in the 1920s?
    1   the phonograph
    2   cinematography
    ③   refrigeration
    4   the automobile

2   Prohibition was a political attempt to
    ①   correct social problems
    2   limit due process rights
    3   fight organized crime
    4   censure academic freedom

3   Writers of the 1920s,
    1   glorified technological achievement
    2   questioned the materialism of the age
    ③   encouraged a return to traditional values
    4   focused on patriotic themes

Constructed Response:

"Sometimes,...[a] whisper in the trombones swings me back into the early Twenties when we drank wood alcohol, and every day in every way we were better, and there was a first abortive shortening of skirts, and girls all looked alike in sweater dresses,...it seemed only a matter of time before the older people would step aside and let the world be run by those who saw things as they were..."

– F. Scott Fitzgerald, *Taps at Reveille*, 1935

1   Who does Fitzgerald claim "saw things as they were"?

2   Why did the mood of the 1920s seem so reckless and rebellious?

    Alot of drugs.

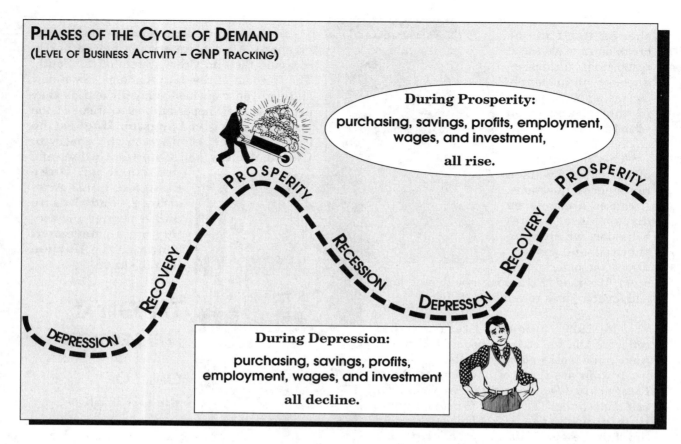

PHASES OF THE CYCLE OF DEMAND
(LEVEL OF BUSINESS ACTIVITY – GNP TRACKING)

During Prosperity:
purchasing, savings, profits, employment, wages, and investment, all rise.

During Depression:
purchasing, savings, profits, employment, wages, and investment all decline.

Herbert Hoover, who became Calvin Coolidge's successor, said, "We in America are nearer to the final triumph over poverty than ever before in the history of any land." Gross National Product (GNP) shot up 50% in the decade and the "American Dream" seemed to have become a reality.

WEAKNESSES IN THE ECONOMY

It is natural to have ups and downs in a market economy, especially one as large and diverse as that of the United States. Demand for goods and services, savings, investments, and employment can never be perfectly in line in a system that allows freedom of choice. Combinations of hundreds of factors cause the economy to soar at times and decline in others. The illustration above is a graphic representation of this **cycle of demand**, or what some economists call the "business cycle."

Industrialization made most Americans aware of the cycle, but there was something very different about the collapse of 1929-1932. It was much worse than ever before. Economists list many reasons for this:

• During the Twenties, the wealth flowed into the hands of only 5-10% of the population. American manufacturers overproduced massive amounts of goods. As the years went by, the number of people who could afford to buy goods actually declined. The number of those who could consider themselves middle class stagnated.

• Wages did not kept pace with the rising GNP. Farmers, miners, and textile workers' incomes declined after the mid-1920s. The number of poor Americans grew rapidly after 1925. Consumer purchasing began to level off.

• Government saw some of the signs, but the Harding-Coolidge-Hoover administrations were locked into a laissez-faire philosophy. They refused to "tamper" with income taxes and interest rates or make use of the regulatory power that government had acquired in the Progressive Era.

• To make matters worse, after the stock market crash, businessmen's fear pressured Congress into raising tariffs even higher with the *Hawley-Smoot Act* (1930). It sealed off American markets from other nations, who reciprocated by raising their own tariffs against the United States. Without U.S. dollars circulating, buying American goods and paying debts to U.S. bankers became impossible. World trade dried up, and other national economies collapsed.

THE STOCK MARKET CRASH

In the 1920s, businesses showed enormous profits, and people rushed to buy shares in the "bull market" (rising stock prices). In the fall of 1929, little more than a year after Hoover had made his optimistic "final triumph" pronouncement, business declines caused public confidence to falter. Edgy stockholders began to sell shares rapidly. The "bear market" (falling stock prices) accelerated down hill. Slimly financed "margin loans" were called in by brokers. Many could not pay. The wave of selling turned into a panic. The economy collapsed so rapidly and completely that it left the nation and the world in a state of shocked disbelief.

THE HOOVER RESPONSE

Herbert Hoover was an accomplished businessman and one of the most talented public administrators ever to be elected to the White House (term 1929-1933). After less than a year in office, his administration had to struggle with the worst economic catastrophe in history. While he basically believed in laissez-faire – the market could repair itself, Hoover also felt government could help to battle the spiraling depression.

There were strong laissez-faire advocates among Hoover's advisors. Although Hoover supported some government spending to relieve suffering, his advisors would not allow any unbalancing of the budget to destroy business confidence. Hoover refused to centralize power. He felt it would take power from state and local governments and destroy individual freedom. Hoover held White House conferences with business leaders to encourage increased production and wage stability, but little improvement came from these meetings.

Hoover did increase expenditures on public works projects. He also put a moratorium (suspension) on war debt payments by European nations to the U.S. He even set up the **Reconstruction Finance Corporation** (RFC) which helped save numerous businesses from bankruptcy.

As the decade of the Thirties opened, Hoover's efforts were too restrained. The economy continued to spiral downward. In 1932, the Gross National Product was half of what it was in 1929. In those same years, more than 5,000 banks closed. Wages and prices continued to fall, and unemployment rose sharply.

Americans were bewildered and shocked by the economic collapse. At first, most people did not expect government to act. There had never been a tradition of large-scale government intervention. However, by 1932, people were clearly expecting more decisive leadership. In June of that year, destitute veterans sought a bonus promised to them by Congress. From all over the nation this **Bonus Army** descended on Washington for mass marches. When the bonus bill failed, a nervous Hoover allowed Army Chief of Staff **General Douglas MacArthur** (1880-1964) to lead U.S. Army troops in dispersing the veterans with bayonets and tear gas, setting fire to their camps.

	LABOR FORCE AND UNEMPLOYMENT: 1929-1941 (NUMBERS IN MILLIONS)		
YEAR	LABOR FORCE	NUMBER UNEMPLOYED	PERCENT UNEMPLOYED
1929	49.2	1.6	3.2
1930	49.8	4.3	8.7
1931	50.4	8.0	15.9
1932	51.0	12.1	23.6
1933	51.6	12.8	24.9
1934	52.2	11.3	21.7
1935	52.9	10.6	20.1
1936	53.4	9.0	16.9
1937	54.0	7.7	14.3
1938	54.6	10.4	19.0
1939	55.2	9.5	17.2
1940	55.6	8.1	14.6
1941	55.9	5.6	9.9

The public was outraged. That summer, farmers tried to organize a general strike to withhold their produce to drive prices up, but it collapsed in disillusion. It was an election year, desperation was growing, and the people began to see Hoover's leadership as timid and frightened. He was soundly defeated at the polls in November.

Franklin Delano Roosevelt

FDR AND THE NEW DEAL

RELIEF, RECOVERY, AND REFORM

In Hoover's place, the nation elected Democrat **Franklin Delano Roosevelt** (1882-1945, served 1933-1945) in a massive **landslide vote** (overwhelming victory). FDR won 59% of the popular votes (23 million to Hoover's 16 million), but 88% of the electoral vote (472-59).

At first glance, it seemed strange that the common people turned to a patrician (upper class) New Yorker, born to wealth, and not at all like the self-made Hoover. Roosevelt's wealthy parents raised him on the family's beautiful estate in Hyde Park, NY and sent him to upper class schools. After a brief private law practice, he entered New York State politics. He was not a social reformer, but he was attracted to the Progressive Movement because of his concern for human suffering.

Roosevelt enthusiastically supported the progressive Woodrow Wilson in 1912, and was named Assistant Secretary of the Navy as a reward. In 1920, he ran for Vice President on the Democratic ticket with James M. Cox. They

---

MINI•ASSESSMENT (6-4)

1   A major reason for the collapse of the American economy after 1929 was
    ① the failure of the prohibition experiment
    2   over-regulation of banking by the Federal Reserve
    3   restriction of the free flow of immigration
    4   wage levels did not keep pace with economic growth

2   Economic thinking which dominated the Republican administrations of the 1920s rested on creating prosperity by
    1   implementing programs favorable to business investment
    ②   stimulation of military spending
    3   setting production incentives for agriculture
    4   expanding the lower class' consumption capacity

3   As the Great Depression deepened, President Hoover

1   refused to launch programs to aid the needy
②   adopted a limited program to aid business investment
3   pressed Congress to lower tariffs
4   demanded European nations pay their war debts

Constructed Response

"You cannot extend the mastery of government over the daily working life of the people without, at the same time, making it the master of people's souls and thoughts."
– Herbert Hoover, 1930

1   According to Hoover, what is the danger of creating massive government agencies to help people? *You cant control ppl.*

2   If new federal agencies would not help in the face of the Great Depression, what approach did Hoover and the Republicans advocate?

---

were soundly defeated by Warren Harding and Calvin Coolidge (404 electoral votes to 127).

A year later, Roosevelt was tragically paralyzed with polio and never regained the use of his legs. In 1928, he narrowly succeeded in winning election as Governor of New York. His willingness to help people cope with the Depression helped him not only win reelection in 1930, but put him in a position to easily gain the Democratic nomination for President in 1932.

He was a vigorous campaigner, displaying confidence with his "Happy Days Are Here Again" theme song. He was an inspiring orator – "I pledge you, I pledge myself, to a new deal for the American people." He criticized Hoover's lack of action, but he was vague about his own programs.

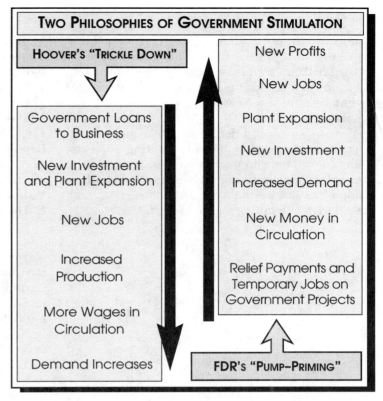

TWO PHILOSOPHIES OF GOVERNMENT STIMULATION

HOOVER'S "TRICKLE DOWN"

Government Loans to Business

New Investment and Plant Expansion

New Jobs

Increased Production

More Wages in Circulation

Demand Increases

New Profits

New Jobs

Plant Expansion

New Investment

Increased Demand

New Money in Circulation

Relief Payments and Temporary Jobs on Government Projects

FDR'S "PUMP–PRIMING"

THE NEW DEAL PHILOSOPHY

Actually, FDR had only a few programs in mind, but he did represent a different philosophy of government's role in the economy. Hoover and the Republicans followed a **trickle-down theory.** They believed in working from the top downward. They reasoned that, if government legislation protected the wealth of big corporations and the well-to-do, their continued investments would expand the economy and a better life would "trickle down" to workers and consumers in general.

FDR and his advisors viewed things differently. They felt that government should use **pump-priming** – that government should take actions that would make the consuming public secure and optimistic. They believed in working from the bottom up. By increasing government programs, business activity would increase, thereby fostering consumer confidence and investment – keeping the economy growing.

Roosevelt felt that in an economic contraction, government must first take **relief** actions to stabilize the economy, then **recovery** actions to stimulate it. From his earlier experiences in the Progressive Movement, Roosevelt felt that the system needed basic changes (**reform**) to keep it functioning. Later, this idea would

become part of a more complex formal theory in British economist **John Maynard Keynes'** (1883-1946) *General Theory on Employment, Interest, and Money* (1936), which would challenge the classical approach to market economics and advocate an activist role for government.

FDR AS GOVERNOR OF NEW YORK

FDR became the new governor of New York State in 1929. He inherited a state which had gone through much social reform under his predecessor, **Alfred E. Smith** (1873-1944). Smith left to run for President as the Democratic Presidential candidate against Herbert Hoover in 1928. In less than a year, Roosevelt was faced with helping his state deal with the **Great Depression**. New York was hard hit with unemployment.

With the federal government reluctant to aid the states, Governor Roosevelt had to take the initiative. With the New York State Legislature's cautious approval, he set up the Temporary Emergency Relief Agency (TERA). He chose a young social worker, **Harry Hopkins** (1890-1946), to be its head. Later, Hopkins became a central figure of President Roosevelt's New Deal.

Many others who were with Roosevelt's administration in Albany later became cabinet officers and White House advisors (**Henry Morganthau, Frances Perkins**). In New York, this influential group laid the groundwork for what became the New Deal. They guided many measures through the state legislature that called national attention to the state and its governor: work-relief on public building projects; minimum wage and maximum hour laws; old-age insurance, unemployment relief; increased school aid; a gas tax to finance road construction; and, regulation of banking and public utilities.

Eleanor Roosevelt, wife of FDR, often helped the president by substituting for him at ceremonial events. (Here she tours a U.S. Army base during World War II.)

Eleanor Roosevelt (1884-1962) strongly influenced FDR's return to public life after he was stricken with polio in the early 1920s. She played a vital role in the years he was governor. She campaigned hard and often made public appearances when it was impossible for her husband. Touring the state, she saw suffering and returned to Albany to press her husband for action. Her sympathy for disadvantaged youth, women, and minorities was enormously influential.

To alleviate unemployment, Governor Roosevelt had his Public Works Commissioner, **Robert Moses**, construct 5,000 new acres of parks, miles of parkways, many connecting bridges, and two new subway lines. In New York City alone, Moses directed the completion of the Triborough Bridge complex, two new subway lines, and a new airport (later to be named in honor of Mayor LaGuardia).

In 1932, the same year that the dynamic FDR won election to the White House, New York City elected a new and equally energetic mayor, **Fiorello LaGuardia** ("The Little Flower," 1882-1947). This son of Italian-Jewish immigrants led an astonishing career as an Ellis Island interpreter, diplomat, criminal prosecutor, WW I combat pilot, and maverick Republican congressman. He became one of the greatest reformers in the city's history. He recruited a tough Police Commissioner, **Lewis Valentine**, and a special prosecutor, **Thomas E. Dewey**, to fight crime and corruption.

Despite the fact that LaGuardia and FDR were of different parties, they worked well together. With one billion dollars in federal aid, LaGuardia put the nearly bankrupt city back on its feet. The activist mayor began the first major publicly-funded housing project in the nation. LaGuardia was also instrumental in arranging federal guarantees for the Metropolitan Life Insurance Company to build the largest privately-funded housing development in the nation, Parkchester (Bronx County).

THE NEW DEAL ADMINISTRATION

"THE BRAIN TRUST"

Roosevelt carried the momentum and high powered personnel from New York to Washington in March of 1933. Louis Howe remained at his side as a personal advisor. Henry Morganthau and Frances Perkins became cabinet members. Raymond Moley and Rexford G. Tugwell headed a brilliant group of personal advisors nicknamed **"The Brain Trust."** They were dynamic, pragmatic thinkers, ready to try new ideas to aggressively attack the problems of the depression. Perhaps the most famous of these was Harry Hopkins, a mid-western social worker, who headed up the work-relief programs. Later, Hopkins was FDR's chief foreign policy advisor and trouble-shooter during World War II.

RELIEF OF HUMAN SUFFERING

Once in the White House, FDR focused on relief, recovery, and reform to get the national economy functioning. In the first three months of his administration, nicknamed the "Hundred Days," he and his staff rushed a mass of "3R's" legislation through Congress. The breathtaking

THE NEW DEAL'S 3-RS

PRESIDENT AND ADVISORS
(SUGGEST LEGISLATION)

↓

CONGRESS
(LEGISLATES PROGRAMS)

↙ ↓ ↘

RELIEF	RECOVERY	REFORM
Immediate Action to Halt the Economy's Deterioration	"Pump- Priming" Temporary Programs to Restart the Flow of Consumer Demand	Permanent Programs to Avoid Situations Causing Contractions and Insurance for Citizens Against Economic Disaster
Bank Holiday Emergency Banking Act Federal Emergency Relief Act Civil Works Administration	Agricultural Adjustment Act National Industrial Recovery Act Home Owners Loan Corp. Works Progress Administration	Securities and Exchange Commission Federal Deposit Insurance Corp. Social Security Administration National Labor Relations Board

scope and pace of "The Hundred Days" raised public confidence. Immediate relief measures had to be taken to stop the downward trend of the economy.

The nation's banking system was on the verge of total collapse. On 5 March 1933, Roosevelt closed all the nation's banks, declared a "Bank Holiday," and called Congress into special session. The *Emergency Banking Act* was passed. Treasury officials, under Secretary Henry Morganthau, examined banks and let solvent ones reopen.

Congress rushed through the *Federal Emergency Relief Act* (FERA) to give direct aid to the poor and starving in the country.

Congress created the **Civil Works Administration** (CWA, 1933-34) to ease unemployment. Under Relief Administrator Harry Hopkins, the CWA created over three million work-relief jobs repairing roads, parks, and pub-

lic buildings. Criticized as wasteful, Congress replaced the CWA with the larger **Works Projects Administration** (WPA) in 1935. Between 1935 and 1941, the WPA employed 8 million workers and spent $11 billion on highway, park, post office, and school construction. Another Congressional measure was the **Civilian Conservation Corps** (1933-1942). The CCC enrolled over 2.5 million unemployed young men in a military-like organization doing reforestation and flood-control work.

ECONOMIC RECOVERY

Relief measures helped people survive, but they were insufficient to move the economy upward. **Recovery** meant short-term programs to generate demand in the marketplace to encourage the natural flow of supply and demand.

Stimulation measures (pump-priming) were passed to start industry and agriculture moving again. To create production incentives, Congress created the *National Industrial Recovery Act* (NIRA) and *Agricultural Adjustment Act* (AAA).

The NIRA was a complex scheme involving voluntary industrial codes (rules) on production quotas, price agreements, and wage guarantees. It was mobilized by the **National Recovery Administration** (NRA) in a vast patriotic campaign with rallies, parades, and its own "Blue Eagle" symbol.

The AAA was a similarly complex program to aid destitute farmers and to manage agricultural production and prices. Legal challenges eventually ended in both of these programs being declared unconstitutional (the NRA in 1935 and the AAA in 1936).

To stimulate the construction industry, Congress created the **Home Owners Loan Corporation** (HOLC) which set up the **Federal Housing Administration** (FHA) to guarantee mortgages and spur home purchasing. It also made money available so people could refinance mortgages, giving more stability to the banking industry.

SEARCH FOR EFFECTIVE REFORM

Amid the whirlwind of New Deal legislation, Roosevelt also led Congress to seek permanent reform of the economic system. These changes made life more secure and helped avoid many of

ECONOMIC POLICY

MINI•ASSESSMENT (6-5)

1   In the campaign of 1932, Franklin Delano Roosevelt
    1   had no previous experience in dealing with the Depression
    2   supported the "trickle-down theory"
    3   made only vague promises about fighting the Depression
    4   denounced Hoover's progressivism

2   During the "Hundred Days" in 1933, Congress
    1   passed many work-relief programs
    2   blocked FDR's New Deal
    3   fought the President to preserve laissez-faire policies
    4   eliminated the unemployment problem

3   Which statement reflects the New Deal approach to social responsibility?
    1   Interaction between buyer and seller is all the consumer protection necessary.
    2   The federal government's power over the economy should be limited.
    3   Moderation of the effects of the business cycle is a federal government function.
    4   Government policies should be approved by the boards of directors of the major corporations.

Constructed Response

Below is an adaptation of a political cartoon which appeared in 1933, in the Salt Lake (Utah) *Tribune*. The cartoon is typical of a conservative reaction to the speed of Congressional action during the New Deal.

1   Who seems to be in charge of government in the cartoon?

    Congress

2   Why is the figure representing the public concerned?

    because ~~Congress~~ Congress lost the brakes

---

the situations that had caused the Great Depression. These included:

- **Banking and Financial Structures**
The *Glass-Steagall Banking Act* (1933) created the **Federal Deposit Insurance Corporation** (FDIC) to insure depositors against bank failures, but it also required banks to undergo frequent examinations of their operations. The Federal Reserve Bank was given more power to oversee banking in general. A **Securities and Exchange Commission** (SEC) was created to watch over the stock market. (In 1999, Congress lifted many of the Depression Era banking restrictions. The changes allowed banks to be more competitive with other financial services in the modern marketplace.)

- **Income Security**
The most far-reaching reform created a financial security program for individuals. It was based on earlier Progressive Era ideas and on the examples already adopted by many European nations. Under the *Social Security Act* (1935), a system of insurance was created to assist people in coping with the loss of income due to old-age, unemployment, and physical handicaps. FDR called it "the cornerstone" of his administration.

- **Workers' Rights**
Basic rights of working people were also established. Congress created the *Fair Labor Standards Act* (1937) to secure reasonable working hours, basic conditions of safety, and a federal minimum wage. The *National Labor Relations Act* (or *Wagner Act*, 1935) established workers' rights to organize as a group to negotiate with employers (**collective bargaining**). The *Wagner Act* also authorized the National Labor Relations Board to investigate contract labor problems and offer mediation of disputes.

- **Government Corruption**
Roosevelt recruited crusading Progressive Republican **Harold L. Ickes** ("Honest Harold," 1874-1952) as Secretary of the Interior. Under FDR and Truman, Ickes brought the notoriously corrupt department under control.

POPULAR RESPONSE

There were mixed reactions to the whirlwind of activity in Washington. To a considerable extent, the New Deal spirit of reform took hold in the country.

In labor, **John L. Lewis** (1880-1969) leader of the United Mine Workers, had tried for years to gain full acceptance for his union in the powerful American Federation of Labor. The AFL took the position that it was an organization of skilled tradesmen and rejected the idea of affiliating with broad-based industry-wide unions. After a stormy three-year dispute, the AFL ejected Lewis' group. In 1938, he formed a separate national organization of industry-wide unions – the **Congress of Industrial Organizations** (CIO). The two organizations then began a long and fierce competition for membership which did not end until they merged into the **A.F.L.-C.I.O.** in 1955.

Like the LaGuardia administration in New York City, most state and local governments responded well to the offers of New Deal aid. Some conservative Democrats in the South opposed federal interference, and many rural Republican communities of the North and Mid-West refused to participate in what they called "FDR's creeping socialism."

In the middle of the New Deal, conservative businessmen formed the American Liberty League to raise funds for Conservative candidates. It was the main backing for Kansas Governor **Alf Landon** (1887-1987), the Republican Party's Presidential candidate in 1936. Landon won 17 million popular votes to FDR's 28 million, but he won only 8 electoral votes (2 states) to FDR's 523.

CONTROVERSIAL ASPECTS: THE NEW DEAL

The United States is a democracy. Although the American public was generally supportive of

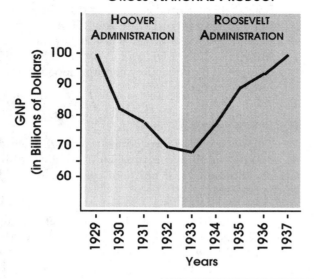

GROSS NATIONAL PRODUCT

HOOVER ADMINISTRATION — ROOSEVELT ADMINISTRATION

GNP (in Billions of Dollars)

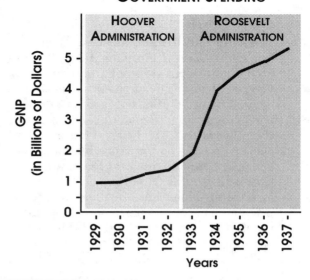

GOVERNMENT SPENDING

HOOVER ADMINISTRATION — ROOSEVELT ADMINISTRATION

GNP (in Billions of Dollars)

the New Deal, no true democracy could go through such alterations of policy without public discussion and opposition. Although Congress was generally in agreement with the President's programs, checks and balances were operating all through the New Deal years.

Critics of the New Deal attacked:

- *The growth in federal spending to finance the New Deal*. Opponents spoke out against the unbalanced government budget. Because raising taxes would have a negative effect on consumer spending and investment, increasing revenues to balance the budget was difficult. Tariff barriers were lowered to increase trade opportunities. With government income low, Treasury Secretary Morganthau felt the only recourse was for the government to use **deficit spending** (government borrowing heavily to finance its operations). Many considered this concept to be poor economic management.

- *The growth of the federal agencies and their staffs*. This unleashed an outcry against "big government." Opponents pointed out that taxes would have to go up to maintain such a large operation. Worse, they said, more clerks and offices meant that the country would be run by a complex and inefficient bureaucracy. The TVA (Tennessee Valley Authority) brought electrification to the heart of poverty-stricken Appalachia, but critics said it was a socialist

program that undermined private enterprise.

- *The liberal stretching of legislative and executive power*. Opponents of many of the hastily devised New Deal programs immediately launched legal challenges. By 1935, the Court was declaring key laws unconstitutional. The Court said that Congress had stretched its power over interstate commerce too far and struck down the AAA in *United States v. Butler*, and the NIRA in ***Schechter Poultry Corp. v. United States****. The Court also ruled that New Deal laws on pensions, bankruptcy, and the minimum wage were questionable.

Riding high on a landslide re-election in 1936, FDR tried to have Congress change the composition of the Supreme Court to make it friendlier to his programs. At the height of his popularity, the operation of checks and balances handed him his most devastating political defeat. The media called it his "**Court Packing Plan**." He proposed legislation that would enable him to name additional federal judges for those over 70 years old who refused retirement. The plan received nationwide criticism and was soundly defeated by Congress.

Another action widely denounced was Roosevelt's decision to run for a third term in 1940. This broke a precedent set 150 years before by George Washington. There was no limit on the number of Presidential terms in the

Constitution, but two terms had become a tradition. Critics were deeply disturbed to see the precedent broken, and felt that FDR was undermining the constitutional principle of limited power. (In 1951, the Twenty-second Amendment to the Constitution was adopted limiting Presidents to two terms.)

THE HUMAN FACTOR

The New Deal had numerous effects on the American people. Some helped to ease the pain and suffering of the Depression, some did not:

FDR

- *Franklin Roosevelt as a Masterful Communicator*
  Undoubtedly, one of the things that helped the New Deal was Roosevelt's own personality. The optimistic and dynamic FDR was able to project a positive attitude toward life in his frequent press conferences, in the short clips people saw weekly in theater newsreels, and most of all, in his radio addresses. The latter became known as "fireside chats," because he talked in a direct, almost personal tone to the radio listener.

- *The Dust Bowl*
  One of the most tragic human stories of the Depression Era occurred in the Midwestern states. Farmers in general were suffering financially long before the collapse of 1929, but in 1932, nature turned tragically against them. A devastating drought that would last more than four years in some areas hit the midsection of the nation from Texas and Oklahoma to the Dakotas. In the area which became nicknamed "the Dust Bowl," winds picked up the parched soil, and destitute farmers watched helplessly as it blew their livelihoods away.

- *Oakies*
  A million or more "Oakies" and "Arkies" packed up their families and possessions and hit the roads. These refugees from the Oklahoma and Arkansas Dust Bowl sought work in the agricultural regions of the West Coast. They often found rejection by Western townspeople who feared their economic competition. **John Steinbeck** (1902-1968) wrote sympathetically about the tragedy in his classic novel, *The Grapes of Wrath.*

- *The New Deal and Women*
  Despite the new status women had achieved during the 1920s, they were to suffer the same discrimination as African Americans when the Depression struck. Women were brought into FDR's administration. Secretary of Labor Frances Perkins became the first female cabinet officer, and women were also appointed to judgeships and foreign service posts. Mrs. Roosevelt used her considerable influence with the President, and her syndicated daily news column, *My Day*, to press for more equal treatment for women under New Deal programs.

- *The New Deal and Minorities*
  The record of the New Deal in helping minority groups is not inspiring. Although the problems plagued all Americans during the Depression, African American wage earners and farmers were particularly hard-hit. Already suffering from discrimination in housing and jobs, they disproportionately felt the economic collapse in increased lay-offs, foreclosures, and evictions. In 1932, they made up nearly 20% of the unemployed. Politically, they backed Roosevelt, but the Democratic leadership was cautious on racial matters.

- *Segregation* was still strong in the North and the South. African Americans were not given equal treatment in the administration of New Deal programs. Since Southern legislators held key positions in Congress, and the success of the New Deal was largely in their hands, FDR was reluctant to challenge their power with reforms for African Americans. The Works Projects Administration (WPA) did have nondiscrimination clauses in its hiring regulations, but still by 1935, three times as many African Americans were on relief as whites. Eleanor Roosevelt became a strong voice for equal treatment of minorities and met frequently with African American leaders including **A. Philip Randolph**, **Ralph Bunche**, **Robert Weaver**, and **Mary McLeod Bethune**, who was a director of the National Youth Administration.

- *Native Americans* did little better than African Americans. The *Indian Reorganization Act* (*Wheeler Act*, 1934) gave them greater control over their lands, and improved educational opportunities for their youth. A special bureau was also created for reservation work under the CCC.

THE CULTURE OF THE DEPRESSION

The New Deal made a significant cultural contribution to American life. Reaching out to help people, programs were designed to assist creative artists. Under Harry Hopkins, the WPA created theater and art projects. Artists worked on building murals and illustrations for federal publications, and dramatists and choreographers created new works which were performed throughout the nation under the **Federal Theater Project**. The WPA also supervised oral history projects, helping to preserve regional folklore. The New Deal also created a dramatic photographic record of rural life in the 1930s through the artistry of **Dorothea Lange** and **Walker Evans**.

Entertainment in the 1930s reflected a desire for escapism. Hollywood films and daily radio shows catered to this desire and both experienced a golden era. Americans flocked to the movies to escape the Depression, watching Fred Astair and Ginger Rogers in glamorous formal wear dancing their cares away, or Dorothy (Judy Garland) flying over the rainbow in the *Wizard of Oz*, or Scarlett O'Hara and Rhett Butler (Vivian Leigh and Clark Gable) facing the problems of the South in *Gone with the Wind*. At home, they escaped from their dismal times with the comedy of George Burns and Gracie Allen, the music of Bing Crosby, melodramas such as *Lights Out* and *Suspense*, or the many soap operas (*The Guiding Light*, *Ma Perkins*) that filled the airwaves.

POLITICAL EXTREMISM

Not everyone was bent on escaping reality in the troubled 1930s. There were many groups that would gain popularity by trying to radically change the American system. As a movement, American communism had suffered greatly in the 1920s, after the "Red Scare." The dark days of the Depression drew new attention to communism. The Communist Party of the U.S. was especially attractive to intellectuals. However, the intense loyalty of leaders **William Z. Foster** and **Earl Browder** to international policies directed by the U.S.S.R. and constant talk of radical revolution alienated many from the communist movement.

The **Socialist Party** also gained a larger following, and its leader, **Norman Thomas**, constantly criticized Roosevelt about being too timid in using government to help the working class. Fascist groups also emerged, admiring the type of system that seemed to be working in Italy and Germany.

Home grown radical movements also arose. **Dr. Francis E. Townsend** attracted thousands to an Old Folks' Crusade. He pressed for a $200 a month pension system. Townsend clubs helped to organize support for the *Social Security Act*, although they saw it as too limited.

From Louisiana came the socialistic "Share Our Wealth" program launched by its powerful Senator, **Huey P. Long** (1893-1935). Long was a hero to some, a **demagogue** (leader who appeals to emotions and prejudices) and potential dictator to others. He wanted to limit individual wealth, guarantee everyone a home, a minimum $2,500 income, a free college education, and a pension by taxing the rich. He began to criticize the New Deal for being too cautious. By 1935, *"Share Our Wealth"* clubs were forming nationally and Long was preparing to launch a challenge to Roosevelt for the 1936 Democratic nomination. The movement declined after Long was assassinated on the steps of the state capitol in Baton Rouge.

A third powerful critic of the Roosevelt administration was Father **Charles E. Coughlin** (1891-1979). The Michigan "Radio Priest" had gained popularity in the early Depression. He began to use his devotional radio broadcasts to denounce the Hoover administration's lack of social conscience. Coughlin advocated a mixture of socialist and populist causes and denounced modern capitalism. At first, he endorsed the New Deal, but later, when FDR ignored his schemes, Coughlin denounced the

---

MINI•ASSESSMENT (6-6)

1 A criticism of President Franklin Roosevelt's programs to combat the Great Depression was that these programs
   1 reduced the power of the federal government
   2 ignored the plight of homeowners with mortgages
   3 provided too much protection for big business
   4 made people dependent on the federal government

2 An immediate result of the Supreme Court decisions in *Schechter Poultry Corporation v. United States* (1935) and *United States v. Butler* (1936) was that

   1 the constitutional authority of the President was greatly expanded
   2 some aspects of the New Deal were declared unconstitutional
   3 state governments took over relief agencies
   4 Congress was forced to abandon efforts to improve the economy

3 Which statement is accurate about American culture during the Great Depression?
   1 The federal government provided money to support the arts.
   2 Most movies featured realistic themes and unhappy endings.
   3 Rock and roll music became popular.
   4 Interest in professional sports declined.

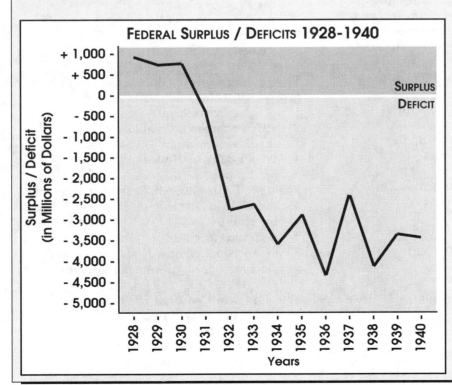

FEDERAL SURPLUS / DEFICITS 1928-1940

Constructed Response

– Source: U.S. Office of Management & Budget

1 How do the figures from 1928-1930 differ from those after 1930?

2 What conditions in the United States during the Depression caused this trend after 1930?

New Deal as communistic. He created a lobby called the National Union for Social Justice. In 1936, he transformed it into the **Union Party** and attracted former supporters of Huey Long's movement. The Union Party did not do well at the polls in 1938 and gradually deteriorated. Coughlin continued to be a Roosevelt critic, but his movement became more and more radical and lost many followers. In 1942, Roman Catholic Church officials ordered him to stop all non-religious broadcasting.

SUMMARY

By 1938, the New Deal was losing momentum. At that point, the economy was inching upward, and attention was focusing more on foreign problems. Historians still argue about whether the New Deal was a success. Supporters feel the New Deal:

• preserved the free enterprise system by remodeling its weakest parts,

• forged a new connection between the individual and government, and

• established the role of government as stimulator of economy.

UNIT ASSESSMENT
MULTI-CHOICE QUESTIONS

1 The chart on page 225 characterizes the U.S. economy during WW I as
   1 laissez-faire
   2 market
   3 command
   4 underdeveloped

2 During World War I, financier Bernard Baruch, labor leader Samuel Gompers, and public administrator Herbert Hoover
   1 managed the transportation systems of the nation
   2 increased taxes and raised funds for the government
   3 helped to mobilize the American economy
   4 assisted Wilson in readjusting the economy after the war

3 Money to finance war expenditures came from
   1 selling liberty bonds
   2 rationing of scarce goods
   3 building and selling ships
   4 increasing tariffs

4 Rapid government demobilization after wars usually causes
   1 public disillusion
   2 a "bull market"
   3 economic expansion
   4 economic contraction

5 Employment in war industries had some positive influence on the status of women and African Americans, because they were
   1 allowed to join unions for the first time
   2 given pay equal to that of white males
   3 performing well in management positions
   4 filling large gaps in the labor force

6 Harding's administration was hurt by
   1 the President's unpopularity
   2 over-regulation of business
   3 unscrupulous behavior by officials
   4 women's suffrage

7 The guiding principle during the Coolidge prosperity of the middle 1920s was
   1 progressive reform
   2 strict commercial regulation
   3 tariff reciprocation
   4 laissez-faire attitudes

8 Farm problems of the 1920s were caused by
   1 scandals in government farm aid programs
   2 high food prices
   3 overproduction and declining demand
   4 slow recovery by European farmers

9 The "Red Scare" of 1919-1920 led to
   1 repression of civil liberties
   2 a new military buildup
   3 a move to the suburbs
   4 more socialist legislation

10 Women in the 1920s
1 returned to pre-World War I social status
2 lost political and economic power
3 were brought into important government positions
4 assumed new social roles

11 The *National Origins Act* of 1929
1 set up specific quotas for countries
2 encouraged the flow of immigrants
3 aided World War I refugees
4 abolished the practice of xenophobia

Base your answer to question 12 on the quote below and your knowledge of U.S. history and government.

"No nation in the history of the world was ever sitting as pretty. If we want anything, all we have to do is go buy it on credit. So that leaves us without any problems whatsoever, except perhaps some day to have to pay for them."

— Will Rogers,1927
(The Will Rogers Company, Claremore, OK)

12 Of which aspect of the 1920s' economy is Rogers being critical?
1 high tariffs
2 installment plans
3 laissez-faire policies
4 over speculation

13 Immediately after taking office, FDR
1 closed the banks temporarily
2 ordered pensions for the aged
3 raised the minimum wage
4 expanded minority rights

14 The tariff policies of the U.S. government in the 1920s led to
1 increased profits for farmers
2 a decrease in world trade
3 over expansion of European industry
4 over-speculation in the stock market

15 FDR tried to have the federal court system revised because
1 the justices needed a better retirement plan
2 he felt life terms were undemocratic
3 the courts were falling behind in their work
4 the courts were dismantling his New Deal programs

16 The *Wagner Act* symbolized reform because it
1 created a old-age pension system
2 focused on reclaiming the "Dust Bowl"
3 established collective bargaining rights
4 provided for unemployment insurance

17 One characteristic that New Deal reformers shared with Roosevelt was their
1 pragmatic approach to problems
2 belief in command economies
3 socialistic philosophy
4 escapist attitude

Base your answer to question 18 on the chart below and your knowledge of U.S. history and government.

| LABOR FORCE AND UNEMPLOYMENT: 1929-1941 | | | |
| (NUMBERS IN MILLIONS) | | | |
YEAR	LABOR FORCE	NUMBER UNEMPLOYED	PERCENT UNEMPLOYED
1929	49.2	1.6	3.2
1930	49.8	4.3	8.7
1931	50.4	8.0	15.9
1932	51.0	12.1	23.6
1933	51.6	12.8	24.9
1934	52.2	11.3	21.7
1935	52.9	10.6	20.1
1936	53.4	9.0	16.9
1937	54.0	7.7	14.3
1938	54.6	10.4	19.0
1939	55.2	9.5	17.2
1940	55.6	8.1	14.6
1941	55.9	5.6	9.9

18 Which generalization can be validly drawn from the chart above?
1 The New Deal restored employment to its 1929 level.
2 Industrial production improved after 1933.
3 New Deal legislation improved working conditions.
4 Employment levels generally improved in the New Deal era.

19 The radio and film industries blossomed in the 1930s, because they
1 offered jobs to the unemployed
2 provided an escape from dismal reality
3 were considered luxuries for the rich
4 received many government subsidies

20 The New Deal reflected the idea that the United States government should
1 regulate and reform the economy
2 restrict its actions to foreign affairs and defense
3 own and operate vital industries
4 reduce the scope of the welfare system

THEMATIC ESSAY QUESTION

Theme:

> **Legislating Change**
>
> Legislation in the New Deal Era had significant effects on American society.

Task:

> Using your knowledge of United States history and government, write an essay in which you choose *three* measures passed by Congress in the New Deal Era. For *each* one chosen:
>
> - describe the existing economic, social, or political conditions that prompted the legislation, and
> - discuss the impact of the change on these conditions.

Suggestions:

You may wish to focus on legislation concerning the old-age pension system, the minimum wage, insurance of bank deposits, collective bargaining for unions, or government-sponsored price, wage, production quota agreements among businesses. **You are not limited to these suggestions.**

DOCUMENT BASED QUESTION

The following task is based on the accompanying documents. The documents may have been edited for the purposes of this exercise. The task is designed to test your ability to work with historical documents. As you analyze the documents, take into account both the source of the document and the author's point of view.

Directions:

Read the documents in Part A and answer the question after each document. Then read the directions for Part B and write your essay.

Historical Context:

As the 1930s progressed, government activities became controversial.

Task:

Using information from the documents and your knowledge of United States history and government, write an essay in which you discuss why President Franklin D. Roosevelt's actions to help the economy were controversial.

Part A - Short Answer

Analyze the documents and answer the questions that follow each document.

Question for Document 1

What improvement do these figures show for the New Deal?

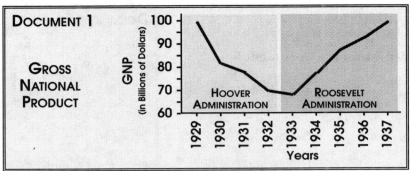

DOCUMENT 1

GROSS NATIONAL PRODUCT

GNP (in Billions of Dollars)

Hoover Administration | Roosevelt Administration

1929 1930 1931 1932 1933 1934 1935 1936 1937

Years

Question for Document 2

What seems to be the major criticism of government in this cartoon?

DOCUMENT 2

Question for Document 3

According to the article, why was the hatred that the rich had for Roosevelt ironic?

DOCUMENT 3

"A resident of Park Avenue in New York City was sentenced not long ago to a term of imprisonment for threatening violence to the person of the President Roosevelt ...it was significant as a dramatically extreme manifestation of the most extraordinary phenomena [of the 1930s]: the fanatical hatred of the President which today obsesses thousands of men and women among the American upper class.

"...this hatred may go down as the major irony of our time. ...the fanatic who went to prison had lost his fortune and, therefore had a direct grievance [reason for complaint], those who rail [make complaints] against the President have to a large extent had their incomes restored and their bank balances replenished since the low point of March, 1933."

– *Harper's Magazine*, May 1936

DOCUMENT 4

RELIEF	RECOVERY	REFORM
Bank Holiday	Agricultural Adjustment Act	Securities and Exchange Commission
Emergency Banking Act	National Industrial Recovery Act	Federal Deposit Insurance Corp.
Federal Emergency Relief Act	Home Owners Loan Corp.	Social Security Administration
Civil Works Administration	Works Progress Administration	National Labor Relations Board

Question for Document 4

Why were the reform actions more apt to change the traditional role of the national government in the economy than relief or recovery measures?

Question for Document 5

How would the 1930s trend in the chart be viewed by workers; by business?

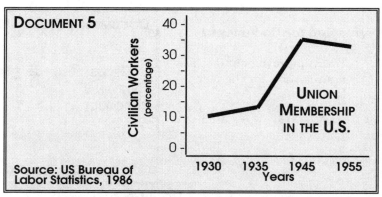

DOCUMENT 5

UNION MEMBERSHIP IN THE U.S.

Civilian Workers (percentage)

Years

Source: US Bureau of Labor Statistics, 1986

Question for Document 6

What role is the cartoonist showing for the National Recovery Administration?

DOCUMENT 6

GO ON TO PART B

Part B - Essay

Directions:
- Write a well organized essay that includes an introduction, several paragraphs, and a conclusion.
- Use evidence from the documents to support your response.
- Do not simply repeat the contents of the documents.
- Include specific related outside information.

Historical Context:
As the 1930s progressed, government activities became controversial.

Task:
Using information from the documents and your knowledge of United States history and government, write an essay in which you discuss why Roosevelt's actions to help the economy were controversial.

Be sure to include specific historical details. You must also include additional information from your knowledge of United States history and government.

THE UNITED STATES IN AN AGE OF GLOBAL CRISIS

1930-

NAZIS COME TO POWER (1933)
GOOD NEIGHBOR POLICY (1933)
U.S. RECOGNIZES U.S.S.R. (1933)

1935-

U.S. NEUTRALITY ACTS (1936-1939)

AXIS PACT (1939)
WW II IN EUROPE (1939)

1940-

DESTROYERS FOR BASES (1940)
ATLANTIC CHARTER (1941)
LEND-LEASE (1941)
U.S. ENTERS WW II (1941)
RATIONING (1942)

D-DAY (1944)

YALTA CONFERENCE (1945)

1945-

HIROSHIMA (1945)
WW II ENDS (1945)

TRUMAN DOCTRINE (1947)

FAIR DEAL (1948)
MARSHALL PLAN (1948)
BERLIN AIRLIFT (1948-1949)

NATO (1949)

1950- McCARTHY ERA (1950-1954)

On 9 August 1945, the United States dropped the 2nd Atomic Bomb of the War, "Fat Man." The photo is of the mushroom cloud as it rose over Nagasaki where 75,000 died from the bomb.
– U.S Air Force Photo

PEACE IN PERIL: 1933-1950

ISOLATION AND NEUTRALITY

PRECEDENTS FOR NEUTRALITY 1790-1917: POST-WW I DIPLOMACY

The Great Depression did not just upset personal lives and national economies. It destroyed a very delicate structure of peace set up at Versailles in 1919 and world conferences in the 1920s. The peace depended on the smooth operation of the major nations' economies. The chaos, bitterness, and disillusion of the Depression years became fertile ground for extremists and radical movements.

By 1929, only a few nations had physically recovered from the devastation of World War I. Germany, saddled with an enormous war debt and forced to pay war reparations to Britain and France, resorted to printing worthless currency. The staggering German economy was finally shattered in the chaotic period that followed the American collapse in 1929. **Adolf Hitler** and the National Socialist Party (**Nazis**) came to power in 1933.

Nearly a decade earlier, Italy had turned to a fascist structure which concentrated economic power in state-directed arrangements under **Benito Mussolini**. Hopes for a lasting peace structure were dashed as nations pursued their self-interest in the Great Depression years.

WASHINGTON'S "STEER CLEAR" POLICY

"It is our true policy to steer clear of permanent alliances with any portion of the foreign world."
– George Washington, *Farewell Address*, 1796

After the U.S. Senate's rejection of President Wilson's pleas for the *Treaty of Versailles* and the League of Nations in 1919, American foreign policy followed a zig-zag course. The Harding, Coolidge, and Hoover administrations made gestures toward international cooperation but refused to commit any military power to peacekeeping. This remoteness was also reflected in anti-immigration policies, stubborn international economic dealings and exorbitantly high tariff policies.

Key Terms

Clear and Present Danger
Storm - Cellar Isolation
Command Economy
Nuclear Deterrent
Loyalty Program
Totalitarianism
Appeasement
Iron Curtain

Summit
Genocide
Cold War
Holocaust
Aggression
Superpower
Containment

Many Americans felt comfortable with **isolationism**. Those who favored it cited the 18th and 19th century traditions of neutrality. Isolationists quoted Washington's *Farewell Address* of 1796. The first President had warned against foreign alliances. From the early struggles of the early Presidents to keep the U.S. out of the Napoleonic Wars to Wilson's neutral stance throughout most of World War I, the advice of Washington appeared to be a cornerstone of American foreign policy.

Italian Fascist leader Benito Mussolini and German Fuehrer Adolf Hitler parade together in Munich, 18 June 1940.   Photo credit: U.S. National Archives

Isolationists also cited the Monroe Doctrine (1823). It warned Europe to stop colonization of the Western Hemisphere, but it also indicated Americans' desire to stay out of European affairs.

In the 1930s, the isolationists argued that this neutral tradition was the safest path for America. To isolationists, the imperialism of President McKinley (1898), the world power vision of Theodore Roosevelt, and the internationalism of Woodrow Wilson were only brief shifts from the mainstream of American isolation policy.

Note: Items marked with an * are listed in the *Landmark Supreme Court Decisions* chart in Appendices.

This oversimplified view was strengthened by the fact that the two oceans still afforded reasonable protection for the U.S. (The true potential of the air age was not yet grasped by most citizens in the 1930s.) The sour feeling of the post-World War I days was amplified in the popular literature of the era. These were strong forces for isolationism. Japan's aggression in Manchuria in 1931, and similar moves by Italy and Germany in the mid-1930s, added even more strength to the isolationists' position – global involvement was a mistake.

The truth was that America always played a much more active role in world affairs than the isolationists believed. Nineteenth century involvement over territorial expansion and trading rights brought Americans into many conflicts with the Barbary States (No. Africa), Spain, France, Britain, Mexico, Germany, and even Tsarist Russia. Late 19th century industrial growth and tipping the balance in World War I had placed the U.S. among the world's great powers. No amount of wishful thinking about the past by isolationists could change these facts.

When it came to foreign policy, Franklin D. Roosevelt understood the strength of the isolationists, but he was a product of 20th century America. He was a Progressive who shared the optimistic outlook of Theodore Roosevelt and Woodrow Wilson. He shared the Progressives' belief that America's rise to power had given it a major role to play in world affairs. He believed in seeking peaceful, economic solutions to problems and was troubled when militarism once again reared its head in Europe and Asia. During the Depression, Roosevelt and his Secretary of State, **Cordell Hull** (1871-1955), sought to boost American trade in world markets by a free trade policy. They refused to be bound by any agreements at the London International Economic Conference (1933), arranged by Herbert Hoover before he left office. They pressed Congress for the *Reciprocity Act* (1934). This gave the President power to negotiate tariff rates with individual nations and gave government aid to American companies seeking more business abroad.

These initiatives led to two major diplomatic changes in the early days of the New Deal – the **Good Neighbor Policy** and the diplomatic recognition of the U.S.S.R. (Union of Soviet Socialist Republics). The Good Neighbor Policy involved Secretary Hull's pledge at the Pan American Union's Montevideo Conference in 1933 to end the long history of U.S. **interventionism** in the internal affairs of Latin American nations. This was followed by FDR's effective use of the *Reciprocity Act* which doubled the trade between the U.S. and Latin America by 1935.

Josef Stalin

Less successful was a similar policy toward the U.S.S.R. Over many congressional protests, FDR officially gave diplomatic recognition to the communist Soviet regime in Russia in 1933. Secretary Hull sent William Bullitt to Moscow as our first ambassador to the U.S.S.R. However, Soviet leader **Josef Stalin** (1879-1953) was more interested in negotiating a defense treaty against the rising threat of Japan than talking about trade, and Bullitt's mission failed.

GENEVA DISARMAMENT CONFERENCE OF 1932-1934

Despite the growing isolationist sentiments and the problems at home, Herbert Hoover's administration had been enthusiastic about a major disarmament conference in Geneva in 1932-1934. Hoover believed that arms manufacturing did not produce real wealth needed for re-establishing a healthy world economy. The Conference was doomed to failure especially since the French were becoming more wary of a rehabilitated arms industry in Germany. While the Conference met off and on for the next two years, and Roosevelt continued support after replacing Hoover as President, it made no headway. French fears remained the chief stumbling block, especially after Hitler began to rearm Germany.

THE NYE COMMITTEE

Isolationism gained even more popularity as a result of the *Nye Committee Report* in 1935. North Dakota Senator Gerald Nye headed the controversial "merchants of death investigation." Nye looked into rumors that U.S. bankers and manufacturers, seeking war profits in 1915-1917, from the British and French, had effectively undermined President Wilson's neutrality position.

This was a major reason why the United States had been drawn into World War I. While the Nye Committee found many financial arrangements had existed, it found no evidence to connect them to government policies. However, the isolationist press ignored the lack of evidence and helped many Americans jump to the conclusion that the arms business had pushed America into war in 1917. The resulting outcry helped pave the way for Congress to pass the *Neutrality Act of 1935*.

NEUTRALITY ACTS 1935-1937

Tension began to mount during 1933, when Japan violated its 1922 pledge (*Nine-Power Treaty*) to keep trade with China open. Japan left the League of Nations when that body censured its aggression in Manchuria. Isolationist sentiments ran even higher in 1935, when Mussolini announced Italy's plan to conquer Ethiopia. Congress responded by passing the first of a series of neutrality acts. In an attempt to avoid the kinds of things that had led the United States into World War I, the sale or shipment of arms to belligerent nations (countries at war) was forbidden.

The following year, Congress forbid private loans to belligerents in the *Neutrality Act of 1936*. Roosevelt was against these restrictions. His foreign policy was centered on spurring economic recovery in the Great Depression, and he viewed the arms trade as important.

SPANISH CIVIL WAR

A year later, Congress again altered the neutrality legislation due to the outbreak of a civil war in Spain. During the summer of 1936, Spain was torn by a savage civil war which became a focus of international attention. The Spanish Republic's forces were attacked by a right-wing, conservative coalition of army officers backed by Catholic Church leaders. Mussolini and Hitler, now joined in the Axis alliance, gave significant aid to this group, led by "El Caudillo," **Francisco Franco** (1892-1975). The weaker, socialist-leaning Republican forces received aid from the Soviet Union, but they fell to the army coalition in 1939. The fascist Franco proclaimed Spain neutral in World War II, but remained sympathetic to Hitler.

Calls came from many corners for the U.S. to assist one of the two warring sides in the Spanish Civil War. Fear of the conflict erupting into another major war led Congress to extend its earlier trade restrictions to include civil wars. In the *Neutrality Act of 1937*, FDR was able to gain some flexibility. Congress added a "cash and carry amendment" to allow belligerents to buy non-military goods in America as long as they made immediate payment and transported them in their own ships.

STORM WARNING DIPLOMACY	
ACT	**PROVISION**
Neutrality Act of 1935	When the President proclaimed that a foreign war existed, no arms could be sold or transported on American ships to the nations involved. No Americans could travel on the ships of warring nations.
Neutrality Act of 1936	When the President proclaimed that a foreign war existed, no loans could be made to the warring nations.
Neutrality Act of 1937	No Americans could travel on ships of warring nations. All provisions of the above *Neutrality Acts* applied to civil wars.
Neutrality Act of 1939	Nations fighting aggression were allowed to buy war material from U.S. manufacturers on a "cash and carry" basis. President could proclaim "danger zones" and forbid U.S. ships to enter the danger zone.

FDR's "Quarantine" Speech Of 1937

FOREIGN POLICY

In July 1937, Japan again tried to expand its Manchurian territory by attacking China. Roosevelt sensed that Americans wished to send aid, but the *Neutrality Acts* stood in his way. Japan's naval control of the Pacific made "cash and carry" too risky for Chinese ships. Early in October, FDR made his famous "quarantine speech" indicating that aggression must be stopped by peace-loving nations. Isolationists loudly denounced him, but it appeared that the public was beginning to change its mind as they watched aggression mount in the world.

The League of Nations tried to use Roosevelt's "quarantine" idea to get members to collectively cut off trade with aggressor nations. However, no one wished to sacrifice their economic welfare for peace. At that same point, a severe recession threatened to push the slowly recovering economy back to its pre-1933 level. The economic slump, mounting aggression, and the League's failure to act allowed the President to convince Congress to agree to an increase in defense spending for naval and air power.

Aggressive Actions: Japan, Germany, & Italy (1932-1940)

Thus, America entered the final days before the outbreak of World War II with an isolationist policy. It was reinforced by neutrality legislation that restricted President Roosevelt's diplomatic

---

Mini • Assessment (7-1)

1 American foreign policies between the two world wars reflected
   1 both isolationism and internationalism
   2 strong faith in the League of Nations
   3 consistent promotion of free trade
   4 aggressive military action

2 Franklin Roosevelt made his "quarantine" speech in 1937, because
   1 congressional neutrality acts prevented him from aiding China
   2 he wished to enter the League of Nations
   3 the U.S. could not trade with Japan
   4 Japanese trade was hurting U.S. business recovery

3 "Storm Warning Diplomacy" is a term indicating that U.S. foreign policy in the late 1930s
   1 abandoned the *Monroe Doctrine*
   2 sanctioned arms sales to belligerents
   3 continued to raise high tariffs to protect home industry
   4 attempted to avoid involvement in foreign wars

Constructed Response

1 When this cartoon appeared in 1938, what memories did Americans have of World War I?

2 Is the cartoonist an isolationist? Explain.

---

capabilities. The President's hands were tied by congressional limitations, and Britain and France were not ready for the speed with which the pattern of aggression grew.

Japan's 1937 push south into China from its Manchurian territory seemed to unleash a rapid unfolding of events. Mussolini simultaneously achieved success in Ethiopia. In 1938, Hitler moved into Austria and threatened the Sudetenland region of Czechoslovakia.

APPEASEMENT: MUNICH CONFERENCE (1938)

No major nation in Europe was prepared to face the combined war machines of Nazi Germany and Fascist Italy. To try to resolve the Czech problem, a fateful international meeting was convened in Germany. At the **Munich Conference** (29 September 1938), France and Britain agreed to let Hitler take the Sudetenland in exchange for a pledge to cease further aggressive claims by Germany and Italy. Britain's Prime Minister **Neville Chamberlain** (1869-1940) claimed the world had purchased "peace with honor" at Munich.

Publicly, Roosevelt reluctantly approved of the Munich Agreement. Privately, he told his Cabinet that such an **appeasement** (granting concessions to potential enemies to maintain peace) of the Axis dictators was shameful. FDR was aware of the Germans' diplomatic activities in Latin America which were undercutting his Good Neighbor policy. With the time purchased by the Munich Agreement, Roosevelt worked intensely to cement friendly relations in Latin America.

Actually, the appeasement at Munich did not buy much time at all. In 1938, German troops occupied Czechoslovakia. In an effort to balance

PRELUDE TO WORLD WAR II		
ACT	RESPONSE	RESULT
1931 Japan Invades North Manchuria	League of Nations reprimand; U.S. issues Stimson Doctrine, refuses to recognize Japanese claim to territory	Japan quits League of Nations, annexes Chinese conquests
1935 Italy Invades Ethiopia	U.S. passes *Neutrality Act*, no arms sales to belligerents. League of Nations reprimand	Italy conquers and annexes part of Ethiopia
1936 Germany Invades Rhineland Region	No response	Germans build fortifications along the Rhine River in violation of Versailles Treaty
1936 Germany & Italy back Franco in Spanish Civil War	U.S. broadens *Neutrality Acts* to include arms trade ban for civil war belligerents	Franco is victorious, becomes "silent partner" for Axis alliance
1937 Japan Invades China	FDR calls for "quarantine" of aggressor nations. League of Nations fails with trade embargo against Japan	Japan conquers and occupies most of N.E. China
1938 Germany Invades Austria	No response	Germany proclaims "Anschluss" – unification of Germany and Austria
1938 Germany Claims Czech Territory	Britain and France appease Hitler, allow Germans to take over the area at Munich Conference	Germany annexes Sudetenland region
1939 Italy Invades Albania	No response	Italy conquers and occupies Albania
1939 Germany & U.S.S.R. Invade Poland	Britain and France declare war; U.S. modifies *Neutrality Acts* to allow "cash and carry"	World War II begins

the Axis' geographic power, France and Britain desperately tried negotiation with the Soviet Union. By this, they hoped to deter Hitler's ambitions. However, Stalin was suspicious of the anti-communist policies of the Western democracies. In a shocking diplomatic move in late August 1939, the Soviet Union and Germany announced a mutual non-aggression treaty.

GERMAN ATTACK ON POLAND – WW II BEGINS

The 1939 pact created a strange alliance between the fascist government of Germany and the communist government of the Soviet Union. This alliance took pressure off Germany's eastern borders and gave Hitler and Stalin the opportunity to advance into the long-coveted nation of Poland. Hitler demanded a return of German territory given to Poland after World War I.

On 1 September 1939, a mere nine days after the Nazi-Soviet pact, Hitler launched his **blitzkrieg** (lightning war). Bound by treaty to defend Poland, Britain and France declared war two days later. World War II had begun in Europe. While France and Britain mobilized, the massive German technological war machine rolled through Poland and conquered the country in three weeks.

Swiftly, the Soviets took a share of eastern Poland, began annexing the tiny Baltic nations of Estonia, Latvia, and Lithuania, and then launched their own lightning invasion of Finland which fell in only four months.

The winter of 1939-1940 was misleadingly calm in Europe, allowing talk of intervention by America to die down and isolationists to regain strength. A frustrated Roosevelt wished to aid victims of aggression, but reluctantly invoked the *Neutrality Acts*.

Unexpectedly, Hitler launched another blitzkrieg against Denmark and Norway in April of 1940. Then in May, German forces rolled through the Netherlands and Belgium, conquering both before the month ended.

The Battle of France opened on 5 June, and Italy attacked from the south on 10 June. Paris fell to the Germans four days later. The Free French government under General **Charles DeGaulle** (1890-1970) fled into exile in Britain. On 22 June, France's Field Marshal Henri Pétain surrendered to the Germans. In a matter of three months, all of Western Europe, except Great Britain, had fallen to Hitler's war machine.

GRADUAL U.S. INVOLVEMENT

The speed and success of the Axis offensive jolted America into action. Roosevelt set up a task force to arrange for the defense of the Western Hemisphere. Plans were approved by the Pan-American Union, and a Joint Defense Board was set up with Canada.

Congress raised taxes and the debt limit to allow for more military purchasing. Congress authorized absorbing National Guard units into the U.S. armed forces and the nation's first peacetime draft. Fear of spy activities led Congress to pass the *Smith Act* (1940) to monitor alien activities. The act also made it illegal to

London in ruins after Hitler's blitz – the relentless series of air attacks and civilian bombing.
(Photo credits: U.S. National Archives)

Children – orphaned, hungry, and homeless – following the German Blitz on London 1940.
(Photo credits: U.S. National Archives)

advocate or teach the forceful overthrow of lawful government in the United States.

The *Neutrality Acts* of the late 1930s hampered Roosevelt's efforts to help Britain. By the end of 1940, the British stood alone under a relentless series of German air attacks. Sensing American public opinion had changed, FDR took a landmark step in September of 1940. By stretching his power as Commander in Chief, Roosevelt took fifty World War I navy ships and gave them to Britain in exchange for the use of naval base sites in Canada, Bermuda, and the Caribbean. This became known as the **Destroyers-for-Bases Deal**.

Roosevelt's worst fears came in that same month when Japan joined the Axis alliance. He angered the Japanese by authorizing an **embargo** (stoppage) of iron and steel shipments outside the Western Hemisphere (except Britain).

In January of 1941, at his precedent-breaking third inaugural, FDR delivered his famous *Four Freedoms* speech ("...freedom of speech, of worship, from want, and from fear..."). The four freedoms framed what became America's war aims. In that same speech, he called for a *Lend-Lease Act* by Congress, to allow the United States to lend and transfer arms and war supplies to Britain and other "victims of aggression."

The passage of the *Lend-Lease Act* in March 1941 defeated the isolationist forces in Congress. *Lend-Lease* overturned much of the 1930s neutrality legislation and committed the United States to become what Roosevelt called the "Arsenal of Democracy." FDR extended the Navy's patrol region in the Atlantic and allowed merchant ships to arm themselves.

In June 1941, while still pounding Britain from the air, Hitler turned on his ally, Stalin, launching an all-out blitzkrieg against the U.S.S.R. Within a few months, Roosevelt extended Lend-Lease to the U.S.S.R.

America's commitment to the survival of Britain took another step in the summer of 1941. Roosevelt and Prime Minister **Winston Churchill** (1874-1965) met off the Canadian coast and drew up an informal set of anti-Axis war aims. Known as the *Atlantic Charter*, this document was eventually signed by 15 nations, including the U.S.S.R. In 1945, it became the basis for the *United Nations Charter*.

ROOSEVELT AND CHURCHILL SET COMMON PRINCIPLES

INSIGHTS ON LIBERTY

"The President of the United States of America and the Prime Minister, Mr. Churchill, representing His Majesty's Government in the United Kingdom, being met together (on the battleship *Prince of Wales* off Newfoundland) deem it right to make known certain common principles ... on which they base their hopes for a better future for the world.

"**First**, their countries seek no aggrandizement, territorial or other;
"**Second**, they desire to see no territorial changes that do not accord with the freely expressed wishes of the peoples concerned;
"**Third**, they respect the right of all peoples to choose the form of government under which they will live; and they wish to see sovereign rights and self-government restored to those who have been forcibly deprived of them;
"**Fourth**, they will endeavor... to further the enjoyment of all States... to the trade and raw materials of the world...;
"**Fifth**, they desire to bring about the fullest cooperation between all nations in the economic field, ... securing for all, improved labor standards, economic advancement, and social security;
"**Sixth**, after the final destruction of the Nazi tyranny, they hope to see established a peace which will afford that ...all the men in all the lands may live out their lives in freedom from fear and want; and,
"**Seventh**, such peace should enable all men to traverse the high seas and oceans without hindrance;
"**Eighth**, they believe that all the nations of the world, for realistic as well as spiritual reasons, must come to the abandonment of the use of force..."

– Franklin D. Roosevelt, Winston S. Churchill, *The Atlantic Charter*, 1941

1 The pattern of response to the acts of Germany, Italy, and Japan in the "Prelude to World War II" (see chart on page 254) shows
  1 quarantining aggressors was the only effective way to stop them
  2 lack of strong response can encourage aggressors
  3 the U.S. was the only nation to stand up to the aggressors
  4 forceful counter-actions deterred continued aggression

2 The Destroyers-for-Bases Deal between Roosevelt and Churchill showed that
  1 a President can bypass legislative restraints in foreign policy
  2 the U.S. focused on problems in the Pacific
  3 Americans were nervous about espionage
  4 the American boycott of trade with Japan was working

3 Before the U.S. actually declared war, FDR stated the nation's war aims in
  1 the New Deal and the Geneva Convention
  2 the Quarantine Speech and the Good Neighbor Policy
  3 the *Atlantic Charter* and the *Four Freedoms* speech
  4 the *Farewell Address* and the *Treaty of Versailles*

Constructed Response

"... Innocent peoples and nations are being cruelly sacrificed to a greed for power and supremacy which is devoid of all sense of justice and humane consideration.

"... If those things come to pass in other parts of the world, let no one imagine that America will escape ... If those days come, there will be no safety by arms, no help from authority, no answer in science. The storm will rage till every flower of culture is trampled and all human beings are leveled in a vast chaos."

– Franklin D. Roosevelt, Address to Congress, July, 1937

1 Where were "innocent peoples and nations" being "cruelly sacrificed to a greed for power and supremacy..."?

2 What connection did Roosevelt make between the problems in Europe and Asia and the future of the U.S.?

THE U.S. IN WORLD WAR II

PEARL HARBOR

In 1940, Japanese-American relations were also reaching a crisis stage. Japan was again seeking oil and rare metals in the Southeast Asia region ("Indochina"), where the fallen France was the chief colonial power. Secretary of State Hull issued a steady stream of warnings to the Japanese.

Just a few months before Hitler turned the full force of his war machine against the U.S.S.R., Stalin was able to convince Japan to sign a non-aggression pact. The Soviet-Japanese tensions in Asia were eased and Stalin could focus attention on defending his European borders. With France out of the picture, the U.S. claiming neutrality, and Britain and the Soviets fighting defensive wars with Hitler in Europe, Japan had no powerful enemies in Asia. The pact with Stalin also allowed Japan to confidently begin conquest of the mineral-rich area of Indochina. In July 1941, Japan attacked Thailand and the nearly defenseless French colonies. Diplomatic protests were issued by

Hull, and FDR embargoed nearly all trade with Japan.

In the late fall of 1941, aggressive militarists under General Tojo took power in Japan. They planned a secret attack against several U.S. naval installations to devastate U.S. military forces and reserves. The majority of American seagoing power in the Pacific was located at the Pearl Harbor naval base in Hawaii, assumed to be far out of range for the Japanese. The main concern was for the forces in the Philippines, which was still a U.S. possession.

The Japanese struck Pearl Harbor on 7 December 1941. The U.S. was totally unprepared. Scholars agree this was not only due to the Americans' disorderly intelligence system, but to their weak analysis and communications. With

over 5,000 casualties, it was probably the single most costly defeat in American history. Six major battleships and many lesser vessels were rendered useless. The attack left Japan nearly invincible in East Asia and the Pacific. Congress declared war on Japan the next day.

Within a week, Japan's Axis partners declared war on the United States. All the internal debates about isolationism were put to rest. The attempts to stay out of Europe's problems had proven useless. America now had to face the reality of World War II.

THE WAR IN EUROPE

Hitler had not been told by his Japanese allies of their plan to attack the U.S. He was angered, because he had not yet disposed of Britain, and his attack on the U.S.S.R. was slowly unraveling. In declaring war in mid-December, he hoped the U.S. would focus on Japan in the Pacific and America's Lend-Lease aid to Europe would slow down.

With public opinion united behind him, Roosevelt became an extremely powerful Commander in Chief and set America's overall strategic goals. His strategy was the opposite of what Hitler had guessed. He ordered American commanders to temporarily "hold the line" in the Pacific and focused attention on the European theater of the war.

To assure this strategy, FDR's brilliant Chief of Staff, General **George C. Marshall** (1880-1959), sent his most talented assistant, General **Dwight D. Eisenhower** (1890-1969), to Europe as Allied Commander. Taking the war to Germany's homeland, "Ike" ordered joint bombing attacks by the Royal Air Force and U.S. Army Air Corps on strategic production centers.

American assault troops of the 16th Infantry Regiment, wait by the Chalk Cliffs for evacuation to a field hospital. During the Invasion, thousands were killed or injured while storming Omaha Beach at Collville-sur-Mer, Normandy, 6 June 1944, "D-day."
(U.S. National Archives)

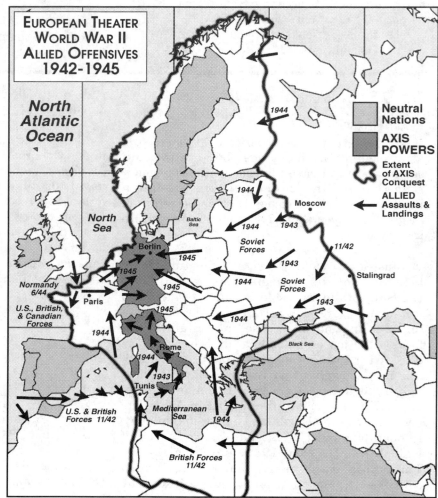

EUROPEAN THEATER
WORLD WAR II
ALLIED OFFENSIVES
1942-1945

North Atlantic Ocean

North Sea

Neutral Nations

AXIS POWERS

Extent of AXIS Conquest

ALLIED Assaults & Landings

Moscow

1944

1944

1943

Soviet Forces

11/42

Stalingrad

Berlin

1945

1945

1944

1943

Soviet Forces

1945

Normandy 6/44

U.S., British, & Canadian Forces

Paris

1945

1944

Black Sea

1943

Rome

1944

1944

1943

Tunis

Mediterranean Sea

1944

U.S. & British Forces 11/42

British Forces 11/42

The Americans then turned their attention to North Africa where British forces, under General **Bernard Law Montgomery** (1887-1976), began to turn the tide. At El Alamein in Egypt, Montgomery defeated the Germans' legendary "Desert Fox," General **Erwin Rommel** (1891-1944). In November 1942, Eisenhower's forces landed in North Africa, and his field commander, General **George Patton** (1885-1945), pushed eastward toward Montgomery, bottling the Germans up at Tunis. Victory in North Africa (May 1943) gave the Allies access to the Mediterranean and a southern staging point for invading Europe. At the same time, the Soviets halted the Axis invasion of their homeland after a brutal six month siege of **Stalingrad**.

With the Allied momentum building, Sicily was invaded in July 1943, followed by the Italian mainland in September. Mussolini fled Rome and the Italians surrendered on 8 September 1943. However, the German forces in Italy fought on, and it was not until June 1944 that the Allies were able to inch their way to Rome.

Eisenhower, now Supreme Allied Commander in Europe, launched **Operation Overlord**, the largest amphibious invasion in history. On 6 June 1944, nearly 200,000 troops, 4,600 ships, and 11,000 planes attacked the beaches of Normandy, France. Its success meant a second European front was now open. The German resistance was ferocious. By the end of that summer, Montgomery's British invasion force liberated the Netherlands and Belgium. A combined Free French, American, and Canadian army, under General **Omar Bradley** (1893-1981), liberated Paris at about the same time.

Hitler was now caught between the Soviets driving from the east and the combined Allied force moving rapidly from the west. In July, some of his general staff attempted to assassinate him. Shaken, he tried to stem the tide by ordering the new **V-2 rockets** launched at Britain in massive incendiary raids. Nearly overcome by Allied air power and with Allied forces already in Germany, Hitler made a last, desperate attempt to protect his homeland. In December, he threw ground forces against a weak section of the Allied line in Belgium. In the Battle of the Bulge (Dec.'44 - Jan.'45), the French-Anglo-American-Canadian forces were thrown back. However, a massive drive toward Germany from Poland by the Soviets, and another from Holland by the British forced the Germans to retreat. The Allies regained their momentum. With Berlin under attack, Hitler committed suicide on 30 April 1945. Germany's Field Marshal **Alfred Jodl** agreed to unconditional surrender on 8 May 1945.

THE WAR IN THE PACIFIC

In 1943, Roosevelt allowed his military advisors to turn their attention to the Pacific theater. By that time, Pacific Commander General **Douglas MacArthur** had evacuated the Philippines, the British and Americans had retreated to Australia, and the Japanese had overrun most of Southeast Asia and Indonesia (Dutch East Indies). The Japanese advance was stopped by tough Navy and Marine resistance in mid-1942, at the battles of the Coral Sea and Midway. A successful Allied attack on Guadalcanal just north of Australia threw the Japanese into a defensive position. The Allies began a vicious "island-hopping" offensive through the Pacific.

Intense cooperation between MacArthur and Admiral **Chester Nimitz** (1885-1966) allowed the Americans to move simultaneously in the South and Central Pacific. Wake and Guam were recaptured by mid-1944. This put the Americans in position to increase the devastating carrier air strikes on Japan itself. The drive toward the Japanese Islands grew more bloody and costly. **Iwo Jima** (18,000 Allied casualties) and **Okinawa** (45,000 Allied casualties) were taken in early 1945.

Iwo Jima Marine Memorial Arlington Cemetery, Virginia   – PhotoDisc ©1994

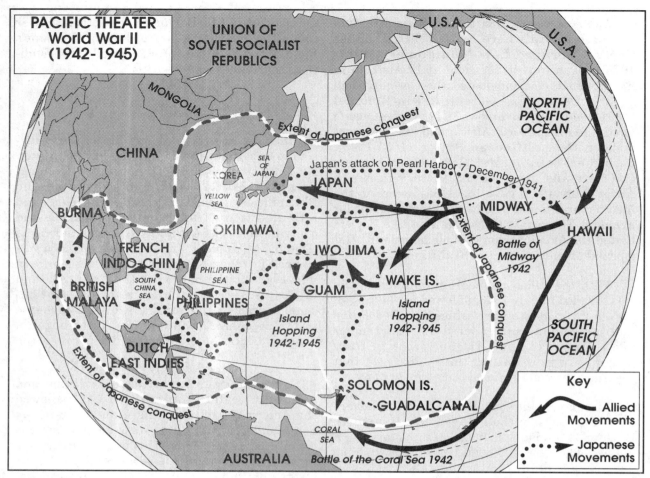

PACIFIC THEATER
World War II
(1942-1945)

UNION OF SOVIET SOCIALIST REPUBLICS

U.S.A.

U.S.A.

MONGOLIA

CHINA

NORTH PACIFIC OCEAN

Extent of Japanese conquest

SEA OF JAPAN

KOREA

YELLOW SEA

Japan's attack on Pearl Harbor 7 December 1941

JAPAN

MIDWAY

HAWAII

BURMA

OKINAWA

IWO JIMA

Battle of Midway 1942

FRENCH INDO-CHINA

PHILIPPINE SEA

WAKE IS.

Extent of Japanese conquest

BRITISH MALAYA

SOUTH CHINA SEA

PHILIPPINES

GUAM

Island Hopping 1942-1945

Island Hopping 1942-1945

SOUTH PACIFIC OCEAN

DUTCH EAST INDIES

Extent of Japanese conquest

SOLOMON IS.

GUADALCANAL

Key

Allied Movements

Japanese Movements

AUSTRALIA

CORAL SEA

Battle of the Coral Sea 1942

Tragically, FDR died of a cerebral hemorrhage on 12 April 1945. Vice President **Harry S Truman** (1884-1972) became the nation's Commander in Chief. Shortly thereafter, the Germans surrendered. Truman focused his attention on the bloodbath in the Pacific. It was felt that the Japanese would not accept unconditional surrender, but would fight to the last. Truman increased air attacks on Japan, hoping for surrender. The President then received word that an atomic weapon had been successfully developed by **J. Robert Oppenheimer** and a team of scientists working on the **Manhattan Project** at Los Alamos in the desert of New Mexico. After much agonizing, the President decided he could end the War quickly and end the bloodletting in the Pacific by authorizing the use of the bomb. On 6 August 1945, the first atomic bomb was dropped on **Hiroshima**, but there was no reply from the Japanese.

On 9 August a second bomb was dropped on the Japanese naval base of **Nagasaki**. The following day, Japanese Premier **Suzuki** offered to surrender if the Emperor **Hirohito** (1901-1989) was allowed to keep his throne. The Allies accepted the Japanese surrender on 14 August 1945. America had over a million casualties in World War II (nearly 325,000 dead and 700,000 wounded).

The Japanese envoy signs the document of surrender on board the *USS Missouri* in Tokyo Bay, September 2, 1945.

(Photo credit: U.S. National Archives)

THE HUMAN DIMENSIONS OF WAR

World War II brought about monumental social and economic changes in Americans lives. America's phenomenal three and one-half year drive to overthrow the Axis was fought equally hard on the **home front**. Roosevelt harnessed the entire economic capacity of the nation to the war effort. He created a number of wartime agencies to manage the home front. Industry was somewhat slow to respond to war needs in 1942, reluctant to give up profits from a booming consumer market.

Roosevelt persuaded industry to patriotically donate the services of their top managers. "Dollar-a-year men," like Sears-Roebuck's **Donald M. Nelson**, ran the **War Production Board** which supervised military production. The WPB forbade production of "nonessential items" (autos, kitchen appliances, toys). Manufacturing conversions were widespread. Nylon had not been developed yet, but silk stocking manufacturers switched to producing parachutes. Ford, Chrysler, and GM built tanks and planes. Kaiser Industries built prefabricated ship hulls and produced cargo transports in less than three months.

ECONOMIC POLICY

NECESSARY SELF-DENIAL

"There is one front and one battle where everyone in the United States – every man, woman, and child – is in action, and will be privileged to remain in action throughout this war. That front is right here at home, in our daily lives, in our daily tasks. Here at home, everyone will have the privilege of making whatever self-denial is necessary, not only to supply our fighting men, but to keep the economic structure of our country fortified and secure during the war and after the war ..."

–Franklin D. Roosevelt, Washington, DC, April 1942 (fireside chat).

1943 Cartoon illustrating humorous side of OPA restrictions. (O.Soglow - National Archives)

even a system for housewives to turn in cooking fat to be converted to glycerine needed for gunpowder. Even fashion changed to conserve fabrics; men's suit jackets were shorter, trousers were cuffless, vests were out, and women's skirts were shorter.

The OPA program called for much self-sacrificing on the part of the public. The people responded when government "We Do Our Part" poster programs urged those on the home front to support those doing the fighting. Comic book characters were given wartime assignments; superhero *Captain America* started off as an Army recruit. Hollywood films such as *Casablanca* and *Sands of Iwo Jima* deepened the support by focusing on the sacrifice of those fighting overseas.

As in World War I, the role of women in the economy expanded. As men were drafted for military service, seventeen million women entered the work force. Many worked in non-traditional jobs. Patriotic posters, animated film shorts, and even a pop song glorified a new American heroine, *"Rosie the Riveter."* Some industries set up day care and nursery schools near their defense plants to assist women workers. More than a quarter of a million also joined newly created women's corps of the Army (WACs), Navy (Waves), Marines, and Coast Guard, relieving men of non-combatant duties.

The nation's GNP tripled by 1945. Federal spending jumped from 20 billion dollars in 1941 to almost 98.4 billion dollars in 1945. The **War Manpower Commission** was able to coordinate the draft of nearly 14 million men into the armed forces while at the same time keeping a steady flow of trained workers moving into the nation's factories. Unemployment stood at 17.2 percent in 1939. By 1945, the figure had dropped to 1.9 percent. Average weekly earnings jumped from $25.25 in 1939 to $47.08 in 1945.

The **War Labor Board** handled labor disputes and kept the country relatively strike-free. The government helped with temporary housing units (barracks and portable, corrugated steel "quonset huts") such as those built in a Beacon (NY) park across the street from Green Fan Company propeller works.

The **Office of Price Administration** (OPA) kept the inflation-prone economy working on a fair basis as consumer goods became scarce due to military production demands. The OPA imposed **price ceilings** and supervised the **rationing program** so that people would be able to get a fair share of goods in short supply (shoes, sugar, coffee, tires, gasoline). There was

World War II cost America more than 300-billion dollars. To finance it, Congress not only

ECONOMIC POLICY

RATIONS

"Each person, regardless of age, will be allowed sixteen points a week for the whole group of new items to be rationed. There will be no exact meat ration, although the amount of meat available will average two pounds per person per week ...

"Blue stamps in War Ration Book No. 2 are used for most canned goods and for dried peas, beans, lentils and frozen commodities like fruit juice. The Red stamps are used for meats, canned fish, butter, hard cheese, edible fats, and canned milk. You have to give up more points when buying scarce food than when buying the same quantity of a plentiful one ..."
– Office of Price Administration, *Directives*, Washington, DC, March 1943.

raised and expanded the income tax system, but also changed the method of collection to require employers to withhold taxes from workers' paychecks. Major **war bond drives** were launched in workplaces and a movie-going public saw filmed appeals to buy bonds at every picture show.

Many famous entertainers such as Kate Smith, Jane Froman, Eddie Cantor, Al Jolson, Frank Sinatra, Bob Hope, and Bing Crosby volunteered to tour the country staging **bond rallies** in major cities. The war bond purchases accounted for nearly two-thirds of government war revenues.

British Prime Minister Winston Churchill, along with U.S. President Franklin Roosevelt and Soviet Premier Josef Stalin, attend the conference at Yalta.
(Library of Congress)

"Rosie the Riveter" – Women welders in Connecticut war production plant, 1943.
(Library of Congress)

PERSONAL DIPLOMACY

In 1943, Roosevelt said he was switching hats from "Dr. New Deal" to "Dr. Win-the-War." Actually, the coming of the European war in 1939 had led Roosevelt to change his leadership role. Especially after Lend-Lease, the problems of the Great Depression began to subside as employment increased in defense industries. In 1942, Roosevelt let the CCC and WPA fade as the War Manpower Commission and the *Selective Service Act* became operative. Some New Deal reforms on working hours and corporate price agreements had to be put aside in order to boost industrial productivity.

As the dangers in Europe and Asia mounted, President Roosevelt became more involved in foreign affairs and less in domestic issues. As chief diplomat and Commander in Chief, he had to meet personally with Allied leaders. With diplomatic groundwork laid by long-time advisor Harry Hopkins, FDR travelled to Africa and Asia to confer with Britain's Prime Minister Winston Churchill, the U.S.S.R.'s Premier Josef Stalin, Free France's General Charles DeGaulle, and China's Generalissimo **Jiang Jieshi** (Chiang Kai-shek). The Allied leaders gathered at summit meetings, usually involving the "Big Three" (U.S., Britain, & Soviet Union), in Casablanca (1943), Cairo (1943), Teheran (1943), and Yalta (1945).

Just after being elected to his fourth term as President, FDR was within a month of his death when he journeyed to Yalta in the Soviet Union in February 1945. At the **Yalta Conference**, in the southern U.S.S.R., FDR met with Stalin and Churchill to plan for the final stage of the war and shape the peace that would come thereafter. Roosevelt has been criticized for making too many concessions to Stalin in Eastern Europe, but the Soviets had been invaded from the west in both world wars and were deeply concerned about their security. By the Yalta Conference, the Soviets had already conquered most of Eastern Europe. Roosevelt and Churchill felt they had made great headway getting a reluctant Stalin to agree to have free elections in Soviet-conquered territories and to help establish the new **United Nations** peace organization. Stalin also promised to join the War against Japan as soon as he could.

In July 1945, a final wartime summit took place at **Potsdam**, Germany. By then, Harry Truman had taken Roosevelt's place. He met with Churchill and Stalin to make agreements on the peacetime treatment of Germany and on the location of Polish borders. Truman came away from the meeting very pessimistic about dealing with Stalin in the future. From World War II on, **summit meetings** and personal diplomacy became an important and burdensome responsibility for Presidents in the modern era.

U.S. MILITARY OCCUPATIONS

Despite all these Allied meetings, the War ended without a general peace treaty. The failure to construct such a general agreement paved the way for the tensions and suspicions that resulted in a **Cold War** between the Soviet Union and the Western democracies. Germany was placed under military occupation by the Allies. It was split into an Eastern Zone with Berlin as its capital, and administered by the U.S.S.R., and a Western Zone with Bonn as its capital, and jointly administered by Britain, France, and the United States. Isolated inside the Soviet Zone, Berlin later became the scene of much post-war tension (see map on page 271).

Treatment of Japan was different. The U.S. tried about 4,000 Japanese officials for war crimes, executing only General Tojo and several other leaders. The Americans occupied and rap-idly reconstructed the nation. Pacific commander General Douglas MacArthur was appointed military governor and created a democratic constitution adopted in 1947. In 1951, the former Allied nations, with the exception of the Soviet Union, signed a formal peace treaty with Japan.

WORLD WAR II: IMPACT ON MINORITIES

The War brought about enormous social change in America. It created numerous problems for minority groups at home and abroad. A panic broke out on the west coast of the United States after Pearl Harbor. Anti-Japanese feelings ran high. Fear of sabotage and espionage caused many unfounded charges to be leveled at Japanese aliens and American citizens of Japanese ancestry (**Nisei**). Japanese-Americans were most densely settled in California.

In the early spring of 1942, on the advice of his Western Defense Commander, FDR issued *Executive Order 9066* and formed the War Relocation Authority. The FBI rounded up 100,000 Japanese Americans, most of them citizens, and shipped them to ten relocation centers in Arkansas, Arizona, Utah and several other Western states. Many remained there for the duration of the War. Americans of Italian and German descent were not treated in a similar fashion.

This apparently racially-motivated denial of due process rights was eventually challenged in

OF JAPANESE ANCESTRY ...

"We were the last group of Japanese-Americans to leave Los Angeles. I was full of deep emotion when I thought that from tomorrow there would be not even one Japanese walking the greater Los Angeles area...
"Roll call started at 6:00 A.M. We all got instructions and boarded the train... In each coach there were two soldiers with rifles and bayonets... At 5:45 P.M., the train crossed the Colorado River and arrived at the station... Buses came ... Finally we arrived at the camp... My family registered and got Block 45-1-C. It was no better than a beggar's hut. We had to make our own mattresses by filling bags with hay... I felt like crying...
– Kasen Noda in *War Relocation Memoirs and Diaries*, 29 May 1942

These young evacuees of Japanese ancestry await their turn for baggage inspection upon arrival at the Assembly Center in Turlock, CA, 2 May 1942.
(photo Dorothea Lange, U.S. National Archives)

the Supreme Court. In the case of **Korematsu v. U.S.** * (1944), the Court upheld the government's actions under the "clear and present danger" rule based on the World War I era *Schenck* decision (1919). Later appeals in the 1950s and 1960s were won by the Nisei and partial compensation was made by the government for their suffering. In 1988, President Reagan signed a bill publicly apologizing to the Japanese American internees during the War and granted each of the 60,000 survivors a tax-free payment of $20,000.

Filmed footage of the Allied liberation of Hitler's concentration camps in Germany, Poland, and Eastern Europe brought home the shocking reality of what prejudice can truly mean. There was knowledge of Nazi atrocities against minorities early in the 1930s, but the world was shocked beyond belief by the documentation of the genocide of six million Jews in the Nazi death camps of Auschwitz, Belzec, and Treblinka. **The Holocaust** could not be brushed aside in dealing with the captured enemy leaders. Gypsies of many nationalities were also part of Hitler's "Final Solution." Approximately the same proportion of Gypsies as Jews was exterminated during World War II. Other victims of Nazis death camps included members of other religious sects, homosexuals, and the physically and mentally handicapped.

The former leaders of Hitler's Third Reich on trial in Nuremberg, Germany. Shown in the photo above - Front Row from Left to Right: Hermann Göring, Rudolf Hess, Joachim von Ribbentrop, Wilhelm Keitel, Ernst Kaltenbrunner, Alfred Rosenberg, Hans Frank, Wilhelm Frick, Julius Streicher, Walther Funk, Hjalmar Schacht.
(Photo credit: U.S. National Archives)

More barbaric Nazi practices were revealed at the **Nuremberg Trials** conducted by the Allies in 1946. Twenty-two major Nazi leaders were placed on trial for violations of the basic rules of war and inhumane treatment of political prisoners. Half of the accused were sentenced to death, half received prison terms.

African Americans also suffered from racial policies during the War. Despite FDR's 1942 orders to end racial restriction, African American servicemen were still assigned to segregated units but more saw combat than in World War I. Many civilian workers migrated north to take advantage of government non-discrimination policies in hiring defense plant workers under the Fair Employment Practices Commission. The number of African Americans in industry tripled between 1940 and 1945, and wages quadrupled. Still, many trade unions in defense industries banned African Americans from membership and protested if minorities received promotions. Mass migrations also caused race riots to break out in Los Angeles, Mobile, New York, and Detroit.

DEMOBILIZATION, INFLATION, AND STRIKES

Truman was a strong-willed man, but many people in his party doubted whether he could fill the shoes of the departed Roosevelt. Some felt that he and his advisors were overreacting to the Soviet moves in Europe, and he was incapable of conducting a sound foreign policy. Congress was not as enthusiastic as it had been in the New Deal days about the liberal reforms that Truman wanted on civil rights, housing, Social Security,

In the Nazi Concentration Camp at Dachau, prisoners were forced to stand without moving for endless hours as a punishment.
(Photo credit: U.S. National Archives)

and labor conditions. Nonetheless, they followed his recommendations and created an **Atomic Energy Commission** (AEC) to supervise military use of nuclear energy and research of its future applications.

The President also convinced Congress to pass the *Maximum Employment Act of 1946*, which incorporated the Keynesian concept of a permanent government role in keeping the economy stable and growing. Wages were not keeping up with inflation. Labor reacted to the problem. In 1946, a United Mine Workers' strike so hurt the economy that Truman had to threaten to use the army to keep coal production up. In the same year, he again threatened to use the army to end a national railroad strike.

In mid-1945, war-weary Americans clamored for a speedy demobilization. Truman, new to foreign policy-making, was suspicious of Soviet moves in Eastern Europe. He wanted a very gradual dismantling of United States power and was criticized by Congress and the public for dragging the process out. The aid Truman began sending overseas to reconstruct war-devastated areas served as an economic stimulus at home, as did continued military spending to provide for the occupation forces in Europe and Asia.

As consumer production gradually increased, the administration ended rationing. The public's cashing of war bonds stimulated the economy even more. The Truman Administration fought with Congress, trying to keep wartime **price controls** while attempting to balance supply with consumer demand to avoid the classic pattern of inflation and post-war recession. Recession was avoided, but inflation increased enormously as people willingly paid high prices for scarce autos and appliances they hadn't been able to purchase during the War.

THE "G.I. BILL"

In 1944, as the fortunes of war began to change, Roosevelt had been farsighted enough to anticipate the domestic problems that would occur as the War moved toward its conclusion. The President wanted to ease the economic conversion from wartime to peacetime. He had the War Production Board let some industries increase their consumer production while cutting back on military production. As a gesture of gratitude to those who had done the fighting, he managed to have Congress pass the *Service-men's Readjustment Act*, commonly called the *"G.I. Bill of Rights."* It provided for physical and vocational rehabilitation of wounded veterans, granted one year's unemployment compensation, and allowed for low cost business and housing loans. It also provided funds for veterans to continue their college and vocational educations – 7.8 million World War II veterans took advantage of the *G.I. Bill*'s educational provisions. The Act helped to ease the impact on the economy of demobilizing thousands of servicemen by avoiding massive unemployment. In the long run, it created a better educated work force and stimulated construction on university campuses.

PROBLEMS WITH CONGRESS

Truman's ability, growing inflation, and the slow demobilization became issues in the 1946 Congressional elections. The Republicans regained control of Congress for the first time in sixteen years. The new 80th Congress was more conservative than in the New Deal days, and Truman's liberal positions on civil rights pushed many Southern Senators and Congressmen toward a **coalition** with the Republicans. The business-oriented Republicans handed him a bitter defeat when they overrode his veto of the anti-union *Taft-Hartley Act* in 1947. The Act outlawed closed-shops, permitted government intervention in strikes, and cancelled many of the collective bargaining gains made under the *National Labor Relations Act* of 1935. Truman was running into a stone wall of opposition on domestic issues, but he was able to reorganize the military. Congress did pass the administration's *National Security Act* of 1947 which consolidated all military affairs under the Department of Defense, coordinated the military command under a **Joint Chiefs of Staff**, and formed the **Central Intelligence Agency** (CIA). His energetic foreign policy of containment, the Truman Doctrine (page 270), also began to earn him popularity. Stalin was breaking the Yalta and Potsdam agreements in Eastern Europe and Iran. Truman's tough diplomatic stance was unexpected.

THE 1948 ELECTION

Perhaps this personal characteristic of scrappy toughness helped Truman win an uphill battle in the election of 1948. It is considered one of the greatest "come-from-behind victories" in the history of presidential elections. The

Democrats nominated him rather unenthusiastically, and the Southern wing of the party, opposed to his civil rights position walked out of the convention. They formed their own **States' Rights Party** (nickname: **Dixiecrats**) and nominated Governor **Strom Thurmond** (SC) as their standard-bearer. A small, left-leaning group of Democrats also left the party in protest to Truman's anti-Soviet policies and nominated former Vice President **Henry A. Wallace** to run on a new Progressive Party ticket.

With the Democrats badly split, the Republicans could sense victory. They renominated their 1944 candidate, New York Governor **Thomas E. Dewey** (1902-1971). The overconfident Dewey ran a slow-paced, lackluster campaign. Truman threw himself into an enthusiastic campaign. Crisscrossing the country by train, he emphasized his down-to-earth style and the lack of cooperation from what he called the "Do-Nothing 80th Congress."

Truman upset Dewey by a surprising two million popular votes on election day 1948. (Electoral results: Truman - 303, Dewey - 189, Thurmond - 39). Truman managed to attract a strong African American vote, the labor vote, moderate liberals, and those who agreed with his tough containment policies. Also, he had a strong enough **"coattail effect"** that voters selected Democratic candidates for U.S. Representatives and Senators, restoring the Democrats' control of Congress.

Harry S Truman

THE FAIR DEAL

With a slightly friendlier Congress, Truman was able to get more of his **Fair Deal** domestic program passed. A new *Federal Housing Act*, a revised *Fair Labor Standards Act* with an increased minimum wage, major expansion of Social Security, and federal assistance for city slum clearance programs were passed in his

---

MINI•ASSESSMENT (7-4)

1 To meet the demands of World War II, the Roosevelt administration nearly converted the U.S. economy to one based on
   1 command
   2 laissez-faire
   3 tradition
   4 free enterprise

2 An economic idea begun in WW II that is still used by the federal government is
   1 rationing of consumer goods
   2 "dollar-a-year men"
   3 the withholding tax system
   4 Lend-Lease

3 At Potsdam in 1945, Truman realized
   1 Churchill would no longer support the U.S. military actions
   2 Stalin would be difficult to deal with in the post-war world
   3 the Western allies would have to move out of Berlin
   4 Germany would not accept unconditional surrender

4 President Truman slowed the process of demobilization to

1 reorganize the armed forces
2 stabilize the economy and monitor Soviet behavior
3 slow down rapidly falling prices
4 delay the production of nuclear weapons

Constructed Response

THE WAR YEARS: WOMEN AS A PERCENTAGE OF THE WORK FORCE SOURCE: U.S. BUREAU OF STATISTICS, 1953			
OCCUPATION	1940	1945	1947
Professional	45.5%	46.5%	39.9%
Managerial	11.7%	17.4%	13.5%
Clerical	52.6%	70.3%	58.6%
Sales	27.9%	54.1%	39.9%
Skilled Craftsman	2.1%	4.4%	2.1%
Factory Operative	25.7%	38.3%	28.1%
Domestic Service	93.8%	93.8%	92.3%
Agriculture	8.0%	22.4%	11.8%

1 By percentage, which three categories had the greatest changes in the war years (1940-1945)?

2 Why do all the percentages decline between 1945 and 1947?

term. The Republican-Southern Democrat coalition still handed him defeats on programs to aid education and the small farmer, health insurance for the elderly, and enforcement of civil rights. As Chief Executive, he appointed a national **Civil Rights Commission** in 1947, issued executive orders to end segregation in the the armed forces and in federal jobs, and had the Justice Department challenge segregation in federal housing projects. Truman was able to show strong leadership in domestic affairs.

PEACE WITH PROBLEMS: 1945-1955

FORMATION OF THE UNITED NATIONS

Despite the friction among the Allies at the War's end and the failure to achieve a general peace agreement, significant efforts were made to build some type of peace structure.

In the 1930s, Woodrow Wilson's great dream of a League of Nations to preserve the peace after World War I had failed. Nations had refused to sacrifice their sovereignty for the sake of stabilizing world order. At the end of World War II, Franklin Roosevelt attempted to renew Wilson's dream by devoting his last diplomatic efforts to a new structure, the **United Nations**. He knew the organization could only stand with the cooperation of the United States and the Soviet Union. At Teheran and Yalta, he bargained intensely with Stalin to make the U.N. a reality.

On 25 April 1945, less than two weeks after FDR's death, President Truman opened a world conference at San Francisco to establish a charter for the United Nations organization. The charter created a **General Assembly** to be the general deliberative body of all member nations. The most powerful unit, the **Security Council**, dominated by the great powers, negotiates peaceful settlements of international disputes or uses force to stop acts of aggression. Because each of the five permanent members of the Security Council (Britain, China, France, U.S.A., and U.S.S.R.) have a great power, the **veto**, the U.N. has often failed to achieve its original goal in settling east-west controversies, especially in the Cold War years.

Although it has not lived up to initial expectations, the U.N. has achieved three major goals in the years since its inception,

* world problems have been rapidly brought to public attention and openly debated,

* significant humanitarian actions have been coordinated under its health and economic cultural aid programs in underdeveloped regions, and

* trusteeship programs have transformed former colonies into independent nations.

UNIVERSAL DECLARATION OF HUMAN RIGHTS

Always a fighter for justice, in 1946, Eleanor Roosevelt accepted an appointment as head of the new U.N.'s Commission on Human Rights. She worked diligently to design a basic statement of the rights all human beings should enjoy. In 1948, the United Nations adopted the *Universal Declaration of Human Rights* created by her committee. It sums up the ideals to which all freedom-loving people have long aspired: that all individuals should be able to live their lives in peace and dignity, free from the oppression of political forces and discrimination. This simple, yet profound document has since become a statement of goals for the establishment and monitoring of justice and human dignity throughout the world.

DISPLACED PERSONS

The War destroyed lives in many ways. Most survivors in war-torn areas began to reconstruct their lives with privately organized relief efforts. However, many in Europe were uprooted and could not return to their homes in Soviet-dominated nations. These **"displaced persons"** looked to the U.S. as a land traditionally open to the world's troubled peoples. The restrictive immigration acts of the 1920s barred large numbers of refugees especially from Eastern European origins from moving to the United States. Plagued with problems of demobilization and economic readjustment, Congress moved slowly to aid such people. In 1948, amendments to the *Immigration Acts* permitted the President to make emergency adjustments in the admission quotas, allowing an additional 200,000 carefully-screened persons to enter the country in the next two years.

EXPANSION AND CONTAINMENT: EUROPE

SUMMITRY: YALTA AND POTSDAM

The failure of the Allies to reach agreements on a world peace structure left the post-war world in a rather chaotic state. Built around the major European states, the old world power structure had dissolved. Only two major industrial states emerged from the war stronger – the

United States and the Soviet Union. These two **superpowers** dominated world politics in the generation that followed. The peace structure rested on their ability to work together.

At the wartime summit meetings, Stalin communicated his goals to Roosevelt and later to Truman. The Soviet Union would maximize its security and protect its extensive borders by setting up friendly governments in the areas that its armies liberated. At the Yalta Summit Conference in early 1945, Churchill and

---

MINI•ASSESSMENT (7-5)

1 The U.N. was to be an improvement over the League of Nations, because the U.N. created a Security Council of major powers to
  1 manage world trade
  2 assist former colonies in becoming full-fledged nations
  3 monitor violations of human rights
  4 solve international disputes

2 The original intent of the U.N.'s Security Council has not been achieved because the great powers tend to
  1 be out-voted by neutral Third World nations
  2 use summit meetings to settle their differences independently
  3 use the veto to block effective police actions
  4 favor economic matters over military ones

3 President Truman's desire to aid World War II's displaced persons was made difficult by
  1 Soviet vetoes in the U.N. Security Council
  2 the restrictive immigration policies of the United States
  3 opposition of senators from segregated states
  4 the *Universal Declaration of Human Rights*

4 The United Nations' most impressive achievements have been in the area of
  1 helping underdeveloped nations
  2 easing the tensions of the Cold War
  3 prosecuting human rights violations
  4 controlling the nuclear arms race

Constructed Response

Security Council
develops policies on situations that threaten world peace

Secretariat
carries out administrative functions for Assembly and Security Council; Assembly elects Secretary-General

General Assembly
each nation has one vote, can bring and discuss issues, and recommend actions

Economic and Social Council
oversees agencies dealing with human rights and social conditions

International Court of Justice
rules on international disputes

1 What official unit of the U.N. carries out the actions approved by the General Assembly and the Security Council?

2 Which two units of the U.N. organization deal most directly with threats to world peace?

Roosevelt understood this to mean conducting free elections in these countries after a brief period of military occupation. To Stalin, it meant something else. In 1945 and 1946, Soviet officials moved quickly to insure the occupied nations would have communist governments. American and British diplomats protested that the Soviets were not living up to the Yalta agreements. The Soviets ignored the protests.

At the Potsdam Summit Conference (July 1945), Churchill and Truman brought up the question of free elections in Poland, but Stalin brushed it aside. The Soviets planned to have a block of communist satellite nations become a buffer between themselves and the West. American policy-makers began to see an inevitable **polarization** of world affairs (the world divided into two armed camps around the superpowers: the Soviets and their allies on one extreme, and the Western democracies on the other). They projected a long, drawn out **Cold War** between the superpowers.

WINSTON CHURCHILL AND THE IRON CURTAIN

In the year that followed World War II's end, Congress and the American people characteristically focused on the problems of returning to peacetime. They knew of the difficult situation with the U.S.S.R., but they had a naive confidence that things could work out with the Soviets. The mood was more ominous within the Truman Administration. Veteran State Department officials and diplomats experienced in dealing with the U.S.S.R., such as **Dean Acheson**, **Averill Harriman** and **George F. Kennan**, were pessimistic.

Truman's own optimism about the Soviets was severely shaken at Potsdam. In February 1946 the Soviets refused to end their occupation of Iran. British oil interests appealed for help. In the U.N., the U.S.S.R. ignored the American and British complaints. Secretary of State **James F. Byrnes** issued a threat of American force, and the Soviets withdrew. The episode convinced Truman that the U.S.S.R. was becoming a real challenge to world peace.

The following month, former British Prime Minister Winston Churchill delivered an address in Missouri. Churchill had become a modern-day folk hero in America, and his **Iron Curtain** speech shocked the public and drew attention to the suspicious behavior of the U.S.S.R. Support for Truman's tough stance began to grow.

IRON CURTAIN

"From Stettin on the Baltic, to Trieste on the Adriatic, an iron curtain has descended across the continent."

– Winston Churchill,
Speech at Fulton College, MO, March 1946

TRUMAN DOCTRINE: GREECE AND TURKEY

A year after the Iranian incident, the Soviets again attempted to influence events on their southern border. The U.S.S.R. put pressure on a weak Turkish government to negotiate control over the Straits of the Dardenelles, leading to the Soviets' Black Sea ports. The U.S. and British sent stern notes, and the Soviets backed off again. At the same time, a stronger Soviet effort aimed at helping communist rebels overthrow Turkey's neighbor, Greece. Nearly bankrupted by World War II, the British indicated to Truman that they could not help the Greeks.

Acheson advised Truman to make a strong showing of American commitment in the Mediterranean. The President went before the Republican Congress. He boldly stated that it was America's obligation to see that democratic nations would not be abandoned to communistic aggression. This idea gradually came to be known as the **Truman Doctrine**. The memory of the disastrous Munich Conference, when the democracies appeased Hitler, was still fresh in most minds.

Congress responded positively to Truman's request, and the first principle of America's new **containment policy** was born: America would give military aid and training to nations resisting communist takeovers. Congress allocated the 400 million dollars that Truman had requested to aid Greece and Turkey, and it eventually added an additional 200 million dollars by 1950.

MARSHALL PLAN

A second great principle of the containment policy was set in place at the urging of Truman's key policy advisors: economic aid to stabilize tottering  FOREIGN POLICY regimes in Western Europe. Former Army Chief of Staff General George C. Marshall served as Truman's Secretary of State from 1947-1949. On 5 June 1947, Marshall unveiled a dramatic program for saving the economies of European nations. *The European Recovery Act*, later known as the **Marshall Plan**. Secretary

Marshall pr_____ that the European economy could be stabilized by joint efforts of the European states and grants-in-aid from the U.S. Again, a reluctant Congress was prodded into action by Truman.

At that point, the communist overthrow of a moderate government in Czechoslovakia brought home the seriousness of the situation in Europe. Congress agreed to fund the Marshall Plan for 12 billion dollars. In the long run, the plan offered $13.15 billion to stimulate the Western European economy. The extra production it stimulated in the U.S. undoubtedly helped to avoid the kind of 1930s style global depression that WW I had caused.

The Marshall Plan also paved the way for a number of cooperative projects among Western European nations. In 1952, French Foreign Minister Robert Schuman organized France, West Germany, Belgium, and the Netherlands into a European Coal and Steel Community. Its purpose was to administer tariffs, prices, and supply vital industrial resources. On this base came the **Common Market**, or the European Economic Community, in 1957. It began to break down tariff barriers and coordinate trade in Western Europe.

The Common Market also created a political assembly whose delegates debated problems of mutual concern. Known as the **European Parliament**, it is modeled after the Council of Europe an idea sponsored by Winston Churchill after World War II. It is a general advisory body and has few legislative authority or enforcement powers. In 1993, voters in the Common Market countries agreed to expand membership and renamed it the **European Union**.

BERLIN BLOCKADE AND AIRLIFT

Friction grew between the United States and the U.S.S.R. as the Truman Doctrine and the Marshall Plan became effective. To strengthen Western Europe, the United States, Britain, and France had earlier agreed to merge the administration of their occupation zones in Germany, into a single Federal Republic of Germany (commonly called West Germany until reunification in 1990). The U.S.S.R. wanted to keep Germany weak. The Soviets would not agree to creating a reunited nation.

Germany
Post
World War II

The Soviets retaliated by making it more and more difficult for the other Allies to administer their half of Berlin, which was deep inside Soviet East Germany. At the end of the War, it was agreed that the German capital would be divided into four zones. However, no provision had been made for guaranteeing land and water access to the city through the surrounding Soviet Zone.

On 24 June 1948, Truman saw some of his worst suspicions about the Soviets realized. To get the other occupying nations to leave, they blockaded all road, railroad, and canal routes to Berlin. Truman could use force or fly over the blockade. He chose the latter. An elaborate **Berlin Airlift**, called "Operation Vittles," was devised. From June 1948 to September 1949, the U.S. and Royal Air Forces kept half of the city alive with round-the-clock air shipments of nearly 12,000 tons of essential goods each day. Stalin, embarrassed by the show of moral strength, lifted the roadblocks in May of 1949.

FORMATION OF THE NATO ALLIANCE

Nearly four years of difficulties with the Soviets in Germany, plus the pattern of their domination of Eastern European nations, convinced Truman that a major break with American

tradition had to take place. Mere economic and emergency military measures would not achieve containment of communism and Soviet aggression.

In its weakened state, Western Europe could not withstand a military move on the part of the Red Army. America had to enter into a permanent, **multilateral** defense alliance for the first time since the French Alliance of 1778. Dean Acheson served as Truman's Secretary of State from 1949 to 1953. Acheson carefully laid NATO's groundwork with Congress and the European allies. **NATO (North Atlantic Treaty Organization)** united ten nations of Western Europe with Canada and the United States. Any attack on one member was considered an attack on all under the concept of **collective security**.

U.S. AND THE THIRD WORLD

Truman also recognized that the U.S. role in containing communism could not focus solely on

Europe. As the old European colonial empires began to break up, new underdeveloped nations were being formed in the "Third World." Communist activities were sparking trouble in these new countries.

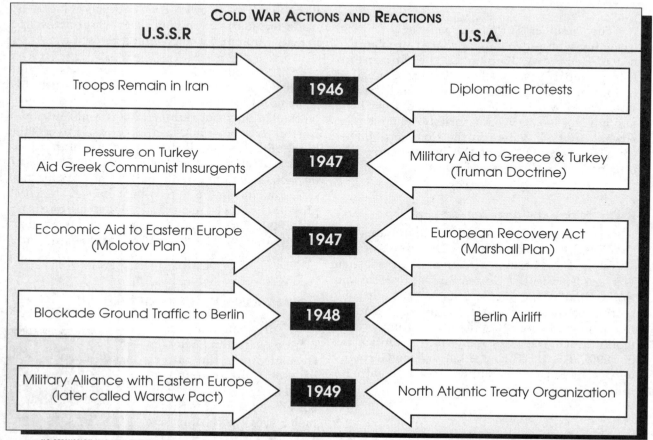

COLD WAR ACTIONS AND REACTIONS		
U.S.S.R		**U.S.A.**
Troops Remain in Iran	1946	Diplomatic Protests
Pressure on Turkey / Aid Greek Communist Insurgents	1947	Military Aid to Greece & Turkey (Truman Doctrine)
Economic Aid to Eastern Europe (Molotov Plan)	1947	European Recovery Act (Marshall Plan)
Blockade Ground Traffic to Berlin	1948	Berlin Airlift
Military Alliance with Eastern Europe (later called Warsaw Pact)	1949	North Atlantic Treaty Organization

In Truman's January 1949 inauguration speech, he made a proposal, now called the **Point Four Program**. He proposed that technological assistance would be given to new and struggling nations to build their economic bases so that they could resist communist insurgency. Out of this proposal came a flow of billions of American dollars for foreign aid to underdeveloped nations which continues to this day.

Jiang Jieshi

By 1949, the essential elements of the containment policy were in place: global economic and military aid to help others resist communist aggression.

CONTAINMENT IN ASIA

THE UNITED STATES AND JAPAN

The general behavior of the Soviet Union in Asia and communist insurgents in China in the post-war period led State Department officials to help rebuild Japan in much more rapid fashion

than originally planned. The U.S. had been supporting the Chinese Nationalists (or Guomindang) under **Jiang Jieshi** (Chiang Kai-shek, 1887-1975) with the hope that the country could be rebuilt into the stabilizing power in East Asia. Difficulties in settling differences between Jiang and the communists under **Mao Zedong** (1893-1976) caused Secretary of State Acheson to convince Truman to shift attention to rebuilding Japan.

Mao Zedong

The Allies stripped Japan of its wartime territorial gains and its military power, but they did not levy harsh reparations. The democratic constitution that General Douglas MacArthur created allowed only a small defensive military. The U.S. provided protection on a large scale. A bilateral (two-sided) defense agreement in 1949 eventually reduced the U.S. occupation forces, but it also allowed the U.S. to maintain bases on Japanese soil. This meant that Japan could devote its resources to peacetime production. U.S. aid was stepped up, paralleling the Marshall Plan in Europe, and a campaign began to convince American business to invest in Japanese industrial growth.

As a result, the U.S. helped create a formidable capitalist democracy with strong trade links to the American market. As economic recovery accelerated, an independent Japanese government took over the reins of power in 1949. This happened just as Jiang's forces were losing their final battle and the communists completed their takeover in China.

THE UNITED STATES AND CHINA

In China, things did not go as well for U.S. policymakers as they had in Japan. Between 1945 and 1949, over two billion dollars was sent to aid Jiang's Nationalist Chinese forces to resist the communist rebels. However, gross mismanagement and corruption plagued the Nationalists. The struggle between Jiang's government and Mao's rebels had been going on from the beginning of Japanese occupation in the 1930s. Some of the U.S. aid money and supplies for Jiang's armies was traded off by his own officers to the communists. After World War II, the U.S. attempted to resolve the Chinese civil war through diplomatic mediation. Truman even sent retired Secretary of State George Marshall. However, Marshall concluded Jiang had lost the people's support.

During the long civil struggle with the communists that began in the 1930s, Jiang's Nationalists became associated with the powerful land-holding aristocratic class. The communists helped the peasants. In the end, the Nationalists defeated themselves. Mao proclaimed victory and established the new **Peoples' Republic of China** on 1 October 1949. The U.S. broke diplomatic relations with China, and the two countries would not speak again for nearly a quarter of a century.

U.S.S.R. TESTS AN A-BOMB (1949)

The loss of China to the communists came on the heels of the announcement that only a month earlier the U.S.S.R. had tested its first nuclear weapon. The American monopoly on atomic weapons was over, and the Cold War power structure changed. These two events,

coming in such rapid succession, were viewed as considerable setbacks for Truman's containment policies. The Republicans, again hoping for victory in the 1950 Congressional elections, loudly criticized the Democrats for allowing such strategic blunders. Secretary of State Acheson came under assault for inept diplomacy. Some even charged that the State Department was riddled with communists who had "sold out" China.

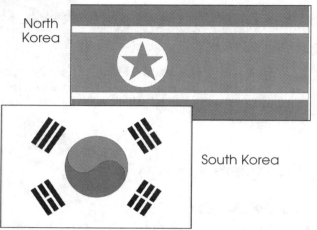

North Korea

South Korea

"HOT WAR" IN ASIA: THE KOREAN CONFLICT

A new side of the Cold War in Asia emerged in the late spring of 1950. On the morning of 25 June, North Korea, a Soviet satellite, attacked U.S.-backed South Korea. The Cold War seemed to be turning hot. After Japan's surrender in 1945, Korea, long dominated by the Japanese, was divided into two occupation zones. The Allies intended to reunify the country. However, the post-war tensions between the U.S. and the U.S.S.R. prevented this. The U.N. was asked to study the question in 1947.

In South Korea, the U.S. set up a democratic constitution. A U.N.-supervised election was held, and the **Republic of Korea** emerged in 1948. Late in that same year, the U.S. withdrew its occupation forces at the request of the U.N. The U.S.S.R. quickly set up the People's Republic of Korea in the northern half of the peninsula. Skirmishes began between the two countries across the 38th Parallel border. Truman sent financial aid to help the South Koreans.

When the June 1950 invasion occurred, the U.S. requested the U.N. Security Council to take action against the aggression by North Korea. With the Soviet Union boycotting the Security Council and unable to veto the Korean resolution, the U.N. voted to assist South Korea.

Truman acted quickly. He termed it a "police action" and placed General MacArthur in command. He ignored Congress, claiming a declaration of war was unnecessary, and ordered U.S. troops into Korea where they were joined by small contingents of other U.N. members.

The speed of North Korea's attack nearly pushed the U.N. and South Korean troops off the peninsula. In September, MacArthur ordered a surprise attack with a brilliant, amphibious landing behind the North Koreans at Inchon. The North Koreans were thrown on the defensive and retreated behind the 38th Parallel. The goal of restoring the border had been achieved.

Truman then took an unexpected step. He authorized MacArthur to enter North Korea, provided the Soviets or Chinese didn't enter the War. Nervous about United Nations' and United States' presence near its border, China invaded North Korea in November and pushed MacArthur's forces back to the 38th parallel.

MacArthur began criticizing Truman and the Joint Chiefs of Staff for restraining him from launching a massive counterattack against the Chinese. In one of the most controversial moves

of his presidency, Truman relieved MacArthur of command. A cease-fire was declared and a round of negotiations began that lasted two years. An armistice was signed on 27 July 1953, restoring the border near the 38th parallel. The War ended in a political as well as military stalemate.

This political cartoon is typical of the news media criticism that President Truman suffered for firing General MacArthur in 1951.

MINI•ASSESSMENT (7-7)

1 After World War II, the U.S. moved to strengthen Japan as an economic power in Asia
  1 as a logical extension of Manifest Destiny
  2 after the disastrous attack on Pearl Harbor
  3 to balance the threat of the Axis alliance
  4 once it appeared a communist government would control China

2 The series of multilateral and bilateral defense agreements set up after 1949 showed that the U.S. desired to
  1 surround the communist nations militarily
  2 send aid to underdeveloped nations
  3 protect its colonies
  4 isolate itself

3 Jiang Jieshi's Nationalist forces lost the 1949 Chinese civil war because
  1 U.S. diplomats misjudged the communists' strength
  2 massive military reinforcements were sent in by the U.S.S.R.

  3 Nationalist leaders were disorganized and sometimes corrupt
  4 the U.S. refused to become involved in China's internal politics

Constructed Response

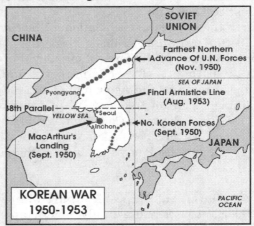

KOREAN WAR 1950-1953

1 At what point shown on the map did the U.N. forces restore the pre-June 1950 border?

2 Why was the Korean conflict a "turning point" for the U.S. in the era of containment?

COLD WAR AT HOME

The post-World War II period was a stormy time domestically. Not only were there economic ups and downs, but adjusting to the new role of the U.S. as the worldwide anti-communist defender of democracy was not easy for Americans. The actions of the Soviet Union in Europe and Asia and the vigor of the Truman Administration's response caused many to grow fearful. In Washington, politicians in both parties were indicating that communist subversion was widespread.

TRUMAN AND GOVERNMENT LOYALTY CHECKS

The anti-communist concern caused Truman to form a **Loyalty Review Board** which investigated thousands of federal employees, some of whom were dismissed or resigned. The country began to show signs of paranoia. Notarized (signed before an official) loyalty oaths were frequently required of public and private employees under threat of dismissal.

THE SMITH ACT AND
CONGRESSIONAL INVESTIGATIONS

In 1947, the House of Representatives authorized its **Committee on Un-American Activities** to investigate the many charges of left-wing activities in the government. The Committee launched its investigation of the American Communist Party by leveling contempt charges against leaders who refused to testify. In the summer of 1948, the Justice Department successfully prosecuted eleven of these leaders for violation of the *Smith Act* (1940). The *Smith Act* made illegal the teaching or advocating of the forceful overthrow of the U.S. government. The communist leaders appealed, claiming the Act violated their First Amendment right of free speech. In *Dennis v. U.S.* (1951), the Supreme Court upheld the *Smith Act* and opened the door for many more prosecutions of Communist Party members in the early 1950s.

Years later, the Supreme Court indicated that the *Smith Act* had actually gone too far. In *Yates v. U.S.* (1957), the Court ruled that speaking, studying, or teaching about theories of forcible overthrow of the government were not the same as participating in an actual conspiracy. In the same year, in *Watkins v. U.S.**, the Court held that witnesses summoned before congressional committees must be properly informed of the nature of the questions to be put

to them and care must be taken to preserve their constitutional rights.

A full-blown anti-Red crusade began as the Committee on Un-American Activities held hearings all over the country. Refusal to answer questions that might incriminate oneself is a basic right protected by Fifth Amendment. Still, "taking the Fifth" cast enough doubt on some witnesses, especially in Hollywood, to cause them to be "blacklisted" and lose their jobs.

THE ALGER HISS CASE

California Congressman **Richard Nixon** achieved national attention as a member of the Committee on Un-American Activities. Nixon was able to gain a U.S. Senate seat as a result. In mid-1948, sensational spy cases began to unfold. The House Committee on Un-American Activities investigated **Alger Hiss** (1904-1994), who had been a State Department official in the Roosevelt years. **Whittaker Chambers**, a *Time* magazine editor and an admitted communist and Soviet agent, openly accused Hiss of espionage. In a shocking move, Chambers involved Rep. Nixon in revealing microfilm of classified State Department documents. Chambers claimed Hiss passed these documents to Soviet officials in the 1930s. Hiss, then head of the prestigious Carnegie Endowment for Peace, vigorously denied the charges before the Committee. Hiss was later charged with perjury and convicted in a series of sensational trials. Hiss served 4 years in prison.

The House Committee on Un-American Activities eventually sponsored legislation designed to stop subversive activities. In 1950, Congress passed the *McCarran Internal Security Act* which essentially allowed the President to arrest and detain persons suspected of any affiliations with groups which might "…contribute to the establishment…of totalitarian dictatorships in the United States."

President Truman vetoed the McCarran bill, saying it would undermine the basic civil liberties of Americans. Congress easily overrode the Truman's veto. At the same time, Truman continued to expand the activities of his own Loyalty Review Board.

The furor caused by the House Committee on Un-American Activities hearings also caused the FBI to broaden its espionage investigations. One of these resulted in the famous **Rosenberg**

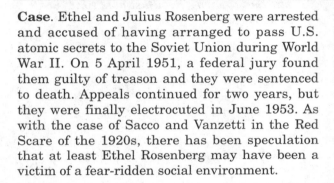

COMMUNISTS IN GOVERNMENT

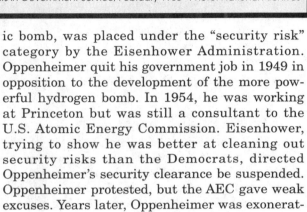

Mr. President (of the Senate), I wish to discuss a subject tonight which concerns me more than does any other subject... It not only concerns me, but it disturbs and frightens me.

About 10 days ago, at Wheeling, W. Va., in making a Lincoln Day speech, I made the statement that there are presently in the State Department a very sizable group of active Communists. I made the further statement, Mr. President, that of one small group which had been screened by the President's own security agency, the State Department refused to discharge approximately 200 of those individuals.

The Secretary of State promptly denied my statement and said there was not a single Communist in the State Department."

– Joseph R. McCarthy, U.S. Senate Speech, *Communists in Government Service*, February 1950   Photo: National Archives

Case. Ethel and Julius Rosenberg were arrested and accused of having arranged to pass U.S. atomic secrets to the Soviet Union during World War II. On 5 April 1951, a federal jury found them guilty of treason and they were sentenced to death. Appeals continued for two years, but they were finally electrocuted in June 1953. As with the case of Sacco and Vanzetti in the Red Scare of the 1920s, there has been speculation that at least Ethel Rosenberg may have been a victim of a fear-ridden social environment.

MCCARTHYISM

The U.S. Senate was not silent in this growing atmosphere of mistrust. Wisconsin Republican **Joseph R. McCarthy** (1908-1957) began to make a series of shocking accusations about communist influence on high government officials which included General Marshall, Dean Acheson, and 1952 Democratic Presidential candidate Adlai Stevenson. As chairman of the Senate Committee on Government Operations, McCarthy led his own anti-communist investigations, making brash charges and ignoring the civil rights of those he subpoenaed to testify. He never unearthed any conspiracy or any communists in government, but he came to symbolize the great anti-communist crusade of the early 1950s. His fellow Republicans had enjoyed his attacks on the Truman Administration but began to change their minds when he began attacking officials of the Eisenhower Administration.

LOYALTY AND DISSENT: THE OPPENHEIMER CASE

Even as eminent a person as Dr. J. Robert Oppenheimer, who had developed the first atom-ic bomb, was placed under the "security risk" category by the Eisenhower Administration. Oppenheimer quit his government job in 1949 in opposition to the development of the more powerful hydrogen bomb. In 1954, he was working at Princeton but was still a consultant to the U.S. Atomic Energy Commission. Eisenhower, trying to show he was better at cleaning out security risks than the Democrats, directed Oppenheimer's security clearance be suspended. Oppenheimer protested, but the AEC gave weak excuses. Years later, Oppenheimer was exonerated.

McCarthyism finally met its match when the Senator pledged to get the communists out of the U.S. Army. Millions of Americans watched the televised hearings. Senator McCarthy was shown to be reckless and irresponsible. His unpopularity became an embarrassment. The U.S. Senate officially censured him in 1954.

SUMMARY

By 1955, Americans were becoming accustomed to the tensions of Cold War, the Korean Conflict was over, and McCarthy was silenced. The hysteria over internal security subsided and the public's attention was drawn to other matters.

MULTI-CHOICE QUESTIONS

1 A basic argument used by isolationists is that the tradition of U.S. neutrality stems from
   1 Lincoln's *Emancipation Proclamation*
   2 Washington's *Farewell Address*
   3 Teddy Roosevelt's "Big Stick Policy"
   4 Wilson's "New Freedom"

2 Public support for congressional neutrality legislation began to change after
   1 the Munich Conference
   2 Italy conquered Ethiopia
   3 Franco was victorious in Spain
   4 France fell to Hitler

3 The *Lend - Lease Act*
   1 effectively ended congressional neutrality
   2 raised high protective tariff walls
   3 set up the defense plan for the Western Hemisphere
   4 nearly threw the U.S. into another depression

4 President Franklin Roosevelt rallied Americans to help Britain and the U.S.S.R. against the Axis nations by stating we must
   1 "make the world safe for democracy"
   2 "remain neutral no matter how costly"
   3 "remember that we have nothing to fear but fear itself"
   4 "become the great arsenal of democracy"

5 Which of the following programs had to be abandoned as America entered the war?
   1 bond rallies
   2 Lend-Lease
   3 Good Neighbor Policy
   4 New Deal

6 The war in the Pacific involved a difficult
   1 co-ordination of British, French, and American forces
   2 intense rivalry between the British and American navies
   3 island-hopping strategy
   4 conquest of mainland China

7 Women made their most significant contribution to the war effort by
   1 administering the rationing program
   2 serving in combat units
   3 filling industrial jobs
   4 acting as diplomatic couriers

8 Truman's decision to use the atomic bomb turned on his desire to
   1 demonstrate U.S. power to Churchill
   2 force Hitler to surrender
   3 halt wartime inflation of the economy
   4 reduce the loss of American lives in the Pacific

9 In upholding the internment of U.S. citizens of Japanese ancestry (*Korematsu v. U.S.* 1944), the Supreme Court used the rule set in the Schenck decision (1919) that individual rights may be suspended when
   1 there is a danger to the society
   2 the economy is in a state of depression
   3 the doctrine of habeas corpus is used
   4 state and national governments are in conflict

10 The *Servicemen's Readjustment Act* (1944) actually helped
   1 end segregation in the U.S. armed forces
   2 increase the number of men being drafted
   3 prevent mistreatment of Axis war prisoners
   4 convert the economy to peacetime

11 Truman was unable to get many of his legislative proposals passed because he
   1 retained wartime price controls too long
   2 had no background in legislative matters
   3 was opposed by a coalition of conservatives and segregationists
   4 condemned Keynesian economic theories as wasteful

12 The term "Cold War" indicates
   1 international disputes over mineral rights in polar regions
   2 intense competition and confrontations between the "superpowers"
   3 "superpower" hostilities were cooled down by United Nations' mediation
   4 Congress became cool toward the President's spending programs

13 Senator Joseph McCarthy's activities were criticized because they
   1 attempted to discredit the Democratic Party at election time
   2 focused narrowly on the U.S. State Department
   3 often violated individuals' constitutional rights
   4 provoked the communist attack on South Korea

Base your answer to question 14 on the chart at the right and your knowledge of U.S. history and government.

THE ELECTION OF 1948				
CANDIDATE	PARTY	POPULAR VOTE	ELECTORAL VOTE	PERCENT OF POPULAR VOTE
Harry S Truman	Democrat	24,105,812	303	49.5
Thomas E. Dewey	Republican	21,970,065	189	45.1
J. Strom Thurmond	States' Rights	1,169,063	39	2.4
Henry A. Wallace	Progressive	1,157,172	0	2.4

14 One reason the election of 1948 is considered one of the greatest upset victories in the history of presidential elections is that
1 the incumbent President lost the election
2 Truman's party splintered into three groups
3 Dewey won the popular vote but lost the electoral vote
4 two third parties received the same percent of the electoral vote

15 The *Taft-Hartley Act* was aimed at
1 curbing the power of labor unions
2 helping World War II veterans readjust to peacetime
3 limiting the number of presidential terms
4 increasing Social Security benefits

THEMATIC ESSAY QUESTION

Theme:

> **Foreign Policy Change**
>
> Several actions taken by the U.S. government after World War II had significant effects on global affairs.

Task:

> Using your knowledge of United States history and government, write an essay in which you select *three* actions taken by the U.S. government after World War II in the field of foreign affairs. For each one chosen:
>
> • describe the existing economic, social, or political conditions that prompted the action, and
> • discuss the impact of the change on global conditions.

Suggestions:
You may use any action from your study of United States history and government. You may wish to include actions such as the Berlin Airlift, the Point Four Program, the NATO Alliance, the Marshall Plan, the Truman Doctrine, or joining the United Nations. **You are not limited to these suggestions.**

DOCUMENT BASED QUESTION

The following task is based on the accompanying documents. The documents may have been edited for the purposes of this exercise. The task is designed to test your ability to work with historical documents. As you analyze the documents, take into account both the source of the document and the author's point of view.

Directions:
Read the documents in Part A and answer the question after each document. Then read the directions for Part B and write your essay.

Historical Context:

War is always disruptive to societies. World War II had significant effects on different groups within the United States.

Task:

Using information from the documents and your knowledge of United States history and government, write an essay in which you describe how life changed for certain groups in American society during World War II.

Part A - Short Answer

Analyze the documents and answer the questions that follow each document.

Question for Document 1

How did young Frankie's life changed when he got his first job in the American Steel foundry.

DOCUMENT 1

"My first job was at the American Steel foundry in Granite City (IL). I worked as a molder's helper. ...It was a great change from Richmond (KY). I had electricity and indoor plumbing. I just walked across the street to the grocery store. I had money to buy any kind of food I wanted. ...We went out to eat, which was brand new to me. ...Meeting people from different places made me see that I actually didn't know about anything else but the little community I was raised in."

– Frankie Cooper quoted in *The War Years*, 1967

Question for Document 2

What effect did military production have on the amount of money middle class Americans had to spend?

source - U.S. Bureau of the Census, *Historical Statistics of the United States*

DOCUMENT 2

	MILITARY EXPENDITURES AND PERSONAL CONSUMPTION	
YEAR	MILITARY EXPENDITURE (IN BILLIONS)	PERSONAL CONSUMPTION (IN BILLIONS)
1938	$ 1.0	$ 64.6
1940	1.6	71.9
1942	22.6	89.7
1944	74.7	109.8

Question for Document 3

How were the lives of Japanese Americans living in this section of Los Angeles affected by this order?

DOCUMENT 3 – *U.S. GOVERNMENT PROCLAMATION*

Instructions to All Persons of Japanese Ancestry Living in the following Area:

All that portion of the city of Los Angeles, State of California, within the boundary beginning at that point at which North Figueroa Street meets a line following the middle of the Los Angeles River; thence southerly and following the said line to East First Street; thence westerly on East First Street to Alameda Street; thence southerly on Alameda Street to East Third Street; thence northwesterly on East Third Street to Main Street; thence northerly on Main Street to First Street; thence northwesterly to Figueroa Street; thence northeasterly on Figueroa Street to the point of beginning.

Pursuant to the provisions of Civilian Exclusion Order No. 33, this Headquarters, dated May 3, 1942, all persons of Japanese ancestry, both alien and non-alien, will be evacuated from the above area by 12 o'clock noon, P.W.T., Saturday, May 9, 1942.

No Japanese person living in the above area will be permitted to change residence after 12 o'clock noon P.W.T., Sunday May 3, 1942, without obtaining special permission from the representative of the Commanding General, southern California Sector, at the Civil Control Station located at Japanese Union Church, 120 North San Pedro Street, Los Angles, California.

Question for Document 4

What changes did manufacturers and consumers have to accept during the War?

DOCUMENT 4

"...Roosevelt's War Production Board started off by banning the production of nonessential items to the war effort, including new automobiles, refrigerators, and bicycles among others. The Ford Motor company began turning out B-24 Liberator bombers instead of cars and by 1944, the plant produced one every sixty-three minutes. General Motors assembled fighter planes and bomber parts instead of Buicks. Chrysler manufactured bomber fuselages..."

– Emert, P.R., "Changing to a Wartime Economy," *World War II: On the Homefront*, 1996

Question for Document 5

What encouragement did women have to take jobs in fields that had previously been "the exclusive domain" of males?

DOCUMENT 5

We Can Do It!

Question for Document 6

Why did some African Americans find it hard to fight fascism overseas?

DOCUMENT 6

"... [African Americans] were extremely concerned over the fact that racism and bigotry and discrimination were a continuing practice...Fascism was not a monopoly of Hitler, or of Mussolini, or of the Japanese. It was something seen everyday on the streets of Baltimore...We did not see much sense in the War unless it was tied to a commitment for change on the domestic scene..."

– Alexander J. Allen quoted in *Democracy and Hypocrisy*, 1976

Question for Document 7

If the country needed war workers so badly, why did men react this way to Adele?

DOCUMENT 7

"... And they said, 'Now Adele, it's going to be a real challenge, because you'll be the only woman in the shop.' I thought to myself, Well that's going to be fun, all those guys and Adele... I walked in there, in my overalls, and suddenly all the machines stopped and every guy in the shop just turned around and looked at me. I think it was two weeks before anyone even talked to me. The discrimination was indescribable. They wanted to kill me."

– Adele Erenberg quoted in *The Home Front – America During World War II*, 1984

GO ON TO PART B

Part B - Essay

Directions:

• Write a well organized essay that includes an introduction, several paragraphs, and a conclusion.
• Use evidence from the documents to support your response.
• Do not simply repeat the contents of the documents.
• Include specific related outside information.

Historical Context:
War is always disruptive to societies. World War II had significant effects on different groups within the United States.

Task:
Using information from the documents and your knowledge of United States history and government, write an essay in which you describe how life changed for certain groups in American society during World War II.

Be sure to include specific historical details. You must also include additional information from your knowledge of United States history and government.

1950-

KOREAN WAR ENDS (1953)
BRINKSMANSHIP (1953)
BROWN V. BOARD OF EDUCATION (1954)

1955-

CIVIL RIGHTS REVOLUTION (1956-1966)
LITTLE ROCK (1957)
SPUTNIK (1957)

1960-

BERLIN WALL (1961)
CUBAN MISSILE CRISIS (1962)

WAR ON POVERTY (1964)
1965-
VIETNAM ESCALATION (1965-1968)
MIRANDA V. ARIZONA (1966)

MOON LANDING (1969)

1970-

WATERGATE (1972-74)
DÉTENTÉ (1972-1976)
VIETNAM WITHDRAWAL (1973)
ROE V. WADE (1973)
ARAB OIL CRISIS (1973-1974, 1979)

1975-

CAMP DAVID ACCORDS (1979)
IRANIAN HOSTAGE CRISIS (1979-1981)

1980-

THE
WORLD IN
UNCERTAIN TIMES

St. Patrick's Cathedral & Sculpture
of Greek Titan, Atlas, NYC, NY
– ©PhotoDisc 1993

Toward A Post-industrial World: Living In A Global Age

After World War II, the pace of global change accelerated. Interdependence among nations grew. Since the isolation of earlier times no longer worked, the United States tried to meet the challenges presented by the changes. America learned that seeking global cooperation was not easy. Conflicts arose frequently. The United States learned to consider the basic desire of all nations for sovereignty and control of their destinies.

Change Within The United States

Modern wars spur technological growth. World War II sparked new advances in science that generated many peacetime applications. Energy, materials, business organizations, and even the basic approach that Americans had to their work, changed rapidly.

Changing Energy Sources

The United States has become the largest consumer of energy in the world. Using traditional fossil fuels to provide enough energy to meet a rising standard of living has caused environmental problems. In addition, petroleum imports have made Americans dependent upon the political and economic whims of other nations.

In 1957, the first nuclear power plant opened. During the 1960s, the number of new facilities grew in number. By 1990, 112 nuclear power plants were in operation in the United States. One quarter of the world's nuclear power plants were in the United States. Nuclear plants generated nearly 20% of the nation's electricity.

However, long-term operational costs are sometimes lower than fossil fuel plants. Nuclear power plant construction peaked in the 1970s. Inflation and safety concerns drove construction costs to over $4 billion per plant. Only one nuclear plant opened during the 1990s, and no new ones are planned. By 2000, the number of operational nuclear facilities had fallen to 104.

Cooling towers for nuclear reactors
(PhotoDisc ©1995)

Many critics question the safety of nuclear reactors. Although rare, plant breakdowns resulted in the leakage of small amounts of radiation. A 1979 nuclear accident at the **Three Mile Island Reactor** near Harrisburg, Pennsylvania heightened awareness of the dangers. The future of nuclear generated energy depends upon the success of researchers to perfect fusion techniques, a more desirable approach.

Changing Materials

Stronger and lighter materials affect every aspect of modern life. New plastics can withstand changes in weather, are lighter than metals, and retain strength for many years. Plastics have widespread applications in the construc-

> Note: Items marked with an * are listed in the *Landmark Supreme Court Decisions* chart in Appendices.

tion industry. Automobiles and airplanes use lighter metals and alloys to reduce weight and fuel consumption. The medical and communications industries now use fiber optics. This process sends light through minute fiber rods. Scientists are also making rapid progress in superconductivity. This process will revolutionize sending electricity over long distances.

Computer Advertisement
MacConnection catalog, May 2000

CHANGING TECHNOLOGY

Computers are a vital part of everyday life in America. In business and industry, computers speed communication, accounting, inventories, and banking. Computers help factories automate operations. In government, computers increased the efficiency of law enforcement and tax collection. Military strategy and pinpoint bombing techniques depend on a wide range of computer guidance systems. On-board computers do millions of split second calculations needed for space exploration. In health and medicine, computers aid in diagnoses and monitor complex equipment.

The computer age has also meant

- **fewer "blue-collar" jobs** when automation and robotics replace human labor,

- **increased need for computer literacy** to qualify for jobs in nearly all fields,

- **reduced individual privacy** due to governments' and private data collecting organizations' greater capacity to access information on individuals, and

- **enhanced information explosion** as widespread access to the internet provides an almost limitless source of material.

CHANGING CORPORATE STRUCTURES

After World War II, many corporations internationalized their operations. Today, **multinational corporations** are common in manufacturing, mining, banking, and petroleum production. Advantages to large scale operations include: access to raw materials, cheap labor, and international markets. Because they operate in many countries, multinationals can avoid the restrictions imposed by individual governments. Smaller corporations doing business within one nation do not have this advantage.

Critics of multinationals fear corporations will interfere in the domestic affairs of nations. They also say **LDCs** (less developed countries) will be dominated by multinationals. American critics denounce multinationals for shifting operations overseas for cheaper labor.

Corporate mergers also changed the structure of American business. Firms that used to sell a single product merged with others into giant **conglomerates**. A typical merged-management conglomerate included operation in diverse fields: manufacturing, transportation, entertainment, travel, communications, and food processing. Some mergers combined two competing firms in the same product line (provided they did not violate the antitrust laws). This gave conglomerates staggering market power.

CHANGING NATURE OF EMPLOYMENT

When the *Constitution of the United States* was written, over 90% of the American population was **agrarian** (made living by farming). The technologies developed in the 19th century shifted the economy to industry. Since World War II, however, many older industries have closed or moved to other countries. Foreign competition and automation resulted in huge drops in the steel and textile industries, mining, and other "blue collar" jobs.

Growth in today's economy is in **service industries**. These industries create jobs in health care, retailing, education, finance, food service, and recreation. Economists cite the decline in manufacturing jobs as a new stage of economic development they call post-industrialism. For the American worker, it means more frequent occupation changes in mid-life, and diminished job security. In addition, many jobs will require more technical education.

CHANGE IN GLOBAL CONDITIONS

In the industrial nations of North America, Western Europe, and East Asia, modern farming techniques enable small numbers of farmers to produce enough food for the entire population. The opposite is true of the LDCs of Asia, Latin America, and Africa. Although most people in LDCs are farmers, starvation is common. Most farms operate on subsistence levels (barely sufficient to maintain life). Cash crops for export (cotton, tobacco) seriously cut the amount of acreage devoted to food production.

AGRICULTURE: TRADITIONAL PATTERNS AND THE GREEN REVOLUTION

Many LDCs have yet to take advantage of the **Green Revolution** – intense scientific effort developed new technology, machinery, and fertilization. Improved strains of food staples (such as disease-resistant wheat) increased production and protein intake in industrialized nations. Some LDCs, such as China and India, have shown progress in adopting Green Revolution methods. Other LDCs, such as those in Saharan Africa, have experienced difficulties for a number of reasons:

- resistance to changes in traditional lifestyle

- unpredictable weather patterns, poor soil, and erosion

- illiteracy

Desertification is evident in the appearance of the emaciated Sahel Cattle around Keur Bibarick, Senegal, Africa.   ©David Johnson, Photographer 1993

- lack of governmental cooperation

- inadequate infrastructures

- lack of financial capital

MANUFACTURING: DEVELOPED NATIONS V. LDCS

Since World War II, the older industrial nations (Britain, France, and the United States) have seen declines in heavy industries (steel, autos). After the War, U.S. aid helped rebuild devastated nations in Western Europe and Asia. This gave them a more technologically advanced industrial base. Japan, South Korea, Taiwan, and China's Hong Kong began producing products competing with those of the United States.

World War II upset the prewar global colonial structure of Western European nations. Independence movements swept through Asia and Africa in the 1950s and 1960s. With the change came the "Revolution of Rising Expectations." It created a hope that LDCs could imitate the higher standards of living of Western nations. Developed nations shared technology and gave loans to former colonies. Some of the multinationals provided technical training and investment capital. Unstable governments, unskilled labor, and lack of capital hindered progress. However, rapid population growth often offset industrial gains. In some cases, skilled workers emigrated from their homelands seeking higher wages in developed nations.

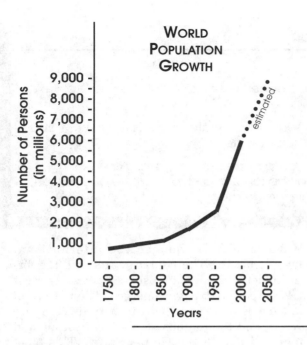

WORLD POPULATION GROWTH

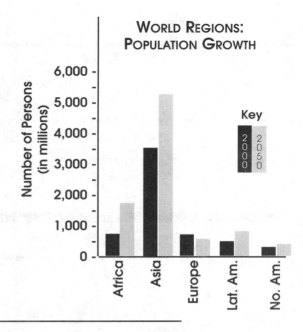

WORLD REGIONS: POPULATION GROWTH

WORLD POPULATION GROWTH: HUNGER AND CONTROL

In recent times, population growth declined in most industrialized nations. Changing social values caused much of the decrease. The growing importance of careers for women and later marriages limit child-bearing years. In most developed nations, people voluntarily reduced family size. The expense of raising children is one major reason for this.

The reverse is true for most LDCs. After World War II, advances in medicine and science reduced infant mortality. Medical advancements increased longevity. Birthrates remain high in LDCs. In many countries, the population doubles every thirty years. Reasons for high birthrates in LDCs include

- working children in traditional agricultural societies

- marriage at a young age

- religious traditions and importance of male heirs

- illiteracy

Poor living conditions and food shortages have resulted from population explosions. Inadequate transportation and lack of communication (especially in Africa) have made the problems worse.

In the 1970s, India and China undertook massive public education campaigns to convince couples to limit child bearing. They have met with limited success.

ENVIRONMENTAL CONCERN

Every human pays a significant price for technological advancement. Industrial wastes pollute the environment.

In environmental matters, the actions of one nation can affect many. Trying to clean up the environment often takes international cooperation. Some examples of international problems include:

- **acid rain** from the effluent of U.S. factories, which hurt both Canadian wildlife and farms

- **chemical dumping** in rivers that flow through several European nations

- **nuclear testing** over oceans that cause widespread radiation fallout

- **lethal pesticide** residues carried by air currents

- **ozone depletion** caused by the release of the chemical compound CFC (used in refrigeration) into the upper atmosphere

The misuse of natural resources and destruction of the land concerns environmentalists. In developed nations, industrial and urban growth

POLLUTION		
TYPES	**CAUSE**	**SOLUTION**
Air	Factories and Automobiles	Burn cleaner fuels; Install pollution control equipment
Water	Factory discharges, municipal sewage waste plants	Conservation of water sources; Treatment and filtration of water
Land	Garbage dumps Buried toxic waste	Recycling paper, metals, and glass; Clean up landfills and toxic waste dumps; Seek safer storage areas

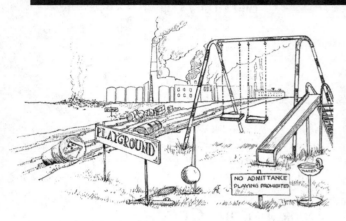

results in more roads, shopping centers, and housing. This reduces farm acreage and forests. The danger of flooding increases. **Strip mining** (tearing up large chunks of land for valuable resources) ruins the ecological balance. Both of these situations have begun to occur in the LDCs.

Over-grazing and poor soil management have turned large areas into deserts. Nations eager for industrialization have not placed very high priorities on environmental protection. The expense has been too high. Meeting consumer demand and protecting nature are often conflicting goals. Governments find it difficult to do both. They have to make too many agonizing trade offs.

CHANGING POWER RELATIONSHIPS

For centuries, the struggle for global leadership took place among the nations of Europe. Shifting alliances constantly changed the European balance of power. In modern times, the main players were England and France. Spain, Germany, Italy, and Russia had varying influences.

World War II changed the international power structure. The United States and the former Soviet Union became superpowers. An East vs. West power struggle emerged. The nations of Eastern Europe and China allied with the Soviets, and the nations of Western Europe and Japan allied with the United States. This bipolar division left out most LDCs. As Western European colonial empires broke up, new nations emerged from independence movements in Africa and Asia. The East-West power structure remained in place until the Soviet Union dissolved in 1991.

LDCs usually have low GDPs. With the exceptions of Australia, New Zealand, and South Africa, and Japan, the more developed nations are in the North America and Western Europe. This is significant. Many of the LDCs have the raw materials needed by the developed nations. Some of the "have not" nations use their economic power to pressure the industrial "haves." The industrial nations suffered economic distress when the **OPEC** (Organization of Petroleum Exporting Countries) cartel's boycotts reduced oil supplies in the 1970s.

CONTAINMENT AND CONSENSUS: 1945-1960

EISENHOWER FOREIGN POLICIES

The rebuilding of Europe and Asia after World War II revealed a lack of cooperation

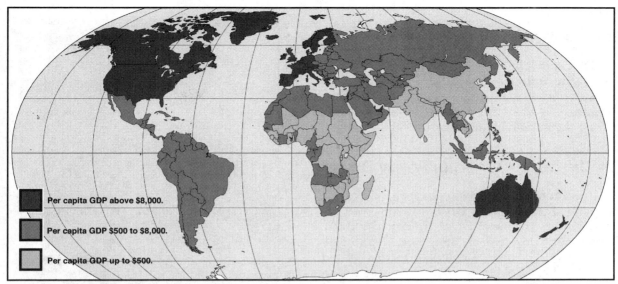

The "Have" and "Have Not" Countries (based on per capita gross domestic product)
In general, the lower the per capita GDP, the lower the standard of living and the poorer the country.
In most cases, the low GDP countries are the "have nots" or LDCs.

Per capita GDP above $8,000.

Per capita GDP $500 to $8,000.

Per capita GDP up to $500.

between the great powers. Soviet-American disputes over Germany, Eastern Europe, the Middle East, and Korea caused bitter and lasting divisions. The decade of the 1950s saw a continuation of the U.S.–U.S.S.R. rivalries. The Eastern and Western Blocs became firmly entrenched. Each side attempted to strengthen its influence among the developing nations.

Under President Eisenhower, the United States attempted to maintain world peace while continuing the campaign to check the spread of communism, especially in Asia. The proliferation of nuclear weapons and the introduction of long-range missiles gave international conflicts the potential for global destruction.

END OF THE KOREAN CONFLICT

The conflict in Korea turned into a stalemate. The **Panmunjom peace talks** bogged down on the question of repatriation of prisoners of war. An armistice was finally signed in July of 1953, leaving the nation divided near the 38th Parallel.

THE DIPLOMACY OF JOHN FOSTER DULLES

President Eisenhower appointed career diplomat **John Foster Dulles** (1888-1959) as his Secretary of State. Dulles held many State Department posts in his long career and had

FOREIGN POLICY

been a delegate to the United Nations. He was a staunch opponent of communism and believed that the United States had to make forceful moves to prevent Soviet advances. Dulles held that war could be avoided only if America was constantly ready to deploy deterrent force. This policy of being on the brink (edge) of war earned Dulles' diplomacy the name **"brinkmanship."** He discouraged the Soviets from risking a direct confrontation with the West with the threat of **massive retaliation** (to destroy an attacking nation with nuclear weapons). To discourage a "first strike," President Eisenhower supported the policy and concept of **mutual destruction** (devastation so great that no country can "win" a war fought with weapons of mass destruction).

Indirect communist aid to insurgents in Asia continued. The poor, weak nations of Southeast Asia were prime targets. The possibility of the nations falling to communism one after another became known as the **domino theory**. Dulles formed a NATO-like organization to strengthen resistance in Asia. In 1954, **SEATO** (the Southeast Asia Treaty Organization) was formed. SEATO lacked the unity and power of the older European alliance and was unsuccessful.

H-BOMB & ATOMS FOR PEACE

By 1949, the U.S.S.R. exploded its first nuclear device, followed by Britain and France. India and China joined these ranks in the 1960s and Pakistan and Israel in the 1970s.

In the early 1950s, both superpowers exploded devices known as **hydrogen bombs**, which

Dwight David Eisenhower
White House Historical Association

were hundreds of times more powerful than the two dropped in 1945.

The possibility of nuclear annihilation became increasingly real. However, the Soviets balked at establishing international inspection teams to verify continued compliance with disarmament agreements.

In 1953, President Eisenhower hoped to increase the peaceful benefits of atomic energy by proposing the **Atoms for Peace** program. Under this international agreement, nations shared knowledge and materials in order to advance peaceful applications of nuclear power. The U.N. approved the plan, which has done much to aid international science, but it did little to curb the arms race.

SUMMITS AND U-2'S

The death of Soviet dictator Josef Stalin in March of 1953 left a power vacuum at the Kremlin. A number of Politburo figures moved in and out of the leadership. **Nikita S. Khrushchev** (1894-1971) emerged as the new First Secretary of the Communist Party, and by 1958 he became Premier. The leaders of the **"Big Four"** (United States, U.S.S.R., Britain, and France) met at a summit in Geneva in 1955. There was little progress on major issues, such as the reduction of nuclear arms and the reunification of Germany.

In 1959, Khrushchev was Eisenhower's guest on a two-week tour of the United States. No specific agreements were reached. However, they pledged to meet at a summit the following year. This gave the world some hope that Soviet-American relations were improving.

The **Paris Summit** in May of 1960 was a disaster. Two weeks before the meeting, the Soviets shot down a U-2 reconnaissance plane of the U.S. Central Intelligence Agency (CIA) 1,000 miles inside the Soviet border. At first, American officials denied the spy charges. An embarrassed Eisenhower later acknowledged the blunder when the Soviets produced the pilot for a public propaganda trial. Khrushchev demanded an apology from Eisenhower. Then he cancelled the Paris summit before any meetings actually took place.

EISENHOWER DOCTRINE: LEBANON INTERVENTION

In reaction to the widening role of the U.S.S.R. in the Middle East, President Eisenhower followed the precedent of the Truman Doctrine in Europe. He requested congressional funds to aid in fighting communist aggression. Under the **Eisenhower Doctrine**, any Middle Eastern nation that suspected a communist takeover could apply for U.S. assistance. When Lebanon was threatened with a revolution in 1958, it asked for U.S. aid. Eisenhower dispatched a force of U.S. Marines. The Soviets protested, but the situation was brought under control, and the Marines were withdrawn. The United States indicated its dedication to the containment policy, but the Soviets were still able to spread their influence in the region.

SPUTNIK: THE SPACE RACE

By the end of 1957, the Soviet Union had orbited two unmanned space satellites (Sputnik

I and II). The U.S. rocket program had not received much priority from the government, and Americans were shocked that Soviet technology seemed superior. In addition to the loss in prestige, there was concern that the Soviets' rockets now gave them intercontinental ballistic missile capability.

Nikita Khrushchev
Soviet Government Photo

In a flurry of activity, the United States launched its first satellite. Congress funded the ***National Defense Education Act*** to help states upgrade school courses in science and mathematics. The rivalry in space occupied the attention of the American public for the next decade.

DOMESTIC POLITICS AND CONSTITUTIONAL ISSUES: THE EISENHOWER PEACE

In both the 1952 and 1956 presidential elections, Eisenhower easily defeated Illinois Governor **Adlai E. Stevenson** (1900-1965). The Republicans rejoiced in putting their first candidate in the White House since Herbert Hoover. In the 1952 election, they also won control of both houses of Congress. The Democrats regained control of Congress in the 1954 elections, but Eisenhower's moderate approach led to broad cooperation between the White House and Capitol Hill during his two terms.

1 When President Dwight D. Eisenhower said "If you knock down the first row of dominoes, all the others will fall in quick order," he was expressing a view that led to
  1 stronger support for United States involvement in Southeast Asia
  2 less restrictive immigration policies toward Africa and Latin America
  3 decreased foreign aid to Western Europe
  4 the end of colonialism in Africa

2 The policy of "massive retaliation" initiated during the 1950s meant that the United States would have to
  1 keep large detachments of ground forces in Europe
  2 discuss disarmament with the Soviet Union
  3 constantly upgrade its nuclear capability
  4 maintain a favorable balance of trade

3 The successful launching of Sputnik by the Soviet Union in 1957 signaled the beginning of
  1 American fears that the Soviets had achieved technological superiority
  2 the Cold War with the United States
  3 Soviet Aggression in Afghanistan and China
  4 disarmament discussions between the superpowers

Constructed Response

"It is also agreed that the principal deterrent to aggressive war is mobile retaliatory power. This retaliatory power must be vast in terms of its potential. But the extent to which it would be used would, of course, depend on the circumstances. The essential is that a would-be aggressor should realize that he cannot make armed aggression a paying proposition..."
— John Foster Dulles, Secretary of State, Address on April 22, 1957.

1 According to Secretary Dulles, how should the United States prevent aggressors from starting a war?

2 Why did some in the United States oppose the policy as stated in the above quote?

RETURNING THE UNITED STATES TO A PEACETIME ECONOMY

As the Korean War ended in 1953, Eisenhower hoped to stimulate the economy by lifting government wage and price controls. Government defense and foreign aid spending renewed inflation during the rest of the 1950s, but was offset by the steady growth of the economy. Eisenhower managed to balance the budget in three of his eight years, but high tax rates continued. As recovery from World War II took hold in Europe, demand for U.S. agricultural products lessened, and profits began to decline. Inflation was not bothersome to most expanding sectors of the economy, but it ate up the small profits farmers were making.

Eisenhower instituted a more flexible system of farm-price supports, hoping to reduce farmers' dependence on government subsidies and reduce overproduction. A federal Soil Bank Plan paid farmers to take land out of production and convert it to pasture or forest. These plans did not solve the farm problem. Surpluses mounted and many farmers lost money. Continued mechanization drove others out of agriculture altogether.

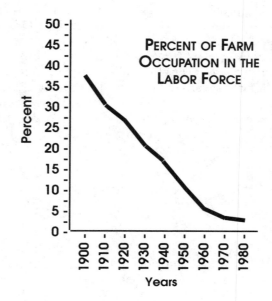

PERCENT OF FARM OCCUPATION IN THE LABOR FORCE

LABOR UNREST

In the years that followed World War II, labor unions experienced much success at the bargaining table. Attracting more members, unions received regular cost-of-living raises, expanded pension benefits, and health insurance. In 1947, the Republican Congress attempted to control the power of organized labor by passing the *Taft-Hartley Labor Management Relations Act* over President Truman's veto (see page 266). Despite its growth and influence, labor was not able to get the *Taft-Hartley Act* repealed during the Eisenhower era.

In 1955, the nation's two giant labor organizations merged. The American Federation of Labor and the Congress of Industrial Organizations – rivals from the days of the Great Depression – formed the AFL-CIO **George Meany** (1894-1980) became the first president of the 15 million member organization.

Corruption plagued many major unions in the 1950s. Congress launched intense investigations against racketeering in the International Longshoremen's Association and the International Brotherhood of Teamsters. Out of these investigations came the *Landrum-Griffin Labor Management Reporting and Disclosure Act* (1957). It required unions to publish financial statements, hold regular elections, use secret ballots, end secondary boycotts, and forbid communists and convicted felons from holding union office.

The Teamsters continued to have problems. They were ejected from the AFL-CIO in the 1960s. In 1967, their long-time president, **James R. Hoffa**, was sent to prison. He mysteriously disappeared after his release in 1972 and was never heard from again. Hoffa's disappearance triggered a long internal struggle. The AFL-CIO readmitted the Teamsters in 1987.

The most serious strike was one by the steelworkers in 1959. After 116 days, Eisenhower invoked the 80-day **injunction** (suspension) provided in *Taft-Hartley*. The strike was settled in 1960 with the workers securing most of their original demands.

THE WARREN COURT

GROWTH OF DEMOCRACY

In 1953, President Eisenhower appointed the governor of California, **Earl Warren** (1891-1974) as the 14th Chief Justice of the Supreme Court. For the next fifteen years, the Warren Court followed a policy of **judicial activism**. This meant that decisions of the Court not only provided interpretations of the Constitution but initiated broad changes in American life. Issues of equality and fairness were being dealt with by Congress, but very slowly. Critics claimed the Court was actually performing legislative tasks and taking power away from the individual (see chart below).

CIVIL RIGHTS

After the Civil War, the Thirteenth, Fourteenth, and Fifteenth Amendments freed former slaves, made them equal citizens, and gave them suffrage. As Reconstruction ended, Southern state leaders found legal ways to avoid

THE WARREN COURT JUDICIAL ACTIVISM	
DECISION	**SIGNIFICANCE**
Brown v. Board of Ed. of Topeka *(1954)	Racial segregation of schools violated the Fourteenth Amendment.
Baker v. Carr *(1962)	"One person, one vote" rule ordered states to set up Congressional Districts on equal basis.
Engel v. Vitale *(1962)	State laws requiring prayers in schools violated the First Amendment.
*Gideon v. Wainwright** (1963)	State laws denying felony suspects legal counsel violated the Sixth Amendment.
*Miranda v. Arizona** (1966)	Authorities must inform accused persons of their "due process" rights under the Fifth and Sixth Amendment.

equal treatment for African Americans. Jim Crow laws established **de jure segregation** throughout the South. In 1896, in a narrow vote, the U.S. Supreme Court upheld the Southern contention that racial separation was legal as long as the facilities for both races were equal (*Plessy v. Ferguson*). The net result was that de jure segregation was considered constitutional. It quickly evolved that transportation, education, dining, and entertainment facilities were always separate, but rarely were they equal.

Jackie Robinson
Sports Magazine, 1947

JACKIE ROBINSON: THE COLOR LINE BREACHED

Condemnations of Nazi racial policies and the service of African Americans in segregated units of the U.S. armed forces in World War II raised consciousness of inequality. African Americans were making progress in educational achievement and gains in political power in Northern cities. They no longer wanted to be treated as second class citizens. Segregation in the military was ended by President Truman in the late 1940s. At the same time, **Jackie Robinson** (1919-1972) became the first African American player in major league baseball. Brooklyn Dodgers' general manager Branch Rickey signed the talented young player in 1946 and brought him into the major leagues the following year. Despite intense prejudice from opposing teams and fans, Robinson calmly managed to break the "color line" of America's national pastime. Robinson's dazzling play helped win the National League championship for Brooklyn and Rookie of the Year honors in 1947.

BROWN V. BOARD OF EDUCATION OF TOPEKA, KANSAS (1954)

Southern senators' use of the **filibuster** (unlimited debate to block legislation) blunted efforts by the Truman and Eisenhower administrations to end racial segregation. The Supreme Court was not subject to the same political pressures as the other two branches. After World War II, the **NAACP** (National Association for the Advancement of Colored People) brought a series of civil cases to the Supreme Court. The Court began applying the Fourteenth Amendment's "equal protection of the laws" phrase against various state segregation laws. In 1954, the Court issued its decision in ***Brown v. the Board of Education of Topeka***, which reversed the doctrine of "separate but equal" put forth in the 1896 *Plessy* case. At the time of *Brown*, racially segregated schools were the norm in nearly 20 states. The Court pronounced racial segregation of schools to be inherently wrong and ordered it ended throughout the nation.

The *Brown Decision* had little immediate effect. Outraged Southern governors and senators claimed that education was a reserved power of the states, and the Supreme Court had no jurisdiction in the matter. In some states, militia and state police kept African Americans from registering at school, while angry mobs threatened violence.

CIVIL RIGHTS MOVEMENT BEGINNINGS FOR AFRICAN AMERICANS

THE MONTGOMERY MOVEMENT

The ruling against separate schools prompted African Americans to demand an end to segregation in all aspects of life. Many African American leaders recognized that court challenges would move slowly against Southern politicians' resistance. They began to take new avenues toward change. In 1955, **Rosa Parks**, an African American seamstress refused to give up her seat to a white passenger on a Montgomery, Alabama bus.

Rosa Parks breaks a Jim Crow Law in 1955 by sitting in the front of a bus.   UPI

Her arrest led to a year-long boycott of city buses organized by a young Baptist minister, **Martin Luther King**, **Jr**. (1929-1968). King rose to national prominence during the incident. The boycott ended in an agreement by the city and the bus company to desegregate the transportation facilities. The Supreme Court later declared such segregation unconstitutional.

Martin Luther King, Jr.

THE LITTLE ROCK CRISIS

Eisenhower was against increasing federal power over the states. However, in 1957, he did take decisive action in civil rights. In Little Rock, Arkansas, Governor Faubus defied federal court orders to admit African American students to Central High School. At one point, the Governor had Arkansas units of the National Guard fix bayonets to keep a handful of students out of the school. Eisenhower could not let such flagrant disregard of federal law go unanswered. On national TV, he ordered the Arkansas National Guard demobilized and sent regular U.S. Army troops to escort the students into the school.

NON-VIOLENT, DIRECT ACTION

African Americans began an intense campaign to overcome the injustice of segregation in all public facilities. In 1960, they began to illegally – but peacefully – sit at segregated lunch counters in restaurants throughout the South. Another group, called the **Freedom Riders**, rode buses to try to desegregate the bus terminals. Their tactics were called **nonviolence**, **direct action,** and **civil disobedience**. Protesters were often arrested and thrown into local jails under the glare of national television cameras. The sometimes brutal tactics of Southern officials in dealing with these "agitators" caused public interest and empathy to grow.

CIVIL RIGHTS LEGISLATION

GROWTH OF DEMOCRACY

In 1957, Congress overcame the Southern filibusters and passed its first *Civil Rights Act* since the Civil War days. The 1957 law created a new Civil Rights Commission to investigate and prosecute injustices. It was also authorized to secure voting rights for African Americans in the South. Another *Civil Rights Act of 1960*, furthered voting rights, but relief was slow and painful, because the full force of the federal government was not put behind enforcement of these laws.

PEOPLE:
PROSPERITY & CONSERVATISM

The 1950s was a time of prosperity. Post war international stress, Korea, and McCarthyism left most Americans desirous of a more stable environment. The Eisenhower domestic policies were conservative by nature, and most people welcomed a lessening of government reform efforts after nearly three decades of upheaval.

POSTWAR CONSUMPTION

The demands for consumer goods boomed during the postwar period. Savings from higher wartime wages gave many Americans disposable income. Nearly 50 million autos were sold between 1950 and 1960, with most families owning a car by the end of the decade. The federal interstate highway system, which began in 1956, made automobile travel faster and easier.

Demand was great, allowing European manufacturers recovering from World War II to profitably export to the United States. The **Volkswagen "Beetle"** from Germany became enormously popular. However, the number of American auto makers declined. Old names, such as Studebaker and Packard disappeared as mergers and reorganizations narrowed the field to the industry's "Big Three" – Ford, General Motors, and Chrysler.

While invented in the 1920s, television was not ready for mass production until after World War II. Postwar prosperity enabled the majority of American families to obtain black and white receivers by the middle 1950s. A wide variety of sports, news programs, and game shows were developed for television. Old Hollywood movies were popular, and many of the comedy and dramatic shows from radio were able to retain audiences for their sponsors by jumping to the video medium.

Critics began to assail TV almost immediately for the violence on popular western and detective shows.

NEW EDUCATIONAL OPPORTUNITIES

Eager young people flooded colleges and universities in search of the higher education needed to qualify for engineering and administrative jobs in expanding American corporations. The 1944 *G.I. Bill* aided returning World War II veterans and continued to aid Korean War veterans with generous education allowances. College enrollment continued to expand through the 1970s. Some state institutions enrolled as many as 25,000 or more students.

THE BABY BOOM

Returning veterans and postwar economic expansion also resulted in a fifteen year surge in

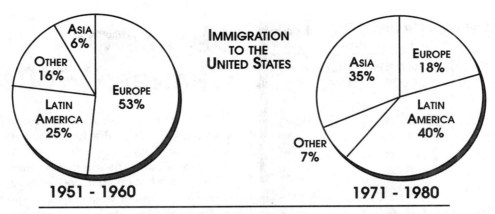

IMMIGRATION TO THE UNITED STATES

1951 - 1960

- ASIA 6%
- OTHER 16%
- LATIN AMERICA 25%
- EUROPE 53%

1971 - 1980

- ASIA 35%
- EUROPE 18%
- LATIN AMERICA 40%
- OTHER 7%

the American birth rate. This "baby boom" created a demand for more schools and teachers. By the end of the 1950s, the economy began catering to the increasing numbers of young people. New forms of dress, entertainment, and music ("Rock 'n' Roll") had a definite youth orientation.

MIGRATION AND IMMIGRATION

NEW IMMIGRATION PATTERNS

Prior to 1965, the *National Origins Quota System* passed in the 1920s, gave preferential quotas to immigrants of "old" ethnic groups from Northern and Western Europe. The *Immigration Act of 1965* abolished the National Origins Quota System altogether. It created a limit for the Eastern and Western Hemispheres and based admission on a first-come, first-served basis. It gave preference to relatives of American citizens and those with needed job skills. Immigration patterns changed as groups fleeing political turmoil in Asia and Latin America began to dominate the ranks of newcomers. Economic instability in Asia and Latin America has led to large numbers of immigrants coming to the United States.

SUBURBS

Americans have always moved in search of a better life. Relatively few new homes were built during the Great Depression and World War II, despite a growth in population. The postwar demand made prices skyrocket. Government officials retained wartime rent control rules. During the 1950s, millions of new, affordable homes were built in suburbs for young families. Shortages of housing and crowding conditions in the cities made commuting from the suburban areas seem more reasonable. Young families flocked to the suburbs in the 1950s. The *G.I. Bill*

aided veterans in securing mortgages and gave even more incentive to construction. The **Levittown** developments in New York and Pennsylvania are examples. Thousands of mass-produced single-family houses were constructed at affordable prices. With employment and shopping at a distance, the convenience of a second automobile often became a "necessity." The mass exodus to the suburbs caused a secondary boom in the construction of shopping centers, roads, water supplies, and sewage systems.

CITIES

The exodus of young middle class families had a devastating economic effect on urban areas. Poorer, unskilled groups from agricultural regions where jobs were declining were moving into the cities. Elderly people on fixed incomes held on to their rent-controlled apartments. War refugees gravitated toward the lower paying job opportunities in city factories as new immigrants had always done. Minority groups could not overcome prejudicial hiring practices and overcrowded slum conditions.

The result was that cities experienced a declining tax base. This made it more difficult for municipalities to meet the need for public housing. Private developers did not want to risk capital in urban housing. They preferred the suburbs or building office complexes for major corporations in downtown areas. Businesses began to leave the cities, too. They fell victim to rising city tax rates and the decline in city services. Many businesses followed the more skilled middle class workers into the suburbs. As businesses left, the resulting unemployment caused conditions of urban decay, bringing many older cities in the Northeast and Mid-West (dubbed "The Rust Belt" by the mass media) to the brink of bankruptcy by the 1960s.

CITY POPULATION CHANGE 1950 – 1990 (SOURCE: U.S. BUREAU OF CENSUS)		
CITY	**POPULATION IN 1990**	**CHANGE 1950-1990**
New York	7,322,564	-569,393
Los Angeles	3,485,398	+1,515,040
Chicago	2,783,726	-837,236
Houston	1,630,553	+1,034,390
Philadelphia	1,585,577	-486,028
San Diego	1,110,549	+776,162
Detroit	1,027,974	-821,594
Dallas	1,006,877	+572,415
Phoenix	983,403	+876,585
San Antonio	935,933	+421,170

As the table above shows, some cities did prosper. Retirees, immigrants, and white urban dwellers of the Northeast moved to the South and West. The "Sun Belt" cities offered warmer climates, expanding job markets, a lower cost of living, and fewer racial problems.

DECADE OF CHANGE: 1960s

The general peace and prosperity of the Eisenhower years disintegrated as the 1960s progressed. Television brought the Vietnam War and urban riots into living rooms and divided public opinion as it had not been since the Civil War. By the end of the decade, the nation soured on social reform programs that had held great promise when the 1960s had dawned.

THE KENNEDY YEARS

In the very close presidential campaign of 1960, Democratic Senator **John F. Kennedy** (MA, 1917-1963) defeated Eisenhower's Vice President, Richard M. Nixon. Kennedy was young, rich, and the first Catholic candidate since Al Smith in 1928. Southern Protestants continued to vote Democratic, because

MINI•ASSESSMENT (8-4)

1   Which is the most valid conclusion that may be drawn from the study of population patterns in the United States since 1950?
    1   Most of the population is concentrated in and around large urban centers.
    2   The number of ethnic groups has declined.
    3   The population of the South has continued to decline.
    4   The Northeast is the fastest growing region in the nation.

2   In the 1950s and the 1960s, a significant factor in the growth of suburbs was the
    1   passage of antipollution laws that closed down urban factories
    2   increase in immigration from Southern and Eastern Europe
    3   building of the interstate highway system
    4   placement of most senior citizen housing in these areas

3   Colleges experienced growth after World War II because
    1   the G.I. Bill provided tuition assistance to returning veterans
    2   there was an influx of foreign students
    3   federal loans were made available to all students
    4   state colleges were converted to federal universities

Constructed Response

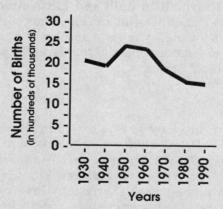

UNITED STATES BIRTH RATE

1   What decade had the highest rate of births?

2   Discuss one cause and one result of the high rate in the years identified in question 1.

THE DEFENSE OF FREEDOM

INSIGHTS ON LIBERTY

"In the long history of the world, only a few generations have been granted the role of defending freedom in its hour of maximum danger. I do not shrink from this responsibility - I welcome it. I do not believe that any of us would exchange places with any other people or any other generation. The energy, the faith, the devotion which we bring to this endeavor will light our country and all who serve it - and the glow from that fire can truly light the world.

"And so, my fellow Americans: ask not what your country can do for you - ask what you can do for your country."

White House Historical Association
Washington, D.C.

– John F. Kennedy, *Inaugural Address*, January 20, 1961

Kennedy's running mate, Senate Majority Leader **Lyndon B. Johnson** (TX, 1908-1973), helped to "balance the ticket."

THE "NEW FRONTIER" PROGRAM

The youth-oriented Kennedy promised to lead a new generation of Americans to a "New Frontier" with energetic proposals for the space program, civil rights, urban renewal, social welfare, and a new image in foreign policy.

DOMESTIC POLICY STALLS IN CONGRESS

To achieve his ambitions, Kennedy convinced the Democratic Congress to pass legislation which lowered tariffs, increased the minimum wage and Social Security benefits, and helped the beleaguered cities. Most of his suggestions ran into opposition from conservative Republicans and Southern Democrats opposed to expanding federal influence, especially in civil rights. Federal aid to education, subsidized medical care for the poor and elderly, tax cuts, and civil rights reforms met with defeat, often through the use of Senate filibusters. Many of these programs did eventually become law, but not until after the young President's tragic assassination in 1963.

CIVIL RIGHTS

The equal protection of the law, guaranteed in the Fourteenth Amendment, was slow to mate-

rialize in the South. Racially prejudiced Americans opposed attempts at integration and equality, but civil rights organizations, old and new, began a new phase of the crusade for justice.

In the decade that followed *Brown v. Board of Education of Topeka*, few Southern schools had actually carried out the Supreme Court's order to integrate "with all deliberate speed." In 1962, **James Meredith** attempted to become the first African American student to register at the University of Mississippi. The scene was a replay of the violent Little Rock Crisis of 1957.

Once again, the governor personally barred Meredith's entry. A riot broke out and two persons were killed before Kennedy sent in federal troops. With the help of federal marshals, Meredith finally enrolled.

The city of Birmingham, Alabama refused to integrate. The Rev. Martin Luther King, Jr. led a series of non-violent marches to protest the stubbornness of city officials. Millions watched on television as police turned fire hoses, tear gas, and attack dogs on the marchers. While under arrest for leading the nonviolent marches, Dr. King wrote his famous *Letter From a Birmingham Jail*. In it, he equated the non-violent struggle of African Americans in America with the struggle of early Christians and the Indian independence movement of Mohandas Gandhi (see pages 300 and 305).

Violence continued in the South while Kennedy's efforts in Washington stalled in

Congress. In the spring of 1963, NAACP leader **Medgar Evers** was assassinated in Mississippi. In August, over 200,000 people marched on Washington and heard Dr. King's "I Have a Dream" speech and sang the battle hymn of the movement, "We Shall Overcome..."

Even as Dr. King spoke, the non-violent movement was losing momentum. In September, in an ugly answer to the March on Washington, four African American children were tragically killed in a Birmingham church bombing. The level of frustration increased among younger civil rights activists. Dr. King began to lose control of the civil rights movement.

ACTION IN FOREIGN POLICIES

CUBAN PROBLEMS

U.S.-Latin American relations had not improved greatly in the period after World War II. Suspicion of U.S. actions remained despite the efforts made by Truman with the **Organization of American States** (OAS). U.S. businesses still supported military Latin American regimes that harshly maintained economic stability.

One such regime, that of Cuban dictator Fulgencio Batista, was overthrown by a small group of rebels with U.S. support led by **Fidel Castro** in 1958. Hopes for a new type of democracy ended shortly afterward, when Castro condemned the United States and announced that Cuba would be a Marxist state, allied with the Soviet Union.

Eisenhower broke off relations with Cuba. He gave approval to a CIA plot to train and assist Cuban refugees in launching a counterrevolution. When Kennedy took over the White House, he allowed the CIA to go forward with the plan.

In April 1961, two thousand Cuban exiles landed at the **Bay of Pigs** in Cuba. An air strike by CIA-trained Cuban fighter pilots, to be launched from Guatemala, never materialized, nor did a planned revolt inside Cuba. Castro's intelligence informed him of the plan. The invaders were captured on the beach, and Castro and Soviet Premier Khrushchev openly denounced the United States.

FOREIGN POLICY

In the fall of 1962, U-2 reconnaissance planes provided pictures of what the U.S. government feared most about the Cuban-Soviet alliance. Missile bases with nuclear capacity were being constructed 90-miles from the Florida Keys.

After verification, Kennedy invoked the Monroe Doctrine and publicly condemned the Soviet intrusion in the Western Hemisphere. Claiming the missiles a threat to the security of the entire Hemisphere, President Kennedy demanded that the U.S.S.R. remove the missiles immediately. Kennedy ordered a naval blockade to stop Soviet ships from delivering any additional nuclear missiles or related supplies. The show of force caused Khrushchev to back down and remove the missiles under U.S. observation. In exchange, the Americans pledged not to launch any further invasions of Cuba. Khrushchev's misjudgment of Kennedy's resolve was a costly personal blunder. Shortly thereafter, the Soviet Politburo forced him to resign as Premier and First Secretary.

The Kennedy administration moved to stem the tide of communism in Latin America by offering a generous aid program called the **Alliance for Progress**. This ten-year program poured over 20 billion dollars into Latin American republics for housing, schools, hospitals, and factories. In return, the governments were to have initiated political reforms to achieve greater economic opportunity for the masses, but few were truly effective.

PEACE CORPS

President Kennedy also created the **Peace Corps** as a unique way for Americans to volunteer to personally help people in the underdeveloped nations. Response was great. Since 1961, the corps has sent more than 135,000 volunteers to serve in more than 100 developing countries, using their skills to help others develop agricultural, educational, and medical facilities.

THE RACE TO THE MOON

After the success of Sputnik, Americans were eager to match the Soviet space accomplishments. In 1961, Kennedy proposed the goal of landing a man on the moon by the end of the decade. In 1962, astronaut **John H. Glenn** became the first American to orbit the Earth. (In 1998, 77 year-old U.S. Senator Glenn of Ohio made another NASA flight to become the oldest person to have flown in space.) Later in the 1960s, two-man Gemini flights brought spacewalks and more technological achievements as the Americans slowly moved ahead of the Soviets in the space race.

THE BERLIN WALL

In the spring of 1961, Kennedy travelled to Vienna to meet Khrushchev at a summit which

did little to ease tensions between the superpowers. The U.S.S.R. continued to demand that the Western democracies leave the city of Berlin which was located inside the communist state of East Germany. Thousands of people escaped to freedom through West Berlin annually. Khrushchev ordered the East German government to seal off the flow of refugees by building a 25 mile long wall between the two sectors of the city. Thousands were cut off from relatives and jobs by the Berlin Wall.

THE NUCLEAR ARMS RACE

Continued atmospheric testing of nuclear weapons threatened to poison the environment with radiation, but the superpowers could not agree on methods of limitation and verification.

In 1963 after years of negotiation, a **Nuclear Test-Ban Treaty** was signed by the United States, U.S.S.R., and 100 other nations. France and China refused to agree. The agreement prohibited testing of nuclear weapons in the atmosphere, underwater, or in outer space. (Another agreement in 1967 prohibited testing on the Moon.) However, underground testing and stockpiling of warheads still continued. In addition, the United States and U.S.S.R. also agreed to establish a direct telephone line (the "**hot line**") between Moscow and Washington to be used to prevent accidental nuclear conflict.

ASSASSINATION IN DALLAS

On 22 November 1963, while in a motorcade through Dallas, Texas, Lee Harvey Oswald shot and killed President Kennedy. Vice President

MINI•ASSESSMENT (8-5)

1 When necessary to achieve justice, which method did Martin Luther King, Jr., urge his followers to employ?
   1 using violence to bring about political change
   2 engaging in nonviolent, civil disobedience
   3 leaving any community in which racism is practiced
   4 demanding that Congress pay reparation to African Americans

2 During the early 1960s, the United States had to deal with the building of the Berlin Wall, the Bay of Pigs invasion, and the Cuban missile crisis. Each of these events was a direct result of the
   1 continued tensions between the United States and the Soviet Union
   2 sustained U.S. support of United Nations' decisions
   3 failure of U.S. to remain permanently involved in world affairs
   4 concern for the safety of Americans living in foreign nations

3 Which statement about the Cuban missile crisis (1962) is most accurate?

1 The crisis showed that the United States and the Soviet Union could agree on total disarmament.
2 The communist government in Cuba was overthrown.
3 The United States wanted to establish missile sites in Cuban territory.
4 The crisis brought the two major world powers very close to war.

Constructed Response

1 What circumstances led to the United States action in the headline on 23 October 1962?

2 What was the outcome of the action taken by the United States?

Lyndon Baines Johnson was immediately sworn in as the nation's leader.

Two days later, Jack Ruby, a Dallas bar owner shot and killed Oswald. President Johnson appointed Chief Justice Earl Warren to head an investigation to determine if the shootings were part of a conspiracy. The **Warren Commission** announced that both Oswald and Ruby had acted alone, then sealed the records from the public. Some critics argued that more than one person had fired at Kennedy. This view was supported (December 1978) when a congressional committee concluded, on the basis of acoustic evidence, that Kennedy had probably been fired at by two assassins.

LYNDON JOHNSON AND THE GREAT SOCIETY

Lyndon Baines Johnson (TX, 1908-1973) had over 20 years of experience in Congress before becoming President. After filling a little over a year of the slain Kennedy's term, he easily won election in his own right in 1964. Johnson polled more than 60% of the popular vote against the conservative Republican candidate, Senator **Barry Goldwater** of Arizona. The Democrats also increased an already substantial margin of seats in Congress that year.

Johnson came to Washington during the New Deal and believed in social reform. He eventually became the Senate Majority Leader (1955-1961). With his legislative skill, LBJ capitalized on the desire to honor the fallen Kennedy. Johnson was able to achieve victory for stalled *New Frontier* programs and used the momentum to work out his own *Great Society* program.

Johnson envisioned a reformed society in which poverty, illiteracy, hunger, and racial injustice would be eliminated. All Americans would enjoy freedom, equality, and prosperity. It would involve substantially expanding the role of the federal government in everyday life.

Lyndon Baines Johnson
White House Historical Association

GREAT SOCIETY PROGRAMS

ECONOMIC POLICY

Johnson used the legislative skill of his new Vice President, former Senate Majority Leader **Hubert H. Humphrey** (MN, 1911-1978). He was able to guide many previously rejected legislative measures through Congress.

POVERTY RATES 1960 - 1980

THE WAR ON POVERTY

Despite the prosperity of the post-World War II years, an estimated 35 million Americans lived below the poverty line in 1960. The highest concentration of poverty existed in inner cities, in Appalachia, on Native American reservations, and in the rural areas of the South. Johnson proclaimed a "War on Poverty" and established the **Office of Economic Opportunity** (OEO) to attack the problems. OEO directed the Volunteers in Service to America program. **VISTA** was touted as a "domestic Peace Corps,"

in which Americans volunteered to use their skills to help people in poverty regions.

OEO also administered two other important programs – the Job Corps and Project Head Start. The **Job Corps** trained school dropouts and unemployed youth. **Project Head Start** prepared young children from disadvantaged families for a more productive early childhood education. By 1969, the number of Americans living below the poverty level had been reduced to 22.5 million. Experts still argue whether this was due to the efforts of the Great Society or the general rise in incomes due to the booming economy.

MEDICARE

During the 1940s, Congress rejected President Truman's proposal for helping the poor and elderly meet medical expenses. Conservatives and the medical profession feared governmental control. In 1965, President Johnson secured passage of the **Medicare** and **Medicaid** bills. Medicare helped defray doctor and hospital expenses for senior citizens. Medicaid helped states pay similar costs for the economically disadvantaged through their welfare systems. Critics of the programs complained of the increasing costs burdening the government and the opportunity for fraud in the system.

Medicare costs rose dramatically from 3 billion dollars per year in the 1970s to over 200 billion dollars in the year 2000. Part of the increase was due to the addition of catastrophic illness insurance coverage. However, experts feel that medical industry costs also soared out of control in recent years.

AID TO EDUCATION

Federal involvement in education became a controversial subject during the Johnson Administration. While the need was great and the quality of education varied from state to state, states were reluctant to give up any reserved power in this area. The *Elementary and Secondary Education Act of 1965* provided more than a billion dollars in federal funding for schools with disadvantaged students. Subsequent programs provided money for efforts to improve nutrition and health conditions. Colleges also received grants and loans for enrollment of minority and educationally and economically disadvantaged students.

ENVIRONMENTAL IMPROVEMENT

The Great Society also launched programs to deal with air and water pollution, as well as toxic waste and sanitary garbage disposal.

- The *Wilderness Act* helped preserve the national forests.

- The *Highway Beautification Act* sought removal of billboards and junk yards.

- The *Water Quality Control Act* provided funds for community waste disposal treatment plants.

- The *Clean Air Act of 1970* ordered auto manufacturers to equip cars with pollution control devices to reduce auto emissions.

Congress also gave permission for the Johnson administration to form two new cabinet-level departments: **Housing and Urban Development** (HUD), and the **Department of Transportation** (DOT).

The Great Society programs helped millions, but the problems addressed did not go away. Its scope was enormous, and so was its cost. The unpopularity of Johnson's foreign policies soon undercut support for his domestic reforms.

MOON LANDING

President Kennedy's earlier pledge to place U.S. astronauts on the Moon was achieved on 20 July 1969. The tragic deaths of three astronauts in a 1967 pre-launch accident delayed the program schedule, but one year later, an Apollo spacecraft orbited the Moon. The following summer, *Apollo 11* astronauts **Neil Armstrong** and **Buzz Aldrin** finally set foot on the lunar surface.

While contributing greatly to scientific, medical, and technical knowledge, as well as launching the age of satellite communication, the space program was again criticized as too costly. Declining public interest and budgetary restraints in the 1970s forced Congress to scale down the space program.

CONTINUED DEMANDS FOR EQUALITY: THE CIVIL RIGHTS MOVEMENT

The movement for racial equality, begun in earnest after the Supreme Court's landmark decision in *Brown v. Board of Education of Topeka, Kansas* (1954), continued in the Johnson years. Never tightly organized, the Civil Rights Movement encompassed a growing variety of organizations. They all sought social justice and political equality, but many differed as to their specific notion of what those ideals meant and what means should be employed to achieve such goals.

NAACP

The National Association for the Advancement of Colored People (NAACP) is the oldest and largest civil rights organization. Founded by W.E.B. DuBois and others in 1909, the NAACP used legislative pressures and legal challenges to actively protest racial injustice. The NAACP became the driving force behind the monumental victory in the *Brown* decision.

NATIONAL URBAN LEAGUE

Another traditional organization, the **National Urban League**, followed the pattern of the NAACP. Founded in 1910, it has worked mainly to assist African Americans migrating to Northern cities from the rural South. It fought constantly to improve urban living conditions and took a leading role in seeking fair treatment for minorities in industry.

SCLC

The **Southern Christian Leadership Conference (SCLC)** was formed by Dr. Martin Luther King, Jr. and other ministers after the Montgomery bus boycott (1956-1957). The SCLC attempted to make churches the focal point of the civil rights movement. Its leaders used non-violent, direct action techniques to confront

LETTER FROM A BIRMINGHAM JAIL

"We will match your capacity to inflict suffering with our capacity to endure suffering. We will meet your physical force with our soul force. We will not hate you, but we cannot obey your unjust laws. Do to us what you will and we will still love you. Bomb our homes and threaten our children; send your hooded perpetrators of violence into our communities and drag us out on some wayside road, beating us and leaving us half dead, and we will still love you. But we will soon wear you down by our capacity to suffer. And in winning our freedom, we will so appeal to your heart and conscience that we will win you in the process."

– Martin Luther King, Jr., *Letter from a Birmingham Jail*, April 16, 1963

injustice through marches and public demonstrations of civil disobedience.

SNCC

The **Student Non-violent Coordinating Committee (SNCC)** was formed in 1960 by college students arranging the sit-in demonstrations at segregated restaurants in the South. The sit-in, a widely used, non-violent, and passive resistance tactic, spread rapidly as a protest form. SNCC's leaders became increasingly militant as frustration with the violent white racist resistance mounted in the middle 1960s.

SNCC leader **Stokley Carmichael** began to openly question the tactics of Dr. King and older civil rights leaders. Carmichael's raised clenched fist and calls for militant **"Black Power"** alienated some political figures as well as some general popular support of the movement among liberals.

CORE

The **Congress of Racial Equality (CORE)** was organized in 1942 to promote peaceful means of calling the public's attention to racial discrimination. CORE organized the Freedom Riders of 1961, which staged demonstrations in segregated buses, terminals, and waiting rooms in the South.

BLACK MUSLIMS

The **Black Muslims**, a fast-growing group of followers of the Islamic faith in the mid-1960s, held that true equality was nearly impossible under the U.S. political system. They began a movement for a separate African American state within the United States. The

popular Minister **Malcolm X** (1925-1965) became the foremost spokesman for the group. Malcolm X was beginning to advocate more active accommodation with U.S. society rather than separatism, when he was assassinated by a rival Muslim faction. This more inclusive approach continued in later decades.

BLACK PANTHERS

The **Black Panthers** were the most radical of the groups of the 1960s. They espoused revolution by the African American population and armed take-over of the country. Because they accumulated weapons and often used them to incite violence, they were under constant surveillance by the FBI. Many Panther leaders were forced to go underground.

ON NONVIOLENCE

"The day of nonviolent resistance is over. If they have the Ku Klux Klan nonviolent, then I'll be nonviolent ...But as long as you've got somebody else not being nonviolent, I don't want anybody coming to me talking any nonviolent talk."

– Malcolm X, 1964

CIVIL UNREST

THE KERNER COMMISSION REPORT

Although many whites supported the goals of equality, others harbored continuing prejudice. Some were wary of changes in traditional ways, while others feared economic competition. After a decade of crusading for reform, the Civil

Rights Movement could point to some progress. Yet, large numbers of African Americans continued to live in poverty in the rural South and in the urban **ghettoes** all over the United States. They were hampered by limited educational opportunities and continuing discrimination in employment.

In the "long, hot summers" from 1965 to 1967, riots broke out in many American cities. The most serious disturbances occurred in Los Angeles (CA), Detroit (MI), and Newark (NJ). In these cities, over 100 persons died, thousands of people were arrested, and millions of dollars in property was destroyed.

President Johnson appointed a special commission to investigate the riots and seek solutions. The **Kerner Commission** reported that "white racism" had caused the riots. The deep-seated prejudice in some sectors of the nation was often the cause of African Americans being denied equal opportunity. The report also concluded that America was still a long way from overcoming segregation and inequality. It suggested more job training, improved schools, increased assistance for the needy, and wider construction of low income housing.

SHOCKING ASSASSINATIONS

To a nation in which vocal protest and tense civil confrontations were more and more frequently followed by episodes of violence, a series of brutal murders of key leaders intensified the shock and bewilderment of the late 1960s.

In April of 1968, Dr. Martin Luther King, Jr. was in Memphis to show support for striking sanitation workers. He was shot and killed by an escaped convict, James Earl Ray. In 1983, the U.S. Congress honored the memory of the slain civil rights leader by declaring a national day of commemoration on each 15 January.

In June 1968, President Kennedy's brother, Senator **Robert F. Kennedy** (NY) was shot and killed by another assassin. Sirhan Sirhan, an Arab sympathizer was unhappy with the presidential candidate's statements in support of Israel.

LEGISLATIVE IMPACT OF THE CIVIL RIGHTS MOVEMENT

The persistent effort of the Civil Rights Movement gradually influenced the legislative and executive branches of the federal government to take actions for justice and equality in America.

The actions of the Civil Rights Movement in the Eisenhower years were directed at racial segregation by law (de jure segregation). As the movement progressed into the 1960s, it became evident that racial discrimination in neighborhoods throughout the country had established **de facto segregation**. All African American and all-white neighborhoods were served by local schools which were, in fact, racially segregated schools.

In *Swann v. the Charlotte-Mecklenburg Board of Education*, 1971, the Supreme Court approved busing of students to schools in different parts of communities to achieve racial balance. The technique was successful in some cities, but triggered violent confrontations in others. It also increased the rate of "white flight" as more and more white middle class families fled the cities for the less turbulent suburbs.

Adding to the civil rights legislation of the Eisenhower years, Congress passed four new actions attempting to achieve equality: the *Civil Rights Acts of 1964* and *1968*, and the *Voting Rights Acts of 1965* and *1970*.

Local officials harassed civil rights demonstrators. Violence marred the civil rights march from Selma to Montgomery in 1963, but it brought the problem to the attention of the nation. President Johnson called on Congress to pass the *Voting Rights Act of 1965*. (A second act was passed in 1970.) As a result, a majority of African American citizens were registered to vote by the mid-1970s. In addition, the number of African American officeholders increased dramatically. Additional legislation in 1975 required bilingual ballots in certain districts, and in 1982, federal protection was continued in areas of the country that had a history of discrimination toward minority voters.

1960s CIVIL RIGHTS LEGISLATION	
LAW	**DESCRIPTION**
Civil Right Acts of 1964	attaches stiff criminal penalties for discrimination in voting and employment, ends segregation in most public facilities, and withholds federal funds from school districts and communities practicing discrimination
Civil Rights Act 1968	bans discrimination in rental units and real estate transactions and gives broader federal protection to civil rights workers; also prohibits the hiring and classification of employees; makes it illegal for unions to discriminate on the basis of race, color, religion, sex, and national origin in their membership practices
Voting Rights Act of 1965	suspends literacy tests in counties where more than half the population cannot vote; provides federal help to register new voters; and, began action to end state use of poll taxes
Voting Rights Act of 1970	ends all literacy tests and establishes 30-day residency requirements

In 1964, Congress proposed, and the states ratified, the Constitution's Twenty-fourth Amendment, which prohibited the **poll tax** in federal elections. Shortly thereafter, the Supreme Court decided that all use of poll taxes was unconstitutional, because it denied citizens equal protection of the law.

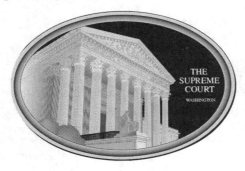

JUDICIAL DECISIONS FURTHERING EQUALITY

In its decisions concerning civil rights, the U.S. Supreme Court moved and shaped public policy when the other two branches of government were not acting in a progressive manner.

In ***Baker v. Carr*** (1962)*, the Supreme Court applied the Fourteenth Amendment to bring about equally-sized election districts. The case dealt with election districts in Tennessee. Population shifts led to urban residents being under-represented in the state legislature, while rural residents were over-represented. The Court ruled that the inequality in representation violated the equal protection clause. As a result, state and local governments now reapportion (redraw) their election districts following each census to guarantee the concept of "one person, one vote."

The *Civil Rights Act of 1964* banned discrimination in public accommodations, but the owner of the Heart of Atlanta Motel still refused to serve African Americans, claiming that Congress had no authority to regulate his business. In ***Heart of Atlanta Motel Inc. v. United States*** (1964)*, the Court ruled that the business in question served those from other states, and that under the interstate commerce clause of the Constitution, Congress has the authority to regulate such activity.

The perceptions of the nation were beginning to change as a result of the civil rights struggle. In an effort to end discriminatory practices, some corporations and educational institutions began **affirmative action programs**. These programs set aside a certain percentage of positions for African Americans and other minorities.

Whites who were denied jobs or school admission because of affirmative action programs complained of **reverse discrimination**. In 1978, the Supreme Court ruled that while the use of such affirmative action quotas was constitutional, they must be administered in such a way that the rights of others are not violated (***Bakke v. the Regents of the University of California****).

1 "...the Great Society is not a safe harbor, a resting place, a final objective, a finished work. It is a challenge constantly renewed, beckoning us toward a destiny where the meaning of our lives matches the marvelous products of our labor..."

– President Lyndon B. Johnson

The statement supports President Johnson's belief that the federal government has a responsibility to
1 protect the national security
2 guarantee the rights of workers
3 assume the responsibilities of state governments
4 improve the general welfare

2 "The Civil Rights Movement would have been vastly different without the shield and spear of the First Amendment."
Based on this quotation, which is a valid conclusion?
1 The Civil Rights Movement used the right to assemble peacefully to its advantage.
2 Armed violence was responsible for the gains made by the Civil Rights Movement.
3 Congress ignored the Constitution in its efforts to speed civil rights gains.
4 The executive branch lacked the power to enforce equal rights legislation.

3 An original purpose of affirmative action programs was to
1 increase educational and employment opportunities for women and minorities that had faced past discrimination
2 improve the American economy by guaranteeing that employees will be highly skilled

3 decrease social welfare costs by requiring recipients of public assistance to work
4 reduce the federal deficit by increasing government efficiency

Constructed Response

Voter Registration Billboard in Los Angles, CA

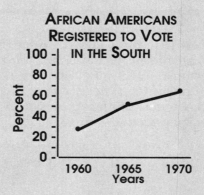

AFRICAN AMERICANS REGISTERED TO VOTE IN THE SOUTH

1 How does the graph show the effect of the *Voting Rights Acts of 1965* and *1970*?
   More ppl. Star red to vote.

2 Discuss two ways in which the information presented above has influenced American politics.
   They present themselves more to minorities.

DEMANDS FOR EQUALITY: WOMEN

As the Civil Rights Movement focused the nation's attention on the subject of racial inequality, other groups also renewed their struggles for equality. Throughout the history of Western civilization, women had traditionally been afforded an inferior status. In America, women were denied political and legal rights, as well.

In 1961, President Kennedy set up a Presidential Commission on the Status of Women. The Commission concluded that legislative and judicial reform was needed to end discriminatory legal practices, allow equal job opportunities, and establish equal pay for equal work. It also recommended increased child care facilities and greater involvement of women in the political process.

BURNING WITH INDIGNATION

"...I have met and talked to women who are burning with indignation at the wastefulness and stupidity of a society that makes second-class citizens of half its population.

"Women, in fact, are 53 percent of the electorate. Yet throughout our history and now, more than one-half century after we won the vote, women are still almost invisible in government, in elected posts, in high administrative decision-making positions, in the judiciary.

"Wherever I go, ...I have found a strong community of interest among huge numbers of American women, a strong commitment to changing the direction of our society."

– U.S. Rep. Bella Abzug (NY), *A New Kind of Southern Strategy*, February 12, 1972.

In 1963, Congress passed the *Equal Pay Act* which provided that men and women doing the same job be paid equally. Incorporated into the *Civil Rights Act of 1964* was **Title VII**, which prohibited discrimination against women in employment and job promotions.

The **National Organization for Women** (**NOW**) was founded in 1966 by **Betty Friedan**, author of the 1963 work, *The Feminine Mystique*. The book made a singular contribution to raising women's consciousness of their inferior status in American society. NOW is usually perceived as representing middle class women and pursues change through legislative and judicial channels. NOW became politically active, supporting or opposing certain candidates and spearheading campaigns for the **Equal Rights Amendment** and on the legal right to abortion.

In the *Higher Education Act* (**Title IX**), passed by Congress in 1972, colleges were forbidden to discriminate against women. By 1980, all public and most private colleges were co-educational.

KEY WOMEN'S ISSUES

Since the turn of the century, the percentage of women in the work force has increased dramatically. In 1900, 17% of the work force was women; in 1980, they made up 43% of the work force, and in 1997, the figure was 46%. Women continue to dominate clerical positions, domestic work, and patient care in hospitals. At the same time, the number of women in professional, managerial, and supervisory positions has also increased.

Working women are more apt to put off marriage and child rearing until later in life, seeking to first develop their careers. Women's groups also seek publicly funded day-care facilities for children of mothers who wish to continue careers while raising a family. Today, many more women must work to meet basic family expenses.

To guarantee equality with men in all circumstances nationwide, many women's groups wanted an Equal Rights Amendment (**ERA**) to the Constitution.

In 1972, the proposed ERA won quick approval in Congress, but failed by 3 states to gain the approval of the 3/4 of the states necessary for it to be included in the Constitution. It fell short of ratification again after reintroduction in the 1980s. Some opponents feared laws which protect women would be nullified and that women might be drafted into the military in wartime. Also, the general terminology of the amendment produced fear that it would be too susceptible to court interpretations.

EQUALITY OF RIGHTS

"Equality of rights under the law shall not be denied or abridged by the United States or any state on account of sex."

CONSTITUTIONAL STRUCTURES

- Proposed Equal Right Amendment to the *United States Constitution*

In *Roe v. Wade** (1973), the U.S. Supreme Court invalidated all state laws which prohibited abortion. Many women's groups saw it as a victory for women's rights, proclaiming that they now had "freedom of choice." Others saw abortion as murder and formed **Right to Life Movements**, with the goal of getting the Court to reverse its decision or prohibit abortion with a new constitutional amendment. While unsuccessful on either of these approaches, Right to Life groups continue to campaign to halt the use of federal Medicaid funds for abortions.

WANTED

| Cleaning Woman $5 per hour | Sanitary Engineer $10 per hour |

Statistics indicate that women earn considerably less than men. Women's groups claim that much of the inequality is due to women being paid less then men even when their jobs are similar in nature. Some states passed *"equal-pay-for-equal-work"* laws, which mandate the same pay scale for jobs requiring similar skills. Critics of this idea cite an increased economic burden on businesses and the subjective way in which different jobs are equated. In a 1981 federal court decision, it was ruled that women could sue for equal pay, even if the work was not identical.

RISING CONSCIOUSNESS OF HISPANIC AMERICANS

THE LATINO MOVEMENT

The Hispanic (or Latino) population of the United States doubled from 1970 to 1990. Some projections indicate that nearly 25% of the population will be of Hispanic ancestry by the year 2050. Hispanics account for much of the immigration to the United States. Exact figures are sometimes difficult to determine. Those immigrants that entered the U.S. illegally are reluctant to be counted in the census, and Hispanics can also classify themselves as either African American or white. Official statistics from the 1990 census show that nearly 60% of Hispanics are of Mexican origin, about 12% are from Puerto Rico, and 5% from Cuba. Significant numbers also come from the Dominican Republic, Central America, and other islands of the Caribbean.

The Civil Rights Movement of the 1960s and 1970s inspired Hispanics to fight for equality and justice. In addition to the goals of equal opportunity in schools, housing and jobs, Hispanics also sought bilingual education and ballots, and opportunities for citizenship (for Puerto Ricans, citizenship was not an issue, as residents of Puerto Rico are already American citizens). Another concern was the exploitation of workers new to the country.

ORGANIZING FARM LABOR

Though large populations of Hispanics live in cities and suburbs, many others found employment as migrant farm workers. These migrant workers often lived in deplorable conditions. During the 1960s, **Cesar Chavez** (1927-1993) fought for the rights of Mexican farm laborers in the Southwest United States. Under the leadership of Chavez, the United Farm Workers organized boycotts of produce to bring attention to the harsh conditions. Over the years, conditions slowly improved as federal, state, and local governments became more involved in the regulation of migrant farm operations.

CUBAN AND HAITIAN IMMIGRATION

Hundreds of thousands have fled Cuba since the takeover by Fidel Castro in 1959, some as "boat people" who came from Cuba to Florida. Most have been welcomed into the United States, and they became American citizens. Miami and South Florida have seen the largest Cuban influx, while areas in the Northeast have smaller Cuban populations. Economically diverse, Cubans range from the middle classes and business people fleeing Marxist rule, to those attempting to escape poverty in Cuba.

Haiti has also experienced political oppression and poverty under a succession of dictators, especially the Duvalier family. As with Cubans, tens of thousands fled the country by boat, seeking entry into the United States. But unlike the Cuban experience, most were captured by the Coast Guard and sent back to Haiti. Some criticized the immigration polices that admitted Cubans (fleeing a communist dictator), but kept out Haitians (fleeing a dictator with no communist leanings).

INCREASING PRESENCE IN AMERICAN POLITICS

Hispanics often have a lower turnout of voters than either African Americans or whites. Some of this can be traced to language barriers and citizenship status. The use of bilingual ballots and an emphasis on the importance of political participation has slowly resulted in an increased Hispanic presence in American politics.

The Congressional delegations from California, Texas, Florida, and New York all have significant Hispanic representation. Many cities have Hispanic elected officials, and there has also been Hispanic representation in the Cabinet. At the same time, non-Hispanic politicians are paying increased attention to issues that are important to the Hispanic community as the Hispanic population and influence grow.

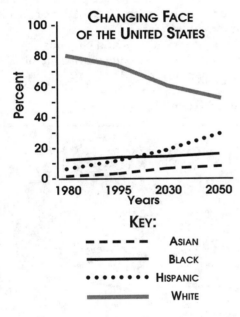

CHANGING FACE OF THE UNITED STATES

KEY:

- – – – – ASIAN
- ———— BLACK
- • • • • • • HISPANIC
- ———— WHITE

Note: numbers do not add up to 100 because of rounding and omission of American Indians and others.

DEMANDS FOR EQUALITY: NATIVE AMERICAN MOVEMENT

Native Americans have been one of the most impoverished groups in modern America. Long subject to the confusing and inept policies of the federal Department of the Interior's **BIA** (Bureau of Indian Affairs), Native Americans have been plagued by high unemployment, poor health, and inferior educational opportunities.

In 1968, the **American Indian Movement (AIM)** was organized by Native Americans demanding equal rights and greater government concern for the problems of Native Americans. AIM developed into a militant organization, using direct and often violent actions to gain publicity and achieve their goals.

Near the end of 1969, several Native American rights groups occupied the empty federal prison on Alcatraz Island in San Francisco Bay. They remained there for over a year, demanding that federal authorities return the island to them as its original owners. Federal marshals removed the remaining demonstrators in 1971. News of the occupation of Alcatraz spurred Native Americans to attempt similar tactics elsewhere to raise the public's consciousness of their problems.

In the Long March of 1972, over 500 Native Americans crossed the country to protest government policies in Washington, DC. Organized by AIM, it was called the **"Trail of Broken Treaties."** The demonstrators occupied the BIA building, doing over two million dollars in damage.

The town of **Wounded Knee** (SD) was the site of a deadly confrontation with federal troops. Early in 1973, members of AIM occupied the town. They demanded that the federal government honor past treaties and reform the BIA. Confrontations with federal marshals left several dead and injured.

A major complaint of Native Americans has been the record of treaty violations by state and local governments. Agreements which gave land to Native American tribes many years ago were broken as the government needed to build highways, reservoirs, and other public facilities. Until recently, such seizures were common, backed by the constitutional provision of "eminent domain" (Fifth Amendment). Since 1970, Native Americans have gone to court over treaty violations and have won most of the time.

PROTECTION OF RIGHTS OF THE ACCUSED

Through a series of Supreme Court decisions, those accused of crimes gained important constitutional protections in the 1960s. These decisions resulted in widespread change in the way the authorities treated criminal suspects. In each case, states were forced to comply with the ruling through the Fourteenth Amendment, which forbade states from depriving citizens of due process and equal protection of law.

In *Mapp v. Ohio** (1961), a suspect was handcuffed by police in her apartment, who then conducted a search. The Court ruled that this was an illegal search because of the Fourth Amendment guarantee against unreasonable search and seizure.

Florida was one of many states that did not require suspects at a trial be provided with a lawyer. One suspect, Clarence Gideon, could not afford counsel and was found guilty. Gideon appealed to the Supreme Court, saying that the Sixth Amendment guaranteed him the right of counsel. In *Gideon v. Wainwright** (1963), the Court agreed, saying that states must provide the accused with a lawyer (public defender) when the accused can not afford one.

Ernesto Miranda had been a suspect in a rape and kidnapping case. The police questioned him, and after incriminating statements made by Miranda, placed him under arrest. Miranda appealed to the Supreme Court, arguing that the police should have told him of his constitutional right against self-incrimination. In *Miranda v. Arizona** (1966) the Court overturned Miranda's conviction. To be sure that suspects know their Fifth and Sixth Amendment rights, those who are detained must be told before any questioning of their right to remain silent, and their right to a lawyer.

MINI•ASSESSMENT (8-7)

1   In the United States today, legal rights specifically guaranteed to women have resulted primarily from
    1   laws adopted during the colonial period
    2   the historic influence of France on United States affairs
    3   the provisions of the original Constitution
    4   many years of political and social activism

2   "For women working outside the home, it is not new opportunities, but rather new necessities, that have made it happen." What is the most valid conclusion based on this quotation?
    1   The feminist movement of the 1960s gained success in promoting many career choices for women.
    2   Because families are smaller, women no longer need to remain at home to care for children.
    3   Whether they are married or not, many women must work to provide support for their families.
    4   The computer age has actually reduced the number of professional and technical jobs for women.

3   In the 1970s, the goal of federal government policies toward Native Americans was to
    1   make Native Americans more dependent on the federal government
    2   give the states more control over Native American affairs
    3   eliminate tribal ties and customs
    4   give Native Americans more control over their own affairs

Constructed Response

1   Why are the individuals standing at the right not in the contest?

2   Describe two ways in which the federal government has attempted to "even the competition" and provide equal opportunity since 1950.

THE LIMITS OF POWER: TURMOIL AT HOME AND ABROAD, 1965-1972

VIETNAM: SACRIFICE AND TURMOIL

The Vietnam War was the longest armed conflict in American history. Except for the Civil War, it was also the most divisive. The War exposed the limitations of American military power when faced with guerrilla warfare. These strains on American society called into question the constitutional limitations on the war-making power of the Executive branch.

REVIEW OF U.S. INVOLVEMENT IN ASIA SINCE 1865

In the latter half of the 19th century, the United States acquired several island possessions in the Pacific (Midway, Wake, Samoa, Hawaii, and the Philippines) to protect expanding trade. Subsequently, Secretary of State John Hay's pursuit of an Open Door Policy in the McKinley-Roosevelt Era brought the U.S. into competition with major European powers in East Asia. Japan's empire crumbled at the end of World War II as did those of the exhausted French, British, and Dutch. Slowly, they withdrew from the region, but France attempted to cling to its possessions in Southeast Asia (Indo-China).

THE FRENCH-INDOCHINESE WAR

While France was under Nazi occupation, a Marxist group headed by **Ho Chi Minh** (1890-1969) organized a nationalist revolution in Indo-China. Non-communist groups joined the independence movement, hoping to end French rule. Eight years of sporadic fighting followed World War II.

In 1954, even with aid from the United States, the exhausted French suffered a final defeat at **Dien Bien Phu**. At a peace conference in Geneva, diplomats worked out a cease-fire agreement. Vietnam was divided at the 17th Parallel. Ho and the communists controlled the North and an anti-communist government ruled the South. The United States was to supervise elections to unite the country in 1956. In that year, the government of South Vietnam, under **Ngo Dinh Diem** refused to participate in the elections. Diem's government was not democratic, but the United States supported it, in the hope of containing communism.

Ho Chi Minh

Ho Chi Minh gave increasing support to a communist insurgent movement (**Viet Cong**) in the South. President Eisenhower gave military supplies, advisors, and financial support to Diem. Diem's government was unpopular, especially in the treatment of religious groups. Buddhists began open demonstrations including ritual suicides by some monks.

President Dwight Eisenhower with Secretary of State Dulles, assures President Ngo Dinh Diem the U.S. will to provide South Vietnam with military assistance.   (National Archive)

The Viet Cong grew into a major threat by the early 1960s, and President Kennedy increased the U.S. commitment by sending 15,000 military personnel as advisors. A coup d'etat in 1963 ended Diem's rule, but the fighting against the Viet Cong continued.

TROOP ESCALATION

FOREIGN POLICY

"The United States regards as vital to its national interest to world peace the maintenance of international peace and security in Southeast Asia ... the United States is prepared, as the President determines, to take all necessary steps, including the use of armed forces, to assist any member or protocol state of the Southeast Asia Collective Defense Treaty requesting assistance in defense of its freedom."

– Joint Resolution of Congress on Gulf of Tonkin Incidents, 24 August 1964, Washington DC

THE DOMINO THEORY

The **Domino Theory** continued to influence policymakers' thinking in the Kennedy and Johnson years. The Theory's premise was that if one weak nation fell to communism, others around it would similarly topple. Foreign policymakers felt that a stand had to be made in Vietnam if the surrounding nations were to survive the communist threat.

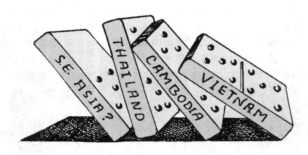

In 1964, U.S. ships were reportedly fired upon by North Vietnamese gunboats in the Gulf of Tonkin. President Johnson ordered bombing of North Vietnamese harbors. In the ***Tonkin Gulf Resolution***, a near unanimous vote in Congress authorized the President to "take all necessary action to protect American interests" in the region. Bombing continued through 1965, but the Viet Cong appeared to be gaining strength. Johnson's advisors indicated a major effort could stem the tide. President Johnson ordered 500,000 U.S. combat troops into South Vietnam.

GUERRILLA WARFARE

Despite heavy bombing, increased troop strength, and high communist casualties, the War seemed to be stalemated. Guerrillas attacked towns and villages with no logical pattern, then retreated into the rain forests. So much of the countryside was infiltrated by both Viet Cong and non-uniformed troops, that Americans could not tell friend from foe.

Even the use of toxic chemical defoliants such as **Agent Orange** had little military effect. Communist forces and supplies from the North seemed to be filtering into the South through Laos and Cambodia.

STUDENT PROTESTS AT HOME

As the Vietnam War escalated an increasing number of Americans, nicknamed "doves," demanded immediate withdrawal. The most vocal doves were often young people on college campuses. By 1969, anti-war protests in major cities drew hundreds of thousands of people.

DRAFT PROTESTERS

As the numbers of young men being drafted for service in Vietnam grew, the draft itself became a hated symbol of the war. Many protested by burning their draft cards at campus rallies, and some fled to Canada and Scandinavia to avoid the draft. Civil rights leaders protested that a disproportionate number of African Americans were being drafted.

RADICAL POLITICS

Radical groups, such as the **Students for a Democratic Society** (**SDS**), organized war opposition. SDS concentrated their activity on the nation's campuses. They helped lead civil rights-like marches and demonstrations aimed at the Pentagon. In 1969, SDS organized a national student strike on **Vietnam Moratorium Day**.

Memorial Stone for the four students who died during an anti-war demonstration at Kent State University on 4 May 1970.
Photo - Kent State History Archives

The **Weathermen**, an extremist offshoot of SDS, engaged in terrorist tactics, burning buildings, and planting bombs. Demonstrations at the University of California at Berkley and at New York's Columbia University became violent and destroyed millions of dollars in property. In 1970, after President Nixon ordered the bombing of Viet Cong supply routes in Cambodia, a demonstration at the **Kent State** campus of the University of Ohio resulted in National Guardsmen killing four students.

CULTURAL RADICALS: HIPPIES AND COMMUNES

As an offshoot of the radical anti-war movement, some of the nation's youth turned to cultural dissent. They rejected traditional American values, often practiced pacifist religions, adopted outlandish clothes, and experimented with drugs. Some of these "hippies" and "flower children" rejected society altogether, going off to live in remote rural areas as hermits or in "back-to-nature" communes. They formed enclaves in San Francisco's Haight-Ashbury section and New York's Greenwich Village.

While relatively few in number, they had a remarkable influence on the nation's youth. The clothing and music industries were especially quick to publicize their activities and capitalized on their hard-driving protest songs and rebellious image.

JOHNSON'S GESTURE: ABDICATION AND PEACE OVERTURES

In 1964, President Johnson garnered over 60% of the popular vote and excited the nation with his vision of the Great Society. In less than two years, Vietnam made Johnson one of the most unpopular Presidents in U.S. history. "Hawks" criticized him for not mounting an all-out invasion of North Vietnam. "Doves" despised his escalation of the War.

Congress continued to appropriate funds for the War, but it was the President who was ultimately accountable for foreign policy. The Viet Cong and North Vietnamese launched the **Tet Offensive** during the 1968 Vietnamese New Year holiday. It showed that the enemy had been little weakened by three years of American effort.

In March 1968, Johnson announced that he would not seek re-election. At the same time, he ordered a cutback in the bombing of North Vietnam and asked Ho Chi Minh to consider peace negotiations. Peace talks began a few months later in Paris, but the War dragged on for another five years.

THE 1968 CHICAGO DEMOCRATIC CONVENTION

With LBJ out of the running, Vice President Hubert Humphrey became the logical candidate for the Democrats in 1968. "Doves" rallied behind anti-war Senator **Eugene McCarthy**, but their ranks were split when New York Senator Robert F. Kennedy (1925-1968), brother of the slain President, joined the race. Robert Kennedy was assassinated in June, and the anti-war faction lost momentum by the riot-plagued summer convention in Chicago.

IMPACT OF THE WAR ON SOCIETY

The Vietnam conflict had a critical impact on America. The Great Society programs suffered as billions of tax dollars were diverted to the military. War spending caused inflation which made everything more costly. Reluctance about the Johnson social program grew as people's incomes became strained.

The American military command was widely criticized for its conduct of the War. Top generals assured the President and the public that the Vietnam War was being won while asking for more and more money and troops. As the public began to doubt their leaders, the ranks of war dissenters grew.

Article I, section 8 of the *Constitution of the United States* specifically gives Congress the responsibility for declaring war, but Article II makes the President the Commander in Chief of the armed forces. Congress never declared war in the Vietnam conflict. Various executive agreements had put America into a position of defending the Indochinese region after France's exodus.

As the War became more and more unpopular, demands grew for legal limits on the President's power to involve the country in such situations. While Johnson was to bear the responsibility, it should be noted that the Congress passed the *Tonkin Gulf Resolution* and continued funding the war effort.

MINI•ASSESSMENT (8-8)

1   The *Tonkin Gulf Resolution* indicated to President Johnson that
    1   his actions in Vietnam were unconstitutional
    2   there was full congressional support for escalation
    3   the United Nations opposed the American intervention
    4   student groups would patriotically rally to the American cause

2   During the Vietnam War, serious questions were raised in the United States concerning the
    1   authority of the Supreme Court in regard to national security
    2   loyalty of United States military leaders
    3   extent of the President's powers as Commander in Chief
    4   role of the North Atlantic Treaty Organization (NATO) in international peacekeeping

3   A major long-term effect of the Vietnam War has been
    1   an end to communist government in Asia
    2   a change in United States foreign policy from containment to imperialism
    3   a reluctance to commit United States troops for extended military action abroad
    4   a continued boycott of trade with Asia

Constructed Response

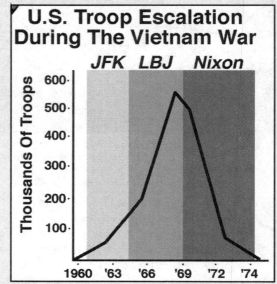

U.S. Troop Escalation During The Vietnam War

1   During what Presidential Administration was escalation of the Vietnam War the greatest?

    LBJ

2   How did America become a divided society during this period of escalation?   *hawks and dove*

    Some people did not want to go to war so they developed drafting groups

A TREND TOWARD CONSERVATISM: 1972 TO 1980

The period of upheaval and change during the 1960s was followed by a more conservative period in the 1970s and 1980s. The protests and civil disorders convinced many Americans that law and order had broken down. The failure in Vietnam led to increased caution in the area of foreign policy. The momentum of the Civil Rights Movement also evaporated in the domestic turbulence of the late 1960s.

Richard Nixon

NIXON AS PRESIDENT 1969-1974

The 1968 Presidential election saw the Democratic Party in terrible disarray. The Republicans, who had leaned too far to the right with Goldwater in 1964, now saw their chance to capitalize on the divisions racking the opposition and nominated Eisenhower's former Vice President Richard Nixon. Promising to restore order to the country, Nixon barely edged Humphrey in the popular vote (43.4% to 42.7%). The results showed a deeply divided electorate, with a staunchly conservative **George Wallace** of Alabama on an American Independent ticket pulling a substantial 13.5% of the popular vote. Analysts indicated that the Wallace vote probably hurt the Democrats more than the Republicans. Once again the Electoral College distorted the true results (Nixon: 301, Humphrey: 191, Wallace: 46). The Democrats retained control of Congress.

DOMESTIC POLICIES AND EVENTS

DISMANTLING THE GREAT SOCIETY

The disorientation of the late sixties led to a pessimistic attitude about Johnson's Great Society. Nixon sensed the public's disenchantment. He claimed Johnson's Great Society programs were ineffective, costly, mismanaged, and had over expanded the federal government's power. Nixon abolished the Office of Economic Opportunity. Through his **"revenue sharing program,"** he shifted welfare responsibility back to the states. Nixon cut urban renewal, job training, and education programs. The Democrats struggled to keep Nixon from cutting even more.

ENVIRONMENTAL AND CONSUMER LEGISLATION

In his State of the Union message in 1970, President Nixon spoke of the need to protect the environment. A major movement gained momentum in the late 1960s. The first **Earth Day** was held in the Spring of 1970 as a means of educating the public to the general erosion of the natural environment.

American young people celebrate the First Earth Day, 22 April 1969.   (United Nations Photo)

Congress authorized Nixon to set up the **Environmental Protection Agency (EPA)** to enforce regulations flowing from the 1970s *Clean Air, Resource Recovery Act*, and the *Water Pollution Control Act*. These measures addressed concerns about offshore oil spills, auto exhaust, industrial discharge, waste disposal, and recycling. The Acts were controversial. They had ecological benefits, but businesses and municipalities found it costly to comply. There was a general concern that the Acts added to the problem of inflation and slowed the economy.

Unsafe products and fraudulent advertising raised the cry for broader consumer protection in the 1960s. The Consumer Products Safety Commission was finally created in 1972. The *Truth-in-Lending Act* (1969) required consistent disclosure of finance charges and annual percentage rates (APR) in consumer credit arrangements. In 1971, a controversial measure banned cigarette advertising on radio and television in addition to "sin taxes."

The consumer rights cause had a strong and intense spokesman in **Ralph Nader**. His legal challenges and writings have exposed a long list of unsafe products and dishonest business practices. His book, *Unsafe at Any Speed* (1965) was highly critical of the lax production methods and unsafe vehicles of the U.S. auto industry. His criticisms resulted in several models being discontinued by GM and Ford.

THE BURGER COURT

The activist decisions of the Supreme Court under Chief Justice Warren redefined many basic rights. However, some critics said that the liberal decisions contributed to the disorder and turmoil of the late 1960s. Explicitly defining the rights of accused persons had raised the ire of law enforcement officials. Some critics said that the rising crime rates were the fault of the Court's actions in the *Gideon* and the *Miranda* decisions. Other critics blamed the moral decay of the nation on the decisions banning school prayer and protecting media obscenity (*Engel v. Vitale* and *Roth v. United States*).

Nixon promised to change the Supreme Court's liberalism and judicial activism. He got his chance when Chief Justice Warren resigned in 1969, followed by three other justices within several years. Nixon appointed **Warren Burger** to the Chief Justice's position, and Harry Blackmun, William Rehnquist, and Lewis Powell as associate justices.

Warren Earl Burger, 15th Chief Justice of the United States. TV Photo

The Court under Burger's leadership exercised **judicial restraint** on controversial cases. Some conservatives were dismayed that the Court did not try to reverse some of the controversial decisions of the Warren years. Conservatives were upset with the new Court decisions on abortion (*Roe*), busing, and the overturning of many states' death penalty laws.

PENTAGON PAPERS

In the 1960s, the Defense Department prepared a confidential study on the progress of the Vietnam War. Daniel Ellsberg, who at one time worked on the study, leaked the information to the *New York Times*. The newspaper published the study, naming it *The Pentagon Papers*. It revealed the misleading and dishonest statements made by the military and the government to gain congressional and public support for the continued escalation of the War. The Nixon Administration went to the Supreme Court to halt publication of the documents, but lost the case. *NY Times Company v. United States** (1971) was considered a major victory for the First Amendment protection of freedom of the press.

SELF-DETERMINATION FOR NATIVE AMERICANS

The Bureau of Indian Affairs' "termination policy" of the 1950s sought to break up tribes and subdivide Native Americans' land. It was a dismal failure. Many Native Americans wished to remain in the tribal setting, protected but not dominated by the federal government. In 1970, President Nixon sent a message to Congress proposing a policy of self-determination for Native Americans. The new policy would turn over the administration of most of the federal programs to the tribes. A final version of the measure did this to some extent, but Native Americans continued to complain of governmental interference. In a similar action, the administration began to name Native Americans to management positions in the BIA.

In 1972, the tribes became eligible for the same revenue-sharing arrangements as the state governments. While this released significant funds for improvements on reservations, at the same time it increased tribal dependence on federal money.

NIXON'S INTERNATIONALISM

On taking office, President Nixon appointed Dr. **Henry Kissinger** as special White House advisor on national security. Kissinger was not part of the Cabinet, but he was able to play a very influential role in shaping foreign policy.

MINI•ASSESSMENT (8-9)

1 The goal of President Nixon's Revenue Sharing Program was to
   1 increase the role of the federal government in poverty programs
   2 provide a system for monitoring the use of foreign aid grants
   3 give state and local government control over programs
   4 provide federal campaign funds to Presidential candidates

2 The goal of both Upton Sinclair in the early 1900s and Ralph Nader in the 1960s was to
   1 limit immigration to those with skills needed by American industry
   2 encourage the growth of American business interests
   3 protect the environment
   4 expose social and economic problems

3 The Burger Court disappointed some conservatives because it
   1 continued the activist role of the Court in certain areas
   2 reversed most of the civil rights decisions of the Warren Court
   3 increased the power of the states at the expense of the federal government
   4 tried to block the impeachment of Richard Nixon

Constructed Response

> **Philadelphia Police Department**
> **STANDARD POLICE INTERROGATION CARD**
>
> **WARNINGS TO BE GIVEN ACCUSED**
>
> We are questioning you concerning the crime of (state specific crime).
>
> We have a duty to explain to you and to warn you that you have the following legal rights:
>
> A You have the right to remain silent and do not have to say anything at all.
>
> B Anything you say can and will be used against you in court
>
> C You have a right to talk to a lawyer of your own choice before we ask you any question, and also to have a lawyer here with you while we ask questions.
>
> D If you cannot afford to hire a lawyer, and you want one, we will see that you have one provided to you free of charge before we ask you any questions.
>
> E If you are willing to give us a statement, you have a right to stop any time you wish.

1 From what Supreme Court case did the requirement for this warning come?

2 What part of the Constitution makes it necessary for the above information to be given to the accused?

3 Why have some Americans been critical of the requirement that the information above be read to the accused?

NIXON'S FOREIGN POLICY	
COUNTRY	**U.S. INTERESTS**
Vietnam	withdraw troops, place burden on South Vietnam
China	economic benefits, eventual diplomatic ties
U.S.S.R.	slowing the arms race through SALT

Not being tied down to running a major governmental department, Kissinger was able to make frequent trips to Red China and the U.S.S.R. Later, he was appointed Secretary of State by Nixon (and continued in that position under President Ford), conducting peace missions to the Middle East.

VIETNAM WITHDRAWAL

Vietnam posed the most immediate problem for Nixon. In the 1968 campaign, he had promised "peace with honor," an end to the War, but with the "mission accomplished." To that end, Nixon began **Vietnamization** of the War – putting more and more responsibility on the South Vietnamese themselves. He began a gradual reduction of U.S. ground forces. The Paris peace talks continued, but no major diplomatic progress seemed to be made.

For years, communist forces used Cambodia as a supply route. In 1970, Nixon ordered secret bombing raids on these supply lines. News of the escalation leaked and triggered numerous demonstrations, including the deadly incident at Kent State. The massive bombing raids continued into 1973, when the Paris talks finally yielded an agreement. A cease fire was effected, American troops were to be completely withdrawn, and prisoners of war were to be returned.

North Vietnam still had over 100,000 troops in the South Vietnamese countryside. American supplies and financial aid not withstanding, South Vietnam and Cambodia were overrun within two years of the American evacuation. After nine years of fighting and more than 50,000 lives sacrificed, America came away disillusioned as to its power and role in the world.

NIXON DOCTRINE

In the middle of the Indochinese quagmire, the President issued a policy statement which became known as the *Nixon Doctrine*. It said that the United States would continue to honor its treaty obligations in Asia, providing military, financial and humanitarian aid, but actual combat troops would have to be provided by the nation directly involved in the conflict. Nixon hoped to maintain foreign friendship, but wished to avoid another unwinnable war.

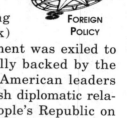

FOREIGN POLICY

OPENING TO CHINA

Twenty years after Jiang Jieshi's (Chiang Kai-shek) Nationalist Chinese government was exiled to Taiwan, it remained officially backed by the United States. Meanwhile, American leaders steadfastly refused to establish diplomatic relations with Mao Zedong's People's Republic on the Chinese mainland. However, early in his presidency, Nixon had Kissinger investigate the possibility of visiting mainland China.

Nixon and Kissinger decided on a daring policy toward both nations. During this period, China and the Soviet Union were having serious diplomatic problems. Communism no longer posed a single, powerful threat to democracy. A new relationship with communist China might force the Soviet leaders to be more accommodating to America.

No significant agreements resulted from Nixon's trip to China in 1972. However, it served to pave the way for negotiations which eventually increased trade and cultural exchanges. In 1979, President Carter opened full diplomatic relations. While trade relations with Taiwan were preserved, the mutual defense treaty with the island was ended. After the Nixon breakthrough, American trade with communist China expanded significantly despite concerns over continuing human rights violations by the Chinese government.

DÉTENTE: SALT AND GRAIN DEALS

After his trip to China, Nixon also visited the Soviet Union. He hoped to relax tensions (**détente**) between the two superpowers and limit the nuclear arms race. This new détenté policy also increased trade and cultural relations between the two superpowers.

One result of Nixon's Moscow visit was an agreement to allow the U.S.S.R. to buy American grain for three years. It was beneficial to American farmers, but smaller supplies in the United States drove up prices in America and added to inflation.

The *Strategic Arms Limitation Treaty* (SALT, 1972) also came out of Kissinger's breakthroughs. The treaty won overwhelming support in the U.S. Senate. It reduced anti-ballistic systems and froze the expansion of Intercontinental Ballistic Missiles (ICBMs). It did not, however, place limits on multiple warheads or slow construction of long-range bombers. It did not prevent construction of new missile systems, nor provide on-site inspections for verification.

The arms race continued in these areas. SALT's supporters hoped these issues could be dealt with in subsequent negotiations. (The *SALT II Treaty* was negotiated in 1979, but the Senate never approved it, citing lack of true compliance by the Soviets with the original agreement and the Soviets' invasion of Afghanistan.) A proposal by the U.N. to prohibit the placement of nuclear weapons on the ocean floor was signed by the United States, the U.S.S.R. and over one hundred other nations in 1972.

THE "IMPERIAL PRESIDENCY" IN TROUBLE

The successes of Nixon's first term were followed by a series of political disasters which would lead to his becoming the first President of the United States to resign from office.

THE ELECTION OF 1972

Despite a shaky domestic record and continued fighting in Vietnam, Nixon and the Republicans were confident in the 1972 elections. Nixon based his fortunes on his foreign policy achievements and the gradual de-escalation in Indochina.

The Democrats had not repaired the deep rifts within their party from 1968. They nominated anti-war candidate Senator **George McGovern** of South Dakota, but his liberal philosophy drew little support.

18-YEAR-OLDS VOTE

"The right of citizens of the United States, who are 18 years of age or older, to vote shall not be denied or abridged by the United States or by any state on account of age."

– Twenty-sixth Amendment, 1971

In November, Nixon overwhelmed McGovern with more than 60% of the popular vote. In the electoral college, McGovern was only able to carry the District of Columbia and one state, while Nixon took 520 of the 538 electoral votes. McGovern was hoping that he could capture the youth vote which had been increased by virtue of the new Twenty-sixth Amendment (1971), allowing 18 to 20-year-olds to vote, but the results were disappointing. The Republicans were not able to capture either house of Congress.

AGNEW'S RESIGNATION

Treasury Department investigations into past activities of Nixon's Vice President, **Spiro Agnew**, found evidence of his taking bribes while a county executive and Governor of Maryland. Instead of going to trial, Agnew plea-bargained the charges down to income tax evasion and a fine, instead of a prison term. The embarrassment for the administration led him to become the second Vice President to resign. (The first was John C. Calhoun who resigned in 1832 in a policy disagreement with President Andrew Jackson.)

PRESIDENTIAL REPLACEMENT

Whenever there is a vacancy in the office of the Vice President, the President shall nominate a Vice President who shall take office upon confirmation by a majority vote of both houses of Congress."

– Twenty-fifth Amendment, 1967

With the Vice Presidency vacant, the Twenty-fifth Amendment (1967) was invoked for the first time. To replace Agnew, Nixon nominated **Gerald R. Ford**, the Republican leader in the House of Representatives. He was quickly approved by the required vote of Congress (House: 387 to 35; Senate: 92 to 3)

THE WATERGATE AFFAIR

In June of 1972, five men were arrested while attempting to electronically "bug" the Democratic Party headquarters in the **Watergate** office-apartment complex in Washington, DC. At first it seemed to be a bizarre incident, but investigators soon discovered a pattern of activities by members of the Republican Committee to Re-elect the President (CREEP) in violation of federal election laws. Nixon repeatedly claimed no knowledge of the activities by anyone in the White House.

In June of 1973, a Congressional investigating committee discovered that President Nixon had routinely made tape recordings of all his conferences and phone conversations. It subpoenaed the tapes. Nixon refused, claiming **executive privilege**, saying there were secret, national security matters on the tapes.

The U.S. Supreme Court ruled (*United States v. Nixon**, 1974) against "executive privilege" and ordered the President to turn over the tapes to investigators. Nixon had discussed ways of preventing a damaging investigation of White House aides being involved in the Watergate burglary. (This later became known as "the Coverup.")

IMPEACHMENT PROCEEDINGS

As Nixon's actions came into question, the Judiciary Committee of the House of

---

MINI•ASSESSMENT (8-10)

1   The purpose of President Richard Nixon's diplomatic initiatives toward China in 1972 was to
    1   end the United States relationship with the government of Taiwan
    2   establish military bases on Chinese territory
    3   eliminate communist rule in China
    4   counteract growing Soviet power and influence

2   Which occurred in Southeast Asia after the withdrawal of U.S. troops from Vietnam?
    1   Democratic governments replaced military dictatorships.
    2   Vietnam was conquered by China.
    3   The United States contributed enough military aid to allow the South Vietnamese government to become a powerful force in the region.
    4   Communist forces took over South Vietnam and several other countries of Indochina.

3   The resolution of the Watergate Affair was significant because it reinforced the idea that in the United States the
    1   government is based on the rule of law, not on the rule of an individual
    2   Chief Executive has nearly unlimited powers
    3   Congress is not effective in dealing with a constitutional crisis
    4   Supreme Court is afraid to make decisions involving the Presidency

Constructed Response

"Above Any Office"

1   What "office" is being referred to in the cartoon?

2   How did rulings of federal courts and the Supreme Court impact the power of this office during 1973 and 1974?

Representatives began to consider impeachment. After publicly televised hearings in the summer of 1974, the committee voted to recommend Nixon's impeachment on charges of obstructing justice and abuse of executive power. According to the Constitution, a majority vote in the House of Representatives is needed to officially bring charges or impeach. The Senate must then hold a trial and vote. (A two-thirds majority in the Senate is needed to remove a federal official from office.)

Jimmy Carter   Gerald Ford

NIXON RESIGNATION

It was apparent that the Democratic House favored impeachment. With the Senate vote predicted as close, Nixon would have little chance of surviving the impeachment and removal process. Rather than going through months of debate and paralyzing the government, Nixon resigned on 9 August 1974. Gerald Ford, who nine months earlier was the first person ever appointed to the Vice Presidency, was elevated to the Presidency.

THE FORD AND CARTER PRESIDENCIES

In the wake of Watergate, both Gerald Ford and **Jimmy Carter** experienced difficult times in the presidency. Ford served the remainder of Nixon's term (August 1974 to January 1977) and Carter served only a single term (1977-1981). Economic woes plagued their tenures, and Carter had the added burden of the **Iranian hostage crisis**. Both men lost their bids for re-election, indicating a deep sense of dissatisfaction and disorientation in the nation.

AN APPOINTIVE PRESIDENCY: FORD AND ROCKEFELLER

President Ford was the first person to occupy the White House by virtue of appointment. When Nixon resigned, Ford nominated former New York Governor **Nelson A. Rockefeller** (1908-1979) to fill the vacant Vice Presidency, and for the second time in a year, the Twenty-fifth Amendment proved its usefulness when Congress approved.

The relationship between the executive and the legislative branches is critical to the success of an administration. Republican Gerald Ford's twenty years of experience in Congress certainly helped him. However, as any President faced with a Congress dominated by the opposing party learns, a working relationship is often modified by partisanship.

DOMESTIC POLICIES

THE NIXON PARDON

Former President Nixon still faced possible criminal indictment and trial for his actions. He never apologized, and many Americans wished to see justice done. Claiming he wanted to "close the book" on Watergate, President Ford used his Constitutional power to grant a general pardon to Nixon. While Ford's intentions appeared honorable, the controversial move cost him votes in the 1976 election.

DRAFT AMNESTY

After the final fall of the South Vietnamese government in 1975, many Americans wished to put Vietnam behind them. There remained thousands of "draft evaders" who had left the United States to avoid military service in the unpopular war. Ford established a **draft amnesty program** which required those who wanted to return home to take an oath of allegiance to the United States and perform community service. Critics charged that Ford's plan asked too much, especially in the wake of his generous pardon of Nixon. Later in the 1970s, President Carter issued an unconditional pardon to those who still remained in exile.

OIL CRISIS

As the largest energy consumers in the world, Americans had been importing oil in ever increasing quantities in the post-World War II period. A seemingly endless supply flowed into the United States at very low cost. In 1973, Arab members of the world's major oil cartel, **OPEC** (Organization of Petroleum Exporting Countries), embargoed oil shipments to nations which supported their enemy, Israel. At the same time, the OPEC nations agreed to increase their prices, eventually raising the price of crude oil from $2.50 to $35.00 a barrel.

While a relatively low percentage of America's oil imports came from the Arab countries, a general disruption in world supplies caused hardships. The shortages caused by OPEC, plus realignment by multinational oil corporations, caused prices to rise sharply in the late 1970s. During the embargo, Americans found a new pastime: waiting on long lines to purchase gasoline. In 1979, the revolution in Iran resulted in a second oil shortage. The oil embargo caused inflation to shoot up (see graph above right).

Measures by federal, state, and local authorities to ease the energy crisis included temporary gasoline rationing, imposing a highway speed limit of 55 miles-an-hour, and temporary school closings. Both Ford and Carter tried to implement comprehensive national plans for dealing with the crises. Neither could win congressional approval for many measures.

The completion of the **Alaskan North Slope Pipeline** and the development of more fuel efficient American cars reduced foreign dependency somewhat. Revitalizing coal generators and allowing more nuclear power projects helped, but each had environmental trade offs.

In the late 1970s, Carter encouraged research on wind and solar power generation, development of synthetic fuels, and voluntary cutbacks on power consumption. Most of these programs met with intense opposition from special interest groups. Many efforts fell by the wayside in the 1980s, when Middle-Eastern oil began flowing more freely. Carter did manage to get Congress to create a cabinet level Department of Energy to plan strategies for the future.

CONSUMER PRICE INDEX INFLATION DURING THE OIL CRISIS

SOURCE: BUREAU OF LABOR STATISTICS

The total federal deficit grew in the 1970s. Efforts by both Presidents to balance the budget failed. As the national debt mounted, economists disagreed as to the deficit's impact on the future. Some blamed the deficits for inflation, while others felt the growing budget shortfalls would lead to an eventual economic collapse. Arguments continued throughout the decade as the annual deficit grew to 100 billion dollars.

THE SPACE PROGRAM

The fears about government deficits and a decline in public interest led to a more modest space program in the 1970s. The *Skylab* space station was in orbit for several years, permitting astronauts to do research. In 1981, NASA launched a reusable shuttle craft, ***Columbia***.

Succeeding shuttle flights placed scientific, commercial, and military satellites in orbit.

Space Shuttle Landing © PhotoDisc, 1998

Act of 1973. It forbade discrimination in jobs, education, and housing. In 1975, Congress required free public education for all physically and mentally disabled students. Many communities began providing special vehicle parking facilities and ramps for the disabled. The ***Americans with Disabilities Act*** (1990) required by law that most public places be accessible to the disabled.

A decade later, the program suffered a serious setback. In 1986 the shuttle ***Challenger*** exploded shortly after takeoff, killing seven astronauts. The tragedy forced NASA to review and refocus America's plan for space exploration. Unmanned space probes (*Explorer, Galileo, Magellan, Hubble Telescope,* and *Voyager)* also reached other planets, sending back important data and pictures from Venus and Mars.

LEGISLATION FOR THE BI-LINGUAL AND THE HANDICAPPED

Several acts passed by Congress during the 1970s provided greater opportunities for foreign language-speaking Americans. The *1975 Voting Rights Act* required bilingual ballots in districts with large populations of non-English speaking voters. The ***Bilingual Education Act*** mandated public schools to teach students in their native languages while they were learning English. However, opposition to such costly programs sprang up in the 1980s, as a growing number of Americans sought but failed to make English the official national language.

To meet the needs of the handicapped and disabled, Congress passed the ***Rehabilitation***

ENVIRONMENTAL CONCERNS

The Environmental Protection Agency was created in the Nixon Administration and made significant progress in cleaning up the nation's water and air in the 1970s. New concerns also arose over the disposal of hazardous chemical wastes.

"Mommy, What kind of icebergs are these?"

In 1977, homes built near a chemical dump called the **Love Canal** near Niagara Falls, New York, had to be abandoned when residents were stricken with illnesses and a high incidence of birth defects. The disaster raised public awareness about the problem of toxic waste. Congress responded with a **"super fund"** of several billion dollars to be used by the Environmental Protection Agency to clean up dangerous sites.

A 1979 accident at the **Three-Mile Island** nuclear power facility near Harrisburg, Pennsylvania increased public awareness of the possible risks of nuclear generators. While no one

---

KEY PROVISIONS OF THE AMERICANS WITH DISABILITIES ACT (1990)

- Properties open to the public must be made accessible to disabled people.

- Employers may not discriminate against disabled people in hiring, advancement, compensation, or training, and must adapt the workplace if necessary.

- Public transportation must be accessible to those in wheelchairs.

---

was killed or injured, and the radioactive release was small, serious concerns emerged. A rash of anti-nuclear demonstrations arose. The **Nuclear Regulatory Commission** (**NRC**) tightened safety procedures, and some plants were denied operating licenses, such as the Shoreham facility on Long Island (NY).

Middle East Power: Oil and Military Weapons

FOREIGN POLICIES

During the 1970s, it sometimes appeared as though the once mighty United States was at the mercy of international forces beyond its control. Third World nations (LDCs) repeatedly joined forces to block U.S. desires in the United Nations. Arab oil countries seemed to be manipulating the economy. The Soviets continued to ignore human rights agreements. Militant Iranian revolutionaries held American officials hostage. American policymakers were lukewarm about containment of communism after the disaster in Southeast Asia. For the struggling President Carter, his brightest and darkest moments came in the area of foreign policy.

OIL CRISIS

The oil crisis following the Arab-Israeli War of 1973 heightened awareness of the strategic importance of the Middle East. It also spotlight-

---

MINI•ASSESSMENT (8-11)

1 The presidency of Gerald Ford was different from all previous presidencies because he was the first President who
  1 won the office by running on a third-party ticket
  2 resigned from the office of the President
  3 ran for office as a nonpartisan candidate
  4 was not elected to either the Presidency or the Vice Presidency

2 Oil prices increased in the 1970s primarily due to
  1 economic actions by OPEC
  2 increased costs of exploration and drilling
  3 U.S. government price regulations
  4 competition between consumer and military interests

3 Under federal laws, Americans with disabilities must be
  1 placed in federally funded institutions near their homes
  2 guaranteed access to public transportation and facilities
  3 educated and supported by their families without governmental help
  4 educated only until they complete the eighth grade

Constructed Response

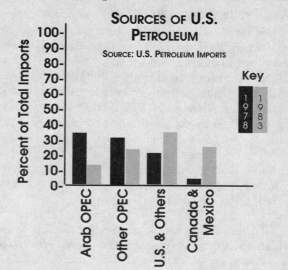

SOURCES OF U.S. PETROLEUM
SOURCE: U.S. PETROLEUM IMPORTS

1 What two sources of petroleum experienced a decline between 1978-1983?

2 What conditions and events in the world made it necessary for Americans to seek the shift indicated in the sources of oil?

---

ed America's reliance on energy imports and the growing interdependence of nations. The Soviet Union also began showing more interest in a role in the Middle East.

HUMAN RIGHTS

During his administration in the late 1970s, President Carter was an outspoken critic of human rights violations. He continually condemned improper and inhumane treatment of political prisoners in Cuba, South Africa, Uganda, and the U.S.S.R.

In 1975, the United States, Soviet Union, and most nations of Europe made several agreements dealing with political boundaries and protocols in Europe. An additional accord was signed which spelled out proper regard for human rights. Under Carter, this *Helsinki Accord* was a constant source of friction between the United States and the Soviet Union.

Even as the United States pointed out violations, the Soviets continued to restrict freedom of speech and the press, and block attempts by those who wished to leave the U.S.S.R., especially Russian Jews.

AFGHANISTAN

Late in 1979, Soviet armed forces invaded neighboring Afghanistan, an impoverished Muslim nation, to support a new Marxist regime fighting a civil war. The move was condemned by Western nations, Third World countries, and China. It was seen as an attempt by the U.S.S.R. to influence events in the Middle East. In diplomatic retaliation, President Carter withdrew the SALT II treaty from the Senate, cut sales of U.S. grain to the Soviets, and ordered a boycott of the 1980 Summer Olympics in Moscow. Soviet leaders ignored all protest actions. The United States sent aid to Afghan rebels in their mountain strongholds. The Soviets left Afghanistan in 1989, and the civil war continued through the 1990s. Many people compared the Soviet experience in Afghanistan to that of the United States in Vietnam.

PANAMA

The United States' continued presence in Panama ignited increasingly violent protest riots in the 1960s and 1970s. The United States began negotiations to turn the Canal and the U.S. Canal Zone territory over to the Panamanian government. In 1977, President Carter signed a treaty which began a phased turnover to be completed in 20 years. In the treaty, the United States retained the right to intervene in the area to maintain the Canal as a neutral international waterway. There was considerable criticism of U.S. security being compromised, but the Senate ratified the treaty later that year.

MIDDLE EAST

FOREIGN POLICY

Efforts begun by Henry Kissinger in the mid-1970s to bring about a peace settlement in the Middle-East had stalled. In 1978, Egyptian President **Anwar Sadat** and Israeli Premier **Menachem Begin** indicated a willingness to renew the quest for peace. President Carter took the initiative and brought the two leaders together at Camp David, the presidential retreat in Maryland. The three leaders worked out a peace agreement that was signed at the White House the following year.

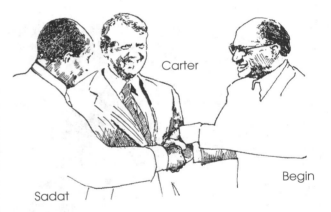

Sadat   Carter   Begin

The *Camp David Agreements* ended thirty years of hostility between the two nations and gave Israel official recognition, as well as access to the Suez Canal. Israel agreed to evacuate areas of the Sinai Peninsula conquered in the 1973 War. Both parties promised to start negotiations regarding self-determination for the Palestinian refugees in Israel.

The peace agreement was President Carter's major achievement in foreign policy. President Sadat was later assassinated by Egyptians who felt he had given in to Israel. The Palestinian question remained unresolved for many years.

HOSTAGES IN IRAN

Carter's most trying experience as President came at almost the same moment as the Israeli-Egyptian accord. Anger with the iron rule of the Shah of Iran boiled over in that country in 1979. A civil war forced the Shah to flee. Resentment grew because of long-time support of the Shah by the United States. The Shah's harsh government had supplied the United States with low cost oil and allowed U.S. military installations. His attempts to "Westernize" the country with the help of U.S. aid had clashed with strong Muslim fundamentalist beliefs. **Ayatollah Rullah Khomeini**, a militant religious leader who had been exiled by the Shah, returned to take control. An "Islamic Republic of Iran" was established which began to purge the Shah's followers and "de-Westernize" the nation.

Khomeini

When the exiled Shah was admitted to the United States for cancer treatment at a New York hospital, furious Iranians demanded his return. When the United States refused, militant students in Iran attacked the U.S. embassy in Teheran and began holding over 50 U.S. employees hostage.

President Carter's attempts to negotiate for the hostages' release proved futile. Iran was in revolutionary chaos, and the government threatened to put the hostages on trial. Daily newscasts showed thousands of Iranians outside the embassy chanting "Death to Carter – Death to America." As the crisis lengthened, Carter's popularity at home began to wane. A secret rescue attempt failed miserably, and Secretary of State Cyrus Vance resigned over the problem.

By the autumn of 1980, Carter's popularity reached an all-time low. Even before the Iranian situation, Carter's inability to deal with the Soviet invasion of Afghanistan, the energy crisis, inflation, and Congress in general were casting doubt on his leadership ability. When the Iranian Revolution brought about a second oil crisis in 1979, Americans were further demoralized.

Ronald Reagan

The Republicans, devastated earlier in the decade by Watergate, sensed victory as they nominated the conservative Governor of California, **Ronald Reagan**. Promising to reduce the federal bureaucracy and make America strong again, Reagan polled eight million votes more than Carter and swept the electoral vote 489 to 49.

The Iranians needed money for their war with Iraq. Facing mounting international criticism, they released the hostages in the same hour that Reagan took his oath of office on 20 January 1981. The United States released frozen Iranian bank accounts in America in return. The hostages were welcomed home with dramatic displays of American patriotism.

SUMMARY

As the 1970s came to a close, Americans had witnessed three decades of enormous change. An abundance of consumer goods helped place a majority of Americans in the comfortable middle class, yet poverty still existed. A lost war in Vietnam and a disgraced President Nixon led many citizens to question the actions of government. The nation's dominance in world affairs became less certain. However, opportunities for those who in the past faced discrimination, especially women and African Americans, increased. By the end of the 1970s, equality and justice for all, though still not fully reached, was becoming a much more realistic goal.

MINI•ASSESSMENT (8-12)

1 In response to the Soviet invasion of Afghanistan in 1979, the United States
   1 sent U.S. troops to the region to engage in a combat role
   2 withdrew from world affairs and sought a policy of isolation
   3 imposed an oil embargo on the Soviet Union
   4 attempted various means of economic and international pressure on the Soviets

2 Since World War II, what has been a major goal of United States relations with the Middle East?
   1 a peaceful resolution to Arab-Israeli conflicts
   2 an end to European influence over Arab nations
   3 establishment of United Nations control over the Middle East
   4 equal access for all nations to the oil reserves in the Middle East

3 The *Camp David Accords* negotiated during President Jimmy Carter's administration were an attempt to
   1 decrease United States control of the Panama Canal
   2 encourage the use of solar and other nonpolluting energy sources
   3 end inflationary oil prices
   4 establish peace in the Middle East between Israel and an Arab nation

Constructed Response

CHART A

Events of the Carter Administration

(late -1977) Panama Canal Treaty signed
(mid-1979) Camp David Accords
(mid-1980) Failed Iranian Hostage Rescue

CHART B

PRESIDENTIAL APPROVAL RATINGS
PRESIDENT JIMMY CARTER
1977-1981

Jan. 1977 - 63%
Jan. 1978 - 50%
Jan. 1979 - 46%
Jan. 1980 - 52%
Jan. 1981 - 32%

Source: Gallup Poll

1 Between which two years of his presidency did Carter's approval ratings *increase* the most?

2 Between which two years did Carter's approval ratings *decrease* the most?

3 How did the events in chart A affect the approval ratings given to President Carter in chart B?

UNIT ASSESSMENT
MULTI CHOICE QUESTIONS

1   Which is the major reason why families in highly industrialized nations are smaller today than in the past?
1   Modern religious beliefs prescribe smaller families.
2   Many governments offer financial incentives for smaller families.
3   Families need fewer children as producers.
4   Agricultural production will not support large families.

2   "We conclude that in the field of public education the doctrine of 'separate but equal' has no place. Separate educational facilities are inherently unequal."

This quotation expresses the Supreme Court decision in the case of
1   *Plessy v. Ferguson*
2   *Engel v. Vitale*
3   *Tinker v. Des Moines, Iowa*
4   *Brown v. Board of Ed. of Topeka, Kansas*

Base your answer to question 3 on the outline below and on your knowledge of U.S. history and government.

I._____
A.   President appearing on major television networks to announce important policies
B.   Candidates for public office spending large amounts on political advertisements
C.   President delivering "State of the Union" addresses to Congress at 9:00 P.M.

3   Which heading would be most appropriate for this list?
1   Political Corruption
2   Reforms in Television
3   Influence of the Media
4   Duties of the President

4   During the "Cold War" of the 1950s, U.S. foreign policy was characterized by
1   a policy of neutrality
2   increasing trade with Eastern Europe
3   numerous compromise agreements with communist nations
4   moves to protect others from communist aggression

5   A major effect of the rapid technological changes since 1945 has been
1   decreased economic competition between producer nations
2   a growing degree of isolationism
3   greater interdependence in the international marketplace
4   a reduction of the influence of democratic nations in world affairs

6   Since the 1960s, the use of automation in United States industry has led to
1   a shortage of consumer goods
2   increased union membership
3   the lowering of the legal minimum wage
4   increased unemployment among unskilled workers

7   A major cause of the growth of state and federal highway systems after World War II was the
1   increased use of mass transit systems
2   growing prosperity of inner-city areas
3   rapid development of suburbs
4   return of city dwellers to farm areas

8   The Great Society programs of the 1960s used the power of the federal government to bring about
1   an all-volunteer military
2   antipoverty reforms
3   deregulation of business
4   reduced defense spending

9   One similarity between the 1920s and the 1960s in the United States is that during both decades
1   traditional standards of dress, conduct, and conformity were challenged
2   involvement in international peacekeeping organizations was rejected
3   economic conditions led to a severe depression
4   civil rights legislation improved conditions for minorities

10 *Uncle Tom's Cabin*, *The Jungle*, and *The Feminine Mystique* are significant books because they all
1   exposed corrupt government practices
2   led to federal legislation to protect the environment
3   led to the adoption of constitutional amendments
4   influenced socioeconomic changes

11 The decisions of the United States Supreme Court in *Miranda v. Arizona*, *Gideon v. Wainwright*, and *Escobedo v. Illinois* all advanced the
   1 voting rights of minorities
   2 guarantees of free speech and press
   3 rights of accused persons
   4 extent of the President's powers as Commander in Chief

12 In the 1960s and 1970s, the Great Society programs and the Vietnam War demonstrated to the American people that
   1 racism can be eliminated through governmental actions
   2 strong Presidents can exercise power without creating public controversy
   3 major problems can be solved without increasing the size and cost of the federal government
   4 spending money and using modern technology do not necessarily solve problems

13 "Let every nation know, whether it wishes us well or ill, that we shall pay any price, bear any burden, meet any hardship, support any friend, oppose any force to assure the survival and the success of liberty."
   – President John F. Kennedy, 1961

   "Clearly there are limits to what outside forces can do to solve the severe internal problems of countries."
   – President William J. Clinton, 1993

   The best explanation for the difference between these two statements is that the United States has
   1 reduced its support for the United Nations
   2 been influenced by its experiences in the Vietnam War
   3 abandoned the policy of terrorism
   4 rejected the principle of collective security

14 The "domino theory," popular in the 1950s and 1960s, assumed the expansion of
   1 South African apartheid into other African nations
   2 totalitarianism throughout Latin America
   3 communism into Southeast Asia
   4 Soviet influence into China

15 President Harry Truman advanced the cause of civil rights for African Americans by
   1 ordering the desegregation of the Armed Forces
   2 appointing the first African American to the Supreme Court
   3 supporting the ratification of the Fourteenth and Fifteenth Amendments
   4 establishing affirmative action policies for industry

16 Which action in United States history is an example of civil disobedience?
   1 The National Association for the Advancement of Colored People (NAACP) filed suit against the state of Kansas for violating the constitutional rights of students in public schools.
   2 The Congress of Racial Equality (CORE) supported efforts to have the courts order the desegregation of buses and trains in the South.
   3 The Southern Christian Leadership Conference (SCLC) organized a boycott in Montgomery, Alabama, until transportation facilities were integrated.
   4 In Montgomery, Alabama, Rosa Parks refused to give up her seat on a bus to a white man.

17 What is the main criticism of affirmative action in recent years?
   1 The program has been extremely costly to the federal government.
   2 Hiring quotas for minorities may have denied opportunities to other qualified persons.
   3 Very few minority persons have been hired.
   4 Most state governments have been unwilling to enforce the program.

18 In the 1960s, Congress met some of the demands of the women's rights movement by
   1 requiring the federal government to hire an equal number of women and men
   2 prohibiting job discrimination on the basis of sex
   3 allowing women to be drafted into combat positions in the military
   4 requiring that professional schools set aside half their places for women

19 Under Chief Justice Earl Warren, the Supreme Court was considered "activist" because of its
  1 reluctance to overturn state laws
  2 insistence on restricting freedom of speech to spoken words
  3 expansion of individual rights in criminal cases
  4 refusal to reconsider the issues of the *Plessy v. Ferguson* case

20 The *Panama Canal Treaty of 1978* reversed earlier U.S. policy in that region because it
  1 ended U.S. isolation through a military alliance with Panama
  2 relinquished control of an area long held by the U.S.
  3 recognized a Marxist government in Panama
  4 accepted European control in the Western Hemisphere

21 Which principle was most weakened as a result of the Watergate controversy?
  1 congressional immunity
  2 executive privilege
  3 judicial review
  4 states rights

22 Constitutional amendments have been proposed to ban forced busing, forbid abortion, and prohibit burning the United States flag. These proposals indicate that
  1 the Constitution is an inflexible document
  2 amending the Constitution is a simple process
  3 some people disagree with certain Supreme Court decisions
  4 American society has been unwilling to deal with complex social issues

Base your answer to question 23 on the cartoon below and on your knowledge of U.S. history and government.

23 The cartoon makes the point that decisions of the Supreme Court
  1 sometimes do not resolve controversial issues
  2 are usually accepted by both sides in a controversy
  3 should avoid dealing with controversial issues
  4 ignore public opinion

24 The outcome of the Watergate scandal reinforced the principle that
   1   national security takes precedence over freedom of the press
   2   the power of executive privilege is greater than the rule of law
   3   the law applies equally to all citizens, including government officials
   4   impeached government officials are immune from criminal prosecution

25 A major achievement of President Jimmy Carter was
   1   the worldwide acceptance of his human rights policy
   2   the balancing of the federal budget
   3   his handling of international terrorist incidents
   4   the signing of the Camp David peace accords

THEMATIC ESSAY

Directions: Write a well-organized essay that includes an introduction, several paragraphs explaining your position, and a conclusion.

Theme:

Foreign Policy
From the period 1950-1980, the United States interacted many times with foreign nations and governments to protect the national interests of the United States.

Task:

Using your knowledge of United States history and government, write an essay in which you select *three* specific occurrences between 1950-1980 when the United States had dealings with a foreign nation in order to protect the national interest of the United States.

For each occurrence

•   identify the country or countries involved,
•   state what the national interest of the United States was, and
•   discuss the extent to which the United States achieved this goal.

Suggestions:
You may use any examples from your study of U.S. history and government within the specified time period. Some suggestions you might wish to consider include: Korean War, Eisenhower Doctrine, Bay of Pigs, Cuban Missile Crisis, Vietnam War, Détente, SALT, Camp David Agreements, or the 1980 Olympic Boycott. **You are *not* limited to these suggestions.**

DOCUMENT BASED QUESTION

The following task is based on the accompanying documents. The documents may have been edited for the purposes of this exercise. The task is designed to test your ability to work with historical documents. As you analyze the documents, take into account both the source of the document and the author's point of view.

Directions: Read the documents in Part A and answer the question after each document. Then read the directions for Part B and write your essay.

Historical Context:

The Preamble indicates the purpose of the U.S. Constitution is to "form a more perfect union, establish justice, promote the general welfare, and secure the blessings of liberty." The second half of the 20th century has seen numerous attempts to make this a reality for all people in the United States. The documents below present information on these efforts.

Task:

Using information from the documents and your knowledge of United States history and government, write an essay in which you

- describe the impact of the government's attempts to further the guarantees of justice, equality and liberty on American society in general, and
- discuss the impact of the government's attempts to increase justice, equality and liberty for some specific groups.

Part A - Short Answer

Analyze the documents and answer the questions that follow each document.

Questions for Document 1

1 What type of tax is prohibited as a result of this Amendment?

2 How did this Amendment benefit a particular group in the United States?

> **DOCUMENT 1**
> "The right of citizens of the United States to vote in any primary or other election for President or Vice President, for electors for President or Vice President, or for Senators or Representatives in Congress, shall not be denied or abridged by the United States or any state by reason of failure to pay any poll tax or other tax."
> – XXIV Amendment (1964)

Question for Document 2

How did the the *Civil Rights Act of 1964* attempt to bring about a more equal society?

> **DOCUMENT 2**
> "All persons shall be entitled to the full and equal enjoyment of the goods, services, facilities, privileges, advantages, and accommodations of any place of public accommodation ... without discrimination or segregation on the ground of race, color, religion, or national origin."
> – Civil Rights Act of 1964

Question for Document 3

How does this decision help to guarantee equal justice to the accused?

> **DOCUMENT 3**
> "The right of one charged with crime to counsel may not be deemed fundamental and essential for fair trials in some countries, but is in ours. From the very beginning, our state and national constitutions and laws have laid great emphasis on ... safeguards designed to assure fair trials before impartial tribunals in which every defendant stands equal before the law. This noble ideal cannot be realized if the poor man charged with a crime has to face his accusers without a lawyer to assist him."
> – Gideon v. Wainwright (1963)

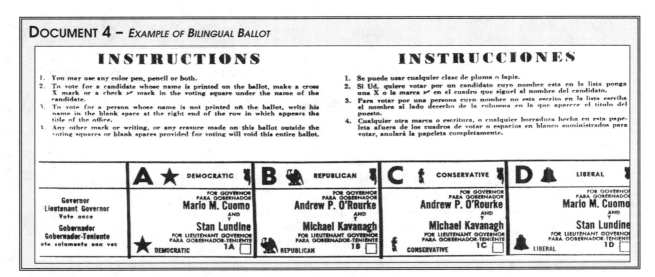

DOCUMENT 4 – *EXAMPLE OF BILINGUAL BALLOT*

Questions for Document 4

1 Why is this an example of a bilingual ballot?

2 How does this ballot open the democratic process to more people?

Question for Document 5

Explain how equality in the education setting was advanced by this act.

DOCUMENT 5

"No person in the United States shall, on the basis of sex, be excluded from participation in, be denied the benefits of, or be subjected to discrimination under any education program or activity receiving federal financial assistance."

– Title IX, Education Amendments of 1972

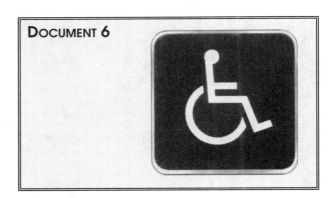

DOCUMENT 6

Questions for Document 6

1 Where would you see this symbol?

2 How is the concept of equal protection of the law furthered by complying with policies related to this symbol?

GO ON TO PART B

Part B - Essay

Historical Context:

The Preamble indicates the purpose of the U.S. Constitution is to "form a more perfect union, establish justice, promote the general welfare, and secure the blessings of liberty." The second half of the 20th century has seen numerous attempts to make this a reality for all people in the United States.

Directions:

- Write a well organized essay that includes an introduction, several paragraphs, and a conclusion.
- Use evidence from the documents to support your response.
- Do not simply repeat the contents of the documents.
- Include specific related outside information.

Task:

Using information from the documents and your knowledge of United States history and government, write an essay in which you

- describe the impact of the government's attempts to further the guarantees of justice, equality, and liberty on American society in general, and
- discuss the impact of the government's attempts to increase justice, equality and liberty for some specific groups.

Be sure to include specific historical details. You must also include additional information from your knowledge of United States history and government.

UNIT

9

PAGE 337

AMERICA ASTRIDE THE MILLENNIUM

NASA Photo

FOREWORD

The United States had to contend with rapid changes that occurred in the world during the last two decades of the 20th century. The Cold War ended, the Soviet Union crumbled, and communism proved to be a failed ideology. New conflicts in various corners of the world kept the United States busy, however. Within the country, many Americans prospered in the strong economy, but some problems remained unsolved. Health care and Social Security concerns, trade deficits, and the uneven distribution of wealth provoked strong debates and controversy.

Ronald Reagan
Presidential Library

THE NEW FEDERALISM

Ronald Reagan's victory in the 1980 presidential election allowed many Republican candidates to ride into office "on his coattails." This resulted in Republican control of the U.S. Senate for the first time in thirty years. Republican victories in congressional races also reduced the power of the Democrats in the House of Representatives. Although some critics denounced Reagan's domestic agenda and foreign policies, his personal popularity remained high. In the 1984 election, he easily defeated the

Democratic challenger, Carter's Vice President, Walter Mondale. Reagan received the largest number of electoral votes in history (525 to 13) and 60% of the popular vote. As with earlier Republicans (Eisenhower, Nixon, Ford), Reagan set a high priority on reducing the growth of the federal government. He had limited success.

President Reagan called his domestic agenda the **New Federalism**. His goal was to shift federal programs in education, health, welfare, and transportation to state and local authorities. State officials welcomed control over such programs, but voiced concern about paying for them. Reagan reduced aid to states for the programs. The New Federalism had mixed results. The federal government cut only a few programs and reduced others. The states were unable to finance most of the programs themselves, and the federal government continued massive funding.

SUPPLY-SIDE ECONOMICS

ECONOMIC POLICY

Reagan inherited a weak economy. It was one of the nation's most pressing problems. As a solution, the Reagan Administration proposed **supply-side economics**. Supply-siders pressed Congress to reduce capital gains taxes, individual income taxes for the rich, and corporate income taxes. Supply-side economists pledged to cut expensive government costs. They hoped to free up new investment capital and spur growth. They claimed this would increase supplies of goods and services.

Supply-siders said the general population would eventually prosper as the new growth "trickled down" in the form of new employment.

Note: Items marked with an * are listed in the *Landmark Supreme Court Decisions* chart in Appendices.

These ideas were similar to those used during Hoover's administration (chart on page 235). Supply-siders theorized the increased employment would expand demand (consumer spending power). Congress supported the basic plan.

At first, the rapid economic changes triggered an 18 month recession. The Federal Reserve Board kept bank interest rates high. It feared inflation from the tax cuts. Reagan argued for lower interest rates. The tax breaks eventually increased investments and corporate growth. Critics claimed that the federal budget cuts harmed millions of poor. They said the rich prospered at the expense of the middle and lower classes.

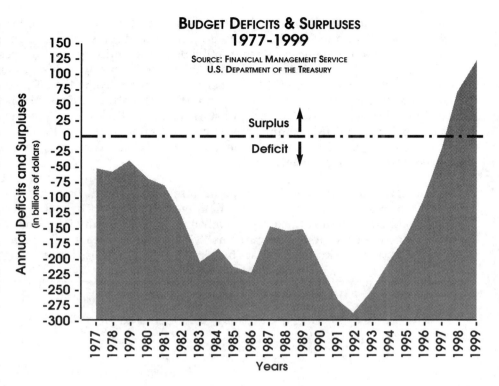

BUDGET DEFICITS & SURPLUSES 1977-1999

SOURCE: FINANCIAL MANAGEMENT SERVICE
U.S. DEPARTMENT OF THE TREASURY

Annual Deficits and Surpluses (in billions of dollars)

Surplus ↑
Deficit ↓

Years

TAX CUTS AND DEFICITS

ECONOMIC POLICY

The Democratically controlled House bowed to the popularity of Reagan's tax cuts. Congress passed a 25% tax reduction for individuals and larger reductions for businesses. A tax simplification program (1986) cut deductions for education, reduced the tax brackets, and simplified payment schedules. Although **revenue** (income from taxes and tariffs) increased, government spending increased at a higher rate. This caused **budget deficits** (annual imbalances when federal spending exceeds revenue). Reagan wanted more military spending and Congress increased domestic social-welfare programs. This caused an even greater deficit, necessitating additional borrowing. The interest on the accumulating debt became a major government expense in itself, and the national debt soared.

The President and Congress shared responsibility for the budget. For political reasons, they often disagreed on where to make necessary cuts in federal spending. Well into the 1990s, annual deficits pushed the **national debt** (the total accumulation of federal borrowing to offset deficits over many years) to over $4 trillion. In the 1990s, the annual interest alone grew to over $100 billion.

Through the 1980s, Congress failed to balance the budget. In the 1990s, its deficit reduction legislation raised taxes selectively, and brought in more revenue. Coupled with the strong economy and more controlled spending, deficit reduction measures produced the first budget surplus (1998) in decades. Even then, Congress and President Clinton disagreed on whether to use the surplus to provide tax relief, pay off some of the debt, increase spending, or strengthen Social Security.

ENVIRONMENTAL & CIVIL RIGHTS POLICIES

In 1981, President Reagan appointed the controversial **James G. Watt** as his Secretary of the Interior. In trying to promote economic growth, Watt weakened or cut laws that provided protection to the environment, endangered wildlife, and national parks. The Reagan Administration also increased the number of permits for offshore oil drilling and strip-mining, both potentially dangerous to the environment.

Administration officials claimed that, under the New Federalism, these policies shifted more responsibility to state agencies. Reagan officials said federal regulations interfered with free enterprise and economic growth. They believed cutting regulations stimulated the economy. Outraged environmentalists railed against Watt and these policies that undermined years of ecological work. They said resources, once destroyed, could never be reclaimed.

For many years, airborne factory pollutants caused by burning fossil fuels (oil, coal) have been carried high into the atmosphere, eventually returning to earth during rainstorms. This **acid rain** destroyed lakes and forests hundreds, even thousands of miles from the factories, often in other states and in Canada. Difficulties in determining the sources of such pollution and lobbying by industry slowed efforts at congressional remedies. In 1986, a meeting between Canadian Prime Minister **Brian Mulrooney** and President Reagan set up an international effort to seek solutions, but deciding responsibility for cleanup costs remained a problem.

Reagan also reduced federal involvement in civil rights. The individual states had to enforce busing, affirmative action, and prosecution of civil rights violations. Civil rights leaders condemned this approach. They said it abolished the progress made since the *Brown* decision.

THE SUPREME COURT AND THE SCHOOLS

In recent decades, the Court has ruled in various cases regarding the constitutional rights of school students.

CONSTITUTIONAL
STRUCTURES

Engel v. Vitale, 1962
(First Amendment – establishment clause)

Parents and students challenged the constitutionality of recitation of a non-denominational prayer in public schools. Opponents of the daily prayer cited the First Amendment requirement of separation of Church and State. The Court ruled the NY State written prayer unconstitutional, saying the practice violated the First Amendment rights of students. Such prayer also conflicted with the establishment clause, which forbids the establishment of religion by government.

Tinker v. Des Moines School District, 1969
(First Amendment – free speech)

Two students were suspended from school for wearing black armbands to protest the Vietnam War. The students said the Constitutional guarantee of free speech protected this form of protest. Agreeing with the students, the Court ruled that this symbolic type of speech is protected by the First Amendment. However, speech that is disruptive of the educational process can be restricted.

New Jersey v. TLO, 1985
(Fourth Amendment – search and seizure)

School officials found a student smoking in school, and conducted a search of the student's purse, in which not just cigarettes, but drugs and and drug related items were found. The student claimed this was an unreasonable search. The Court ruled in favor of the school authorities, saying that in a school, only "reasonable suspicion" (instead of probable cause) is necessary for a search. Schools have a duty to promote a safe environment for learning.

Veronia School District v. Acton, 1995
(Fourth Amendment – search and the right of privacy)

A school required drug testing for all students participating in athletics. One student refused, citing his right of privacy and his guarantee against unreasonable search and seizure. The school's policy was upheld by the Supreme Court. Student athletes do not have the same privacy rights as adults. The "search" was constitutional and the importance of reducing drug use make such testing reasonable.

Supreme Court Justice Sandra O'Connor
Photo: Supreme Court

SOCIAL ISSUES: AN ACTIVIST COURT

Reagan's actions encouraged a growing conservative movement called the **New Right**. It tried to overturn controversial Supreme Court decisions of the Warren Court. The banning of prayer in public schools (see *Engel*, Supreme Court and the Schools chart, page 340), and abortion-by-choice (*Roe v. Wade*, 1973) were major targets of New Right activists. They also sought stricter censorship of pornographic materials and defeat of the Equal Rights Amendment.

GROWTH OF DEMOCRACY

President Reagan supported attempts to pass constitutional amendments allowing school prayer and banning abortions. These proposals did not receive the necessary two-thirds vote in Congress. However, Reagan did manage to reinforce the Supreme Court's conservative direction. He named Associate Justice **William Rehnquist** to replace retiring Chief Justice Warren Burger in 1986. Reagan also named three additional conservatives to Court vacancies: **Sandra O'Connor** (the first woman to serve on the Court), **Antonin Scalia**, and **Anthony Kennedy**.

NEW APPROACHES TO OLD PROBLEMS
POVERTY IN AN AFFLUENT SOCIETY

The uneven economic recovery and growth in the 1980s failed to check poverty. Some African Americans and members of other minorities achieved middle class status. However, a significant percentage of the population remained below the poverty line. Growing numbers of elderly people on fixed incomes found it increasingly difficult to survive.

Many critics blamed the problems on the New Federalism. Federal authorities cut many social welfare programs designed to help the poor. Supply-side economics seemed to benefit the rich rather than the poor.

At the end of Carter's Administration (1980) unemployment was 7.1%. By the end of Regan's term, it had fallen to 5.5% (1988). However, unemployment remained especially high among minorities in the inner cities. Federal cuts ended job retraining programs. The new job market provided few opportunities for those with limited education and skills. Poorly administered state programs and inadequate educational systems in many areas also shared the blame.

The Reagan cuts forced many states to reduce the patient population and staffs of mental institutions. Many former patients became homeless, could not afford expensive urban housing, and were turned onto the streets. Drug and alcohol addictions added to the problem. Local governments struggled with ways to find housing for the homeless.

FEAST AND FAMINE: THE FARMERS' DILEMMA

During the 1970s, inflation drove farm prices to record levels. Demand for food expanded in overseas markets. (Repeated crop failures in the U.S.S.R. drove demand up.) Many farmers expanded. They borrowed money for new machinery. However, during the 1980s, inflation slowed, domestic and overseas demand fell, and farmers' overproduction caused prices to drop.

These factors made it difficult for farmers to pay debts. Foreclosures and bank failures grew in the agricultural regions of the country. The government renewed farm subsidy programs, but they provided little relief. In addition, the scientific and technological developments of the **Green Revolution** affected farming. Increased crop yields resulted in greater production, but reduced the number of small farms and family farmers annually (see graphs on page 342).

FORTY YEARS OF FARMING IN THE UNITED STATES

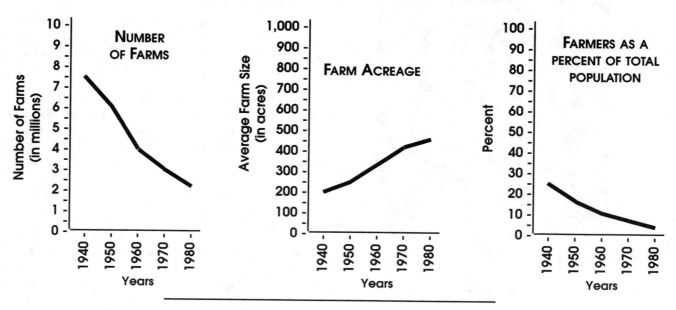

NUMBER OF FARMS — Number of Farms (in millions) vs. Years (1940–1980)

FARM ACREAGE — Average Farm Size (in acres) vs. Years (1940–1980)

FARMERS AS A PERCENT OF TOTAL POPULATION — Percent vs. Years (1940–1980)

NEW SOURCES OF IMMIGRATION

From 1967-1990, American immigration underwent dramatic changes. The *Immigration Act of 1965* ended the national origins quota system and tried to deal with newcomers fairly. Congress gave preference to immigrants with needed technical and professional skills. Despite such regulations, millions of illegal aliens continued to enter the country. Most came in search of political freedom and economic opportunity.

To stem the tide of illegal entrants, Congress passed the *Immigration Reform and Control Act of 1986*. The law granted legal status to "illegals" who had entered the U.S. before 1982. However, it also provided strict punishment for employers who continued to hire illegal aliens. Supporters hoped that fewer people would enter if they could not find work. Critics claimed the law was unfair and discriminated against poorer Hispanic groups, especially Mexican workers.

GROWING NUMBERS OF ELDERLY

In 1900, people over 65 made up four percent of the nation's population. By 1960, the figure doubled. In 2000, it doubled again. There are many reasons for the rise in the senior citizen population: improvements in medicine, better nutrition, safer working conditions, and the availability of hospital care.

By 2020, larger numbers of elderly will pressure the Social Security System to pay more benefits than it collects in taxes. Such a situation could bankrupt the system by the middle of the 21st century. Society will also have to find ways to deal with the problems of affordable medical care and housing for the elderly.

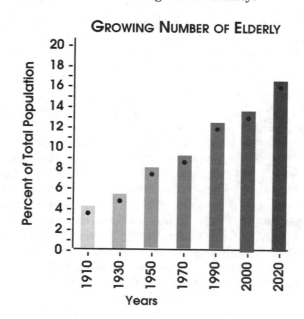

GROWING NUMBER OF ELDERLY — Percent of Total Population vs. Years (1910–2020)

RENEWED U.S. POWER IMAGE

Reagan promised to restore America's strength and pride on the international front. The President hoped to reverse some of the foreign policy humiliations of the previous decade.

1 The term New Federalism refers to a plan to change the relationship
  1 among the fifty states
  2 between the states and the federal government
  3 among the three branches of the federal government
  4 between the President and the cabinet

2 According to the supply-side economic principles promoted by President Ronald Reagan, economic growth would occur when
  1 corporate business taxes were reduced
  2 business was regulated by antitrust legislation
  3 unemployment benefits were increased
  4 investment in capital goods was decreased

3 During the 20th century, agriculture in the United States experienced a decrease in the
  1 average size of farms
  2 total output of farm products
  3 productivity of farm workers
  4 number of farm workers

Constructed Response

"We always must ask: Is government working to liberate and empower the individual? Is it creating incentives for people to produce, save, invest, and profit from legitimate risks and honest toil? Is it encouraging all of us to reach for the stars? Or does it seek to compel, command, and coerce people into submission and dependence? Ask these questions, because no matter where you look today, you will see that development depends on economic freedom."
– President Ronald Reagan, 15 October 1981

1 According to President Reagan, what is the role of government?

2 What are two specific ways in which the Reagan administration attempted to implement this role of government?

CENTRAL AMERICA AND CARIBBEAN

President Reagan opposed communist expansion in Latin America. During the 1970s and 1980s, Cuba secretly supported Marxist revolutions in Nicaragua and Grenada. President Reagan denounced Nicaragua and Grenada as centers of Cuban and Soviet communist influence.

In 1973, as the U.S. began to withdraw from Vietnam, Congress moved to cut back the war-making power of the President. It passed the *War Powers Act* over the veto of President Nixon. As a result, the President must report in writing to Congress within 48 hours the movement of troops into areas where hostilities are occurring. Congress must vote within 60 days to continue U.S. military action. If the vote is to discontinue, the President must remove the troops. In addition, the President would have to secure periodic congressional approval if the troops were to remain in a combat role.

In 1983, reluctantly complying with the *War Powers Act*, Reagan ordered 1,900 U.S. troops to join 300 troops from six Latin American nations to stop a Soviet-Cuban communist coup in Grenada. The invading forces quickly defeated the communists, occupied the island, and set up a new, friendly government.

Reagan also struggled with Congress over sending aid to the Nicaraguan **contras** (anti-communist guerrilla group based in Honduras). U.S. aid was sporadic. However, international pressure forced the Nicaraguan government to hold elections. Nicaraguans voted to oust Daniel Ortega's communist Sandinistas in 1990. The new democratic leadership under Violeta de Chamorro improved relations with the United States. Reagan also sent aid and advisors to El Salvador as that nation struggled to resist communist insurgents.

MIDDLE EAST: WAR AND HOSTAGES

In the 1980s, Lebanon's civil war between the Muslims and Christians, begun in 1975, continued. Israel, Syria, the PLO (Palestine Liberation Organization), and various armed Islamic groups entered the struggle. President Reagan sent

Marine units to aid the U.N. peace-keeping efforts. On 21 October 1983, Muslim extremists crashed a bomb-laden truck into the Marine headquarters, killing 241 U.S. servicemen.

Warring Muslim factions also took Western diplomats, educators, and newsmen hostage at an alarming rate. Through the 1980s, normal diplomatic channels failed, and the captors released only a few hostages. Tentative peace in Lebanon and shifting relations in the Middle East helped most hostages regain freedom in 1991 and 1992.

Nearly a decade of war between Iran and Iraq dragged on until the summer of 1989. Both sides bombed oil tankers to hamper petroleum shipments. President Reagan sent American naval forces to the area in 1987. Other European nations followed the American lead and sent forces to the Persian Gulf region. U.S. Navy ships escorted oil tankers of friendly Kuwait. Reagan arranged for the tankers to fly the American flag while passing through the region. Iranian attacks on the "reflagged" tankers nearly brought the United States into the war.

TERRORISM

With the exceptions of the 26 February 1993 terrorist bombing of the World Trade Center in NYC (6 killed, 1,000 injured, and $600 million in damage) and the 19 April 1995 bombing of the Alfred P. Murrah Federal Building in Oklahoma City (168 killed, including 19 children, 500 wounded), relatively few terrorist attacks have occurred within the United States. However, Americans traveling abroad have experienced violent episodes since the 1980s.

In the 1980s, Muslim religious extremists, backed by the PLO, Libya, and/or Iran, commit-

ted terrorist acts throughout Western Europe. In 1986, terrorists bombed a Berlin nightclub, massacred civilians at Rome's airport, and hijacked a TWA plane, holding the passengers hostage for two weeks. A brutal killing of an American took place when terrorists took over the Italian cruise ship *Achille Lauro* in 1985. Although terrorists usually evaded capture, U.S. jets managed to catch the *Achille Lauro* terrorists as they attempted escape.

For many years Libya's head of state, **Muammar Qaddafi**, was known as a supporter of terrorist activity and had been allowing terrorist organizations to train in Libya. In 1986, in an internationally controversial move and as a warning that terrorist support would not be tolerated, President Reagan ordered U.S. planes to bomb Qaddafi's headquarters in Tripoli.

In 1988, 270 died (mostly Americans), when Libyan-Iranian backed extremists blew up a Pan Am jet over Lockerbie, Scotland. In 1991 both the United States and the United Kingdom indicted two Libyan intelligence agents for the bombing. Finally, in 1999 after years of U.N. sanctions, the Libyan People's Congress handed over the two accused to the International Court of Justice in The Hague for trial that began in the year 2000.

DRUG TRAFFICKING

During the 1980s, there was a increase in the quantity of illegal drugs entering the United States. Several foreign governments routinely allowed illegal drug shipments to leave their countries. In 1989, President Bush traveled to Colombia and met with several Latin American leaders. He pledged to aid efforts to stem the flow of drugs from their Latin American sources.

American law enforcement officials in most communities failed to halt the flow of drugs. FBI anti-crime task forces and drug enforcement units joined police from local areas. Federal agencies worked together to stop drugs from entering the country. President Reagan also sponsored **drug-testing** of federal employees, a practice that has spread to local governments and private industry.

REASONS FOR RAPID GROWTH OF TRADE DEFICIT

- a high value for the dollar made imports less expensive and American exports more costly

- lower production costs in foreign nations drove many American manufacturers out of business

- "dumping" of excess products by foreign nations in the United States

- trade barriers set up against U.S. products by other nations

- exceptionally high prices of foreign oil in the early 1980s

TRADE IMBALANCE AND DIVESTING

U.S. foreign trade experienced a mounting **trade deficit** (the value of imports exceeds exports) in the 1980s. Essentially, money flows out of the country. Domestic demand slumps, production slows, and jobs disappear. The U.S. trade deficit grew alarmingly in the 1980s.

JAPAN: TRADE IMBALANCE

Japan exported a flood of autos, cameras, and electronic equipment to the United States but refused to lower its own restrictions on U.S. goods. President Reagan was usually an advocate of free trade (no restrictions). However, in the mid-1980s Reagan placed import quota restrictions on some Japanese goods.

The quota restrictions were too weak to alter the trade deficit. Foreign companies simply cut profits to stay competitive in America. The big foreign automakers (VW, Honda, Toyota) skirted the restrictions. By building auto plants in California, Kentucky, Ohio, Pennsylvania, and Tennessee, they could sell their cars in the U.S. and avoid tariff and quota restrictions.

U.S. consumers benefited from the greater choice of goods at lower prices. However, American workers faced unemployment as domestic producers cut back or ceased production. Reagan and Bush resisted pressure from business and unions for stronger retaliation against foreign governments. They feared an international trade war with detrimental consequences.

UNITED STATES AND SOUTH AFRICA

South Africa's domestic policy of **apartheid** (racial separation by law) made relations between the United States and South Africa a problem. Over 70% of South Africa's population was black, yet they were second class citizens. Apartheid policies restricted their living and working conditions. It limited their civil and voting rights. Throughout the 1980s, the white controlled government continued to resist reforms. This led to many violent confrontations.

Nearly all nations condemned apartheid. Some Americans believed that all U.S.-based corporations should cease operations in South Africa until the government ended the inequality. They urged stockholders of corporations doing business in South Africa to **divest** (sell off their stock) and demanded that the U.S. government sever trade relations to force the abandonment of apartheid.

Others believed that it was best for American corporations to stay in South Africa. These foreign companies were more likely to treat black Africans as equals and provide economic opportunity. The Reagan and Bush Administrations imposed limited economic sanctions on South Africa, but resisted demands to end all ties.

In 1990, the South African government released African National Congress leader **Nelson Mandela** after 28 years in prison. A new white minority government headed by **F.W. de Klerk**

Nelson Mandela

gradually repealed many apartheid restrictions. In early 1992, a 68% victory in a referendum by white voters encouraged de Klerk, Mandela, and other African leaders to end racial inequality and expand suffrage. In April 1994, the nation's first all-race elections resulted in Mandela becoming President and de Klerk, Vice President. A new cabinet and parliament began implementation of a new constitution based on racial equality for Africa's most prosperous nation.

U.S. – SOVIET RELATIONS

President Reagan opposed the 1970s policy of détenté. He took a strong position against Soviet expansionism, and he promoted rebuilding U.S. military strength as a deterrent. He spent billions researching the **Strategic Defense Initiative** (nicknamed "Star Wars"). Star Wars' supporters claimed high tech defensive shield could be built to defend successfully against an enemy missile attack.

FOREIGN POLICY

During his first term, Reagan's "hard-line" anti-communism stand led to a deterioration of relations between the two superpowers. He soundly criticized the shooting down of a Korean airliner which strayed into Soviet airspace, the imposition of martial law in Poland, and Soviet involvement in the war in Afghanistan.

GORBACHEV
By Reagan's second term, three Soviet leaders had died. Relations improved in the mid-1980s when **Mikhail Gorbachev** emerged as the Soviet leader/reformer. He started economic reform (**perestroika**) and political openess (**glasnost**) at home. He reduced the Soviet military presence in Eastern Europe and allowed the Soviet satellite countries greater autonomy. These changes ushered in a wave of political upheavals in Eastern Europe and the Soviet Union culminating in 1989.

The reforms also signaled a new relationship between the superpowers. Both sides sought new agreements on arms control. Reagan and Gorbachev held frequent summits, and the two superpowers moved vigorously toward significant arms reduction, especially in Europe.

"If the President looks for me, tell him he can reach me at 1-800-TEHERAN"

IRAN-CONTRA AFFAIR

In 1986, congressional investigators revealed that members of the Reagan Administration illegally sold weapons to Iran. The officials then diverted the funds to the contra rebels in Nicaragua. Federal courts convicted several White House staff members of violating federal laws which prohibited such clandestine aid.

Congress criticized President Reagan for his inattention to these illegal activities. President Reagan came under severe criticism for his lax administrative procedures and lack of knowledge about the activities of

President Reagan & General Secretary Gorbachev signing the INF Treaty in the East Room of the White House, 8 December 1987. (National Archives and Record Administration)

1 The Reagan Administration became involved in Latin American affairs because the U.S. desired to
   1 protect the rights of U.S. citizens living abroad
   2 trade in an area that is strategically vital
   3 block communist expansion
   4 reduce the financial debt of the Latin American nations

2 Why do authorities find it difficult to prevent terrorism?
   1 Terrorists are better armed than the American military.
   2 Terrorists usually outnumber law-abiding citizens.
   3 Some countries give aid and sanctuary to terrorist groups.
   4 Under a United Nations agreement, terrorists have diplomatic immunity.

3 The Iran Contra affair involved the selling of weapons to Iran, then diverting the money from the sales to
   1 the United Nations peacekeeping forces in Africa
   2 the rebels fighting the communists in Nicaragua
   3 the Republican Party Campaign Committee
   4 those fighting apartheid in South Africa

CONSTRUCTED RESPONSE

1 What difficulty is Uncle Sam experiencing?

2 What is the cartoonist's point of view regarding the foreign policy of the United States?

3 Cite some specific instances of American involvement in these areas during the 1980s.

his staff. Reagan broke no laws, but many critics questioned his lack of control over staff and foreign policymakers.

AMERICA IN THE 1990S: THE BUSH PRESIDENCY

In the 1988 Presidential election, Reagan's Vice President, **George Bush** (TX) defeated Democratic nominee, Governor Michael Dukakis (MA). Bush became the first sitting Vice President elected to the presidency since Martin Van Buren in 1836.

In foreign affairs, the breakup of the Soviet Union and downfall of communism in Eastern Europe ended a generation of Cold War. This presented the Bush Administration with new opportunities and new problems. In the Middle East, Iraq's dictator, **Saddam Hussein**, began a new threat to the stability of the region.

President George Bush and his wife Barbara
National Archives

In domestic affairs, Bush supported most of Reagan's programs. However, he promised some changes. He pledged greater emphasis on child care, education, and the war on drugs. Bush's domestic programs received lukewarm attention from the Democratic controlled Congress. A recession in 1991-1992 caused high unemployment (7-8%). Economic uncertainty, budget deficits, the **S&L crisis** (see below) and Congress' own bank scandals nearly stopped legislative activity in the 102nd Congress.

Bush followed the Reagan lead in appointing conservative justices to the federal bench. Liberals, minorities, and some women's groups criticized these appointments. The Senate approved two Bush nominees to the Supreme Court (Justices **David Souter**, 1990 and **Clarence Thomas**, 1991 only after long and bitter debate.

DOMESTIC ISSUES

THE AIDS CRISIS

AIDS (**Acquired Immuno-Deficiency Syndrome**) will continue to impact U.S. society into the 21st century. The Federal Center for Disease Control estimated that in the U.S. over a million persons have contracted AIDS (40+ million worldwide). The U.S. expects up to 100,000 new cases each year. More than 30,000 people are dying each year from AIDS-related disease. A vaccination against the **HIV virus** (human immunodeficency virus) has eluded researchers. Education on HIV testing, safe sex, and avoidance of contaminated blood is currently the best defense. Once the disease progresses to "full-blown" AIDS, the prognosis is death. Many controversies surround the disease and its victims, including

- methods of testing to prevent the spread of the disease,

- payment for AIDS sufferers treatment, and

- rights of confidentiality of individuals with AIDS vs. rights of those with whom they come in contact.

SAVINGS AND LOAN FAILURES

Deregulation and lax enforcement of banking rules during the Reagan Administration led to unwise and sometimes dishonest banking practices. Federal investigators implicated several U.S. Senators and many federal and state officials in banking fraud.

By the early 1990s, hundreds of savings and loan associations went bankrupt. The **FSLIC** (Federal Savings & Loan Insurance Corporation) collapsed under the strain of paying off S&L depositors and reorganizing troubled banks. To avoid a banking crisis such as that of the Great Depression years, Congress created the **RTC** (Resolution Trust Corporation).

Similar problems affected commercial and savings banks. The **FDIC** (Federal Deposit Insurance Corporation) absorbed the FSLIC and paid billions to insured depositors of failed banks. Banking officials closed some banks, while others merged with healthier institutions. The bill to taxpayers was over 500 billion dollars in adjustments before the RTC and FDIC completed work on the the problems in 1995.

HEALTH CARE PROBLEMS

Affordable health care became a major issue in the 1990s. About half of America's workers received some form of health insurance protection through their employers. Government sponsored Medicare and veterans' programs provided coverage to some others. Still, a significant number of individuals had no health insurance. As the 1990s progressed, more working families lost insurance protection. The increasing costs of hospitalization and prescription drugs forced insurance premiums to rise dramatically.

Experts debated over the best way to provide affordable health care to all Americans. Some preferred expansion of current programs to cover the uninsured. Others called for a complete overhaul of the insurance system. They believed government should provide universal health coverage. Insurance companies, medical associations, pharmaceutical companies, and consumer advocates took different sides of the issue. Providing affordable medical care while containing costs remains an elusive goal.

SOCIAL CONCERNS

The abortion debate continued with additional rulings by the Supreme Court. Another controversy before the Court involved decisions about the withdrawal of life support systems for the terminally ill, and the broader issue of the right to die.

In ***Planned Parenthood v. Casey**** (1992), the Supreme Court upheld its 1973 *Roe v. Wade* ruling that legalized abortion. However, it allowed certain restrictions by the states. Among these restrictions was the requirement for a 24-hour waiting period for the abortion, parental consent for minors, and certain record-keeping procedures.

In ***Cruzan v. Director, Missouri Dept. of Health*** (1990)*, the Supreme Court ruled on the case of Nancy Cruzan (an auto accident left her in a coma with severe brain injuries). The Court ruled that the patient had not clearly expressed her wish to remove life support ahead of time, and that the state had a legitimate concern in protecting life. However, the Court also said each state was free to develop its own policies, and in many instances, life support may be removed in terminal cases.

Also controversial in the 1990s was the issue of assisted suicide. A Michigan doctor, **Jack Kervorkian**, became nationally known for helping dozens of terminally ill patients to commit suicide. After numerous prosecutions and acquittals, Kervorkian was found guilty of murder in 1999 for his active participation in a suicide that was shown on television. In Oregon, however, voters and the legislature approved the *Death With Dignity Act*, which permits physician-assisted suicide in carefully defined circumstances.

FOREIGN ISSUES
THE PERSIAN GULF CONFLICT

In August 1990, Iraqi dictator Saddam Hussein vowed to annex Kuwait. Saddam's well-equipped army quickly overran the tiny, oil rich country. Exiled Kuwaitis and leaders of other Persian Gulf states appealed to the United States for help. With congressional approval, Bush sent 500,000 troops to the region in a campaign called **Operation Desert Shield**. He persuaded the U.N. Security Council to condemn Saddam's aggression and set up an economic blockade of Iraq.

FOREIGN POLICY

President Bush organized a **coalition** (alliance) of 23 nations to block any additional Iraqi aggression. He intensified diplomatic pressure to force Iraq to withdraw from Kuwait.

By early 1991, the international pressure weakened Iraq, but Saddam stubbornly refused to negotiate. In mid-January, coalition air forces began an intensive bombing campaign of Iraqi positions (**Operation Desert Storm**). Iraq launched Scud missile attacks on Saudi Arabia and Israel with little success. The delicate stability of the entire Middle East, with its vast strategic oil reserves, was in jeopardy.

After five weeks of the most intense bombing since World War II, Bush ordered ground forces led by General Norman Schworzkopf into action. American-led coalition forces invaded southern Iraq and Kuwait. In four days of fighting, the Iraqis suffered an estimated 100,000 casualties. Large segments of the Iraqi Army surrendered, and coalition troops liberated Kuwait. President Bush ordered a truce, but Saddam Hussein remained in power in Baghdad.

PROBLEMS IN PANAMA

Progress on the return of the Canal Zone proceeded well until early 1988, when Panamanian military leader **Manuel Noriega**, who had been indicted by U.S. officials for drug trafficking, overthrew the civilian government. Panama was wracked by general unrest, strikes, and demonstrations. The Reagan Administration levied economic trade sanctions, and Congress cut off aid. Noriega announced a state of war existed with the United States.

In December 1989, after U.S. military personnel were harassed, injured, and one shot by Noriega's forces, President Bush authorized an invasion. In the ensuing skirmishes, a number of Panamanian civilians and U.S. combatants were killed or wounded. Within days, Noriega's forces were dispersed, the dictator surrendered. He was remanded for trial in the United States, convicted on drug-related charges, and sentenced to a 40-year prison term.

INTERVENTION:
SOMALIA AND THE BALKANS

On the strategic "Horn of Africa," long-time Somalian dictator Mohammed Siad Barre's regime collapsed in 1991. A civil war broke out among the local warlords that produced 50, 000 casualties in less than a year. Banditry hampered U.N. relief efforts as drought, starvation, and disease threatened the population. Responding to pressure from the world press, the U.N. approved a Bush Administration plan for limited military action (**Operation Restore Hope**). American troops made up two-thirds of the 48,000 member international force. Coalition troops landed in the Somalian capital of Mogadishu in December 1992 and began pacification. By spring 1993, the Pentagon withdrew most of the U.S. contingent as planned. Local warlords renewed harassment of remaining U.N. troops. Compromises with the warlords led to a truce and U.N. withdrawal in 1995 without a solution.

A bloody civil war also erupted in the Balkans as the "original" Yugoslavia disintegrated. Timeless ethnic and religious conflicts fueled the breakup of the former communist nation. Serbian nationalists of the "new" Yugoslavia fought Croats and Muslims for power in the west central state of Bosnia. As the deaths, destruction, and dislocation of people mounted, the

SOUTHWEST ASIA & NORTH AFRICA

European Community, NATO, and the U.N. all sought to end the fighting. In June 1993, the United States reluctantly agreed to military participation in a peacekeeping mission. A 1995 truce led to elections the following year.

Yugoslav-Serbian repression and brutal "ethnic cleansing campaigns" against ethnic Albanians living in the southern Kosovo Province erupted into another civil war in 1997. The earlier scenario repeated itself, this time involving U.S. and NATO bombing campaigns, until another truce was negotiated in 1999.

THE IRON CURTAIN FALLS

During the 1980s, Mikhail Gorbachev's *glasnost* (political) and *perestroika* (economic) reform programs spread to the U.S.S.R's Eastern European satellites. Inside the Iron Curtain, Eastern European nations (Poland, Hungary, Czechoslovakia, Rumania, Bulgaria, and Albania) ousted communist leaders. Democratic governments and market reforms blossomed.

Berlin had been a physically divided city since Khrushchev had the Wall erected in 1961. In November of 1989, a vast movement for democratic reform swept through Eastern Europe. In East Germany, the reforms resulted in the ruling communist group's resignation. Gorbachev allowed the Wall to be torn down. In 1991, the two halves of Germany reunited into a single democratic nation.

COLLAPSE OF THE SOVIET UNION

Inside the U.S.S.R., Gorbachev's economic reforms floundered. He lost support among the ruling politburo and Soviet people. Several republics (Ukraine, Lithuania, Latvia, Georgia, and Armenia) demanded self-government.

In the summer of 1991, anti-reform Politburo members launched a coup against Gorbachev. While Gorbachev was a prisoner, resistance rallied around the Russian Federation President **Boris Yeltsin**. Yeltsin led public demonstrations defying the coup. Red Army commanders and troops refused to fire on their own people. The coup disintegrated. Gorbachev returned, resigned from the Communist Party, and agreed to share power with Yeltsin.

Boris Yeltsin

Gorbachev recognized the independence of Estonia, Latvia, and Lithuania in 1991. Ukraine, Belarus, and other republics prepared to leave the Soviet Union. Yeltsin took action on his own. He negotiated a loose military and economic alliance of republics called the **Commonwealth of Independent States (CIS)**. After this, Gorbachev resigned. The CIS became a loose alliance of former Soviet republics with little central control. Critics compared it to the weak United States government under the *Articles of Confederation* (1781-1789) because CIS members agreed on very few policies.

The U.N. gave Russia the Security Council seat that belonged to the U.S.S.R. Other republics applied for U.N. membership. Yeltsin continued Gorbachev's pattern of foreign policy. He shared some control of the nuclear arsenal with other CIS members. However, the former republics oversaw the bases on their soil. Problems about the military, foreign policy, currency, and trade relations remained difficult to resolve. In 1997, the CIS set up a mediation board to help settle border and water rights among former Soviet republics.

Throughout the 1990s, new governments in Ukraine, Belarus, Kazakhstan, and other republics were unstable. Civil struggles plagued the Transcaucasian and Central Asian regions. Economic chaos concerned leaders. Market systems usually work on trial and error. It takes time before consumers and producers achieve price equilibrium. In Russia, the government ended many price controls, but unstable currency and shortages of most products existed. Crime and black market activities increased. Some Russians demanded a return to the communist system. Some nations sent humanitarian aid. Yeltsin sought more. Private foreign investors lacked the confidence to risk long term investment in the region's development.

In 2000, Yeltsin stepped aside and Russians elected a new President, **Vladimir Putin**. He represented a new generation's more organized approach to economics and politics. In his inaugural speech, Putin pledged to continue what Gorbachev and Yeltsin had begun – transformation to a "modern democratic state."

DOWNSIZING THE ECONOMY

While the public supported President Bush's foreign policies, domestic problems plagued his administration. A serious economic recession hit the country during his second year in office. Overuse of credit by consumers and businesses in the Reagan years peaked. Purchasing and production began to decline. Fear gripped the banking and financial markets. Downsizing of bloated corporate conglomerates led to rising unemployment. The Federal Reserve loosened the money supply and interest rates dropped.

A sluggish recovery began, but was slowed by concern over astronomical federal budget deficits. The Bush Administration took some steps to lower unemployment and stimulate the economy, but they were mostly unsuccessful.

MINI•ASSESSMENT (9-3)

1   How did the banking crisis of the late 1980s and early 1990s avoid the widespread public panic experienced in the 1930s?
  1   By 1985, most people invested their savings in stocks.
  2   Foreign banks intervened to rescue the American banks.
  3   Federal deposit insurance protected most depositors.
  4   The federal government nationalized the banking system.

2   A major reason for the ending of the Cold War Era was that
  1   a recession forced the United States to cut military spending
  2   the United States and the Soviet Union were unable to destroy one another
  3   the Soviet Union was seriously weakened by internal conflict and economic difficulties
  4   Vietnam became a united country

3   One direct result of the Persian Gulf War was that the United States
  1   gained control of oil resources in the Middle East
  2   liberated Kuwait from Iraqi control
  3   brought about peaceful relations between Israel and its neighbors
  4   obtained overseas colonies in the Middle East

Constructed Response

The Soviet "Ship of State," the U.S.S.R. sinks into history, as the former S.S. Republics are set adrift into the "Sea of Uncertainty."

1   To what event in the early 1990s does this cartoon refer?

2   How did this event affect United States foreign policy?

THE CLINTON PRESIDENCY

In 1992, President Bush lost his bid for reelection to Arkansas Democratic Governor **William J. ("Bill") Clinton**. Clinton took only 43% of the popular vote, but garnered 370 electoral votes to Bush's 168. An independent candidate, businessman **H. Ross Perot** (TX) managed to siphon conservative popular votes from Bush, allowing Clinton to take the electoral vote in key states.

In the 1992 congressional elections, the Democrats edged the Republicans for control of both houses. (It was the first time in 12 years that one party controlled both the legislative and executive branches.) The economy remained sluggish with unemployment and welfare expenses rising. Sensing a "grass roots rebellion" against federal spending and debt, Congress rejected Clinton's programs, especially on national health insurance. With Republican help, Clinton did get approval of **NAFTA** (North American Free Trade Association), a 1994 economic alliance with Canada and Mexico that reduced tariffs and trade restrictions.

In the 1994 congressional elections, voters gave the Republicans their first majorities in both houses in 40 years. **Newt Gingrich** (GA) became Speaker of the House, and **Robert Dole** (KA) became Senate Majority Leader. Gingrich promoted a "Contract With America" reform program for balanced budgets, tax cuts, and welfare reform. Only some of these ideas became law, because the Republicans did not have the two-thirds majority to override Clinton's vetoes. The reform spirit did lead to deficit reduction, gun control, childhood disease immunization, family sick leave, and some tax reform.

CAMPAIGN FINANCE REFORM

The 1990s saw a large increase in the amount of money flowing into the parties. Part of this was due to the popularity of a specific type of special interest group: the **PAC** – Political Action Committee. (PACs are formed by a variety of organizations to influence the decisions made by government officials.) While individuals and businesses face strict limits on the amount that can be contributed to a candidate, PACs encounter far fewer restrictions. Another source of contributions was "soft money" – virtually unlimited amounts given to political parties (instead of directly to candidates) for general use. Courts have usually ruled that mandatory spending limits are unconstitutional, because such limitations restrict the free speech rights of candidates. In March 2002, President George W. Bush signed the ***Campaign Finance Reform Act***, urged on by Senator John McCain (R-AZ). This act attempted to limit the campaign contributions of wealthy individuals, corporations, and labor unions. It also tried to restrict the use of soft money contributions.

FOREIGN POLICY ISSUES

Clinton's foreign policy was uneven. He was slow to withdraw troops from Somalia, slow to take action in Bosnia, and delayed helping restore President Aristide's democratic regime in Haiti. Clinton was more effective convincing Congress to ratify the **GATT** (General Agreement on Trade and Tariffs). The GATT treaty created the 116 member **World Trade Organization** (WTO) to moderate trade disputes, environmental issues, labor standards, and questions arising from foreign investment.

Clinton was also successful in pressing Israelis and the Palestinians to restart peace negotiations, and in convincing the North Koreans to halt nuclear weapon development. In 1997 and 1998, Clinton called for firm action against Iraq's blocking of the U.N. weapons inspection program.

In 1994, Israel and the PLO (Palestine Liberation Organization) agreed on Palestinian self-rule in the Gaza Strip and sections of the West Bank, including Jericho. Israel hoped the compromise would quell Palestinian violence. Palestinians wanted this to be the first step to an independent Palestinian state. In June 2000, Israeli troops pulled out of southern Lebanon and the slow process of negotiation continued.

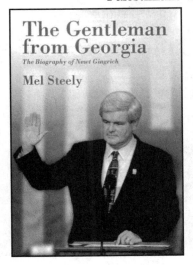

The Gentleman from Georgia
The Biography of Newt Gingrich
Mel Steely

PRESIDENTIAL CAMPAIGN 1996

Despite a spotty record of achievement and personal and party ethical problems, the strong economy helped Clinton receive 49% of the popular vote in his 1996 reelection bid. Republican Senator Dole received 159 electoral votes to Clinton's 379, but the Republicans held their majorities in the House and Senate.

ECONOMIC TRENDS AND PROBLEMS

By the end of 1997, American economic indicators were the best they had been in decades. Unemployment and inflation were down. Interest rates remained stable, and the stock market reached record highs. Gasoline cost less than it had nearly 20 years earlier. Because of the strong economy, federal, state, and local governments collected billions in added revenue, and budget surpluses were common. Yet, trade deficits remained, as the American people's appetite for imports greatly exceeded the value of American exports.

The "wonder-growth economies" of Asia (Japan, Singapore, Taiwan) faltered in 1997 and 1998. Clinton helped shore up the Asian economy in June of 1998 by jumping into the currency market and buying 2 billion dollars in Japan's yen.

The strong U.S. economy led many Americans to ignore Clinton's personal problems and campaign finance investigations. Then came convictions of former Clinton associates in Arkansas for illegal banking and real estate deals (the "Whitewater Scandal"). A sexual harassment suit against Clinton by Paula Jones, a former Arkansas state employee, was dismissed, but he agreed to pay her a monetary settlement. Later, the same judge fined Clinton for contempt of court for giving "misleading" testimony.

IMPEACHMENT AND ACQUITTAL

The most serious situation arose from the President's perjury before Special Prosecutor Kenneth Starr regarding an improper relationship with White House intern Monica Lewinski. In the summer of 1998, Clinton admitted he had lied about the liaison. The House of Representa-tives' Judiciary Committee drew up four articles of impeachment.

In December 1998, the full House voted for two articles, accusing the President of lying under oath and obstructing justice. Clinton became the second President in U.S. history to be impeached. (Andrew Johnson was the first in 1868.) In January 1999, the Senate began the trial to remove the President. With Chief Justice William Rehnquist presiding, several weeks of testimony ended with an unusual three day closed-door session. The Senate failed to muster the necessary two-thirds majority, and Clinton remained in office.

INTERVENTION IN YUGOSLAVIA

In the spring of 1999, a new crisis in the Balkans gave the embattled Clinton some respite from the constant focus on domestic scandals. In Yugoslavia, ethnic Albanians in the **Kosovo** Province intensified their resistance to the Serbian-led government's ethnic cleansing policies. The Albanians were met with brutal repression. Whole villages were evacuated, and many inhabitants slaughtered. Kosovar refugees streamed into Albania and Macedonia. Clinton authorized U.S. participation in an intensive NATO air campaign to drive Serbian troops out of Kosovo. The air strikes pounded Yugoslavia for more than two months. Finally, Serbian leaders agreed to withdraw in the summer of 1999.

ELECTIONS OF 2000

In 2000, Republican Governor **George W. Bush** (TX) challenged Vice President **Albert Gore** (TN). Voter apathy translated into the closest election since 1876.

Vice President Gore actually won the total popular vote, but he did not gain a majority of electors. However, it was unclear if Bush had an electoral majority either. It was unclear which candidate had won in Florida, and that state's 25 electoral votes would tip the balance. At first, Bush appeared to be the winner, but state authorities ordered recounts due to voting irregularities and flawed ballots. Some local courts ordered recounts that narrowed Bush's leads, but Florida state courts halted further recounts.

The Washington Post

Clinton Impeached

House Approves Articles Charging Perjury, Obstruction

Mrs. Clinton, the president, Vice President Al Gore and House Minority Leader Richard Gephardt after the House voted to impeach Clinton. On the South Lawn, the president told Democratic House members, "We must stop the politics of personal destruction."

The Washington Post

Clinton Acquitted

2 Impeachment Articles Fail to Win Senate Majority

The president on February 12, 1999, walks to the Rose Garden after the Senate acquitted him of the impeachment charges. "I want to say again to the American people how profoundly sorry I am for what I said and did to trigger these events," he said, adding, "I believe any person who asks forgiveness has to be prepared to give it."

After a month of confusion, the U.S. Supreme Court ruled on an appeal (***Bush v. Gore***) that the Florida state courts had acted questionably in reexamining only certain ballots and ordered all recounts stopped. Gore conceded. Florida officials certified Bush as the winner. According to later (10 May 2001) independent studies of the news media, Bush would have won a hand recount of all disputed ballots in Florida's presidential election by a margin of 1,183 votes.

In congressional races, the Republicans maintained their narrow advantage in the House, while they held the Senate by the barest majority. (Several months later, Vermont Republican Senator Jeffords left the Party to become an independent, and the Democrats took control of the Senate – they lost it again in the 2002 election.)

A SECOND BUSH IN THE WHITE HOUSE

George W. Bush became the second son of a President to serve (John Quincy Adams was the first in 1825). At his inauguration, Bush called on the nation to unite after the bitter election struggle and live out the nation's promise of justice and opportunity "through civility, courage, compassion, and character." In the first half of his term, President Bush exceeded expectations, achieving a controversial and historic tax cut and reorganizing the nation's strategic defenses. Bush won reelection in 2004 in a close, high spending contest against Democratic Senator John Kerry (MA) in which the Republicans solidified their hold on Congress.

MINI•ASSESSMENT (9-4)

1   The General Agreement on Tariffs and Trade (GATT) and the North American Free Trade Agreement (NAFTA) are both based on the belief that
   1   protective tariffs raise the standard of living
   2   the economies of member nations benefit from an unrestricted flow of goods and services
   3   foreign imports contribute to increased employment in the United States
   4   the United States must be self-reliant in producing strategic products

2   The main reason that the United States sent troops to Bosnia in 1995 was to try to
   1   bring a peaceful end to a civil war
   2   contain the spread of communism
   3   take over the area as a protectorate
   4   resettle refugees in North America

3   In situations where the President is suspected of wrongdoing, such as the Watergate scandal and the questions over the testimony of President Clinton, the official role of the House of Representatives is to
   1   determine the punishment if the President is convicted
   2   conduct the impeachment trial
   3   provide an attorney to defend the President
   4   investigate and bring charges against the President

Constructed Response

Document A

U.S. Trading Partners (ranked by value of exports, 1997; in billions of dollars)			
Nation	**Imported from U.S.**	**Exported to U.S.**	**Deficit for U.S.**
Canada	151	168	- 17
Mexico	71	85	- 14
Japan	65	121	- 56

Document B

> **PUNITIVE TARIFFS ARE APPROVED ON IMPORTS OF JAPANESE STEEL**
> WASHINGTON, June 11, 1999 (AP) –
> United States steel producers won an important ruling today when the International Trade Commission, a federal agency, approved punitive tariffs to combat low-priced Japanese shipments.
>
> Tariffs ranging from 18 percent to 67 percent will be ordered by the Clinton Administration within weeks. These tariffs will effectively make Japanese steel more expensive to sell in the United States, a move intended to offer domestic producers some relief.

1   For all three countries in Document A, what is true when comparing the value of exports with the value of imports?

2   How is the action referred to in Document B an attempt to solve, in part, the deficit numbers in Document A?

TERRORIST ATTACKS ON SEPT. 11

On September 11, 2001, nineteen extremists belonging to the terrorist group **Al Qaeda** (Arabic for "the base") hijacked four American commercial airliners. One plane went down in western Pennsylvania, and a second slammed into the Pentagon near Washington, D.C. The greatest damage occurred when the hijackers flew the other two planes directly into the twin towers of the World Trade Center in New York City. The mammoth buildings collapsed from the enormous fires resulting from the impact. Over 3,000 people died in these attacks. Over 2,000 of the deaths occurred at the World Trade Center and included 343 New York City firefighters, rescue workers, and law enforcement officials that rushed to the disaster scene to assist.

While all of the actual hijackers died, President Bush vowed to punish those who had ties to Al Qaeda, both at home and abroad. With worldwide cells, and funded and led by Saudi millionaire **Osama bin Laden**, Al Qaeda's main bases were in Afghanistan. It had previously been suspected of bombing U.S. embassies in Kenya and Tanzania and tragically attacking the *USS Cole* at anchor in Yemen.

The **Taliban**, a radical Islamic group ruling Afghanistan, provided vital support and protection for Al Qaeda training bases. Vowing to rid Afghanistan of these groups, President Bush ordered U.S. troops to the area and started aerial attacks and raids on the terrorist strongholds. Afghan opponents of the Taliban – loosely organized as the Northern Alliance – plus Canada, Great Britain, and other allies contributed troops and financial resources. The Taliban was driven from power, and new leadership was installed for Afghanistan. American troops captured hundreds of suspected Al Qaeda terrorists and camps. Afghans began a struggle to form a new government in the fragmented, war torn Asian nation.

While the Taliban was ousted and Al Qaeda was in disarray by 2002, the Sept. 11 attacks affected the U.S. in other ways. A wave of patriotism swept the country. The government increased security at airports, at public events, and at the borders. It tightened immigration controls. The attacks altered the economy. With the economy already in a mild recession, the attacks deepened unemployment. With people scared to fly, the airline industry lost billions and imposed staff layoffs. Tax revenues declined and the government dipped into budget surpluses for billion dollar military and security operations. State and local governments struggled in the face of declin-

President George W. Bush speaks to a Joint Session of Congress February 27, 2001.
Behind: Vice President Richard Cheney (left) and Speaker of the House J. Dennis Hastert (right)
WHITE HOUSE PHOTO BY PAUL MORSE

ing revenues and federal assistance. Stock prices fell too, but this was due largely to corporate financial manipulations and scandals not related to the attacks.

However, during the succeeding years President Bush pushed congress for tax cuts and his economic stimuli package helped the economy rebound. Unemployment dropped, the stock market made back its losses, new housing starts rose to a new record, and the public's confidence in the nation's economy and future increased.

THE SECOND WAR AGAINST SADDAM

At the UN, the Bush Administration charged Iraq with violations of post 1991 Gulf War UN resolutions that prohibited dictator Saddam Hussein's Baath Party power group from amassing nuclear, chemical, and biological weapons. After many delays and denials, the Saddam readmitted UN weapons inspectors, but circumvented and compromised their efforts. In early 2003, France, Germany, and Russia blocked a U.S.-sponsored resolution in the UN Security Council authorizing military action against Iraq. A determined President Bush and Britain's Prime Minister Blair formulated what eventually became a 68-nation international coalition remove the dictator's regime.

In March of 2003, coalition forces launched a coordinated sea-land-air attack on Saddam's weapons sites throughout the country. Saddam's totalitarian regime disintegrated in less than a month. Coalition forces had moved up the Tigris and Euphrates river valleys and captured Baghdad. In northern Iraq, joint operations between U.S. Special Forces and Kurd nationalists gradually secured most of the region. Iraqi military units put up uneven resistance, but massive surrenders led to the country's rapid military collapse. Coalition forces suffered only 229 deaths. There were 115 U.S. military deaths during the official combat phase.

Coalition investigations unveiled suspected sites of weapons of mass destruction, but no actual chemical and biological WMDs were unearthed in the immediate period after the combat phase ended. In May 2003, coalition reconstruction efforts began in earnest. Sporadic but intense attacks by insurgents and escalating terrorist bombings hindered the U.S.-led reconstruction efforts. This contributed to a higher loss of lives than in the official combat phase of the war. While Saddam and most of his staff were captured and bound over for trial, suspected caches of weapons of mass destruction were not found.

Occupation officials labored with new Iraqi leaders, such as interim prime minister **Iyad Allawi**, to establish full sovereignty through a stable, democratically elected government guaranteeing human rights. After months of obstinate disputes, the U.N. Security Council voted in June 2004 to support the interim government and authorized the continuance of American military reinforcement for Iraqi security forces. In the January 2005 election – the country's first free election in 50 years – Iraqis chose members of a new national assembly amidst minimal violence.

By June 2006, a new Iraqi government was established as a result of free national elections, but sectarian discord between the majority Shi'a and Sunni Muslim groups continued to compromise national unity. U.S., Coalition, and newly trained Iraqi forces continued efforts to provide safety and stability but met continued violence from opponents of a democratic state (Saddam loyalists, insurgents, and foreign religious and political zealots). Casualties increased and a few nations in the coalition began to withdraw forces in the face of growing criticism from opponents and terroristic atrocities at home.

SUMMARY

As the Cold War faded into history, the United States became the world's leading power. As part of the global community, numerous conflicts in foreign countries drew America's interest. As part of a global economy, interdependence broadened U.S. interests in the world marketplace. Prosperity grew, but not without problems. Poverty was reduced, but still affected more than 12% of the population. With people living longer, the aging required a greater share of the nation's resources. Moving into a new millennium precipitated unprecedented issues at home and abroad.

UNIT ASSESSMENT
MULTI CHOICE QUESTIONS

1 The "supply side" economics of Presidents Reagan and Bush favored
   1 raising tariffs to increase the number of imports
   2 increasing federal taxes to support social welfare programs
   3 providing incentives to stimulate business growth
   4 establishing government programs to provide jobs for the unemployed

2 A major difference between the presidencies of Lyndon Johnson and Ronald Reagan was that President Reagan
   1 had a good relationship with labor unions
   2 followed an isolationist foreign policy
   3 called for the states to assume a larger role in domestic programs
   4 supported the strengthening of civil rights legislation

3 In the United States in the 1990s, cuts in defense spending were proposed because
   1 Japan assumed the peacekeeping responsibilities of the United Nations
   2 military technology became less expensive
   3 the United States returned to an isolationist foreign policy
   4 communist governments in Eastern Europe and the former Soviet Union collapsed

4 In the United States, most new jobs created during the 1980s were jobs that
   1 were classified as managerial
   2 provided services rather than produced goods
   3 depended on heavy manufacturing
   4 were farm related

5 The fundamental problem facing U.S. farmers since the end of WW II has been
   1 the disappearance of fertile farmland
   2 overproduction of agricultural goods
   3 a steady rise in prices of agricultural products
   4 a shortage of modern farm equipment

Base your answer to question 6 on the headlines below and your knowledge of U.S. history and government.

> *"Johnson Decides Not to Run"*
> *"Nixon Resigns Presidency"*
> *"Bush Defeated by Clinton"*

6 Based on these headlines, which is a valid conclusion about the presidency since the 1960s?
   1 Incumbent Presidents are guaranteed success in the next election.
   2 Vice Presidents seldom become President.
   3 The people hold a President accountable for his performance.
   4 Presidential power has become nearly unlimited.

7 Which caused the recession during 1991-1992?
   1 long-term overuse of credit
   2 mergers of defense industry corporations
   3 the activities of political action committees
   4 failure to establish a national health insurance program

8 Since the end of the Cold War, the most persistent problem facing United States foreign policy has been
   1 using higher tariffs to protect United States' markets
   2 dealing with the conflicts in other nations and regions
   3 supporting command economies in Western Europe
   4 increasing the preparedness of the armed forces

9 Since the Russian people abandoned communism in the early 1990s, the United States has provided support to the new nation by
   1 creating a military alliance with Russia
   2 destroying most United States nuclear weapons
   3 giving foreign aid to Russia in the form of low-interest loans
   4 opposing the independence of the other Russian republics

10 One important conclusion that can be drawn as a result of the United States experience in the Spanish American War (1898), the Persian Gulf War (1991), and the NATO campaign in Kosovo (1999) is that
   1 only the President should decide issues of war and peace
   2 the media are a powerful influence in shaping U.S. public opinion toward war
   3 the public has little confidence in the ability of the American military
   4 international organizations play a decisive role in determining the outcome of a war

Base your answer to question 11 on the cartoon below and on your knowledge of U.S. history and government.

11 The cartoon's main point is that Fidel Castro
1 tried to spread communism to the United States
2 failed to influence U.S. foreign policy
3 allowed many Cuban refugees to come to the United States
4 frustrated many presidential administrations

12 Health care issues in the 1990s included concerns about
1 the establishment of national standards for licensing all doctors
2 the shortage of hospitals in urban areas
3 the lack of qualified applicants for medical school
4 the difficulty for many to find available and affordable health care

13 During the 1990s, which issue led to the greatest tension between the United States and Japan?
1 trade policies
2 immigration quotas
3 military preparedness
4 use of natural resources

Base your answer to question 14 on the table below and on your knowledge of U.S. history and government.

ELECTORAL VOTES CAST BY LARGE STATES IN 1984 AND 1996		
State	1984 Electoral Votes	1996 Electoral Votes
California	47	54
Florida	21	25
New York	36	33
Pennsylvania	25	23
Texas	29	32

14 Which trend is illustrated by the information provided in this table?
1 a decline in importance of the electoral college in presidential elections
2 the growing importance of special interest groups in presidential politics
3 a shift in population from the Northeast to the South and the West
4 the increasing cost of presidential election campaigns

15 In 1999, President Clinton was impeached by the House of Representatives, but not removed from office by the Senate. A similar action and result occurred during the presidency of
1 Thomas Jefferson   3 Richard Nixon
2 Andrew Johnson   4 Ronald Reagan

THEMATIC ESSAY

Directions:
Write a well-organized essay that includes an introduction, several paragraphs explaining your position, and a conclusion.

Theme:

Divisive Issues of American Society

A number of issues have divided American society into opposite sides in recent years, with each side presenting strong arguments to support their beliefs.

Task:

Using your knowledge of United States history and government, write an essay in which you select *three* [3] specific controversial issues that have divided American society since 1970. For *each* issue:

• identify the issue involved and the opposing sides,
• present the arguments put forth by opposing sides, and
• discuss attempts that have been made by individuals, groups, or government to resolve the issue or bring about a compromise.

Suggestions:
You may use any examples from your study of U.S. History and Government within the specified time period. Some suggestions you might wish to consider include: abortion, the death penalty, gun control, flag burning, prayer in public school, or immigration. **You are *not* limited to these suggestions.**

DOCUMENT BASED QUESTION

The following task is based on the accompanying documents. The documents may have been edited for the purposes of this exercise. The task is designed to test your ability to work with historical documents. As you analyze the documents, take into account both the source of the document and the author's point of view.

Directions:
Read the documents in Part A and answer the question after each document. Then read the directions for Part B and write your essay.

Historical Context:
Change has taken place since 1980 in both domestic and foreign affairs. These changes have often been accompanied by controversy. The documents below present information on these efforts.

Task:
Using information from the documents and your knowledge of United States history and government, write an essay in which you

* describe changes that have taken place in U.S. society since 1980,
* discuss the controversial issues involved in the changes, and
* evaluate the impact of the changes on American society.

Part A - Short Answer

Analyze the documents and answer the questions that follow each document.

Question for Document 1

Identify two areas that saw an increase.

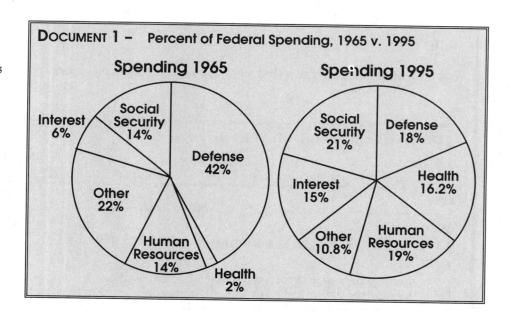

DOCUMENT 1 – Percent of Federal Spending, 1965 v. 1995

Spending 1965

Spending 1995

Questions for Document 2

1 What was President Reagan's goal in the approach shown in the cartoon?

2 What is the cartoonist's view of Reagan's policies?

DOCUMENT 2

RICH

MIDDLE CLASS

POOR

Question for Document 3

According to Clinton, what gives the United States a chance to improve peoples' lives?

DOCUMENT 3

"The world is no longer divided into two hostile camps. Instead, we are building bonds with nations that once were our adversaries. Growing connections of commerce and culture give us a chance to lift the fortunes and spirits of people the world over. And for the very first time in all of history, more people on the planet live under democracy than dictatorship."

– President Bill Clinton, *Second Inaugural Address*, 1997

Question for Document 4

What geographic pattern can be noted from looking at the gains and losses?

DOCUMENT 4

CHANGES IN THE ELECTORAL COLLEGE: 1980-1990
(Gain or loss of 2 or more electors)

States Gaining Electors	States Losing Electors
California . . . . +7	New York . . . . -3
Florida . . . . +4	Pennsylvania . . . . -2
Texas . . . . +3	Ohio . . . . -2
	Illinois . . . . -2
	Michigan . . . . -2

Question for Document 5

What overall change took place in U.S.-Chinese trade between 1980 and 1997?

DOCUMENT 5

U.S. TRADE WITH THE PEOPLE'S REPUBLIC OF CHINA
(in millions of dollars)

Year	Exports	Imports	Balance
1980	3,755	1,054	+2,701
1997	12,862	62,557	–49,695

Questions for Document 6

1　Identify the change shown by the information in this chart.

2　Why has this trend proved disturbing to some in the United States?

| DOCUMENT 6 |

DEATH PENALTY IN THE UNITED STATES
– Source: U.S. Dept. of Justice, 2000

Prisoners Executed	Inmates on Death Row Subsequently Acquitted or Charge Dropped
1980 0	
1985 18	
1990 23	1980 2
1995 56	1985 0
1999 98	1990 4
	1995 5
	1999 8

Part B - Essay

Historical Context:
Change has taken place since 1980 in both domestic and foreign affairs. These changes have often been accompanied by controversy.

Directions:
• Write a well organized essay that includes an introduction, several paragraphs, and a conclusion.
• Use evidence from the documents to support your response.
• Do not simply repeat the contents of the documents.
• Include specific related outside information.

Task:
Using information from the documents and your knowledge of United States history and government, write an essay in which you

• describe changes that have taken place in U.S. society since 1980,
• discuss the controversial issues involved in the changes, and
• evaluate the impact of the changes on American society.

Be sure to include specific historical details. You must also include additional information from your knowledge of United States history and government.

FORWARD

During the 3rd session of the 2nd Continental Congress, Richard Henry Lee of Virginia proposed, and John Adams of Massachusetts seconded, a resolution declaring the United Colonies free and independent states. Thomas Jefferson, John Adams, Roger Sherman, and Robert Livingstone were appointed a committee to draw up a declaration of independence to be presented to the British Crown. The declaration, composed almost entirely by Jefferson, was adopted unanimously on July 4, 1776.

IN CONGRESS, JULY 4, 1776

The unanimous Declaration of the thirteen united States of America.

When in the Course of human events, it becomes necessary for one people to dissolve the political bands which have connected them with another, and to assume among the Powers of the earth, the separate and equal station to which the Laws of Nature and of Nature's God entitle them, a decent respect to the opinions of mankind requires that they should declare the causes which impel them to the separation.

We hold these truths to be self-evident, that all men are created equal, that they are endowed by their Creator with certain unalienable Rights, that among these are Life, Liberty, and the pursuit of Happiness. That to secure these rights, Governments are instituted among Men, deriving their just powers from the consent of the governed, That whenever any Form of Government becomes destructive of these ends, it is the Right of the People to alter or to abolish it, and to institute new Government, laying its foundation on such principles and organizing its powers in such form, as to them shall seem most likely to effect their Safety and Happiness. Prudence, indeed, will dictate that Governments long established should not be changed for light and transient causes; and accordingly all experience hath shown, that mankind are more disposed to suffer, while evils are sufferable, than to right themselves by abolishing the forms to which they are accustomed. But when a long train of abuses and usurpations, pursuing invariably the same Object evinces a design to reduce them under absolute Despotism, it is their right, it is their duty, to throw off such Government, and to provide new Guards for their future security. Such has been the patient sufferance of these Colonies; and such is now the necessity which constrains them to alter their former Systems of Government. The history of the present King of Great Britain is a history of repeated injuries and usurpations, all having in direct object the establishment of an absolute Tyranny over these States. To prove this, let Facts be submitted to a candid world.

He has refused his Assent to Laws, the most wholesome and necessary for the public good.

He has forbidden his Governors to pass Laws of immediate and pressing importance, unless suspended in their operation till his Assent should be obtained; and when so suspended, he has utterly neglected to attend to them.

He has refused to pass other Laws for the accommodation of large districts of people, unless those people would relinquish the right of Representation in the Legislature, a right inestimable to them and formidable to tyrants only.

He has called together legislative bodies at places unusual, uncomfortable, and distant from the depository of their Public Records, for the sole purpose of fatiguing them into compliance with his measures.

He has dissolved Representative Houses repeatedly, for opposing with manly firmness his invasions on the rights of the people.

He has refused for a long time, after such dissolutions, to cause others to be elected; whereby the Legislative Powers, incapable of Annihilation, have returned to the People at large for their exercise; the State remaining in the mean time exposed to all the dangers of invasion from without, and convulsions within.

He has endeavoured to prevent the population of these States; for that purpose obstructing the Laws of Naturalization of Foreigners; refusing to pass others to encourage their migration hither, and raising the conditions of new Appropriations of Lands.

He has obstructed the Administration of Justice, by refusing his Assent to Laws for establishing Judiciary Powers.

He has made Judges dependent on his Will alone, for the tenure of their offices, and the amount and payment of their salaries.

He has erected a multitude of New Offices, and sent hither swarms of Officers to harass our People, and eat out their substance.

He has kept among us, in times of peace, Standing Armies without the Consent of our legislature.

He has affected to render the Military independent of and superior to the Civil Power.

He has combined with others to subject us to a jurisdiction foreign to our constitution, and unacknowledged by our laws; giving his Assent to their acts of pretended legislation:

For quartering large bodies of armed troops among us:

For protecting them, by a mock Trial, from Punishment for any Murders which they should commit on the Inhabitants of these States:

For cutting off our Trade with all parts of the world:

For imposing taxes on us without our Consent:

For depriving us in many cases, of the benefits of Trial by Jury:

For transporting us beyond Seas to be tried for pretended offenses:

For abolishing the free System of English Laws in a neighbouring Province, establishing therein an Arbitrary government, and enlarging its Boundaries so as to render it at once an example and fit instrument for introducing the same absolute rule into these Colonies:

For taking away our Charters, abolishing our most valuable Laws, and altering fundamentally the Forms of our Governments:

For suspending our own Legislature, and declaring themselves invested with Power to legislate for us in all cases whatsoever.

He has abdicated Government here, by declaring us out of his Protection and waging War against us.

He has plundered our seas, ravaged our Coasts, burnt our towns, and destroyed the lives of our people.

He is at this time transporting large armies of foreign mercenaries to compleat the works of death, desolation and tyranny, already begun with circumstances of Cruelty & perfidy scarcely paralleled in the most barbarous ages, and totally unworthy the Head of a civilized nation.

He has constrained our fellow Citizens taken Captive on the high Seas to bear Arms against their Country, to become the executioners of their friends and Brethren, or to fall themselves by their Hands.

He has excited domestic insurrections amongst us, and has endeavoured to bring on the inhabitants of our frontiers, the merciless Indian Savages, whose known rule of warfare, is an undistinguished destruction of all ages, sexes and conditions.

In every stage of these Oppressions We have Petitioned for Redress in the most humble terms: Our repeated Petitions have been answered only by repeated injury. A Prince, whose character is thus marked by every act which may define a Tyrant, is unfit to be the ruler of a free People.

Nor have We been wanting in attention to our British brethren. We have warned them from time to time of attempts by their legislature to extend an unwarrantable jurisdiction over us. We have reminded them of the circumstances of our emigration and settlement here. We have appealed to their native justice and magnanimity, and we have conjured them by the ties of our common kindred to disavow these usurpations, which, would inevitably interrupt our connections and correspondence. They too have been deaf to the voice of justice and of consanguinity. We must, therefore, acquiesce in the necessity, which denounces our Separation, and hold them, as we hold the rest of mankind, Enemies in War, in Peace Friends.

We, therefore, the Representatives of the United States of America, in General Congress, Assembled, appealing to the Supreme Judge of the world for the rectitude of our intentions, do, in the Name, and by Authority of the good People of these Colonies, solemnly publish and declare, That these United Colonies are, and of Right ought to be Free and Independent States; that they are Absolved from all Allegiance to the British Crown, and that all political connection between them and the State of Great Britain, is and ought to be totally dissolved; and that as Free and Independent States, they have full Power to levy War, conclude Peace, contract Alliances, establish Commerce, and to do all other Acts and Things which Independent States may of right do. And for the support of this Declaration, with a firm reliance on the Protection of Divine Providence, we mutually pledge to each other our Lives, our Fortunes and our sacred Honor.

THE DECLARATION OF INDEPENDENCE
4 JULY 1776

...WE MUTUALLY PLEDGE TO EACH OTHER OUR LIVES, OUR FORTUNES AND OUR SACRED HONOR.

And for the support of this Declaration, with a firm reliance on the protection of Divine Providence, we mutually pledge to each other our Lives, our Fortunes and our sacred Honor.

[signatures]

John Hancock

New Hampshire
Josiah Bartlett
Matthew Thornton
William Whipple

Massachusetts Bay
Samuel Adams
Elbridge Gerry
John Adams
Robert Treat Paine

Rhode Island
Stephen Hopkins
William Ellery

Connecticut
Roger Sherman
William Williams
Samuel Huntington
Oliver Wolcott

New York
William Floyd
Francis Lewis
Philip Livingston
Lewis Morris

New Jersey
Richard Stockton
John Hart
John Witherspoon
Abraham Clark
Francis Hopkinson

Pennsylvania
Robert Morris
James Smith
Benjamin Rush
George Taylor
Benjamin Franklin
James Wilson
John Morton
George Ross
George Clymer

Delaware
Caesar Rodney
Thomas McKean
George Read

Maryland
Samuel Chase
Thomas Stone
William. Paca
Charles Carroll of Carrollton

Virginia
George Wythe
Thomas Nelson, Jr.
Richard Henry Lee
Francis Lightfoot Lee
Thomas Jefferson
Carter Braxton
Benjamin Harrison

North Carolina
William Hooper
John Penn
Joseph Hewes

South Carolina
Edward Rutledge
Arthur Middleton
Thomas Heyward, Jr.
Thomas Lynch, Jr.

Georgia
Button Gwinnett
George Walton
Lyman Hall

Preamble

We the People of the United States, in Order to form a more perfect Union, establish Justice, insure domestic Tranquility, provide for the common defense, promote the general Welfare, and secure the Blessings of Liberty to ourselves and our Posterity, do ordain and establish this Constitution for the United States of America.

ARTICLE I

Establishes Congress as a bicameral legislative branch (House of Rep. & Senate); how members are chosen and terms; lists 17 specific powers plus the "elastic clause;" presidential veto and override; actions prohibited

Section 1. All legislative Powers herein granted shall be vested in a Congress of the United States, which shall consist of a Senate and House of Representatives.

Section 2. 1. The House of Representatives shall be composed of Members chosen every second Year by the People of the several States, and the Electors in each State shall have the Qualifications requisite for Electors of the most numerous Branch of the State Legislature.

2. No Person shall be a Representative who shall not have attained to the age of twenty five Years, and been seven Years a Citizen of the United States, and who shall not, when elected, be an Inhabitant of that State in which he shall be chosen.

3. Representatives and direct Taxes shall be apportioned among the several States which may be included within this Union, according to their respective Numbers, which shall be determined by adding to the whole Number of free Persons, including those bound to Service for a Term of Years, and excluding Indians not taxed, three-fifths of all other Persons. The actual Enumeration shall be made within three Years after the first Meeting of the Congress of the United States, and within every subsequent Term of ten Years, in such Manner as they shall by Law direct. The Number of Representatives shall not exceed one for every thirty Thousand, but each State shall have at Least one Representative; and until such enumeration shall be made, the State of New Hampshire shall be entitled to choose three, Massachusetts eight, Rhode-Island and Providence Plantations one,

---

SUMMARY VERSION:

THE UNITED STATES CONSTITUTION

PREAMBLE

We the people of the United States, in order to form a more perfect union, establish justice, insure domestic tranquility, provide for the common defense, promote the general welfare, and secure the blessings of liberty for ourselves and our posterity, do ordain and establish this Constitution of the United States of America.

ORIGINAL CONSTITUTION

Article I: Establishes Congress as a bicameral legislative branch (House of Rep. & Senate); how members are chosen and terms; lists 17 specific powers plus the "elastic clause;" presidential veto and override; actions prohibited

Article II: Establishes executive branch with President and Vice-President; duties of office; how elected; appointment power; checks on power, including impeachment procedure

Article III: Establishes judicial branch, with Supreme Court and its jurisdiction; how Congress sets up lower Federal courts; defines treason

Article IV: Declares equality among the states, extradition, admission of new states, Congress' authority over territories; requires republican form of government in all states

Article V: Establishes procedure for amending the Constitution

Article VI: Declares Constitution the Supreme law of the land

Article VII: Establishes procedure for the 13 states to ratify the new Constitution

CONSTITUTIONAL AMENDMENTS

Bill of Rights (1791)

1st Amendment - freedom of speech, press, assembly, free exercise of religion

2nd Amendment - right to bear arms

3rd Amendment - forbids government from quartering of troops in peacetime

4th Amendment - protects against unwarranted search

5th Amendment - protects rights of accused to due process; eminent domain

6th Amendment - protects rights to fair trial & counsel

7th Amendment - right of jury trial in civil cases

8th Amendment - protects against cruel punishment & excessive bail

9th Amendment - rights not specifically mentioned still exist

10th Amendment - powers not specified in Constitution left to states and people

---

Connecticut five, New-York six, New Jersey four, Pennsylvania eight, Delaware one, Maryland six, Virginia ten, North Carolina five, South Carolina five, and Georgia three.

4. When vacancies happen in the Representation from any State, the Executive Authority thereof shall issue Writs of Election to fill such Vacancies.

5. The House of Representatives shall choose their Speaker and other Officers; and shall have the sole Power of Impeachment.

Section 3. 1. The Senate of the United States shall be composed of two Senators from each State, *chosen by the Legislature* thereof, for six Years; and each Senator shall have one Vote. (changed by 17th Amendment)

2. Immediately after they shall be assembled in Consequence of the first Election, they shall be divided as equally as may be into three Classes. The Seats of the Senators of the first Class shall be vacated at the Expiration of the second Year, of the second Class at the Expiration of the fourth Year, and the third Class at the Expiration of the sixth Year, so that one third may be chosen every second Year; and if Vacancies happen by Resignation, or otherwise, during the Recess of the Legislature of any State, the Executive thereof may make temporary Appointments until the next Meeting of the Legislature, which shall then fill such Vacancies. (Changed by 17th Amendment)

3. No Person shall be a Senator who shall not have attained to the Age of thirty Years, and been nine Years a Citizen of the United States and who shall not, when elected, be an Inhabitant of that State for which he shall be chosen.

4. The Vice President of the United States shall be President of the Senate, but shall have no Vote, unless they be equally divided.

5. The Senate shall choose their other Officers, and also a President pro tempore, in the Absence of the Vice President, or when he shall exercise the Office of President of the United States.

6. The Senate shall have the sole Power to try all Impeachments. When sitting for that Purpose, they shall be on Oath of Affirmation. When the President of the United States is tried, the Chief Justice shall preside: And no Person shall be convicted without the Concurrence of two thirds of the Members present.

7. Judgment in Cases of Impeachment shall not extend further than to removal from Office, and disqualification to hold and enjoy any Office of Honor, Trust or Profit under the United States: but the Party convicted shall nevertheless be liable and subject to Indictment, Trial, Judgment and Punishment, according to Law.

Section 4. 1. The Times, Places and Manner of holding Elections for Senators and Representatives, shall be prescribed in each State by the Legislature thereof; but the Congress may at any time by Law make or alter such Regulations, except as to the Places of choosing Senators.

2. The Congress shall assemble at least once in every Year, and such Meeting shall be on the first Monday in December, unless they shall by Law appoint a different Day.

Section 5. 1. Each House shall be the Judge of the Elections, Returns and Qualifications of its own Members, and a Majority of each shall constitute a Quorum to do Business; but a smaller Number may adjourn from day to day, and may be authorized to compel the Attendance of absent Members, in such Manner, and under such Penalties as each House may provide.

2. Each House may determine the Rules of its Proceedings, punish its Members for disorderly Behavior, and, with the Concurrence of two thirds, expel a Member.

3. Each House shall keep a Journal of its Proceedings, and from time to time publish the same, excepting such Parts as may in their Judgment require Secrecy; and the Yeas and Nays of the Members of either House on any question shall, at the Desire of one fifth of those Present, be entered on the Journal.

4. Neither House, during the Session of Congress, shall, without the Consent of the other, adjourn for more than three days, nor to any other Place than that in which the two Houses shall be sitting.

Section 6. 1. The Senators and Representatives shall receive a Compensation for their Services, to be ascer-

---

SUBSEQUENT AMENDMENTS – SUMMARY VERSION

11th Amendment (1795) - suits by citizens of one state against a particular state must be heard in the latter's courts not in Federal ones

12th Amendment (1804) - electors must use separate ballots for President and Vice President

13th Amendment (1865) - abolishes slavery

14th Amendment (1868) - defines citizenship, application of due process, and equal protection

15th Amendment (1870) - defines citizens' right to vote

16th Amendment (1913) - allows Federal income tax

17th Amendment (1913) - direct popular election of United States Senators

18th Amendment (1919) - manufacture, sale, importation, & transportation of alcoholic beverages forbidden in U.S. (repealed by 21st Amend.)

19th Amendment (1920) - right of women to vote

20th Amendment (1933) - redefines term of President & sessions of Congress

21st Amendment (1933) - repeal of prohibition amendment(18th)

22nd Amendment (1951) - limits Presidential terms

23rd Amendment (1961) - provides presidential electors for District of Columbia

24th Amendment (1964) - abolishes poll taxes: Fed. elections

25th Amendment (1967) - defines succession to presidency & disability of president

26th Amendment (1971) - eighteen year-old citizens may vote in Federal elections

27th Amendment (1992) - sitting Congress may not raise own salary

---

tained by Law, and paid out of the Treasury of the United States. They shall in all Cases, except Treason, Felony and Breach of the Peace, be privileged from Arrest during their Attendance at the Session of their respective Houses, and in going to and returning from the same; and for any Speech or Debate in either House, they shall not be questioned in any other Place.

2. No Senator or Representative shall, during the Time for which he was elected, be appointed to any civil Office under the Authority of the United States, which shall have been created, or the Emoluments [payment for an office or employment; compensation] whereof shall have been increased during such time: and no Person holding any Office under the United States, shall be a Member of either House during his Continuance in Office.

Section 7. 1. All Bills for raising Revenue shall originate in the House of Representatives; but the Senate may propose or concur with Amendments as on other Bills.

2. Every Bill which shall have passed the House of Representatives and the Senate, shall, before it become a Law, be presented to the President of the United States; if he approve he shall sign it, but if not he shall return it, with his Objections to that House in which it shall have originated, who shall enter the Objections at large on their Journal, and proceed to reconsider it. If after such Reconsideration two thirds of that House shall agree to pass the Bill, it shall be sent, together with the Objections, to the other House, by which it shall likewise be reconsidered, and if approved by two thirds of that House, it shall become a Law. But in all such Cases the Votes of both Houses shall be determined by Yeas and Nays, and the Names of the Persons voting for and against the Bill shall be entered on the Journal of each House respectively. If any Bill shall not be returned by the President within ten Days (Sundays excepted) after it shall have been presented to him, the Same shall be a Law, in like Manner as if he had signed it, unless the Congress by their Adjournment prevent its Return, in which Case it shall not be a Law.

3. Every Order, Resolution, or Vote to which the Concurrence of the Senate and House of Representatives may be necessary (except on a question of Adjournment) shall be presented to the President of the United States; and before the Same shall take Effect, shall be approved by him, or being disapproved by him, shall be repassed by two thirds of the Senate and House of Representatives, according to the Rules and Limitations prescribed in the Case of a Bill.

Section 8. The Congress shall have Power

1. To lay and collect Taxes, Duties, Imposts [taxes or duties] and Excises, to pay the Debts and provide for the common Defense and general Welfare of the United States; but all Duties, Imposts and Excises shall be uniform throughout the United States;

2. To borrow Money on the credit of the United States;

3. To regulate Commerce with foreign Nations, and among the several States, and with the Indian Tribes;

4. To establish an uniform Rule of Naturalization, and uniform Laws on the subject of Bankruptcies throughout the United States;

5. To coin Money, regulate the Value thereof, and of foreign Coin, and fix the Standard of Weights and Measures;

6. To provide for the Punishment of counterfeiting the Securities and current Coin of the United States;

7. To establish Post Offices and post Roads;

8. To promote the Progress of Science and useful Arts, by securing for limited Times to Authors and Inventors the exclusive Right to their respective Writings and Discoveries;

9. To constitute Tribunals inferior to the Supreme Court;

10. To define and punish Piracies and Felonies committed on the high Seas, and Offenses against the Law of Nations;

11. To declare War, grant Letters of Marque and Reprisal, and make Rules concerning Captures on Land and Water;

12. To raise and support Armies, but no Appropriation of Money to that Use shall be for a longer Term than two Years;

13. To provide and maintain a Navy;

14. To make Rules for the Government and Regulation of the land and naval Forces;

15. To provide for calling forth the Militia to execute the Laws of the Union, suppress Insurrections and repel Invasions;

16. To provide for organizing, arming, and disciplining, the Militia, and for governing such Part of them as may be employed in the Service of the United States, reserving to the States respectively, the Appointment of the Officers, and the Authority of training the Militia according to the discipline prescribed by Congress;

17. To exercise exclusive Legislation in all Cases whatsoever, over such District (not exceeding ten Miles square) as may, by Cession of particular States, and the Acceptance of Congress, become the Seat of the Government of the United States, and to exercise like Authority over all Places purchased by the Consent of the Legislature of the State in which the Same shall be, for the Erection of Forts, Magazines, Arsenals, dock-Yards, and other needful Buildings;—And

18. To make all Laws which shall be necessary and proper for carrying into Execution the foregoing Powers, and all other Powers vested by this Constitution in the Government of the United States, or in any Department or Officer thereof.

Section 9. 1. The Migration or Importation of such Persons as any of the States now existing shall think proper to admit, shall not be prohibited by the Congress prior to the Year one thousand eight hundred and eight, but a Tax or duty may be imposed on such Importation, not exceeding ten dollars for each Person.

2. The Privilege of the Writ of Habeas Corpus shall not be suspended, unless when in Cases of Rebellion or Invasion the public Safety may require it.

3. No Bill of Attainder or ex post facto Law shall be passed.

4. No Capitation, or other direct, Tax shall be laid, unless in Proportion to the Census or Enumeration herein before directed to be taken.

5. No Tax or Duty shall be laid on Articles exported from any State.

6. No Preference shall be given by any Regulation of Commerce or Revenue to the Ports of one State over those of another: nor shall Vessels bound to, or from, one State, be obliged to enter, clear or pay Duties in another.

7. No Money shall be drawn from the Treasury, but in Consequence of Appropriations made by Law; and a regular Statement and Account of Receipts and Expenditures of all public Money shall be published from time to time.

8. No Title of Nobility shall be granted by the United States: And no Person holding any Office of Profit or Trust under them, shall, without the Consent of the Congress, accept of any present, Emolument, Office, or Title, of any kind whatever, from any King, Prince, or foreign State.

Section 10. 1. No State shall enter into any Treaty, Alliance, or Confederation; grant Letters of Marque and Reprisal; coin Money; emit Bills of Credit; make any Thing but gold and silver Coin a Tender in Payment of Debts; pass any Bill of Attainder, ex post facto Law, or Law impairing the Obligation of Contracts, or grant any Title of Nobility.

2. No State shall, without the Consent of the Congress, lay any Imposts or Duties on Imports or Exports, except what may be absolutely necessary for executing it's inspection Laws: and the net Produce of all Duties and Imposts, laid by any State on Imports or Exports, shall be for the Use of the Treasury of the United States; and all such Laws shall be subject to the Revision and Control of the Congress.

3. No State shall, without the Consent of Congress, lay any Duty of Tonnage, keep Troops, or Ships of War in time of Peace, enter into any Agreement or Compact with another State, or with a foreign Power, or engage in War, unless actually invaded, or in such imminent Danger as will not admit of delay.

Article II
Establishes executive branch with President and Vice-President; duties of office; how elected; appointment power; checks on power, including impeachment procedure

Section 1. 1. The executive Power shall be vested in a President of the United States of America. He shall hold his Office during the Term of four Years, and, together with the Vice President, chosen for the same Term, be elected, as follows:

2. Each State shall appoint, in such Manner as the Legislature thereof may direct, a Number of Electors, equal to the whole Number of Senators and Representatives to which the State may be entitled in the Congress: but no Senator or Representative, or Person holding an Office of Trust or Profit under the United States, shall be appointed an Elector.

The Electors shall meet in their respective States, and vote by Ballot for two Persons, of whom one at least shall not be an Inhabitant of the same State with themselves. And they shall make a List of all the Persons voted for, and of the Number of Votes for each; which List they shall sign and certify, and transmit sealed to the Seat of the Government of the United States, directed to the President of the Senate. The President of the Senate shall, in the Presence of the Senate and House of Representatives, open all the Certificates, and the Votes shall then be counted. The Person having the greatest Number of Votes shall be the President, if such Number be a Majority of the whole Number of Electors appointed; and if there be more than one who have such Majority, and have an equal Number of Votes, then the House of Representatives shall immediately choose by Ballot one of them for President; and if no Person have a Majority, then from the five highest on the List the said House shall in like Manner choose the President. But in choosing the President, the Votes shall be taken by States, the Representation from each State having one Vote; A quorum for this Purpose shall consist of a Member or Members from two thirds of the States, and a Majority of all the States shall be necessary to a Choice. In every Case, after the Choice of the President, the Person having the greatest Number of Votes of the Electors shall be the Vice President. But if there should remain two or more who have equal Votes, the Senate shall choose from them by Ballot the Vice President. (changed by 12th Amendment)

3. The Congress may determine the Time of choosing the Electors, and the Day on which they shall give their Votes; which Day shall be the same throughout the United States.

4. No Person except a natural born Citizen, or a Citizen of the United States, at the time of the Adoption of this Constitution, shall be eligible to the Office of President; neither shall any Person be eligible to that Office who shall not have attained to the Age of thirty five Years, and been fourteen Years a Resident within the United States.

5. In Case of the Removal of the President from Office, or of his Death, Resignation, or Inability to discharge the Powers and Duties of the said Office, the Same shall devolve on the Vice President, and the Congress may by Law provide for the Case of Removal, Death, Resignation or Inability, both of the President and Vice President, declaring what Officer shall then act as President, and such Officer shall act accordingly, until the Disability be removed, or a President shall be elected.

6. The President shall, at stated Times, receive for his Services, a Compensation, which shall neither be increased nor diminished during the Period for which he shall have been elected, and he shall not receive within that Period any other Emolument from the United States, or any of them.

7. Before he enter on the Execution of his Office, he shall take the following Oath or Affirmation:—"I do solemnly swear (or affirm) that I will faithfully execute the Office of President of the United States, and will to the best of my Ability, preserve, protect and defend the Constitution of the United States."

Section 2. 1. The President shall be Commander in Chief of the Army and Navy of the United States, and of the Militia of the several States, when called into the actual Service of the United States; he may require the Opinion, in writing, of the principal Officer in each of the executive Departments, upon any Subject relating to the Duties of their respective Offices, and he shall have Power to grant Reprieves and Pardons for Offenses against the United States, except in Cases of Impeachment.

2. He shall have Power, by and with the Advice and Consent of the Senate, to make Treaties, provided two thirds of the Senators present concur; and he shall nominate, and by and with the Advice and Consent of the Senate, shall appoint Ambassadors, other public Ministers and Consuls, Judges of the supreme Court, and all other Officers of the United States, whose Appointments are not herein otherwise provided for, and which shall be established by Law: but the Congress may by Law vest the Appointment of such inferior Officers, as they think proper, in the President alone, in the Courts of Law, or in the Heads of Departments.

3. The President shall have Power to fill up all Vacancies that may happen during the Recess of the Senate, by granting Commissions which shall expire at the End of their next Session.

Section 3. He shall from time to time give to the Congress Information of the State of the Union, and recommend to their Consideration such Measures as he shall judge necessary and expedient; he may, on extraordinary Occasions, convene both Houses, or either of them, and in Case of Disagreement between them, with Respect to the Time of Adjournment, he may adjourn them to such Time as he shall think proper; he shall receive Ambassadors and other public Ministers; he shall take Care that the Laws be faithfully executed, and shall Commission all the Officers of the United States.

Section 4. The President, Vice President and all civil Officers of the United States, shall be removed from Office on Impeachment for, and Conviction of, Treason, Bribery, or other high Crimes and Misdemeanors.

Article III
Establishes judicial branch, with Supreme Court and its jurisdiction; how Congress sets up lower Federal courts; defines treason

Section 1. The judicial Power of the United States, shall be vested in one supreme Court, and in such inferior Courts as the Congress may from time to time ordain and establish. The Judges, both of the supreme and inferior Courts, shall hold their Offices during good Behavior, and shall, at stated Times, receive for their Services, a Compensation, which shall not be diminished during their Continuance in Office.

Section 2. 1. The judicial Power shall extend to all Cases, in Law and Equity, arising under this Constitution, the Laws of the United States, and Treaties made, or which shall be made, under their Authority;—to all Cases affecting Ambassadors, other public Ministers and Consuls;—to all Cases of admiralty and maritime Jurisdiction;—to *Controversies to which the United States shall be a Party*;—to Controversies between two or more States;—between a State and Citizens of another State;—between Citizens of different States;—between Citizens of the same State claiming Lands under Grants of different States, and between a State, or the Citizens thereof, and foreign States, Citizens or Subjects. (changed by 11th Amendment)
2. In all Cases affecting Ambassadors, other public Ministers and Consuls, and those in which a State shall be Party, the supreme Court shall have original Jurisdiction. In all the other Cases before mentioned, the supreme Court shall have appellate Jurisdiction, both as to Law and Fact, with such Exceptions, and under such Regulations as the Congress shall make.
3. The Trial of all Crimes, except in Cases of Impeachment, shall be by Jury; and such Trial shall be held in the State where the said Crimes shall have been committed; but when not committed within any State, the Trial shall be at such Place or Places as the Congress may by Law have directed.

Section 3. 1. Treason against the United States, shall consist only in levying War against them, or in adhering to their Enemies, giving them Aid and Comfort. No Person shall be convicted of Treason unless on the Testimony of two Witnesses to the same overt Act, or on Confession in open Court.
2. The Congress shall have Power to declare the Punishment of Treason, but no Attainder of Treason shall work Corruption of Blood, or Forfeiture except during the Life of the Person attainted [disgraced].

Article IV
Declares equality among the states, extradition, admission of new states, Congress' authority over territories; requires republican form of government in all states

Section 1. Full Faith and Credit shall be given in each State to the public Acts, Records, and judicial Proceedings of every other State. And the Congress may by general Laws prescribe the Manner in which such Acts, Records, and Proceedings shall be proved, and the Effect thereof.

Section 2. 1. The Citizens of each State shall be entitled to all Privileges and Immunities of Citizens in the several States. (see 14th Amendment)
2. A Person charged in any State with Treason, Felony, or other Crime, who shall flee from Justice, and be found in another State, shall on Demand of the executive Authority of the State from which he fled, be delivered up, to be removed to the State having Jurisdiction of the Crime.
3. No Person held to Service or Labor in one State, under the Laws thereof, escaping into another, shall, in Consequence of any Law or Regulation therein, be discharged from such Service or Labor, but shall be delivered up on Claim of the Party to whom such Service or Labor may be due. (see 13th Amendment)

Section 3. 1. New States may be admitted by the Congress into this Union; but no new States shall be formed or erected within the Jurisdiction of any other State; nor any State be formed by the Junction of two or more States, or Parts of States, without the Consent of the Legislatures of the States concerned as well as of the Congress.
2. The Congress shall have Power to dispose of and make all needful Rules and Regulations respecting the Territory or other Property belonging to the United States; and nothing in this Constitution shall be so construed as to Prejudice any Claims of the United States, or of any particular State.

Section 4. The United States shall guarantee to every State in this Union a Republican Form of Government, and shall protect each of them against Invasion; and on Application of the Legislature, or of the Executive (when the Legislature cannot be convened) against domestic Violence.

Article V
Establishes procedure for amending the Constitution

The Congress, whenever two thirds of both Houses shall deem it necessary, shall propose Amendments to this Constitution, or, on the Application of the Legislatures of two thirds of the several States, shall call a Convention for proposing Amendments, which, in either Case, shall be valid to all Intents and Purposes, as Part of this Constitution, when ratified by the Legislatures of three-fourths of the several States, or by Conventions in three fourths thereof, as the one or the other Mode of Ratification may be proposed by the Congress; Provided that no Amendment which may be made prior to the Year One thousand eight hundred and eight shall in any Manner affect the first and fourth Clauses in the Ninth Section of the first Article; and that no State, without its

Consent, shall be deprived of its equal Suffrage in the Senate.

Article VI
Declares Constitution the Supreme law of the land

1. All Debts contracted and Engagements entered into, before the Adoption of this Constitution, shall be as valid against the United States under this Constitution, as under the Confederation. (see 14th Amendment)

2. This Constitution, and the Laws of the United States which shall be made in Pursuance thereof; and all Treaties made, or which shall be made, under the Authority of the United States, shall be the supreme Law of the Land; and the Judges in every State shall be bound thereby, any Thing in the Constitution or Laws of any State to the Contrary notwithstanding.

3. The Senators and Representatives before mentioned, and the Members of the several State Legislatures, and all executive and judicial Officers, both of the United States and of the several States, shall be bound by Oath or Affirmation, to support this Constitution; but no religious Test shall ever be required as a Qualification to any Office or public Trust under the United States.

Article VII
Establishes procedure for the 13 states to ratify the new Constitution

The Ratification of the Conventions of nine States, shall be sufficient for the Establishment of this Constitution between the States so ratifying the Same.

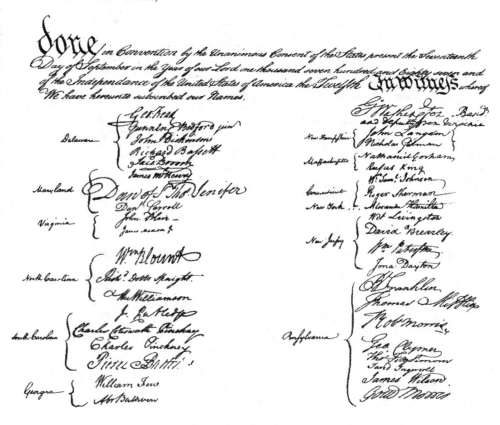

SIGNERS OF THE CONSTITUTION

resident of the Convention and deputy from Virginia
George Washington

Delaware
George Read
Gunning Bedford, Jr.
John Dickinson
Richard Bassett
Jacob Broom

Maryland
James McHenry
Daniel of St. Thomas Jenifer
Daniel Carroll

Virginia
John Blair
James Madison, Jr.

North Carolina
William Blount
Richard Dobbs Spaight
Hugh Williamson

South Carolina
John Rutledge
Charles Cotesworth Pinckney
Charles Pinckney
Pierce Butler

Georgia
William Few
Abraham Baldwin

New Hampshire
John Langdon
Nicholas Gilman

Massachusetts
Nathaniel Gorham
Rufus King

Connecticut
William Samuel Johnson
Roger Sherman

New York
Alexander Hamilton

New Jersey
William Livingston
David Brearly
William Paterson
Jonathan Dayton

Pennsylvania
Benjamin Franklin
Thomas Mifflin
Robert Morris
George Clymer
Thomas FitzSimons
Jared Ingersoll
James Wilson
Gouverneur Morris

AMENDMENTS TO THE CONSTITUTION

Amendments I-X (1791) collectively known as the

"BILL OF RIGHTS"

Amendment I

Congress shall make no law respecting an establishment of religion, or prohibiting the free exercise thereof; or abridging the freedom of speech, or of the press; or the right of the people peaceably to assemble, and to petition the Government for a redress of grievances.

Amendment II

A well regulated Militia, being necessary to the security of a free State, the right of the people to keep and bear Arms, shall not be infringed.

Amendment III

No Soldier shall, in time of peace be quartered in any house, without the consent of the Owner, nor in time of war, but in a manner to be prescribed by law.

Amendment IV

The right of the people to be secure in their persons, houses, papers, and effects, against unreasonable searches and seizures, shall not be violated, and no Warrants shall issue, but upon probable cause, supported by Oath or affirmation, and particularly describing the place to be searched, and the persons or things to be seized.

Amendment V

No person shall be held to answer for a capital, or otherwise infamous crime, unless on a presentment or indictment of a Grand Jury, except in cases arising in the land or naval forces, or in the Militia, when in actual service in time of War or public danger; nor shall any person be subject for the same offense to be twice put in jeopardy of life or limb; nor shall be compelled in any criminal case to be a witness against himself, nor be deprived of life, liberty, or property, without due process of law; nor shall private property be taken for public use, without just compensation.

Amendment VI

In all criminal prosecutions, the accused shall enjoy the right to a speedy and public trial, by an impartial jury of the State and district wherein the crime shall have been committed, which district shall have been previously ascertained by law, and to be informed of the nature and cause of the accusation; to be confronted with the witnesses against him; to have compulsory process for obtaining witnesses in his favor, and to have the Assistance of Counsel for his defense.

Amendment VII

In Suits at common law, where the value in controversy shall exceed twenty dollars, the right of trial by jury shall be preserved, and no fact tried by a jury, shall be otherwise re-examined in any Court of the United States, than according to the rules of the common law.

Amendment VIII

Excessive bail shall not be required, nor excessive fines imposed, nor cruel and unusual punishments inflicted.

Amendment IX

The enumeration in the Constitution, of certain rights, shall not be construed to deny or disparage others retained by the people.

Amendment X

The powers not delegated to the United States by the Constitution, nor prohibited by it to the States, are reserved to the States respectively, or to the people.

****

Amendment XI [1795]
Suits by citizens of one state against a particular state must be heard in the latter's courts not in federal ones.

The Judicial power of the United States shall not be construed to extend to any suit in law or equity, commenced or prosecuted against one of the United States by Citizens of another State, or by Citizens or Subjects of any Foreign State.

Amendment XII [1804]
Electors must use separate ballots for President and Vice-President.

The Electors shall meet in their respective states and vote by ballot for President and Vice-President, one of whom, at least, shall not be an inhabitant of the same state with themselves; they shall name in their ballots the person voted for as President, and in distinct ballots the person voted for as Vice-President, and they shall make distinct lists of all persons voted for as President, and of all persons voted for as Vice-President, and of the number of votes for each, which lists they shall sign and certify, and transmit sealed to the seat of the government of the United States, directed to the President of the Senate;—The President of the Senate shall, in the presence of the Senate and House of Representatives, open all the certificates and the votes shall then be counted;—the person having the greatest number of votes for President, shall be the President, if such number be a majority of the whole number of Electors appointed; and if no person have such majority, then from the persons having the highest numbers not exceeding three on the list of those voted for as President, the House of Representatives shall choose immediately, by ballot, the President. But in choosing the President, the votes shall be taken by states, the representation from each state having one vote; a quorum for this purpose shall consist of a member or members from two-thirds of the states, and a majority of all the states shall be necessary to a choice. And if the House of Representatives shall not choose a President whenever the right of choice shall devolve upon them, before the fourth day of March next following, then the Vice-President shall act as President, as in the case of the death or other constitutional disability of the President. The person having the greatest number of votes as Vice-President, shall be the Vice-President, if such number be a majority of the whole number of Electors appointed, and if no person have a majority, then from the two highest numbers on the list, the Senate shall choose the Vice-President; a quorum for the purpose shall consist of two-thirds of the whole number of Senators, and a majority of the whole number shall be necessary to a choice. But no person constitutionally ineligible to the office of President shall be eligible to that of Vice-President of the United States.

Amendment XIII [1865]
Abolishes slavery.

Section 1. Neither slavery nor involuntary servitude, except as a punishment for crime whereof the party shall have been duly convicted, shall exist within the United States, or any place subject to their jurisdiction.

Section 2. Congress shall have power to enforce this article by appropriate legislation.

Amendment XIV [1868]
Defines citizenship, application of due process, and equal protection.

Section 1. All persons born or naturalized in the United States, and subject to the jurisdiction thereof, are citizens of the United States and of the State wherein they reside. No State shall make or enforce any law which shall abridge the privileges or immunities of citizens of the United States; nor shall any State deprive any person of life, liberty, or property, without due process of law; nor deny to any person within its jurisdiction the equal protection of the laws.

Section 2. Representatives shall be apportioned among the several States according to their respective numbers, counting the whole number of persons in each State, excluding Indians not taxed. But when the right to vote at any election for the choice of electors for President and Vice President of the United States, Representatives in Congress, the Executive and Judicial officers of a State, or the members of the Legislature thereof, is denied to any of the male inhabitants of such State, being twenty-one years of age, and citizens of the United States, or in any way abridged, except for participation in rebellion, or other crime, the basis of representation therein shall be reduced in the proportion which the number of such male citizens shall bear to the whole number of male citizens twenty-one years of age in such State.

Section 3. No person shall be a Senator or Representative in Congress, or elector of President and Vice President, or hold any office, civil or military, under the United States, or under any State, who, having previously taken an oath, as a member of Congress, or as an officer of the United States, or as a member of any State legislature, or as an executive or judicial officer of any State, to support the Constitution of the United States, shall have engaged

in insurrection or rebellion against the same, or given aid or comfort to the enemies thereof. But Congress may by a vote of two-thirds of each House, remove such disability.

Section 4. The validity of the public debt of the United States, authorized by law, including debts incurred for payment of pensions and bounties for services in suppressing insurrection or rebellion, shall not be questioned. But neither the United States nor any State shall assume or pay any debt or obligation incurred in aid of insurrection or rebellion against the United States, or any claim for the loss or emancipation of any slave; but all such debts, obligations and claims shall be held illegal and void.

Section 5. The Congress shall have power to enforce, by appropriate legislation, the provisions of this article.

Amendment XV [1870]
Defines citizens' right to vote.

Section 1. The right of citizens of the United States to vote shall not be denied or abridged by the United States or by any State on account of race, color, or previous condition of servitude.

Section 2. The Congress shall have power to enforce this article by appropriate legislation.

Amendment XVI [1913]
Allows federal income tax.

The Congress shall have power to lay and collect taxes on incomes, from whatever source derived, without apportionment among the several States, and without regard to any census of enumeration.

Amendment XVII [1913]
Allows direct popular election of United States Senators.

The Senate of the United States shall be composed of two Senators from each State, elected by the people thereof, for six years; and each Senator shall have one vote. The electors in each State shall have the qualifications requisite for electors of the most numerous branch of the State legislatures.

When vacancies happen in the representation of any State in the Senate, the executive authority of such State shall issue writs of election to fill such vacancies: Provided, That the legislature of any State may empower the executive thereof to make temporary appointments until the people fill the vacancies by election as the legislature may direct.

This amendment shall not be so construed as to affect the election or term of any Senator chosen before it becomes valid as part of the Constitution.

Amendment XVIII [1919]
Prohibited manufacture, sale, importation, & transportation of alcoholic beverages in U.S.
(repealed by 21st Amendment)

Section 1. After one year from the ratification of

this article the manufacture, sale, or transportation of intoxicating liquors within, the importation thereof into, or the exportation thereof from the United States and all territory subject to the jurisdiction thereof for beverage purposes is hereby prohibited.

Section 2. The Congress and the several States shall have concurrent power to enforce this article by appropriate legislation.

Section 3. This article shall be inoperative unless it shall have been ratified as an amendment to the Constitution by the legislatures of the several States, as provided in the Constitution, within seven years from the date of the submission hereof to the States by the Congress.

Amendment XIX [1920]
Declares right of women to vote.

The right of citizens of the United States to vote shall not be denied or abridged by the United States or by any State on account of sex.

Congress shall have power to enforce this article by appropriate legislation.

Amendment XX [1933]
Redefines term of President & sessions of Congress.

Section 1. The terms of the President and Vice President shall end at noon on the 20th day of January, and the terms of Senators and Representatives at noon on the 3d day of January, of the years in which such terms would have ended if this article had not been ratified; and the terms of their successors shall then begin.

Section 2. The Congress shall assemble at least once in every year, and such meeting shall begin at noon on the 3d day of January, unless they shall by law appoint a different day.

Section 3. If, at the time fixed for the beginning of the term of the President, the President elect shall have died, the Vice President elect shall become President. If a President shall not have been chosen before the time fixed for the beginning of his term, or if the President elect shall have failed to qualify, then the Vice President elect shall act as President until a President shall have qualified; and the Congress may by law provide for the case wherein neither a President elect nor a Vice President elect shall have qualified, declaring who shall then act as President, or the manner in which one who is to act shall be selected, and such person shall act accordingly until a President or Vice President shall have qualified.

Section 4. The Congress may by law provide for the case of the death of any of the persons from whom the House of Representatives may choose a President whenever the right of choice shall have devolved upon them, and for the case of the death of any of the persons from whom the Senate may choose a Vice President whenever the right of choice shall have devolved upon them.

Section 5. Sections 1 and 2 shall take effect on the 15th day of October following the ratification of this article.

Section 6. This article shall be inoperative unless it shall have been ratified as an amendment to the Constitution by the legislatures of three-fourths of the several States within seven years from the date of its submission.

Amendment XXI [1933]
Repealed 18th Amendment (prohibition).

Section 1. The eighteenth article of amendment to the Constitution of the United States is hereby repealed.

Section 2. The transportation or importation into any State, Territory, or possession of the United States for delivery or use therein of intoxicating liquors, in violation of the laws thereof, is hereby prohibited.

Section 3. This article shall be inoperative unless it shall have been ratified as an amendment to the Constitution by conventions in the several States, as provided in the Constitution, within seven years from the date of the submission hereof to the States by the Congress.

Amendment XXII [1951]
Limits Presidential terms.

Section 1. No person shall be elected to the office of the President more than twice, and no person who has held the office of President, or acted as President, for more than two years of a term to which some other person was elected President shall be elected to the office of the President more than once. But this Article shall not apply to any person holding the office of President when this Article was proposed by the Congress, and shall not prevent any person who may be holding the office of President, or acting as President, during the term within which this Article becomes operative from holding the office of President or acting as President during the remainder of such term.

Section 2. This article shall be inoperative unless it shall have been ratified as an amendment to the Constitution by the legislatures of three-fourths of the several States within seven years from the date of its submission to the States by the Congress.

Amendment XXIII [1961]
Provides presidential electors for District of Columbia.

Section 1. The District constituting the seat of Government of the United States shall appoint in such manner as the Congress may direct:

A number of electors of President and Vice President equal to the whole number of Senators and Representatives in Congress to which the District would be entitled if it were a State, but in no event more than the least populous State; they shall be in addition to those appointed by the States, but they shall be considered, for the purposes of the election of President and Vice President, to be electors appointed by a State; and they shall meet in the District and perform such duties as provided by the twelfth article of amendment.

Section 2. The Congress shall have power to enforce this article by appropriate legislation.

Amendment XXIV [1964]
Abolishes poll taxes in federal elections.

Section 1. The right of citizens of the United States to vote in any primary or other election for President or Vice President, for electors for President or Vice President, or for Senator or Representative in Congress, shall not be denied or abridged by the United States or any State by reason of failure to pay any poll tax or other tax.

Section 2. The Congress shall have power to enforce this article by appropriate legislation.

Amendment XXV [1967]
Defines succession to presidency & disability of President.

Section 1. In case of the removal of the President from office or of his death or resignation, the Vice President shall become President.

Section 2. Whenever there is a vacancy in the office of the Vice President, the President shall nominate a Vice President who shall take office upon confirmation by a majority vote of both Houses of Congress.

Section 3. Whenever the President transmits to the President pro tempore of the Senate and the Speaker of the House of Representatives his written declaration that he is unable to discharge the powers and duties of his office, and until he transmits to them a written declaration to the contrary, such powers and duties shall be discharged by the Vice President as Acting President.

Section 4. Whenever the Vice President and a majority of either the principal officers of the executive departments or of such other body as Congress may by law provide, transmit to the President pro tempore of the Senate and the Speaker of the House

of Representatives their written declaration that the President is unable to discharge the powers and duties of his office, the Vice President shall immediately assume the powers and duties of the office as Acting President.

Thereafter, when the President transmits to the President pro tempore of the Senate and the Speaker of the House of Representatives his written declaration that no inability exists, he shall resume the powers and duties of his office unless the Vice President and a majority of either the principal officers of the executive department or of such other body as Congress may by law provide, transmit within four days to the President pro tempore of the Senate and the Speaker of the House of Representatives their written declaration that the President is unable to discharge the powers and duties of his office. Thereupon Congress shall decide the issue, assembling within forty-eight hours for that purpose if not in session. If the Congress, within twenty-one days after receipt of the latter written declaration, or, if Congress is not in session, within twenty-one days after Congress is required to assemble, determines by two-thirds vote of both Houses that the President is unable to discharge the powers and duties of his office, the Vice President shall continue to discharge the same as Acting President; otherwise, the President shall resume the powers and duties of his office.

Amendment XXVI [1971]
Sets eligibility of eighteen year-old citizens to vote in federal elections.

Section 1. The right of citizens of the United States, who are 18 years of age or older, to vote shall not be denied or abridged by the United States or any State on account of age.

Section 2. The Congress shall have the power to enforce this article by appropriate legislation.

Amendment XXVII [1992]
Forbids sitting Congress to raise its own salary.

No law varying the compensation for the services of the Senators and Representatives shall take effect, until an election of representatives shall have intervened.

LANDMARK COURT DECISIONS

CHRONOLOGICAL LISTING

Throughout U.S. history, decisions of the Supreme Court have altered American law and public policy. Interpretations of the *Constitution of the United States* ripple through our legal, social, religious, and political systems. The decisions affect everyday life on issues from prayer to pregnancy. What follows is a partial study list of major decisions made through out the Court's history.

Case 1:   ***Marbury v. Madison*** (1803)
Key Word: Judicial review
Reference: page 96
Issue: Separation of Power; checks and balances the power to interpret the constitutionality of laws passed by Congress
Decision: The Court decided part of a 1789 Congressional law contradicted the Constitution and declared it void. (First time the Court checked the power of Congress.)

☆☆☆☆☆

Case 2:   ***McCulloch v. Maryland*** (1819)
Key Word: Federalism
Reference: page 105
Issue: State v. national power; implied power
Decision: The Court decided that federal agencies could not be taxed by state government since "the power to tax is the power to destroy."

☆☆☆☆☆

Case 3:   ***Gibbons v. Ogden*** (1824)
Key Word: Federalism
Reference: page 96
Issue: State v. national power; Interstate commerce
Decision: The Court decided that only Congress could make rules on commerce between states.

☆☆☆☆☆

Case 4:   ***Worcester v. Georgia*** (1832)
Key Word: Native Americans
Reference: page 107
Issue: State v. national power; judicial supremacy
Decision: The Court decided that only the federal government had jurisdiction to deal with Indian nations.

☆☆☆☆☆

Case 5:   ***Dred Scott v. Sanford*** (1857)
Key Word: Citizenship; slavery; property
Reference: page 117
Issue: Property rights; citizen rights
Decision: The Court decided that slaves were personal property of their owners protected by the Fifth Amendment and that Congress could not make laws prohibiting slavery.

☆☆☆☆☆

Case 6:   ***Civil Rights Cases*** (1883)
Key Word: Citizenship
Reference: page 146
Issue: Congressional power; Fourteenth Amendment; discrimination
Decision: In a group of five related cases, the Court decided that Congress could make laws to control discriminatory actions by states but not by private individuals.

☆☆☆☆☆

Case 7:   ***Wabash, St. Louis & Pacific RR v. Illinois*** (1886)
Key Word: State regulatory power limits
Reference: pages 156, 174
Issue: Interstate commerce
Decision: The Court decided that Congress must the general rules on interstate commerce and that states were very limited in actions to control interstate transportation.

☆☆☆☆☆

Case 8:   ***United States v. E.C. Knight Co.*** (1895)
Key Word: Anti-trust; interstate commerce
Reference: pages 156, 174
Issue: State regulation of commerce; Congressional power
Decision: The Court reasserted that Congress has the power to make rules on activities directly linked interstate commerce, but that under the Tenth Amendment, states could regulate activities of interstate corporations that take place within the state.

☆☆☆☆☆

Case 9: ***In Re Debs*** (1895)
Key Word: Commerce clause
Reference: page 159
Issue: Freedom of speech; support for general welfare
Decision: The Court ruled that the federal government has the power to halt a strike that affects the nation's general welfare (in this case mail delivery).

☆☆☆☆☆

Case 10: ***Plessy v. Ferguson*** (1896)
Key Word: Separate but equal
Reference: page 145
Issue: *14th Amendment's* equal protection of the law clause
Decision: The Court ruled that state laws providing "separate but equal" accommodations for the black and white races did not violate the Fourteenth Amendment's equal protection of the law clause, and that these laws did not conflict with federal regulation of interstate commerce.

☆☆☆☆☆

Case 11: ***Northern Securities Co. v. U.S. (1904)***
Key Word: Antitrust
Reference: page 192
Issue: Commerce; restraint of trade
Decision: The Court ruled that it was constitutional to apply Congress' antitrust laws to a holding company set up to eliminate interstate railroad competition.

☆☆☆☆☆

Case 12: ***Lochner v. New York*** (1905)
Key Word: Use of personal property; contracts
Reference: page 192
Issue: Employer/employee contracts; property rights; substantive due process; public welfare
Decision: The Court ruled that a New York State law went beyond its "police power" to protect the public welfare and violated the employer's economic rights ("liberty to contract with employees").

☆☆☆☆☆

Case 13: ***Muller v. Oregon*** (1908)
Key Word: Working conditions for women
Reference: page 192-193
Issue: Contracts; state's interest in worker protection; equal protection of law
Decision: The Court ruled that an Oregon law to protect women from overwork was within the state's "police power" to protect the public welfare and did not violate the equal protection for employer's economic rights to make contracts with employees.

☆☆☆☆☆

Case 14: ***Schenck v. United States*** (1919)
Key Word: Clear and present danger; war powers
Reference: page 211
Issue: Freedom of speech; Congressional war power
Decision: The Court ruled that the First Amendment did not protect a citizen's freedom of speech if a public statement posed a "clear and present danger" to the nation's security during a world war.

☆☆☆☆☆

Case 15: ***Schechter Poultry Corp. v. U.S. (1935)***
Key Word: New Deal economic legislation
Reference: page 240
Issue: Executive v. legislative power; Federalism
Decision: The Court ruled that a Congressional act unconstitutionally gave the President power (to regulate interstate commerce) that belonged only to Congress.

☆☆☆☆☆

Case 16: ***Korematsu v. United States*** (1944)
Key Word: Forced relocation
Reference: page 265
Issue: Executive power; war power; Fourteenth Amendment equal protection; Fifth Amendment right to "life, liberty, and property"
Decision: The Court ruled that a military situation permitted Congress and the President to deprive an entire race of basic Fifth and Fourteenth Amendment rights in the interest of national security.

☆☆☆☆☆

Case 17: ***Brown v. Board of Education of Topeka*** (1954)
Key Word: Racial segregation of schools
Reference: pages 293-294
Issue: Equal protection; state's rights to educate
Decision: The Court ruled that the mere act of legally segregating schools by race violated the concept of equal treatment (Fourteenth Amendment) no matter how equal a state made the physical facilities in the schools.

☆☆☆☆☆

Case 18: ***Watkins v. United States*** (1957)
Key Word: Un-American activities
Reference: page 276
Issue: Self-incrimination; due process; congressional power
Decision: The Court ruled that citizens testifying before Congressional investigating committees must be granted the same civil rights under the Bill of Rights they would have in any legal proceeding.

☆☆☆☆☆

Case 19: ***Mapp v. Ohio*** (1961)
Key Word: Unwarranted search; privacy
Reference: page 312
Issue: Right to privacy; unwarranted search and seizure
Decision: The Court ruled that the use of evidence seized in an unwarranted search of an individual's home violated the Fourth and Fourteenth Amendments.

☆☆☆☆☆

Case 20: ***Baker v. Carr*** (1962)
Key Word: Reapportionment; representation
Reference: page 307
Issue: Equal voting rights; equal protection
Decision: The Court ruled that, under the Fourteenth Amendment, seats in a state legislature must be apportioned on a population basis.

☆☆☆☆☆

Case 21: ***Engel v. Vitale*** (1962)
Key Word: School prayer; state religious requirement
Reference: page 319
Issue: First Amendment: establishment of religion
Decision: The Court ruled that requiring students to recite a non denominational New York State Board of Regents prayer, violated the First Amendment's prohibition on the establishment of religion.

☆☆☆☆☆

Case 22: ***Gideon v. Wainwright*** (1963)
Key Word: rights of accused, due process
Reference: page 312
Issue: right to attorney; state v. individual rights; due process
Decision: The Court ruled that the Sixth Amendment's due process guarantee of the right to counsel applied to all felony cases (not just in federal courts) and that the state government must provide a defense attorney for indigent accused persons.

☆☆☆☆☆

Case 23: ***Heart of Atlanta Motel v. U.S.*** (1964)
Key Word: discrimination
Reference: page 307
Issue: property rights; commerce clause
Decision: The Court ruled that the commerce clause of the Constitution justified the *Civil Rights Act of 1964* prohibition of racial discrimination in "any place of public accommodation" whose operations affect interstate commerce.

☆☆☆☆☆

Case 24: ***Miranda v. Arizona*** (1966)
Key Word: Rights of accused
Reference: pages 293, 312
Issue: Self-incrimination (Fifth Amendment), due process (Sixth Amendment), equal protection (Fourteenth Amendment)
Decision: The Court ruled that unless a criminal suspect is informed of the right to counsel and the right against self-incrimination during police interrogation, evidence so obtained may not be used to prosecute the suspect.

☆☆☆☆☆

Case 25: ***Tinker v. Des Moines*** (1969)
Key Word: Symbolic silent speech
Reference: page 340
Issue: Freedom of speech; state's right to educate
Decision: The Court ruled that the wearing of arm bands to make a political statement was protected by the First Amendment as "symbolic speech." As long as there was no substantial or material interference with the educational process, it could not be interfered with by school officials.

☆☆☆☆☆

Case 26: ***New York Times v. U.S.*** (1971)
Key Word: Free press, prior restraint, Pentagon Papers
Reference: page 318
Issue: Executive power v. free press
Decision: The Court ruled that "prior restraint" (prohibiting information from being published) inhibits freedom of the press (First Amendment) and that the government bore a "heavy burden" of justifying such restraint.

☆☆☆☆☆

Case 27: ***Roe v. Wade*** (1973)
Key Word: Abortion rights; personal liberty, right-to-life
Reference: page 318
Issue: Privacy; abortion rights; personal choice reserve power of the state
Decision: The Court ruled with some qualification that state laws prohibiting abortions were unconstitutional. (first 3 mos. = no state interference; second 3 mos. = state could interfere based on mother's health; third 3 mos. = state could interfere to protect unborn child)

☆☆☆☆☆

Case 28: ***United States v. Nixon*** (1974)
Key Word: Separation of power
Reference: page 322
Issue: Impeachment; executive privilege, separation of power
Decision: In the issue of the president withholding information from a Congressional investigation, the Court ruled that the president's executive privilege cannot "prevail over the fundamental demands of due process of law in the fair administration of criminal justice."

☆☆☆☆☆

Case 29: ***New Jersey v. TLO*** (1985)
Key Word: Student rights; right to privacy; unwarranted search
Reference: page 340
Issue: Unwarranted search (Fourth Amendment)
Decision: The Court ruled that because of a school's educational mission, school officials need only "reasonable suspicion" of a student's unlawful behavior to conduct a reasonable search (as opposed to the police needing more specific "probable cause").

☆☆☆☆☆

Case 30: ***Cruzan v. Director, Missouri Dept. of Health*** (1990)
Key Word: Right to die; police power
Reference: page 349
Issue: Right to die; police power; due process, equal protection (Fourteenth Amendment)
Decision: The Court ruled that due process under the Fourteenth Amendment entitled a "clearly competent" person to refuse life-prolonging medical treatment (artificial life support).

☆☆☆☆☆

Case 31: ***Planned Parenthood of Southeastern Pennsylvania v. Casey*** (1992)
Key Word: Privacy; abortion
Reference: pages 348-349
Issue: Privacy; abortion; due process, *Roe Decision*
Decision: The Court ruled that states could seek to control abortion through reasonable waiting periods and parental consent for minors as long as the controls were not unduly burdensome and did not present substantial obstacles to procedures protected by the *Roe Decision* of 1973.

☆☆☆☆☆

Case 32: ***Veronia School District v. Acton*** (1995)
Key Word: Privacy; abortion
Reference: page 340
Issue: Student search and seizure
Decision: The Court ruled that, to maintain student safety and to fulfill the educational mission of the school, drug testing of student athletes was constitutional.

PRACTICE FINAL EXAM
NUMBER ONE

PART I : 50 QUESTIONS (55 PTS.)
ANSWER ALL QUESTIONS

Base your answer to questions 1 and 2 on the map below and your knowledge of United States history and government.

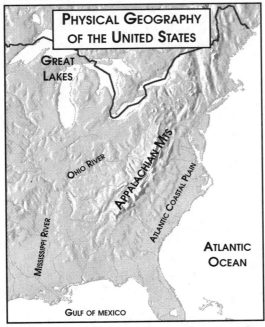

PHYSICAL GEOGRAPHY OF THE UNITED STATES

GREAT LAKES

OHIO RIVER

APPALACHIAN MTS

ATLANTIC COASTAL PLAIN

MISSISSIPPI RIVER

ATLANTIC OCEAN

GULF OF MEXICO

1   In the early period of European colonialism, the mountain chain running inland but parallel to the Atlantic Seacoast
1   acted as a barrier to westward settlement
2   drew prospectors because of its rich minerals
3   discouraged settlement because of volcanic activity
4   delayed western settlement until the railroad era

2   The great river systems of the central plains region
1   had high falls and cataracts that deterred settlement
2   leached the prairie soil of its fertility
3   discouraged settlement because of constant flooding
4   became arteries of commercial growth

3   Under colonial mercantilist policies, a goal was to obtain a favorable balance of trade. To do so, the mother country would
1   allow the colonies to trade with colonies of other nations
2   forbid or severely restrict colonial manufacturing
3   encourage the colonies to produce finished manufactured products
4   discourage new settlers from going to the colonies

4   New England town meetings and the *Fundamental Orders of Connecticut* were attempts by colonists to
1   break away from British rule
2   control all colonial trade
3   establish official state religions
4   introduce aspects of democracy into the colonies

5   The major objection that British colonists in North America had to English rule was that the colonists were
1   denied the right to arm themselves for defense
2   denied the rights of citizens who live in England
3   forced to settle in wilderness areas
4   forced to farm crops ordered by England

6   The Battle of Saratoga proved to be a turning point in the Revolutionary War because the British
1   withdrew from North America immediately after the battle
2   navy no longer had any impact on war activities
3   failed to divide the 13 states
4   Loyalists joined the Patriot cause after this battle

U.S. CONSTITUTION LIMITS POWER BY DIVIDING IT BETWEEN THE NATIONAL AND STATE GOVERNMENTS.

Delegated Powers
(national government only)

Interstate & foreign commerce
foreign relations
declares war
coins money
immigration
postal service

&

Implied Powers
Congress can stretch
the delegated
powers

Concurrent Powers
(both governments)

taxation
borrowing
court systems
penal systems
law enforcement agencies
general welfare of citizens
charter banks and
corporations

Reserved Powers
(state governments only)

Intrastate commerce
local governments
public health
voter qualification
supervise elections
supervise education
license occupations

AMERICANS ARE CITIZENS UNDER TWO GOVERNMENTS:
NATIONAL (U.S. FEDERAL) GOVERNMENT AND THE STATE IN WHICH THEY RESIDE

Base your answer to questions 7 and 8 on the diagram above and your knowledge of United States history and government.

7   What is the primary constitutional principle exemplified by the diagram?
1   federalism
2   checks and balances
3   States rights
4   executive privilege

8   Which traditional phrase sums up the powers shown in the diagram as concurrent powers?
1   "The Trickle-Down Theory"
2   "The Power of the Purse and the Sword"
3   "The Open Door Policy"
4   "Clear and Present Danger"

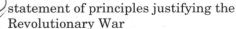

9   Which fundamental political idea is expressed in the *Declaration of Independence*?
1   The government should guarantee economic security to every citizen.
2   The central government and state government should have equal power.
3   If the government denies its people certain basic rights, that government can be overthrown.
4   Rulers derive their right to govern from God and are bound to govern in the nation's best interest.

10   The *Articles of Confederation* are best described as a
1   statement of principles justifying the Revolutionary War
2   plan of union for the original 13 states
3   set of arguments supporting ratification of the Constitution
4   list of reasons for the secession of the Southern states

11   Which belief was generally held by the delegates to the Constitutional Convention of 1787?
1   A strong central government is necessary to maintain order.
2   Slavery should be abolished.
3   The principle of government should be firm and unchangeable.
4   Rule of men is superior to rule of law.

12   An example of the unwritten constitution in the United States is the
1   right of citizens to vote if they are 18 years old or older
3   right to freedom of speech
2   use of the electoral college system
4   rise of the two party political system

13   The majority of cases heard by the United States Supreme Court come to the Court because of its constitutional power to
1   act on decisions appealed from lower courts
2   mediate disagreements between states
3   advise Congress on the legality of bills
4   exercise jurisdiction in legal situations involving foreign governments

14 The *Constitution of the United States* requires that a census be taken every ten years to reapportion
1 membership in the House of Representatives
2 the number of delegates to national nominating conventions
3 federal aid to localities
4 agricultural subsidies

15 The most valid generalization about the U.S. Supreme Court under Chief Justice John Marshall is that it
1 reduced the delegated powers of Congress
2 usually supported the doctrine of states rights
3 made decisions that strengthened the power of the National Government
4 followed a doctrine of strict interpretation of the Constitution

16 Adherence to a strict interpretation of the Constitution would have prevented President Thomas Jefferson from
1 making the Louisiana Purchase
2 writing "State of the Union" messages
3 receiving ambassadors
4 commissioning military officers

17 A major reason for the growth of sectionalism during the 1820s was the
1 treatment of Native Americans by the federal government
2 differing economic activities of each section
3 inequality created by the electoral college system
4 dispute over the active role of the United States in world affairs

18 *Compromise Enables Maine and Missouri to Enter the Union* (1820)

California Admitted to Union as a Free State (1850)

Kansas-Nebraska Act Sets Up Popular Sovereignty (1854)

Which issue is common to these headlines?
1 protective tariffs
2 voting rights for minorities
3 extension of slavery
4 universal public education

19 In his writings, Henry David Thoreau supported an individual's right to
1 own slaves in the territories
2 vote directly for President
3 engage in polygamy
4 disobey unjust laws

20 The passage of the Thirteenth, Fourteenth, and Fifteenth Amendments in the period following the Civil War showed that
1 the states had increased their power at the expense of the federal government
2 segregation would no longer be allowed in the United States
3 federal power could be expanded to protect the rights of minorities
4 the political and economic rights of women were protected

Base your answer to question 21 and 22 on the diagram below and your knowledge of United States history and government.

21 Which group would strongly disagree with the cartoonist's point of view?
1 urban dwellers
2 farmers
3 former slaves
4 industrialists

22 The cartoonist believes that during the Age of Industrialization, the U.S. Senate was
1 being taken advantage of by the trusts
2 passing strong legislation to control big business
3 more powerful than the Presidency
4 less effective than the House of Representatives in dealing with trusts

23 The passage of Jim Crow laws in the South in the late 19th century is evidence that
1 the Supreme Court refused to hear civil rights cases
2 the federal government had increased its commitment to civil rights
3 Southern legislators were determined to keep African Americans in an inferior position
4 African Americans in the South were satisfied with their legal and economic status

24 During the 1860s and 1870s, the federal government's policies toward Native Americans were generally
1 intended to improve economic opportunities for Native American tribes
2 based on the view that Native Americans were obstacles to white settlement
3 identical to federal policies toward African Americans
4 based on Native American values

Base your answer to question 25 on the poem below and your knowledge of United States history and government.

"Give me your tired, your poor,
Your huddled masses yearning to breathe free,
The wretched refuse of your teeming shore.
Send these, the homeless, tempest-tost to me,
I lift my lamp beside the golden door!"

EMMA LAZARUS
"The New Colossus," 1883

25 An American who agrees with the information above would likely be in favor of
1 severe restrictions on immigration
2 immigration only for those who show a political need
3 liberal immigration policies
4 a ban on all immigration

26 In the late 19th century, what was a problem of American farmers that led to government regulation of business?
1 high railroad rates
2 high tariffs on imported products
3 high wheat prices
4 scarcity of farmland

27 AFL president Samuel Gompers said,"The American worker is primarily interested in his real wages." Real wages represent the
1 minimum wages demanded by a union
2 dollars the worker receives weekly
3 dollars the worker receives annually
4 goods and services the worker's dollars will buy

28 The main purpose of a progressive income tax is to
1 base tax rates on a person's ability to pay
2 increase government spending on welfare programs
3 tax everyone at the same percentage rate
4 ensure a balanced budget

29 Which argument was used to support United States acquisition of overseas possessions in the late 1800s?
1 The spread of Marxist ideas had to be stopped because they threatened world peace.
2 The United States should be the first world power to build a colonial empire.
3 The United States needed to obtain raw materials and new markets.
4 The doctrine of Manifest Destiny had become obsolete.

30 The activities of the muckrakers led Congress to pass laws that
1 curbed the power of labor unions
2 protected the consumer
3 placed strict limits on immigration
4 increased taxes on imports

31 President Woodrow Wilson's *Fourteen Points* were intended to
1 punish Germany for causing World War I
2 create a foundation for a lasting peace after World War I
3 redistribute Germany's colonies among the Allied nations
4 make the United States, Great Britain, and France into leading world powers

Base your answer to question 32 on the cartoon below and your knowledge of U.S. history and government.

32 The cartoon shows the United States Senate's support for a foreign policy of
1 isolation
2 appeasement
3 internationalism
4 collective security

33 "The business of America is business." President Calvin Coolidge's 1924 statement expressed his support for the idea that
1 workers should have a greater role in influencing business decisions
2 the United States should end trade with other countries and become economically self sufficient
3 basic industries should be owned by the federal government
4 the economy functions best if government allows business to operate freely

34 One reason for the economic decline in the United States in the late 1920s was
1 a drastic reduction in tariffs
2 industrial and agricultural overproduction
3 excessive government regulation
4 new sources of investment capital

35 Two important New Deal measures that were declared unconstitutional were the
1 Civilian Conservation Corps and the Works Progress Administration
2 National Industrial Recovery Act and the Agricultural Adjustment Act
3 Fair Labor Standards Act and the National Labor Relations Act
4 Social Security Act and the Home Owners Loan Corporation

36 A major impact of New Deal legislation has been
1 a reduction in the power of the federal government over the states
2 the dominance of the judiciary over the legislative and executive branches
3 a strengthening of the President's influence in lawmaking
4 more separation between the national and local levels of government

37 In arguments before the Supreme Court in Korematsu v. U.S. (1944), the United States government justified the forced relocation of Japanese Americans during World War II on the grounds that
1 Japanese Americans refused to serve in the armed forces
2 Japanese Americans should be treated in the same way as German Americans
3 most of the relocated people were not United States citizens and thus had few legal rights
4 the wartime need to assure national security was more important than the protection of individual rights

Base your answer to question 38 on the map below and your knowledge of United States history and government.

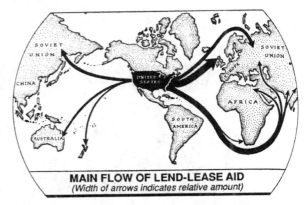

MAIN FLOW OF LEND-LEASE AID
(Width of arrows indicates relative amount)

38 The situation shown in the map occurred as part of the United States effort to
1 help the Allies fight the Axis powers
2 persuade other nations to join the United Nations
3 provide technical assistance to economically developing nations
4 force other nations to pay their debts to the United States

39 An important effect of World War II on United States foreign policy was a
1 refusal to become involved in world affairs
2 stronger commitment to collective security and world leadership
3 smaller role for the President in foreign policy and national security issues
4 willingness to intervene only when the national economy is involved

40 Which statement best summarizes economic conditions in the United States since the end of World War II?
1 The economy has been in a depression for most of the period.
2 The United States has had the world's highest unemployment rate.
3 The United States has come to depend more heavily on imports to meet its economic needs.
4 The legal minimum wage has steadily declined.

41 The chief objective of President Lyndon Johnson's Great Society programs was to
1 increase foreign aid to developing nations
2 unite democratic nations and contain communist nations
3 reform society through expanded government social welfare programs
4 make the states rather than the federal government responsible for supporting social programs

Base your answer to question 42 on the illustration below and your knowledge of United States history and government.

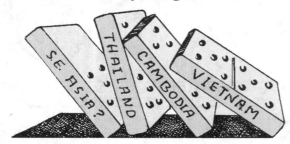

42 President Lyndon Johnson tried to stop the situation in the illustration by
1 escalating the war in Vietnam
2 withdrawing all U.S. troops from Vietnam
3 forming an alliance with communist forces in Vietnam
4 imposing a limited trade embargo on Thailand and Cambodia

43 One difference between World War II and the Vietnam War is that the Vietnam War
1 involved direct armed conflict with China
2 was formally declared a war by Congress
3 was a decisive military victory for the United States
4 caused a significant amount of protest in the United States

44 The women's movement was strengthened in the 1960s chiefly because
1 job discrimination against women and minorities was eliminated
2 women were angered by the failure of voters to elect them to Congress
3 women became increasingly dissatisfied with their status and their roles in society
4 the radical liberation movements of the 1950s had failed

Base your answer to question 45 on the graphs below and your knowledge of United States history and government.

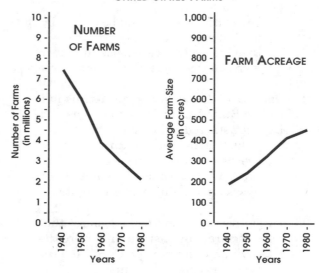

45 Since the end of World War II, agriculture in the United States has experienced a decrease in the
1 total output of farm products
2 productivity of farm workers
3 average size of farms
4 number of farms

46 The Supreme Court in *Planned Parenthood v. Casey* (1992) decided that
1 the right to an abortion guaranteed in *Roe v. Wade* (1973) should be overturned
2 individual states could pass legislation to ban abortion
3 though states can impose some restrictions, individuals still have the legal right to an abortion
4 only Congress can change the abortion laws

Base your answer to question 47 on the quotations below and your knowledge of United States history and government.

• "Separation of the races does not place a badge of inferiority upon one group over another, thus it is not a violation of the Fourteenth Amendment." (1896)

• "To separate (children in grade school and high school) from others of similar age and qualifications solely because of their race generates a feeling of inferiority as to their status ... that may affect their hearts and minds in a way unlikely ever to be undone." (1954)

47 The difference in opinion between these two rulings best shows
1 a change in judicial philosophy and public attitudes
2 the persistent efforts of the major political parties to increase equal opportunity
3 a recognition that democracy depends on economic equality for all citizens
4 the refusal of the Supreme Court to deal with controversial issues

48 Demographic shifts in the late 20th century resulted in
1 Northeastern states regaining power in the Electoral College
2 new immigration quotas being placed on Western Hemisphere countries
3 less economic equality for elderly citizens
4 electoral votes shifting to western and southern states

49 One way in which some environmentalists want the United States government to protect lakes and forests from acid rain is by
1 requiring factories to use coal rather than other forms of energy
2 spraying lakes and forests with protective chemicals
3 replacing nuclear energy with fossil fuels
4 requiring industries to reduce their smokestack emissions

Base your answer to question 50 on the graphs below and your knowledge of United States history and government.

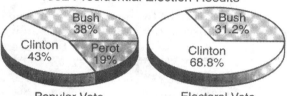

1992 Presidential Election Results

50 Which generalization is supported by the information provided by the graphs?
1 The electoral vote often fails to reflect the popular vote.
2 The House of Representatives settles presidential elections in which third party candidates participate.
3 The electoral college system weakens the two party system.
4 Electoral college members often vote against their party's candidates.

End of Part I.

Continue on to Part II on the next page.

PART II – ANSWER ALL QUESTIONS
THEMATIC ESSAY: (15 PTS.)

Directions: Write a well-organized essay that includes an introduction, several paragraphs explaining your position, and a conclusion.

Theme: Reform Movements in American society

> Throughout American history, reformers have attempted to correct abuses and unfair features in American society. Some attempts have taken the form of writings, speeches, protests, legislative pressure, and court action.

Task:

> Using your knowledge of United States history and government, write an essay in which you select *three* specific reform movements in American history.
> For *each* reform movement:
>
> - describe the goals of the movement,
> - discuss the activities of one individual in the movement, and
> - evaluate the success of the movement in achieving its goals.

Suggestions:
You may use any examples from your study of U.S. history and government. Some suggestions you might wish to consider include: abolition, treatment of mental illness, prohibition, educational reforms, civil rights, women's rights, and rights of the disabled. **You are *not* limited to these suggestions.**

DOCUMENT BASED QUESTION: (30 PTS.)

The following task is based on the accompanying documents. The documents may have been edited for the purposes of this exercise. The task is designed to test your ability to work with historical documents. As you analyze the documents, take into account both the source of the document and the author's point of view.

Directions: Read the documents in Part A and answer the question after each document. Then read the directions for Part B and write your essay.

Historical Context:
Since 1789, the federal government has grown in terms of power and influence in the United States. This growth has been accompanied by controversy. Not everyone approves of the growth. The documents below present information regarding this growth.

Task:
Using information from the documents and your knowledge of United States history and government, write an essay in which you

- describe the way in which the power and influence of the federal government has grown,
- discuss controversy that has accompanied the growth, and
- evaluate how that change has helped or harmed American society.

Part A – Short Answer [15 pts.]
Analyze the documents and answer the questions that follow each document in the space provided.

Question for Document 1

On what basis is Maryland's law "unconstitutional and void"?

DOCUMENT 1

"The question is, in truth, a question of supremacy; and if the right of the states to tax the means employed by the general government be conceded, the declaration that the Constitution and the laws made in pursuance thereof, shall be the supreme law of the land, is empty and unnecessary declamation...We are unanimously of opinion, that the law passed by the legislature of Maryland, imposing a tax on the Bank of the United States, is unconstitutional and void."

– Chief Justice John Marshall - *McCulloch v. Maryland* (1819)

Question for Document 2

Corporations and contracts are created by powers reserved to states, does this act take those powers away? Why or not?

DOCUMENT 2

"Every contract, combination in the form of trust or otherwise, or conspiracy, in restraint of trade or commerce among several states or with foreign nations, is hereby declared illegal."

– *Sherman Antitrust Act* (1890)

Question for Document 3

Under what conditions did the *Schenck* ruling increase federal control over speech?

DOCUMENT 3

"The most stringent protection of free speech would not protect a man in falsely shouting fire in a theater and causing a panic...The question in every case is whether the words used are used in such circumstances and are of such a nature as to create a clear and present danger that they will bring about substantive evils that Congress has a right to prevent...When a nation is at war many things that might be said in time of peace are such a hindrance to its effort that their utterance will not be endured so long as men fight and that no Court could regard them as protected by any constitutional right."

– Justice Oliver Wendell Holmes - *Schenck v. U.S.* (1919)

Question for Document 4

How does the chart show a change in government roles in the 20th century?

DOCUMENT 4 – FEDERAL INDEPENDENT REGULATORY AGENCIES

1890	1990
Interstate Commerce Commission	Interstate Commerce Commission Federal Reserve Board Federal Trade Commission Securities and Exchange Commission Federal Communication Commission National Labor Relations Board Federal Maritime Commission Civil Aeronautics Board Consumer Products Safety Commission Nuclear Regulatory Commission Commodities Futures Trading Commission Federal Energy Regulatory Commission

Question for Document 5

Why was it necessary for federal troops to take action at Central High School, Little Rock, AK in 1957?

DOCUMENT 5

Question for Document 6

How did the role of the government change when it switched from the "Trickle Down" philosophy to the "Pump-Priming" philosophy?

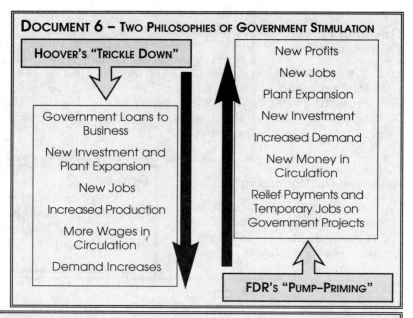

DOCUMENT 6 – TWO PHILOSOPHIES OF GOVERNMENT STIMULATION

HOOVER'S "TRICKLE DOWN"

Government Loans to Business

New Investment and Plant Expansion

New Jobs

Increased Production

More Wages in Circulation

Demand Increases

New Profits

New Jobs

Plant Expansion

New Investment

Increased Demand

New Money in Circulation

Relief Payments and Temporary Jobs on Government Projects

FDR'S "PUMP-PRIMING"

Question for Document 7

What roles does General Hoover say that Congress and taxpayers play in regard to nuclear weapons?

DOCUMENT 7

"The nuclear development and production programs are unique in government in that they constitute a government-owned industry...From the air, our production plants would look like a cross section of American industry:...strategic weapons...battlefield nuclear systems...fleet air defense...You [members of Congress] should consider yourselves the Board of Directors...The record of this testimony will serve as our report to the stockholders – the American taxpayers."

– Maj. Gen. William Hoover, Director of the Office of Nuclear Military Application, Department of Energy in a 1982 report to the House Subcommittee on Procurement and Military Nuclear Systems.

GO ON TO PART B

Part B - Essay [15 pts.]
Directions:
- Write a well organized essay that includes an introduction, several paragraphs, and a conclusion.
- Use evidence from the documents to support your response.
- Do not simply repeat the contents of the documents.
- Include specific related outside information.

Historical Context:
Since 1789, the federal government has grown in terms of power and influence in the United States. This growth has been accompanied by controversy. Not everyone approves of the growth.

Task:
Using information from the documents and your knowledge of United States history and government, write an essay in which you
- describe the way in which the power and influence of the federal government has grown,
- discuss controversy that has accompanied the growth, and
- evaluate how that change has helped or harmed American society.

Be sure to include specific historical details. You must also include additional information from your knowledge of U.S. history and government.

GLOSSARY & INDEX

Anti-Federalists (opponents of U.S. Constitution's ratification c. 1788-89), 73

Anti-Imperialist League (prominent Americans opposed the acquisition of colonies), 203

Anti-Klan Law (see Ku Klux Klan), 145

Anti-Saloon League (prohibitionist group; national scale in 1895), 190

Anti-trust suits (stopping monopolies), 157, 192

Antiquities Act (1906; federal land preservation), 193

Apartheid (19th - 20th C. South African policy of total separation of races), 345

Apollo 11 (moon landing mission, 1969), 304

Appalachian Mountains, 13, 15, 16, 17, 47

Appeasement (European countries concede to Hitler's aggressive acts, c. 1938-40), 254, 270

Arbitration (third party dictates settlement in labor-management or international disputes), 159

Aristotle (384-322 BC; ancient Greek political philosopher influenced ideas on U.S. gov't.), 69

"Arkies" (victims displaced by 1930s Dust Bowl disaster in AR), 241

Armour, Philip (1832-1901; industrialist active in building the meat-packing business), 154

Armstrong, Louis (1900-1971; musician; greatly influenced the development of jazz), 231

Armstrong, Neil (1930 - ; *Apollo 11* commander; 1st human to set foot on Moon, 1969), 304

"Arsenal of Democracy" (FDR pre-WW II preparation speech), 256

Articles of Confederation (first U.S. national gov't structure, 1778-1789), 66-68, 351

Assimilation (process whereby a minority group gradually adopts the customs and attitudes of the prevailing culture), 168

Astair, Fred (1899-1987; Hollywood entertainer; 1930s musicals), 242

Atlantic Charter (WW II aims for U.S. and Britain), 256 [+box]

Atomic Energy Commission (1946-1975; independent gov't. agency regulates civilian uses of nuclear materials; succeeded the Manhattan Project; became Nuclear Regulatory Commission, 1975), 266, 277

Atoms for Peace Program (Eisenhower era research control and cooperation), 290

Austin, Stephen (1793-1836; colonizer and political leader; helped Texas settlers gain their independence, 144

Axis Alliance (1936 informal cooperation between Italy and Germany, formalized in 1939, Japan joined in 1940), 252, 254, 255, 258, 259, 260

Aztec (people of central Mexico whose civilization was at its height at the time of the Spanish conquest in the early 16th century), 24-25

Baby boom (post WW II population explosion), 296-297

Backlash (negative reaction usually to civil rights campaigns), 143

Bacon, Nathaniel (1647-1676; VA colonist who led frontiersmen in a 1676 rebellion against royal governor Berkley to gain political reforms), 41

Baker v. Carr (1962; equity in Congressional district apportionment), 307, 379

Bakke v. the Regents of the University of California, (1978; Supreme Court ordered care in the use of racial quotas in affirmative action programs to avoid reverse discrimination), 307, 379

Bank Holiday (Mar.-April 1933; FDR suspended banking operations to stop runs and collapses and restore public's confidence), 237

Bank of the United States (Jackson's controversial veto), 105-106

Barnard, Henry (1811-1900; educator-reformer; sought higher standards in public schools; the first U.S. Comm. of Ed., 1867-1870), 108

Barry, John (1745-1803; Revolutionary naval commander), 55

Baruch, Bernard (1870-1965; stock broker, public official, and advisor for Presidents from Wilson to Kennedy; key manager of WW I economy), 224

Baseball (professional sports emerge in the 19th c. industrial era), 164

Batista, Fulgencio (dictator ousted by Castro), 300

Battle of Bunker Hill (Boston, MA; 1st major Revolutionary War battle on nearby Breed's Hill on 17 June 1775), 52

Battle of the Bulge (WW II battle in France, 1944-45), 259

Bay (body of water partially enclosed by land but with a wide mouth, affords access to the sea), 11

Bay of Pigs in Cuba (CIA attempt overthrow Castro), 300

Beecher, Lyman (1775-1863; fiery Calvinist theologian; militant abolitionist, temperance crusader), 110

Begin, Menachem (1913-1992; Israeli prime minister, 1977-1983), 327

Bell, Alexander Graham (1847-1922; inventor of the telephone in 1876), 154

Bellamy, Edward (early socialist reform work: *Looking Backward*, 1888), 176

Berlin Blockade and Airlift (1948-1949; Soviet blockade of city relieved by Allies air supplies), 271

Berlin Wall (1961-1989; Soviets ordered blocking off of E. Berlin; divided communist and free sections of Berlin), 301, 351

Bessemer Process (see Kelly-Bessemer)

Bethune, Mary McLeod (1875-1955; educator sought improved racial relations and educational opportunities for African Americans; advisor to FDR; delegate to first U.N. meeting, 1945), 242

BIA (Bureau of Indian Affairs - an agency of the U.S. Department of the Interior set up to handle Indian affairs), 311

Bicameral legislature (lawmaking body divided into two-houses), 57, 71, 78

"Big Four" (U.S., U.S.S.R., Britain, and France post WW II powers), 290

"Big Stick, The" (T. Roosevelt's foreign policy), 205

"Big Three" (U.S., Britain, & U.S.S.R.-WW II summit meetings), 263

"Big Three" of American auto industry (Ford, GM, and Chrysler), 261, 296

Bilateral (two-sided diplomatic agreement, e.g., Soviet-Nazi NonAggression Pact, 1939; multilateral = many sided, e.g., NATO, 1949), 275

Bilingual Education Act (1975 mandate that children be taught in their native language while learning English), 325

Bill (draft of a proposed law presented for approval to a legislative body), 80

Bills of attainder (laws declaring persons guilty without right of trial), 79-81

Bill of Rights (1791 - U.S. Constitutional Amendments 1-10 stating fundamental personal rights of citizens), 75-76, 367, 373

bin Laden, Osama (Saudi-born millionaire, financed and led Islamic terrorist Al Qaeda organization), 356

Black Friday (financial panic of 1869), 144

Black Muslims (Nation of Islam; founded in 1930s; anti-integrationist in the 1960s; main group dissolved in 1970s to blend with worldwide orthodox Islam; 1970s Detroit-based Farrakhan group advocates of male solidarity and intensive work with youth in inner-city communities), 305

Black Panthers (1960s militant civil rights group), 305-306

Black Power (post 1966 militant civil rights activities), 305

Blacklist (lists of undesirable employees circulated among an industry's producers), 160

Blackmun, Harry (1909-1999; U.S. Supreme Court justice, 1970-94; *Roe* decision), 318

Blitzkrieg (swift, sudden military offensive, usually by combined air and mobile land forces; Nazis - WW II attack on Poland), 255, 256

Blue collar jobs (industrial workers; ["white collar" usually means clerical/managerial jobs]), 285

Blue Eagle (symbol of the New Deal's NRA programs; see *National Industrial Recovery Act*), 238

Bolsheviks (communist group led late 1917 revolution in Russia), 210, 211, 229

Bond rallies (raised money; WW II home front), 263

Bonus Army (1932 veterans' march on Washington , lobby for military pensions), 233

Border states (slave states that did not rebel against the Union), 121, 122

Boss (professional politician who controls a party or a political machine), 144

Boston Massacre (1770; squad of British troops fired into an unruly crowd killing three men outright and mortally wounding two others), 50

Boston Tea Party (1773; colonial protest against Parliament's *Tea Act*), 50-51

Boxer Rebellion, The (anti-imperialist movement in China, 1900), 200-201

Boycott (organized abstaining from doing business with someone to force them to accept a condition), 48-49

Braddock, Edward (1695-1755; British general in America during the French and Indian War), 46

Bradley, Omar (1893-1981; U.S. commander WW II; liberated Sicily, Italy, and Paris), 259

Bragg, Braxton (1817-1876; Confederate general in the Civil War; defeated in the Chattanooga Campaign, 1863), 123

"Brain Trust, The" (New Deal advisors), 236

Brandeis, Louis (1856-1941; judicial activist associate justice of the Sup. Ct., 1916-1939), 192-193

"Brinkmanship" (confrontational Cold War diplomacy; see Dulles), 290

Brooklyn Bridge (1869-83; first great suspension bridge in the U.S.), 137, 161

Browder, Earl (U.S. communist leader, 1930s-1940s), 242

Brown, John (1800-1859; abolitionist; aborted raid on U.S. arsenal at Harper's Ferry, VA to liberate Southern slaves), 118

Brown v. Board of Ed. of Topeka (1954 - school desegregation), 145, 293 [chart], 294, 299, 304, 379

Bryan, William Jennings (1860-1925; Populist/Democratic leader; unsuccessful bids for the presidency in 1896, 1900, 1908; "Cross of Gold" speech advocating free silver, 1896; defense of fundamentalism in the Scopes Trial, 1925), 175, 230

Buchanan, James (1791-1868; 15th President, 1857-1861; could not prevent the South from seceding), 119

Budget deficit (amount by which gov't. revenue falls short of meeting expenses; a shortage of income), 339 [+graph]

Budget surplus (amount by which gov't. revenue exceeds meeting expenses; an overabundance of income), 339 [+graph]

"Bull Market" (wild speculation before 1929 stock market crash), 233

Bunche, Ralph (1904-1971; 1940s civil rights leader; U.N. activist; Nobel Peace Prize, 1950), 242

Bureaucracy (power concentrated in an immense hierarchy of gov't. agencies), 85, 240

Burger Court (1969-1986; judicial restraint), 318

Burger, Warren E. (1907 - 1995; Chief Justice, 1969- 1986; advocate of judicial restraint), 318

Burns, George & Gracie Allen (20th century radio / TV entertainers), 242

Bush, George H.W. (1924- ; 41st President, 1989-93; ambassador to the U.N. and China; CIA Director; Vice Pres., 1981-1989), 347-353

Bush, George W. (1946- ; 43rd President, 2001- ; 46th Governor of Texas (1995-2001), son of George Bush, 41st President), 355

Business cycle (see cycle of demand)

Byrnes, James F. (1879-1972; U.S. Rep. and Senator in New Deal; Supreme Court, 1941-42; War Mobilization Board, 1943; with FDR at Yalta Conference; Secretary of State, 1945-47), 270

Cabinet (collective heads of the various executive agencies functioning as an advisory group to the President), 94

Cabot, John (1450-1498; Italian-born explorer [Giovanni Caboto]; commanded English expedition that discovered the North American mainland in 1497), 28, 29

Calhoun, John C. (1782-1850; Senator, Vice-President, Southern rights spokesman), 99, 103-104, 321

Calvert, Cecil (1605-1675; recipient of the Maryland proprietorship, 1634), 35

Call of the Wild, The (Jack London story - realism of industrial era writers), 165

Camp David Agreements (1979 Egyptian-Israeli accords), 327

Capitalism (system in which the means of economic production and distribution are privately owned; development is balanced by accumulation and reinvestment of profits), 148

Carmichael, Stokley (1941-1998; militant "black power" civil rights leader of SNCC), 305

Carnegie, Andrew (1835-1919; industrialist and philanthropist who amassed a fortune in the steel industry), 155

Carter, Jimmy (James E., 1924- ; 39th President, 1977-1981; negotiated the Camp David accords between Egypt and Israel, 1979; Gov. GA 1971-1975), 323, 326-328

Cartels (international trade organizations with monopolistic power), 149, 288, 324

Cartier, Jacques (1491-1557; French explorer who navigated the St. Lawrence River in 1535 and laid claim to the region for France), 28, 29

Castle Garden (a.k.a. Castle Clinton, 1811 fortress served as early U.S. immigration depot in NYC until 1892), 165

Castro, Fidel (1936- ; Cuban rebel leader; created communist state, 1959), 300

Catt, Carrie Chapman (1859-1947; major role in the ratification of the *19th Amendment* giving women the vote; founded the League of Women Voters), 197

Caucuses (small leadership group within a political party; sometimes picks candidates), 106

Central Intelligence Agency (CIA; U.S. espionage agency created in 1947; coordinates other agencies in the intelligence community), 266

Central Pacific Railroad Company (transcontinental railroad built eastward from San Francisco; joined Union Pacific in 1869), 152

Central Powers (Austria, Germany, Turkey WW I alliance), 208, 215, 224

Challenger (25th space shuttle mission; exploded on take-off 1/1986, killed crew of 7), 324

Chamberlain, Neville (British Prime Minister, 1937-1940; advocated a policy of appeasement toward the fascist regimes of Europe), 254

Chambers, Whittaker (1901-1961; journalist; communist; testified before Committee on Un-American Activities; implicated Alger Hiss), 276

Chamorro, Violeta Barrios de (1929- ; president of Nicaragua, 1990-1996; ended 8-year civil war), 276, 343

Champlain, Samuel de (1567-1635; French explorer; founded Nova Scotia and Quebec), 30

charter (document issued by a sovereign, legislature, or other authority, creating a public or private corporation; colonies were often chartered as private enterprises), 32, 33, 34, 35

Chavez, Cesar (1927-1993; organized farm workers into the United Farm Workers (UFW), 310

Checks and Balances (system that grants power to various branches to keep the other branches within specific bounds), 6, 69, 72

Cherokee Nation (Native American people formerly inhabiting the western Carolinas, eastern TN, and northern GA; gov't. removed them to Indian Territory in the 1830s), 27 map, 107, 171

Chicago, Milwaukee & St. Paul Railway Co. v. Minn. (1889), 174 [box]

Chief Diplomat (presidential role of carrying out foreign policy), 81-82

Chief Executive (presidential role of implementing and administering laws of Congress), 81-82

Chief Jurist (constitutional presidential role of enforcing decisions made by the Supreme Court), 81-82

Chief Legislator (unofficial presidential role of suggesting laws and programs to Congress), 81-82

Chief of Party (unofficial presidential role of representative of a political faction), 81-82

Chief of State (presidential role of ceremonial head of gov't.), 81-82

Chinese Exclusion Act (1882; immigration restriction), 168

Chinese Nationalists (also Guomindang; party of Jiang Jieshi; ruling power group in China 1924-1947), 263, 273-274, 320

Chiang Kai-shek (see Jiang Jieshi)

Choctaw (Native American people inhabiting central and southern Mississippi and southwest Alabama, with present-day populations in Mississippi and southeast Oklahoma), 26-27

Christian Crusades (military expeditions undertaken by European Christians in the 11th, 12th, and 13th centuries to recover the Holy Land from the Muslims), 27

Chrysler Corporation (1925; Walter P. Chrysler converted the Maxwell Motor Company absorbing Dodge Brothers in 1928 later adding Plymouth, De Soto, and Jeep), 261

Churchill, Winston (1874-1965; British prime minister, 1940-1945 and 1951-1955; led Great Britain through WW II), 256, 263, 270

CIA (see Central Intelligence Agency)

Cities (center of population, commerce, and culture; a town of significant size and importance; urban areas of the U.S.), 14, 41, 161, 297-298

Civil disobedience (intentional public breaking of laws deemed unjust), 295, 300 [box], 305

Civil liberties (basic personal rights and protections in *U.S. Constitution, Bill of Rights,* and other Amendments), 74

Civil Rights Acts (1875, 1964, 1968; laws guaranteeing and elaborating rights belonging to an individual by virtue of citizenship, especially the freedoms and privileges guaranteed by the *13th* and *14th Amendments*; include due process, equal protection of the laws, and freedom from discrimination.), 147, 295, 306, 307 [box], 309

Civil Rights Cases (1883; Supreme Court held the *13th* and *14th Amendments* did not allow Congress to legislate on private or social actions of citizens), 146 [box], 377

Civil Rights Commission (1957; evaluates federal laws and policies on equal rights and the effectiveness of equal opportunity programs; makes recommendations to the president and Congress), 268, 295

Civil Rights Movement (1957-1965 intense public pressure and massive demonstrations produced congressional legislation to overcome local and state obstruction to the exercise of citizenship rights by African Americans), 294, 300, 304-306, 308, 310, 317

Civil service (distribute gov't. jobs through fair competitive examinations; see *Pendleton Act*), 187

Civil War (U.S.; 1861-1865 war between the Union and the Confederacy; also called The War Between the States; [general: a war between factions or regions of the same country]), 118-129

Civil Works Administration (CWA, 1933-34, provided construction employment for destitute), 237 [+chart]

Civilian Conservation Corps (CCC; 1933-1942; unemployed, unmarried young men enlisted to work on conservation and resource-development projects), 237, 263

Clark, George Rogers (1752-1818; raids on British troops in the Northwest Territory during the Revolutionary War), 57

Clay, Henry (1777-1852; U.S. Representative, KY; Speaker of the House; Senator; Sec'y of State; Presidential candidate, 1824, 1832, 1844), 99, 105, 115, 116

Clayton Anti-Trust Act (1914; made up deficiencies in the *Sherman Anti-Trust Act* of 1890 in combatting monopolistic practices), 195-196

Clean Air Act (1970; curbed auto emissions), 304, 318

"Clear and present danger rule" (gov't. can suspend civil liberties in time of national stress), 211, 265

Clemenceau, Georges (1841-1929; French news correspondent and politician; WW I leader), 141 [quote], 213

Cleveland, [Stephen] Grover (1837-1908; 22nd and 24th President, 1885-1889 and 1893-1897), 201

Clinton, Bill (William J., 1946- ; 42nd President, 1993-2001; Gov. AR, 1978-80 & 1983-93), 353-355

Clinton, George (1739-1812; Vice Pres. [Jefferson & Madison]; NY Gov., 1777-1795), 73

Coalition (alliance of small groups to achieve majority control of a gov't. or organization), 266, 267 349

Coattail effect (election success of a strong, popular candidate may pull votes for other candidates in the same party), 267, 338

Collective bargaining (labor-management negotiation on wages and working conditions), 158, 237

Collective security (mutual defense agreement among several nations pledged to come to the aid of any member attacked; e.g., NATO), 272

Cold war (political tension and military rivalry between nations that stops short of full-scale war), 264, 270-277

Columbia (1981; 1st space shuttle launched: reuseable craft designed to be launched by rockets and land on a runway), 324

Columbian Exchange (early contacts between Native Americans and Europeans), 29

Columbus, Christopher (1451-1506; Italian explorer in the service of Spain; attempted to reach Asia by sailing west from Europe, encountered America in 1492; made three other voyages to the Caribbean), 28-29

Commander-in-Chief (official role of the president as head of the U.S. military forces), 81-82, 256, 258

Command economy (arrangement for exchange of goods and services following decisions by gov't. agencies), 18-19, 224

Commerce clause (Constitutional grant of power to Congress to regulate trade among various states), 156-157

Commerce Department (cabinet dept. created in 1903 to aid business development), 192

Committee on Un-American Activities (1938-1975; House of Representatives investigations on communism and subversive activities; renamed Internal Security committee, 1969-1975), 276

common law (system of laws originated and developed in England based on court decisions, on the doctrines implied in those decisions, and on customs and usages rather than on codified written laws), 37, 69

Common Market (see European Union)

Commonwealth of Independent States (CIS – economic/military cooperative body of former Soviet republics, 1991), 351

Communism (state plans and controls the economy; social order in which all goods are equally shared by the people; Marxist-Leninist version advocates the overthrow of capitalism by the revolution of the proletariat), 210, 211, 212, 242, 276-277

Compromise of 1850 (an omnibus bill of five laws enacted by Congress aimed at ending sectional disputes that threatened the Union), 116

Computers, 285

Concurrent power (power shared by several divisions of gov't.), 79

Confederate States of America (name adopted by the states that seceded from the U.S. in 1860-61 to form an independent nation, also "The Confederacy"), 118, 119, 121, 122, 123-130

Confederation (union of sovereign states retaining power locally), 21, 66-68, 70

Conglomerates (large, highly diversified corporations), 285, 352

Congress, The (federal legislative body of U.S.), 77-81

Congress of Industrial Organizations (CIO; 1930s-1950s, major national labor union; rival of AFL, merged with AFL in 1955), 293

Congress of Racial Equality (CORE- 1940s civil rights organization; active in the 1960s), 305

Conscription (see draft)

Conservation (attempts to preserve the natural environment), 193-194

Conspicuous consumption (lavish indulgence by the very rich seen as a duty of status, c. industrial era), 162

Constitution (fundamental law), 21, 54, 66-86, 94-96, 367-376

Constitutional Convention (1787), 68-72

Consumer Products Safety Commission, 318

Consumers' Union (private non-profit consumer rights organization; publishes *Consumer Reports* magazine), 160

Containment policy (post WW II foreign policy to restrain growth of communism on global scale), 270-275, 288-290

Continent (principal land masses), 11

Continental Congress (delegates from the 13 original American colonies /states; U. S. gov't., 1774-1789; declared independence, fought Am. Revolution, managed country under the *Art. of Confederation*), 51-57, 66-68

Continental divide (line in Rockies; divides rivers that run east from those that flow west), 15

Contraction (economic decline; see depression, recession), 225, 226

Contract With America (Republicans' reform platform in 1994 Congressional elections), 353

Coolidge, President (1872-1933; 30th President, 1923-29), 216, 227-228, 232, 250

Cooper, James Fenimore (1789-1851; novels of frontier life – *The Last of the Mohicans*), 109

Cooperatives (late 19th C. farmers' organizations to combat high railroad shipping charges), 174

Copperheads (Northerners who sympathized with the South during the Civil War), 121

Cornwallis, Charles (1738-1805; British commander in NC during the Am. Rev.; surrendered at Yorktown in 1781), 56

Corporations (business organization drawing capital from large group of share holding owners), 150 [chart], 151, 227

Cotton, John (1584-1652; English Puritan leader; fled to Boston, Massachusetts Bay; became a civil and religious leader; shaped the colony's early development), 34

Coughlin, Charles E. (1891-1979; isolationist, antisemitic, and profascist "radio priest" of the 1930s-40s; broadcasts critical of New Deal), 243-244

Council of National Defense (Wilson's primary WW I wareffort management organization), 224

County (territorial division of a state or colony exercising administrative, judicial, and political functions), 38

Court Packing Plan (FDR's 1937 attempt to influence Supreme Court decisions), 240

Coureurs de bois (15th-16th C. fur trappers of New France / Canada), 30

Craft unions (labor organizations for skilled trades), 157, 158

Crane, Stephen (1871-1900; realist author of industrial era), 164

Credit Mobilier Scandal (Grant era RR scandal), 144

Creek (confederacy of Native American people formerly inhabiting eastern Alabama, southwest Georgia, and northwest Florida), 27

Creel, George (WW I propagandist), 225

Crime of '73 (refusal of gov't. to increase silver coinage issue aroused farmers groups), 175

"Critical Period" (1781 to 1789 - near collapse under Articles of Confederation), 67

Crop lien system (mortgaging future crops to pay for present expenses), 142

Crosby, Bing (singer-actor, radio, cinema, TV), 242

"Cross of Gold" (William. J. Bryan's 1896 campaign speech in favor of free silver), 175

Crow (Native American people formerly inhabiting northern Great Plains between the Platte and Yellowstone Rivers), 26, 27

Cruzan v. Director, Missouri Dept. of Health (1990 decision on life support issue), 349, 380

Cuba (U.S. protectorate after Spanish American War; 1962 missile crisis), 202-205, 310

Cullen, Countee (1903-1946; Harlem Renaissance poet; collections: *Colors, Copper Sun*), 231

Cultural pluralism (society made up of a blend of numerous cultures), 168 [box]

Cumberland Road (also National Road; authorized by Congress in 1806; built from Cumberland, MD., to Vandalia, IL, between 1811 and 1852), 101

Cumming v. County Board of Education (1899 - Southern school racial segregation upheld), 146

Cycle of demand (ebb and flow of demand; causes the economy to expand and contract at intervals; also business cycle), 232 [+chart]

Darrow, Clarence (1857-1938; lawyer known for highly publicized defense of "lost causes"; Scopes evolution trial (1925), 230

Dartmouth College v. Woodward (1819, legal sanctity of contracts), 96

Davis, Jefferson (1808-1889; president of the Confederacy, 1861-1865), 118, 119 [photo]

Dawes General Allotment Act (1887 - attempt to distribute tribal lands and resettle Native Americans), 172

Debs, Eugene V. (1855-1926; industrial era labor union and Socialist Party leader), 159, 211

Deciduous (shedding or losing foliage at the end of the growing season), 13

Declaration of Independence (summary of the reasons the colonies revolted against Britain in 1776; employs the natural-rights theories of John Locke), 53-54, 186, 364-366

Declaration of Sentiments (Elizabeth Stanton's proclamation at the 1848 Seneca Falls women's rights convention), 111, 186

Declaratory Act (1766; Parliament asserted Britain's supremacy over America), 48

De facto segregation (racial separation by informal means; neighborhood settlement patterns), 306

Deficit spending (spending of public funds obtained by borrowing rather than by taxation), 240

De Gaulle, Charles (1890-1970; French WW II leader), 255

De Klerk (1936- ; President of South Africa, 1989-1994; abolished apartheid), 345

De jure segregation (racial separation by legal statutes), 145, 294, 306

Delaware (Native American peoples formerly inhabiting the Delaware and Hudson river valleys and the area between), 26, 27 [map]

Delegated power (specifically assigned in Constitution), 6, 78, 79 [chart]

Demagogue (leader who obtains power by means of impassioned appeals to the emotions and prejudices of the populace), 242

Demand (amount of a commodity or service that people are ready to buy for a given price), 19

Demobilize (disband military structures), 18, 232

Democratic Party (evolved in early 19th C. from Democratic-Republicans; modern party tends to be more liberal of the two major parties; support comes from the lower and middle class, urban dwellers, ethnic minorities, and unions; generally in favor of welfare, and gov't. economic intervention), 95, 96, 214, 235, 239, 267, 291, 317, 321, 328, 338, 353

Democratic republic (gov't. decisions made by popularly elected representatives), 76

Dennis v. U.S. (1951 decision questioned freedom of speech rights for communists; upheld the 1940 *Smith Act* on modified freedom of speech rights for communists), 276

Department of Transportation (DOT, est. 1966), 304

Depression (severe and prolonged economic slow down characterized by low production and high unemployment), 104-105, 232 [chart], 231-244, 250, 263, 293, 297

Destroyers-for-Bases Deal (1940; FDR's executive order for indirect aid to Britain), 256

Détenté (a relaxation of tense diplomatic relations between adversaries), 320, 346

De Tocqueville, Alexis (1805-1859; French politician, traveler, and historian), 107

Dewey, George (1837-1917; naval commander in the Spanish-American War), 203

Dewey, John (1859-1952 philosopher and educator; exponent of philosophical pragmatism), 203

Dewey, Thomas E. (1902-1971; NY Governor 1943-1955; Republican nominee for President, 1944, 1948), 237, 267

Diaz, Porfiro (1830-1915; Mexican general and dictator; dominated Mexico from 1876 to 1911; catered to the rich and foreign investors), 207

Dickinson, John (1732-1808; Revolutionary politician and pamphleteer), 49, 50, 66

Dien Bien Phu (battle in which French were forced out of Vietnam, 1954), 313

Dime novels (inexpensive adventure stories popular c.1900), 164

Disabled (see *Rehabilitation Act of 1973*)

Displaced persons (WW II refugees), 268-269

Dissidents (one who disagrees in opinion or belief; a dissenter), 34

Divest (to sell off or otherwise dispose of), 345

Dix, Dorothea (1802-1887; pioneer in specialized treatment of the mentally ill), 111

Dixiecrats (see States' Rights Party)

Doctrine of Nullification (see nullification)

Dole, Robert (1923- ; KA Rep., 1960-68; U.S. Sen., 1969-1996; Sen. Majority Leader, 1985-87, 1995-96; Republican pres. candidate 1996), 353-354

Dollar Diplomacy (Taft administration approach to using business investment to further U.S. foreign policy interests), 207

"Domino Theory" (1950s-1960s foreign policy underpinning that if one small country in a region succumbs to communist insurgency, others will quickly fall), 289, 314

Douglas, Stephen A. (1813-1861; U.S. rep. and senator from IL; proposed legislation that allowed individual territories popular sovereignty on the slavery issue), 116

Douglass, Frederick (1817-1895; abolitionist / journalist; escaped from slavery; became an influential lecturer in the North and abroad), 111

Downsize (reduction of large corporations in the early 1990s), 352

Evers, Medgar (1925-1963; assassinated MS civil rights leader), 300

Excise Tax (tax on luxuries), 95, 97

Ex parte Milligan (1866- limits of Presidential power in wartime), 121

Ex post facto laws (retroactive legislation - making something a crime after the act has been committed - forbidden in Constitution), 81

Executive branch (branch of gov't. charged with putting into effect a country's laws and the administering of its functions; in U.S. national gov't., the Presidency), 81-84, 94-95, 97-101

Executive privilege (claim by presidents refusing to share information with Congress or the courts that disclosure would compromise either national security or the principle of separation of powers; see *United States v. Nixon*), 96, 322

Fair Deal (domestic program of Truman), 267

Fair Labor Standards Act (1937- federal minimum wage, other labor rights), 239

Fall, Albert (Sec'y. Interior for Harding; Teapot Dome scandal), 227

Fascist (system of gov't. marked by centralization of authority under a dictator; suppression of opposition through terror and censorship), 250

FDIC (see Federal Deposit Insurance Corporation)

"Fed" (see Federal Reserve System)

Federal Deposit Insurance Corporation (1933; FDIC- New Deal agency protects depositors by insuring their bank accounts; absorbed FSLIC in 1989), 239, 348

Federal Emergency Relief Act (FERA- New Deal relief measures), 237

Federal Housing Administration (FHA, 1934; insures mortgages, providing banks with a guarantee of secured housing loans), 238

Federal Reserve Board (administers Federal Reserve Banking System), 196-197

Federal Reserve System (1913; "The Fed"; central bank of the U.S.; holds deposits of the commercial banks and operates a nationwide check-clearing system; serves as the basic controller of credit in the economy), 196-197, 339, 352

Federal Savings & Loan Insurance Corp. (FSLIC; est. 1932; provided credit reserves for savings & loan associations; dismantled by Congress' 1989 savings-and-loan bailout and reorganization legislation; became the Savings Association Insurance Fund run by FDIC), 348

Federal System (see federalism)

Federal Theater Project (New Deal aid for arts), 242

Federal Trade Commission (maintains free and fair competition in business; takes action against monopoly, restraints on trade, and unfair or deceptive trade practices), 195-196, 227

Federal union (see federalism)

Federalism (political union with a strong central gov't. with some power shared among smaller components), 6, 72, 76, 104, 377

Federalist Papers, The (essays in defense of new U.S. Constitution by Hamilton, Jay, and Madison, 1788), 73

Federalists (supporters of the Constitution in ratification struggle, also early political party founded by Hamilton and John Adams), 72-73, 95

Ferdinand, Franz (1863-1914; Austrian Archduke; assassination caused WW I), 208

Field, Marshall (1834-1906; Chicago merchant; organized largest wholesale and retail dry goods establishment of the late 1800s), 151

Fifteenth (15th) Amendment (1870; states could not deny citizens suffrage because of race or previous slavery), 139, 143, 147

Filibuster (U.S. Senate's privilege of unlimited debate to block legislation), 294, 295, 299

Finney, Charles Grandison (1792-1875; religious leader and educator; key figure in the Second Great Awakening), 108

"Fireside Chats" (FDR's radio messages), 241

First Continental Congress (see Continental Congress)

Fisk, Jim (industrial era speculator), 144

Fitzgerald, F. Scott (1896-1940; writer who epitomized the Jazz Age disillusion), 231

Five Power Naval Armaments Treaty (1922; at Washington Naval Conference, nations pledged to stop building major warships and limit production of lighter ones), 215

Fletcher v. Peck (Federal courts can review state laws), 96

Flexibility (responsive to change; adaptable), 6

Flynn, Elizabeth G. (1890-1964; Populist / Progressive reform leader; a founder of the American Civil Liberties Union), 159

Foraker Act (Puerto Rican colonial status, 1900), 204

Force Acts (early anti-KKK laws, c. 1870), 145

Ford, Gerald R. (1913- ; 38th President; 1974-1977; appointed Vice President in 1973; became President after Nixon's resignation), 320, 322, 323-325

Ford, Henry (1863-1947; automobile manufacturer; developed a gasoline-powered automobile in 1893; founded the Ford Motor Company in 1903), 155, 227, 229

Ford Motor Company (1903- ; automotive corporation founded by Henry Ford in 1903), 261, 296, 318

Fort Sumter (Union installation in Charleston, SC surrendered 12 April 1861 in first action of the Civil War), 120

Foster, William Z. (1881-1961; leader of American Communist Party, 1945-1956), 242

Four Freedoms Speech (1941 - FDR voiced WW II aims), 256

Four Power Treaty (1921; U.S., Britain, France and Japan agreed to keep peace upon among imperial powers in the Pacific, 215

Fourteen (14) Points, The (Wilson's plan for post-WW I world peace), 209-210

Fourteenth (14th) Amendment (1868 former slaves and African American males receive citizenship and equal protection of the law), 139, 143, 145, 146 [chart], 147, 368, 374, 377-380

Franco, Francisco ("El Caudillo" - Fascist dictator of Spain, 1937-73), 252

Franklin, Benjamin (1706-1790; diplomat, public official, writer, scientist, and printer; played major part in the Am. Rev.; negotiated French support for the colonists and the *Treaty of Paris of 1783*; helped draft the *U.S. Constitution*), 44, 45, 53, 57, 70, 71

Free enterprise (freedom of private businesses to operate competitively for profit with minimal gov't. regulation; see laissez-faire and capitalism)

Free Soil Party (1848 opposed extension of slavery into newly acquired territories from Mexican War; by 1850s members moved into the Republican Party), 117

Free trade (no national restrictions on international commerce), 199

Freedmen's Bureau (federal agency set up at the end of the U.S. Civil War to aid refugees and ex-slaves), 138

Freedom Riders (civil rights voting registration campaigns of 1960s), 295, 305

Frelinghuysen, Theodorous (17th C. NJ Dutch Reformed minister; active in Great Awakening), 43

French and Indian War (1756-63: Extension of 18th C. imperial rivalry between England and France; French driven out of North America), 39, 40 [chart], 46

Frick, Henry C. (1849-1919; industrial era steel magnate), 159

Friedan, Betty 1921- ; (feminist activist, 1960s Women's Liberation Movement), 309

FSLIC (see Federal Savings and Loan Insurance Corp.)

Fugitive Slave Act (required capture and return of runaway slaves), 116

Fundamental Orders of Connecticut (1st written body of laws in the American colonies), 38

Gable, Clark (1930s-1950s film actor; *Gone with the Wind*), 242

Gadsden Purchase (area in extreme southern NM and AZ purchased from Mexico in 1853); 113

Gage, General Thomas (1721-1787; British general and colonial administrator, 1774-1775; suppressed resistance), 52

Gandhi, Mohandus K. (1869-1948; non-violent independence leader in India), 299

Garfield, James A. (1831-1881, 20th President, assassinated, 1881), 187

Garland, Hamlin (1860-1940; agrarian writer), 164

Garland, Judy (1930s-60s film actress, singer; *The Wizard of Oz*), 242

Garrison, William Lloyd (1805-1879; abolitionist leader; published the antislavery journal *The Liberator*, 1831-1865), 111, 116

Garvey, Marcus (1887-1940; civil rights-separatist leader in 1920s), 190

GATT (see General Agreement of Trade and Tariffs)

GDP (see Gross Domestic Product)

General Agreement on Tariffs and Trade (GATT; overseer of world trade 1948-1995; see World Trade Organization), 199, 353

General Assembly (U.N.'s main deliberating body), 268

General Motors Corporation (founded in 1908 by Wm. Durant to manufacture Cadillac, Oldsmobile, Pontiac, merged with Chevrolet in 1911; reorganized in 1920s by Alfred P. Sloan; acquired Buick to become the largest auto maker), 261

Gentlemen's Agreement (1907- restrictions on Japanese immigration), 168

George, David Lloyd (British WW I leader), 213

George, Henry (industrial era philosopher / author), 176

George III (English monarch during American Revolution), 51, 54

Geographic terms, 11

Ghana (6th -11 C. medieval West African kingdom on the trans-Saharan caravan routes), 27

Ghetto (section of a city occupied by a minority group who live there especially because of social, economic, or legal pressure), 306

G.I. Bill of Rights (aid for returning veterans and post WW II economic recovery), 266, 296, 297

Gibbons v. Ogden (1824 - upheld Congressional power to regulate interstate commerce), 96 [chart]

Gideon v. Wainwright (1963- Sup. Ct. ruled on rights of poor to legal defense), 293 [chart], 312, 318

Gilded Age (term coined by Mark Twain to characterize the post-Civil War period as an era by the ruthless pursuit of profit, gov't. corruption, conspicuous consumption, and vulgarity in taste), 162, 164, 188

Gingrich, Newt (1934 - ; conservative Republican congressman, GA, 1979-1999; Speaker of House, 1995-1999), 353

Glass-Steagle Banking Act (sets up federal bank examinations, FDIC), 239

Glasnost (U.S.S.R.; Gorbachev internal political and economic reform program initiated by), 346, 351

Glenn, John H. (1921- ; 1st U.S. astronaut to orbit Earth; U.S. Sen., OH, 1974-1998), 301

Glorious Revolution (Parliament's 1688 overthrow of Roman Catholic James II and the accession of his daughter Mary II and her Dutch Protestant husband, William III), 37, 44

GM (see General Motors)

GNP (see Gross National Product)

Goldman, Emma (WW I radical dissenter), 211

Goldwater, Barry (1909-1998; U.S. Sen., AZ, 1953-1987; ultraconservative Republican pres. candidate, 1964), 302, 317

Gompers, Samuel (1850-1924; labor leader; president of the American Federation of Labor, 1886-1924), 158, 224

Good Neighbor Policy (1930s; FDR's efforts to improve U.S.-Latin Am. relations), 251, 254

Gorbachev, Mikail (1931- ; Soviet leader 1985-1990; dissolved U.S.S.R.), 346, 351

Gospel of Wealth (Carnegie's social philosophy), 162

Gould, Jay (1836-1892; American financier and speculator of industrial era), 144

Graduated income tax (scaled individual tax rates to income levels; see *16th Amendment*)

Grandfather clauses (South's voting restrictions on former slaves), 143

Grange Movement (agrarian reform group), 174

Grant, Ulysses S. (1822-1885; 18th President, Civil War commander), 123, 126, 127, 128, 129, 144

Great Atlantic & Pacific Tea Company, The (A&P; mass marketing of food products - evolved into the supermarket), 151

Great Awakening (1720-1750; widespread revival of interest in Calvinist religion; also Second Great Awakening: 1840s revival challenged Calvinist dogma), 43-44, 108

Great Compromise (1787; settled issue of representation in the national legislature), 70-71

Great Depression (1929-1941; global economic collapse of the 1930s), 231, 235, 250, 251, 263

Great Plains (large, grassland grain-producing region in central North America, stretching from Canada to Texas), 13, 15 [map], 16, 17 [map]

Great Society (Lyndon Johnson's social welfare reform program), 303-304, 316, 317

Greeks (classical influence on American constitutional gov't.), 69

Green Revolution (popular 1960s term to describe transfer and diffusion of agricultural technology from the developed countries to LDCs), 286, 341

Grimke (sisters Angelina, 1792-1873 and Sarah, 1805-1879; abolitionist crusaders), 111

Gross Domestic Product (GDP; post-1980s basic statistical indicator of economic activity; measures the total value of all nation's production of goods and services [excluding national firms' overseas installations] in a given year), 289

Gross National Product (GNP; pre-1980s basic statistical indicator of economic activity: measures the total value of all nation's production of goods and services [including national firms' overseas installations] in a given year), 232 [+chart], 240 [chart], 261

Guadalcanal (1942-43 WW II battle; s.w. Pacific island), 259

Guerrilla warfare (small band hit-and-run fighting tactics), 55, 204, 313, 314

Gulf (large area of a sea or ocean partially enclosed by land, especially a long landlocked portion of sea opening through a strait), 11

Hamilton, Alexander (1755-1804; soldier and politician; first U.S. secretary of the treasury, 1789-1795; established the national bank and public credit system), 68, 73, 94, 95 [chart], 97, 156

Hancock, John (1737-1793; Revolutionary leader; president of the Continental Congress; first to sign the *Declaration of Independence*; served nine terms as governor of MA), 48, 51

Harding, Warren G. (29th President, 1921-1923; corrupt administration) 216, 225-227, 228, 232, 250

Harlem Renaissance (1920s and early 1930s composers, novelists and poets renewed racial pride; emphasis on African cultural heritage), 231

Harriman, Averill (1891-1986; diplomat of WW II and Cold War era, ambassador to U.S.S.R., Governor of NY), 270

Harris, Joel Chandler (1848-1908; post Civil War southern author), 164

Harte, Bret (1836-1902; western journalist), 164

Haudenosaunee Union (see Iroquois Confederacy)

Hawaii, 201-202, 313

Hawley-Smoot Act (1930; kept protective tariffs high), 228, 233

Hawthorne, Nathaniel (1804-1864; writer; moralistic and spiritual novels and short stories), 110

Hay, John, (1838-1905; public official / writer; Sec'y. of State, 1898-1905), 201 [+box]

Haymarket Riot (1886; violent labor confrontation at Chicago's McCormick Reaper Co. strike), 158

Hayes, Rutherford B. (1822-1893; 19th President, 1877-1881), 145, 187

Hayne, Robert Y. (1791-1839;U.S. senator from SC, 1823-1832; states' rights advocate), 104

Haywood, William "Big Bill" (1869-1928; socialist who helped found the Industrial Workers of the World, 1905), 159, 211

Hearst, William Randolph (1863-1951; newspaper and magazine publisher; built the world's largest publishing empire; see yellow journalism), 164

Heart of Atlanta Motel Inc. v. United States (1964; Court upheld Civil Rights Act of 1964's prohibition of racial discrimination in places of public accommodation if operations affect interstate commerce), 307, 379

Helsinki Accords (agreements on human rights and defense perimeters of Europe, 1975), 327

Hemingway, Ernest (1899-1961; post WW I author; work: *The Sun Also Rises*), 231

Hemisphere (northern or southern half of the earth as divided by the equator or eastern or western half as divided by a meridian), 11

Henry, Patrick (1736-1799; Revolutionary leader and orator; member of the VA House of Burgesses and the Continental Congress; Gov. of Virginia, 1776-1790), 46, 73

Hepburn Act (1906 - continued earlier interstate commerce reforms), 192

Higher Education Act (1960s; expanded minority rights, opportunities), 309

Highway Beautification Act (improvement of national landscape), 304

Hill, A.P. (1825-1865; Confederate officer; his charge began the Battle of Gettysburg, 1863), 123, 129

Hirohito, Japanese Emperor (1901-1989; Emperor of Japan, 1926-1989; advocated unconditional surrender that ended WW II; renounced his divine status), 260

Hiroshima (city of southwest Honshu, Japan; US nuclear bombing, 1945), 260

Hiss, Alger (1904 -1996; public official; accused of espionage at the height of the 1950s Communist scare; convicted of perjury in controversial case), 276

Hitler, Adolf (1889-1945; leader of Nazi Germany), 213, 250, 251, 252, 254, 255, 256, 257, 258, 259, 270

Ho Chi Minh (1890-1969: communist rebel leader; N. Vietnamese leader), 313, 315

Hoffa, James R. (controversial Teamster's Union president, 1960s), 293

Holding companies (special stock pool designed to indirectly monopolize an industry), 156

Holocaust, The (genocide of European Jews and others by the Nazis during WW II), 265

Home front (civilian activities of a country at war), 261-263

Home Owners Loan Corp. (HOLC - New Deal housing assistance), 238

Homestead Act (1862; free land to induce settlement of the American West), 170

Homestead Strike (l892; bloody strike against Carnegie Steel Co. in PA), 159

Homesteaders (western pioneer settlers), 172-175

Hood, John Bell (1831-1879; Confederate commander: Atlanta Campaign, 1864; defeated at Nashville later that year), 123, 129

Hooker, Thomas (1586-1647; Massachusetts Bay cleric; clashed with authorities and left to found Hartford, Connecticut in 1636), 34

Hoover, Herbert (1874-1964; 31st President, 1929-1933), 233, 234, 235, 250, 251, 339

Hopkins, Harry (1890-1946; head of successive New Deal relief agencies and wartime advisor to President FDR), 235, 237, 263

Horizontal integration (near monopolistic control over one basic aspect of an industry; cf. vertical integration), 154

Hot Line (direct telephone line between U.S. and U.S.S.R. to be used to prevent accidental nuclear war), 301

House of Burgesses (colonial VA legislature, c. 1619), 37, 46

House of Representatives, U.S. (lower chamber of U.S. national legislature), 77-78 [chart], 367-368

Housing and Urban Affairs, Department of (HUD; 1965; federal programs relating to housing and city improvement), 304

Houston, Sam (1793-1863; led the Texan struggle for independence; president of the Republic of Texas, 1836-1844; served as U.S. senator and governor), 114

How the Other Half Lives (1890- analysis of urban poverty, Jacob Riis), 189

Howe, Louis (political manager and aide to FDR), 236

Huckleberry Finn (1884- Mark Twain's novel of Mississippi boyhood), 164

Mexican War (1846-1848 conflict fomented by U.S. annexation of Texas), 114-115

Midway (Pacific battle- WW II turning point), 260 [map]

Middle-class (usually the average level of economic or social status), 160, 164

Middle Passage (trip from Africa in slave ships), 42, 165

Military Reconstruction Plan (1867; Radical Republicans set up harsh post-Civil War occupation), 139, 145

Minutemen (rebels pledged to be ready to fight on a minute's notice just before and during the Revolutionary War), 51

Miranda v. Arizona (1966; Sup. Ct. clarified rights of criminally accused persons), 293, 312, 318, 379

Mission Oak (industrial era furniture style), 165

Mississippi river (chief river of the U.S., rises in the lake region of northern MN and flows generally southward about 2,350 mi.; enters the Gulf of Mexico through a huge delta in S.E. Louisiana), 15, 16, 100, 123, 125, 127

Missouri Compromise (1820; an attempt to solve the sectional disputes between free and slave states), 115-116, 118

Mixed economy (exchange of goods and services combining market and command structures), 19

Model T (mass production popular middle class Ford auto), 155

Mohawk (Native American people formerly inhabiting northeast NY along the Mohawk and upper Hudson valleys north to the St. Lawrence River), 26

Molasses Act (1733; Parliament imposed mercantilist taxes on molasses, rum, and sugar imported into British North America), 40

Moley, Raymond (Brain Trust aide to FDR), 236

Mondale, Walter (1928- ; Vice Pres., 1977-1981; U.S. Senator, MN, 1964-1977; Democratic pres. candidate, 1984), 339

Monopoly (company or group having exclusive control over a commercial activity), 156

Monroe Doctrine, The (1823; declared U.S. opposition to European interference in the Americas), 101-102, 205, 206, 250, 300

Monroe, James (1758-1831; 5th President, 1817-1825; acquisition of FL, 1819; Missouri Compromise, 1820; Monroe Doctrine, 1823), 101-102

Montesquieu, Baron de la Brede et de (1689-1755; philosopher and jurist of French Enlightenment; wrote The Spirit of the Laws, 1748), 69

Montevideo Conference, (1933; U.S. pledged to end intervention in Latin America), 251

Montgomery, Bernard L. (1891-1976; British supreme commander, WW II), 259

Montgomery Movement (1955-1956; bus desegregation led by Dr. King), 294-295

Montgomery Ward (early mail-order business, 19th C.), 151, 173

Moon Landing (U.S. 7/20/1969), 304

Morgan, J.P. (John Pierpont Morgan, 1837-1913; Wall St. financier - philanthropist), 152, 154, 155, 192

Morgenthau, Henry, Jr. (189-1967; chair of the Federal Farm Board, 1933; Treasury Sec. , 1934-45), 236, 237

Mormonism (way of life practiced by members of the Church of Jesus Christ of Latter-day Saints), 108

Morrill Land Grant Act (1862; created agricultural colleges), 173

Morse, Samuel F.B. (1791-1872; artist and inventor; refined and patented the telegraph [1854]), 154

Moses, Robert (1888-1981; planner of many important public works, parks, highways and buildings in NYC and NY state), 236

Mott, Lucretia (1793-1880; feminist social reformer; active in the antislavery movement), 111

Mountain (natural elevation of the earth's surface having considerable mass, generally steep sides, and a height greater than that of a hill), 11

Muckrakers (journalists who expose corruption and scandal), 188-189

Muir, John (1838-1914; naturalist who promoted the creation of national parks and reservations), 194

Muller v. Oregon (1908, gov't. limits on women's working hours upheld), 192-193, 378

Mulrooney, Brian (1939- ; Conservative, business oriented Canadian Prime Minister, 1984-1993), 340

Multilateral (multi-sided agreement; e.g., NATO, 1949), 272

Multinational corporations (one that owns plants or business enterprises in more than one country), 285

Munich Conference (1938 - Britain and France gave in to Hitler's demand for German occupation of the German-speaking Sudetenland in w. Czechoslovakia), 254, 270

Munn v. Illinois (1877 - states could regulate railroads), 156, 174

Mussolini, Benito (1883-1945; fascist dictator of Italy), 250, 252, 259

NAACP (see National Association for the Advancement of Colored People)

Nader, Ralph (1934 - ; consumer rights spokesman since the 1960s), 318

NAFTA (see North American Free Trade Agreement)

Nagasaki (city of western Kyushu, Japan; nuclear bombing by U.S., 1945), 260

Napoleon I (1769-1821; Napoleon Bonaparte, military commander, and consul, Emperor of the French [1804-1814]), 100

Napoleonic Wars (1803-1815 European wars with France; U.S. tried to remain neutral), 99, 250

Nast, Thomas (1840-1902; Grant Era political cartoonist; anti-corruption crusader), 144

Nat Turner Uprising (1831 rebellion in VA, killed 50 whites), 42, 117

National Association for the Advancement of Colored People (NAACP; major civil rights group, 1909-), 146, 294, 304

National nominating convention (formal meeting of members, representatives, or delegates of a political party as method of selecting presidential candidates; began c. 1830), 106

National debt (money owed by a gov't. to investors -individuals, businesses, nonprofit organizations, and other gov'ts.; finances budget deficits when spending exceeds tax revenues), 339

National Defense Education Act (1959; authorized $887 million to upgrade educational programs in science, mathematics, and modern foreign languages), 291

National Industrial Recovery Act (1933, NIRA - New Deal regulation/stimulation of industry; permitted businesses to draft "codes of fair competition" [subject to presidential approval] that regulated prices, wages, working conditions, plant construction, and credit terms; administered and better known by initials NRA [Nat. Recovery Admin.]), 237 [chart], 238, 241

National Labor Relations Act (1935 - *Wagner Act*: assured right of organization and collective bargaining for unions; set up National Labor Relations Board for oversight), 239

National Organization for Women (1966; NOW; works to achieve "full equality for women in truly equal partnership with men."), 309

National Recovery Administration (NRA; see *National Industrial Recovery Act*)

National Road (see Cumberland Road)

National Origins Act (1924-1965; immigration system based on preference quotas for certain groups), 230, 297

National Security Act (1947; reorganized military after WW II), 266

National Union for Social Justice (see Coughlin)

National Urban League (civil rights group founded in 1910 to provide jobs for southern African Americans in industry and aid southern migrants moving into northern cities), 304

Nationalists (see Chinese Nationalists)

Native Americans (member of any of the aboriginal peoples of the Western Hemisphere; see also American Indian or Amerindian), 24-27, 70, 101, 107, 170-172, 242, 318-319

Nativist (organized opposition to immigrants), 168

NATO (see North Atlantic Treaty Organization)

Navigation Acts (17th C. series of statutes by the English Parliament, formed the basis of the mercantilist trading system in the early British Empire), 40, 47 [chart]

Nazis (National Socialist German Workers' Party, founded in Germany in 1919 and brought to power in 1933 under Adolf Hitler), 250, 255, 265

Nelson, Donald (industrialist managed WW II military production), 261

Neutrality Acts of 1935, '36, '37 (pre-WW II isolationist sentiment; see chart for differences), 252, 256

New Deal (FDR's reform programs to help in Great Depression), 235-244, 263, 265

New England Town Meeting (assembly of the qualified voters of a community to conduct public business), 38

New Freedom (Wilson's domestic Progressive reform program), 195

New Federalism (Reagan's policy - shift more welfare responsibilities on local gov't.), 338

New Frontier (JFK's legislative program), 309

"New" Immigration (S. and E. Europeans coming in larger numbers after 1890), 166

New Jersey v. TLO (1985; school authorities search & seizure powers), 340, 380

New Nationalism (Theodore Roosevelt's general legislative program; also Square Deal), 191

New Right (ultra conservative groups in 1980s politics), 252, 341

"New South" (post Civil War industrialization), 142

Newlands Act (1902 - national parks), 193

Newton, Sir Isaac (1642-1727; English mathematician and scientist; invented differential calculus; formulated the theories of universal gravitation, terrestrial mechanics, and color), 44

New York Times Co. v. United States (1971; "Pentagon Papers case"; federal power to prohibit publication of gov't. documents), 318, 380

Ngo Dinh Diem (1901-1963; South Vietnamese leader 1954-63, assassinated), 313

Niagara Movement (founding of NAACP), 146

Nicaragua (anti-communist containment in Reagan Administration), 343, 346

Nimitz, Admiral Chester (1885-1966; WW II Pacific naval commander), 259

Nine-Power Treaty (1922; reduction of naval armaments), 215

19th Amendment (1920; provides men and women with equal voting rights), 187, 197

Nisei (person born in America of parents who emigrated from Japan), 264-265

Nixon Doctrine (curtailed American use of power against communist insurgency after the Vietnam withdrawal), 320

Nixon, Richard M. (1913-1994; 37th President, 1969-74; Watergate scandal; resignation, pardon), 276, 298, 317-323

Non-violent, direct action (protest tactics of the civil rights movement), 295, 299, 304-305

Noriega, Manuel (1934- ; Panamanian dictator, 1983-89; indicted and imprisoned by U.S. for drug trafficking and overthrowing the elected Panamanian gov't., 1992), 350

Normalcy (normality – state or fact of being typical; Warren Harding's 1920 campaign misnomer for wanting the country to return to normal, pre-Progressive and pre-war conditions); 225-227

Norris, Frank (early 20th century muckraking writer; works include: *The Octopus*, *The Pit*), 188

Norse (the people of Scandinavia), 27

North American Free Trade Agreement (1994 NAFTA – U.S., Can., Mex. phased out trade barriers over 15 yr. period), 353

North Atlantic Treaty Organization (1949; NATO - 12 nation defense alliance; first permanent peacetime military alliance for the U.S; now 18 nations are members), 271-272, 355

North Korea (Soviet satellite attacked South Korea, 1950 to begin the Korean War), 274-275

Northern Securities Co. v. U.S. (1904, first Federal prosecution and breakup of a monopoly), 192, 378

Northwest Ordinance (1787; procedures for admission of states), 67, 171

NRA (see *National Industrial Recovery Act*)

Nuclear family units (smaller family in industrial society households as opposed to larger extended families in rural areas), 163

Nuclear power plant (first opened, 1957), 284, 326

Nuclear Regulatory Commission (NRC, 1975; independent U.S. gov't. agency responsible for licensing and regulating civilian uses of nuclear materials; successor to Atomic Energy Commission), 326

Nuclear Test-Ban Treaty (1963, U.S.-U.S.S.R., plus 100 other nations pledged no more atmospheric testing), 301

Nullification (individual states declaring a federal law is invalid and refusing to enforce it), 104

Nuremberg Trials (Allied trials of Axis war criminals, 1945-1946), 265

Nye Committee (1935 report led to new neutrality laws), 252

Oakies (farmers displaced by 1930s Dust Bowl disaster; focus of Steinbeck's *Grapes of Wrath*), 241

OAS (see Organization of American States)

Ocean (any principal division of the body of salt water that covers 70% of the Earth, including the Atlantic, Pacific, and Indian Oceans), 11, 16

O'Connor, Sandra Day (1930 – first woman associate justice of the U.S. Supreme Court), 341

Office of Economic Opportunity (OEO- major Great Society job retraining and anti-discrimination agency), 303

Office of Price Administration (OPA – administered WW II rationing), 262 [+box & cartoon]

Oglethorpe, James (1696-1785; English soldier, philanthropist; secured a charter for the colony of Georgia in 1732), 36

Oil Crisis (1973, 1978, Arab and OPEC nations used economic embargo and supply manipulations against Western nations, 1973), 324, 327

Okinawa (WW II Pacific battle [4-6/1945] 650 mi. s.e. of Japan), 259

Old Folks' Crusade (New Deal Era campaign by Dr. Francis Townsend), 242

"Old" Immigrants (predominance of WASP-related groups before Civil War), 166

Olney, Richard (Sec'y. of State / Attorney Gen. for Pres. Cleveland), 206

Olympics (U.S. boycott of the 1980 Summer Games in Moscow), 327

O'Neill, Eugene (1888-1953; 20th C. plays: *Emperor Jones, Mourning Becomes Electra*), 231

OPA (see Office of Price Administration)

OPEC (see Organization of Petroleum Exporting Countries)

Open Door Policy (1900; U.S. call for equal trading rights in China be guaranteed to all foreign nationals), 201

Operation Desert Shield (1990-91 protection of Saudi Arabia, preparation for invasion of Kuwait), 349

Operation Desert Storm (1991 invasion of Kuwait – Persian Gulf Conflict), 350

Operation Overlord (code name for WW II - Allied invasion of Europe 6/6/44), 259

Operation Restore Hope (Dec. 1992, U.S. / U.N. action to protect humanitarian aid in Somalia), 350

Oppenheimer, J. Robert (1902-1967; physicist directed development of the first atomic bomb, 1942-1945), 260, 277

Organization of American States (Western Hemisphere peace & mediation organization; formerly the Pan American Union, 1910-1948) 251, 255, 300

Organization of Petroleum Exporting Countries; OPEC cartel created by 5 oil producing countries in 1960 to counter oil price cuts of American and European oil companies; oil boycotts of the mid-1970s; now 12 members), 288, 324

Orlando, Vittorio (Italian Premier at Versailles, 1918-19), 213

Oswald, Lee Harvey (1963 JFK assassin), 301

Owen, Robert (1771-1858; Scots manufacturer and social reformer; attempted to establish a cooperative community in Indiana), 111

PAC (see Political Action Committee)

Paine, Thomas (1737-1809; Anglo-American revolutionary; wrote the pamphlets *Common Sense* and *The Crisis* in 1776; published *The Rights of Man* in 1792 defending the French Revolution), 52 [box], 53

Palestine Liberation Organization (PLO; umbrella organization founded in 1964 for several groups of Palestinians seeking to liberate their homeland; recognized in 1974 by U.N. as sole representative of Palestinian people), 344, 353

Palmer, A. Mitchell (1872-1936; U.S. Attorney General, 1919-21; staged the 1919-20 raids against alleged radicals and subversives during the Red Scare period following WW I), 169, 212, 229

Palmer Raids (see Palmer)

Pan-American Union (see Organization of American States)

Panama Canal Zone (1903-1999; 648 sq.mi. U.S. corridor that ran through the middle of the Republic of Panama from the Atlantic to the Pacific Ocean), 206, 327

Panama Invasion (December 1989, U.S. armed forces remove dictator Manuel Noriega and restore elected gov't.), 351

Panmunjom peace talks (negotiated truce in Korean War, 1950-53), 290

Parallel (imaginary lines representing degrees of latitude that encircle the earth parallel to the plane of the equator), 11

Paris summit (1960 Big Four meeting aborted because of U-2 incident), 291

Parish (administrative subdivision in southern states that corresponds to a county in other U.S. states), 38

Parks, Rosa (defiance of racially segregated bus seating triggered Montgomery Movement, 1955-56), 295

Parkchester (privately-funded Bronx, NY housing project during Great Depression), 236

Partnership (limited business contract arrangement entered into by two or more persons in which each agrees to furnish a part of the capital and labor for a business enterprise, and by which each shares a fixed proportion of profits and losses), 150 [box], 151

Patroon (under Dutch colonial rule: New Netherland granted proprietary and manorial rights to a large tract of land in exchange for bringing 50 settlers to the colony), 31

Patton, Gen. George S. (1885-1945; U.S. WW II 3rd Army commander in Europe), 259

Paul, Alice (1885-1977; suffragist; founded National Woman's Party in 1916; wrote the first equal rights amendment considered by Congress, 1923), 197

Peace Corps (JFK's international volunteer program to aid people in underdeveloped nations), 301

Pearl Harbor (naval base in Hawaii- 1941 attack by Japan drew U.S. into WW II), 257

Pendleton Act (1883; initiated federal civil service examination system), 187

Peninsula (piece of land that projects into a body of water and is connected with the mainland by an isthmus), 11

Penn, William (1644-1718; English Quaker colonizer in America; received proprietary rights to the colony of Pennsylvania in 1681), 35

Pentagon Papers, The (1960s secret study by Dept. of Defense; stated gov't. had falsified Vietnam War reports; intensified anti-Vietnam War demonstrations), 189, 318

Peoples' Republic of China (name adopted by Mao's communists after defeating the Nationalist forces in 1949), 274

Perestroika (Gorbachev's internal political and economic reform program in U.S.S.R.), 346, 351

Perkins, Frances (1882-1965; FDR's Secretary of Labor; 1st female cabinet member), 236, 241

Perot, H. Ross (1930- ; TX businessman; independent, "grass roots" presidential challenges in 1992, 1996; formed the Reform Party), 353

Perry, Matthew C. (1794-1858; U.S. naval commander opened trade with Japan 1854), 200

Perry, Oliver Hazard (1785-1819; U.S. naval commander in War of 1812), 99 [illus.], 100

Pershing, John (1860-1948; U.S. general; WW I commander), 207, 210

Persian Gulf (U.S. involvement in protecting oil shipping), 344, 349-350

Persian Gulf Conflict (see Operations Desert Shield and Storm)

Pétain, Henri (French field marshal surrendered to Nazis, 1940), 255

Phillips, Wendell (1811-1884; abolitionist; American Antislavery Society president, 1865-1870), 117

Philanthropy (charitable aid to increase the well-being of humankind), 154, 162

Philippines (U.S. possession after Spanish-American War 1898-1946; fell to Japan in WW II; independent 1946), 202-205, 260 [map]

Philosophe (French or Continental European intellectuals during the 17th C. Enlightenment Era), 37, 44, 69

Picketing (group of persons stationed outside a place of employment, usually during a strike, to express grievance or protest and discourage entry by non-striking employees or customers), 160

Pilgrims (English Separatists from the Anglican Church who founded the Plymouth colony in 1620), 33, 38

Pillsbury, Charles (1842-1899; industrialist, flour milling), 154

Pinchot, Gifford (1865-1946; conservationist and politician; served as chief of the U.S. Forest Service, 1898-1910), 194

Pinckney, Thomas (1750-1828; Gov. of SC; U.S. Rep.; War of 1812 commander; minister to Great Britain and Spain), 99

Pinckney's Treaty (Treaty of San Lorenzo, 1795; gained right of deposit from Spain for western farmers), 99

Pinkerton guards (agency notorious for breaking strikes and disrupting labor union efforts late 19th and early 20th C.), 99

Pit, The (1903 muckraking novel by Norris), 189

Plain (extensive, level area of land), 11

Planned Parenthood v. Casey (1992 decision upheld Roe), 348-349, 380

Plateau (elevated, comparatively level expanse of land), 11

Platt Amendment (1901 - U.S. grants Cuban independence), 204

Plato (427-347 B.C.; classical Greek influence on gov't. institutions), 69

Plessy v. Ferguson (1896 - allowed de jure segregation, sets "separate but equal" rule), 145, 294, 378

PLO (see Palestine Liberation Organization)

Pluralistic society (multiple ethnic and cultural groups), 168

Poe, Edgar Allan (1809-1849; writer known especially for his macabre poems and short stories), 109

Point Four Program (1949 containment policy to strengthen LDCs against communist insurgency through technical-assistance to improve living standards in underdeveloped countries), 273

Poland (freedom in question at Yalta Conference), 254 [chart], 255

Polarization of world affairs (U.S.-U.S.S.R. Cold War rivalry forced many nations into the allied camp of one superpower or the other), 270

Political Action Committees (organizations established by private, special interest groups to support candidates for public office – labor unions, corporations, trade associations [e.g., 4,500 PACs distributed $201.4 million to congressional candidates in the 1995-96 election]), 353

Political boss (professional politician who controls a party or a political machine), 144, 162

Political parties (organizations of common political interest), 94-95 [+chart], 106

Political science (study of principles & structures of gov't.), 19

Poll taxes (fees charged in order to vote, see 24th Amendment), 143, 307

Pools (combination of firms for monopolistic ends), 156

Popular Sovereignty (status of slavery decided by each new state), 116

Populism (see Populist Party)

Populist Party (People's Party; c. 1892 - western / midwestern agrarian reform group), 174

Post-war contraction (1919-21: natural recession when stimulus of war production ceases; see reconversion), 225, 227

Potsdam (1945, WW II summit; Stalin-Truman-Churchill / Attlee), 263, 270

Powderly, Terence V. (1849-1924; idealist reform leader of Knights of Labor; mayor of Scranton, PA), 158

Power of the purse (essential power of any gov't.: finance, revenue), 20-21, 38, 67

Power of the sword (essential power of any gov't.: enforcement, police power), 20-21, 38, 67

Powhatan (16th and 17th c. confederacy of Native American peoples of eastern VA), 27

Prairie (extensive area of flat or rolling, predominantly treeless grassland, especially the large tract or plain of central North America), 13, 16

Preamble (preface to U.S. Constitution), 72, 367

Precedents (initial actions in gov't. that become basic pattern for subsequent actions of similar nature), 73, 94-102

Presidency, The (executive branch of gov't.), 81-84

Presidential Disability and Succession Amendment (25th Amend., 1967), 84, 376

Presidential election process (see Electoral College)

Presidential powers, 81-84

Presidential Succession Act (1947, order of officials to take over after VP; modified by 25th Amend.), 84

Price ceilings (WW II gov't. economic management; limits on prices to control inflation), 262

Price controls (gov't. sets ceilings and floors for specific goods and services to stabilize economy), 266

Primary source (document or artifact created at the same time as historical period being examined), 8

Primogeniture (all inheritance rights given to first-born son), 186

Prisoners of war (problems of return after Vietnam War), 290, 320

Proclamation of 1763 (British stopped settlement beyond Appalachian Mts), 47, 171

Proclamation of Neutrality (1793- Washington sought isolation from European wars), 97

Proclamation of Neutrality (1914, Wilson sought isolation from WW I in Europe), 209

Progressive Era (period from 1900 to WW I; age of reform:trust-busting, railroad legislation, pure food and drug acts), 187-197

Progressive income tax (see 16th Amendment)

Progressivism (general reform spirit c. 1900 to readjust society to industrial era), 187-197

Prohibition (1920-1933 period when the *18th Amendment* forbade the manufacture and sale of alcoholic beverages), 190, 230

Project Head Start (1960s Great Society program for preschool help for minority children), 303

Propaganda (information managed and disseminated by an agency to promote a particular set of ideas), 225

Proprietary colony (private ownership of a large tract of land granted by a sovereign, then developed as a commercial real estate enterprise), 35-36, 37 [box]

Proprietorships (single-owner businesses), 150 [box], 151

Protectionists (high-tariff advocates), 199

Protective tariffs (high import duties to insure competitive pricing for domestic producers; e.g., Tariff of Abominations, Fordney-McCumber, 1922), 97 103-105, 228

Protestant Reformation (16th C. movement in W. Europe aimed at reforming some doctrines and practices of the Roman Catholic Church; resulted in the establishment of Protestant churches), 29, 33, 36, 43

Pueblo (some 25 Native American peoples, including the Hopi, Zuñi, and Taos, living in established villages in northern and western NM and northeast AZ; descendants of the cliff-dwelling Anasazi peoples), 26

Puerto Rico (central Caribbean island taken as U.S. colony in Spanish-American War), 202, 203, 204

Pulitzer, Joseph (1847-1911; NY newspaper publisher; endowed the Pulitzer Prizes; yellow journalism), 164

Pullman Boycott (1894- bloody nat'l railroad strike), 159

Pullman, George M. (1831-1897; industrialist who developed the railroad sleeping car), 152, 159

Pump-priming theory (gov't. stimulation of economy through assistance to the poor to stimulate market demand; also demand-side economics), 235

Pure Food and Drug Act (1906- Progressive consumer reform), 192

Puritans (a Calvinist reform faction in the Anglican Church in the 16th and 17th century; populated Massachusetts Bay Colony in 1630s), 33-34, 155

Putin, Vladimir (1953-...; former intelligence operative; appointed prime minister in 8/1999, became acting head of Russia when Yeltsin resigned in 12/1999; elected president of Russia 4/2000), 352

Qaeda, Al (Arabic for "the base"; Islamic terrorist group emerged in 1990s under leadership of a radical Saudi businessman Osama bin Laden and responsible for the Twin Tower attack), 356

Qaddafi, Muammar (1942 -...; Libyan leader, 1969- , proponent of terrorism; attacked by U.S. under Reagan), 344

Quarantine Speech (FDR's Oct. 1937 anti-aggression address met with isolationist reaction), 253

Quotas (ethnically biased immigration restrictions of 1920s), 168-169, 230

Radical Republicans (extreme wing of Republican Party bent on punishment of the South; led Reconstruction Era), 138-141

Raleigh, Sir Walter (1552-1618; English, navigator and colonizer of VA; introduced tobacco and the potato to Europe), 31

Randolph, A. Philip (1889-1979; labor and civil rights leader, 1920s-1960s; organized FDR's Fair Employment Practices Committee), 242

Randolph, Edmund (1753-1813; Revolutionary leader; member of the Constitutional Convention, 1787; served as U.S. attorney general and secretary of state), 69, 71, 94

Rankin, Jeannette (1880-1973; leader in the women's suffrage movement; first woman U.S. representative, 1917-1919 and 1941-1943; pacifist), 189-190, 197, 210

Ratification (1787-88 battle to accept the *U.S. Constitution*), 72-73, 372

Rationing program (WW II gov't. controlled consumer supplies of critical goods), 262

Ray, James Earl (assassin of Martin Luther King, Jr.), 306

Reagan, Ronald (1911-2004 ; 40th President, 1981-1989; improved relations with the U.S.S.R.), 265, 328, 338-347

Real cost (actual expenditure of an economic decision in resources and in opportunities sacrificed because of the decision), 18

Real wages (actual purchasing power of dollars earned), 142, 158

Recall (a public election to remove an official from office; reform sought by Populists & Progressives), 191

Recession (economic slowdown characterized by declining production and rising unemployment for more than 9 straight months of falling GDP), 232 [chart], 348

Reciprocation (other countries retaliate against high tariffs with increased tariffs of their own), 103

Reciprocity Act (1934, New Deal action to reduce international trade barriers), 251

Reconstruction (1865-1877; Congressional program for reform of South after Civil War), 138-145

Reconstruction Finance Corporation (RFC - Hoover's attempt to stimulate economy through business loans), 233

Recovery (short-term gov't. actions to stimulate slow economic activity), 235, 237-238

Red Scare (1918-1919; paranoiac response socialist and anarchist activities after WW I; see Palmer), 211-212

"Redeemer" governments (white supremacist control in South after Reconstruction), 144

Redemptioners (colonial emigrant from Europe who paid for the voyage by serving for a specified period as a bond servant), 41, 165

Referendum (deciding public issues in a general election; democratic reform sought by Populists and Progressives), 191

Reform (actions to abolish abuse or malpractice; improve by alteration, correction of error, or removal of defects; put into a better condition), 110-112, 186-197, 235, 237 [chart], 238-239

Region (large, indefinite portion of the earth's surface), 11

Rehabilitation Act (1973; federal law providing improved public access and facilities for the handicapped and forbidding discrimination against them), 325

Rehnquist, William (1924- ;. associate justice of Supreme Court 1972-1986; chief justice, 1986 -), 341, 354

Relief (gov't. actions to relieve economic misfortune), 235, 236-237 [+chart]

Renaissance (humanistic revival of classical art, architecture, literature, and learning that originated in Italy in the 14th C. and later spread throughout Europe), 27

Reparations (compensation required from a defeated nation as indemnity for damage or injury during a war; especially as a cause of economic difficulties in Europe after WW I), 226, 250

Representative government (see republic; republican forms), 72

Representatives, House of, (lower chamber of U.S. national legislature), 77-81, 367-368

Republic (political order in which the supreme power lies in a body of citizens who are entitled to vote for officers and representatives responsible to them), 76

Republic of Korea (democratic southern half of Korea, created in 1948; attacked by North Korea in 1950), 274-275

Republican Party (emerged in the 1850s from anti-slavery, free-soil wing of the Whig Party; the more conservative of the two major modern parties; support comes from the upper middle class, suburban and rural populations, and corporate, financial, and farming interests; generally favors laissez-faire, free enterprise, and fiscal responsibility and opposes the welfare state and expansion of state power), 117-118, 138-141, 143 [box], 145, 194-195, 214, 235, 239, 267, 291, 317, 321, 328, 338, 353, 354

Reserved powers (by virtue of the *10th Amendment*, powers not specifically assigned or delegated to the national gov't., are left to the states), 76, 79, 367, 373

Resolution Trust Corporation (RTC; 1989-1995; created by Congress to replace the collapsed FSLIC and cure the S&L Crisis), 348

Resource Recovery Act (1971; environmental action under Nixon), 328, 318

Revenue (sources of income for a gov't.; e.g., taxes, tariffs), 97, 339

Revenue Act (1913; began Fed. income tax under the 16th Amendment), 195

Reverse discrimination (claims that affirmative action preferences seeking to alter discrimination are discriminatory of themselves by creating inequity based on race), 307

Right of deposit (privilege granted by Pinckney's Treaty; Spain allowed U.S. farmers to transfer goods shipped down the Mississippi through Spanish New Orleans to export ships), 99

Right to Life and "freedom of choice" (opposing sides in abortion question), 309

Riis, Jacob (investigative journalist of the industrial-Progressive Era), 189

River (large natural stream of water emptying into an ocean, a lake, or another body of water and usually fed along its course by converging tributaries), 11

Robber barons (derogatory name for ruthless industrialists), 154

Robinson, Jackie (1919-1972; 1st African American player in Major League Baseball, 1947), 294

Rockefeller, John Davison (1839-1937; oil industry monopolist), 153, 154

Rockefeller, Nelson A. (1950s-60s Governor of NY, appointed Vice-President under Ford, 1974), 323

Roe v. Wade (1973 - controversial abortion decision), 309, 318, 341, 380

Rogers, Ginger (1930s-'40s Hollywood film actress / dancer), 242

Rolfe, John (1585-1622; English colonist; cultivated tobacco as an export crop; husband of Pocahontas), 31

Romans (classical influences on American gov't.), 69

Rommel, Erwin (1891-1944; WW II German tank commander, "Desert Fox"), 259

Roosevelt Corollary to the Monroe Doctrine (1903; U.S. to act as protector of the Western Hemisphere, adopts interventionist approach), 206

Roosevelt, Eleanor (1884-1962; diplomat, writer, and 1st Lady of the U.S., 1933-1945; delegate to the UN, 1945-1952 / 1961-1962), 236, 268

Roosevelt, Franklin D. (1882-1945; 32nd President, 1933-1945; Governor of NY, 1929-1932), 234-244, 251, 252-254, 255, 256-260, 261 [box], 263, 264, 265, 266, 268

Roosevelt, Theodore (1858-1919; 26th President, 1901-1909; hero of the Spanish-American War; Governor of NY, 1899-1900; U.S. Vice President, 1901), 191-195, 205-206, 250

Rosenberg case (atomic secrets spy case of early 1950s; 1st U.S. civilians executed for espionage), 277

"Rosie the Riveter" (fictional American heroine - symbolic of women's home front role in WW II), 262

Roth v. U.S. (1957 - obscenity ruling), 318, 263

Rousseau, Jean-Jacques (1712-1778; 18th C. French philosopher / writer held humanity is essentially good but corrupted by society; work: *The Social Contract*), 37, 70

Royal colony (large tract of land owned and operated by a sovereign, with revenues going to the monarch or national gov't.), 31, 33, 37 [chart]

Roycroft Movement (anti-industrial craft movement in NY), 165

Ruby, Jack 1963; (murdered JFK assassin Lee Harvey Oswald, 1963), 302

Russian Revolutions (1917, overthrow of Tsar, and subsequent overthrow of provisionals by Bolsheviks), 210, 211, 229

"Rust Belt, The" (decaying industrial centers of Northeast and Mid-west in 1960s-80s), 297

Sacajawea (1787-1812; guide and interpreter for Lewis and Clark Expedition, 1805-1806), 101

Sacco-Vanzetti trial (1920s; due process questions in case of 2 anarchists' accused of murder), 230

Sadat, Anwar (1918-1981; President of Egypt, 1970-1981), 327

Saddam Hussein (Iraqi dictator, 1980- ; defeated in Persian Gulf Conflict), 349-350

St. Augustine (Spanish settlers established the first permanent European settlement in North America in Florida in 1565), 30

St. Lawrence River (major river of S.E. Canada/ N.E. U.S., flowing N.E. from Lake Ontario to the Atlantic Ocean), 16

"Salary Grab" (1873 - Grant Era scandal), 144

SALT Treaty (1972 U.S.- Soviet strategic arms limitation agreement), 321

Sanger, Margaret (1883-1966; nurse who campaigned widely for birth control; 1929 founded organization that became Planned Parenthood Federation in 1942), 189

S & L Crisis (see Savings & Loan failure)

Saturday Evening Post, The (weekly periodical popular in 20th C.), 164, 229

Savings & Loan Failures (bank deregulation crisis - 1985-1995), 348

Sault Sainte Marie Canals (canals of upper MI opened Great Lakes raw materials for industrial trade), 150

"Scabs" (worker who refuses membership in a labor union; employee who works while others are on strike; a strikebreaker; person hired to replace a striking worker), 159

Scalia, Antonin (1936- ; appointed associate justice of the U.S. Supreme Court in 1986), 341

Schechter Poultry Corp. v. United States (1935 - Court struck down New Deal's NIRA), 240, 378

Schenck v. United States (1919- civil rights in wartime; see clear and present danger rule), 211, 265, 378

Scopes Monkey Trial (1925 - controversy over teaching evolution), 230

Scott, Winfield (1786-1866; officer in War of 1812; commander in Black Hawk, Second Seminole, and Mexican Wars; Lincoln's 1st Civil War chief-of-staff), 114, 123

Sea (tract of water within an ocean; relatively large body of salt water completely or partially enclosed by land), 11

Sears, Roebuck & Co. (early mail-order business, 19th C.), 151, 173, 260

SEATO (see Southeast Asia Treaty Organization)

Second Continental Congress (see Continental Congress)

Secondary source (document or artifact created after the historical period being examined), 8

Secret ballot (reform sought by Populists & Progressives), 191 [box]

Secretariat (U.N. executive branch for the General Assembly and the Security Council)

Secretary of State (cabinet officer in charge of U.S. foreign affairs), 94, 96, 101

Sectionalism (loyalty to one's state or region surpassing one's nation), 103

Securities and Exchange Commission (1934; SEC -protects investors against malpractice in the securities and financial markets), 239

Security Council (major power arm of U.N.), 268

Sedition Act (1918; concern for wartime security and dissent), 211

Segregation (racial separation), 241-242, 294-295, 305

Selective Service acts (military conscription, draft laws), 210, 263, 293 [box], 294, 295, 306, 307 [box]

Senate (upper chamber of U.S. national legislature), 71, 77, 78 [chart], 80 [chart]

Senators, direct election of U.S. (see 17th Amendment)

Seneca Falls Convention (1848, first U.S. women's rights meeting), 111, 186

Separation of Power (three branches of U.S. gov't. to avoid tyranny), 38, 69-70, 72, 96

Service industries (industries involved in transportation, communications, and public utilities; wholesale and retail trade, finance, insurance, real estate, and gov't. and professional and personal services such as health care, accounting, entertainment, education, and food services), 286

Servicemen's Readjustment Act (see "G.I. Bill")

Settlement houses (late 19th and early 20th C. aid for immigrants, industrial poor), 189

Seven Years' War (18th C. Anglo-French imperial struggles world wide), 46

Seventeenth (17th) Amendment (direct election of U.S. Senators), 78 [chart], 368, 374

Shakers (Quaker reform sect originating in England in 1747, practicing communal living and observing celibacy), 108

"Share Our Wealth" (slogan of LA Sen. Huey Long in Great Depression), 243

Sharecropping (payment of land rent with agricultural produce), 142

Shays, Daniel (1747-1825; raided gov't. arsenal in Springfield, MA to protest the state legislature's indifference to the plight of farmers, 1787), 68

Shays' Rebellion (see Daniel Shays)

Sheridan, Philip (1831-1888; Union general; active in the Chattanooga, and Wilderness campaigns; routed Confederate forces at the Battle of Five Forks, 1865), 123, 129

Sherman, Roger (1721-1793; CT Revolutionary patriot and politician; helped draft Declaration of Independence; delegate to Constitutional Convention - Great Compromise), 53, 71

Sherman, William T. (1820-1891; Union general; commander of all Union troops in the West, 1864; captured Atlanta in 1864 and led a destructive March to the Sea), 123, 129

Sherman Anti-trust Act (1890; 1st gov't. attempt to regulate monopolies), 157, 159, 160, 195

Significance of the Frontier in American History, The (F.J. Turner's historical theory positing westward expansion as key force on American experience), 169

Sinclair, Upton (1878-1968 ; muckraking writer and reformer; novels include The Jungle, 1906), 188

Sioux (Native American peoples, also known as the Dakota, inhabiting the northern Great Plains from MN to eastern MT and from southern Saskatchewan to NE), 26, 172

Sirhan, Sirhan (assassin of Sen. Robert F. Kennedy, 1968), 306

Sit-ins (non-violent civil rights protest tactic; occupying the seats or an area of a segregated establishment to protest racial discrimination.), 305

Sixteenth (16th) Amendment (gives Congress the power to "lay and collect taxes on incomes, from whatever source derived"), 195, 368, 374

Skylab (1st U.S. manned orbiting laboratory; launched 1973), 324

Skyscrapers (tall, industrial era urban architecture), 161

Slater, Samuel (1768-1835; textile manufacturing pioneer in 1790s New England), 151

Slaughterhouse Cases (late 19th C. question of federally guaranteed rights on state level), 146 [chart]

Slavery (social institution based on ownership, dominance, and exploitation of one human being by another), 29, 33, 41-42, 71, 72, 110-111, 115-118, 120, 121, 122, 139

Smith Act (1940 Alien Registration Act required registering of all aliens residing in the U.S.; made it a crime to advocate or teach the violent overthrow of the U.S. gov't. or to belong to a group advocating or teaching it), 255, 276

Smith, Adam (see Wealth of Nations)

Smith, Alfred E. (1873-1944; 1920s Democratic reform Governor of NY; 1st Catholic pres. candidate, 1928), 235

Smith, Bessie (1894-1937; leading jazz and blues singer in the 1920s), 231

Smith, Joseph (1805-1844; founder of the Mormons or Latter-day Saints), 108

SNCC (see Student Non-violent Coordinating Committee)

Social Darwinism (application of "survival of fittest" to human behavior, justification for ruthless business practices of industrial era), 162

Social Security System (1935; gov't. program provides economic assistance to persons faced with unemployment, disability, or agedness, financed by assessment of employers and employees), 239, 265

Socialism (social system in which means of producing and distributing goods are owned collectively and political power is exercised by the whole community), 211

Socialist Party (1900s coalition of worker interests weakened after WW I; regained some strength during the Depression of the 1930s; abandoned presidential campaigns after 1948; Socialist Workers Party, more militantly allied with international communism, was founded in 1937), 242

Soil Bank Plan (farm conservation), 292

Solid South (predominance of Democratic Party in region after Civil War into the late 20th C.), 147

Somalia (U.S. part of 1992 U.N. peacekeeping mission), 350

Songhai (8th -16th C. West African Berber empire on the trans-Saharan caravan routes), 27

Sons of Liberty (secret intercolonial organization founded in 1765 to oppose the *Stamp Act*), 48

Souter, David (1939 - ; appointed associate justice of U.S. Supreme Court, 1990), 348

South Africa (problem of apartheid), 345-346

South Carolina Exposition and Protest (Calhoun's 1830 statement on states rights), 104

Southeast Asia Treaty Organization (SEATO - U.S. backed regional collective security arrangement, 1953), 290

Southern Christian Leadership Conference (SCLC, 1957 - Dr. King's group intended to broaden the civil rights effort through peaceful demonstrations), 304-305

Sovereignty (complete independence and self-gov't.), 21, 67

Soviet Union (U.S.S.R.; Union of Soviet Socialist Republics; lands of the old Russian Empire governed by the Communist Party of the U.S.S.R., 1917-1991), 251, 255, 256, 257, 259, 263, 264, 268, 269, 270, 271, 272, 274, 277, 288, 289, 290, 291, 300, 301, 320, 321, 327, 328, 346, 338, 346, 351-352

Spanish-American War (1898; marked emergence of the U.S. as a great power; advent of overseas imperialism), 191, 202-203, 204

Spanish Civil War (an internal struggle that began in 1936 and ended with the defeat of the Spanish republic in 1939 and the rise of dictatorship of Franco), 252

Speaker of the House (presiding officer of the U.S. House of Representatives), 78 [chart]

Spencer, Herbert (1820-1903; British philosopher who attempted to apply the theory of evolution to philosophy and ethics), 162

Sputnik I and *II* (Soviet challenges to American technology), 291

Square Deal (Theodore Roosevelt's Progressive program), 191-192, 193

Stalin, Josef (1879-1953; successor to Lenin, dictator/premier of the U.S.S.R., 1926-1953), 251, 255, 257, 263, 269, 270, 290

Stalingrad (1941, turning point of Nazi invasion of U.S.S.R.), 259

Stamp Act (1765-66; first direct tax imposed by Britain on its American colonies), 47 [+chart], 48

Stamp Act Congress (intercolonial conference; met in 1765 in NYC; issued a declaration of American rights and grievances), 48

Stanton, Elizabeth Cady (1815-1902; feminist and social reformer), 111, 186, 187

Stanton, Edwin (Secretary of War under Lincoln and Johnson), 139

Star Wars (see Strategic Defense Initiative)

States' rights (opposition to power of Federal gov't.), 103-104, 117

States' Rights Party (nicknamed the Dixiecrats; 1948 Southern opposition to Truman's civil rights program), 267

Steffens, Lincoln (1866-1936; journalist. As managing editor of *McClure's* Magazine, 1902-1906), 188

Steinbeck, John (1902-1968; novelist; *The Grapes of Wrath*), 241

Stephens, Uriah (early U.S. labor leader; Knights of Labor), 158

Stereotyping (form of prejudice; to give a fixed, unvarying form to a person or group), 168

Steuben, Baron Friedrich Wilhelm Ludolf Gerhard Augustin von (1730-1794; Prussian-born American Revolutionary military leader troops under Washington), 55

Stevenson, Adlai (1900-1965; Gov. of IL; Democratic presidential candidate, 1952, 1956), 277, 291

Stewardship Theory of Presidency, The (Theodore Roosevelt's concept that the president acts in the interests of the people as a whole), 191

Stickley, Gustav (1858-1942; designer of Mission Oak furniture), 165

Stone, Lucy (1818-1893; social reformer; founder of the American Woman Suffrage Association, 1869), 187

Strategic Arms Limitation Treaty (SALT; 1972 U.S.-U.S.S.R. agreed to limit the number of ABM sites), 321

Strategic Defense Initiative (Reagan's "Star Wars" space missile defense system proposal), 346

Streetcars (industrial era mass transit), 161

Strict constructionists (believers in precise interpretations of the Constitution), 79, 95 [chart], 97

Strike (to cease working, in support of demands made upon an employer), 158-160

Strip mining (clearing a natural covering or growth for extracting minerals near the earth's surface, especially coal), 288

Strong, Rev. Josiah (1847-1916; social justice advocate and pro-imperialist of 1880s), 199

Student Non-violent Coordinating Committee (SNCC; founded 1960 to coordinate sit-ins and voter-registration campaigns in the South), 305

Students for a Democratic Society (SDS- radical anti-Vietnam group), 315

Submarine warfare (as a cause of U.S. entry into WW I), 208, 209

Suburbs (residential region around a major city; growth after WW II), 229, 297

Subversion (to plot and take secretive actions to overthrow a gov't.)

Subway systems (urban mass transit system), 161

Sudetenland (region of Czechoslovakia taken by Hitler in 1939), 254

Suffrage (the right to vote), 186-187, 197

Suffragist (crusader for women's right to vote ["suffragette" was used in Britain, not in the U.S. movement]), 186-187, 197

Summit meetings (personal diplomacy among world leaders), 263, 269-270, 291, 301, 346

Sumner, William Graham (1840-1910; sociologist; social Darwinist theories), 162

"Sun Belt" (Southern and Western states developing in the 1970s), 298

Superpower (powerful and influential nation, especially a nuclear power that dominates its allies or client states in an international power bloc), 269

Supply (Economics: amount of a commodity available for meeting a demand or for purchase at a given price), 18

Supply side economics (gov't stimulus through tax incentives to industry and richer classes; similar "trickle down" concept), 338-339

Supreme Court (highest court in the U.S. federal system; exerts a commanding influence on public and legal policies of the U.S.; currently consisting of nine justices), 84-85, 96, 105, 107, 117, 141, 145, 146 [chart], 154, 156, 159, 171, 174 [chart], 192, 205, 211, 227, 240, 265, 276, 294, 295, 306, 307 [+box], 309, 311, 318, 322, 340 [box], 341, 348

Suzuki (Japanese premier, surrendered in WW II), 260

Swan v. the Board of Education of Charlotte-Mecklenburg (1971- upheld busing as desegregation technique), 306

Sweatshops (factory with poor working conditions), 159, 163

Taliban (militant 1980s-90s Islamic fundamentalist group arose during Soviet occupation of Afghanistan; governing body until 2002 U.S. invasion), 356

Taft, William Howard (1857-1930; 27th President, 1909-1913; chief justice of the Supreme Court, 1921-1930), 194-195

Taft-Hartley Labor Management Relations Act (1947; cut power of labor unions), 266, 293

Talented Tenth (W.E.B. DuBois' theory for social equality), 146

"Talkies" (talking motion pictures introduced in the late 1920s), 229

Tammany Hall (19th & early 20th C. NYC Democratic political club), 167

Tarbell, Ida (1857-1944; muckraker: *History of the Standard Oil Co.*, 1904), 188

Tariff of Abominations (1828 - exceptionally high duties became subject of Southern protests), 103-104

Tariffs (duties, taxes on imports), 72, 97, 103-104, 199, 228

Taylor, Zachary (1784-1850; 12th President, 1849-1850; commander in Black Hawk , 2nd Seminole , and Mexican Wars), 114

Tax revenue (see revenue)

"Tax simplification" program (1986-Reagan reform of income tax system), 339

Taylor, Frederick Winslow (1856-1915; inventor, engineer, and efficiency expert noted for his innovations in industrial engineering and management), 227

Tea Act (1773 - Parliament tried to force Americans to buy East India Co. tea.), 51-52

Teapot Dome Affair (1920s Harding era scandal), 227

Teller Resolution (1898 - promise of Cuban independence), 204

Temperance (restraint in the use of or abstinence from alcoholic liquors), 110, 190

Tenement (run-down, low-rental apartment building whose facilities and maintenance barely meet minimum standards), 161

Tennent, Gilbert (1703-1764, NJ/PA Presbyterian leader of America's first widespread religious revival, the Great Awakening), 43

Tennent, William (1673-1746: PA Presbyterian minister; active in Great Awakening), 43

Tennessee Valley Authority (TVA, 1933 independent agency provides integrated flood-control system on the Tennessee, Ohio, and Mississippi Rivers; gov't. production and sale of electric power), 240

Tenure of Office Act (Radical Republican law used as ploy to impeach Andrew Johnson), 139-141

Terrorism (use of acts of violence for political purposes), 344

Tet Offensive (massive Viet Cong attack 1968 leads to questions about U.S. role), 315

Textiles (first major U.S. industry), 150-151

Third Reich (Adolf Hitler's Nazi regime in Germany, 1933-45; Third Reich identified the Nazi Empire, as 3rd in succession to the Holy Roman Empire and the German Empire of 1871-1918), 213

"Third World" Countries (underdeveloped nations of Asia & Africa; see LDCs), 327

Thomas, Clarence (1948 - ; sworn in as associate justice of the Supreme Court in 1991), 341

Thomas, George H. (1816-1870; Union general renowned for his defense during the Union defeat at Chickamauga, 1863), 123, 128

Thomas, Norman (1884-1968; 1920s-1940s socialist leader; a founder of the American Civil Liberties Union), 242

Thoreau, Henry David (1817-1862; writer; *Walden, On Civil Disobedience*), 109

Three-Fifths Compromise (slavery question in Constitutional Convention), 71

Three R's (Relief, Recovery, Reform programs [in New Deal]), 236, 237 [chart]

Three Mile Island (1979, PA nuclear accident), 326

Thirteenth (13th) Amendment (1865 addition to the Constitution abolished slavery), 139, 143, 186

Thurmond, Strom (1902 – ; SC Governor, U.S. Sen.; led opposition wing of Democrats - Dixiecrats - against Truman in 1948), 267

Tilden, Samuel (Gov. of NY, Democratic Presidential candidate, 1876), 145

Tinker v. DesMoines (1969 - symbolic speech protected by *1st Amendment*), 340 [chart], 379

Title VII (section of the *Civil Rights Act of 1964* prohibiting job discrimination against women), 309

Title XI (equal educational access - women, minorities), 309

Tojo Hideki, (1884-1948; general; leading advocate of Japanese military conquest; prime minister, 1941-44), 257, 264

Tom Sawyer (1876 - work by Mark Twain), 164

Toomer, Jean (1894-1967 writer: *Cane*, 1923, on lives of Southern rural blacks and their Northern urban migration; Harlem Renaissance), 231

Tonkin Gulf Resolution (Congressional permission for Johnson to escalate troops in Vietnam), 314 [+box], 316

Topography (surface features of a place or region), 13

Tories (American colonists who favored the British side during the American Revolution; also Loyalists), 56

Townsend, Francis E.(1867-1960; social reformer; plan for gov't.-sponsored old-age pension), 242

Townshend Acts (1767- Parliament levied repressive mercantile duties on imports to the American colonies), 47 [chart], 48-50

Trade deficit (the value of a nation's imports exceeding that of its exports), 345

Trade quotas (one country restricts the quantity of a good that another country can export to it), 345

Traditional economy (exchange of goods and services followed by a people continuously from generation to generation; governed by custom or usage), 18, 19 [chart]

"Trail of Broken Treaties" (1970s civil rights protest by Native Americans), 311

"Trail of Tears" (forced gov't. relocation of Native Americans under President Jackson, 1830s), 171

Transcendentalist thought (mid-19th C. literary and philosophical movement; asserts an ideal spiritual reality surpasses observed scientific knowledge); 109

Transportation, Dept. of, (DOT; 1966; responsible for policies aimed at an efficient national transportation system that can also facilitate national defense), 94 [chart], 304

Treaty of Alliance (1778 - France recognized the gov't. of the U.S. during the Revolution; committed financial and military aid), 57

Treaty of Ghent (1814; settled War of 1812), 100

Treaty of Guadeloupe-Hidalgo (1848: ended U.S.-Mexican War and provided considerable western territory to the U.S.), 115

Treaty of Paris (1783 - ended American Revolution), 57, 67

Treaty of Paris (1898 - ended Spanish American War), 202, 203

Treaty of Tordesillas (1494 - Spain & Portugal divided Western Hemisphere colonial rights), 29

Treaty of Versailles (ended WW I, created League of Nations, rejected by U.S. Senate), 213-214, 250

Triangle Shirtwaist Co. fire (1913 disaster in NYC; 146 women garment workers died; spurred factory safety reforms), 158

Trickle-down theory (gov't. stimulation of economy through business assistance and tax cuts for the rich to spur investment; also supply-side economics), 235

Triple Alliance (WW I alliance of the Central Powers: Germany, Austria-Hungary, and Italy), 208

Triple Entente (WW I alliance: France, Great Britain, Russia), 208

Truman Doctrine (U.S. aid to contain communist expansion in Europe), 270, 271

Truman, Harry S (1884-1972; 33rd President, 1945-1953; authorized the use of the atomic bomb against Japan; implemented the Marshall Plan, NATO; U.S. involvement in Korean War, 1950-1953), 260, 263, 265-268, 272, 273

Trust (combination of firms or corporations for the purpose of reducing competition and controlling prices throughout a business or an industry), 156, 192; 195

Truth, Sojourner (1797?-1883; abolitionist and feminist; leading preacher against slavery and for the rights of women), 111

Truth-in-Lending Act (1969 - consumer protection: banking, installment buying), 318

Tubman, Harriet (1820?-1913; abolitionist. escaped MD slave who became the most renowned conductor on the Underground Railroad), 117

Tudor (ruling dynasty of England; 1485-1603; included Henry VII and his descendants Henry VIII, Edward VI, Mary I, and Elizabeth I), 31

Tugwell, Rexford G. (advisor to FDR), 236

Turner, Frederick Jackson (1861-1932; historian; emphasized the importance of the frontier in American history), 169

Turner, Nat (led VA slave revolt in 1830s), 42, 117

Tuskegee Institute (Booker T. Washington's technical training school for blacks), 146

TVA (see Tennessee Valley Authority)

Twain, Mark (1835-1910; pen name of industrial era author, humorist Samuel L. Clemens; works: Tom Sawyer, Huckleberry Finn, Gilded Age), 162, 164, 188, 203

Tweed Ring (NYC political corruption in Grant Era), 144

Twenty-fourth (24th) Amendment (outlawed poll taxes in federal elections, 1964), 307

Two Treatises on Government (17th C. British enlightenment philosopher John Locke's work - influenced framers of the Constitution), 44

Tydings-McDuffie Act (1946; U.S. granted Philippines independence), 205

U-2 incident (U.S. spy plane shot down in U.S.S.R.), 290-291

Uncle Remus' Stories (post Civil War Southern literature - Joel Chandler Harris), 164

Uncle Tom's Cabin (Harriet Beecher Stowe's abolitionist novel, 1852), 117

"Underground Railway" (secret, organized efforts by northerners to help escaped slaves find safe shelter in the free states or Canada), 117

Underwood Tariff (1913; Progressive Era attempt to lower tariffs), 195

Unicameral legislature (having only one house in legislative branch), 67

Union Pacific Railroad Company (transcontinental railroad built westward from St. Louis; joined Central Pacific in 1869), 152

Union Party (opponents of the New Deal organized ran Wm. Lempke for president in 1936), 244

United Nations (post-WW II international peace organization), 21, 263, 268, 290, 327, 345, 351

United States Constitution (1789- present; system of fundamental laws and principles that outlines the functions and limits of the U.S. gov't.), 38, 67, 69-86

United States v. Butler (1935; Supreme Court struck down New Deal's agricultural program), 240

United States v. Cruikshank (1876 interpretation of 14th Amendment), 146 [chart]

United States v. E. C. Knight Co. (1895; Supreme Court limited power of Congress to regulate monopolies under the Sherman Antitrust Act, saying "commerce" did not include manufacturing), 156, 377

United States v. Nixon (1974; Supreme Court ruled against "executive privilege"), 322, 380

Universal Declaration of Human Rights (1947; backing for basic rights; see Eleanor Roosevelt), 269

U.S.S.R. (see Soviet Union)

Unsafe at Any Speed (1968; Ralph Nader book on U.S. auto industry), 318

Unwritten constitution (precedents, judicial decisions, expansions of legal power and procedure not in the Constitution), 94

Urban League (see National Urban League)

Urbanization (process of the society's central activities taking place in cities), 131

V-2 rockets (Germany's Vengeance Weapon 2; liquid-propellant rocket; more than 4,300 were launched against London, southeastern England, & Antwerp, 1944-1945), 259

Valentine, Lewis (crusading NYC Police Commissioner under Mayor LaGuardia, 1930s-'40s), 236

Van Buren, Martin (1782-1862; 8th President, 1837-1841; U.S. Sen., NY, 1821-1828; Sec'y. of State, 1829-1831; Vice Pres., 1833-1837), 106

Veronia School District v. Acton (1995; upheld school authorities' power to require drug testing of athletes), 340 [box], 380

Versailles Peace Conference (ended WW I), 213-214, 250

Vertical integration (near monopolistic control over all the basic aspects of an industry; cf. horizontal integration), 155

Verrazano, Giovanni (1485-1528; Italian explorer of the Atlantic coast of North America), 29

Veto power (executive power to nullify legislation), 79, 81, 139 [+chart], 266

Victorian ideal, The (idealized vision of women as delicate, weaker members of the society c. 1890s), 163, 230

Viet Cong (communist insurgent forces in Vietnam War), 313, 314, 315

Vietnam Moratorium Day (1969- massive anti-war rally), 315

Vietnam War, 313-316, 320

Vietnamization (Nixon's idea of placing more and more responsibility on the South Vietnamese to win the war), 320

Vigilante groups (sought unofficial law and order in old west), 172

Villa, Pancho (Mexican revolutionary leader c. 1913), 207

VISTA (see Volunteers in Service to America)

Voice of the People (unofficial presidential role when he speaks on national concerns), 81

Volkswagen "Beetle," (imported cars popular in U.S. in 1950s), 296

Voltaire (18th C. French Enlightenment thinker whose views influenced framers of Constitution), 69

Volunteers in Service to America (VISTA; Great Society program to aid underprivileged), 303

Voting Rights Acts (1965, 1970, 1975 insured proper procedures against racial discrimination), 306, 307 [box]

Wabash, St. Louis, and Pacific Railway v. Minn. (1886 - states could regulate railroads), 156, 174 [box], 377

Wade-Davis Bill (Lincoln vetoed this 1864 attempt of Congress to run Reconstruction), 138

Wallace, George (Gov. of AL: 1963-1967, 1971-1979, and 1983-1987; ran for President in 1968 and 1972), 317

Wallace, Henry A. (FDR's 2nd Vice President; ran for President against Truman in 1948), 267

Wanamaker, John (1838-1922; PA merchant whose men's clothing business grew into one of the first department stores), 151

War of 1812 (fought between the U.S. and Great Britain from June 1812 to the spring of 1815), 99-100

War bond drives (WW II patriotic pressures to finance war effort), 263

War Hawks (land-hungry pro-war Congressmen in 1812 era), 99

War Labor Board (WW I and WW II management of labor force), 225, 262

War on Poverty (see Great Society)

War Manpower Commission (WW II management of labor), 262

War Powers Act (1973; post Vietnam Congressional move to limit Pres. power), 343

War Production Board (WPB; WW II economic command structure for industry), 261

War reparations (vindictive penalties assessed against Germany after WW I), 226

Warren Commission (1963-64; investigated JFK assassination), 302

Warren Court (followed a policy of judicial activism), 293

Warren, Earl (Chief Justice of the Supreme Court, 1953-1969), 293

Warsaw Pact (1950s Soviet alliance of Eastern European nations; gave Soviet commanders control over the satellite's armies; ended in 1991), 272 [chart]

Washington Conference (1921-1922; diplomatic attempt to stop naval arms race after WW I), 215

Washington, Booker T. (post Civil War civil rights leader), 146

Washington, George (1732-1799; Commander of American forces in the Revolutionary War, 1775-1783; presided over Constitutional Convention, 1787; first President of the U.S., 1789-1797), 52, 55, 56, 74, 94-98, 208, 250

Washington's *Farewell Address* (1796; recommended neutrality), 97, 250

Watt, James (1938 - ; controversial Sec'y. of Interior under Reagan, 1981-83), 339

Water Quality Control Act (1970s anti-pollution and environmental reform), 304

Watergate Affair (1973-1974 election scandal - Nixon resignation), 189, 322-323

Watkins v. U.S. (1957; federal witness protection stipulations in Congressional hearings; further clarified right of free speech position on the *Smith Act* after *Dennis* decision), 276, 379

Wealth of Nations (1776, Scottish philosopher Adam Smith's attack against mercantilism and outline of the market economic system), 148, 156

Weathermen (a radical extremist offshoot of SDS in Vietnam era), 315

Weaver, Robert (1907-1997; first African American to hold a cabinet post), 242

Webster, Daniel (1782-1852; U.S. Rep., NH, 1813-1817 and MA, 1823-1827; Sen., MA, 1827-1841 and 1845-1850; advocated preservation of the Union; secretary of state twice), 104

Webster-Ashburton Treaty (1842; negotiation settled disputes the U.S.-Canadian boundaries), 113 [map]

Westinghouse, George (1846-1914; engineer / manufacturer; 400 patents, including the air brake), 152

Whiskey Rebellion, The (PA farmers' protest of Hamilton's excise tax, 1794), 95

Whiskey Ring (scandal in Grant era), 144

White Armies (anti-communist Russian groups aided by Allies in 1918), 211

White House (official residence of the President since 1800; also journalistic phrase denoting executive branch of the U.S. gov't.), 81 [photo], 233, 236, 291, 300, 319, 322, 327, 346, 354

Whitefield, George (1714-1770; English religious leader; follower of Methodist John Wesley; preached widely in the American colonies; was a central figure in the Great Awakening), 44

Whitman, Walt (1819-1892; poet who used unconventional meter and rhyme), 110

Wilderness Act (1960s Great Society environmental preservation measure), 304

Willard, Emma (1787-1870; educator; early proponent of higher education for women), 109

Williams, Roger (1603-1686; Puritan cleric expelled from MA; founded Providence in 1636; obtained a royal charter for Rhode Island in 1663), 34 [+box]

Wilson, James (1742-1798; PA delegate influential at Constitutional Convention), 69

Wilson, [Thomas] Woodrow (1856-1924; 28th President, 1913-1921; WW I; prohibition; Treaty of Versailles; established the League of Nations; won 1919 Nobel Peace Prize; governor of NJ), 194-195, 209-210, 213-214, 250, 251, 252, 268

Winthrop, John (1588-1649; English Puritan colonial administrator; first governor of Massachusetts Bay Colony 1629-1649), 34

"Wobblies" (see Industrial Workers of the World)

Women, 109, 111, 158, 159, 163, 186-187, 189, 262, 308-310

Women's Christian Temperance Union (1876 - prohibitionists), 190

Women's International League for Peace and Freedom (WW I pacifists), 210